IMAGES *of* DEV
and SOCIAL CONTROL

◆

A Sociological History

SECOND EDITION

Stephen Pfohl

Professor of Sociology
Boston College

McGRAW-HILL, INC.

New York   St. Louis   San Francisco   Auckland   Bogotá   Caracas
Lisbon   London   Madrid   Mexico City   Milan   Montreal   New Delhi
San Juan   Singapore   Sydney   Tokyo   Toronto

**To the many students with whom I've worked.
Your questions and concerns have given form
to words that follow.**

This book was set in Palatino by Better Graphics, Inc.
The editors were Phillip A. Butcher, Katherine Blake, and Linda Richmond;
the production supervisor was Louise Karam.
The cover was designed by Joseph A. Piliero.
The illustrations were done by Joseph LaMantia and Stephen Pfohl.
R. R. Donnelley & Sons Company was printer and binder.

IMAGES OF DEVIANCE AND SOCIAL CONTROL
A Sociological History

Acknowledgments appear on page xiv, and on this page by reference.

This book is printed on acid-free paper.

12 13 14 15 DOC/DOC 0 9 8 7 6 5 4 3

ISBN 0-07-049765-6

Library of Congress Cataloging-in-Publication Data

Pfohl, Stephen J.
    Images of deviance and social control : a sociological history /
Stephen J. Pfohl.—2nd ed.
        p.   cm.
    Includes index.
    ISBN 0-07-049765-6
    1. Deviant behavior.   2. Social control.   3. Power (Social
sciences)   4. Deviant behavior—History.   I. Title.
HM291.P4849   1994
302.5′42—dc20

93-25803

CONTENTS

PREFACE

This is a text about other texts and their context. The texts it examines are those used to explain nonconformity and justify its control. Their context is a changing landscape of power within western history. Economic power, gendered power, heterosexualized power, racialized power, state power—these and other forms of social hierarchy have long guided the production and consumptions of images of the deviant "outsider." As structured arrangements of power have changed, so have society's images of those whom it fears. These people, whether we call them "criminals," "witches," "rebels," or "lunatics," have deviated from the dominant order. They stand outside the common sense of society and its relations of power. Whether by anguish, accident, or desire, they resist falling in line with that power. For some, resistance may be primarily symbolic. This, however, may be no less threatening than the nonconformity of those who strike out with their fists or checkbooks. Think of the considerable fear generated by people who feel different sexually, think different politically, or wear skin of a different color. In a world constructed as much by symbolic action as physical behavior, this may be reason enough to call in the forces of control.

The forces of control—they sweep in upon us in three waves. The first consists of a host of everyday social rituals. By these, individuals are born and bound into the collective life of society. If such rituals are successful, individuals will feel at home, both with themselves and with the "natural," or commonsensical, character of a social order. They will be engulfed by what Émile Durkheim referred to as a sense of collective conscience. They will be surrounded both from within and from without. Such rituals come in many forms. E. A. Ross's 1901 text *Social Control* pioneered the study of these matters by surveying such order-producing rituals as parenting, religion, education, the mass mediation of public opinion, ceremonial-like expressions of style and fashion, and the social organization of music, art, and visual imagery. The power of such rituals to produce conformity is, however,

xi

circumscribed by the distribution of power in society at large. In a society in which power is unequally distributed, conformity is undermined by the resistance of those less blessed by the existing order. Such deviance ushers in a second wave of control. On its crest ride various agents of containment— priests, police, doctors, judges, therapists, and the like. Whether by prayer, punishment, counseling, or surgery, these control agents strive to wash clean the shores of the dominant social order.

Behind the first two waves there rolls a third. It is constituted by explanations as to why certain forms of control are necessary and how they can best be executed. It provides a justification for certain arrangements of power and for the controls which secure their reign. This third wave consists of theorists and the conceptual images they produce about nonconformity. This text is about them and the knowledge they claim about deviants. It is a text about knowledge and its relationships to power.

The story told within this text is a sociological story. It is the story of how powerful theoretical images of deviance and social control blossom in the historical soil of one social landscape and languish in another. It employs a social-historical perspective to describe and analyze the theory, methods, and control policies associated with nine major ways of conceiving deviant behavior. The theoretical images examined span a wide variety of religious, legal, medical, psychological, social, economic, and political concerns. Materials pertaining to "Critical Perspectives" are presented in two separate chapters (Chapters 10 and 11). This is due both to the complexities of these important perspectives and to the fact that a critical orientation guides the construction of this text as a whole. By examining how theoretical perspectives are related to programs of empirical research and practical public policy and by considering the continued importance of each in today's world, it is hoped that theory will come alive in the imagination of the reader. Rather than look at theories as dry, abstract, or highly technical propositions, this text locates these "ways of seeing" deviance in the politically charged social contexts in which they arise.

ACKNOWLEDGMENTS

The book you are reading is now in its second edition. As such, the work involved in producing this text has spanned nearly two decades, and those to be thanked for their support, encouragement, and criticism are many. The questions it pursues were first raised for me by Simon Dinitz and a cohort of exceedingly capable and creative graduate students with whom I studied sociological criminology at Ohio State University. There my interest in the historical study of social theory was also nurtured by Gisela and Roscoe Hinkle and Clyde Franklin. In preparing the first edition I am particularly indebted to feedback from Richard Quinney and Charles Sarno. Charles worked tirelessly as my research assistant throughout the project. Thanks also to my many other colleagues at Boston College, particularly Sandra

Joshel, John Williamson, Andrew Herman, Avery Gordon, David Karp, Lynda Holmstrom, Benedict Alper, John Donovan, Diane Vaughan, Susan Guarino Ghezzi, Michael Rustad, Cheryl Boudreaux, Javier Trevino, Phyllis Meaghan, Maria Pavlaki, Mary Brady, Robert Lavizzo-Mourey, Michele Garvin, Jennifer Wilton, Steven Dolliver, Kate Stout, Delia Johnson, Tom Shamshack, Jeanne Chislom, Dick Batten, Nancy Frankel, Ann Marie Roucheleau, and Laura Carr (who assisted in the preparation of the footnotes). Also acknowledged is the periodic input of Ray Michalowski, Ron Kramer, Malcolm Spector, Jim Thomas, and Peter Conrad, and the substantive support for this project provided by a grant from the National Institute of Mental Health and by Yale University, where I spent the 1981–82 academic year as a postdoctoral fellow in the sociology of social control. In New Haven the regular comments of Albert J. Reiss, Harry Mika, Kirk Williams, and Robert Holden proved invaluable. In Boston conversation with Theresa Burns provided a continuous source of care and inspiration, while thanks also go to David Serbun, Christina Mediate, Barry Benjamin, Eric Munson, and Rhona Robbin, editors at McGraw-Hill, and to Gary Jensen, John DeLamater, and James MacIntosh, whose thoughtful review comments helped guide this book into final form. My gratitude extends as well to Alice Close, Shirley Urban, and Sara White for their ceaseless assistance in converting my scribbling into a completed manuscript.

In preparing the second edition, in addition to those already mentioned, particular thanks to my Boston colleagues and friends: Jackie Orr, Emily Kearns, Janet Wirth-Cauchon, Marc Driscoll, Alex Wirth-Cauchon, David Croteau, Julie Rosen, Michael Walker, Jeremy Grainger, Pelle Lowe, Patrick Withen, Mary Murphy, William Coughlin, Glyn Hughes, Platon Coutsoukis, Tracy Stark, Maureen Whalen, and Denis Culhane; and to others whose engagement have helped shaped the concerns resulting in these pages, including Peg Bortner, Kathleen Ferraro, Nancy Jurik, Gray Cavender, Dorothy Smith, Kathy Acker, Drew Humphries, Richard Dello Buono, Susan Caringella-MacDonald, Josef Mendoza, Charles Penderhughes, Marjorie Zatz, and Nancy Wonders. Thanks also go to my current McGraw-Hill editors, Kathy Blake, Phil Butcher, and Linda Richmond; to my copy editor, Georgia Kornbluth; and to reviewers—Richard Block, Loyola University of Chicago; Jackie Eller, Middle Tennessee State University; Michael Givant, Adelphi University; Eric Hickey, California State University–Fresno; Gary Kiger, Utah State University; Esther Madriz, CUNY–Hunter College; and Richard Rosenfeld, Skidmore College—whose comments made valuable contributions to the form and content of the revisions themselves. Thanks also to Eunice Dougherty, Roberta Pasternak, and Maureen Eldridge for assistance in bringing these words before you.

A final note of gratitude to Joseph LaMantia. Joseph and I created the photomontages that open most of the following chapters. These visual images were constructed from a variety of original drawings, photographic materials, and paintings. Each collage represents key elements of the theoretical images considered in this book. The process of collaboratively designing and producing these images was a particularly rewarding way of completing this manuscript.

For permission to include material from copyright works, I owe thanks to the following authors and publishers. Specific citations are included in footnotes.

Theresa Burns. "The Sociology Room" from *Seven Dreams,* copyright © 1981, Theresa Burns. Used by permission of author.

Michel Foucault. Excerpt from pp. 3–5, *Discipline and Punish: The Birth of the Prison,* translated by Alan Sheridan, translation copyright © 1977 by Alan Sheridan. Reprinted by permission of Pantheon Books, a division of Random House.

Jon King and Andrew Gill. Excerpt from lyrics of "Why Theory," from album *Solid Gold* by Gang of Four, copyright © 1981, Gill-King Inc. Excerpt from lyrics of "Muscle for Brains," from album *Songs of the Free* by Gang of Four, copyright © 1982, Gill-King Inc. Reprinted by permission of publisher.

Joseph LaMantia and Stephen Pfohl. Chapter opening illustrations: *Shadow Control, Cool Man Calculated, Normalizing Relations Remix, Adrift Chicago, The Social Machine, It Turns Me On, Suicidal Walkman, Enforced Imitation, Lining Labels,* and *Make-Over,* copyright © 1984, Marty Martin Productions Inc. Used by permission of publisher.

Stephen Pfohl. Chapter opening illustrations: *Sin, Dangerous Differences,* copyright © 1993 Parasite Cafe Productions. Used by permission of publisher.

St'ng. Excerpt from lyrics of "Every Breath You Take," from album *Synchronicity* by the Police, copyright © 1983, Regetta Music Ltd. Reprinted by permission of publisher.

Mark Twain. Excerpts from "The War Prayer," pp. 394–398, *Europe and Elsewhere,* copyright © 1923, 1951. Used by permission of Harper and Row, Publishers, Inc.

Lesley Woods, Paul Ford, Pete Hammond, and Jane Monroe. Excerpts from lyrics of "Headache for Michelle," from album *Playing with a Different Sex* by Au Pairs, copyright © 1981, CBS Songs Ltd. Reprinted by permission of publisher.

Stephen Pfohl

IMAGES *of* DEVIANCE *and* SOCIAL CONTROL

◆

A Sociological History

Shadow Control By Joseph LaMantia and Stephen Pfohl

CHAPTER 1

IMAGES OF DEVIANCE AND SOCIAL CONTROL:
An Introduction

We equate sanity with a sense of justice, with humaneness, with prudence, with the capacity to love and understand other people. We rely on the sane people of the world to preserve it from barbarism, madness, destruction. And now it begins to dawn on us that it is precisely the sane ones who are the most dangerous.

It is the sane ones, the well-adapted ones, who can without qualms and without nausea aim the missiles and press the buttons that will initiate the great festival of destruction that they, the sane ones, have prepared. . . . No one suspects the sane, and the sane ones will have perfectly good reasons, logical, well-adjusted reasons for firing the shot. They will be obeying sane orders that have come sanely down the chain of command. And because of their sanity they will have no qualms at all. . . . The ones who coolly estimate how many millions of victims can be considered expendable in a nuclear war, I presume they do all right with the Rorschach ink blots too. On the other hand, you will probably find that the pacifists and the ban-the-bomb people are, quite seriously, just as we read in Time, *a little crazy.*

Thomas Merton[1]

The scene is a crowded church during the American Civil War. "It was a time of great and exalting excitement. The country was up in arms, the war was on, in every breast burned the holy fire of patriotism." So says Mark Twain in his short and searing parable—*The War Prayer*.[2] Amidst the clamor of beating drums, marching bands, and toy pistols popping, Twain describes an emotional church service. A passionate minister stirs the gallant hearts of eager volunteers; bronzed returning heroes; and their families, friends, and neighbors. The inspired congregation await their minister's every word.

And with one impulse the house rose, with glowing eyes and beating hearts, and poured out that tremendous invocation—

God the all-terrible!
Thou who ordainest,
Thunder thy clarion
and lightning thy sword!

Then came the "long" prayer. None could remember the like of it for passionate pleading and moving and beautiful language. The burden of its supplication was that an ever-merciful and benignant Father of us all would watch over our noble young soldiers and aid, comfort, and encourage them in their patriotic work; bless them, shield them in the day of battle and the hour of peril, bear them in His mighty hand, make them strong and confident, invincible in the bloody onset; help them to crush the foe, grant to them and to their flag and country imperishable honor and glory.

Wars come and go. Words vary. Nonetheless, the essential message of this sermon remains alarmingly the same: "God is on our side." Before continuing with Twain's story, I ask you to consider a more contemporary version of this age-old narrative—the 1991 Gulf War between Iraq and the United States-led coalition of "New World Order" forces demanding an Iraqi withdrawal from Kuwait. Claiming it to be its moral imperative to repel an act of international aggression, the United States pictured Iraqi President Saddam Hussein as a Hilter-like character bent on world domination. Iraq in turn cited contradictions in the U.S. position (its long-term support for Israeli occupation of Palestinian territories, for example) as evidence of both U.S. hypocrisy and what Iraq alleged to be the true motives for the attack on Iraq—namely, "American" efforts to police the price of oil. Each side in this conflict represented the other as evil, treacherous, and power-mongering. Each side claimed to be righteous and blessed by God. This is typical of societies engaged in war.

Returning to Twain's story, what is untypical about this thoughtful tale is what happens next. It is not only untypical, but "deviant." After the minister completes his moving prayer, an "unnaturally pale," aged stranger enters the church. He is adorned with long hair and dressed in a full-length robe. The stranger motions the startled minister aside and informs the shocked parishioners that he is a messenger from Almighty God. He tells the congregation that God has heard their prayer and will grant it, but only after they consider the full import of their request. In rephrasing the original sermon the mysterious messenger reveals a more troubling side to the congregation's prayer. When they ask blessing for themselves they are, at the same time, praying for the merciless destruction of other humans (their enemies). In direct and graphic language the old man portrays the unspoken implications of their request, as follows:

help us to tear their soldiers to bloody shreds with our shells;
help us to cover their smiling fields with the pale forms of their patriotic dead;
help us to draw the thunder of the guns with shrieks of their wounded,
    writhing in pain;
help us to lay waste their humble homes with a hurricane of fire;
help us to wring the hearts of their unoffending widows to unavailing grief;
help us to turn them out roofless with their little children to wander
    unbefriended the wastes of their desolated land.

The strange old man continues—talking about blighting their lives, bringing tears, and staining the snow with blood. He completes his war prayer with a statement about the humble and contrite hearts of those who ask God's blessings. The congregation pauses in silence. He asks if they still desire what they have prayed for. "Ye have prayed it; if ye still desire it, speak! The messenger of the Most High waits." We are now at the final page of Twain's book. The congregation's response is simple and abrupt. As suggested previously, the old stranger was clearly a social deviant. In Twain's words: "It was believed afterward that the man was a lunatic, because there was no sense in what he said."

The stranger in *The War Prayer* directly threatens the normal, healthy, patriotic, and blood-lusting beliefs of the embattled congregation. Yet it is with ease that they contain and control this threat. They do not have to take seriously the chilling implications of his sermon. Their religious and patriotic senses are protected from his disturbing assault. Why? The reason is as simple as their response. They believe that he is a lunatic. They believe that he is a deviant. By classifying the old man as a deviant they need not listen to him. The congregation's beliefs are protected, even strengthened. The lunatic's beliefs are safely controlled. *The War Prayer* is thus a story of how some people imagine other people to be "deviant" and thereby protect or isolate themselves from those whom they fear and from that which challenges the way in which "normal" social life is organized. It is a story of how people convince themselves of what is normal by condemning those who disagree. It is a story of both deviance and social control. So is the book you are reading.

CONTROLLING NORMAL AND DEVIANT SOCIAL LIFE

The story of deviance and social control is a battle story. It is a story of the battle to control the ways people think, feel, and behave. It is a story of winners and losers and of the strategies people use in struggles with one another. Winners in the battle to control "deviant acts" are crowned with a halo of goodness, acceptability, normality. Losers are viewed as living outside the boundaries of social life as it ought to be, outside the "common sense" of society itself. They may be seen by others as evil, sleazy, dirty, dangerous, sick, immoral, crazy, or just plain deviant. They may even come to see themselves in such negative imagery, to see themselves as *deviants*.

Deviants are only one part of the story of deviance and social control. Deviants never exist except in relation to those who attempt to control them. Deviants exist only in opposition to those whom they threaten and those who have enough power to control against such threats. The outcome of the battle of deviance and social control is this. Winners obtain the privilege of organizing social life as they see fit. Losers are trapped within the vision of others. They are labeled deviant and subjected to an array of current social control practices. Depending upon the controlling wisdom at a particular moment in history, deviants may be executed, brutally beaten, fined, shamed, incarcerated, drugged, hospitalized, or even treated to heavy doses of tender loving care. But first and foremost they are prohibited from passing as normal women or men. They are branded with the image of being deviant.

When we think of losers in the battle to control acceptable images of social life, it may seem natural to think of juvenile gang members, serial killers, illegal drug users, homosexuals, and burglars. Indeed, common sense may tell us that such people are simply deviant. But where does this common sense come from? How do we come to know that certain actions or certain people are deviant, while others are "normal"? Do people categorized as deviants really behave in a more dangerous fashion than others? Some people think so. Is this true?

Think of the so-called deviants mentioned above. Are their actions truly more harmful than the actions of people not labeled as deviants? In many cases the answer is no. Consider the juvenile gang. In recent years the organized drug dealing and violent activities of gangs have terrorized people living in poverty-stricken and racially segregated urban neighborhoods. Gang-related deviance has also been the focal point for sensational media stories and for social control policies ranging from selective "stop-and-search" police tactics to the building of new prisons and (in Los Angeles) even the criminalization of alleged gang members' parents.

But what about the people most responsible for the oppressive inner-city conditions that lie at the root of many gang-related activities? What about the "gangs" of bankers whose illegal redlining of mortgage loans blocks the investment of money in inner-city neighborhoods? What about the "gangs" of corporate executives whose greed for short-term profits has led to the "offshoring" of industrial jobs to "underdeveloped" countries where labor is cheap and more easily exploitable? Aren't the actions of such respectable people as costly as, if less visible than, the activities of most inner-city gangs? Yet, there is an important difference: unlike gangs of elite deviants, inner-city youths have little or no real access to dominant institutions in which contemporary power is concentrated.

A related question may be posed concerning serial killers. The violence of serial killers haunts our nightly news broadcasts. Indeed, the seemingly random character of serial killings —although they are most commonly directed against women and children—instills a deep and alarming sense of dread within society as a whole. Nevertheless, the sporadic violence of serial murderers, no matter how fearful, is incomparable in terms of both scope and number to the much less publicized "serial killings" perpetrated by United States-supported *death squads* in countries such as El Salvador and Guatemala. The targets of such death squads are typically people who dare to speak out in the name of social justice. From 1980 to 1991, for instance, approximately 75,000 Salvadoran civilians were secretly killed or made to "disappear" by paramilitary executioners. Why is it that such systematic murders are rarely acknowledged as true serial killings? Why, moreover, do such cold-blooded killings provoke so little U.S. public outrage in comparison to the attention given to the isolated violence of individual murderers, such as Ted Bundy or Jeffrey Dahmer? Is it because the people who authorize them are respectable persons, sometimes even publicly elected officials? Is it because, though we feel vulnerable to other serial killers, we ourselves—at least those of us who are white, male, North American, and economically privileged to live at a distance from the violence that historically envelops the daily lives of others—feel protected from death squads?

Similar questions might be raised about drug users. When we speak of the abuse of drugs, why do we often think only of the "controlled substances" that some people use as a means of achieving psychic escape, altered consciousness, and/or bodily pleasure? True, we as individuals and as a society may pay a heavy price for the abuse of such drugs as cocaine and heroin. But what about other—legal—substances that many of us are "on" much of the time? Some of these drugs are even more dangerous than their illicit counterparts. In addition to alcohol, tobacco, chemical food additives, and meat from animals that have been fed antibiotics and hormones, our society openly promotes the use of prescription and over-the-counter drugs for everything from losing weight, curing acne, and overcoming anxiety to building strong bodies, fighting depression, and alleviating allergies caused by industrial pollution. Certainly many of these substances have their salutary effects and may help us adjust to the world in which we live. However, even legal substances can be abused; they too can be dangerous. The effects can be direct, jeopardizing an individual's health or fostering addiction, or they can be indirect and more insidious. For example, consider the role drugs play in creating and sustaining our excessively image-conscious, age-conscious environment and in promoting our tendency to avoid dealing with personal conflicts and everyday problems in a thoughtful and responsible manner. Also—not to belabor the issue—just think of what we are doing to our planet, to our future, with our use of pesticides, fertilizers, and other industrial products and by-products. To raise such concerns is not to claim that legal drugs are more dangerous than illegal drugs, but simply to suggest that what is officially labeled illegal or deviant often has more to do with what society economically values than with whether the thing is physically harmful per se.

Further consider the actions of sexist heterosexuals. Such persons may routinely mix various forms of sexual harassment with manipulative patriarchal power and an intolerance of alternative forms of sexual intimacy. Despite the harm these heterosexist individuals cause, they are far less likely to be labeled deviant than are gay, lesbian, or bisexual lovers who caress one another with affection. The same goes for corporate criminals, such as the executives recently implicated in the savings and loan scandal. The stealthy acts of such white-collar criminals have cost the U.S. public as much as $500 billion. Yet the elite deviance of the upper echelon of rule breakers is commonly less feared than are the street crimes of ordinary burglars and robbers.

From the preceding examples it should be evident that many forms of labeled deviance are not more costly to society than the behaviors of people who are less likely to be labeled deviant. Why? The answer proposed in this book is that labeled deviants are viewed as such because they threaten the control of people who have enough power to shape the way society imagines the boundary between good and bad, normal and pathological, acceptable and deviant. This is the crux of the effort to understand the battle between deviance and social control. Deviance is always the flip side of the coin used to maintain social control.

THEORETICAL PERSPECTIVES

The book you are reading tells the story of one important aspect of the battle between deviance and social control. It is a story about the telling of other stories. It is a historical and sociological story about the invention and use of various theoretical perspectives on deviance. Such perspectives guide the ways we both think about and act toward deviance. Throughout history, priests, philosophers, politicians, police, therapists, activists, social scientists, and others have produced a variety of perspectives on these matters. This book will examine the dominant theoretical imagery, research strategies, and practical control policies associated with nine perspectives which have, at various points in time, captured the theoretical imagination of western society.

All theoretical stories of deviance are told from historically specific standpoints. They embody the perspectives of particular authors within contradictory and often politically charged social contexts. The words you are reading are no exception. In an examination of the social contexts in which theories about deviance are produced and consumed, two issues become particularly relevant: the disciplinary character of various perspectives and the relationship between each theoretical framework and social power.

Disciplinary Images of Deviance: Toward an Interdisciplinary Perspective

There are today numerous specialists in the study and control of deviance, professionals who provide expert opinions regarding the causes, consequences, and cures of nonconformity. Not all such specialists view deviance in the same way. Indeed, specialists often divide their vision along disciplinary lines. Psychiatrists, sociologist, psychologists, criminologists, medical researchers, and other specialists frequently present divergent and even contradictory images of deviance. In this sense, images of deviance are commonly organized according to the selective vision of the disciplines in which specialists are trained. The images of deviance which someone is trained to see in the police academy vary greatly from those learned in medical school, in the psychology lab, the historical archive, the anthropological field study, the seminary, or the sociology classroom. Each of these sites of training may literally discipline the perceptions, moral judgments, and controlling outlooks of people who study deviance. This point is well illustrated in the following poem:

The Sociology Room
   by Theresa Burns

In the sociology room the children learn
that even dreams are colored by your perspective.

I toss and turn all night.

   The overspecialized division of theoretical images between competing disciplines is unfortunate. Some of the most fertile insights about deviance are those born in the cracks between disciplinary perspectives. There we are forced to confront such things as the rich and complex relationships between material and spiritual forces; between the economy and culture; between life today and life yesterday; between the body, the mind, and the social environment; or between society as we know it and society as it is organized in other places and times. Because of these things I have tried in this book to draw upon the diverse viewpoints of numerous disciplines. This is true in terms of the topics selected for study and the materials used to examine these topics. The topics, nine distinct theoretical images of deviance and social control, span the concerns of several disciplines: theology, law, medicine, psychology, anthropology, social work, special education, psychiatry, and sociology.
   The materials used to examine these diverse theoretical images are also drawn from numerous disciplines. I have been trained as a sociologist, but in reading this book you will learn that I place great value on insights gathered from other, related fields of study. Throughout, I have attempted to combine the vision of sociology with that of history. Other perspectives are used as well, those listed above and some that are considered more as "arts" than "sciences." In referring to materials from poetry, films, music, novels, paintings, I mean to do more than provide cute "arty" examples. By pointing to parallels between the images of deviance produced by scientific experts and those portrayed by various sorts of artists, I mean to suggest that both types of imagery arise out of a pool of common experience—the experience of people in history attempting to make sense of the long human struggle for control over ways of thinking, feeling, and behaving.

Power-Related Images of Deviance:
A Deconstructive Viewpoint on Theory

In addition to interdisciplinary concerns, this text is guided by the deconstructive viewpoint of a *power-reflexive* perspective. This is a critical approach to deviance, rooted in the recognition that every act of naming, theorizing, or translating lived experience into language is, by its very nature, also an act of exclusion, displacement, or sacrifice. In other words, when you or I rel _____ theoretical story about an experience, certain aspects of that experie _____ singled out while others are marginalized, silenced, or made unthi _____ me
   The ability to discriminate between different interpretations _____ ries event is part of the constructive power of any theoretical pra _____ What inevitably frame what we perceive in certain ways but n _____

makes a power-reflexive perspective deconstructive is its attempt to situate its own claims to knowledge as themselves contingent upon their theorists' personal and historical relations to power. This is to act upon the recognition that all theoretical constructions, including power-reflexive theoretical constructions, are never divorced from the complex and contradictory scenes of power in which they are materialized in certain ways but not others. In this way, a power-reflexive viewpoint attempts to work with, rather than suppress, the awareness that the observer (or theorist) always plays an active role in the selective framing of meaningful knowledge.

Using a power-reflexive approach involves inquiring not only about the dynamics of deviance and its control but also about how theorists' own social positioning may influence the kinds of questions they ask and the range of answers they imagine as possible. Does it make a difference that most influential theories of deviance have been constructed by economically advantaged, selectively educated, and heterosexually oriented white men working in prestigious university settings or well-funded research institutes? If theories about nonconformity were constructed by people whom society labels as deviants rather than by others who fear and attempt to control deviants, how different might the resulting conceptual understandings be?

Theoretical perspectives on deviance are never neutral scientific matters. They are always political as well as scientific concerns, connected to the historical organization of both power and knowledge. Who gains and who loses as certain perspectives take on the accent of truth? To ask this question is to begin theorizing, not only about deviance, but also about how various theories of nonconformity contribute to or challenge existing relations of power. When deviance is opposed by individuals in power, it is because deviance threatens the way things are. Sometimes this threat is economic. It affects the social organization of material resources. At other times deviance may threaten the dominant organization of sexual, spiritual, racially marked, or culturally specific resources. At all times it is political. By this I mean that deviance affects the ways that power is socially organized and used.

The recognition that all theories of deviance are also political theories means that certain segments of society are likely to prefer some theoretical perspectives over others. Thus, it is no surprise that scholars who believe in the desirability of a particular political order may view deviance very differently from the way people who think the same order is unjust view it. Indeed, individuals who fit comfortably into an existing political system typically seek to explain deviance so as to more efficiently control deviant people. Such scholars may be well rewarded for their work. They may receive lucrative research grants and prestigious chairs in elite universities. Others, who are less comfortable with the way things are, may find their theoretical viewpoints less profitable. Persons who conceptualize deviance as a symptom of [socia]l inequality may encounter difficulty in obtaining adequate research [grants,] publication outlets, and classrooms to teach in.

[How] do you view our society? How do your professors and fellow stu[dents vie]w the current political order? Such power-reflexive questions are discussed at length in Chapter 11. They are raised here only to preview some of the issues presented throughout the book. At first glance, such concerns may seem ridiculously complex. Yet, upon further reflection, I believe they suggest the simplest of sociological truths: how you and I construct ideas about deviance is at all times contingent upon the scenes of power in which we find ourselves in history. In our society such scenes are typically hierarchical. They are dramatized by social inequality. They support the power of men over/against women, whites over/against nonwhites, and people who have greater economic resources over/against people who are impoverished.

It is within such contradictory social scenes that we come to *partially* theorize problems posed by deviance and its control. I am here using the term *partial* in a dual sense. On one hand, I mean to suggest that all forms of knowledge are forever incomplete and that even the most truthful theories will be haunted by the shadows of what they leave out. This in no way implies abandonment of an ongoing search for scholarly objectivity. The materials presented in this book are intended to aid our search for objectivity. They do so, not by pretending that we can become fully detached from political commitments, but by systematically exploring the ways that our inevitable political attachments filter how we perceive deviance. Thus, in searching for objectivity we must also consider the ways that objective standards are themselves partially shaped by the changing historical contexts in which they are produced.

Our investigations are *partial* in a second sense as well. They are partial because, as suggested above, they cannot escape being political. By directing attention to some things but not others, all theories politically empower (if only temporarily) certain viewpoints over others. To work with, rather than deny, the *partiality of theory* is a challenge for all students of deviance and social control. To accept this challenge means that we must be vigilant about the ways in which our own social positions both shape and are shaped by what we study. This demands a willingness to continually revise our theoretical viewpoints in accordance with what we learn and unlearn. Otherwise the end point of our scholarly journey will be no different from its beginning. How will you respond to such a power-reflexive challenge? It is my hope that you will develop both a historically informed perspective on some of the most powerful ways of conceiving deviance and a reflexive (if partial) theoretical viewpoint of your own.

Uneasy Questions: Substantive and Personal Concerns

There is little escape from the questions raised in the preceding p'
Whether we are dealing with a strange-acting roommate, an unfaithf' ce,
a frightening mugger, or a politician promising to support the deat' arsh
we are confronted daily with questions of deviance and the quite
realities of social control. Nor are such questions easy. In f' In subse-
uneasy. They are uneasy in two senses. They are uneas'
about what causes deviance and its control are diffict'

quent chapters we will examine a range of proposed answers. Some place the burden of deviance on the free choice of nonconformists. Others view deviance as biologically or psychologically determined. Another views it as something which is learned. Still another sees deviance as primarily a problem of overly repressive social control. Which, if any, of these views are correct? By what standards is correctness measured? The task before us is an uneasy one. It requires that we dig deeply into the social, political, and economic landscapes out of which images of deviance are born and upon which they implant their vision of social control.

What are the major perspectives that humans have used to make sense of deviance and to make sensible certain programs of social control? Where do these perspectives come from? Like acts of deviance and strategies of social control, theoretical images are produced at certain moments of history. Put into practice, they create history as well. What are their consequences? How well have they stood the tests of time, experience, and systematic research? How exactly have they been translated into social control policy and practice? What are their social, political, or economic implications? What should we think of them? Are they sound or unproven, helpful or useless, good or bad? These are central substantive questions which will occupy us during our journey through this book. They are not easy questions to answer. They require that we combine questions of theory with questions of research and practice.

Questions about deviance and social control are uneasy at a second level as well—the level of our own personal choices, feelings, and political commitments. At this level, questions about deviance and social control challenge us to go beneath our surface thoughts and feelings, to become reflective and critical about things we have come to take for granted as acceptable and things we oppose or are even repulsed by. How is it that we have come to accept or reject certain ways of thinking, feeling, and acting? How have we been influenced or shaped by the processes which promote social control and/or deviance? What are the consequences for others and for ourselves of living within the confines of our present social, economic, and political realities?

How do we benefit or lose by accepting or deviating from the dominant realities of our time? How are the lives of others directly or indirectly influenced by the way we presently endorse normality and oppose deviance? Could we do better? Should we seek to alter the images of deviance produced in the context of present social, political, and economic arrangements? Would we be deviants if we did? This is the second set of uneasy questions that confront us. These questions will not and should not make us feel comfortable. They ask us not only about who we are but about whom we could me as well.

uneasy nature of our questions about deviance and social control is
m. It is not an uncommon experience for the serious student of such
abo experience an initial sense of dizziness, a sense of lost innocence
tural" character of things that were previously taken for granted

as being simply deviant. If you are unwilling to risk having this discomforting experience, stop reading now. If, on the other hand, you are willing to examine critically the simultaneous formation of deviant and normal realities, including the ways that your own personal realities have been shaped by the ever-present processes of social control, the end experience can be quite exhilarating.

Our worlds can become wider and deeper. This expansion will lead behind and below the ordinary surface of everyday social life by taking a hard look both at deviants—who they are and what they do—and at control processes—who or what gets controlled, how, and why. This expansion can provide us with the freedom of greater personal and social movement. Some of the old, "seemingly natural" binds, bonds, taboos, and rules may loosen up. This new awareness may permit us greater space within which to celebrate the dance that is human life. It may also present us with new senses of human responsibility for our actions and the actions of our fellow deviants and controllers alike. Now that I have said all this, it may be useful to provide a brief overview of the form and content of the present book. I will begin with some additional thoughts on the meaning of theoretical perspectives and their relationship to the study and control of deviance.

Conceiving and Controlling Deviance

Any "theory" of deviance is much more than a set of abstract notions about its causes, nature, and consequences. . . . An image of deviance determines one's action in concrete instances. It underlies the individual's pronouncements and it even determines what he considers deviant.

J.L. Simmons[3]

I walk into the darkened room. It is late and I am weary. I click on the light. From the shadows leans a coiled shape. A snake poised to strike! I jump back, grabbing for something to ward off the attack. My eyes blink. I look again. My frozen posture yields to a sigh of relief. I laugh. A snake? The coiled object is simply my garden hose. How could I have forgotten that I left it there? Its sight sent me into such a state of alarm. Only now do I recognize the tension that had gripped my whole body, the hammer that I had reflexively clenched in my fist. Why had I perceived the hose as a snake? Perhaps it was the mood I was in, the movie I just saw, or my apprehension about tomorrow. Whatever it was, once I defined the object as a snake, as a danger, I instantaneously mobilized my defenses against it.

The term *theoretical perspective* may sound rather abstract and boorishly academic. It is, however, no more abstract than the snake in the preceding narrative. Theoretical perspectives are ways of naming, ways of conceptually ordering our senses of the world. They are tools with which we decide what we experience, why something is the way that it is, and how we might act or react. Having defined the shape as a snake, I direct my action toward it in a particularly defensive manner. Why? Because coiled snakes are dangerous to one's health. The coiled shape was, from my perspective, a real danger that demanded defense. Cast into another perspective, its meaning and my actions toward it change. This was the case when I redefined it as a hose. The shape didn't change. What changed was my perspective on it. That change made all the difference.

Theoretical perspectives provide us with an image of what something is and how we might best act toward it. They name something as this type of thing and not that. They provide us with the sense of being in a world of relatively fixed forms and content. Theoretical perspectives transform a mass of raw sensory data into understanding, explanations, and recipes for appropriate action. Without them we would be lost in space and time. Everything would be undefined, in flux, without order, chaotic. Without theoretical perspectives we would have no control over what we experience. Such chaos is the stuff of nightmares. In a nightmare, terrifying changes of perspective are beyond our control. Our kind mother becomes a vampire, our pet dog a hideous monster, our room a darkened void in space. Without the guidance of theoretical perspectives we are lost, unable to define, explain, or know how to act toward the objects of our experience.

The link between theoretical perspectives and the sense of having control over a world of ordered experience is important. To have a theoretical perspective on something, to name it in a certain fashion, is the first step in gaining control over it. To cast something into a theoretical perspective is to control it by restricting it to being a certain type of thing. By its being named a snake, the coiled object was trapped in the theoretical imagery in which I conceived it. For the moment it could be nothing else. It was caught in a web of names: frozen in a perspective. In the words of philosopher Jean-Paul Sartre, to cast something into a theoretical perspective is "to catch living things in the trap of phrases." Describing this naming process as one of "persistent illusion," Sartre suggested that by combining words ingeniously, "the object would get tangled up in the signs. I would have hold of it."[4]

Sartre may have correctly described the illusionary quality of theoretical perspectives. They are nonetheless powerful illusions. They exert control over that which they name. This, biblical scholars inform us, is the reason that the God of the Old Testament never revealed his name to his followers. He was known only as the unnameable Yahweh or "he who is." He refused to be cornered into a name by the followers who professed to be his servants.

Deviants have been less fortunate. Throughout history they have been the subject of numerous namings, numerous theoretical perspectives. Each provided explanatory images regarding why people deviate and images of control, images suggesting strategies for restoring conventionality. Some of these theoretical perspectives have been simple, relatively unreflected upon, and, for the most part, taken for granted. They may be called *commonsense theoretical perspectives*.

There are today a variety of competing commonsense perspectives on deviance. As J. L. Simmons points out, one may alternatively consider the deviant as sick, as a boat rocker, as immoral, as statistically rare, as a hero, or as just another human being. Each perspective sheds light on some aspects of deviance while casting a shadow on others. Moreover, most people think and act on the basis of different perspectives in different concrete situations. According to Simmons, "a person will usually have different attitudes toward different kinds of deviants; he sees the drug addict as sick, the promiscuous woman as depraved, the rowdy neighborhood youth as a disturber of the peace, his spiritualist friend as curiously different, the hobo he passes as semiheroic, and his adulterous brother as understandably human and male."[5]

While recognizing the importance of commonsense theoretical perspectives, the present book is concerned with another type of theoretical imagery—the *formal theoretical perspective*. Formal theoretical perspectives are generally more elaborate, more explicitly stated, and subject to a continuous process of refinement and validation. It is upon formal theoretical perspectives that society erects its public policies for dealing with deviance. While this is true, one should not exaggerate the distinction between common sense and formal theories. These two ways of theorizing are at all times interrelated. Formal theories grow out of and feed back upon theories grounded in the "common sense" of a particular period in history. The various spiritual, social, political, and economic forces affecting common sense influence and are influenced by the formal theories of a given age. As a result, in examining formal theories we must remain attentive to the various ways that such perspectives are grounded in the material and spiritual realities of everyday social existence.

Formal Theories of Deviance in the West

We all have opinions. Where do they come from? Each day seems like a natural fact and how we think changes how we act.

Jon King and Andrew Gill[6]

Any one human act can be conceptualized in terms of literally hundreds of formal theoretical perspectives. Each names the act in a particular way, directing attention to certain of its aspects while selectively ignoring others. Consider the police officer blowing a whistle. This act could be conceptualized in terms of physical principles explaining the generation of whistle sound waves, biological principles of human breath exhalation, psychological principles associated with a need to assert authority, anthropological principles suggesting the cultural meaning of whistle blowing among advanced primates in North America, sociological principles related to the norms governing police-citizen encounters, etc. This list could go on and on. The same can be said of perspectives on deviance and social control.

Throughout the remainder of this book we shall take an in-depth look at what I believe to be nine of western society's more important theoretical perspectives on deviance and control. Each offers a distinctive theoretical image of what deviance is, how it can best be studied, and how it should be controlled. Why nine perspectives? There is nothing magical about the number. This is simply how I have categorized, or lumped together, the major strands of thought, study, and action directed regarding deviance and social control. Had I arranged these matters somewhat differently, perhaps we would be talking about four, twelve, or twenty perspectives. Several of the nine perspectives contain a variety of subthemes or subperspectives. Each is considered in somewhat chronological fashion. The first, the supernatural or demonic perspective, is certainly the oldest way of making sense out of nonconformity. The last, a synthesis of several critical viewpoints, is perhaps the most controversial of perspectives today. Yet there is considerable overlap. They are ordered in terms of the general time periods in which each emerged as influential or dominant. Each, however, is still alive and important in today's world.

Why consider only western images of deviance? The choice is purely pragmatic. I am writing primarily for an audience of American and western European students. As such I am writing about the perspectives that have been used to conceive and control deviance in the times and places that are closest to home. To include perspectives originating in the historical lives of Asian, African, and other nonwestern peoples would require a volume much larger than this one. If, by chance, this book should encourage some reader to explore comparative or cross-cultural theoretical developments, I trust that we would all be richer for the experience. On the other hand, there are good practical reasons why nonwestern readers might be interested in this story of western perspectives on deviance. In the hearts and minds of western colonizers, imperialists, and missionaries, these perspectives have frequently been used to control the behaviors of indigenous peoples the globe over.

HOW THIS BOOK IS ORGANIZED

The next ten chapters explore competing images of the deviant and how she or he might be controlled. Each image is attached to a constellation of theoretical research and practical human concerns. Of what do these images consist? Where do they come from? To whom do they appeal? How do they get translated into research? How are they related to practical social control policy? How useful are they in terms of research, policy, and the promotion of a just human order? These are the central questions raised in each of the following chapters.

The nine perspectives on deviance and control cover a wide range of thought and action. Each is considered with three general objectives in mind:

(1) describing the basic theoretical imagery, research strategies, and social control policies associated with the perspective; (2) locating the perspective within a general sociohistorical framework, and (3) developing a sense of critical evaluative thinking regarding the perspective's strengths and weaknesses.

Basic Theoretical Imagery, Research Strategies, and Control Policies   An in-depth description of these issues is the primary objective of this book. Remember that the way we look at deviance shapes our reaction to it. This is true in terms of both public policy and personal response. Deviance is not one thing. It is as many things as there are ways of looking at it. The same is true for methodological strategies for identifying and studying deviance. The same is true for social control.

As suggested previously, how we conceive of deviance influences and is influenced by our methods of research and our ideas about appropriate strategies of social control. Each of the perspectives discussed in this book is aligned with a particular methodology for identifying and studying deviance. Each is also associated with a unique vision of social control. A detailed description of the theory, methods, and control policies related to the particular perspective is the first objective of each of the following chapters.

Sociohistorical Context   Different perspectives have dominated different periods in history. What factors contribute to the popularity or predominance of one perspective over another? How is it that each perspective remains influential today? Perspectives do not live or die on their scientific merits alone. Some fit better into particular historical constellations of political, economic, cultural, and social forces. Others are rejected precisely because they do not. To adequately understand the development and acceptance of a given perspective we must locate its emergence and use within a particular social-historical landscape. Why does it blossom in the soils of one landscape and languish in another? This is a second objective of the following chapters—to provide a historical framework in which to view theoretical images of deviance and the research and control strategies with which they are connected.

Development of the "Conceptual Tools" of Critical Assessment   Competing perspectives on deviance may be valued highly by the people who advocate them. This does not mean that each is equally valuable as a tool for research, an instrument of public policy, or a contributor to a just human order. Each has its strengths and weaknesses, its theoretical, methodological, and practical advantages and disadvantages.

Which is best? I cannot answer this for you. Some perspectives you will like. Others you will not. The important thing is to develop an informed critical sense of your own. I will try to assist you by evaluating what I believe to be the merits and drawbacks of each perspective. My own preferences will undoubtedly shine through. I have attempted to ground these preferences in sound logic and an assessment of all the available evidence. It is my hope that you will do the same.

I will not tell you what to think about this approach to deviance. There are too many people telling you that already. Day in and day out we are bombarded with their opinions. The television, radio, newspaper, classroom, dormitory, and workplace are full of messages about why people should act in a certain fashion and what happens to the deviants who don't. Campaigning politicians, concerned parents, teachers, landlords, bosses, and lovers all hit us with similar messages. They tell us who and what is considered deviant, and why deviance is to be controlled in some specific way.

How are we to think, feel, and act about such matters? As mentioned previously, there is no easy answer to this question. Yet, think, feel, and act we must. We must make decisions about deviance and its control. If we don't, others will make them for us. The third objective of the following chapters involves learning a critical approach to such decision making. As you adopt this approach, the task of evaluating various perspectives will become yours as well as mine. We may agree. We may not. If you believe my analysis is correct, it will be because you have thoughtfully arrived at the same conclusion. If you disagree, your dissent will be similarly grounded. As author and reader we will enter into a dialogue that is informed, responsible, and articulate.

With these things in mind, let us begin our journey into competing images of deviance and control. Our consideration of each perspective is divided into five sections: (1) basic theoretical image, (2) dominant strategies for identifying and/or studying deviance, (3) related strategies of social control, (4) the perspective today, and (5) an assessment of the adequacy of the perspective. We will start with the "demonic perspective." This perspective envisions deviance as sin and social control as a matter of religious duty.

NOTES

1 Thomas Merton, "A Devout Meditation in Memory of Adolph Eichmann," as excerpted in Edward Rice, *The Man in the Sycamore Tree: The Good Times and Hard Life of Thomas Merton*, Doubleday, Garden City, N.Y., 1970, p. 89.
2 All the excerpts from Twain's parable are taken from Mark Twain, *The War Prayer*, Harper & Row, New York, 1970.
3 J. L. Simmons, *Deviants*, Glendessary, Berkeley, Calif., 1969, pp. 12–13.
4 Jean-Paul Sartre, *The Words*, Braziller, New York, 1964, p. 184.
5 Simmons, *Deviants*, p. 24.
6 Jon King and Andrew Gill, lyrics from "Why Theory?" Gang of Four album, *Solid Gold*, 1981.

Sin   By Stephen Pfohl

CHAPTER 2

THE DEMONIC PERSPECTIVE: *Otherworldly Interpretations of Deviance*

I have seen the grim statistics on divorce, broken homes, abortion, juvenile delinquency, promiscuity and drug addiction. I have witnessed firsthand the human wreckage and the shattered lives that statistics can never reveal in their totality. I am convinced that we need a spiritual and moral revival in America if America is to survive the twentieth century.

The Reverend Jerry Falwell[1]

Pilate went back into the palace and called Jesus to him. "Are you King of the Jews?" he asked. . . . "Indeed I am a King," Jesus replied; "the reason for my birth and the reason for my coming into the world is to witness to the truth. Every man who loves truth recognizes my voice." . . . To which Pilate retorted, "What is 'truth'? . . . Won't you speak to me? Don't you realize that I have the power to set you free, and the power to have you crucified?" "You have no power at all against me," replied Jesus, "except what was given to you from above."

John 18:33, 37–38; 19:10–11

INTRODUCTION

On February 16, 1980, a fight broke out between Arne Johnson and his best friend, Alan Bono. The 19-year-old Johnson had gone over to Bono's house to help repair a broken radio. With him were his two teenage sisters and his girlfriend. Within a short time an event occurred which radically altered the course of Arne Johnson's life and ended the life of his friend. Alan had been drinking. He started talking rudely to the young women. Arne took offense. A fight broke out. A knife flashed—a 5-inch folding knife. It belonged to Arne Johnson. Alan Bono died. In the fall of 1981 Arne Johnson stood trial for Bono's death.[2]

The trial of Arne Johnson was a puzzling and dramatic event. I suppose any trial of a shy, gentle small-town Connecticut boy who had delivered papers and captured Little League trophies would be somewhat puzzling and dramatic. But Arne's trial was more puzzling and dramatic. This was not simply because he was known as "such a nice boy," an all-American boy, a boy who had once used his "Newsboy of the Year" prize money to buy his mother a much-needed secondhand car. Nor was it because he had been "such a religious boy," a boy who had been honored by his local minister for bringing in the most students to his Bible class. What made Arne Johnson's trial so puzzling and dramatic was the basis for his plea of not guilty. Without challenging the facts of the stabbing, Arne's attorney argued that he should not be held criminally responsible for Bono's death. Why? The reason, we are told, is because at the time of the stabbing Arne Johnson had been possessed by a demonic spirit.

A demonic spirit? This sounds like something out of a "made-for-TV" horror movie. So do the other "facts" of Arne's case. These involve what, in Connecticut, has become known as the strange case of the "Brookfield demons." The case begins in the home of the Glatzel family. Debbie Glatzel was Arne Johnson's girlfriend. Arne was around when Debbie's younger brother began acting strangely. The 11-year-old Glatzel reported seeing frightening apparitions. He had been helping Debbie move into her new apartment when he suddenly felt a shove from behind. When he turned around he saw the shape of an elderly man pointing an ominous finger in his direction. He heard the voice of the old man warning him to beware. The old man disappeared as quickly as he had come. The frightened boy asked his mother to take him home. Later that evening he experienced a second vision, this one more terrifying than the first. It was the old man again. This time he had cloven feet and was accompanied by two hideous-looking "helpers." The first appeared to have a bullet hole in his forehead. His face dripped with blood from the open wound. The second was a dark figure—burned and blackened. This nightmarish trio would return several times to frighten and harass the young Glatzel boy. They would shortly be joined by some forty other "demons."

Several weeks after seeing the initial apparitions, Debbie Glatzel's younger brother was plagued by all the classic symptoms that experts associate with demonic possession. Two such experts, psychic researchers Lorraine and Ed Warren, were recommended to the Glatzel family by their parish priest. The Warrens were well known in psychic circles for their previous investigations of the so-called Amityville Horror. During the first ten minutes of the Warrens' visit to the Glatzel home they heard loud knocking and banging beneath their feet. Within a short time they decided that the Brookfield case fit a known pattern of what they understood as demonic possession.

The Warrens joined with Catholic priests from the diocese of Bridgeport in trying to aid the afflicted 11-year-old boy. Arne Johnson also tried to help. He was there as the "possessed" child's symptoms multiplied. The child began to quote esoteric passages from Milton's *Paradise Lost*. The child had no prior knowledge of these texts. How is it that he recited them precisely? How was he able to report accurately on events that occurred in rooms beyond his sight and hearing? Was it the same way in which he foretold events that were yet to happen? He once told a young woman that the demons were going to "fix" her; that they were going to do something to her eye. The next day her own child "accidentally" poked his thumb into her eye, and she had to be taken to an emergency room for treatment. He told of an auto accident that subsequently occurred and accurately predicted that a neighborhood dog would be hit by a car. He also informed Arne Johnson that Arne was to die the next day. Arne fell out of a 70-foot tree. His fall was partly broken when his foot became ensnared in one of the branches. He was injured but did not die.

A team of Catholic priests performed four religious rituals aimed at freeing the boy from his possession. Arne Johnson was present at two of these ceremonies—a high mass celebrated at the Glatzel home and an all-night vigil conducted at a local convent. Johnson assisted in restraining the boy while his body shuddered under one or another of his strange "attacks." On one occasion he did more than that. He challenged the "demons" to substitute his body for that of the afflicted boy. According to Ed Warren, "He saw this little boy choking, strangling, being beaten and thrown across the room. He screamed out, 'Don't do it to him. Do it to me. Take me on. I'm stronger.' Nobody, not the priests nor the nuns nor Lorraine nor myself would ever say anything like that, because we know the consequences."[3]

The consequences—? According to the Warrens and other observers, Arne Johnson also began to display symptoms of possession. At least four times between August and the following February Johnson exhibited signs of "being taken over." One time he fell into a seizure of violent shaking. In another instance he smashed his fist through a chest of drawers. The next day he recalled nothing of the incident. A third time he was presented with a vision of a figure which proceeded to slap and shake him. The fourth time was the night of Alan Bono's murder. When Arne Johnson's case went to court, Ed and Lorraine Warren were prepared to testify that, at the time of his argument with Bono, Arne was again seized by demons and the demons directed his hand in the brutal stabbing of his friend.

The case of the Brookfield demons, including the murder of Alan Bono, is most extraordinary because it occurred in a time and place far from those in which demonic possession was viewed as a plausible interpretation of deviant behavior. Perhaps it would be less extraordinary if it had occurred during the Middle Ages or in bewitched Salem, Massachusetts, during the seventeenth century or in some tribal society which even today experiences the "reality" of the spirit world as equal to or greater than the "reality" of the natural world. In such contexts the "demonic perspective" functions as a powerful explanation of the causes, consequences, and control of deviant behavior. In our own western society such a perspective is apt to be viewed as little more than superstition.

It has been several centuries since western society operated under a "sacred canopy" of supernatural understanding. Historians of religious thought trace our own "breakthrough" into essentially secular, naturalistic, or nonreligious explanations of the world to a constellation of events between the fifteenth and nineteenth centuries. Such scholars point to the fracturing of a unitary Christianity under Protestantism, the spread of secular economic rationality under capitalism, the primacy of reason during the eighteenth-century Enlightenment, and the development of modern science and technology as forces of secularization.[4]

What does it mean to have a secularized as opposed to a supernatural or "demonic" view of the world? According to the sociologist Peter Berger, secularization refers to "the process by which sectors of society and culture are removed from the domination of religious institutions and symbols. . . . Put simply, this means that the modern West has produced an increasing number of individuals who look upon the world and their own lives without the benefit of religious interpretations."[5]

If western society has become increasingly secularized, why begin a consideration of theoretical perspectives on deviance with a perspective whose dominance is largely in the past? The answer is severalfold. First, as seen in the case of the Brookfield demons, our contemporary world is not entirely devoid of demonic or supernatural theories about what causes people to act deviantly. Additional evidence for this position is presented later in this chapter. Second, in order to fully appreciate the form and content of what are currently more acceptable or more plausible theories of deviance, it is important to understand that which went before and that against which these secular understandings do battle. Third, critics of certain modern secular perspectives have recently argued that some of these are little more than the same old demonic explanation under a new guise. In order to understand and evaluate such a critique we must first examine the nature of the demonic perspective in its original form.

THEORETICAL IMAGES

To go against the order of society as religiously legitimated . . . is to make a compact with the primeval forces of darkness.

Peter L. Berger[6]

The demonic perspective is the oldest of all known perspectives on deviance. It suggests that we look for the cause and cure of deviant behavior in the realm of the supernatural. Deviance is equated with sin. It is viewed as a transgression against the will of God (or the gods). According to the demonic perspective the human world is but a battleground for the forces of another, more powerful world—the world of the supernatural. We humans are pictured as constantly torn between the supernatural forces of good and evil. When we succumb to the influence of evil forces we are drawn into deviant behavior. This happens in one of two ways: through temptation or through possession.

The road of temptation is the first route to demonic deviance. Along this road we are seduced by the alluring temptations of evil. The biblical story of Adam and Eve's fall from grace into the domain of Satan is the prototype of all such seductions into deviance. Lured on by the promise of God-like knowledge, our biblical parents eat the forbidden fruit and are thereafter weakened and forever susceptible to the dark forces of evil. As the story goes, we inherit their weakness. Also seducible by the devil, we must fight a constant battle to stay on the straight and narrow path of the good.

The first road to demonic deviance, the road of temptation, is one in which we humans are afforded some measure of choice. We can, in principle, say no to Satan (or whichever demonic figure our particular religious tradition employs to symbolize the forces of evil). Yet, following our ancestral fall from grace, we are said to be weakened and seducible by the multiple forms taken by the devil—sloth, anger, lust, pride, envy, gluttony, greed, or however else one might catalogue the "deadly sins" of deviance.

The second road to demonic deviance is more determinant. This is the road of possession. A possessed person is believed to be literally taken over by the devil or by some evil spirit. Once possessed, a person may be viewed as no longer responsible—as no longer able to choose between good and evil, sin and conformity. But could an essentially good or innocent person ever become possessed? The demonic perspective is not entirely clear about this. It does suggest, however, that the possession of innocents may, on occasion, be possible. A case in point involves the outbreak of witchcraft in the Massachusetts Bay Colony in 1692. This case will be considered in greater detail later. For now it is sufficient to point out that the religious officials who attempted to control the manifestation of the devil in Salem made a clear distinction between a small cadre of possessed girls who had been "taken over" by Satan and the accused witches who were believed to have been seduced into acting as "mediums" or "handmaidens" for Satan's demonic mischief. The girls were to be given spiritual assistance. The witches were to be burned.

In summary, there are two roads to demonic deviance—temptation and possession. The first is less deterministic than the second. Yet, in neither does a deviant ever act entirely on his or her own. Behind every act of deviance lurks the devil. Viewed from this perspective, the deviant might quite literally employ the language of comedian Flip Wilson in proclaiming: "The devil made me do it."

One other thing should be considered when describing the theoretical image of deviance under the demonic perspective. This involves what might be called the "cosmic consequences" of any deviant act. From the demonic viewpoint, deviant acts are believed to harm more than a particular or immediate victim. Each act of sin or deviance is also a transgression against God. Beyond that, it is also an act against the whole order of nature itself, against the entire cosmos. Every creature in the cosmos—every plant, rock, animal, or fellow human—is affected by the deviant behaviors of others. In this sense the vested interests of all are clearly linked to the control of deviance. This sense of deviance as "cosmic disruption" is found in numerous religious and literary depictions. Deviance brings the storm or the shadow over the whole of the earthly world and human community.

In performances of Shakespeare's *Macbeth*, theatrical imagery effects are often used to convey this sense of the cosmic consequences of deviance. Macbeth and Lady Macbeth tragically succumb to the temptations of ambition and greed. They set out to kill King Duncan in order to gain his throne. In doing so, they not only assume the bloody stains of their own deviance but radically upset the whole balance of nature itself. As the murderous knife strikes, so does the sound of thunder. In the background we hear the terrified sounds of screeching horses and baying dogs. All of creation feels the consequences of this deviance. Peace and order will not be restored until the guilty pay the price for their demonic acts.

Instigated by the devil and affecting the entirety of the cosmos—these are the essential features of the demonic perspective. How are the perpetrators of such deviance to be identified and controlled? In examining these issues, the next two sections, after a brief side trip to present-day Africa, take a step backward into western history, back to a period in which the demonic perspective reigned supreme. The demonic perspective continues in the west today but not to the extent it did during the Middle Ages. Thus, my description of the identification and control of demonic deviance is drawn largely from past history.

IDENTIFYING DEMONIC DEVIANCE

Demonic Deviance among the Kabré

Anthropologist Raymond Verdier provides us with a fascinating account of what might be called the identification of demonic deviance among the Kabré tribe of northern Togo.[7] For the Kabré, justice means two things: conformity to the plan of the creating God, and respect for the God-given ways of tribal custom. The "justice of men" must then always reflect the "justice of God" in a society organized around what are predominantly supernatural beliefs. But how exactly is this form of justice accomplished? The Kabré employ a form of public trial or a tribunal of "notable elders" who attempt to hear evidence and reconcile disputes between tribal members who cannot settle allegations of wrongdoing in private. Judicial decisions, however, may not always be so simple. How is guilt assessed when alleged acts of deviance involve matters in which there are no visible witnesses? Of particular concern is witchcraft or the hurting of others by casting an evil spell.

When accusations of witchcraft are put forward, the tribe consults a diviner. Such a person is believed to possess a God-given "second sight" such that he or she can trace the origins of evil spirits and spells. The expert testimony of a diviner is, however, open to challenge. In this sense the role of the diviner is much like that of a psychiatrist in a contemporary criminal trial within our own society. The opinion of the diviner may be very damaging. Yet, if it is denied by the accused, the tribal judges must seek a clearer reading on deviance by consulting God. This is done by subjecting the accused to a very painful trial by ordeal. An accused person who overcomes this ordeal is declared innocent. One such diagnostic ritual consists of having the accused plunge his or her hand into a pan of blazing oil in an effort to retrieve an iron ring without being burned. Of the person who succeeds, it is said *bi li sa i*, "it got him out"; of the one who fails, *bi kpa i*, "it took him."

Discovering Medieval Deviance

The Kabré trial by ordeal closely resembles the inquisitional methods used to identify deviants during the medieval heyday of the demonic perspective within our own society. These pain-producing diagnostic techniques were once satirized on the popular television program *Saturday Night Live* by comedian Steve Martin. Dressed like a medieval monk and brandishing an array of weaponlike "tools" for discovering "evidence of the devil," Martin proceeded to inflict torture on a group of accused sinners. Laughable by today's standards, Martin's grotesque satire was not far from the "facts" of the trial by ordeal as once practiced in the name of God. Such ordeals relied upon the correct reading of supernatural signs provided by God to sort the good from the bad, deviants from the rest of the faithful. These identification strategies were often equivalent to or as painful as the punishment for deviance. This, however, was of little importance to a society immersed in otherworldly concerns.

Trial by ordeal quite frankly meant trial by torture. Such trials were presided over by priests or other ordained representatives of the divine will here on earth. Admissions of deviance were literally produced by the disembodiment of deviants from their present sinful state. The reactions of suspected deviants to the searing pain of inquisitorial torture were studied as a sign from above as to whether the accused was guilty of a particular act. While the guilty eventually cried out admissions, it was believed that God fortified the innocent to persevere during the ordeal of their diagnosis. Thus it was entirely possible that the innocent might ultimately be vindicated only by the steadfast endurance of pain until death.

While such torturous diagnostic practices may today seem horrific, during the demonic period there was nothing particularly sacred about the body. In a world which gave primacy to supernatural imagery there was little profit in preserving the body at the expense of the soul. The ordeal of subjecting the body to religious authority was symbolic of the true supernatural order of things. Thus, divinely ordained inquisitioners were carefully trained to "find the tenderest point through which to assail the conscience and the heart."[8] In the words of the historian H. C. Lea, they were "relentless in inflicting agony on body and brain; . . . using without scruple the most violent alternatives of hope and fear. . . . Yet through all this there shines the evident conviction that they were doing the work of God."[9]

Trial by battle was another method commonly used to identify demonic deviance during the Middle Ages. The image most associated with this strategy is that of two knights jousting. Since it was believed that the justice of God was mirrored in natural events, the good person would be victorious, while the deviant would fail. Strength in combat was thus a sign of innocence. Although trial by battle was reserved more for those of wealth than was trial by ordeal, both methods used natural means to achieve supernatural ends. Both served to diagnose the handiwork of the devil.

Discerning the Devil in Colonial America

While trial by ordeal was common in continental Europe, inquisitional techniques of extracting evidence of the devil were largely absent in England. There, and in the American colonies, a system of common law evolved which emphasized such things as trial by jury, separation of prosecution and judge, and the rights to confront one's accusers and to appeal a verdict of guilt. How then, during the reign of a demonic world view, did the British system identify the "hand of the devil"? An answer is provided by the historical record of the Salem witch trials of 1692.

The "facts" of the Salem case are clear evidence of the continued dominance of demonic theorizing right up until the end of the seventeenth century. The story begins in the colonial home of the Reverend Samuel Parris. There, several young girls (ages 9 to 20) spent play time with Tituba, a mysterious "kitchen slave" from Barbados who was reputedly skilled in the art of magic. The story ends with the deaths of twenty-two convicted witches. What exactly happened may never be known. What was alleged to have happened involves the gradual possession, or "taking over," of the young girls by a demonic spirit. "They would scream unaccountably, fall into grotesque convulsions, and sometimes scamper along on their hands and knees making noises like the barking of a dog."[10] Who was it that had conspired with the devil to cause such an outrage? Colonial magistrates demanded an answer. They implored the possessed maidens to identify their assailants.

The names Tituba, Sara Good, and Sara Osburne were spewed from the mouths of the possessed. One could not have imagined a more likely and more vulnerable trio of defendants: Tituba, the strange dark foreigner; Sara Good, the pipe-smoking, leather-faced village hag; Sara Osburne, a woman of higher social standing but also of scandalous reputation, a woman who had shocked the Puritan community of Salem by "living with a man" without being married to him. These three were brought to trial, convicted, sentenced to death, and executed. But the epidemic of witchcraft did not end there. More signs of the devil appeared. Animals died suddenly. Children were born dead. Good people, such as Ann Putnam, lost several children at birth. The search for more witches continued. The possessed girls were asked to name more names and did. Soon the whole Salem community was caught up in a mania of witches. The devil and his disciples were everywhere. Such deviants were to be identified and put to death. But how, lacking a tradition of inquisitional torture, were Puritan magistrates to properly sort out evidence of the devil?

Five types of evidence were accepted to identify the Salem witches. The first was a trial by clever test, if not exactly by painful ordeal. It involved making accused witches say the Lord's Prayer in public. Since witches were believed to say this prayer backward, it was believed that they would slip up when asked to say it in the correct God-fearing manner. Any slips of the tongue were then taken to mean that those tongues belonged to demonic deviants. A second form of evidence simply involved the testimony of those who attributed their own bad fortune to the demonic activities of the accused. A third directed examiners to search for "physical marks of the devil": warts, moles, scars, or other bodily imperfections through which the devil might have penetrated the alleged deviant. The fourth was confession of guilt. Of the hundreds of persons tried, *only* fifty confessed. Ironically they were among those who by their repentance were spared the gallows. Of the twenty-two who died (nineteen were put to death by formal execution, one was pressed to death after remaining mute before the inquiries of examiners, and two died in jail), none had publicly confessed. So much for this fourth form of "hard evidence." The fifth, the most commonly relied upon, entailed what has been described as "spectral evidence." This involved reports of persons who had supposedly seen "floating specters," or ghostly forms which had taken on the shape or appearance of one of the accused. The basis for this particular identification strategy was the belief that the devil cannot assume the shape of an innocent person.[11]

It is very unlikely that any of the five types of evidence mentioned above would be taken seriously in a court of law today. In fact, two of them (mistakes in saying the Lord's Prayer and contested accusations by afflicted parties) were precluded by Puritan officials themselves as the number of witch trials expanded into the hundreds. Two others (physical marks and confessions induced under a situation of great stress) also came to be viewed with suspicion. In actuality it seems that "spectral evidence" became the central tool used to diagnose witches as the trials dragged on to their deadly completion.[12] Can you imagine putting someone to death because of spectral evidence? In today's world someone who sees specters is likely to be put in a mental hospital, but this was far from the case during the reign of the demonic perspective. Spectral evidence was, after all, supernatural evidence, and this was the truest form of evidence available to God's community on earth.

The Confession

The Lateran Council of 1215 was of great significance in shaping the future of the demonic perspective. A centralized gathering of leading church officials, this "fatherly" assembly banned the use of trial by ordeal and battle as methods for determining the guilt or innocence of accused sinners. It also moved dominant western understandings of deviance in the direction of individualized rather than collective responsibility. This it did by instituting the sacrament of penance, or confession. This ritual paved the way for the focus on individual responsibility that would become a key aspect of classical theorizing during the eighteenth century. By shifting the locus of deviant action from the community to the mind of the sinner, confession altered the social and spiritual geography of rule breaking. It also fostered a modern sense of personal autonomy, freed from the cosmic interconnectedness that characterized demonic theorizing.

The ability and obligation of people to confess is today so common that it may be difficult to appreciate the historical importance of the cultural changes set in motion by the sacrament of penance. Indeed, as Michel Foucault points out, whether in the courtroom or in the bedroom, whether in a therapist's office or on a TV talk show, since the late Middle Ages the obligation to confess has become so widespread that "we no longer perceive it as the effect of a power that constrains."[13] The omnipresent confessing of crimes, secrets, and passions is no neutral matter. It is indicative of a powerful shift from group-centered to individually focused senses of moral responsibility.

SOCIAL CONTROL OF DEMONIC DEVIANCE

If your right eye leads you astray, pluck it out and throw it away; it is better for you to lose one of your members than that your whole body should be thrown on to the rubbish-heap.

Matthew 5:29

The demonic perspective differentiated little between various types of deviants. Insomuch as all were seen as demonically inspired, each (whether a murderer, an adulterer, or a heretic) was subject to the same general strategy of control—a religiously administered ritual of public punishment. The purpose of such punishment was to purge the sinner's body of traces of the devil and thereby to restore the body of the community as a whole to its proper relation to God. Rituals are highly patterned actions which, when performed correctly, connect people to a mythic or transcendental sense of what things are and should be, of what is real and how they should act in accord with that reality. Rituals of religious punishment remind participants of the supreme reality of God's will and, by purging evil, restore humans to their proper relationship as servants of the divine.

During the reign of medieval Christianity obedience to God meant obedience to the church. Priests acted as official mediators between God, the sinner, and a spiritual community afflicted with the devil. In presiding over the ritual sacrament of penance, priests granted God's forgiveness and prescribed punishments which cleansed an infested body of evil. Church officials also acted to prevent demonic temptations, particularly those associated with heresy and sins of the flesh. In the years following the Protestant Reformation, for instance, the Roman Catholic Church unleashed its army of Jesuits to combat heretics by a fearsome preaching of the papal gospel. So, likewise, was the spread of unorthodox religious thought countered by church censorship. Of particular importance was the papal Index of Prohibited Books, which forbade believers to tempt their eyes with devilish reading matter. No control policies, however, were as feared or as symbolically important as the supernatural sanctioning of physical punishment. Often intense, brutal, and searingly painful, the ritual execution of such punishments symbolized the supremacy of spirit over matter. Think of the imagery evoked by burning a demonically infested body. Burning was a form of punishment which reached its peak during the high point of demonically generated deviance—the Spanish Inquisition. Why? Burning evoked an image of hell as the ultimate resting place for unpurged sinners. The act of burning the heretic or infidel symbolized this aspect of the "true" nature of the supernatural world. Thus burning functioned as a "divine reflective punishment . . . to give the living a taste of hell before he passed on."[14]

Another symbolic aspect of religious punishment was found in the principle of *lex talionis*, or "an eye for an eye, a tooth for a tooth, stroke for stroke, burning for burning." This principle was used to justify the mutilation of sinners. Thus the thief had a hand cut off, while the penis of a rapist, the tongue of a liar, or the heart of a traitor might be ritually excised. Such punishments underscored the subordination of natural bodies to supernatural struggles between good and evil.

What would become of the demonic spirit which had previously lived within the body of the dead sinner? Fear of such spirits led to a variety of apotropaic rituals—rituals which accompanied the use of the death penalty and which served as a means of warding off evil spirits. Such rituals provided "practical" protection against spirits that might be lingering in or around the body of the condemned. They also served as symbolic reminders of the primacy of the supernatural.

Consider the apotropaic function of that particularly brutal punishment known as "breaking on the wheel." This form of purging may be traced back to the practice of *apotympanismos* in ancient Greece. After the deviant was pegged to a board with irons, an executioner proceeded to break all his or her major bones with a heavy metal bar. Later variations of the "sacred punishment" included such things as tying someone to the broad side of a wheel and then rolling it down an incline, and pegging a person to the ground and running him or her over with a spiked wheel. Why such elaborate means of death? Because in breaking the bones of a sinner one breaks the hold that an evil spirit exercises over an earthly body. As Graeme Newman suggests, "The bones are seen as the most enduring, lasting part of the body, so by breaking the bones it is believed the culprit's spirit will be prevented from getting around too easily."[15]

A similar logic has been used to explain such other practices as casting the ashes of a burned sinner to the wind, drawing and quartering, sinking a drowned body into a bog, staking a body into a fixed position, beheading, and even hanging. For instance, it was not until comparatively modern times that the body of a hanged deviant was taken down and buried. In a world enchanted by all kinds of spirits there was fear that demons within the body of the executed might seep into the earth and thereby endanger its fertility. Hence during the earliest periods of known hangings the dead body would remain swinging between heaven and earth until it decayed and was safely "returned to dust."[16]

Another symbolic consequence of religious punishment was the way in which certain supernaturally ordained control rituals provided a divine blessing for hierarchical class distinctions between humans. Compare the ritual of beheading with death by hanging. Beheading was largely reserved for offenders of the highest status. William the Conqueror first introduced this type of "noble punishment" into England when, in 1076, he ordered the execution of the earl of Northumberland. Over the next six centuries the lives claimed by beheading generally included the God-ordained elite of deviants. In 1644 Archbishop Laud actually petitioned to be beheaded rather than hanged. To behead someone is to strike him or her dead with a sword or an axe to the throat, both symbols of valor since ancient times. On the other hand, "Hanging and other lesser forms of execution were appropriate to a class that was held in disdain. . . . In contrast to beheading, throughout history being hanged has been a disgrace, particularly if one were also stripped naked."[17]

Public Executions: "Rituals of a Thousand Deaths"

The purgative and symbolic dimensions of demonic punishment were nowhere more evident than in that spectacle of spectacles—the public execution. This elaborate ceremony of religiously sanctioned pain was neither swift nor efficient. Known as the "ritual of a thousand deaths" it involved the application of purifying pain inch by inch to the demonically infested body, with death but the last step in the restoration of supernatural order.

Michel Foucault describes the torturous detail of one such execution.

Bouton, an officer of the watch, left us his account: "The sulphur was lit, but the flame was so poor that only the top of the hand was burnt, and that only slightly. Then the executioner, his sleeves rolled up, took the steel pincers, which had been especially made for the occasion, and which were about a foot and a half long, and pulled first at the calf of the right leg, then at the thigh, and from there at the two fleshy parts of the right arm; then at the breasts. Though a strong, sturdy fellow, this executioner found it so difficult to tear away the pieces of flesh that he set about the same spot two or three times, twisting the pincers as he did so. . . .

"After these tearings with the pincers, Demiens, who cried out profusely, though without swearing, raised his head and looked at himself; the same executioner dipped an iron spoon in the pot containing the boiling potion, which he poured liberally over each wound. Then the ropes that were to be harnessed to the horses were attached with cords to the patient's body. . . .

"Monsieur Le Breton, the clerk of the court, went up to the patient several times and asked him if he had anything to say. He said he had not; at each torment, he cried out, as the damned in hell are supposed to cry out, 'Pardon, my God! Pardon, Lord.' . . . Several confessors went up to him and spoke to him at length; he willingly kissed the crucifix that was held out to him; he opened his lips and repeated: 'Pardon, Lord.'

"The horses tugged hard, each pulling straight on a limb, each horse held by an executioner. After a quarter of an hour, the same ceremony was repeated and finally, after several attempts, the direction of the horses had to be changed, thus: those at the arms were made to pull towards the head, those at the thighs toward the arms, which broke the arms at the joints. This was repeated several times without success. He raised his head and looked at himself. Two more horses had to be added to those harnessed to the thighs, which made six horses in all. Without success.

". . . After two or three attempts, the executioner Samson and he who had used the pincers each drew out a knife from his pocket and cut the body at the thighs instead of severing the legs at the joints; the four horses gave a tug and carried the two thighs after them . . . ; then the same was done to the arms, the shoulders, the arm-pits and the four limbs; the flesh had to be cut almost to the bone, the horses pulling hard carried off the right arm first and the other afterwards.

"When the four limbs had been pulled away, the confessors came to speak to him; but his executioner told them that he was dead, though the truth was that I saw the man move, his lower jaw moving from side to side as if he were talking."[18]

Other Rituals of Religious Control: More Shame than Pain

While the ritual application of physical pain remained a primary symbol of social control during the demonic period, other control rituals were more representational in nature. These punishments symbolized the supernatural subjugation of the body without taking pain to its human limits.[19] Thus, the baker who short-weighted his loaves was punished by having bread tied around his neck, while a fishmonger convicted of selling bad fish might be fitted with a collar of decayed smelts. In medieval Europe heretics accused of advocating Judaism were forced to feed on pork in public, while gossiping "scolds" in the American colonies had their tongues cooled by a good public dunking. At other times scolds and such "mouthy" sinners as drunkards, swearers, and noisy schoolchildren were treated to the "scold's bridle," an iron cage placed over the head, with a sharp frontal plate, frequently spiked, protruding into the mouth. A remnant of this religiously inspired ritual of ridicule continued in Providence, Rhode Island, until the eighteenth century. There a "cleft stick" or "whispering stick" was inserted into the mouth of children caught swearing or talking in school.[20]

Other symbolic rituals of religious penance were self-imposed. These included rituals of mild self-degradation in which a penitent sinner might parade barefoot, clad only in a white sheet, publicly begging God's forgiveness. Other rituals, such as the brutal self-whippings of medieval flagellants, were far more dramatic. Most rites of public humiliation were less voluntary.

Like the shaved head or the "scarlet letter" placed over the garments of the adulterous woman or the **T** branded upon the forehead of the English thief, the shameful stigma of demonic deviance was forced upon the sinner as she or he journeyed through this world to the next. Yet, regardless of whether punishment was more painful or shameful, two additional elements of religious control were invariably present: a reliance upon centralized authority, and the local or community nature of control practice.

In the Name of Centralized Authority

The demonic perspective centralized the control of deviance in the hands of religious authorities. Divinely ordained officials administer ritual punishments that purge offenders of demonic influence and restore God's blessing upon the entire community of the faithful. Most traditional histories of social control view this centralization of the authority to punish as a progressive development. Prior to the rule of religious authority, harm was said to beget more harm, as the kin of an offended party retaliated against a deviant clan in a direct and often brutal manner. The practice of blood revenge could lead to a spiraling cycle of ad hoc violence and prolonged periods of social instability. With the institution of centralized religious authority, the primitive practice of feuding came to an end, or so the story is usually told. Religious laws restricted the arbitrary nature of revenge, while religious officials tempered the horrors of private bloodshed by granting "asylum" to persecuted rule breakers and declaring "the truce of god" (*treuga dei*), a temporary peace for fugitives from divine justice.

Today anthropologists recognize that these progressive consequences are only part of the story. Some things were lost as well as gained in the birth of centralized religious authority. Lost was a legacy of reconciliatory control rituals, used to solve problems in the "headless," or *acephalous*, societies which characterized the first 30,000 of our 40,000 years as the species Homo sapiens.[21] The rudimentary level of technology in these societies required the full-time work commitment of each member simply to secure the conditions of material survival for the group as a whole. In these collectively cooperative social units nobody was in charge; nobody was authorized to organize life for others. Power was reciprocally shared among group members in a manner which is hard for most of us to imagine today. While we typically imagine that centralized authority is a natural social condition, acephalous peoples imagined the opposite. In those times nobody legitimately commanded others. A cooperative sharing of power was seen as both necessary and natural.

A full discussion of acephalous societies is beyond the scope of our present project. Suffice it to say that the radical social and economic equality of such groups was complemented by a diffuse role structure (providing for a high degree of common experience), a kin-based social organization (creating familial blood ties between all members), and a belief system emphasizing the collective nature of success and failure. Together these organizational characteristics produced a high level of cooperation and a significantly different style of social control. While blood revenge was one mechanism used to control wrongdoing between acephalous groups, it was not as common as once imagined, nor was it typically used as a form of control within acephalous groups. The reasons are simple. Between groups revenge might engender a cycle of feuding dangerous to the survival of these highly interdependent, collectively organized social units. Within groups the idea of personal revenge made no sense, given the close identification of each member with the group itself. The group rather than the individual per se was perceived as both the true offender and the victim. Trouble within or between groups must be resolved. It was not sufficient for action to be taken against a troublemaker or an individual deviant. As such, the most common control rituals of acephalous societies were directed at reconciling parties in troubling situations rather than at exorcising trouble out of particular individuals. This later practice awaited the birth of centralized religious authority. In acephalous societies ceremonial mechanisms of group reconciliation were more creative.

Often the reconciliatory control practices of acephalous communities involved the mediative efforts of skilled negotiators, such as the *monkalun* among the acephalous Ifugao tribe of the Philippines[22] and the "leopard skin" mediator of the Nuer in southern Sudan.[23] Such mediators possess no legal authority. Their only power is their ability to bring deviating parties back together.[24] Ordinarily this is accomplished by means of symbolic rituals designed to dissolve the trouble between deviating parties. One such ritual is observed among the Tiwi of Australia.[25] Tiwi society is composed of large polygamous households in which older men are surrounded by many younger wives. This leads to a scarcity of young unattached females. Imagine the trouble this presents for young heterosexual males. Older males commonly accuse the young of seducing their women. How are such accusations of deviance resolved? Troubling situations of this kind are defused by an elaborate and dramatic simulation of deadly duel. In this ritual of reconciliatory control, an agile young man (unarmed or armed only with a stick) dodges spears thrown by a less threatening elder. This continues for about five to ten minutes as the younger man retains his honor. The ritual reaches its climax when the younger man permits himself to be hit. The old man thus regains honor without dishonoring his younger "opponent." The ceremony ends. Reconciliation is complete. Both parties are symbolically satisfied. Neither totally wins nor totally loses. Neither is advantaged by deviantizing the other. Neither is excluded from a return to honorable life within the group.

A similar reconciliatory outcome occurs in the "song duels" of troubled Eskimos.[26] A complaining victim and an accused deviant join in a sharp-tongued battle of song. In the course of exchanging derogatory verses about each other, both deviating parties are at once honored and humiliated. Trouble is dissolved. It is replaced by reconciliation. This is the most common product of diverse rituals of symbolic satisfaction. "Similar solutions can be reached through wrestling matches or other contests of strength in which no lasting damage is done."[27] In acephalous groups possessing a common medium of economic exchange, victim restitution, a ceremonial paying back of harm, is another common means of reconciliation. No matter the form, acephalous control rituals typically result in the reunion of members and the defusing of trouble within the community as a whole.

All this changed as changes in technology permitted groups to create an economic surplus above and beyond what was needed for simple material survival. This enabled some members of the group to become full-time managers of the labor and social activities of others. For the first time in history, power was hierarchically arranged such that a few people were able to legitimately command the deference of everyone else. This marked the transition from acephalous to centralized state rule, and with it came a whole new strategy of social control. No longer was the reconciliation of troubled parties a primary concern. Why? Because the institution of centralized authority was itself a source of trouble. It drove an institutional wedge through the equalitarian cooperation which was so prominent a feature of acephalous life. The benefits and liabilities of group life were now no longer equally distributed. Some people were in authorized positions of greater power than others. They could announce rules and enforce them. But why? Why some people instead of others? In its earliest forms, centralized authority was justified by divine precept. Just at that moment in history when technological changes made centralized rule a material possibility, God's voice was heard by "his" prophets. They were chosen, God said, set above others to rule in "his" name. This historical link between material and spiritual developments is well documented by students of acephalous society such as the anthropologist E. E. Evans-Pritchard.[28] His analysis of the end of acephalous rule among the Nuer of the Sudan suggests that the appearance of prophets was occasioned by an intrusion of Arabs and Europeans into the traditional life of the group. Threatened by the power of other state-organized societies, the Nuer suddenly found "sky spirits" gracing certain of their members (and eventually the offspring of these members) with the previously unknown mantle of divinely authorized leadership.

I am not here suggesting that material changes cause spiritual changes. I am suggesting that material changes are commonly accompanied by spiritual changes; that each impacts upon the other; that each provides a condition for the existence of the other. It is important to note that centralized religious authority is conditioned by the existence of an economic surplus which enables some people to gain an upper hand over others, just as it provides a condition for hierarchical rule by justifying this unequal power in the name of God. This, of course, is exactly what happens as the charismatic voice of a prophet becomes institutionally transformed into the lawful authority of priests. Soon an elaborate religious organization arises, complete with authorized "organizational agents" and an official code specifying who can do what, when, where, and why. Such codes also specify what is to be done to the deviants who violate them. As such, these codes legitimately define the institutionalized social inequalities which are ushered into history with the advent of centralized authority. I shall further examine this troubling feature of centralized authority in Chapter 10. For now it is sufficient to recognize that the blessings of religious control rituals are mixed. On one hand, they reduce the arbitrary nature of revenge. On the other, they provide a justification for the authorized domination of some people by others.

Community Control of the Demonic

Although justified by the principle of centralized religious authority, supernaturally ordained control rituals were practically administered within local geographic communities. Thus, during the dominance of demonic thinking in the medieval west, there were no "out of sight and out of mind" institutions to remove deviants from the public eye. People who violated the laws of God, as written into the ecumenical laws of the church, were to be dealt with locally, purged in public as visible reminders of the ever-present struggle between God and the devil.

Except for a handful of sixteenth- and seventeenth-century "workhouses" in several of Europe's early industrialized cities, the control of demonic deviance was largely the responsibility of local communities and their families. Each community had its mentally afflicted "lunatics" and feebleminded "idiots" who wandered the streets. The care of such persons was, for the most part, a family or neighborhood matter. Although the proper recognition of deviance was viewed in terms of centralized religious authority, the practical control of deviants was generally accomplished by informal local initiative. Moreover, no clear distinctions were made regarding an undifferentiated assembly of deviants, most of whom we presently classify and control separately.

What "care," as distinct from punishment, was provided for the dependent (i.e., lunatic, sick, poor, etc.) members of the above-described deviant class was not the effort of any organized religious or secular response. It was provided by the individuals who were intimately connected to the deviant and was generally guided by spiritual concern both for their fellows and for their own souls. It was only exceptionally burdensome deviants and people who lacked any supportive ties to family or friends who were housed under the same roof with others of their kind. Two sorts of roofs provided for the control of these exceptional cases—the small religious hospital and the jail. Both, however, were locally based and bore little resemblance to the centralized institutions which would later separate deviants from the local community.

While medieval religious hospitals sometimes provided a shelter for both the seriously sick and the honestly poor, jails housed a much wider range of deviant clientele. These early "prisons," however, should not be confused with the houses of correction and the penitentiaries of a later age. It was not until the nineteenth century that imprisonment became a major form of punishment. As mentioned previously, demonic deviants were largely subject to physical punishment or fines. Nor were jails typically administered by the state or the church. In general, jails were small, privately administered places which housed deviants within the geographical and visual boundaries of the local community. According to Andrew Scull,

> Frequently housed in ramshackle buildings, gaols [jails] were private speculations run on behalf of municipalities, or ecclesiastical dignitaries. The inmates found themselves crammed together in a single heterogeneous assemblage. As well as lunatics and debtors, some were there "as a means of securing the payment into the Exchequer of debts due to the Crown," while others were held as punishment for various minor infractions. But most were in custody simply to ensure their appearance at their trials or their executions.[29]

The public administration of punishment was likewise a manifestation of the commitment to community control during the "demonic" period. All were invited and frequently required to witness the ceremonies of bodily penance by which the entire community was restored to grace. The exceptions to this were the deviants who had come from other communities. They were to be controlled properly in the community of their origin. Such outside deviants were generally punished and sent packing. Ceremonial punishments, such as tar and feathering, were reserved as warnings for those who broke local rules but who were themselves not "local folks."

The sentence of death would, of course, remove the body of the deviant from its earthly ties to the local "community of the faithful." Bodily removal from the community was, in this sense, the ultimate in punitive sanctions. Interestingly enough, a form of symbolic bodily removal, "outlawry," was considered almost as severe. This form of punishment emerged during a time in the late Middle Ages in which epidemic plagues reduced vast proportions of the laboring population, thus making the extensive use of mutilations and executions a severe hardship on the bodily needs of an agrarian workforce. Fines and various forms of economic compensation to victims of deviants' acts were instituted as punishment substitutes. These economic punishments exacted from convicted lawbreakers the fruits of the body's work, if not the agony of the body's pain. Fines were calculated, moreover, on the believed social-community value of the victims. Thus, even in communities guided by demonic visions of deviance, not all members were equally valued in the "eyes of the Lord." Greater compensation was demanded if one offended a person of higher social standing. Thus it was safer then, as it is today, to victimize the poor than to disturb the rich.

In any event, if a fined deviant was unable to pay the demanded compensation, he or she fell under the sentence of outlawry. Bodily present within the community, outlaws were condemned to be outside the protected lawful body of "those faithful gathered together." It was as if they were legally dead. Unguarded and unprotected, outlaws were literally outside the law which bound others together.[30] Should harm be committed against them, the community of "insiders" would no longer respond. A feared punishment, outlawry symbolized the importance of the local community in its immediate and direct responsibility for its own body of deviants—punishing most, while physically or symbolically removing the bodies of the worst.

In the Name of the Father: Heterosexist Patriarchy and Religious Control

To this point I have been discussing demonic control rituals as if they applied equally to both men and women. Following the lead of feminist historical scholarship it is today evident that western uses of demonic imagery have been considerably more biased. Indeed, since their historical origins the most dominant strands of Judaic-Christian thinking about deviance have valued abstract male ideas about the purity of spiritual forms over the sacredness of women's bodily experiences. This is not to condemn all Judaic-Christian thought as inherently sexist. The historical record is at once more complex and more contradictory. Indeed, many advocates of gender equality have emerged from within the confines of the Judaic-Christian heritage. Nevertheless, as disturbing as this may prove to those of us reared under the theological sign of the Judaic-Christian "God the Father," when western religious uses of demonic imagery are placed in a historical perspective it becomes undeniably apparent that certain of the most powerful forms of western religious thinking have for far too long favored the viewpoints of men over those of women.

The male or *phallocentric* bias of dominant western religious thinking is evident in many of the founding texts of the Judaic-Christian tradition, but nowhere is this male bias more evident than in the religiously inspired mass murders of suspected pagan witches that took place between the fifteenth and the eighteenth centuries. While historical estimates concerning the extent of this genocide range from 1 million to 9 million, one fact appears certain: approximately 80 percent of the people who were hunted down, tortured, and burnt were women. This is evidence of a terroristic patriarchal logic at work within dominant forms of western religion.

Paganism, the avowed target of the witch hunts, is a religious practice which honors the earth as the "Great Mother" (or the "Goddess"). Pagan rituals also emphasize the spiritual significance of women. Since the late Middle Ages, the rites of pagan peoples have been ruthlessly attacked, destroyed, or driven underground by zealous Christians. Christians who attack the religion of the Great Mother picture God in almost exclusively male terms. Indeed, for many Christians the earth is but a waiting room for the future revelation of supernatural truths. Christian zealots have often confused paganism's reverence for the earth with Satanism or devil worship.

In the third chapter of Genesis, the first book of the Bible, it is written that the Lord said to Eve, "Let your urge be for your husband, and he shall rule over you." Following this edict, a central target of the bloody European witch-hunts was pagan women who had rejected heterosexual marriage (spinsters, including lesbians, who are discussed below) and women who had survived marriage (widows). Also high on the list of Christian targets were peasant women who practiced herbal medicine and rites of "natural healing" and midwives who delivered children outside the auspices of the emerging male medical profession. Accused of such alleged "superstitions" as necromancy, geomancy, and hydromancy (the unauthorized study of death, the earth's cycles, and water), such women were feared because they lived outside heterosexual hierarchies and the logical imperatives of patriarchal social control.[31]

The wrath of Christian inquisitors was also directed at gay men, lesbians, and others who refused to honor the heterosexist inequalities of "blessed" family life. Indeed, large numbers of men whose "sin" involved nothing but the sharing of sexual intimacies with other men were also tortured and burnt at the stake. This is the tragic origin of the association between the term "faggot" and male homosexuals. In the name of the Christian God, gay men were often bound together as kindling or "faggots" and used to ignite the pyres used to burn witches.[32] This link between gay men and pagan women was no accident. In the religion of the Great Mother both were afforded a freedom and respect subsequently denied them by Christian authorities from the late twelfth century onward. Indeed, it was not uncommon for Christian judges to combine charges of witchcraft with accusations of lesbianism and male homosexuality. Writing of pagan assemblies in 1619, Henry Boguet, a judge responsible for the death of many "sorceresses," commented:

> You may well suppose that every kind of obscenity is practiced there, yea, even those abominations for which Heaven poured down fire and brimstone on Sodom and Gomorrah are quite common.[33]

Although condemned as heretical, paganism represented a primary form of religion for the vast majority of Europeans until the late Middle Ages. Christianity, with its official Latin language and organizational hierarchy, remained a religion of the elite. Peasant masses, on the other hand, practiced the "old religion" and honored its ancient agricultural Goddess. At the core of pagan beliefs was a ritual recognition of the sacred character of the ever-changing earth, which was poetically imagined as the Mother who periodically changed forms, like the phases of the moon, the seasons of the year, or the cycles of life itself. What was sacred for pagans was that which was materially in touch with the rhythms of nature. This image of the sacredness of natural processes contrasts greatly with the supernatural imagery of the Judaic-Christian tradition. The Father God of Jews and Christians calls upon his humble servants to bring profane nature under "man's" spiritual control.

From the fall of the Roman Empire until the late Middle Ages, pagan and Judaic-Christian religious practices existed side by side. It was not until the twelfth century that Christianity was in a military position to launch an all-out attack on pagans. Following several centuries of Christian crusades, aimed at seizing the "Holy Lands" of Palestine from Muslims and Moorish-pagan "infidels," Christians began to turn their arms against threats closer to home. By the early thirteenth century a sustained war against the pagan masses was well under way. During the fifteenth and sixteenth centuries the war against pagans reached genocidal proportions. Theological justifications for the wholesale violence were already an established part of Judaic-Christian belief. Consider the first several chapters of Genesis, the epistles of St. Paul, and the writings of early Christian church fathers. Each values the pure word of the orderly male sky God over the supposed chaos and impurities of women's bodies.

In Genesis, creation is pictured as transcendent over nature's cycles—as coming from the supernatural voice of God speaking from the outside. This places the Judaic-Christian understanding of creation at odds with existing Mesopotamian pagan sacred stories of the serpentlike Goddess who gave birth to all forms of life from the womb of earth itself. In the Judaic-Christian scriptures the creative role of the Goddess is suppressed. Creation comes from the word of the male God as he erects an expanse that cuts her chaotic fluidity in half. In so doing, he is said to enlighten her darkness and fix what appears unformed by the power of his speech. If God's actions here appear both *logocentric* (operating through the words that ideally subordinate messy female matters) and *phallocentric* (as his expanse is thrust between her waters), perhaps this is because "unlike many deities of the ancient Near East, the God of Israel shared his power with no female divinity, nor was he the divine husband or lover of any. He can scarcely be characterized in any but masculine epithets: king, lord, master, judge, and father. Indeed, the absence of feminine symbolism for God marks Judaism, Christianity, and Islam in striking contrast to the world's other religious traditions."[34]

The masculine bias of Genesis is further revealed in examining its depiction of the creation of male and female humans. Of particular interest is the fact that Genesis contains two separate accounts of the creation story. In the first (Genesis 1:26–28), God is said to make "man" in his image, and "male and female created he them." Here man and woman come into being at the same time. Both are charged with ruling over "the fish of the sea, the birds of the sky, the cattle, the whole earth, and all the creeping things that creep on the earth." Then, in the second passage (Genesis 2:18–23), the story is retold . It is as if the first is canceled by the second. The often-cited second passage begins with God saying, "It is not good for man to be alone." What follows is an account of the creation of woman from man's rib. Thereafter, Adam (the first man) names the woman just as he names the rest of nature—the cattle, the birds of the sky, and the wild beasts. "The man named his wife Eve, because she was *the mother of all the living*" (Genesis 3:20; italics added).

Why this doubled story of the creation of man and woman? What happened to the first woman, who was created at the same time as man? The answer may lie in a variety of supplemental Jewish texts that were never officially incorporated into the Old Testament. Known as the Midrash and interpreted as a kind of allegorical commentary on the meaning of the canonical scriptures, texts such as *Alpha Bet Ben Sira* suggest that ancient Hebrews may have once recognized the creation of a first woman prior to the creation of Eve. This was Lilith, a dark and powerful female figure who militantly refused subordination to Adam's phallic demands. Accordingly, "Adam and Lilith never found peace together. She disagreed with him in many matters and refused to lie beneath him in sexual intercourse, basing her claim on the fact that each had been created from earth. When Lilith saw that Adam would overpower her, she uttered the ineffable name of God and flew up into the air of the world. Eventually she dwelt in a cave in the desert on the shores of the Red Sea."[35] After escaping from Adam's claims on her body, Lilith is said to have lived a life of "unbridled promiscuity," consorting with demons and posing a continuous threat to the orderliness of "man's" God-given world. In western legends of Lilith we are presented with destructive, chaotic, and erotically charged images of a dark femininity cut off from its previous pagan connections to cycles of creative regeneration and spiraling rebirth.

The legend of Lilith is associated with frightening tales (or male fantasies) of female vampirism, unbridled feminine sexuality, and seduction. Lilith, like the enigmatic winged serpent that embodies her image, was transformed from a woman of power, equal to man, into a man's witchy nemesis—a kind of "bitchy" figure born of male dread and fear of castration. Later, she was replaced by Eve who, unlike Lilith, was not created alongside man but out of man's own body. "This one at last," says Adam, "is bone of my bone and flesh of my flesh. This one shall be called Woman, for from man she is taken" (Genesis 2:22–23) But what happened to Lilith after she was replaced by Eve? She was exiled to the darkly sexualized margins of western culture. There she haunts man's self-righteousness in but a disguised and shadowy form. There she is forced to assume a kind of pornographic image—an alluring, if uncanny, threat to male power that men have long sought to recapture, tie down, and domesticate.

The imaging of women in Genesis doesn't improve much with the story of the fall from the Garden of Eden. Since this tale is well known within our culture, I will not repeat it in detail. Suffice it to say that the "tree of knowledge of good and evil" which lay in the center of the Garden and from which the Lord God forbade Adam and Eve to eat was itself an ancient pagan symbol of ecstatic wisdom. To eat of the fruit of this tree was (for pagans) to participate in the sacredness of life itself.[36] And who was it that tempted the woman to transgress God's spoken commands not to eat of this tree? It was none other than the serpent, that symbolic figure of the once sacred Goddess, now transformed into a demonic figure of sin itself. When the Lord inquired about how all this had come to pass, "The man said, 'The woman you put at my side—she gave me of the tree, and I ate.' And the Lord God said to the woman, 'What is this you have done!' The woman replied, 'The serpent duped me, and I ate'" (Genesis 3:1–13).

As a punishment, the Judaic-Christian God condemned woman to painful childbearing and commanded her perpetual subordination to man, saying, "Your urge shall be for your husband, and he shall rule over you." He also condemned all humans to suffer from the obligation to work and the (animal) certainty that we must someday die. Behind all this travail lies a shameful image of woman as a conduit of evil. As St. Paul declared, "Adam was not deceived, but the woman being deceived was in . . . transgression" (1 Timothy 2:14). In the words of the early church fathers, she was "the devil's gateway," a pushover for Satan and his demons.[37]

As negatively as woman was presented in these canonical texts of the Judaic-Christian tradition, worse still was her fate as a central target of the Christian Inquisition. As a theological justification for mass murder and the use of such severe tortures as "the pear" (a metallic device that operated like forceps; it was heated to red-hot and then inserted into the mouth, vagina, or anus of an accused witch), those who persecuted accused witches commonly cited passages from Genesis, such as those discussed above. Indeed, in constructing the *Malleus Maleficarum*, the infamous 1486 manual for the identification of witches, Dominican priests Heinrich Kramer and Jakob Sprenger wrote: "For though the devil tempted Eve to sin, yet Eve seduced Adam. And as the sin of Eve would not have brought death to our soul and body unless the sin had afterwards passed on to Adam, to which he was tempted by Eve, not by the devil, therefore she is more bitter than death."[38]

The violence directed against accused witches was a cruel manifestation of the patriarchal religious control. Such violence continues today in less dramatic forms. Indeed, many aspects of Judaic-Christian ritual still subordinate the body of women to the word of men, often prohibiting women from participating equally as ministers, priests, rabbis, and other religious officials. Furthermore, both the Roman Catholic Church and a variety of conservative Protestant groups today appear committed to restricting a woman's right to make private choices concerning pregnancy and abortion. Basing their attacks on feminism on alleged Christian doctrine and a defense of "traditional family values," some conservative religious leaders have gone so far as to picture advocates for women's rights as demonic agents inspired by Satan. Indeed, even as I write, the United States has yet to pass an equal rights amendment (ERA) to the Constitution guaranteeing women the same public and private privileges enjoyed by men. A symptom of patriarchal forces still very much alive within today's society, the defeat of the ERA suggests the continuing power of heterosexist religious beliefs as ritual mechanisms of social control.

THE DEMONIC PERSPECTIVE TODAY

Originating in antiquity and continuing as the predominant interpretation of deviance until the time of the eighteenth-century Enlightenment, the demonic perspective may seem far removed from the secular and scientific world views that are so influential in contemporary society. Yet, for more than a few people demonic explanations remain the only true explanations. Indeed, judging from the popularity of stories about demonic possession, satanic cults, and exorcism that are regular features of both sensational tabloid newspapers and TV talk shows, the demonic perspective remains alive and well in the spiritual imaginings of many contemporary people. Moreover, given the abstract, bureaucratically indifferent, and technologically guided rationality governing much of everyday life, it is not surprising to find a huge market of people buying into the mysterious, emotionally charged, and seductive logic of demonic theorizing. Evangelical preachers fill football stadiums and amass large radio and television audiences with sermons suggesting that behind rising crime rates, the spread of acquired immune deficiency syndrome (AIDS), sexual immorality, and family breakdown lies the malicious hand of the devil. Few of us who own a TV set, listen to the radio, open our mail, or walk in public places have not been confronted by the "word" of those who tell us that deviance is sin and that giving ourselves (or our money) to a holy cause is the best form of social control.

Recent advocates of the demonic perspective have made particular forms of deviance targets of highly organized moral and media crusades. Many such crusades are aligned with the conservative religious politics of the Christian right. In the United States well-funded moral campaigns have been directed toward the prohibition of abortion, the elimination of liberal social welfare programs, the censorship of sexually explicit and politically motivated forms of art, a retreat from advances in the areas of civil rights (particularly the rights of women, gays and lesbians, and peoples of color), and the advocacy of a foreign policy dedicated to the worldwide spread of capitalism and the "American way." Some contemporary forms of demonic theorizing are even more dramatic. Calling for the implementation of Christian public policy by using such homophobic slogans as "God's plan for man was for Adam and Eve and not Adam and Steve," right-wing religious and political leaders have even blamed the AIDS epidemic on the "sins" of homosexuals. Others have targeted rock music as a "degenerate" form of entertainment inspired by Satan.[39]

Attacks on homosexuals have been a recurrent aspect of contemporary demonic crusades. This is a major reason few U.S. states have yet to pass legislation guaranteeing the public rights of gays and lesbians. While I was a graduate student in Columbus, Ohio, a gay rights bill was presented to the mayor. A group called the Full Gospel Christian Businessmen's Association parked itself outside City Hall. Led by a Bible-quoting car dealer, this group of wealthy fundamentalists cited passages from scripture "proving" that homosexuality was sinful and demanded that the mayor veto the proposed ordinance. The bill was vetoed. Several years later the popular singer and orange juice promoter Anita Bryant led a national "Christian" campaign against a gay rights referendum in Dade County, Florida. Bryant proclaimed that homosexuality was the devil's doing and that her own prayers have turned numerous "sinful gays" away from their demonic deviance.

Over a decade later, religious opposition to homosexuality is still strong. Although a number of "liberal" congregations have come out in favor of accepting gays and lesbians, mostly compulsively refuse to sanction the blessedness of anything but church-ordained heterosexual unions. In June 1992, for instance, 18,000 delegates from Southern Baptist congregations (the largest Protestant denomination in the United States), meeting in Indiana's Hoosier Dome, voted to both bar homosexuals and withdraw from "fellowship" with churches that permitted the participation of gay and lesbian members. According to the delegates' resolution, homosexual actions "are contrary to the teaching of the Bible on sexuality . . . and are offensive to Southern Baptists."[40]

In numerous state legislatures debates over the ERA have also had an "otherworldly" religious tone. Arguments opposing guarantees of legal equality for women have suggested that the ERA would lead to a deviant state of affairs, out of keeping with the will of God. Yet, perhaps the most focused religious opposition to "deviance" involves militant campaigns aimed at denying women the right to abortion. For those who organize under the slogan "Right to Life," abortion is perceived as something demonic or sinful. Defending the "sanctity" of an unborn fetus in opposition to the difficult moral choices faced by women who experience unwanted pregnancies, various groups—including the male-led hierarchy of the Roman Catholic Church and Operation Rescue, a militant organization known for its efforts to block entrance to abortion clinics—make continued use of demonic theorizing in their attempts to restrict women's control over their own reproductive options.

Contemporary Televangelism and the Moral Majority

If you are still unconvinced of the contemporary political clout of groups organized around a demonic perspective on deviance, consider the recent impact of the so-called Moral Majority. In the late 1970s and early 1980s this group, spearheaded by the Reverend Jerry Falwell, was instrumental in the political defeat of numerous liberal-leaning legislators and in the election of conservative President Ronald Reagan. The extremely well-financed Moral Majority views such things as homosexuality, abortion, sexual permissiveness, and even the rights of women as demonically inspired deviance. In the words of Falwell, a Baptist minister from Lynchburg, Virginia, whose TV program *The Old Time Gospel Hour* reaches millions of Americans weekly:

> It is now time to take a stand on certain moral issues. . . . We must stand against the Equal Rights Amendment, the feminist revolution, the homosexual revolution. We must have a revival in this country. It will come if we will realize the danger and heed the admonition of God found in II Chronicles 7:14, "If my people which are called by my name, shall humble themselves and pray, and seek my face and turn from their wicked ways; then will I hear from heaven, and will I forgive their sin, and will heal their land."[41]

The extent and influence of groups like the Moral Majority as new voices for the demonic perspective are today enormous. In 1980 this resurgence in demonic thinking was being broadcast nationwide by thirty-six separate "religious" television stations, 1,300 "religious" radio stations, and dozens of programs that bought time on mainstream commercial airwaves. Moreover, during that same year an assembly of 18,000 fundamentalist pastors who gathered in Dallas, Texas, for the "Religious Roundtable Conference" were urged to turn their parishes into political precincts in order to bring America back to God.[42] The political objectives of this curious blend of "old-time religion" and new-time electoral politics are described by critics as a "New Prohibitionism."[43] Much of its theological base is rooted in a selective use of the Scriptures. According to the editors of the periodical *Christian Century*, while using the Bible to attack gays and women and to defend the free enterprise system, the new religious right conveniently overlooks scriptural references to matters such as social justice. "They are not accurate and they are not fair. But they are effective."[44]

In the late 1980s the power of televangelist ministries—such as those of Falwell and other well-known TV preachers, including Pat Robertson, Jim and Tammy Bakker, Robert Schuller, Jimmy Swaggart, and Oral Roberts— underwent contradictory twists and turns. With the announced Republican presidential candidacy of Pat Robertson, host of the influential *700 Club* TV show, it appeared as if the demonic message of televangelism was stronger than ever. A skilled communicator and defender of a Christian "will to empire," Robertson showed surprising strength in running against George Bush in the Michigan Republican caucuses. Then came the lurid news of sex scandals involving prominent televangelists such as Jim Bakker and Jimmy Swaggart. These were followed by allegations of financial misdealing on the part of the Bakkers. Televangelist power seemed for a moment shaken.

Today, the dramatic fall of TV prophets appears to have been short-lived. In the 1990s, the airwaves are again filled with televangelists calling for a national moral revival and the marketing of all kinds of "Christian" merchandise. This involves the promotion of religion as something to consume at home via broadcasts, call-in phone banks, prerecorded audiocassettes, and a host of other items that can be bought with credit cards. Moreover, since the summer of 1989, Pat Robertson and other conservative religious leaders have joined forces to form the Christian Coalition, a grass-roots organization boasting over 175,000 members in forty-five states.

Attracting enormous sums of money and the most prominent figures of the Christian right, including former Lt. Col. Oliver North, Jr., Paul Weyrich, and the Reverend James Dobson, the Coalition aims to exert "low-profile" but massive and "tax-free" influence on the U.S. electoral process. Indeed, as evidenced during the 1992 Republican Presidential Convention in Houston, Texas, by the spectacular attacks on feminists, gays and lesbians, and anyone else who dares to question the sacredness of patriarchal family values, the religious right has gained more than a small share of power in mainstream electoral politics. However, the contradiction inherent in this movement is that while most televangelists decry the evils of materialism, secular values, and self-interested consumption, they market with one hand what they condemn with the other. Thus, although they operate in the name of traditional Christian values, many televangelists interpret the accumulation and consumption of wealth as a sign of God's blessings. Indeed, as "the 1987 PTL scandal transparently revealed, it is the same logic of capitalist exchange with its peculiar dynamics of corporate concentration and relentless growth that has guided the various televangelists' quests for bigger market shares, not to mention their defensive moves against hostile takeovers by their competitors."[45]

Progressive Uses of Religious Imagery

To see Reality in our time is to see the world as crucifixion. . . . The revolutionary is the man [or woman] of conscience in today's world.

James W. Douglas[46]

Much of this section so far may have left you with the impression that contemporary political uses of the demonic perspective have been conservative in nature. This is not always the case. In recent years we have also witnessed the change-oriented, or progressive, use of religious imagery to "deviantize" certain forms of social oppression, domination, or injustice.

Think, for instance, of the role played by black ministers and other religious leaders in combating racism during the U.S. civil rights movement. The Reverend Martin Luther King, Jr. and others were clear in viewing racism as a form of spiritual malaise and as a social blot covering this nation's soul. During the height of the civil rights movement, the National Council of Churches denounced segregation and racism as a violation of the Gospel and called upon the church "to confess her sin of omission and delay, and to move forward to witness to her essential belief that every child of God is a brother of every other."[47] Through prayer, fasting, and other forms of non-violent protest, King and other religiously informed dissidents hoped to eradicate the national sin of racism.

Religious imagery was also a vital part of certain persuasive sectors in the antiwar movement of the Vietnam era. Consider the religious motivations of the "Plowshares Eight" and people like Daniel Berrigan and William Sloane Coffin, who violated draft headquarters and destroyed draft records in an attempt to end U.S. participation in the war. The dissenting voices of Catholic priests, brothers, and nuns as well as Protestant clergy, Jewish rabbis, and Buddhist disciples all rendered spiritual as well as political judgment on what may be described as the demonic nature of U.S. foreign policy in that era.

Even with the alleged ascendancy of the "New Religious Right" in the 1980s, progressive uses of what might be considered a demonic perspective are still having a significant impact in the world today. The Protestant and Catholic churches, for example, act together as a major force in the nuclear weapons freeze movement that is sweeping both the United States and Europe. Leaders of all the major religious groups have taken strong stands against the "idolatry" of the arms race.

Perhaps most innovative and radical of all is the work currently being done in the area of "liberation theology," particularly by the Catholic church in Latin America. Theologians such as Gustavo Gutiérrez and José Miranda have combined Marxian social analysis with traditional Catholic social teaching in order to help realize the "Kingdom of God" for the poor, oppressed, and dispossessed of Latin America and the entire third world.[48] Meeting in Medellin in 1968, Latin American bishops declared that "God has sent his Son so that in the flesh he may come to liberate all men from slavery which holds them subject, from sin, ignorance, hunger, misery, oppression—in a word, from the injustice and hate which stem from human egoism.[49] In the words of Camilo Torres, a revolutionary priest from Colombia: "If the good of all mankind cannot be achieved except by changing the temporal structures of society, it would be sinful for Christians to oppose change.[50]

This commitment to revolutionary Christian action is no easy task. It has cost numerous priests and members of Catholic religious orders the support of their own church. Under orders from the Pope, some politically active Roman Catholic priests have been forced to choose between their official religious ministries and their call to serve the poor. Still others have been the target of brutal right-wing assassinations and "disappearances."

The recent history of "liberation theology" in El Salvador represents a tragic case in point. El Salvador is a Central American country where U.S.-backed elites have long exercised tyranny over the nation's massive population of peasants. Beginning around 1969, liberation theology began to play an increasingly important role in the spiritual and political lives of El Salvador's peasants and Church workers. Forming a network of *communidades eclesiales de base*, or "grass-roots Christian communities," Salvadorans began mixing heartfelt religious beliefs with aspirations for social justice. In November 1974, for instance, a Christian community in La Cayetana occupied an idle parcel of land, beseeching the land's wealthy owner to rent it to local peasants. The result was an attack by government troops. Six peasants were killed and another twenty-six arrested. Of these, thirteen were "disappeared," or secretly made to vanish without being officially recognized as murdered.

Struggle escalated thereafter. Increasing Christian resistance met with unprecedented levels of governmental violence and the terror of right-wing death squads, many of whose members were actually soldiers in disguise. In January 1977 the government began rounding up influential priests and torturing them. In February 1980, the day after telling soldiers that they should refuse government orders to kill their peasant brothers and sisters, Cardinal Oscar Romero, the Catholic archbishop of San Salvador, was himself gunned down while saying mass. A decade later, over 70,000 more struggling

Salvadorans had been killed as, under the leadership of Ronald Reagan and George Bush, the U.S. administration poured over $1.4 million per day into El Salvador to ensure that this small country would not fall into the hands of its own peasant peoples. Reagan and Bush claimed to be protecting El Salvador from communists, not from Christians. In November 1989 the distorted truths about this aspect of U.S. foreign policy were made more manifest than ever, as military commandos (probably acting upon orders from El Salvadorean government officials) entered the Jesuit University of El Salvador and brutally assassinated four priests, all leading exponents of liberation theology, along with the priests' cook and her daughter.

A tragic testimony to progressive use of religious imagery in a world in which power appears to be more allied with conservative theological positions than with progressive causes, the death of so many committed Christians in countries such as El Salvador is also a reminder that religious perspectives on social control are not the exclusive prerogatives of the Moral Majority, the Christian Coalition, Operation Rescue, and other conservative organizations.

ASSESSMENT OF THE DEMONIC PERSPECTIVE

How adequate is the demonic explanation of social deviance? How are we to assess its adequacy? Judged by the naturalistic standards of the secularized modern world, the demonic perspective is very inadequate. It relies on belief rather than on observable fact and is thus said to be totally untestable. More correctly, one might say that the demonic perspective relies on beliefs that are no longer believed as much as other beliefs. That is, a belief in the primacy of supernatural explanations has been superseded by a belief in the primacy of naturalistic explanations. This has not happened worldwide. Indeed there are numerous places in the world where supernatural or demonic explanations still prevail. Spokespersons of our modern western perspective often refer to the "primitive" character of such beliefs. Yet, when viewed from the opposite direction, the western world may appear to be little more than a wasteland of godless infidels. Indeed, for many of the spiritual leaders in certain Islamic countries, such as Iran and Iraq, it is not uncommon to find the United States referred to in supernatural terms as the land of "the Great Satan."

Nor is the use of naturalistic explanations entirely dominant even within a largely modernized nation like the United States. Recall the previous discussion of the rise of the Moral Majority. Consider as well the current controversy over what has come to be referred to as "creationism" or "creation science." As late as the mid-1980s an Arkansas state law required a balanced treatment for creationism and evolution theory in public schools.

Creationism involves belief that the universe and human life were brought into being in a sudden instance of creation, that humans and apes are of distinctly separate ancestry, that there once was a worldwide flood, and that the earth is of relatively recent origin (e.g., that it was created several thousand years ago, at a time corresponding to biblical estimates, and not several million years ago, as suggested by the most modern techniques of carbon dating). All this, of course, is contradicted by the evolutionary tenets of conventional science. Creationism attempts to reconstruct the "facts" of science to fit the "facts" of the Bible.

The Arkansas law which required that creationism be taught in a balanced manner alongside teaching about evolution was successfully challenged by the American Civil Liberties Union (ACLU) on the grounds that creationism is religion and not science, and that the U.S. Constitution guarantees a separation of church and state. ACLU attorneys argued that creationism is not a science because science requires a commitment to materialistic causation which is at once tentative and testable. Scientific theory, in other words, is always open to the possibility of being proved wrong or revised. This is not the case with creationism. It is based upon unchangeable beliefs rather than verifiable naturalistic observations. In the words of one scientific expert called to testify, "It's religion, it doesn't invoke natural laws. It invokes miracles."[51]

Both sides in the debate over creationism raise issues that are as important as they are disturbing. While it may be true that creationism and other forms of supernaturalist or demonic interpretations of the world are essentially untestable, it is also true that natural science implies a certain commitment to looking at the world in a particular way. Without challenging anyone's religious faith or trying to come to a final resolution of this issue, I believe that there are distinct analytic advantages to suspending a supernatural view of the world in order to take a rigorous naturalistic look at the study of deviance and social control. The advantages of this approach are straightforward and simple. By suspending belief in the primacy of the supernatural interpretation, we are able to critically examine the way that things in this world impact on one another. By taking a naturalistic approach to the study of deviance and social control, we can consider such things as whether or not certain characteristics of the body make it more likely that a person will engage in certain acts of deviance, or whether a particular form of social organization is related to a specific type of social control strategy. These things are valuable to find out regardless of the nature of our religious beliefs. We cannot, however, truly discover much about them until we suspend our commitment to a demonic perspective. Otherwise we are forever stuck with saying that God or the devil caused our bodies or our forms of social organization to be this or that way. We learn nothing beyond the beliefs we start with. For these reasons the remainder of this book employs an essentially naturalistic focus on deviance and social control.

Some Naturalistic Observations about Spiritual Perspectives

Some naturalistic accounts of the demonic perspective have tried to explain away events which the perspective itself attributes to supernatural causes. The Salem witchcraft epidemic is a case in point. In a 1949 book, *The Devil in*

Massachusetts, M. L. Starkey substitutes a psychoanalytic interpretation for a demonic one. According to Starkey, the young colonial girls were not possessed by the devil but by "hysteria." Their suffering was caused not by Satan but by sexual repression and boredom.[52]

Starkey's interpretation of the events in Salem attempts to explain away invisible things which most people no longer believe in (e.g., demonic possession) but substitutes an account based upon a new order of invisible things (e.g., psychologically induced hysteria) that are more acceptable to the modern mind. How is it that the invisible things of psychology or psychiatry are today more believable than the invisible things of demonology? This question is raised by contemporary critics of psychiatric explanations of deviance, such as the psychiatrist Thomas Szasz. According to Szasz there are numerous parallels between the untestable belief systems of religious explanation and those of medicine or psychiatry.

> For millennia, men and women escaped responsibility by theologizing morals. Now they escape from responsibility by medicalizing morals. Then, if God approved a particular conduct, it was good; and if he disapproved it, it was bad. How did people know what God approved or disapproved? The Bible—that is to say, the Bible experts, called priests—told them so. Today, if medicine approves a particular conduct, it is good; and if it disapproves it, it is bad. And how do people know what medicine approves or disapproves? Medicine—that is to say, the medical experts, called physicians—tells them so.[53]

Not all naturalistic accounts of demonic deviance attempt to explain away the supernatural world view. Hansen's analysis of the events at Salem contrasts sharply with that of Starkey. Hansen assumes that, since witches were a part of the belief system of people in the seventeenth century, and since witchcraft was known to have been practiced in New England, the 1692 outbreak of demonic possession was a serious social reality which both fit within and threatened the spiritual life of the Salem community as a whole.[54]

But why did the devil make his appearance in 1692? This question is examined by sociologist Kai Erikson in his book *Wayward Puritans*. Erikson relates the appearance of witches to social disruptions within the Puritan community. According to Erikson, "No other form of crime in history has been a better index to social disruption and change, for outbreaks of witchcraft mania have generally taken place in societies which are experiencing a shift of religious focus—societies . . . confronting a relocation of boundaries.[55]

Erikson's contention that witchcraft appears at times of social and religious disruption is well illustrated in his own analysis of the witchcraft in Salem. In 1692 a new British government had revoked the once-secure charter of the Puritans in Massachusetts Bay. The entire community was enveloped in doubt and confusion. The once-proud leaders of a rigorous experiment in religious orthodoxy were becoming isolated from a new wave of religious tolerance sweeping through Europe and their mother country. Moreover, the internal religious beliefs of the community had been undergoing a radical shift. The original Puritan settlers believed that their destiny was totally in the hands of God, who personally supervised their every action on earth. Yet, after decades of fighting for survival on the fierce frontiers of America, there was born a new breed of Puritans. The sense of mystique which had accompanied the piety of a previous generation was being transformed into a sense of mastery which accompanied the power of their descendants.

The changes described above were compounded by the onset of extensive internal dissension. The once-unified followers of the "New England Way" had become divided by quarreling factions, land disputes, personal feuds, greed, jealousy, and a mass of litigation and counterlitigation. According to Erikson, "At the time of the Salem witchcraft mania, most of the familiar landmarks of the New England Way had become blurred by changes in the historical climate, like signposts obscured in a storm."[56]

The onslaught of the changes described by Erikson produced what he refers to as a "new wilderness" of religious turmoil and confusion. The old wilderness of thick forests and frightful storms gave way to a new wilderness of mythical beasts and flying spirits. As this happened, so too did the devil change his shape. He was no longer embodied in the form of the Native Americans, who, for the moment, had been defeated and driven westward. Nor was he experienced in the new waves of unorthodox "heretics." Treated with previously unknown tolerance, such persons were permitted to live in peace. Nor did the devil present himself in the shape of the attacking armies of the Counter-Reformation. Such armies remained far from the distant shores of Massachusetts Bay. The devil came instead out of the new wilderness of spiritual malaise. He came in the form of demonic spirits. He came in the form of the witch.

Erikson's analysis suggests that even in a world dominated by demonic thinking the specific shape of the devil is dependent upon how religious communities are organized or disorganized at a given point in time. But why did the devil so often come in the form of a woman? As suggested previously, from the earliest of Judaic-Christian perspectives on the sacred to the present there remains a discernable masculine bias in the formulation of western religious experience and what it renders taboo. As mentioned previously, some scholars estimate that of the 1 million or more persons executed for witchcraft throughout history, 80 percent were women. Indeed, beginning with the scriptural tale of Eve seducing Adam, women have been blamed for luring men into evil. The religious traditions which make such charges are, of course, dominated by men; men who theorize about their own roles as instrumental providers, and masters of nature, and about the roles of women as expressive receptacles of nature, sensuous earth mothers, and the like. Given this imprisonment of gender within the stereotypical confines of male language, it is hardly surprising that during times in which the great male mastery over nature seemed least secure, times of economic hardship and political instability, the priestly finger of men often found bewitching women to blame. Indeed, the 1484 *Malleus Maleficarum*, the authorative theological guide to witch-hunting in the west, makes reference to "normal female witch behavior" which "spirits away" male sex organs "resulting in impotence or castration."[57] Such projections of male inadequacy onto allegedly evil women are today the stuff of many a popular song. During the reign of the demonic perspective the classification of women as witches led to such ritual punishments as baths in boiling water, crushing by heavy weights, tearing the flesh from the breasts with searing-hot pincers, and torture of the female sex organs. Historians even recount incidents where the entire female populations of peasant villages were put to death in order to drive away the devil.[58]

The hunting of witches also distracted people from noticing the contributions of church officials to the perpetuation of medieval poverty. Convicted "witches were mainly peasant and lower-class women who opposed the existing authority structure and thus represented a political, religious, and sexual threat to the dominant class, particularly to men.[59] In the ritual of the witch-hunt, religious leaders diverted attention from themselves while putting the lower rungs of the social order in fear and suspicion of each other. Thus the shape of the devil may be seen as influenced by social stratification as well as social disorganization.

Elliot Currie's analytic comparison of witchcraft in England and on the European Continent suggests that witchcraft is "shaped" by the organization of social control machinery as well. For years Continental Europe experienced huge outbreaks of witchcraft, while in England rates were considerably lower. Why? According to Currie, the answer is found in the contrast between the Continent's "repressive control" machinery and the more "restrained control" mechanisms available in England.[60]

On the Continent, control was organized according to an inquisitional approach wherein "accusation, detection, prosecution and judgment" were concentrated in the hands of the same officials. The trial, rather than being a matter of accusation and defense, was more of an attack pointed toward obtaining a confession. It usually involved a trial by ordeal. It included something else as well—the prerogative of the court to confiscate the property of an accused witch. The processing of witches was, then, not only efficient but also profitable. It resulted in what Currie describes as a "witchcraft industry." Control agents were paid well for their work. Moreover, the more witches they "discovered," the bigger the problem appeared to be. As a result, the unique organization of repressive control machinery guaranteed that both the "problem" and the "solution" would continue at high levels in somewhat of a self-fulfilling manner.

England's restrained control apparatus was much different. Witches, like all other demonic deviants, were assured some form of accusatorial rather than inquisitorial trial as I mentioned in the discussion of the witch trials in Salem. Moreover, England never developed a system for confiscating the property of the accused. As a result, control agents in England, as contrasted with those on the Continent, "had no continuous vested interest in the discovery and conviction of witches. . . . They had neither the power nor the motive for large scale persecution."[61]

Currie's analysis, like Erikson's, indicates that without explaining away demonic beliefs, it is possible to understand them in a different way by situating these beliefs within the social and historical context in which they are used. This is done by suspending judgment about the truth of the demonic perspective and by naturalistically considering it as something which is influenced by and which also influences a wide range of other cultural, political, and economic "things" by which the social world is organized. Once we apply a naturalistic perspective to the study of demonic theorizing, a number of new and exciting questions present themselves. We may ask, for instance, why at this point in time the United States is experiencing such a revival in demonic imagery. Why have groups such as the Moral Majority risen to such importance in recent years? Such groups see modern-day demons and witches behind nearly all forms of secular humanism. One wonders whether Erikson's analysis of the explosive appearance of witches in seventeenth-century Massachusetts can provide clues to the widespread belief in a new wave of demons in our own age. Erikson posited a relationship between the disrupted society and the society which sees demons. Is this what is going on in the United States today? Is it possible that the cultural disruptions of the late 1960s and early 1970s, the political disruptions of the post-Vietnam and post-Watergate era, and the economic disruptions of recession and never-ending inflation are producing a spiritual malaise not unlike that experienced by the Puritans in the late seventeenth century? A naturalistic view of the demonic perspective directs our attention to questions such as this.

Some Spiritual Observations about Naturalistic Perspectives

I hope that what has been said above has convinced you of the advantages of taking a naturalistic perspective on spiritual issues. In closing, however, I think it is important to mention that in recent years there have been several calls by noteworthy scholars of deviance and social control to do the opposite—to reexamine naturalistic analysis in terms of its supernaturalistic dimensions. These scholars, at least the ones I have in mind, are in no way suggesting that we return to the primacy of the demonic or supernatural viewpoint. They are asking instead that we "transcend" or expand the confines of a purely naturalistic perspective, a perspective which often becomes so preoccupied with testable explanations of the "things" in this world that it forgets to consider their moral, spiritual, or cosmic dimensions. This call for transcendence of a purely naturalistic perspective is raised in a variety of recent works of critical sociological scholarship.

In his book *The Seven Deadly Sins* Stanford Lyman argues that a major deficit in most sociological studies of deviance is the lack of any perspective by which to judge the evils of the modern world. According to Lyman,

> Evil is a term that is rarely found in a modern sociology text. . . . To the extent that sociological thought embraces the study of evil today, it does so under the embarrassing, neutered morality of "deviance." Adopting for the most part an uncritical stance toward the normative structure of any given society, the . . . sociologist of

deviance takes his cue from whatever the forces of law and restriction define as evil. Hence, the concerns of the vocal and powerful elements of a society become the resources for a sociological investigation of evil.[62]

Guided toward their fields of study by the "forces of law and restriction," most students of deviance have been content to examine what Alex Liazos once referred to as "the sociology of nuts, sluts, and perverts."[63] Lyman calls upon sociologists to transcend the limits of a research diet prepared for them by the most vocal and powerful chefs of our modern day. The most important evils, suggests Lyman, are to be found at a deeper level, evils entrenched in the foundational bedrock of our society itself, evils rooted in "the corporate structure of modern society."[64]

One sociologist of deviance whom Lyman need not remind to look for the deeper structures of evil in society is Richard Quinney. Quinney's early critical analysis of crime, deviance, and social control linked the impersonal forces of corporate dominance to the political and economic structures of modern capitalist society. More recently Quinney has suggested that the material problems of capitalism are multiplied by its "sacred" (i.e., spiritual) void. In Quinney's words:

> The contemporary world is caught in . . . a sacred void, the human predicament on both a spiritual and sociopolitical level. Among the characteristics that contribute to this void are a mode of production that enslaves workers, an analytic rationalism which dissipates the vital forces of life and transforms everything (including human beings) into an object of calculation and control, the loss of feeling for the bond with nature and the sense of history, the demotion of our world to a mere environment, a secularized humanism that cuts us off from our creative sources, the demonic quality of the political state, and the hopelessness of the future. . . . The void is historical, beginning with the emergence of capitalism and the breakdown of religious tradition under the . . . enlightenment.[65]

How is this sacred void to be overcome? Quinney urges us to move away from a purely naturalistic critique of society to one that incorporates the concerns of "prophetic theology." He argues for a form of "religious socialism" which will both promote social justice and heal the void found in contemporary existence. "By integrating into a Marxist materialist analysis a critical and prophetic theology of culture," Quinney believes, we will "develop an understanding of the world and a way of transcending the contemporary historical condition."[66] This cannot be done by a purely naturalistic critique or secular socialism. According to Quinney: "A socialism without the sacred would become a system as materialist and alienating as that of capitalism. What is emerging in the transition to socialism is a new religious concern, a concern which not only repudiates the essential secularity of capitalism, but one that makes socialism whole by integration of the sacred void."[67]

A third call for a type of spiritual transcendence of the purely naturalistic approach to deviance and social control is found in Larry Tifft and Dennis Sullivan's book *The Struggle to Be Human*. Tifft and Sullivan articulate an "anarchist" approach in which the rule of law or "external authority" is viewed as a villain which separates us from direct responsibility for the good and bad we create for one another. Once this happens we are said to "become the historical ghosts from whom we are struggling to free ourselves."[68] We forget that the world which seems to rule us is "in reality" a world of our own making. According to Tifft and Sullivan, "We deny ourselves our spiritual homes and our ability to become part of the process we create."[69]

Tifft and Sullivan reject an approach to social control which permits the state to act on our behalf in containing the legally defined deviant. When this happens, as it does in our own modern society, we lose the "cosmic sense" of ourselves as humans struggling together.[70] Approaches to the study of crime or deviance which accept the existence of state authority as something natural, as something given, are said to be guilty of a "warped spirituality." Just as impersonal control by state institutions should be replaced by strategies of mutual aid, direct personal resistance, and communal reconciliation, so also do Tifft and Sullivan urge that we "turn scientific inquiry over to the community" and that our research be guided by a sensitivity "to the mystery of life, the mystery of human experience, the mystery of a world of mutual aid."[71]

Bridges between sacred understandings and naturalistic control processes are also embodied by people committed to maintaining or reexamining the values of pagan world views and practices. While driven underground in the west from the late Middle Ages to the present, paganism has remained a material aspect of the religious lives of many so-called third-world peoples. This is particularly true with regard to a wide variety of religious rituals of Africans and of the indigenous peoples of what we today call the "new world." Indeed, whether in Caribbean voodoo, or in the continuing shamanism of various North, Central, and South American "native" peoples, or even in the lineages of Afrocentric religious practices that constitute what Zora Neale Hurston once called the "Sanctified Church" of the black diaspora living in the United States, the resistance of pagan forms to the disembodying male violence of modern western religious controls continues.[72] A recognition of this resistance by people who would pave the world over with modern white-male-oriented economies based on western moral logic and belief is evident in their continuing demand for conversion of others whose pagan spiritualities refuse a clear-cut distinction between pure spirit and the impurities of living bodily in a world that is itself sacred. Where conversion is resisted politically—for instance, in Guatemala, where native peasant opposition to U.S.-based economic domination typically draws spiritual strength from shamanistic religious counselors and healers—figures of "the old religion" have been systematically targeted for "disappearance" by paramilitary death squads. In other settings, such as Puerto Rico, where "ecstatic" pagan undertones mix with a surface adherence to the ways of Christianity, conservative Protestant evangelists have recently used the appeal of new television-based ministries in gaining "Christian access" to practitioners of *Santeria* and other pagan-influenced religious forms.

Even as the future of pagan practices is today being contested in the third world, there is, in the United States and in other overdeveloped countries, a resurgence of interest in Goddess-directed "feminist spirituality" and other pagan spiritualities.[73] This is occurring, in part, because of a growing feminist critique of and dissatisfaction with the silencing or marginalization of both women and non-male-identified religious awareness within the dominant western religious organizations. For a great many women and for some men, paganism is attractive today also because of its reverence for nature in a time of great ecological catastrophes; its relatively reciprocal approach to power in an age of democratic questioning; and its respect for the sacredness of the body in an era in which the body is everywhere profaned, commodified, and pornographized. Paganism offers an immanent understanding of the sacredness of interdependent life (and death) processes and a vision of social control as an ever-changing ritual dialogue between humans and the rest of nature. The fluid, poetic, and power-reciprocal promise of contemporary pagan perspectives is articulated by the feminist witch Starhawk in the following manner:

> Witchcraft offers a model of a religion of poetry, not theology. It presents metaphors, not doctrines, and leaves open the possibility of reconciliation of science and religion, of many ways of knowing. It functions in those deeper ways of knowing which our culture has denied and for which we hunger. The worldview of Witchcraft is cyclical, spiral. It dissolves dualities and seeks opposites as complements. Diversity is valued, both poles of any duality are always valued because between them flows the on-off pulse of polar energy that sustains life. The cycle is the rhythm of the dance. . . . Finally, the Craft provides a structural model, the coven, the circle of friends, in which there is leadership but no hierarchy, small enough to create community without loss of individuality. The form of ritual is circular, not an altar or a podium or a sacred shrine, because it is in each other that the Goddess is found. . . . There are no hierophants, no messiahs, no avatars, no gurus.[74]

In different ways the writings of Lyman, Quinney, Tifft and Sullivan, and various pagan and feminist theorists remind us to temper the naturalistic analysis of deviance and social control with an awareness of the moral, spiritual, or cosmic nature of this subject matter. This reminder is a fitting way to close the chapter on the demonic perspective. After all, the demonic perspective informs us that control of deviance is first and foremost a battle between good and evil. It is a battle over who gets to name the good and control the bad. This is often overlooked (or perhaps covered up) by the neutral-sounding language of some of our more "modern" perspectives. Let us not be fooled by this "devilishness." Deviance is and always has been a moral battle in which the winners are declared saints and the losers sinners.

NOTES

1 Jerry Falwell, *Listen America!* Bantam, New York, 1980, from back cover.
2 My account of the "facts" of this case is drawn from Tom Killen, "By Demons Possessed," *Connecticut Magazine*, September 1981, pp. 47 ff.

3 Ibid., p. 50.

4 For a systematic review of the different processes contributing to secularization, see N. J. Demerath III and Phillip E. Hammand, *Religion in Social Context: Tradition and Transition*, Random House, New York, 1969, esp. pp. 103–114.

5 Peter L. Berger, *The Sacred Canopy: Elements of a Sociological Theory of Religion*, Anchor Books, Garden City, N.Y., 1969, pp. 107–108.

6 Ibid., p. 39.

7 Raymond Verdier, "Ontology of the Judicial Thought of the Kabré of Northern Togo," in Laura Nader (ed.), *Law in Culture and Society*, Aldine, Chicago, 1969, pp. 145–146.

8 H. C. Lea, *The Inquisition of the Middle Ages*, Harper & Row, New York, 1969, p. 168.

9 Ibid.

10 Kai T. Erikson, *Wayward Puritans*, Wiley, New York, 1966, p. 142.

11 Ibid., p. 151.

12 Ibid.

13 Michel Foucault, *History of Sexuality: Volume I*, Robert Hurley (trans.), Vintage, New York, 1980, p. 60.

14 Graeme Newman, *The Punishment Response*, Lippincott, Philadelphia, 1978, p. 46.

15 Ibid., pp. 38–39.

16 Ibid., p. 37.

17 Ibid., pp. 33–35.

18 Michel Foucault, *Discipline and Punishment: The Origins of the Prison*, Alan Sheridan (trans.), Pantheon, New York, 1978, pp. 3–5.

19 John Lewis Gillin, *Criminology and Penology*, rev. ed., Appleton-Century, New York, 1926, pp. 203–205.

20 Newman, *The Punishment Response*, pp. 98–99.

21 The following discussion of social control in acephalous societies is based upon the analysis of Raymond J. Michalowski in *Order, Law and Crime: Introduction to Critical Criminology*, Scott, Foresman, Glenview, Ill., 1984. See also Michael Taylor, *Community, Anarchy and Liberty*, Cambridge, London, 1982; and Stephen J. Pfohl, "Labeling Criminals," in H. Laurence Ross (ed.), *Law and Deviance*, Sage, Beverly Hills, Calif., 1981, pp. 65–97.

22 R. F. Barton, *Ifugao Law*, University of California Press, Berkeley, 1919.

23 E. E. Evans-Pritchard, *The Nuer: A Description of the Modes of Livelihood and Political Institutions of a Nilotic People*, Oxford University Press, New York, 1940.

24 Donald Black, *The Behavior of Law*, Academic, New York, 1976, p. 129.

25 C. W. M. Hart and A. R. Pilling, *The Tiwi of North Australia*, Holt, New York, 1962.

26 J. Friedl and J. E. Pfeiffer, *Anthropology: The Study of People*, Harper & Row, New York, 1977, p. 476.

27 Ibid.

28 Evans-Pritchard, *The Nuer*, pp. 184–191.

29 Andrew Scull, *Decarceration: Community Treatment and the Deviant—A Radical View*, Prentice-Hall, Englewood Cliffs, N.J., 1977, p. 17.

30 Gillin, *Criminology and Penology*, p. 203.

31 Mary Daly, "European Witchburning: Purifying the Body of Christ," in *Gyn/Ecology: the Metaethics of Radical Feminism*, Beacon Press, Boston, 1978, pp. 178–192.

32 See, for instance, Monica Sjöö and Barbara Mor, *The Great Cosmic Mother: Rediscovering the Religion of the Earth*, Harper and Row, San Francisco, 1987, pp. 298–314; and Arthur Evans, *Witchcraft and the Gay Counterculture*, Fag Rag Books, Boston, 1978, pp. 88–99.

33 Henry Boguet, "Discours des Sorciers," quoted in Evans, *Witchcraft and the Gay Counterculture*, p. 77.

34 Elaine Pagels, "The Suppressed Gnostic Feminism," *The New York Review of Books*, vol. 26, no. 18, Nov. 22, 1979, p. 22.

35 This passage from *Alpha Bet Ben Sira* is found in Barbara Black Koltuv, *The Book of Lilith*, Nicholas-Hays, York Beach, Maine, 1986, pp. 19–20. Koltuv's book is an excellent source for materials pertaining to the various legends of Lilith. See also John A. Phillips, *Eve: The History of an Idea*, Harper and Row, San Francisco, 1984, pp. 39–40.

36 See, for instance, Sjöö and Mor, *The Great Cosmic Mother*, p. 171.

37 Phillips, *Eve*, pp. 55–77.

38 Heinrich Kramer and Jakob Sprenger, *Malleus Maleficarum*, Montague Summers (trans.), Pushkin Press, London, 1951, p. 47.

39 The demonic interpretation of rock and roll is not new. For a review of conservative Christian criticism of rock, see Benjamin R. Epstein and Arnold Foster, *The Radical Right: Report on the John Birch Society and Its Allies*, Vintage, New York, 1967.

40 Associated Press, "Southern Baptists Move to Bar Gays," *Boston Globe*, June 10, 1992, p. 12.

41 Quoted in "The New Right Comes of Age," *Christian Century*, Oct. 29, 1980, pp. 995–996. For an extended presentation of Falwell's views, see Falwell, *Listen America!*, p. 17.

42 See also Peggy L. Shriver, *The Bible Vote*, Pilgrim, New York, 1981.

43 Allan J. Lichtman, "The New Prohibitionism," *Christian Century*, Oct. 29, 1981, p. 1029.

44 "The New Right Comes of Age," p. 996.

45 Timothy W. Lukes, *Screens of Power: Ideology, Domination, and Resistance in Informational Society*, University of Illinois Press, Urbana and Chicago, 1989, p. 96.

46 James W. Douglas, *The Non-Violent Cross: A Theology of Revolution and Peace*, Macmillan, London, 1966, p. 3.

47 Quoted in Benjamin Muse, *The American Negro Revolution*, Citadel, New York, 1970, p. 49.

48 For examples of the work which has been done by liberation theologians, see Gustavo Gutiérrez, *A Theology of Liberation*, Orbis, Maryknoll, N.Y., 1973; José (Bonino) Miguez, *Doing Theology in a Revolutionary Situation*, Fortrees, Philadelphia, 1976; and José P. Miranda, *Marx and the Bible: A Critique of the Philosophy of Oppression*, Obris, Maryknoll, N.Y., 1974. For a general overview of the movement, see Arthur F. McGovern, *Marxism: An American Christian Perspective*, Orbis, Maryknoll, N.Y., 1980, esp. chap. 5.

49 Quoted in Peter Hebblethwaite, *The Christian-Marxist Dialogue*, Paulist, New York, 1977, p. 43.

50 Ibid., p. 41.

51 Daniel McShea, "The Nature of Science Is on Trial in Scopes II Case," *Boston Globe*, Dec. 14, 1981, p. 3.

52 M. L. Starkey, *The Devil in Massachusetts*, Knopf, New York, 1949.

53 Thomas Szasz, *The Theology of Medicine: The Political and Philosophical Foundations of Medical Ethics*, Louisiana State University Press, Baton Rouge, pp. viv–xv.

54 Chadwick Hansen, *Witchcraft in Salem*, Braziller, New York, 1969.

55 Erikson, *Wayward Puritans*, p. 153.

56 Ibid., pp. 139–140.

57 Barbara Yoshika, "Whoring after Strange Gods: A Narrative of Women and

Witches," *Radical Religion*, vol. 1, no. 2, spring 1974, p. 7; a publication of Radical Religion Collective. Excerpted in Sheila Balken, Ronald J. Berger, and Janet Schmidt, *Crime and Deviance in America: A Critical Approach*, Wadsworth, Belmont, Calif., 1980, p. 232. See also Nancy van Vuuren, *The Subversion of Women*, Westminster, Philadelphia, 1973.

58 Barbara Ehrenreich and Deidre English, *For Her Own Good: 150 Years of the Experts' Advice to Women*, Anchor, Garden City, N.Y., 1978, pp. 35–39. See also Jules Michelet, *Satanism and Witchcraft*, Citadel, Secaucus, N.J., 1939; and Margaret Alice Murray, *The Witch-Cult in Western Europe*, Oxford University Press, New York, 1921.

59 Balken, Berger, and Schmidt, *Crime and Deviance in America*, p. 231. See also Marvin Harris, *Cows, Pigs, Wars and Witches*, Random House, New York, 1974, p. 237.

60 Elliot P. Currie, "Crimes without Criminals: Witchcraft and Its Control in Renaissance Europe," *Law and Society Review*, vol. 3, August 1968, pp. 7–32.

61 Elliot P. Currie, "Crimes without Criminals," as excerpted in Edwin M. Schuer, *Interpreting Deviance*, Harper & Row, New York, 1979, p. 173.

62 Stanford M. Lyman, *The Seven Deadly Sins: Society and Evil*, St. Martin's, New York, 1978, p. 1.

63 Alex Liazos, "The Sociology of Deviances: Nuts, Sluts and Perverts," *Social Problems*, vol. 20, summer 1972, pp. 103–120.

64 Lyman, *The Seven Deadly Sins*, p. 4.

65 Richard Quinney, *Providence: The Reconstruction of Social and Moral Order*, Longman, New York, 1980, pp. 8–9.

66 Ibid., p. x.

67 Richard Quinney, *Capitalist Society*, Irwin, Homewood, Ill., 1979, p. 127.

68 Larry L. Tifft and Dennis Sullivan, *The Struggle to Be Human: Crime, Criminology and Anarchism*, Cienfuegos Press, Orkney, Scotland, 1980, p. 39.

69 Ibid.

70 Ibid., p. 2.

71 Ibid., p. 20.

72 For a discussion of Native American spiritualities, see Stan Steiner (ed.), *Spirit Woman: The Diaries and Paintings of Bonita Wa Wa Calachaw Nunez*, Harper and Row, San Francisco, 1980; and John G. Neihardt, *Black Elk Speaks*, University of Nebraska Press, Lincoln, 1961. For a discussion of the spirituality of voodoo, see Zora Neale Hurston, *Tell My Horse: Voodoo and Life in Haiti and Jamaica*, Harper and Row, New York, 1990; Maya Deren, *Divine Horsemen: The Living Gods of Haiti*, Documentext/McPherson, New Paltz, N.Y., 1953; Alfred Metraux, *Voodoo in Haiti*, Hugh Charteris (trans.), Schocken Books, New York, 1972; Milo Rigaud, *Secrets of Voodoo*, City Lights, San Francisco, 1953; and Karen McCarthy Brown, *Mama Lola: A Vodou Priestess in Brooklyn*, University of California Press, Berkeley, 1991.

73 For a discussion of the contemporary resurgence of paganism in the United States, see Margot Adler, *Drawing Down the Moon: Witches, Druids, Goddess-Worshippers and Other Pagans in America Today*, Beacon Press, Boston, 1986.

74 Starhawk, *The Sprial Dance: A Rebirth of the Ancient Religion of the Great Goddess*, Harper and Row, San Francisco, 1979, p. 179.

Cool Man Calculated By Joseph LaMantia and Stephen Pfohl

CHAPTER 3

THE CLASSICAL PERSPECTIVE:
Deviance as Rational Hedonism

Laws are the conditions, under which men, naturally independent, united themselves in a society. Weary of living in a continual state of war, and of enjoying a liberty which became of little value, from the uncertainty of its duration, they sacrificed one part of it, to enjoy the rest in peace and security. . . . But it was not sufficient only to establish this deposit; it was also necessary to defend it from the usurpation of each individual, who would always endeavor not only to take away from the mass his own portion, but to encroach on that of others.

Cesare Beccaria[1]

If the expected cost of crime goes up without a corresponding increase in the expected benefits, then the would-be criminal—unless he or she is among that small fraction of criminals who are utterly irrational—engages in less crime.

James Q. Wilson[2]

INTRODUCTION

Several years ago I had the privilege of accompanying a criminal court judge from the Netherlands on a tour of a large, newly constructed maximum-security prison in Ohio. The Dutch jurist was flabbergasted by the cold, impersonal magnitude of the huge steel cage. This penitentiary closed its cell doors upon approximately 1,300 inmates—a number equal to about one-third of the entire prison population of Holland.

We had been given special permission from the governor's office for a "no-holds-barred" view of the entire facility. We observed its central video control room. Each main corridor was constantly "on the air," being watched by guards who manned electronic gate-release switches controlling movement between each cell block and subdivision of the mammoth "correctional center." We were shown its isolation units (these barren cells used to be called "the hole"), its underground intervention tunnels (designed for a speedy militarylike restoration of order in the event of a possible riot), and its ominous-looking electric chair. Its purpose needed no explaining. We spent hours examining the institution and talking with the prisoners who had been sentenced to "do time" within its walls.

Our tour guide was the captain of the guards, who is now referred to as the "chief correctional officer." At numerous points along the tour the Dutch judge appeared to be amazed, even disturbed, by what he saw. The Netherlands incarcerates a far smaller percentage of its criminal population in much smaller facilities for a considerably shorter time. In broken English the judge would exclaim, "This is, how do you say, fantastic." I translated his message to mean, "I can't quite believe this." The guard captain must have interpreted him differently. He responded by saying, "Yeh, if you think that's somethin', judge, wait'll you see this next thing."

Upon completing our tour, the judge, the captain, and I sat down over coffee in the staff cafeteria. The judge had many questions: "Why do you build such large prisons? Why do you incarcerate people for such a long time? Don't inmates get angry and disillusioned locked up for such a long time like so many head of cattle; idle with little to do but pass time talking, sitting, playing cards, playing games of power and intimidation just as games of power and intimidation are played on them?" The captain was surprised by the judge's questions: "You're a judge. You must see these kind of people in your court. Don't you do the same thing with them in your country?" The judge explained that he did not. He explained that in the Netherlands few convicted criminals were locked up. He explained that most offenders there, as in the United States, were property offenders. His country relied much more on a system of costly fines and community-based approaches designed to make such offenders pay back their victims and society. Prison terms were reserved for hard-core and violent offenders. Even for these, sentences were short. Most served under a year. Three years was viewed as an extraordinarily long period of time. After that, said the judge, incarceration worked against itself. It hardened rather than softened deviants. How else could a human being survive such a place?

All this amazed the captain. "I can't believe it. You don't mean it. Say I come to your country. Say I plan this bank robbery. Say I get a gun; shoot somebody; the whole works. Then I get caught, but before I do I stash the loot. Say half a million dollars or whatever you call them over there."

"Guilders," replied the judge.

"Yeh, OK. Guilders. Say I stashed all those guilders so that when I got out I'd get my hands on them. How long would you give me if I came before your court?"

"Well, since you say you shot somebody, probably two years."

The captain shook his head in amazement. "You gotta be kiddin'! Two years. Two years ain't nothin'. Do you know how much I make in two years?

Man, two years—that's worth it. You're kiddin' me, aren't you? No! Hey I'm comin'. I mean it. Just figure it out. Two years. It's like an investment. I'll take the two years, then I'll be rich. Just tell me how to get there, Judge."

Not wanting to get in the middle, I tried to wiggle diplomatically out of the conversation. I mumbled something about the Netherlands being a very different place. What I really thought was that in an odd way both the captain and the judge were voicing ideas that could be pulled directly from the pages of a treatise on the classical perspective on deviance and social control. At the heart of this perspective lies the notion that deviance involves a process of rationally calculated choice to achieve maximum pleasure at the cost of minimum pain. Clearly this is what the captain had in mind in fantasizing his criminal excursion to the Netherlands. In terms of social control the perspective emphasizes an equally rationally calculated approach to punishment. The judge appeared concerned with the same. What would really happen if the calculating captain got caught within the judge's rationalized system of social control? In this chapter we shall explore, at least in principle, the classical perspective's answer to this question.

THEORETICAL IMAGES

The classical perspective represented a radical departure from the long tradition of demonic or supernaturalistic explanation. It may be thought of as the first "modern" perspective on deviance and social control. It appeared first in the eighteenth-century writings of scholars such as Cesare Beccaria and Jeremy Bentham. These theorists viewed themselves as enlightened reformers, guiding society away from a dark age of superstitious and arbitrary social control toward a new order based upon the rational, fair, and consistent application of human reason.

Whereas demonic thinking emphasized the influence of supernatural forces, classical theorists conceived of humans as uninfluenced by anything but the calculative rationality of human reason. Deviance, like any other human act, was viewed as a freely calculated choice to maximize pleasure and minimize pain. Classical thought also departed from the idea of "cosmic connectedness" which lay behind the demonic perspective's understanding of the supernaturally ordained character of human society. Gone was the notion that people were in some mysterious way bound to each other in spirit. This was replaced by a view of society as a contract, a legalistic agreement between people regarding how each should or should not act toward others.

The classical perspective's vision of human nature as a free and rationally calculated choice for pleasure and of society as a consensual social contract permeates everything it has to say about deviance and social control. Where does this particular vision come from? The answer is found in the intimate historical connection between classical thought and a host of major social, economic, political, and intellectual developments.

Sociohistorical Background

It is no accident that classical thought emerged when it did. For historical purposes we mark its birth with the 1764 publication of Cesare Beccaria's important work, *An Essay on Crimes and Punishments*. In reality this new, highly rational way of seeing deviance was the offspring of massive transformations in the social landscape of Europe over the preceding several centuries. Several interconnected developments were particularly important in sowing the seeds of classical theorizing. These included major shifts in the size and shape of Europe's population, the transformation of the feudal economy into early forms of capitalism, the emergence of the modern nation-state, and the intellectual impetus of scholasticism and the Enlightenment. Together these changes broke the back of the local community structures which had contained deviance during the demonic period. Gone were the cosmic connections between saints and sinners and the collective social, economic, and political ties between people who shared a common supernatural destiny. These were replaced by the naturalistic principles of classical reasoning with its stress upon individual responsibility, free choice, and hedonistic calculation.

The story of how major demographic, economic, political, religious, and intellectual changes altered European society's conception of deviant behavior is a complex one. Its outline is briefly sketched in the following pages.

Demographic Changes   With regard to demographic shifts it is important to note that from the sixteenth century through the eighteenth century there was a great growth in the size, density, and heterogeneity of Europe's population.[3]

England, for instance, had grown from a population of 2.8 million in 1500 to 8.9 million in 1800. During that same time France grew from 16 million to 27 million, while the population of Italy expanded from 6 million to 17.2 million. More important, the shape and distribution of the European population were becoming more dense and more heterogeneous than previous generations of people living within small, well-defined feudal kingdoms. The gradual redistribution of Europe's population followed new paths of social and economic development, opened initially by the armies of crusaders and subsequently by the merchants of a new commercial order of international trade. Cities began to grow in size, and this growth was accompanied by development of an anonymity unknown to the small local communities of the Middle Ages. Over several centuries London had mushroomed to a population of 750,000, while Paris had grown to 600,000 inhabitants.

Changes in the structure of the European population disrupted the community-based strategies of social control that were associated with the demonic period. Increases in population size increased the scope of the kinds of problems that during the Middle Ages had been dealt with swiftly and directly by small communities of people who knew each other as kin or neighbors. As density increases it becomes more likely that people who meet one another will be anonymous strangers. Anonymity increases the potential for deviance in that it loosens bonds of informal control which people experience in the presence of well-known others.

The same happens as populations increase in heterogeneity. Heterogeneous populations lack a common history, a common juncture of beliefs, perceptions, and values. As such they are more prone to disagreement and less able to invoke the weight of collectively experienced tradition as a device for controlling deviance.

Political and Economic Changes   Similar problems arose in the economic and political spheres, where centuries of collective communal responsibility were exchanged for an individualist ethic of atomized citizenry. In the economic sphere this happened as the complex interdependent obligations of feudal reciprocity were replaced by the simple cash-for-labor contract of the capitalist marketplace. This is not to romanticize the structures of feudalism and the unequal system of economic exchange in which feudal lords and vassals dominated the material lives of serfs and their families. During the era of feudalism, a vassal, by birth and divine precept, was the rightful controller of a feudal manor, or estate, a collection of lands inhabited and tilled by serfs. Vassals were landlords to whom serfs paid a portion of their crops or agricultural labor. In exchange, serfs were guaranteed protection by the vassal's army. By these traditional arrangements families of vassals and serfs were bound across generations. The ties of fealty, however, were more than economic. Vassals and serfs were also linked by "companionage," a set of mutually binding social obligations rooted in the idea of collective responsibility and the principle that "harm falling upon one fell upon all."[4]

The interdependent controls of companionage were dissipated first by the trade economy of mercantilism and subsequently by the full development of capitalism. These new economic forms stressed private rather than collective ownership of property and the exchange of labor for a fixed, impersonal wage rather than out of personal loyalty to a vassal. This significant and drastic departure from communal control gave rise to an ethic of *individualism*. The new merchant classes were committed to the business of making a profit and called unsympathetically for the rejection of anyone who might lose heavily in trade relations. Individuals, in other words, must go it alone in the new economic marketplace. In the words of Karl Marx, the new capitalist economy "left no other nexus between man and man than naked self-interest, than callous cash payment."[5]

Economic individualization was accompanied by political individualization. In part this was true because the rise of the capitalist economic mode was historically interconnected with the rise of the modern nation-state. Indeed the birth of centralized state power in the west may be told as the story of a "squeeze play" in which an early capitalist-merchant class linked itself to the armed forces of national monarchs in an effort to secure fertile, safe, and consistent conditions for large-scale production and international trade. Squeezed out of power were legions of vassals, many of whom had forfeited mortgages on their feudal manors to merchants who had bankrolled ill-fated military adventures. Thus just as this new economic class triumphed over the old class of vassals, so did it become the monetary backbone of the emerging nation-state.

The political consequences of this triumphant coalition were enormous. Just as the emergence of a market economy destroyed the complex web of mutually binding feudal economic ties, the rise of the nation-state meant a dismantling of a host of collectively oriented medieval political institutions, in particular political power residing in kin, the church, and the local guild. Each of these was an intermediary institution, a link between individuals and the local community, another manifestation of community-oriented social control. With the growth of centralized state power these institutions were replaced by the concept of the "citizen," an atomized individual owing political allegiance to none but the state and its laws. Like the anonymity generated by population changes and the isolated individualism induced by wage-labor relations, this atomization contributed further to a breakdown in old control structures and to the necessity for a new way of envisioning the problem of deviance.

Religious Changes   As discussed in Chapter 2, the late Middle Ages were marked by a patriarchal Christian assault upon the "Great Mother"-focused paganism and upon the witches who were said to represent this supposedly sinful way of life. This contributed to the perception of individual human life as rationally abstracted from the periodic cycles of nature "herself." While pagans celebrated festive rites symbolizing human-animal participation in the spiraling folds of nature, by the early modern period, people schooled in Christian belief alone envisioned themselves to be somewhat anxiously positioned as if outside of or above nature looking down. In combination with the institution of the rite of confession in 1215, which fostered a shift in responsibility for deviant actions from the group to the individual, the outlawing of pagan practices contributed greatly to a modern historical disconnection between idealized individual experience and the material reality of communal interdependence.

During the sixteenth century the Protestant Reformation furthered this atomization of individuals.[6] The "spiritual" revolt against the authority of Roman Catholic religious rule was intimately connected to the more "material" changes described above. Although formally a division in theological understanding, this fracturing of western Christianity during the sixteenth century was buttressed by such other historical developments as the growing dissatisfaction of the laboring poor—serfs and local priests—with the ostentatious lifestyle of the bishops and abbots who occupied privileged seats of influence in the courts of powerful lords and monarchs. Also important were the religious desires of the successful merchant classes whose growth in such places as Germany, Switzerland, and the Netherlands fostered an increased autonomy in relation to the economic and political structures of the old feudal order. These precursors of capitalism were inclined to administer their spiritual affairs as they did their businesses, as unmediated relations between individuals, in this case between God and the solitary believer. So, likewise, was the Reformation fostered by conflict between the secular kings and princes of the emerging nation-states and the centralized religious power of the pope in Rome. For years many of the new monarchs had quarreled with the Roman church over matters related to property, taxation, and legal jurisdiction. With the Reformation the rule of papal authority was dealt a deadly blow. Secular monarchs gained the power to determine which of several Christian churches would become the official religion of their land. Thus, the Church of England was nationally separated not only from the Church of Rome but also from the Lutheran and Calvinist churches, which were allied with the secular state authority of other monarchs.

Once under way the Reformation had significant consequences for social control in western Europe. It tore asunder the appearance of a unitary set of religious standards by which to judge deviance. In countries won over by Protestantism it did far more. It stripped believers of a host of intermediary channels of salvation. Gone was the mediation of Catholic church officials, saints, guardian angels, and the Blessed Virgin. In their place was "faith alone," the naked individual's personal relation to the grace of God the Almighty. This was most evident in the Protestant denial of the efficacy of the sacrament of penance. When Martin Luther hammered his ninety-five theses onto the door of the castle church at Wittenberg in 1517, chief among his contentions was that a sinner was cleansed not by the power of priestly absolution, but *sola gratia*, by the grace of God alone. This emphasis on the total dependence of individuals on the will of the divine was taken to the extreme by the Calvinists, who argued that people were predestined from birth for either salvation or damnation. But how could someone know if he or she was saved? Within a short time Protestants answered this question by coming to view worldly success and self-disciplined rationality as exterior signs of the interior working of God's grace. Thus, those who adhered to the highly constrained "work ethic" of Protestantism revealed in this world their status as God's chosen in the world which is to come. In this fashion Protestantism not only fostered an individualistic approach to the problem of sin but also, by its emphasis on disciplined rationality, nurtured the development of capitalism, a force productive of individualization on its own.

Intellectual Changes: Scholasticism and the Enlightenment   Along with demographic, economic, political, and religious changes, two intellectual developments also contributed to the new rationalist perspective on nonconformity. The first was theological. Its most dramatic form was the way in which Protestant theology encouraged the equation of goodness with disciplined rationality. For Catholics an emphasis on the goodness of the rational was provided by scholastic theology. Given the Catholic educational background of Cesare Beccaria, this emphasis is of particular interest. Scholasticism provided a conceptual bridge for the transition between the supernaturalistic and naturalistic viewpoints. Exposure to scholasticism provided Beccaria and others with theological teachings which emphasized human rationality, free choice, and a logically deducible natural law that justified obedience to secular state authority.

Scholasticism represented somewhat of a fusion between Christian doctrine and the philosophies of Plato and Aristotle.[7] At its core was a deep belief in the power of reason. Scholastic theologians believed that humans could use reason to deductively arrive both at a proof for the existence of God and at the "natural laws" governing correct Christian morality. Natural laws, the benign product of God's infinite wisdom, were discovered by reason rather than through miraculous supernatural signs. This belief in the beneficence of reason was a key part of the teaching of scholastic church fathers such as Thomas Aquinas. Aquinas believed that humans freely choose to do good when they allow their will to be guided by reason, or the "rational intellect." Free choice, moreover, "is possible only where there is knowledge of alternatives and the power of will to make choices."

Aquinas and other scholastic thinkers agreed with Aristotle that the virtues of "natural man" are fully realized only when appetites for such things as riches, pleasure, power, and knowledge are tempered, or controlled, by will and reason. But why should "natural" men (and women by implication) temper their immediate appetites? The answer is found in the "reasonable" deduction that all good human action must direct itself toward the common good. This principle of common good paved the way for a scholastic justification of the state. The state arises naturally to secure a lawful order which would be agreed to by any reasonable person.

Scholastic theology equated sin with a failure to make free and calculably reasonable choices for the common good. This is a long step from a strictly supernatural interpretation of deviance. The will of God and the calculated choice of the reasonable "natural man" become one and the same. The task for morality is thus to establish a rule of reason, a rule of calculated rationality. This was the task chosen by Beccaria and other classical theorists. Schooled in scholastic theology, they borrowed heavily from its emphasis on the goodness of rational choice and obedience to the natural laws of the state. Although first developed in the Middle Ages, scholastic theology rose in preeminence during the same time in which the previously described forces of demographic, economic, and political change were altering the social and material life of European society. How interesting it is that we find a theological justification for such ideas as the importance of free individual choice, calculated rationality, and the naturalness of state authority at precisely those moments in which dramatic population shifts, the emergence of the capitalist marketplace, and the development of the modern state were also occurring. This is not to suggest that these changes "caused" a shift in theological thought. It does suggest that ideas never exist in an historical vacuum. They are influenced by and in turn influence the events in the social and material world in which they are located. The same is true of the philosophy of the Enlightenment.

Scholastic theology prepared religiously educated thinkers such as Beccaria to break with previous supernaturally dominated accounts of deviance and evildoing. In the philosophy of the Enlightenment classical theorists discovered a related set of secular intellectual assumptions. Enlightenment philosophy also emphasized the primacy of reason and the role of calculated rational choice in realizing a state of natural human order. Yet, the most distinctive contribution of the Enlightenment to the classical perspective is the notion of the "social contract." Enlightenment thinkers viewed society as a legalistic contract between freely consenting human individuals. Whether individuals were motivated by what Montesquieu conceived of as the four innate desires of peace, hunger, sex, and sociability, or by Rousseau's posited need for companionship, or by Hobbes's conceptualized need to avoid perpetual conflict, the origin of society was commonly conceived of in terms of a freely entered upon contract of individuals.

Of all the enlightened social contract theorists, Hobbes appears to have had the most influence in the development of the classical perspective. Hobbes believed that without the lawlike restraints of the sovereign state, social life would collapse into an ongoing war between people with conflicting self-interests. Any reasonable person could recognize this. Hobbes's arguments regarding the naturalness of the state are laid out in his renowned treatise *Leviathan*. The influence of this manuscript is felt on nearly every page of Cesare Beccaria's own major life work, *An Essay on Crimes and Punishment*. *Leviathan* spells out what Hobbes considers to be the essential elements of the natural political community: monopoly of force by the state, the naturalness of centralized sovereignty, the supremacy of national values, and the atomlike character of the individual citizen. How did Hobbes arrive at these natural principles? Like other Enlightenment scholars, Hobbes argued that his "discoveries" were the logical deductions of disciplined reason. Maybe. Yet, as Robert Nisbet points out, the natural law which Hobbes articulated in the seventeenth century was, in actuality, little more than an updated transmutation of the principles of law of the ancient Roman state.[8] Both justified central state authority. Both arose at precisely those points in history in which the practical rule of the state demanded a kind of corresponding intellectual defense. Again we find an affinity between theoretical thought and practical social context. As Nisbet points out, Hobbes wrote at a time in which the emerging British nation-state was facing a political crisis of tremendous importance. The followers of the Stuarts were locked in a treacherous civil war with Cromwell and his army of Puritans. The countryside was being ravaged by more conflict than England had seen in centuries. Looting, pillaging, burning, and robbing had become daily occurrences. The monarch Charles I had been beheaded in public. The fate of the modern state appeared in doubt. In the midst of this widespread conflict Hobbes sought to provide firm intellectual footing for the strict imposition of centralized state authority.

Beccaria and Bentham inherited from theorists such as Hobbes a conviction about the naturalness of the "social contract" and the rational rule of state law. Combined with a belief in free will and in the goodness of calculable rationality, these doctrines were a major impetus for classical thought. How did all these factors express themselves in classical theorizing? Let us answer this by first turning to the work of Beccaria.

Cesare Beccaria: Controlling the Rational Calculation of Deviant Pleasure

Born to noble parentage in Milan in 1738, Cesare Beccaria inherited the title Marchese di Beccaria. His upper-class Italian background provided him with the advantages of a rigorous education at the Jesuit College at Parma. Although he was an undistinguished student in his early years, this exposure to the dogmatic demands of Jesuit thought may have influenced Beccaria's later rebellion. In any event, his most influential education occurred after college. Only then did Beccaria become seriously interested in the critical thought of the Enlightenment. He read Montesquieu's *Lettres persanes* and the writings of the Encyclopedists. Convinced of the power of disciplined reason, he turned to the study of law at Pavia.

In 1761 Beccaria married Teresa di Blasco, the daughter of a relatively impoverished military officer. About the same time he entered into another marriage—this one to the "Academy of Fists," a talented, articulate, and radical group of Milanese youth. Its members were disenchanted with the archaic nature of European society. Their strident push for far-reaching social reform earned them the nickname "punch-hards."

The young members of the Academy of Fists saw themselves as "Northern Encyclopedists," as so many Voltaires and Diderots joined in opposition to the antiquated abuses of the current regime. Each was expected to study, master, and report on some specialized subject calling for inquiry and reform. Within this group Beccaria was most influenced by two brothers, Pietro and Alessandro Verri. Pietro, an abstract and dispassionate thinker, was an intellectual inspiration. Alessandro, a man of action, provided Becarria with a practical vision. Through Alessandro, who held a government post as the protector of prisons, Beccaria was exposed to the brutal and undifferentiated remnants of demonic social control. Beccaria witnessed a penal system ridden with corruption and dependent on the idiosyncratic discretion of individual judges. The irrationality and injustice of this system moved Beccaria into the stance of a reformer. In a short time he became a spokesperson for a new vision of social control. It was Pietro, however, who urged him to write down his thoughts and to develop a systematic plan for making legal social control more humane and more rational. Encouraged by Pietro, Beccaria began to scribble his ideas onto scraps of paper. The result was the major treatise of the classical perspective—*An Essay on Crimes and Punishments*.

Fearful of condemnation by those who wielded control over Italy's antiquated system of law and criminal justice, Beccaria first published his work anonymously in 1764. Not only was Beccaria's name omitted, but the first edition of *An Essay on Crimes and Punishments* was distributed without even listing the name of the printer. Such caution proved unnecessary. The book was an explosive success, and almost immediately became a landmark of reform. Beccaria was invited to France to "commune" with such revolutionary thinkers as D'Alembert, Diderot, Helvetius, and D'Holbach. He was publicly praised by Catherine the Great of Russia and Maria Theresa of Austria-Hungry and was quoted with admiration by such luminaries as the philosopher Voltaire, the legal theorist Blackstone, and those architects of the new American republic, Thomas Jefferson and John Adams.

Why was *An Essay on Crimes and Punishments* such an immediate success? The book appealed almost instantaneously to a curious mix of conservatives, who defended the continuance of monarchy, and radicals, such as D'Alembert and Diderot, who were setting in motion forces that would topple it. Both sides had a common stake in preserving the power of the absolute state. Their differences concerned how the state should be organized and who should control it. Both abhorred the continuation of antiquated demonic control policies, viewing them as harsh and arbitrary reminders of the previous days of Inquisition and holy terror. Beccaria's book represented a masterful stroke of timing, an opportunity to bring dark, medieval penal practice into the age of Enlightenment. According to historian Mary Peter Mack, "It was Beccaria's genius . . . to gather up all those poignant cries and shape them into a simple, rational, elegant and passionately human theory, moving and persuasive to all men of good will."[9] This theory is summarized in the six principles discussed below.

The Necessity of Rational Punishment in Preserving the Social Contract

Beccaria followed the lead of Hobbes and other Enlightenment thinkers in arguing for a naturalistic theory of social contract. But what happens when someone steps outside the terms of this contract? What happens when someone breaks the law of the sovereign state? Beccaria argued that a system of rational punishment was necessary in order to remind individuals of their common interest in preserving social order. Such punishments "were necessary to prevent the despotism of each individual from plunging society into its former chaos."[10] In defending the prerogative of the state to punish, Beccaria was careful to distinguish between tyrannical punishments, involving arbitrary efforts by individuals to gain positions of advantage, and rational punishments, aimed at "defending the public liberty . . . from the usurpation of individuals."[11]

Legislative Determination of Law; Judicial Determination of Guilt
During the demonic period, punishment was largely controlled by judges. Judges held enormous discretion both in discerning whether someone was guilty and in deciding the fate of convicted offenders. Little had changed by the eighteenth century. "Secret accusations, *lettres de cachet*, 'confessions' extracted by brutal tortures, mere charges considered prima facie evidence of guilt, convictions without appeal, arbitrary pardons, and tyrannical punishments were all commonplace."[12]

This dark side of demonic justice was revealed to Beccaria by his friend Alessandro Verri, an administrator of prisons. Outraged by the irrational and often abusive nature of judicially administered punishments, Beccaria, in his classical reforms, called for a strict differentiation between the punishment-setting responsibilities of the legislature and the lesser role of judges. As sovereign representatives of the entire social contract, legislators were to determine which acts endangered the common good and assign to each a particular punishment. Judges were to have no role in deciding upon punishment. Once a person was found guilty of breaking the law, a fixed, legislatively determined punishment was to be assigned automatically. In the words of Beccaria, "Judges have no right to interpret the penal law. . . . When the code of laws is . . . fixed (by the legislature), it should be observed in the literal sense, and nothing more is left to the judge than to determine whether an action be, or be not, conformable to the written law."[13]

The Hedonistic Psychology of Deviance: Maximizing Pleasure and Minimizing Pain A third principle of the classical perspective concerns the utilitarian calculus that was believed to govern human motivation. Humans were described as rational hedonists whose actions were based on a rational assessment of the available alternatives for maximizing pleasure and minimizing pain. Deviant action was no exception. It was calculatively chosen over conformity because it would most likely yield the greatest amount of pleasure at the least cost. Thus, for theorists such as Beccaria, who viewed "pain and pleasure [as] the only springs of [human] action," deviance was essentially no different from any other form of human conduct.[14] One deviated for the same reasons that one made other reasonable investments—to reap the profits of maximum pleasure.

Social Control as Rationally Calculated Punishment If humans were indeed rational hedonists, then the control of deviance would require the certain administration of punishment that was slightly more painful than the pleasure of nonconformity. This meant that the irrational cruelty of demonic retribution must be replaced by a rational system of measured punishment, each calculated to exceed the pleasure expected from a specific act of deviance. This system, moreover, must be known to all and administered evenly and without exception. Thus, if burglary produces six units of pleasure, its punishment should involve seven units of pain. In this fashion Beccaria proposed a precise "political arithmetic" of rational sanctions. He argued that specific types of punishment should be rationally fixed by "a calculation of [pleasure-pain] probabilities to mathematical exactness."[15]

Deterrence as the Object of Social Control   The purpose of the calculated punishment was to deter future acts of deviance. Deterrence would at once be specific and general, affecting both those who were caught and sanctioned and those who witnessed the certain application of rational punishment. Yet, for rational deterrence to operate effectively, several conditions must be met. According to Beccaria punishment must be certain, swift, and slightly more severe than the fruits of deviation would be pleasurable. Most important were the criteria of certainty and swiftness (or celerity). If these conditions were not met, there was no reason to expect that people would reasonably be deterred from seeking the pleasures of lawbreaking. The same might be true if punishments were too severe. Overly severe punishments were said to "outdistance" the calculable frameworks which reasonable people use in weighing advantages and costs of action. For this reason Beccaria opposed the death penalty and other forms of extreme penal cruelty.

Control of Acts, Not Actors   This final principle of classical thinking is extremely important. It is also that which offered most of the practical problems. The entire classical system was directed toward reducing deviant acts but paid little attention to deviant actors. According to Beccaria, "they err who imagine that a crime is greater or less according to the intention of the person by whom it is committed."[16] All actors were assumed to be endowed with free will and with a similar rational calculus. Thus, for classical theorists, it was important to know only whether a deviant act had occurred. Once this was ascertained, it was believed that the pleasure of similar acts could be deterred by a simple application of slightly more painful punishment. Accordingly, classical theory showed a total disregard for other aspects of an actor's life and for the circumstances surrounding a particular deviant occurrence. Treat no deviant as an exception. Forget about whether an offender had a bad home, a bad night, or a bad self-concept. If the act occurred, deliver the punishment.

Jeremy Bentham: Extending the Utilitarian Calculus of Rational Punishment

Jeremy Bentham (1748–1832) was, like Beccaria, both a thinker and a reformer. Whereas Beccaria was repulsed by the continuance of harsh demonic control strategies in Europe, Bentham was repelled by the archaic state of eighteenth-century British common law.[17] In his books *Fragment on Government* (1776) and *An Introduction to the Principles of Morals and Legislation* (1789) Bentham laid out a scheme for rational legal reform which closely parallels that of Beccaria. He too believed that human actions were motivated by a utilitarian or hedonistic calculus of pleasure and pain. Bentham's personal passion for quantitative method led him to formulate a mathematics of rational punishments aimed at deterring offenses against the "common good." The common good was, moreover, said to be calculable in terms of acts which ensured the greatest happiness for the greatest number of people.

Because Bentham's ideas so closely resemble those of Beccaria we shall not examine his classical theories in greater detail. It is sufficient to conclude that Beccaria and Bentham shared a common vision regarding a new, rational approach to deviance. Their proposals for legal reform and calculable punishment assumed that deviants were rational actors, responsive to enlightened state policies directed toward the deterrence of lawbreaking and the preservation of the social contract.

IDENTIFYING CLASSICAL DEVIANCE

The classical perspective has shown very little concern for the study of deviant behavior or deviant people. It assumes that deviants are no different from anyone else, that their actions are reflective of efforts to maximize pleasure while minimizing pain. The reason for this is simple. The system of lawful social controls is not rational enough to deter people from choosing pleasure beyond the prescribed boundaries of the social contract. Nothing more. Nothing less. The problem of deviance is thus not a problem of bad or inadequate people but of bad or inadequate laws. In consequence, the highly legalistic classical perspective directs our attention not so much toward the study of deviation as toward the study of law.

What little the classical perspective does tell us about the identification of deviance has already been described in the preceding section. In summary, classical theorists such as Beccaria and Bentham contend that the proper identification of deviant acts is the responsibility solely of the legislature. Judges are to ascertain only whether someone actually committed an illegal act. Neither legislators nor judges are to be concerned with deviants as people. Classical theory is concerned exclusively with deviant acts and with the punitive strategies of rational punishment which are believed to deter such acts.

One question remains. How are legislators to decide which acts are deviant and which acts are acceptable? Beccaria provides guidance on this matter. Like the scholastic theologians who preceded him, he appears to trust the wisdom of the sovereign state to regulate social life in the interest of the common good. But what will state officials perceive as the "common good"? In reviewing the background of the classical perspective, we noted the interdependent connectedness of the early capitalist economy and the modern centralized state as both emerge together in history. Does this mean that the state would be likely to equate the market values of capitalism with the good of society as a whole? A growing number of critical theorists suggest that this was the case. As Mark Kennedy points out, "the State created new crimes and punishments directly as the institutions of capitalism advanced."[18] This contention will be examined in greater detail in Chapter 10 of this book. For the present, it is enough to note that Beccaria's relative silence regarding exactly how state legislators will "naturally" and "reasonably" discern the common good is a silence that rings loudly and disturbingly in the ears of people who are concerned with the role of powerful economic, political, and social interest groups in shaping the style and context of law.

Bentham was not so silent on this issue. His principle of social utility presented a simple ethical command for those who ruled. Act always to ensure the greatest happiness for the greatest number! His inclinations toward rationally quantifying social and legislative policies provided him with a hopeful vision that this principle of the "greatest happiness" would someday be converted into a computable mathematical formula. But even if this could be done, what would happen to minorities, to people whose pleasurable desires fell outside the statistical boundaries of the greatest numbers?

While not resolving this question entirely, Bentham argued that a principle of "demonstrable social harm" was a necessary condition for legislatively prescribed sanctions. If there were no demonstrable victims there should be no punishment. Thus, homosexuality, even if it offends the moral vision of a large segment of people, should not be subject to penal sanction simply because it presents no demonstrable harm to the individuals involved. This principle of demonstrable harm differentiates the classical approach from the demonic. The demonic perspective recognizes no difference between immorality and deviance. The classical perspective offers a somewhat tougher test—does observable harm result? This, perhaps, is the major contribution of classical thought to the methods for discerning deviance.

SOCIAL CONTROL OF CLASSICAL DEVIANCE

On March 9, 1762, Jean Calas, a 60-year-old French Huguenot merchant, was tried, convicted, and executed for the murder of his son. During two hours of "legal torture" the old man repeatedly protested his innocence. The prosecutor meanwhile alleged that Calas, a Protestant, had killed his son because the boy had converted to Catholicism. Calas refused to confess. The judge, convinced more by the prosecutor's emotional arguments than by Calas's cries, sentenced him to death. He was "broken on the wheel." His family was arrested. All his property was confiscated by the state. A short time later the real facts of the case became public. The son had committed suicide. His father had been falsely and mercilessly and savagely tried and executed under a demonic social control system that had dominated Europe for centuries. Critics and reformers called for an end to such antiquated control practices. The reform-minded philosopher Voltaire joined with others critics in obtaining a postmortem reversal of Calas's conviction. Although Calas was not given a proper Christian burial, in the natural order of things the reversal represented a victory that was more symbolic than real.

Two years after Calas's death Cesare Beccaria published his famous *An Essay on Crimes and Punishments*. The publication of the manuscript signified that the dominance of demonic control strategies was nearing an end. Beccaria's treatise quickly resulted in major changes in European social control policy. Its consequences were as practically real as they were symbolically important. Three of the more important practical control policies resulting from classical thinking include: (1) the highly rationalistic French Penal Code of 1791; (2) neoclassical modifications, and (3) the centralized control of deviants in state institutions.

The French Penal Code of 1791

The French Penal Code of 1791 was perhaps the most celebrated instance of applied classical thinking. French progressives were still fuming over the Calas case when Beccaria's book hit the intellectual marketplace. The French edition of *An Essay on Crimes and Punishments* contained a laudatory introduction prepared by Voltaire. Its influence was enormous. French legislators soon came to accept many of Beccaria's ideas as their own. These were incorporated into the famous French Penal Code of 1791.

The new French code read much like the rational control policy Beccaria had dreamed of. It made strict use of the doctrine of uniform punishment for specific crimes. It provided a scale of crimes arranged by seriousness, with punishments proportioned accordingly. It specified that all penal sanctions must be determined legislatively and that the role of judges be limited to determination of guilt. As John L. Gillin has suggested, "In this code there was an attempt not only to legislate on every crime, but to fix by statute the penalty for each degree of each kind. Nothing was left to the judgment of the court, except the question of guilt. There could be no abatement for extenuating circumstances, no added penalty for the heinousness of the way in which a particular crime was committed."[19]

The French code of 1791 came as close as any in history to incorporating a purely classical viewpoint. It was both extremely legalistic and administratively simple. If someone was found guilty, he or she was given the legislatively prescribed punishment, no matter what. This was its greatest advantage. It represented "an exact scale of punishments for equal acts without reference to the individual involved or the special circumstances in which the crime was committed."[20] This was also its greatest disadvantage.

The 1791 code engendered enormous practical problems for which it had no legal answer. It was soon criticized for providing no just recourse for persons committing the same act under very different social circumstances. Shouldn't the law look differently upon someone who plans a crime with calculated premeditation than upon someone who acts criminally in the heat of passion? Was it fair to assign the same punishment to the passionately violent spouse reacting to marital infidelity as to the well-rehearsed murderer executing a prearranged killing for profit? Critics demanded that exceptions should be made. Yet no exceptions were available in the purely classical code of 1791. Similar questions were raised regarding the identical handling of first-time and repeat offenders. Both were assigned the same "rational" punishment. Nor did the code make exceptions for children, the insane, the retarded, or other persons whose capacity for rational choice might be impaired or underdeveloped. Critics demanded reasonable changes. This resulted in a host of neoclassical modifications of an otherwise highly rationalistic control policy.

Neoclassical Modification

In response to criticisms regarding its overly rigid rationality, the 1791 French Penal Code underwent a series of step-by-step revisions. In 1810 a certain discretion was returned to judges in order to deal with hardened repeat criminals. In 1819 exceptions were provided for certain "objective" circumstances affecting the seriousness of a particular act. These ambiguous revisions, while they reopened the door to a certain measure of judicial discretion, did not satisfy critics whose primary objections concerned the classical perspective's inability to consider the unequal "subjective" circumstances or mental state of deviant actors. These critics included the philosopher Paul Johann Anselm von Feuerbach and that pioneer of modern law enforcement, Sir Robert Peel. They pushed for and achieved a wider set of modifications, which included attention to (1) the premeditation of the deviant act, (2) the possibility of extenuating or mitigating circumstances, and (3) the suggestion that some deviant actors should not be held accountable for their acts by virtue of their insanity.

The neoclassical modifications were intended to strengthen rather than replace the central tenets of classical theory. Like other classical theorists, the advocates of neoclassical reform believed that social control policy should, on the whole, be based upon the certain, swift, and proportionate application of rational punishment. Yet, in the areas described below, classical control strategies were said to need more flexibility.

Premeditation   This refers to the prior planning of the act and was considered to be an indicator of the free will. The introduction of this concept during the neoclassical period, however, raised more questions than it answered. Consider the neoclassical assertion that first-time offenders were "freer in will" because their actions lacked the force of "habit." Should they be treated more severely? This matter remained an issue in neoclassical scholastic theory.

Mitigating Circumstances   This concept implies that both physical and social-environmental factors need to be assessed in determining a deviant's responsibility. Such physical factors as the weather might impact upon the freedom of a deviant's choice. Unencumbered free will could hypothetically be eroded by heat and humidity. Socially, such factors as stress, pressure, and situational passion were allowed to be considered as well. This kind of reasoning was viewed as an exception to, and not a replacement of, the classical assumption of rationally based free choice as the basis for deviance. It began, however, to soften the shell of the free will doctrine. Conceptions of deviance moved closer to the determinism that would characterize the later pathological perspective.

Insanity   The institution of the insanity defense, heralded by the 1843 trial of Daniel McNaughtan, is a third example of the neoclassical modifications. McNaughtan was brought to trial for the highly publicized murder of Mr. Drummond, secretary to the London police commissioner, Sir Robert Peel. Upon investigation it appeared that McNaughtan hardly fit the classical stereotype of the rational, calculating deviant. McNaughtan was a character who (in his own mind) experienced direct communication with God. In the course of their conversations, God had apparently informed McNaughtan that a demonic plot was afoot by which agents of the devil, masked as members of Britain's Tory (Conservative) party, were conspiring to establish a reign of Satan on earth. God further informed McNaughtan that this conspiracy could only be stopped by killing Sir Robert Peel, a noted leader of the Tories. What choice did the God-fearing McNaughtan have? He procured a weapon and tried to act in God's name by assassinating the demonic figurehead. The one problem was that McNaughtan did not know what Peel looked like. He staked out Peel's office and mistakenly gunned down Peel's secretary, Drummond. A saintly hero in his own mind, McNaughtan was quickly arrested and charged with murder. But was he guilty? Had he really intended wrong? Wasn't he guided (if admittedly a bit crazily) by what he believed to be the lawful and holy orders of the Most High?

McNaughtan's lawyers felt that whatever he was, he was not guilty of the crime of murder as traditionally defined. He had not intended murder as such. He had intended only to carry out what he (by virtue of some rather nonordinary mental processes) had honestly perceived as the orders of God. He was insane and should not be subject to the same punitive social controls as "rational" criminals. A panel of noted judges commissioned to rule on the controversial case agreed. McNaughtan was declared not guilty by reason of insanity because it was established that "at the time of the committing of the act, the party accused (in this case McNaughtan) was laboring under such a defect of reason, from disease of the mind, as to not know the nature and quality of the act he was doing; or if he did know it, that he did not know what he was doing was wrong.[21] This highly rational, highly cognitive test became, and, with modifications, continues to be, the basic standard for judging criminal insanity. As with the other modifications introduced in the neoclassical era, it suggests that there may be more to some deviance than rationally calculated free choice. Insanely calculated choices were of a different order and should be controlled differently.

As a result of the precedent set by the McNaughtan case, those declared "criminally insane," while not convicted of a crime, have been traditionally committed involuntarily and for "indefinite periods of time" to mental institutions (hospitals for the criminally insane) until "restored to reason." The insane were, in principle, to be "treated" rather than punished. This revision of classical thinking foreshadows what would become the predominant mode of social control under the subsequent pathological perspectives—belief in the "corrective treatment" of deviants.

The McNaughtan case also points to an area of important convergence between classical and pathological theorizing—the strict individualization of accounts concerning deviance. Both classical and pathological thought direct attention to the actions of nonconformers without seriously considering the social and historical context in which deviance takes place. This individualization of deviant actions is particularly troubling in a consideration of the case of McNaughtan. As Richard Moran has recently demonstrated, the traditional legal interpretation of McNaughtan as an isolated and delusional deviant fails to consider the political setting in which the attempted assassination of Peel, the prominent Tory leader, actually took place.[22] Moran points to historical evidence of McNaughtan's involvement with Chartism, a political movement that opposed the exploitative industrialization of the British Empire. In what ways were McNaughtan's "delusions" of persecution by "Tory devils" historically grounded in the unequal realities of nineteenth-century British power? Why, moreover, did British prosecutors, knowledgeable of McNaughtan's Chartist associations, not raise questions about this allegedly insane man's political associations at the time of his trial? In examining the strategic silence of McNaughtan's prosecutors about his passionate political commitments, Moran raises important questions about the individualization of deviance as an outgrowth of both classical and pathological thought.

Centralized Control of Deviants in State Penitentiaries

The primary objective of classical social control was to deter future deviance by the application of rationally calculated punishment. How practically was such punishment carried out? The answer is found in the invention and use of large, centralized state prisons. These first appeared in history just as the classical viewpoint was capturing the intellectual fancy of western society. From a contemporary vantage point this may seem odd. Large state prisons are today criticized as irrational and dehumanizing environments, as schools for crime. During the late eighteenth and early nineteenth centuries, the promise of such institutions was different. Since deviant actors were seen as essentially rational, it was believed that by "doing time" in such places they would learn to "correct" their characters to fit with the calculatively rational demands of life in the modern world, which is dominated by the complementary powers of the capitalist marketplace and the laws of the centralized state.

How did supporters of the classical control model arrive at such an optimistic view of the state penitentiary? The best answer is that institutional confinement originally had more to do with practical circumstances than with intellectual conviction. According to the historian Michel Foucault, there was something contradictory about this from the beginning. The calculative principles behind rational punishment should have meant that each specific crime would be met by some other specific measure of proportionate deterrence. The nearly exclusive reliance on prison as punishment meant that different crimes received essentially the same punishment. The only thing which differed was the time spent within a penitentiary's walls. As Foucault points out, classical theorists envisaged imprisonment "but as one among other penalties."[23] The problem, however, was that "within a short space of time, detention became the essential form of punishment. . . . The theatre of punishment of which the eighteenth century dreamed and which would have acted essentially [as a deterrent] on the minds of the general public was replaced by the great uniform machinery of the prisons. . . . The diversity, so solemnly promised, is reduced in the end to this grey, uniform penalty."[24]

Why this shift from the diverse, public nature of classical punishment to the uniform and secluded mechanics of incarceration? Although there is no easy answer to this question, Foucault suggests an intriguing possibility—that the "total control" potential of prison technology resonated so well with the power structures of a society dominated by the capitalist marketplace and the centralized state that prison soon usurped all other forms of punishment. As a total institution, prison captures not only the body but the "soul," or personality, of the inmate. The penitentiary enables the state to isolate, observe, and then, based upon observation, manipulate and change the offender into a person whose calculated rationality and improved "self-control" would fit better with the inner discipline demanded by the mass marketplace of modern society. In this sense, Foucault suggests that prisons were initially filled up with persons who had been sentenced to receive rational punishment, but that the raw power of prison technology soon produced a new theory of social control, one based upon strategies of manipulative change, one suggesting that deviance results not from free rational choice but from observable and changeable defects or pathologies.

Is Foucault correct about this? Did the control technology of prison have such a great affinity with the disciplinary demands of capitalist and centralized state power that it "took in" classically sentenced rational deviants and "turned out" a new breed of nonconformer—the pathological deviant? Much of Foucault's argument rests on his examination of Jeremy Bentham's plans for constructing the "Panopticon"—the total prison, the ultimate in enforced penal control. Bentham anticipated that convicted offenders would be rationally sentenced to do time in this huge, rounded, glass-roofed "inspection house." At its center would be a central guard tower. There the watchful eyes of state authority could gaze at incarcerated inmates twenty-four hours a day. Each prisoner would pass time by being subject daily to the same monotonous routine of compulsive, dreary work and rigid discipline. The Panopticon was more than a planner's dream. Bentham drafted architectural specifications and obtained a government permit to build this model prison in Tothill Fields, England. Only when the British government defaulted on its agreement to finance the venture were plans for the Panopticon finally laid to rest.

Although the formal purpose of the Panopticon was simply to rationally punish, Foucault reads much more into its environmental design. He sees wider appeal in its possibility for constant surveillance and manipulative transformation. This was its greatest attraction to capitalist society and to the centralized rational state that secured the conditions for its survival. Bentham's own description of the Panopticon seems to suggest that Foucault may be correct about this matter. In describing the ideal prison Bentham appears to have gone well beyond the notion that prison would be strictly a place for rational punishment. In Bentham's own words, the Panopticon would be "a mill to grind rogues honest and idle men industrious."[25]

David Rothman's detailed history of the origins of the U.S. prison system suggests essentially the same thing as Foucault's—that the implementation of classical control philosophy resulted in widespread reliance upon incarceration. Rothman's interpretation of this matter is nowhere near as bold or as suggestive as Foucault's. He argues simply that U.S. reformers, caught up in the "immediate and widespread appeal" of Beccaria's classical proposals, did not think about the contradictions involved in relying upon prison as punishment. In many ways prison seemed like a practical way to implement the classical schema. "Prisons matched punishment to crime precisely: the more heinous the offense, the longer the sentence."[26] According to Rothman, it was the "fact of imprisonment, not its internal routine," that was important to the early U.S. reformers.[27] Convinced of the rational strength of their proposals and of the advantages of classical thought over the remnants of demonic control, advocates of the classical perspective in the United States were said to have paid little attention to what prison really was or what incarceration really meant. The results, however, were the same as those described by Foucault. The late-eighteenth-century experimentation with classical control strategies promoted the construction and use of state penal institutions. These same buildings would later be justified as laboratories for the rehabilitative strategies of pathological theory. Their historical origins, however, are rooted in the blind enthusiasm of early classical thought.

THE CLASSICAL PERSPECTIVE TODAY

In many ways classical theorizing may seem nearly as outdated as the demonic perspective. Ideas about things which cause or determine deviance have, for over a century, replaced the emphasis on free will and rational hedonism. Efforts to treat or rehabilitate deviants have generally superseded an emphasis on rational punishment and its deterrent characteristics. Yet, today we are witnessing a resurgence of classical thinking, a return to the rationalistic and punishment-oriented thinking of the late eighteenth century. Even more than the demonic perspective, the classical perspective is alive and very well in the modern world.

My first exposure to a strong dose of contemporary classical thought came when I was a graduate student. I was attending a lecture by the well-known University of Pennsylvania criminologist, Marvin Wolfgang. Wolfgang was reporting on the results of his recently completed study, *Delinquency in a Birth Cohort*.[28] In that study Wolfgang and his colleagues, Robert Figlio and Thorsten Sellin, tracked the "criminal careers" of nearly 10,000 boys who had been born in 1945 and were living in Philadelphia, between their tenth and eighteenth birthdays. Using records of official police contacts, school reports, and Selective Service registration information, these researchers sought to determine the percentage of boys apprehended for some violation of the criminal law. The boys they studied came from all walks of Philadelphia society.

The extent of the delinquency uncovered by Wolfgang and his associates was striking. By age 18, 35 percent of the Philadelphia birth cohort had been apprehended for a criminal offense. By age 26, this figure grew to 50 percent. This was the percentage who had committed at least one offense. What about repeaters? After the first recorded offense, 47 percent of the boys had no subsequent record. This was the case no matter what was done with or to them. It mattered little, in other words, whether they were dealt with leniently or severely. They simply ceased committing delinquent acts. Or at least they ceased getting caught. Another large percentage, 35 percent, stopped after the second offense. An additional 29 percent stopped after the third. Thereafter the percentage who stopped repeating leveled out to a very small figure, less than approximately 5 percent for each subsequent apprehension.

What are the policy implications of Wolfgang's findings? In addressing himself to this question Wolfgang made reference to the classical control ideas espoused by Beccaria and Bentham. Wolfgang used a baseball metaphor in speculating about what might be called a "three-strike" model of rational deterrence. Let us assume, suggested Wolfgang, that the vast majority of all potential criminals are rationally calculative actors. Let us also assume that people do make mistakes and slip up sometimes. Wolfgang thus aligned himself with what might best be described as a tradition of neoclassical thought. Since the data show that most offenders fall out of the pool of delinquents after one or two offenses, why not devise a crime control policy in which very little is done with people until they arrive at a third offense? This would both save costs and target scarce resources toward that small group of offenders who would repeat acts of delinquency again and again. According to Wolfgang, out of the initial cohort of nearly 10,000, only 627, or 6 percent, committed five or more offenses. Yet this small group of "chronic offenders" was responsible for over half of the total number of all offenses recorded for the cohort as a whole and for about two-thirds of all violent offenses. Given this fact, Wolfgang speculated about whether a truly rational crime control policy should not provide swift, certain, but not very severe admonishments for those caught a first or second time and reserve the full force of its sanctions for offenders who strike out a third time. This latter group, he reasoned, was on a course toward becoming chronic offenders. In order to deter people from this course, why not announce publicly that not much will happen for initial offenses, but once offenders cross over into their "third strike" they will automatically be dealt with in a severe fashion, with severity escalating heavily for each subsequent offense. And perhaps, suggested the noted criminologist, if people commit as many as five offenses they should be locked up forever. Moreover, since everyone would know this would happen without exception, such a policy would maximize the potential deterrence of the criminal law.

Wolfgang paused at this point in his presentation. He said that he was unsure whether his speculative proposal was liberal or conservative. His proposal for the permanent removal of chronic offenders from society sounded very tough. It reminded one of Beccaria, who had once advocated long-term penal slavery as a rational deterrent far superior to that of the death penalty.[29] On the other hand, the suggestion for relative leniency for first- and second-time offenders might appeal to liberals who believe that delinquents should be given a chance to reform themselves. What was clear about Wolfgang's reflections was the manner in which they drew upon the central tenet of the classical perspective.

Wolfgang's comments were, during the course of the 1970s, joined by an ever-widening chorus of criminal justice thinkers with renewed interest in classical thought. The reason for this involved the perceived failure of subsequent "more scientific" perspectives to produce workable solutions to the problem of crime. This issue will be dealt with in greater detail later. For now, it is enough to say that the recent swing backward toward classical thought is often justified by descriptions of the alleged practical inadequacies of the theories that had once replaced it. As Leon Sheleff points out, "As disillusionment sets in about the capacity to fully understand the etiology [causes] of crime, as reservations are increasingly being expressed about the rehabilitative goals of penal philosophy and correctional practices . . . so the basic framework . . . of Beccaria's and Bentham's ideas is slowly infiltrating back into criminological studies."[30]

One need only peruse the professional journals or attend a single criminal justice conference to learn that Sheleff is correct; faith in rehabilitative treatment is dead, or nearly so, and a concern with certain nondiscretionary and uniform systems of rational punishments is at the top of criminal justice priorities. Forget about trying to explain and treat the causes of crime. Deal with criminal deviance as a rational choice. Devise a fixed and certain system of punishments. Warn everyone that, if caught, offenders will be punished without exception. Eliminate the widely disparate discretion of judges in handing out sentences. Emphasize sentences that are fixed and mandatory. Do away with indeterminate minimum and maximum sentences, enabling judges to gear punishment to the correctional needs of the individual actor. Return to the act. Treat all actors alike. Get rid of parole. Release prisoners when the time of punishment is complete, not when it is estimated that they are cured or rehabilitated. Eliminate the insanity plea. Deal with serious juvenile offenders in the same fashion as adults. Punish and punish rationally. These are all current slogans and issues being debated in criminal justice circles. Each sounds remarkably similar to arguments made by Beccaria and the other proponents of the early classical perspective. Consider, for instance, the recent findings of the well-financed, four-year interdisciplinary investigation by the Committee for the Study of Incarceration. These are reported by Andrew von Hirsch in the book *Doing Justice*. According to von Hirsch:

> Some of our conclusions may seem old-fashioned. To our surprise, we found ourselves returning to the ideas of such Enlightenment thinkers as . . . Beccaria—ideas that antedated notions of rehabilitation that emerged in the nineteenth century. . . . We argue, as . . . Beccaria did, that severity of punishment should depend chiefly on the seriousness of the crime. We share Beccaria's interest in placing limits on sentencing discretion.[31]

Perhaps the foremost representative of the revival of classical thinking about deviance is James Q. Wilson. In his book *Thinking about Crime*, Wilson totally denies the value of searching for the causes of crime.[32] Criminal justice policies should, instead, be based upon what Wilson calls a "new realism," a platform of rationality by which criminals will know simply that they will be punished if caught. According to Wilson, "The radical individualism of Bentham and Beccaria may be scientifically questionable but prudentially necessary."[33] Thus Wilson argues that criminals ought to be viewed as rational actors who will get the message if it is made known that their crimes will be met by a swift and certain punitive response. For every conviction for a nontrial offense, penalties should be assigned which "fit the crime" and which permit only a small amount of judicial discretion regarding such matters as mitigating and exacerbating circumstances. According to Wilson, penalties need not be long and severe as long as they are swift and certain. This will maximize their potential for deterrence.

On the surface Wilson's position sounds much like an update of Beccaria's. Yet, his arguments also betray a fundamental political conservatism which undermines the full rationality of his neoclassical platform. A major inconsistency in Wilson's proposals involves what he has to say or what he fails to say about corporate, organizational, or white-collar crime. Such crime is generally committed by highly calculating individuals in the rational pursuit of illegal profit. It is, moreover, among the most costly forms of lawbreaking to society as a whole. The annual economic toll of corporate crime totals billions of dollars, far exceeding that from any form of conventional or street crime. Yet the punishments for such crime remain among the lowest and most lenient. As criminologists Marshal Clinard and Robert Meir point out, "It is ironic that the penalties for white-collar crime are the least severe, while they are given to the very persons who might be the most affected by them. . . . In other words, if these offenders are potentially the most deterred, an increase in punishments and the intensity of enforcement might result in the greatest benefit to society."[34] Surely then the white-collar offender would be a logical target for the revived classical control strategies of Wilson and others. Wilson, however, dismisses this topic. His book, he argues, does not deal with white-collar crimes because it reflects his "conviction" and "the conviction of most citizens, that predatory street crime is a far more serious matter than consumer fraud, antitrust violations," and other varieties of corporate theft.[35] As a result, the "new realism" of Wilson appears more conservative than consistent, more selective than uniform in its return to classical thought.

While the above-described reemphasis of classical thinking sounds quite conservative, it is shared, to some degree, by liberal reformers. These persons are concerned with the rights of individuals under the sanctions of the law. Today, they argue, treating the causes of crime has meant, in practice if not on paper, more time spent under the control of the state. Waiting for the parole board to decide on one's rehabilitative status creates enormous uncertainty, anxiety, and the omnipresent possibility of the discriminatory use of discretionary powers. Most prisoner-rights and ex-offender groups share the desire of conservative "law-and-order" factions to eliminate the open-endedness of indeterminate sentencing and to establish a more fixed set of uniformly applied sanctions. Moreover, such groups have increased their opposition to the "noble lie" of nonvoluntary treatment and recognition of punishment as the primary object of the penal system. By viewing the offender as responsible for his or her actions, as a bearer of punishment rather than the subject of treatment, it is argued, dignity is restored to those convicted. This is the dignity of the rational actor that was an essential component of the classical perspective.

The return to classical thinking is signaled by the replacement of rehabilitation with deterrence and rationally administered punishment as the primary goals of social control over criminality. Yet, even among the continued advocates of treatment, a renewed rationality has shown itself. "Reality therapy," one of the most popular of the contemporary modes of rehabilitation, places an extraordinary emphasis on the individual's acceptance of the consequences of his or her own freely chosen actions.[36] Clients are denied acceptance of "excuses" for their behaviors. It is demanded that they own up to their actions and accept the outcomes accordingly. Indeed, the assumptions of the classical perspective, while shelved for some time in favor of perspectives which replaced the concept of choice with that of cause, have reentered and reclaimed their place in the contemporary marketplace of social control.

ASSESSMENT OF THE CLASSICAL PERSPECTIVE

At the core of the classical perspective lies the claim that rational punishment deters deviant behavior. In this closing section we will sort through a variety of evidence that has recently been gathered to test the adequacy of this claim. The chapter concludes with a short comment on another question of adequacy—the adequacy of the perspective to realize the rational justice it upholds as a goal.

Does Punishment Deter?

According to classical theorists, rationally calculated punishment reduces future deviance by instilling a fear of sanctions both in the punished offender (specific deterrence) and in the public at large (general deterrence). To fully realize this effect, it is argued, punishment must be swift and certain, and the severity of its calculated pain must outweigh the perceived pleasure associated with a given act of deviance.

Are classical theorists correct in their assessment of the deterrent effect of punishment? At a commonsensical level the principle of deterrence has a great deal of appeal. Don't we encounter situations each day in which we might have acted differently if we believed our actions would be met by a swift, certain, and severe stroke of social sanction? Think about something as simple as a parking violation. I pull up to the meter. I plan to run into the store for one item I forgot while shopping for tonight's dinner. I know I'll be gone only a minute. Yet, I know also that the likelihood of my dropping the required coins in the meter is dependent upon whether I think that I might have to pay a costly fine if I don't. I'm sure that seeing a police officer ticketing the car ahead of me will make a difference.

Aside from its commonsensical appeal, is there any substantive evidence that deterrence is an effective principle for social control policy as a whole? Until recent years there has been very little research on this important question. Why? The reason involves the short-lived dominance of the classical perspective as a tool for interpreting deviance and constructing control policy. As will be pointed out in Chapter 4, the popular appeal of classical theorizing lasted less than a full century. It was soon replaced by the pathological perspective, with its promise to scientifically explain the cause of deviance and to clinically produce the cure. As the precepts of pathological theorizing and other deterministic perspectives gained ascendency over the free-will tenets of classical thought, such ideas as the belief in the deterrent power of punishment were dismissed without ever being fully tested.

In *The Criminological Enterprise* Don Gibbons documents this lack of concern with testing the principle of deterrence by examining what is said about punishment by some of the leading texts in the field of crime, deviance, and social control.[37] According to Gibbons, the subject of deterrence is a virtually ignored topic for inquiry. The value of punishment was dismissed as a matter of "emotional" rather than "scientific" procedure,[38] as being a "relatively inefficient method" of dealing with criminals and other deviants,[39] as representing a "child-like faith"[40] in something which was believed to have little causal relationship to deviant behavior.[41] Such criticisms were strong. Yet, they were not based on "hard scientific tests" of the evidence. In Gibbons's words: "The idea of punishment went against the grain, so that criminologists either expressed great hostility toward it or were uninterested in research on deterrence, opting instead for 'scientific' efforts to treat and rehabilitate offenders."[42]

Today things are different. As mentioned previously, the classical perspective has been "born again" in recent years. With the rebirth of classical thinking the study of deterrence has become a veritable "growth industry" within the field of criminology.[43] In the last decade we have witnessed dozens of published reports assessing the deterrent effect of punishment. Many have attempted to refine the meaning of deterrence so that policymakers can better estimate the practical benefits of various strategies of punitive social control. Distinctions arise, for instance, between such notions as "partial" and "marginal" deterrence.[44] Measures of partial deterrence assess reductions in the level of deviance threatened by this or that rationally calculated form of punishment. Measures of marginal deterrence seek to compare such reduction rates with those achieved by other forms of punishment or social control.

The rapidly expanding body of research on deterrence is filled with technical distinctions of this kind. Without burdening the reader with an array of specialized terminology, I would like to provide a simple overview of three of the most important topics emerging from the new literature on deterrence. These include studies of (1) specific deterrence, (2) general deterrence, and (3) the role of perception in mediating the effect of punitive sanctions. I shall conclude with some general reservations about the nature and findings of the research on this topic.

Specific Deterrence Does punishment reduce the likelihood of future offenses for offenders so sanctioned? This is a difficult question to answer. Its ideal test would seemingly involve a comparison between offenders who are punished and those who break similar laws in a similar fashion but whose deviant acts go unpunished. This, however, is a comparison that is not practically possible. Records of subsequent offenses are highly imperfect for punished offenders. The only known offenses are those for which a person actually gets caught. Records are virtually nonexistent for the unpunished offender. Hence, studies of specific deterrence tend to compare subsequent offenses of persons assigned to various levels or degrees of punishment. Those who are imprisoned for a long time are compared with those imprisoned for a short time. Incarcerated offenders are compared with those placed on probation. Such comparisons are methodologically flawed. The people sentenced with the most severe punishments are generally the ones who have the longest records or who have committed the most severe crimes. They may also be persons who systematically suffer social discrimination due to race and class and who, once released with a "record," are more susceptible to police surveillance and future arrest. A comparison of such persons with those in lesser punishment conditions is thus made problematic from the outset. The findings of such studies are problematic as well. They appear to contradict the notion of specific deterrence. According to Jack Gibbs, a noted deterrence researcher, as the severity of punishment increases so does the likelihood that a specific offender will commit an offense again.[45] This, of course, is the opposite of what would be predicted by people who are convinced of the practical utility of punishment.

In order to get around some of the methodological problems encountered in many specific deterrence studies, some researchers have opted for self-report measures of deviation. The work of Martin Gold and Jay R. Williams is a case in point.[46] Using a self-report questionnaire Gold and Williams were able to develop two matched groups of 35 pairs of adolescent delinquents. Each group was similar to the other in terms of past offense histories between matched pairs (measured by the seriousness and frequency of self-reported offenses). What made them different was that the members of one group had been apprehended and sanctioned, while the members of the other had remained "uncaught." By constructing such comparison groups Gold and Williams hoped to control for the impact of prior offenses and the possibility that being apprehended increases the likelihood of being caught again in the future. The results of this study contradict what might be expected from a specific deterrence standpoint. In 20 matched pairs the apprehended delinquent had a higher level of subsequent offending than the nonapprehended delinquent. In 5 other pairs the levels were nearly identical. Apprehended offenders showed lower levels of subsequent offenses in only 10 of the 35 pairs.

The negative findings of most specific deterrence studies have led some researchers to entertain quite different hypotheses. Liska suggests, for instance, that "an equally good case may be made for the opposite conclusion: punishment increases future law violations."[47] Liska directs our attention to what may be referred to as the "socialization" and "stigmatization" effects of certain forms of punishment. By "socialization" Liska refers to the possibility that sentenced offenders may learn "prodeviant" values, attitudes, and behaviors from persons with whom they associate in prison. By "stigmatization" he considers the possibility that the postprison social environment is one in which an ex-con is denied entrance into certain acceptable or conventional social groups or avenues of economic opportunity. Blocked in nondeviant opportunity, the stigmatized deviant may fall back into a social group in which deviant options are both permitted and rewarded. In other words, it is possible for punishment to have the opposite effect from that envisioned by advocates of specific deterrence. This possibility has recently been acknowledged by deterrence researchers such as Charles Tittle. Tittle and others have suggested that future research efforts attempt to include measures of inprison and postprison social environments to better assess the deterrent effect of punitive sanctions.[48]

General Deterrence   Studies of specific deterrence, although methodologically flawed, have generally resulted in negative findings. The results of general deterrence research are more mixed. Measures of general deterrence seek to assess the impact of certain forms of punishment on the level of offenses committed by the public at large. One of the pioneer studies in this area was Jack Gibbs's comparative examination of homicide rates among states with different levels of punitive sanctions for the years 1959–1961.[49] Gibbs's index of the level of punishment involved measures of the certainty and severity with which punishment was delivered. His findings support the thesis of general deterrence. As the certainty and severity of sanctions increased, the rate of homicide was found to decrease.

Gibbs's research was extended by Tittle to include the seven forms of major crime indexed in the FBI's *Uniform Crime Reports*. In addition to homicide these include rape, aggravated assault, robbery, larceny or theft of over $50, burglary, and auto theft. Tittle's findings both support and modify the conclusions drawn by Gibbs.[50] Tittle discovered that certainty of punishment, as estimated by the percentage of convicted offenders sentenced to state prisons, was negatively related to offense rates in various states. As certainty increased, offense rates decreased. Such was not the case with severity of punishment. This variable was measured by the median of months served in prison for a given offense. Except in the case of homicide, increases in severity were not related to decreases in crime rate. The same general results have been confirmed in a number of subsequent studies.[51]

Certainty appears to count more heavily than severity. Research by Charles Logan goes so far as to suggest that the predominant influence of certainty may, in certain cases, obscure the potential influence of severity.[52] Logan discovered that the states which issued the most severe punishments were also the states in which punishment was the least certain. He interprets this finding to suggest that, when the available punishments are most severe, judges and juries may be more reluctant to find persons guilty and thus incarcerate them for lengthy periods of time. Severity may thus work against certainty in states where severity is highest. Because certainty is reduced in high-severity states, and because the impact of severity may depend upon a high level of certainty, a true test of the independent impact of severity is thus said to be missing. Logan attempted to correct for this by assessing the influence of severity only after controlling for levels of certainty. Controlling for certainty, Logan discovered that severity had a consistent, if admittedly small, relationship to lowered rates of crime. Even then, however, the relationship between severity and lower crime rate was nowhere near as high as that between certainty and lower crime rate. Indeed, of the twelve major studies of general deterrence conducted since Gibb's 1968 research, eight have reported very strong negative correlations between rates of crime and certainty of punitive sanction. That is, as certainty increases, the crime rate decreases.

Why has certainty of punishment been found to be so consistently related to lower rates of crime? The most obvious answer is that how one is punished may not be as important as whether one is punished. Several recent studies suggest that the issue may be more complicated. Research by Logan indicates that the impact of certainty is to some degree mediated by the level of severity. He concludes that just as certainty influences the rate of severity, the impact of certainty is itself greatest when the level of severity is highest.[53] Other studies have attended to the role of the so-called tipping effect and to the "overload hypothesis" in interpreting the observed negative relationship between certainty and crime rate. The tipping effect suggests that certainty must reach a specific level before it has a significant impact on crime rate. This effect is reported in Charles Tittle and Allan Rowe's study of municipal and county crime rates in Florida.[54] According to Tittle and Rowe, certainty has a measurable negative impact on crime rate only after the certainty of arrest for crime rises past a cutoff point of 30 percent.[55]

The tipping effect qualifies the suggested impact of certainty on crime rate. The overload hypothesis, however, questions the interpretation of the negative correlation between certainty and crime as one of deterrence. It asks, instead, about the way that the crime rate affects certainty of sanctioning. The overload hypothesis assumes that the general level of policing remains constant during periods of high and low crime. The difference is that police resources will be scattered during periods of high crime, thereby reducing the certainty of arrest and sanction. During periods of low crime the opposite happens. The police may have more time to investigate each case, and this increases the probability that offenders will be sanctioned. Which is the case? Does increased certainty reduce the crime rate, or does a reduction in the crime rate increase certainty? The answer to this question, as to so many others in the burgeoning field of deterrence research, awaits further, more careful, and more controlled investigation.

Perceptions of Punishment   We have to this point been concerned with objective measures concerning such things as the severity and certainty of punishment. But what about the subjective perception of punishment? This would seemingly be at the heart of the classical perspective on deterrence. Beccaria's and Bentham's notion of a utilitarian calculus of pleasure and pain suggests that individuals size up the magnitude and likelihood of possible punishment before freely deciding to engage in deviant behavior. How, then, does the perception of possible punishment impact on the likelihood of deviant behavior?

There have to date been few studies of perception of punishment as it relates to deterrence. This is unfortunate, since according to the principles of the classical perspective, punishment will deter deviance only to the extent that individuals are aware of the price they may pay for straying from the straight and narrow path of conformity. This deficiency in deterrence research has recently been recognized, and new work is under way to explore the relationship between perceptions of possible punishment and the decision to deviate. Two things emerge, however, from the studies that have been completed to this point. The first is a consistent finding that perceptions of punishment are indeed negatively related to the likelihood of committing an act of crime or deviance. That is, as individuals' estimates of the likelihood of being sanctioned increase, the likelihood that they will deviate decreases.[56]

The second finding is more problematic and also less certain. It emerges in two recent self-report studies and is disputed by a third. It suggests that the observed negative relationship between perceived punishment and likelihood of deviation may be mediated by or explained away by the presence of a third variable—perceived level of social condemnation. Perceived social condemnation concerns what somebody thinks others think or feel about a certain action. This factor appears in the research of Matthew Silberman.[57] Silberman examined self-reported crime among a sample of college students. He concluded that reports of criminality were related not only to the perceptions of certainty and severity of punishment (in the negative way suggested by the deterrence thesis) but also to measures of a person's moral commitment to certain legal norms and to his or her associational ties to others who share a similar moral orientation. Hence, while perceptions of punishment may serve as deterrents, Silberman concluded that they are only part of a larger package of social factors affecting the likelihood to deviate.

Similar findings were reported by Maynard Erickson, Jack Gibbs, and Gary Jensen in 1977. These researchers collected self-report and perceptual data on 1,700 Arizona high school students.[58] They found that the perceived certainty of punishment and the perceived seriousness of certain acts (a measure they equate with perceptions of social condemnation) are so interwoven that it is impossible to say whether perceived punishment operates as a deterrent factor in its own right. Supporters of the so-called deterrence doctrine could, of course, argue that perceived punishment causes people to view acts as serious or as socially condemned. If they were not so serious, why would they be severely and certainly punished? Erickson, Gibbs, and Jensen argue that their "findings clearly cast doubts on the deterrence doctrine," and that until proponents of the doctrine demonstrate that "the relation between properties of legal punishments and the crime rate holds independently of the social condemnation of crime, then all purported evidence of general deterrence is suspect."[59]

Jensen, Erickson, and Gibbs answered their own call for more refined research in a publication a year later,[60] in which they reported on an expanded sample of self-reports for 5,000 Tucson, Arizona, high school students. Using more rigorous measures of social condemnation—indexes of both personal disapproval and involvement with others who deviate—they found no support for the position that perceived certainty of punishment is a derivative of social condemnation. The two factors appear to operate independently, although the strength with which perceived punishment relates to likelihood of deviation is bolstered by the perceived seriousness of the act in question. Thus the deterrence relationship is strongest for such offenses as grand theft, robbery, and burglary, and weakest for perceivably more minor offenses, such as drinking, truancy, and marijuana use. This later piece of research both preserves and modifies the deterrence perspective. The perceived anticipation of punishment is seen as an important but not an exclusive factor in an individual's choice to deviate or conform.

Deterrence: Some Concluding Comments and Reservations

What have we learned in examining research related to specific and general deterrence and to the role of perception in mediating the effect of punitive sanctions? We have learned that a better case can currently be made for the value of general deterrence than for the efficacy of specific deterrence; that certainty of punishment appears to weigh more heavily than severity; that perceptions of the certainty and severity of punishment appear to be related to whether or not someone will deviate; and that perceptions of punishment do not operate in a vacuum but are modified, if not directly mediated, by such factors as the perceived seriousness, moral meaning, and peer assessment associated with particular acts of deviance. We have also learned that further research needs to be done on each of these topics before the scorecard on deterrence can be fully tallied.

Given the tentative nature of much current knowledge of deterrence, we should view this central precept of the classical perspective with a certain reserve. Several things prompt this reserve. These include (1) the real-world conditions of punishment, (2) the lack of public awareness about actual punishments, (3) the differential effects of punishments on certain types of people, and (4) the differential effects of punishments in different social contexts.

Real-World Conditions of Punishment   Even if the deterrence thesis were totally confirmed in principle, it still would stumble in practice. Why? The reason is simple. For deterrence to function effectively as a means of social control, there must be some guarantee that a high percentage of offenders either really will be punished or at least believe that they will be punished. Law enforcement today is very different from this ideal situation of deterrence. Most criminal lawbreakers are never caught. Consider the crime of robbery. Of all robberies known to the police and voluntarily reported by the police for the FBI's *Uniform Crime Reports* in 1977, only 27 percent ever resulted in arrests. Moreover, of every 100 persons arrested, it can be expected that only about 36 will go to court and 20 will serve time in prison. The small percentage of offenders punished becomes even smaller when we consider that recent surveys of persons victimized indicate that only 53 percent of all robberies are reported to the police in the first place. For various crimes against property the chance of being caught and punished is even less. Only 16 percent of all known burglaries, 20 percent of all known larceny-thefts, and 15 percent of all known motor vehicle thefts result in arrest. Hence, whether one measures punishment by its certainty, by its severity, or by its swiftness (a factor not yet incorporated into the investigations of contemporary deterrence researchers), the "real-world" conditions of punishment are not very conducive to a workable control policy based upon the principle of deterrence.

Lack of Public Awareness about Actual Punishments   One of the central themes in the writings of Beccaria and Bentham was that the public should be duly informed about the specific nature of the sanctions that will be delivered to individuals convicted of lawbreaking. By any standard of measurement the contemporary American public is ignorant of all but the most general features of possible criminal punishment. Recent surveys in the states of Nebraska and California confirm this fact.[61] In California only 16 percent of the surveyed public had accurate knowledge of punishments related to rape and burglary with bodily injury. Thirty-nine percent knew the punitive cost of being convicted for drunken driving, but even in this area more than half were ignorant of possible sanctions. Perhaps it is enough to know simply that something bad could happen to you if apprehended for such an offense. Surely most people would know that. Maybe, but such a general level of awareness would seemingly undermine the specific, precise, and calculative nature of sanctioning which underlies the classical perspective's advocacy of deterrence.

Differential Effects of Punishment on Different Types of People
Punishment may work differently for different people. Why should we assume that the same punishment will be equally effective for a person who is very future-oriented and for someone who lives for the moment? We shouldn't. And yet the classical perspective on deterrence asks us to do just that—to eliminate a concern with individual differences so as to devise punishments which deter the greatest mass of the public at large. Sociologists Marshall Clinard and Robert Meir identify certain types of offenders who can reasonably be expected not to be as deterred by the threat of formal punishment as others.[62] These include persons who commit emotionally charged acts of violence, persons who commit offenses (such as traffic offenses) which are commonly known to be committed by broad and respectable segments of the public, individuals who have strong motives or heavy personal investment in illegal activity (whether they be drug addicts who need to "score" in order to survive or political revolutionaries whose value commitments lead them beyond the law), and young people who may be more worried about positive peer-group assessment than about the outcomes of getting caught. The suggestion that some persons are better deterred by punishment than others does not mean that the deterrence principle should be abandoned. It does mean, however, that the classical perspective's conception of deterrence needs to be expanded or made more flexible.

Differential Effects of Punishment in Different Social Contexts   In 1970 Richard Salem and William Bowers sought to test the effectiveness of various levels of punitive sanctions among students at 100 colleges for such campus-related offenses as violating alcohol-use rules, getting drunk, stealing library books, marking up books, and cheating.[63] They initially discovered a negative relationship between the severity of a college's punishments and the rate of such offenses on campus. Yet, upon closer examination Salem and Bowers discovered that, after controlling for the effect of peer disapproval, much of the original relationship posited between tough sanctions and conformity simply disappeared. It appeared that student attitudes and various aspects of the immediate social environment (e.g., whether or not the school had an honor-system approach to the problem of possible cheating) were more important determinants of rates of deviance than were types of sanctions per se. The work of Salem and Bowers directs our attention to various nonpunitive aspects of deterrence. It suggests that unlike the pleasure-pain calculations involved in classical thinking, such things as moral values and the influence of one's family, friends, or associates in defining acceptable social reality may be key factors in deterring one's move into deviance. Think about college students who choose not to "get high." Is this because they fear getting punished? Maybe. But it may also be because "smoking dope" is no longer valued by their preppie friends. This fourth area of reservation about the deterrence doctrine asks us to thoroughly consider the situational context in which the threat of punishment is experienced before making inferences about the independent impact of punitive sanctioning.

Realizing Rational Justice: Another Problem of Adequacy for the Classical Perspective

In the preceding pages I have reviewed what is currently known and what remains to be discovered about the adequacy of classical ideas about deterrence. In closing this chapter I would like to raise a few additional questions about another aspect of the classical perspective—its commitment to the goal of realizing rational justice. The early classical theorists, it should be remembered, were reformists as well as thinkers. As Leon Sheleff points out, "The classical school represents an attempt to ensure the maximum expression of a rational system of justice. . . . Both Beccaria and Bentham were . . . humanists and liberals. . . . Theirs was a humanism that sought to do away with the influences and the inequities of earlier times; it was a humanism that sought to put all people on an equal basis, at least in terms of their intrinsic worth, their basic rights, and, specifically, their treatment in the courts of law."[64]

There is certainly much to be said for the rational dignity accorded the deviant by the classical perspective. As the examination of the pathological perspective in Chapter 4 will show, most contemporary understandings of deviants have portrayed them as "creatures subject to causation," as "abnormal human beings, unlike ourselves," as "persons in need of involuntary treatment because they are unable to help themselves." The classical perspective avoids such debasing imagery. It also attempts to avoid the inequalities inherent in a highly discretionary system of social control. If an act is done, its doer, regardless of social position, regardless of the positive or negative "feelings" of some judicial agent, will be punished in accordance with the set prescriptions of the law. Nobody, in principle, will escape the sanctions of rational punishment. As such, the classical perspective holds some appeal for people who are concerned with fairness and individual equality before the law.

Despite its emphasis on rational dignity and individual fairness, the classical perspective has been criticized for reinforcing socially structured inequities in our system of social control.[65] In principle, everyone stands an equal chance of avoiding or being subject to punishment. In practice, some social groups have always been subject to closer scrutiny and closer social control than others. Poor thieves have always been more carefully policed than rich thieves. But even if this were not the case, would the classical perspective be fair? Abstractly, all citizens have an equal chance not to steal; but concretely, are the chances of the poor citizen, in a society that equates human worth with the possession of property, really equal to those of the rich citizen? Are the chances of a relatively powerless citizen, in a society that places an exaggerated emphasis on being powerful, really equal to those of a powerful citizen? I think not.

The abstract equality of the classical school breaks down in confrontation with the concrete inequality of everyday living. In an unequal society, isn't an exclusive commitment to an equally punitive system of rational social control an avoidance of basic social contradictions? How free is "free choice" in an unfree world? These questions are simply not addressed by a strictly classical approach to deviance. Why? The reason lies, in part, in the extreme individualism of classical thought. Insomuch as classical theorizing strips individuals of all but the most instrumental forms of calculative judgment, good intentions aside, the question must be asked: Is there not something sadistic about the isolated individual application of classical reasoning?

The term *sadism* is historically derived from the pornographic writings of the Marquis de Sade, who was a contemporary of Bentham and Beccaria, the founding fathers of the classical perspective. A French pornographer and a criminal convicted of a series of sexual assaults against women, de Sade, like Bentham and Beccaria, was also a theorist of the rationality of both crime and crime control. In 1791 de Sade was imprisoned for publishing the pornographic novel *Justine*. This occurred in the same year in which France enacted the most classical and excessively rational of all criminal codes to date, which was discussed earlier in this chapter. In what ways is sadism an unacknowledged and shadowy double of classical reasoning's abstract commitment to rational hedonism? Both classical theorizing and sadism reduce the social contradictions of deviance to matters of individual choice. Both also advocate the calculative application of swift and certain punishment. As a theorist of crime, de Sade reasoned that, in contrast to the uncertain and disappointing effects of pleasure, "pain must be preferred, for pain's telling effects cannot deceive."[66]

De Sade's arguments concerning the rational benefits of systematically administered pain resemble the arguments of his early criminological counterparts. Like sadistic pornography, classical criminology advocates the application of strict disciplinary punishments in isolation from the complex, contradictory, and often unequal social landscapes within which people make choices between conformity and deviance. This is not to reduce the logic of classical thought to the logic of sadism. It is, however, to note disturbing historical connections between these two excessively rational modes of thought. Each in its own way seeks to pin punishment onto individuals in isolation from the historical complexities of their social context.[67] Does this mean that the logic of classical reasoning and the logic of sadism are historically intertwined? This much may be said for sure: without some commitment to equalizing the human social conditions in which choices for or against deviance are actually made, the classical perspective will favor a very specialized form of rationality—the rationality of the advantaged, the rich, and the powerful. The rationality of the disadvantaged, the poor, and the powerless will be either denied or classified as deviant.

NOTES

1 Cesare Beccaria, *An Essay on Crimes and Punishments*, Philip H. Nicklin, Philadelphia, 1819, as excerpted in Sawyer F. Sylvester Jr. (ed.), *The Heritage of Modern Criminology*, Schenkman, Cambridge, Mass., 1972, p. 12.

2 James Q. Wilson, *Thinking about Crime*, Vintage, New York, 1975, p. 197.

3 Demographic data here cited are drawn from R. R. Palmer and Joel Colton, *A History of the Modern World to 1815*, 5th ed., Alfred A. Knopf, New York, 1978, pp. 433–437.

4 Mark Kennedy, "Beyond Incrimination," in C. E. Reasons (ed.), *The Criminologist: Crime and the Criminal*, Goodyear, Pacific Palisades, Calif., 1974, pp. 106–135. For a related analysis, see Joan Smith, *Social Issues and the Social Order: The Contradictions of Capitalism*, pp. 3–52.

5 Karl Marx and Frederick Engels, "The Communist Manifesto," in *Selected Works*, International Publishers, New York, 1968, p. 37.

6 See, for instance, R. R. Palmer and Joel Colton, *A History of the Modern World to 1815*, Alfred A. Knopf, New York, 1978, pp. 70–88.

7 See, for instance, Samuel Enoch Stumpf, "The Apex of Medieval Philosophy: The Scholastic System of St. Thomas Aquinas," in *Socrates to Sartre: A History of Philosophy*, McGraw-Hill, New York, 1966, pp. 185–211.

8 Robert Nisbet, *The Social Philosophers: Community and Conflict in Western Thought*, Crowell, New York, 1973, p. 139.

9 Mary Peter Mack, "Cesare Beccaria," in *International Encyclopedia of the Social Sciences*, Macmillan, New York, 1968, vol. 2, pp. 37–38.

10 Cesare Beccaria, *An Essay on Crimes and Punishments*, Henry Paolucci (trans.), Bobbs-Merrill, Indianapolis, 1963, pp. 5–6.

11 Ibid., p. 12.

12 Mack, "Cesare Beccaria," pp. 37–38.

13 Beccaria, *An Essay on Crimes and Punishments* (Paolucci trans.), pp. 13, 17.

14 Ibid., p. 31.

15 Ibid., p. 29.

16 Ibid., p. 26.

17 Mary Peter Mack, "Jeremy Bentham," in *International Encyclopedia of the Social Sciences*, Macmillan, New York, 1968, vol. 2, pp. 55–58.
18 Kennedy, "Beyond Incrimination," p. 116.
19 John L. Gillin, *Criminology and Penology*, 3d ed., Appleton-Century-Crofts, 1945, p. 229.
20 George B. Vold, *Theoretical Criminology*, 2d ed., prepared by Thomas S. Bernard, Oxford University Press, New York, 1979, p. 26.
21 As cited in Paul W. Tappan, *Crime, Justice, and Correction*, McGraw-Hill, New York, 1960, pp. 403–404.
22 Richard Moran, *Knowing Right from Wrong: The Insanity Defense of Daniel McNaughtan*, The Free Press, New York, 1981.
23 Michel Foucault, *Discipline and Punish: The Birth of a Prison*, A. Sheridan (trans.), Vintage Books, New York, 1979, p. 115.
24 Ibid., pp. 116–117.
25 Jeremy Bentham, *Works*, vol. X, J. Bowering (ed.), Tait, Edinburgh, 1843, p. 226.
26 David Rothman, *The Discovery of the Asylum: Social Order and Disorder in the New Republic*, Little, Brown, Boston, 1971, p. 62.
27 Ibid.
28 Marvin E. Wolfgang, Robert Figlio, and Thorsten Sellin, *Delinquency in a Birth Cohort*, University of Chicago Press, Chicago, 1972.
29 For a critical discussion of Beccaria's opinions on this matter, see Ysabel Rennie, *The Search for Criminal Man*, Lexington Books, Heath, Lexington, Mass., 1978.
30 Leon Shaskolsky Sheleff, "The Relevance of Classical Criminology Today," in Israel L. Barak-Glantz and C. Ronald Huff (eds.), *The Mad, the Bad, and the Different: Essays in Honor of Simon Dinitz*, Lexington Books, Heath, Lexington, Mass., 1981, pp. 3, 6.
31 Andrew von Hirsch, *Doing Justice: The Choice of Punishments*, Hill & Wang, New York, 1976, p. 6.
32 Wilson, *Thinking about Crime*.
33 Ibid., p. 62.
34 Marshall Clinard and Robert F. Meir, *Sociology of Deviant Behavior*, 5th ed., Holt, New York, 1979, p. 252.
35 Wilson, *Thinking about Crime*, p. xx.
36 William Glasser, *Reality Therapy*, Harper & Row, New York, 1965.
37 Don Gibbons, *The Criminological Enterprise: Theories and Perspectives*, Prentice-Hall, Englewood Cliffs, N.J., 1979, pp. 121–126.
38 Edwin H. Sutherland, *Criminology*, Lippincott, Philadelphia, 1924, p. 360.
39 Ibid.
40 Harry Elmer Barnes and Negley K. Teeters, *New Horizons in Criminology*, 3d ed., Prentice-Hall, Englewood Cliffs, N.J., 1959, p. 286.
41 Walter C. Reckless, *The Crime Problem*, 4th ed., Prentice-Hall, Englewood Cliffs, N.J., 1967, p. 504.
42 Gibbons, *The Criminological Enterprise*, p. 122.
43 Ibid.
44 Franklin E. Zimring, *Perspectives on Deterrence*, National Institute of Mental Health, Washington, D.C., 1971.
45 Jack P. Gibbs, *Crime, Punishment, and Deterrence*, Elsevier, New York, 1975. In the studies reviewed by Gibbs, punishment severity was most commonly measured by length of sentence.

46 Martin Gold and Jay R. Williams, "National Study of the Aftermath of Apprehension," *Prospectus*, vol. 3, 1969.

47 Alan Liska, *Perspectives on Deviance*, Prentice-Hall, Englewood Cliffs, N.J., 1981, p. 98.

48 Charles R. Tittle, *Sanctions and Social Deviance: The Question of Deterrence*, Praeger, New York, 1980.

49 Jack Gibbs, "Crime, Punishment, and Deterrence," *Social Science Quarterly*, vol. 48, March 1968, pp. 515–530.

50 Charles R. Tittle, "Crime Rates and Legal Sanctions," *Social Problems*, vol. 16, spring 1969, pp. 408–423.

51 See Louis N. Gray and T. David Martin, "Punishment and Deterrence: Another Analysis," *Social Science Quarterly*, vol. 50, September 1969, pp. 389–395; and William Bailey, T. David Martin, and Louis Gray, "Crime and Deterrence: A Correlation of Analysis," *Journal of Research in Crime and Delinquency*, vol. 11, July 1974, pp. 124–143.

52 Charles H. Logan, "General Deterrence, Effects of Imprisonment," *Social Forces*, vol. 51, September 1972, pp. 63–72.

53 Ibid.

54 Charles R. Tittle and A. Rowe, "Certainty of Arrest and Crime Rates: A Further Test of the Deterrence Hypothesis," *Social Forces*, vol. 52, June 1974, pp. 455–462.

55 A related study by Don Brown of California counties and towns suggests that the tipping effect may be applicable only to small cities. See Don W. Brown, "Arrest Rates and Crime Rates: When Does a Tipping Effect Occur?" *Social Forces*, vol. 57, December 1978, pp. 671–682.

56 Among the first studies to report this negative relationship were Gary F. Jensen, "Crime Doesn't Pay: Correlates of Shared Misunderstanding," *Social Problems*, vol. 17, fall 1969, pp. 189–201; and Gordon P. Waldo and Theodore G. Chiricos, "Perceived Penal Sanction and Self-Reported Criminality: A Neglected Approach to Deterrence Research," *Social Problems*, vol. 19, spring 1972, pp. 522–540. See also Charles R. Tittle, "Sanction, Fear and the Maintenance of Social Order," *Social Forces*, vol. 55, March 1977, pp. 579–596.

57 Matthew Silberman, "Toward a Theory of Criminal Deterrence," *American Sociological Review*, vol. 41, June 1976, pp. 442–461.

58 Maynard L. Erickson, Jack P. Gibbs, and Gary F. Jensen, "The Deterrence Doctrine and the Perceived Certainty of Legal Punishments," *American Sociological Review*, vol. 42, April 1977, pp. 305–317.

59 Ibid., p. 317.

60 Gary F. Jensen, Maynard L. Erickson, and Jack P. Gibbs, "Perceived Risk of Punishment and Self Reported Delinquency," *Social Forces*, vol. 57, September 1978, pp. 37–38.

61 For the results of the California survey, see Social Psychiatry Research Associates, *Public Knowledge of Criminal Penalties? A Research Report*, State of California Assembly Research Office, Sacramento, 1968. For the results of the Nebraska poll conducted for the Center for Studies in Criminal Justice at the University of Chicago, see Zimring, *Perspectives on Deterrence*, p. 57.

62 Clinard and Meir, *Sociology of Deviant Behavior*, pp. 248–249.

63 Richard G. Salem and William J. Bowers, "Severity of Formal Sanctions as a Deterrent to Deviant Behavior," *Law and Society Review*, vol. 5, August 1970, pp. 21–40.

64 Sheleff, "The Relevance of Classical Criminology Today," p. 5.
65 See, for instance, Ian Taylor, Paul Walton, and Jock Young, *The New Criminology*, Harper & Row, New York, 1973, pp. 1–10.
66 Marquis de Sade, *Justine, Philosophy in the Bedroom, Eugenie de Franval and Other Writings*, Richard Seaver and Austryn Wainhouse (trans.), Grove Press, New York, 1966, p. 252.
67 For an extended examination of the relations between classical criminological theory and sadism, see Stephen Pfohl and Avery Gordon, "Criminological Displacement: A Sociological Deconstruction," *Social Problems*, vol. 33, October/December 1986, pp. s94–s113.

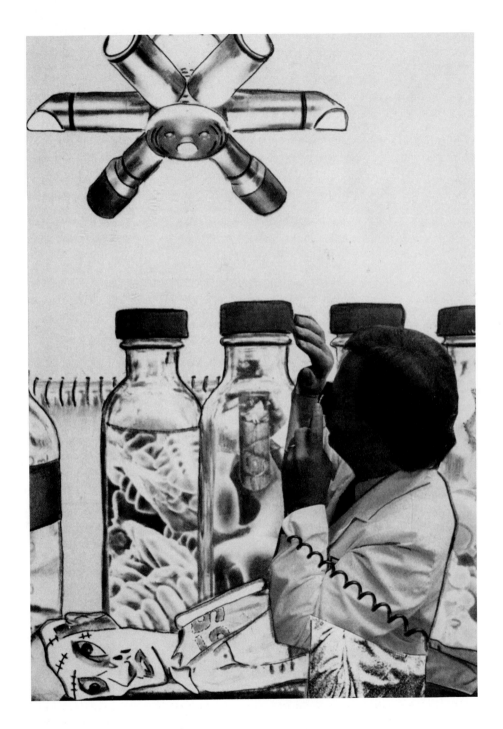

Normalizing Relations   By Joseph LaMantia and Stephen Pfohl

CHAPTER 4

THE PATHOLOGICAL PERSPECTIVE:
Deviance as Sickness

A slow but steady transformation of deviance has taken place in American society. . . . Deviant behaviors that were once defined as immoral, sinful, or criminal have been given medical meanings. Some say that rehabilitation has replaced punishment, but in many cases medical treatments have become a new form of punishment and social control.

Peter Conrad and Joseph Schneider[1]

Everybody and certainly sociologists should know that some things that come to be medicalized or pathologized as disease, especially mental diseases or disorders, are potentially other social forms—forms of moral protest, of imaginary and physical escape from uninhabitable social relations, . . . a symbolic and material response to a profoundly social disease.

Jackie Orr[2]

INTRODUCTION

Imagine going to work and finding yourself surrounded by fellow employees whose distressed actions suggested that they were wrestling with invisible forces. Imagine hearing some of these visibly shaken workers shout out phrases such as, "I will kill you!" and "Let me go!" During the 1970s such strange events began to take place within factories operated by U.S.- and Japanese-based transnational corporations. At the center of these "deviant" episodes were Malay women who migrated from peasant villages to so-called free trade zones. There they became a source of cheap factory labor, particularly for the fast-growing microelectronics industry. In 1975 over 40 women working in a single factory began to manifest such strange disoriented symptoms. What lay behind these women's "dark visions" and fearful sensations?

In 1978 a second large-scale outbreak of such disturbing behaviors took place. This time over 120 operators in a Sungai Way electronics plant appeared to be "possessed" by visions and voices unheard by their supervisors.

The workers were all female operators in the company's high-tech microscope division. The plant was closed down for three days as frightened women reportedly struck out at both invisible spirits and their male managers. In 1978, a Penang-based microelectronics firm was disrupted for three consecutive days as 15 women displayed related forms of behavior. According to a personnel officer at the plant: "Some girls started sobbing and screaming hysterically and when it seemed like it was spreading, the other workers in the production line were ushered out."[3]

What prompted such alarming behaviors? According to medical experts hired by the companies involved, the answer was simple. The women were sick. This is typical of a pathological perspective on deviance—a theoretical explanation of nonconformity as abnormality or disease. The women were diagnosed as "mentally ill," suffering from "epidemic hysteria," "hysterical seizures," and mass hysterical "trance states." The doctors prescribed Valium and other drugs to calm their patients' nerves. The agitated Malay women workers were said to be experiencing psychological difficulties in making the transition from rural to urban culture. Other medical factors cited included the women's weakened physical state, lack of proper food, and inadequate amounts of sleep.[4] After a few days of "sick leave" and the use of sedatives, doctors reasoned that the deviant female workers would soon be back to "normal."

Such medical logic is the not only way to interpret the Malay women's deviance. In some instances, traditional Malay "spirit healers," or *bomohs*, performed rites aimed at ridding the factories of ghosts. These healers pointed to concerns overlooked by a strictly medical viewpoint. The women workers came from villages where a belief in possession by spirits was understood as a sign of moral concern rather than as pathology. To be haunted by a dark spirit, such as a *datuk*, was a sign of moral pollution, a transgression of traditional cultural norms. The exploitative character of employment in the free-trade-zone factories had radically altered the peasant women's moral and economic situations. In traditional Malay villages peasant women conducted their daily chores relatively free of male control or supervision. When women left their villages to work for transnational corporations such freedoms were suddenly lost. In the new factories women were constantly subject to inspection by male managers.

Perhaps, as suggested anthropologist Aihwa Ong, the Malay factory spirits represented a form of unacknowledged social resistance to the women's new and troubling economic situation. Ong's historical enthnography of the disrupted Malay factories found in "the vocabulary of spirit possession" something suppressed by the language of pathology—"the unconscious beginnings of an idiom of protest against labor discipline and male control in the modern industrial situation."[5] In this sense, the spirit possessions spoke of "danger and violation as young Malay women intrude into hitherto forbidden spirit or male domains. Their participation as an industrial force is subconsciously perceived by themselves and their families as a threat to the ordering of Malay culture, . . . as a moral disorder in which workers are alienated from their bodies, the products of their work, their own culture."[6] This possibility is ignored by a pathological perspective on deviance. Moreover, as Ong points out, "In Malaysia, medicine had become part of the hegemonic discourse, constructing a 'modern' outlook by clearing away the nightmarish visions of Malay workers. However, as a technique of both concealment and control, it operates in a more sinister way than native beliefs in demons. Malay factory women may gradually become dispossessed of spirits and their own culture, but they remain profoundly dis-eased in the 'brave new world workplace.'"[7]

Despite the importance of questions raised by traditional Malay healers and by anthropologists such as Ong, the managers and doctors charged with restoring order to the shop floors of Malaysia relied almost entirely on a pathological perspective for their plan of medicalized control. Why this focus on alleged "biomedical" causes to the virtual exclusion of other viewpoints? The answer, it seems, lies in what might be called the "alchemical power" of pathological theorizing—its ability to transform other possible explanations into a singular focus on abnormality, sickness, or disease.

Alchemists are persons who attempt to transform one type of substance into another. The term *alchemy* is often associated with the activities of a secretive group of medieval chemists who labored to transform base metals into gold. Pathological theorizing involves a related transformation. Employing the language of medicine, pathological theorists attempt to transform images of deviance from badness to sickness. In this, pathological theorists have succeeded where other alchemists have failed. Nobody has convincingly demonstrated that any of a variety of cheap metals can be transformed into gold. Indeed, many modern historians regard medieval alchemists as little more than magicians in scientists' clothing. Pathological theorists, on the other hand, have convinced much of the world that deviants are no longer to be considered bad but sick—and that deviant behavior may be explained as the result of physical, mental, or emotional abnormalities.

The image of deviant people as sick people is today extremely widespread. Indeed, by the late nineteenth century, advocates of pathological theory had successfully transformed the classical perspective's emphasis on free choice into an image of medicalized causation. Why do people deviate? They do so as the result of an illness of the body or mind. Unlike medieval alchemists, pathological theorists were successful in clothing their transformations in the garb of science. This is not to say that their work is all science and no magic. As critics such as Ong suggest, there may be more than a bit of magic in the "concealment and control" strategies associated with medicalized explanations of deviance. Are pathological theories today successful because they offer compelling scientific evidence that nonconforming actions are diseased action? Or, are they accepted because they offer theoretical images that are attractive to a particular historical audience—an audience thirsty for simple solutions to complex problems? To ask such questions is to invite criticism concerning the pathological viewpoint. What is the truth of this perspective? Is it found in the vision of its theorists or in that of its critics? These questions are pursued in the following pages.

THEORETICAL IMAGES

The pathological perspective rose to prominence in the late nineteenth century. It represented a dramatic break with both the demonic and the classical traditions. Deviance was pictured as sickness, not sin, and as caused rather than chosen. It was the product of a disease which infected the body or mind. Its control demanded a medical-like cure rather than either penance or punishment.

Early Instances of Pathological Theorizing

Most historians date the origins of pathological theorizing to the 1876 publication of Cesare Lombroso's *The Criminal Man*.[8] Lombroso, an Italian physician, was performing an autopsy on the body of the dreaded brigand Vilella when he was struck by what he perceived as the apelike structure of the criminal's skull. Vilella's skull had two unusual depressions, the *median occipital fossa*, a condition observable in certain lower primates. This led Lombroso to hypothesize that Vilella was an evolutionary throwback—an *atavist*, a born criminal.

Lombroso reasoned that the premodern bodies of atavists were ill-suited for the civilized demands of contemporary life and were thus prone to crime and deviation. He sought to test this thesis by comparing the bodies of some 400 Italian prisoners with the bodies of a group of soldiers. Each was measured for evidence of such physical anomalies as unusual head size, eye defects, receding forehead, large ears, excessive jaws, fleshy and swollen lips, wooly hair, and long arms. According to Lombroso's measurements, 43 percent of the prisoners had five or more "atavistic" anomalies. None of the soldiers had five. Only 11 percent had more than three. This was taken as evidence that, at least for some criminals, biology was destiny; that inferior or pathological bodies produced pathological behavior.

Lombroso's ideas about the pathological origins of crime and deviance were extremely influential. Together with his students Raffaele Garafalo and Enrico Ferri, Lombroso founded the important *Archives of Psychiatric and Anthropological Criminology*, a journal dedicated to the scientific study of the causes of deviance. Yet, despite the seminal nature of Lombroso's contributions, there are those who trace the origins of pathological theorizing to the *humoral theory* of ancient Greece.[9] Humoral theory suggested that human behavior was affected by the balance of the body's four essential fluids: blood, phlegm, black bile, and yellow bile. According to the physician Hippocrates, imbalanced humors may produce madness. *Melancholia,* or depression, resulted from the liver's excess production of black bile. Similar explanations were used to explain other forms of pathological deviance. One unruly or "choleric" temperament was, for instance, believed to be caused by a sudden influx of yellow (liver) bile into the brain.

Other historians credit the origins of pathological theorizing to the writings of Giovanni Battista Della Porta (1535–1615). In his 1586 work *The Human Physiognomy* Della Porta posited a relationship between human facial characteristics and criminal behavior. He argued that criminal types such as the thief could be diagnosed by the presence of small ears, bushy eyebrows, small nose, mobile eyes, sharp vision, and large, open lips.[10] Similar observations were elaborated in 1775 in the four volumes of Johann Casper Lavater's *Physiognomical Fragments*.[11] For Lavater, a Swiss scholar of theology and physiology, shifty eyes, weak chins, and arrogant noses betrayed the criminal type. Other deviance-prone traits included beardlessness in men and beardedness in women.

Of related concern were the *phrenology* theories of the Austrian anatomist Franz Joseph Gall (1758–1828)[12] and his student collaborator, Johann Kasper Spurzheim (1776–1853). Spurzheim, a talented lecturer, was extremely influential in persuading European and American audiences that human behavior was explainable by the shape of the skull. According to the principles of phrenology, the exterior of the human skull was said to conform to the shape of the brain. The brain (equated with the mind) consisted of a set of faculties, each governing a particular aspect of human behavior. The faculties of the normal person were dynamically balanced. The faculty for openness was balanced by a faculty for secretiveness, and acquisitiveness was balanced with generosity. Problems arose when certain faculties were disproportionately developed. The individual would be unbalanced, driven perhaps toward deviance. The overdevelopment of the propensity for "amativeness" (the erotic faculty) was said to lead to rape and crimes of sex. An overdevelopment of acquisitiveness produced thievery and robbery. Too much secretiveness fostered things like treason. Murder was said to be related to an overexpanded faculty for combativeness. Such overdeveloped faculties produced protrusions of the brain, bumps and lumps shaping the exterior portion of the skull. By studying such bumps on the head, trained phrenologists believed, they could distinguish normal people from deviants.

Still other historians trace the beginning of the pathological perspective to the writings of the American physician-reformer Benjamin Rush.[13] In 1812 Rush, a signer of the Declaration of Independence, authored the first American text on psychiatry. Rush suggested that severe mental disorders were caused by an arterial disease of the brain. As a cure he prescribed a regime of hot and cold showers, purgatives, dietary changes, and bloodletting. Rush's definition of pathologically caused and medically curable deviance was extremely broad. His list of behavioral diseases included lying, crime, drunkenness, and "revolutiona," a sickness characteristic of opponents of the American Revolution.[14]

The Essential Components of Pathological Theorizing

All the theories mentioned above viewed nonconformity as resulting from some physical or mental defect. For analytic purposes, however, we shall date the full development of the pathological perspective to the late-nineteenth-century work of Lombroso. Lombroso's work combines the three essential components of pathological theorizing: (1) determinism, (2) positivism, and (3) an image of organismic infection.

Determinism   Pathological theorists see deviance as the product of natural causes. This reflects a thorough acceptance of a scientific viewpoint on human life. In the late nineteenth and early twentieth centuries this was a matter of great controversy. Scientific determinism likened the life of humans to that of other species. The origins and organization of each were to be explained by the forces of nature.

The spread of deterministic, or causal, thinking was spurred by popularizations of the thought of Charles Darwin. Darwin's 1859 *On the Origin of Species by Means of Natural Selection* suggested the evolutionary development of the plant kingdom in accordance with deterministic laws of natural selection. In his 1871 *The Descent of Man*, Darwin suggested that natural laws governed the development of the human species as well.[15] Within a short time, applications of Darwinism were made to nearly all aspects of human life. Some applications were more careful than others. Some, linked to Darwin only by popular inference, were haphazard, erroneous, and racist. Certain forms of human behavior (generally those close to the conventions of white Anglo-European society) were said to be naturally superior. Other types of behavior were viewed as less developed and inferior. All, however, were determined or caused. Each was allegedly ordered or determined by some natural law. Evolutionary theorist Herbert Spencer, for instance, argued that human life was governed by the law of "survival of the fittest." Superior forms were believed to naturally prevail over those less in harmony with the laws of evolution.

Much pathological theorizing carries the shadow of evolutionary thinking. All pathological theorizing is deterministic. Deviance is transformed from a moral choice into a dependent variable. Pathological theorizing replaces classical concern with deviant acts with a preoccupation with the deviant actor and those factors (independent variables) which cause deviant behavior.

Positivism   The pathological perspective contends that the causes of deviance can be known only through the canons of positivistic science. For positivists, valid knowledge is obtainable only through controlled observation and scientific experimentation. The causes of deviance will be known only when nonconformists are placed under the microscope of modern physiological or behavioral science. This, of course, is a radical break from previous ways of studying deviance. As Gideon Fishman points out, the positivist approach represented an "antithetical critique of classical attempts to explain crime as the willful, premeditated and controllable act of a rational human being."[16]

Positivism enters into the study and control of deviance through pathological theorizing. Nevertheless, as a methodological strategy, positivism is not unique to a medical viewpoint. Positivist methods also dominate most forms of modern social science. Indeed, Auguste Comte (1798–1857), the founding father of positivism, is commonly viewed as the first modern sociologist. Comte characterized positivism as the evolutionary successor to previous religious and philosophical viewpoints. From a positivist viewpoint, human life was explained in terms of a system of natural laws. By carefully observing and precisely classifying the dynamic and static aspects of such laws, positivism was said to foster an awareness of the timeless "unity" of human "continuity in change" and to give theoretical order to a "fixed series of successive transformations [by which] the human race, starting from a state not superior to that of the great apes, gradually led to the point at which civilized Europe finds itself today."[17] By the late nineteenth century Comte's positivist outlook formed a general methodological background for pathological theorists such as Lombroso.

Organismic Infection   Pathological theorists view society as an "organism" composed of interrelated parts. Society is likened to the human body. Deviance is likened to a diseased or sick part of that body. It weakens the whole body. Like the cancerous cell, untreated deviance is said to spread its sickness to other cells and dissipate the strength of the organism as a whole.

The History of Pathological Theorizing: Cycles of Optimism and Failure

The history of the pathological perspective is cyclical. From Lombroso to the present it has followed a course marked by optimism, then failure, then optimism again. In its optimistic phase the perspective is confident about scientific advance and humanitarian progress. In its phase of failure, previously promising images of pathology are undercut by an awareness of the faulty research methods which produced them. Humanitarian hopes fade. Little difference is seen between therapeutically tested cures and therapeutically justified controls. Yet, within a short time a new optimism is born, and the cycle of pathological investigations renews itself.

Subsequent sections on research methods and social control indication account for this cyclical optimism by linking modern pathological theorizing to the dominant social forces which have transformed the material and cultural landscape of contemporary western society. The remainder of this section reads like a short history of the rise and fall of major physiological and psychological pathology theories from Lombroso's day until our own. Its purpose is to provide a familiarity with most important variations on the pathological theme, and to underscore the fact that pathological theorists have studied much but proved little.

The Physiological Pathology Tradition: From Body Types to Chromosomes

The enthusiasm for Lombroso's theory of the "born criminal" was dampened by the 1913 publication of research by the English physician Charles Goring.[18] Goring, a medical officer in the British penal system, compared the bodies of approximately 3,000 repeat offenders with a large control group of university students, hospital patients, and soldiers. His rigorous examination of thirty-seven types of physical anomalies failed to support Lombroso's thesis. For a short time the idea that deviance was caused by physiological inferiority was put to rest.

Hooton: The Ghost of Lombroso   Lombroso's ideas did not lie dormant for long. Within a few years American researchers were to revive the physical-inferiority thesis. Leading this revival was Harvard University anthropologist Earnest Hooton. In 1939, Hooton published *The American Criminal*, a twelve-year study comparing a sample of 13,873 incarcerated criminals with 3,203 controls from ten different states.[19] Each had been subject to no fewer than 107 separate physical measurements. Hooton concluded that criminals were "organically inferior," marked by such things as low foreheads, high, pinched nasal nerves, excessive nasal deflections, and compressed faces. These "organic weaknesses" were said to make people unable to cope with their environment and thereby to produce deviant behavior. Hooton offered a bold classification of criminals by their body types. Tall, thin men were said to be predisposed to murder and robbery; tall, heavy men to forgery and fraud; undersized men to thievery and burglary; short, heavy types to assault and sex crimes. As a strategy of control Hooton advocated the elimination, or at least the "complete separation," of the "physically, mentally and morally unfit."

Hootons's findings were only slightly more reputable than Lombroso's. His methods were soon the subject of numerous critiques. Many of these are applicable to research within the pathological tradition in general.[20] In the first place, Hooton's sample of prisoners cannot be equated with criminals. Prisoners are criminals who have been caught. They are unsuccessful criminals. How representative are they of criminals in general? This cannot be answered without studying uncaught criminals as well. Hooton, like most pathological researchers, was content to erroneously equate prisoners with criminals.

A second critique was directed at Hooton's control groups. The attempt to compare criminals with controls was a good idea. Yet, Hooton's controls were hardly representative of the population at large. They were a strange conglomeration of Nashville firemen, Boston hospital outpatients, members of a state militia, patrons of a bathing beach, college students, mental patients, and others. Furthermore, Hooton's comparisons between criminals and controls were highly problematic. His data suggest greater differences between his Nashville and Boston samples than between prisoners and controls. No explanation was provided by Hooton, who glossed over such glaring contradictions.

Hooton's work is also suspect regarding the meaning of physical inferiority. Why is a compressed face inferior to a rounded face or a high forehead superior to a low one? These are value judgments. Hooton disguised them as a scientific fact. Even if they were signs of inferiority, Hooton did not prove that they were biologically inherited. Unhealthy bodies can result from poor nutrition, stress, lack of medical resources, and even prenatal trauma. Such things are social in origin. Preoccupied with individual pathology, Hooton failed to see the importance of a more complex analysis. Nor did Hooton realize that many repeat offenders had been previously incarcerated for some other type of crime. People classified as robbers may have been previously incarcerated for assault. This undermined Hooton's claim that certain body types were indicative of particular criminal types. Despite the excitement it generated, Hooton's work was soon thoroughly discredited. The only thing it reliably demonstrated was that prisoners had slightly smaller helixes and longer necks than controls.

Sheldon and the Study of Deviant Somotypes   Only a few years separated the controversy surrounding Hooton's research and the reintroduction of physiological pathology in the writings of William Sheldon. Sheldon did not equate a particular body type with inferiority. He suggested instead that certain body types predispose people to certain types of deviant behavior.

Sheldon's book *Varieties of Delinquent Youth: An Introduction to Constitutional Psychiatry*[21] drew upon the earlier work of the German scholar Ernst Kretschmer.[22] Kretschmer coined the term *constitutional personality* to refer to a relationship between behavioral disposition and body type. While Kretschmer's constitutional personality types were vague and imprecisely measured, Sheldon's "somotypes" were more defined. According to Sheldon, the adult body structure corresponds to the differential development of the three layers of embryonic tissue: the endoderm, which develops into digestive viscera; the ectoderm, which produces the skin and nervous system; and the mesoderm, which converts into bones, muscles, and tendons. Early embryonic structures mature at different rates or in different proportions. Hence one person's body may represent the disproportionate growth of the endoderm, and another's, of the ectoderm or mesoderm. More importantly, Sheldon believed that each resultant body type was accompanied by a particular personality type.

A disproportionate development of endodermic tissue produced the endomorphic body. This Sheldon characterized in terms of a relatively great development of digestive viscera; a tendency to put on fat; a soft roundness of the body; short tapering limbs; small bones; and a soft, smooth, velvety skin. The plump, rounded body of the "endomorph" was accompanied by a "viscerotonic" personality, a craving for the soft things in life, luxury, and relaxation. In a similar fashion, Sheldon described disproportionate maturation of the ectoderm and mesoderm as resulting in "ectomorphs" and "mesomorphs." The latter were dominated by muscle and bone development, by large trunks, chests, and wrists. Their bodies were hard and rectangular. As "somotonic" personalities they were active, dynamic, and assertive. They walked and talked aggressively. On the other hand, ectomorphs were frail, skinny persons. Their delicate bodies were characterized by the prominence of skin and appendages and by relatively little body mass spread over a great surface area. Their introverted personalities were "cerebrotonic"; oversensitive; and plagued by chronic fatigue, skin trouble, and bodily complaints.

Sheldon's categories emerged out of his measurements of the bodies and temperaments of 200 boys housed in the Hayden Goodwill Institute in Boston. Each was scored on a seven-point scale measuring relative endomorphic, mesomorphic, and ectomorphic development, and examined in terms of 650 temperament or psychological attributes. Sheldon concluded that boys who were disproportionately mesomorphic were characterized by the aggressive somotonic personality and more prone to a life of delinquency.

Sheldon's findings gave new life to the idea that body structures produce deviance. His research methods and analytic techniques were, however, full of holes.[23] His definition of delinquency was extremely vague. Rather than characterize delinquents by what they did (i.e., break the law), Sheldon relied on psychological measurements of failure, or "disappointedness." Drug use, "insufficient" IQs, homosexuality, psychosis, and psychoneurotic tendencies were lumped together as measures of delinquency. This approach led Sheldon to categorize one "really healthy looking tom cat" as a nondelinquent. The individual in question scored well on mental and physical indices and was said to be a strong young man from "good physical stock." Ignored was the fact that the boy had committed several violent sexual assaults.

Sheldon's poor measurements of delinquency undermined his claims to have scientifically linked body type to deviant behavior. The same cannot be said of the more careful work of Sheldon and Eleanor Glueck.[24] The Gluecks used Sheldon's measurement techniques to compare the bodies of 500 adjudicated delinquents with a matched sample of nondelinquents. They concluded that delinquents were more likely to be mesomorphic.

Without arguing with the Gluecks' research methods, it is easy to think of several sociological reasons that explain why adjudicated delinquents have stronger-looking bodies. In the first place, maybe one needs a tough body to be a tough delinquent. A weak-looking, soft, or fat kid is less likely to be accepted as a delinquent than the tough, ready-to-fight street kid. Recall that the Gluecks' delinquents had been officially judged so by the juvenile court. How large a factor is perception of threat in such determination? It is commonly known that physical appearance plays a prominent role in interpersonal assessments. Does this happen in the juvenile court? The Gluecks' data raise more questions than they answer. Why interpret the findings in terms of physiological pathology? It seems that if you look for physical explanations, you'll find them everywhere.

Searching for the Feebleminded Deviant   The English physician Goring is credited with the critique of Lombroso's theory of atavistic criminality.[25] While his measurement of convict bodies suggested no patterns of physical anomaly, Goring nonetheless claimed that heredity was a central cause of deviance. Using the recently developed methods of modern statistics, he compared criminality between brothers and between fathers and sons. Using imprisonment as a measure of criminality, he suggested that correlations between male siblings and between fathers and male children were as high as those for ordinary physical traits. Goring employed two controls for environmental impact. He compared boys living in their father's homes with boys living elsewhere. One group was as criminal as the other. He attempted comparisons between highly visible crimes, which might be imitated, and relatively invisible crimes, which fathers might conceal from sons. Stealing was an example of visible crime, whereas invisible crimes were things like sex crimes. Once again, correlations were as high for one as the other. To Goring, this meant that hereditary factors outweighed environmental factors.

Goring's work led to speculation about just what hereditary mechanisms controlled the relationship between heredity and crime. He hypothesized that an inheritance of poor mental ability might predispose one to a life of deviance. Goring, however, offered no evidence either that intelligence was inherited or that it was specifically related to deviance. Nor were Goring's environmental controls adequately constructed. No information was obtained regarding the environment of boys not living with their fathers. This was unfortunate in that separation from one's parents may have caused increased deviance among controls in Goring's study. Also problematic was the assumption about the invisibility of sex crimes. Such acts attract much public attention. It is hard to imagine them as less visible than crimes such as stealing. Despite such inadequacies, Goring's research opened a new Pandora's box of pathological research aimed at showing the link between heredity and deviance.

The Jukes   The work of Goring was pale compared to the excitement generated by two sensational studies of degenerate families appearing in the late nineteenth and early twentieth centuries. The first, *The Jukes: A Study in Crime, Pauperism, and Heredity*, was published in 1877 by Robert L. Dugdale, a prison investigator in New York.[26] Dugdale was struck by the number of blood relatives he observed behind bars. In order to examine links between heredity and crime, he gathered 150 years of information on a family he considered to be particularly degenerate—the Jukes. Beginning with Mas, "a hard drinker" who was "averse to steady toil," Dugdale allegedly found evidence of hereditary poverty and crime. Of 709 family members studied,

180 had received welfare, while 140 were convicted criminals, including 7 murderers, 60 thieves, and 50 prostitutes, 40 of whom were said to have passed venereal disease to some 440 customers. Thirty others had been charged with bastardy, the bearing of illegitimate offspring. Without comparing such lurid data with any control group, Dugdale drew inferences about the hereditary nature of deviancy. It was not until a critical-minded journalist compared the degenerate Jukes with the respectable Jonathan Edwards family that the "scientificity" of Dugdale's research was undermined. Both families had about the same proportion of deviants.[27]

Goddard: The Kallikaks and the IQ Test   A second famous degenerate-family study was produced by Henry H. Goddard.[28] Goddard's history begins during the American Revolution when Martin Kallikak, a respectable young soldier in the colonial army, developed a sexual liaison with a feeble-minded barmaid. The affair resulted in a child, whom Martin soon abandoned along with its mother. He returned home and married a "good girl" with "normal" intelligence and proper upbringing. By digging through family, town, and court records, Goddard sought to trace the comparative lineages of these two couplings: Martin and the feebleminded barmaid versus Martin and the good girl. The result was predictable. The feebleminded side was filled with deviant offspring—progeny classified as feebleminded, illegitimate, sexually unmoral, alcoholic, and the like. Only forty-six were rated as normal. On the good-girl side there was only respectability. For Goddard this pointed in the direction of heredity.

The Kallikak study, despite its feebleminded bad girl versus normal good girl comparison, is hardly a model of objective research. Goddard admitted to difficulty in obtaining full and unbiased family records. Furthermore, one doesn't have to be Dick Tracy to realize that the dice were loaded against the offspring of the poor, abandoned barmaid. Goddard applied other family-history techniques in tracing the lineages of 327 residents of the Vineland School for Feebleminded in New Jersey. The results again pointed toward heredity.[29] Goddard, however, recognized the limits of research such as his own. Previous ratings of intellectual capacity were too subjective to be considered scientifically valid. In searching for more objective measurements, Goddard pioneered the U.S. use of the Binet-Simon IQ test. Developed in France in 1905, this "intelligence quotient" exam converted answers to a set of pencil-and-paper questions into an alleged measure of "native intelligence."

Was feeblemindedness (or what we today call "mental retardation") related to criminal behavior? Goddard tried to find out by administering IQ tests to the residents of the Vineland School and comparing their scores with those of inmates in several New Jersey jails and prisons. Ignoring the possibility that many residents of the Vineland School might have been previously misclassified, he found that nobody tested higher than a mental age of 13. He therefore set a mental age of 12 as the cutoff point for feeblemindedness. A median of 70 percent of the prisoners scored below this point. For Goddard this meant that low intelligence was a key factor in determining crime. Feebleminded persons were said to be unable to handle complex social conditions, and he suggested that hereditary feeblemindedness might account for as much as 50 percent of all criminal activity.

Goddard's findings were interpreted as support for the pathological perspective. The strength of this support was broken in 1926 by the publication of Carl Murchinson's *Criminal Intelligence*, the first large-scale assessment of IQ scores for noninstitutionalized populations.[30] Murchinson compared IQ data for all World War I recruits with scores from a composite of prison samples. Over 47 percent of the recruits fell below the mental age of 13, and over 30 percent were below the mental age of 12. By comparison, only 20 percent of the prison samples were so low. Something had to be wrong. Either Goddard's findings had been falsely interpreted or over a third of the army was feebleminded. In a gesture of intellectual honesty, Goddard admitted his error and reduced the upper mental age of feeblemindedness from 12 to 9. With this new yardstick, significant differences between prisoners, soldiers, and anyone else disappeared.

Intelligence and Deviance: A Critical Evaluation   Although Murchinson's research put a damper on the equation between low IQ and deviance, there is today a resurgence of interest in this topic. Comparisons between prison samples and the population at large again point to a relationship between being incarcerated and having a low IQ score. What are we to make of such reports? While it is true that prisoners test lower, there are important methodological reasons to distrust causal inferences based upon such findings. These include such matters as the wide variation in IQ scores among both criminals and noncriminals; evidence that good schooling (something uncommon for most prisoners) is related to high IQ test scoring, while low motivation (a characteristic typical of in-prison test takers) is associated with low scoring; and information suggesting that the gap between prisoner scores and those of the general population is greatly reduced when comparisons are made with people of similar economic, linguistic, and educational backgrounds.

This last point is of particular importance. The vast majority of prisoners come from the lower class or from families discriminated against by virtue of color, ethnicity, or language. On the other hand, it is well known that standardized IQ tests contain questions and linguistic constructs which favor middle-class, suburban, white test takers. Given this awareness it is senseless to suggest that lower prisoner IQ scores reflect the primacy of biological factors. The absurdity of this position is underscored by the poor IQ scores of middle-class children who took the so-called "chitling" test developed by black sociologist Adrian Dove. Dove's counterbalance intelligence test was modeled closely after other IQ tests with one exception. It was written in the street language of the urban ghetto. The results (blacks did much better than whites) reversed the ordinary patterning of IQ testing. One suspects that a similar thing would happen if such tests were administered within prisons. This provides an additional reason to question the validity of the posited relationship between low IQ and deviance.[31]

Other Hereditary Theories: Studies of Twins and Adoptees   Studies of intelligence fail to isolate genetic factors which are independent of environmental influence. Studies of twins and adoptees have tried to overcome this limitation. Beginning in 1929 with the research of German geneticist Johannes Lange,[32] a series of studies have claimed significant differences between the criminality of identical twins when compared to that of fraternal twins, born into the same families but without the same genetic makeup. While Lange's twin samples were too small to generate reliable generalization, subsequent research by Legras in 1932 and Kranz in 1936 was cited as evidence of the same general pattern.[33] In 1968 the most extensive twin study was compiled by Christiansen, who compared 7,000 identical and fraternal twins born in Denmark between 1880 and 1910.[34] Like previous researchers, he discovered higher levels of concordance in criminality among identicals than among fraternals. That is, when one identical twin was found to be criminal, it was more likely that his or her sibling would also be criminal than was the case for fraternals. While suggestive of a pattern, Chrisitiansen's findings were hardly proof of a truly deterministic thesis. Identical males had the highest criminal concordance rate, 35.8 percent. This meant that persons with exactly the same genetic composition varied together in a little more than a third of the cases. While higher than the 21.3 percent concordance for fraternals, the difference between these two groups was in no way overwhelming. The difference was slightly greater for female identicals, whose concordance outdistanced fraternals by a rate of 21.4 to 4.3 percent.

What can be said of such small but consistent differences? If heredity really caused crime, we would expect 100 percent concordance. Perhaps the social environment simply affects identical twins more harshly than fraternals. Identical twins are often mistaken for each other. Attempts are made to blur their identities. Parents may dress them in similar clothes and give them similar hairstyles. This may breed resentment. Many identical twins find it difficult to establish independent identities and complain about the unfairness of being constantly compared.[35] For such people experimentation with deviance may offer a social way out of this experience of forced identification. This, unfortunately, is rarely discussed by genetic researchers committed to the discovery of physiological pathology.

Other pathologically oriented researchers have compared the deviance of biological and adoptive parents to that of adoptees. Schulsinger, for instance, analyzed the psychiatric records of the biological parents of adoptees diagnosed as psychopaths.[36] A small but higher percentage of disturbance was discovered in biological as opposed to adoptive relatives. Since the adoptive family was assumed to exert the greatest environmental impact, the greater proportion of disturbed biological relatives was taken as support for the idea that deviance is genetically transmitted.

Crowe approached this topic from another perspective.[37] He compared fifty-two adopted children whose natural mothers were female offenders with a matched sample of adoptees from noncriminal biological mothers. While adoptees from criminal mothers had slightly more arrests, convictions, and incarcerations, the actual differences between the two groups were quite small. Only eight children of criminal mothers and two of noncriminal mothers became criminals. In a study of over 1,000 Danish male adoptees, Hutchings and Mednick found only a 6 percent difference between the offspring of criminal versus noncriminal parents.[38] Moreover, the percentage of criminal adoptees whose adoptive fathers were criminal was higher than that of those whose biological fathers were criminals. These results deflate the notion that genetic predisposition is a primary determinant of future deviance.

In summary, while adoptee studies find a small but consistent trend suggesting that some adopted children reproduce the criminality of their biological parents, this finding may be more indicative of flawed research methods than actual genetic disposition. Consider Schulsinger's discovery that biological parents of psychopathic adoptees were more disturbed than adoptive parents. Think about why people give children over for adoption. Often this is done because parents lack the physical or emotional resources to raise children. It is thus hardly surprising that a slightly higher percentage of such parents may be more disturbed than those screened by adoption agencies as good placements. Other methodological problems include a general lack of data indicating (1) whether the adoptive parents knew of the criminality of the biological parents and whether this influenced their childraising, (2) the amount of time children spent with their biological parents before adoption, and (3) the criminal records of both fathers and mothers. These problems undermine confidence in such pathological research efforts and represent yet another line of scientifically unconvincing inquiry.

XYY Chromosomes: Continuing the Search for Hereditary Pathology

Each cell in the human body normally contains within its nucleus forty-six chromosomes. These microscopic filaments are found in pairs. One chromosome from each pair is transmitted from each parent at the time of conception. Through these pairs hereditary traits are passed from parents to child. Chromosomes governing sex-linked characteristics are labeled XX for females and XY for males. On rare occasions individuals are born with three of these sex-linked chromosomes.

The earliest discovery of such a chromosomal abnormality was the so-called Klinefelter's syndrome. The XXY syndrome refers to males with an extra "female" chromosome. Such persons are late in developing sexual characteristics and may have small testes and enlarged, "femalelike" breasts. Although a disproportionate number of XXY people are labeled mentally retarded, this may not be a purely biological phenomenon. What looks like retarded behavior may be a reaction to other people's negative reactions to unusual sexual characteristics. Moreover, there is no evidence linking Klinefelter's syndrome to criminality.

In 1961 evidence of another chromosomal abnormality was splashed from medical journals to the crime columns of newspapers worldwide. Scottish researcher Patricia Jacobs and her colleagues had isolated an extra male chromosome in 1 of 550 individuals tested.[39] This XYY pattern was soon labeled the "supermale syndrome" and hypothetically associated with an abnormal propensity for violence. The evidence for this was meager. Comparisons between the chromosomal structure of infants and a sample of maximum-security male patients in a Scottish hospital for the criminally insane revealed that 3 percent of the patient prisoners but only 0.15 percent of the newborns were XYY's. Early studies of XYY were extremely expensive and were generally limited to small, highly biased prison samples, such as very tall maximum-security inmates.

Despite a paucity of solid research, this new form of pathological theorizing quickly captured the public and legal imagination.[40] In 1968 the XYY syndrome was introduced as mitigating evidence in the highly publicized French murder case of Daniel Hugon. Hugon had brutally murdered a 65-year-old Paris prostitute. A court-appointed panel of experts recommended that his sentence be reduced as a result of his being XYY. Shortly thereafter an Australian court allowed the syndrome to be used as the basis for a plea of not guilty by reason of insanity.

In the United States the XYY defense fared less well. In 1969 a Los Angeles judge ruled that there was no clear scientific link between this abnormality and criminal behavior. Nonetheless, the most publicized court case involving the XYY concerned Richard Speck, the convicted murderer of eight student nurses in a Chicago apartment. Speck's attorney hinted that his client may have been an XYY. Headlines depicting Speck as a "supermale" appeared everywhere. Had the XYY made him do it? This question was debated in the popular media for several weeks. When actually analyzed, however, Speck's chromosomes appeared normal.

Following the rash of publicity surrounding the XYY syndrome, the National Institute of Mental Health commissioned a costly program of research and a survey of all known studies.[41] Was the XYY linked with higher levels of deviance? Apparently not! After an examination of thousands of people worldwide, it was found that 1 in every 1,500 to 3,000 males is an XYY. Although rates were highest among maximum-security prisoners, no evidence was found to link the XYY with higher rates of violence. The only characteristic with which the XYY syndrome was consistently paired was tallness. Once again we witness the rise and fall of a costly search for pathological deviance.[42]

Psychological Pathology: The Abnormal Mind of Nonconformity

The second major pathological tradition emphasized sick minds rather than sick bodies. Its root may be traced to the early Italian school of positivistic criminology founded by Lombroso. Law professor Raffaele Garofalo, a student and colleague of Lombroso, extended the idea of physiological atavism into the psychological realm. Garofalo hypothesized that certain criminals were "psychological degenerates [who] lacked the natural sentiments of probity and pity [altruism and sympathy] that were normally present in their civilized brethren.[43] Although Garofalo claimed that degenerate persons could be diagnosed by the trained clinical eye, his ideas were never validated by the canons of positivistic science. In recent years, however, several other interpretations of psychological pathology have risen to prominence. Three of the most influential include psychoanalysis, psychometric assessment, and the theory of psychopathy.

Psychoanalysis and Deviance: Unconscious Resistance to Social Control

From a psychoanalytic perspective, deviance is a matter of unconscious desires, fears, or conflicts operating beneath the conscious surface of everyday experience. In this sense, deviance represents what is culturally forbidden—a disruptive return of what is repressed. Why are certain forms of experience consciously recognized while others are censured? For psychoanalysis, everyday life is never entirely rational nor conscious. Meaningful experience is viewed as distorted by fantasies that filter our remembered perceptions of real events. The selective character of such distortions is made manifest (symptomatically) in our dreams; in what we find humorous, fearful, or desirable; and in such "uncanny" occurrences as slips of the tongue. This suggests that there is more to psychic life than meets the conscious "I"—that mundane experience is haunted by unconscious forces which police the borders between what is permitted and what is taboo. In this way, unconscious processes may set the stage for dramatic psychic and bodily crises—crises that may manifest themselves in the form of sickness or an inability to conform to social rules. By giving symbolic recognition to the power of unconscious forces, psychoanalysis attempts to both understand and heal contradictory aspects of human experience.

Psychoanalytic theory originated in the late nineteenth and early twentieth centuries through the research and clinical practice of the Austrian physician Sigmund Freud. Freud's writings opened the doors of science for a serious study of the unconscious. Freud's self-analysis and his therapeutic work with (mostly female) hysterics convinced him of the importance of early childhood experience, much of which may be lost to or repressed from the conscious mind. Psychoanalysis was intended as a science of partial recoveries, a "talking cure" whereby what was banished from memory might return in the form of interpretive symbolic constructions. In this way, psychoanalysis was envisioned as enabling people to work through (rather than be worked over by) unconscious psychic processes.

As a clinical technique, psychoanalysis is laborious and time consuming. Within a web of relational transferences to the analyst, the patient (or analysand) is encouraged to reflect upon a wide range of memories, dreams, fantasies, and feelings, and to "free-associate" to whatever comes to mind. Serving as a kind of projective mirror for a patient's desires and resistances, the analyst listens for symptomatic traces of what has been repressed, and may offer interpretations of experiences that elude conscious understanding. By giving symbolic form to repressed experiences, psychoanalysis endeavors to release its patients from psychic pathologies engendered by unconscious distortions. As such, psychoanalysis is theoretically attuned to the dynamic exchange between subjective experience and objective cultural constraints.

The cultural importance of psychoanalysis extends well beyond the clinical couch. By the mid-1950s psychoanalysis had become a perspective on life in general. Sociologist Peter Berger even likened it to a new religious movement. Its influence was everywhere. Films, literature, paintings, and newspapers bristled with psychoanalytic imagery. Moreover, as a conceptual tool for both social criticism and social control, psychoanalysis has been associated with both progressive and conservative politics. What follows here is an overview of some of the most dominant institutional uses (or abuses) of psychoanalysis as an aspect of pathological theorizing.

Psychoanalytic Theories of Crime and Deviance   Following Freud's 1909 journey to the United States, psychoanalysis became an increasingly important component of pathological theorizing about deviance. Under the auspices of U.S. psychiatry, mainstream psychoanalysis became a kind of "ego psychology," emphasizing the importance of a balanced and socially adjusted personality. The application of this type of psychoanalytic thinking to deviance generally takes one of two forms. The first views deviance as an imbalance in key components of the supposedly normal personality—the *id*, the *ego*, and the *superego*. Freud's observations of repressed sexuality in many of his Victorian patients led him to picture the id as a warehouse of instinctual energies dominated by sexual drives and desires. These are part of a larger package of life energies called the *libido*. After witnessing the massive carnage of World War I, Freud suggested the possibility of another set of energies within the id—the destructive forces of *thanatos*. Whereas libido pushes toward the fertile celebration of life, thanatos pulls toward the grave. Together they compose the unconscious tug between life and death that characterizes the id.

The superego, the second psychoanalytic component of personality, arises in childhood socialization as a control over the chaotic forces of the id. Through the superego, id energy is subordinated to the authority of social rules, contained by an internalized checklist of dos and don'ts. Popularly equated with conscience, the working of the superego sometimes involves conscious moral choice or acts of self-restraint. Other times it operates unconsciously through guilt, fear, or involuntary physiological reactions. The uneasy stomach which a child may feel just before stealing candy is an example of the superego at work.

Between the id and the superego is the ego, or reality principle. In wide-awake, conscious action, a strong ego mediates between the internal desires of the id and the external demands of the superego, balancing the instinctual drives of the individual with the normative dictates of society.

A lack of balance between the key personality components is said to cause deviance. Of particular psychoanalytic concern are the overdeveloped id and the underdeveloped superego. In both cases the ego is weak, unable to mediate between drives and restraints. In the case of the uncontrolled id, individual desires take precedence over societal responsibility. Repeated episodes of antisocial behavior may result. On the other hand, someone dominated by an overexaggerated superego may one day explode in an outburst of overly constrained deviant impulses.

A second application of psychoanalytic thinking is concerned with problems incurred in major stages of personality development. Freud posited three such stages: oral, anal, and phallic. Each revolves symbolically around a critical life experience associated with a particular part of the body. The oral stage involves adjustments associated with weaning, the breakaway from feeding at the mother's breast. The anal stage is associated with control over one's bowel movements, with toilet training. The phallic stage involves the genitals and the management of sexual feelings. Freud's famous description of the *Oedipal complex* is at the core of the phallic stage. Here, Freud asserts an almost primitive sexual desire for the opposite-sex parent that is censured by the strong assertive presence of the same-sex parent. Thus, a boy's alleged lust for his mother is repressed by the "threat of castration" that a father's adult male power symbolizes. Although less clearly described in Freud's own writings, the opposite is generally said to happen to the young (already "castrated") female.

According to Freud, a successful passage through the three developmental stages is a prerequisite for the healthy adult personality. If someone fails to adequately pass through one or more stages, the likelihood of deviance increases. In such cases deviance assumes a symbolic relationship to some aspect of the unresolved developmental crisis. Hence, fast-talking con artists are seen as fixated at the oral stage, symbolically unable to let go of maternal nuturance. Unless they are lucky enough to become radio announcers or college professors, their inadequately weaned mouths will lead them to deviance. Thieves, on the other hand, are psychoanalytically associated with poor anal control. Unable to smoothly let go of their own feces, the thieves become endlessly involved in the deviant acquisition and retention of property. The same is true for those who fail the tests of the genital stage.

Inappropriately formed relations to sexual desire and parental power are said to produce acts of sexual deviance and/or violence. The rapist and the murderer are so cataloged psychoanalytically.

Applications of Psychoanalysis   There have been numerous applications of psychoanalytic thought to the study of deviance. One classic example is *Roots of Crime*, a 1935 work by Franz Alexander and William Healy.[44] Following Freud, Alexander and Healy described how unconscious guilt may drive people to violate the law in order to get caught and punished. According to Freud, "In many criminals . . . it is possible to detect a very powerful sense of guilt which existed before the crime, and it is therefore not its result but its motive."[45] Alexander and Healy agree that efforts to alleviate Oedipal guilt are important unconscious determinants of crime. As evidence they cite the case of a 20-year-old man whose stealing was allegedly a substitute for the "forbidden sexual act." Other unconscious criminal motives were said to include overcompensation for a sense of inferiority, spite reactions toward a rejecting mother, and a desire for dependency. Psychoanalytic knowledge of these matters was drawn from clinical sessions with a small number of convicted criminals. By analyzing dreams, slips of the tongue, and free verbal associations, psychoanalytic theorists created a continuing story of the unconscious dimension of deviance. Manifest motives (such as stealing to obtain money) were supported by latent motives, such as acting out a legacy of repressed childhood trauma.

Psychoanalytic themes are also found in the work of August Aichhorn, a Viennese educator and friend of Freud.[46] Aichhorn suggested that juvenile delinquents bore the unconscious scars of too little parental love. As a corrective, he instituted a permissive therapeutic milieu where wayward youths could act out their troubles while being observed by staff trained in psychoanalytic interpretation. Of related concern is Bowlby's deprivation theory, which argues that parental rejection accounts for most cases of intractable delinquency,[47] and the work of Johnson and Szurek, which blames delinquency on the permissiveness of parents seeking unconscious gratification of their own id impulses in the deviance of their children.[48]

The psychoanalytic perspective appears to account for nearly everything. If one probes deep enough, unconscious motives can be found beneath any form of misbehavior. How adequate is this explanation of deviance? Although psychoanalytic reasoning has sparked the imagination of many, there are serious problems with this type of theorizing. The person who exposes his genitals to old ladies with green eyes and red dresses may be acting out some hidden trauma of his childhood. Perhaps he is subtly reminded of sexual feelings aroused by once seeing his mother and father making love under a green Christmas tree with red lights. But such cases are few and far between. Despite the apparent willingness of much of the public to equate deviance with psychological disturbance, there is simply no sound evidence that most deviance is rooted in the unconscious. When considering the psychoanalytic perspective one must remember several important criticisms, which are discussed below.

The Circularity of Many Psychoanalytic Interpretations How do psychoanalysts know that unconscious impulses lie behind deviance? Such impulses are inferred from behavior. Since people are said to deviate because they are driven by unconscious forces, evidence of deviance is read by most psychoanalysts as a symptom of deep unconscious disturbance. There is, unfortunately, much circularity in this logic. To the degree that psychoanalytic insight rests on speculative inference it is nearly impossible to prove or disprove. A good example occurred several years ago when a group of Muslim activists seized several buildings in Washington, D.C., and refused to release their hostages until the U.S. government met a series of political demands. When asked to explain the actions of these political deviants, one noted American criminologist resorted to the crudest form of circular psychoanalytic conjecture. Without even meeting the Muslim protesters, this expert announced to newspapers across the nation that their activities represented a subconscious male reaction to the growing power of women in Muslim society. The seizure of phallic-looking buildings was explained as a symbolic assertion of displaced masculinity. In a single stroke of psychoanalytic reasoning the political meaning of the Muslim protest was rewritten as a story of psychopathology. Recall, however, that the only evidence of inner psychological disturbance was an external display of deviant action. Inferences about sexual anxiety and displaced masculinity are based on nothing but the circular logic of psychoanalysis. Such circularity undermines the usefulness of psychoanalytic explanations. But then, my objections might be explained as nothing more than my own unconscious fears. The circular nature of psychoanalytic thought goes round and round.

The "Normalization" of Male Heterosexuality The model of ego adjustment offered by mainstream psychoanalysis is based on a relatively unquestioned acceptance of modern male heterosexuality as a timeless cultural norm. This is another failing of many psychoanalytic interpretations of deviance. Such heterosexist biases may be traced back to certain of Freud's writings, particularly his discussions of the *Oedipal complex* and his essay entitled "Femininity." In theorizing the Oedipal complex, Freud universalizes processes that may be historically specific to his own society. He contends that, in the course of normal ego development, a young boy must repress early childhood sexual desires for his mother. Such alleged desires bring a boy into competition with his father. He represses these desires because he fears his father's power. Behind such fear lurks the terror of "castration"—the belief (or the fantasy) that if he does not relinquish his incestuous desires he will be robbed of (the most precise symbol of) his manhood. Such fears are said to be founded upon a little boy's discovery that his mother is already "castrated"—that she lacks a penis, that most powerful of all male symbols. Fearing that unless he complies with his father's demands he too will be castrated, the "normal" male child is said to transfer his identifications to his father. In doing this, he becomes a potential castrator of others as well as becoming a future heterosexual husband.

But what of little girls? And what of children who do not identify with heterosexual norms? Why, moreover, should either girls or boys imagine that their mothers are castrated in the first place? Freud's answers to these questions are problematic. Concerning the assumption of "female castration," he states that children "have learnt from the sight of the female genitals that the organ which they value so highly need not necessarily accompany the body."[49] They have learned, in other words, that something of great value is missing from women's sexual organs. But why should this be the case? Why are female genitals viewed as lacking in value? In pagan cultures, which were violently suppressed to produce that modern, straight-male-dominated culture within which Freud was writing, female genitals were typically revered as symbols of the earth's fecundity, fullness, and periodic change. Given this historical awareness, it is important not to regard the pathological devaluing of the female body as some quasi-natural rite of psychic passage. Such a devaluation is symptomatic, not of something natural, but of modern patriarchal practices that simultaneously construct and subordinate women's sexual difference from men.

Despite his own warnings against "underestimating the influence of social customs," the ahistorical character of Freud's theories is here most evident. This is particularly true when we consider his assertion that, upon catching "sight of the genitals of the other sex," little girls are faced, not simply with the fear of castration, but with the "fact" that they are castrated.[50] This supposed "fact"—the recognition that, in comparison to men, they are severely lacking—may prove a source of great pain and female resistance. In a compulsively heterosexual society, such as Freud's and our own, young girls are normatively expected to transfer their affections away from their mothers' bodies and toward the bodies of men. Since a woman manifestly lacks what Freud theorized as the most desirable of objects, what may she give a man when he offers her his penis? Speaking of (and for) the "female sex," Freud notes that women "feel seriously wronged, often declaring that they want to 'have something like it too,' and fall a victim to 'envy for the penis.'"[51]

Burdened with this alleged "wish to get the longed-for penis," what is the young female child to do? According to Freud, she has three options: (1) to remain in an anxious state of neurotic unease, as she hysterically searches to make up for in fantasy what she lacks in reality; (2) to deny her supposed lack and thereby become a masculinized woman, maybe even a lesbian; or (3) to accept her "castration" by suppressing her "envy" and turning the "aggressive" feelings this lack engenders back upon herself. In this last scenario, she will become a "normal" female "masochist," the passive recipient of her husband's precious penis. The woman, lacking a penis of her own, thus gives "her man" a phallic substitute: a child. In this, she both confirms his (heterosexual) manliness and her masochistic receptivity. Thus, concludes Freud, "masochism as people say, is truly feminine."[52]

Are Freud's remarks about the seeming naturalness of the *Oedipal complex, penis envy,* and *masochistic female heterosexuality* all that psychoanalysis has to say about sexuality? If so, it is hardly surprising that psychoanalysis may appear of little value to anybody but culturally privileged straight men. Unfortunately, this is often how Freud's ideas have been interpreted. Thus, clinician Elizabeth Moberly speaks in almost theological terms when she contends that "heterosexuality is the goal of human development."[53] This sentiment is echoed by Freudian Sandor Feldmen, who, claiming loyalty to Freud, interprets homosexuality as a "devious detour" from normal sexual development. "As a practitioner," writes Feldman, "I have learned that, essentially, homosexuals want to mate with the opposite sex. In therapy my intention is to discover what kind of fear or distress diverted the patient from the straight line."[54]

Such reasoning had led some feminists, as well as gay and lesbian critics, to regard psychoanalysis with considerable suspicion. This is unfortunate, given the suggestive complexity of other aspects of Freudian thought. Indeed, a number of influential early psychoanalysts, including Ernest Jones, Melanie Klein, and Karen Horney,[55] were quick to admonish the masculine and heterosexual biases in certain of Freud's pronouncements. In a related manner, many contemporary theorists of sexualities and gender are returning to psychoanalytic discourse, less out of respect for the content of Freud's original observations than in search of a method for critically examining the network of unconscious repressions that give dominant forms of sex or gender relations their seeming naturalness.[56]

In contrast to his more conservative pronouncements, Freud's *Three Essays on the Theory of Sexuality* may be read as a more provocative starting point for theorizing the force of unconscious sexual processes. Here, rather than assuming the "naturalness" of heterosexual identifications, Freud contends that human sexual aims are initially open-ended, bisexual, or polymorphously perverse. As such, the psychoanalytic story of "becoming sexed" is presented as a contradictory tale of culturally enforced repressions and sublimations, a story haunted by psychic gaps and leftovers, a story whose normative climax is realized only by the compulsive sacrifice of other possible pleasures. This is a story of modern civilization and its resulting discontents. It is also a story of the always imperfect cultural construction of sexual "normality" as a kind of ideological formation that is "precariously achieved and precariously maintained," and of a conflictual process of "psychosexual development from the polymorphous perverse to normality which is less a process of growth and more one of restriction."[57] This aspect of Freudian thought provides a theoretical opening by which psychoanalysis might be used to subvert rather than reinforce straight-male-oriented models of ego development. For the most part, however, this critical possibility remains outside the dominant institutional uses of psychoanalysis as a technology of social control.

The Exaggerated Importance of Childhood Experience   Significant childhood experiences undoubtedly shape later thoughts, feelings, and actions. But so do a wide range of other social, political, and economic experiences. Why is a bad relationship with one's parents more important than a bad relationship with one's employer, peers, or government? Traumatic psychological experiences are not evenly divided between different racial, class, gender, age, or ethnic categories.

Unfortunately, few psychoanalytic theorists address the conscious or unconscious consequences of socially engendered adult trauma. For the most part, psychoanalytic theory has been confined to an analysis of the psychic scars of childhood. According to a recent survey of professional psychiatric articles on crime appearing between 1966 and 1971, only three of thirty-nine examined social factors other than those directly related to the events of childhood.[58] Once again we note a severe limitation of psychoanalytic theorizing as a general explanation of deviant behavior.

Measuring Deviant Personality Traits

Psychological tests are designed to measure aspects of the human personality. Clinicians who use such assessment instruments to diagnose deviance assume that certain personality traits dispose people toward deviant action. There is, however, little evidence to support this assumption. Extensive reviews of the clinical literature on this matter fail to provide evidence that psychological testing successfully distinguishes deviants from those who conform.[59] Two notable exceptions involve studies using either the Minnesota Multiphasic Personality Inventory (MMPI) or the California Personality Inventory (CPI). The MMPI contains over 500 questions, clusters of which are broken into scales measuring various dimensions of personality. One of these, the Pd scale, measuring "psychopathic deviation," consistently differentiates criminals from nonoffenders. The socialization scale of the CPI claims similar results. Is it possible that these scientific measurements of personality have at last isolated the pathological determinants of deviance? A closer look at each deflates faith in this possibility. The Pd scale solicits information about how someone views deviant activity. People convicted of criminal acts are found to respond in a more positive manner than noncriminals. This is hardly surprising. It is more surprising that pathological theorists interpret this as evidence of a crime-prone personality. In actuality such responses may result from the fact that someone has acted criminally and was caught. On the CPI criminals score as more hostile to authority. Again, this is hardly surprising. Convicted criminals, after all, are subject to the long and often harsh arm of the law. Authority is not on their side. No wonder they are more negative. Thus, despite predictive claims, neither the MMPI nor the CPI gives us much hard scientific information about alleged personality characteristics which cause deviance.

Despite past failures there have been numerous recent efforts to nail down a measurable deviant personality. Two of the most notable include Eysenck's theory of genetic personality deficiency and Yochelson and Samenow's idea of the criminal personality.

Eysenck: Genetic Personality Deficiencies For British psychologist Hans Eysenck, criminals are persons who have neither learned to be deterred by punishment nor acquired the internal controls of "conscience."[60] According to Eysenck criminals possess certain personality deficiencies whereby they resist the control of others while having no internal controls of their own. This is evidenced by the fact that convicted criminals score higher on psychological measures of "extroversion" and "neuroticism." Eysenck speculates that this is the result of neurobiological weaknesses, such as a low level of cortical arousal and an autonomic nervous system that is highly susceptible to pain. From this Eysenck goes beyond the available evidence to suggest that the criminal personality may be genetically disposed toward deviance.

There are serious problems with Eysenck's theory. The first concerns his assumption regarding a neurobiological relationship between extroversion, neuroticism, and criminal behavior. There need be nothing genetic about this relationship. It is a well-known fact that body chemistry may be conditioned by how someone behaves. People who behave extrovertedly or neurotically may have different biochemistry from people who don't. We know about such matters from studying the behavior of people who develop ulcers or have early heart attacks. This means that neurobiological differences can be social rather than biological in origin. To forget this is to fall prey to sloppy circular reasoning about the pathological origins of all physical differences.

A second trouble with Eysenck's theory concerns the way he conceives of the relationship between extroversion, neuroticism, and actual criminal behavior. According to critics such as Feldman, the relationship between reported criminality and neuroticism may reflect less about an alleged personality deficiency than about the tendency for anxious people to admit more deviant behavior.[61] On the other hand, extremely extroverted people may place themselves in situations where the opportunity for nonconformity is greater. The assumption that this is the result of a deficient personality is empirically unsupported. Both crime and certain personality traits may be the result of other, more complex patterns of social learning. This challenges the core of Eysenck's theory. As Michael Nietzel points out, "Eysenck has not been able to separate a differential predisposition to be conditioned from the different quality of conditioning opportunities which children will experience."[62] Consider learning that takes place in the lower-class urban ghetto. A high percentage of children may learn crime, extroversion, and neuroticism as normal aspects of everyday life. No genetic or pathological deficiencies are needed to explain how such children may learn deviant adaptations to a harsh and often conflictual social environment.

Yochelson and Samenow: The Criminal Personality   According to psychologists Samuel Yochelson and Stanton Samenow, authors of *The Criminal Personality*, a decision to break the law is the result of abnormal thought patterns characteristic of the "criminal mind."[63] In place since early childhood, this abnormal mode of thinking remains fixed unless confronted with Yochelson and Samenow's unique brand of psychotherapy (a disciplined mix of group therapy, sexual abstinence, and unquestioned acceptance of the therapist's "objective" description of one's own criminal profile). Little is said about how such patterns originate, only that once operative they make criminals a manipulative and self-serving lot.

For the authors of *The Criminal Personality*, criminality is defined, not by unlawful behavior, but by one's state of mind. Thus, "the consequences of a lie told by a criminal and of a lie told by a non-criminal are very different."[64] But if two people act similarly, how can we say that one set of actions results from a criminal mind and the other does not? For Yochelson and Samenow, one needs only to know whether the people in question have a criminal record. If so, the criminal mind must be at work. The circularity of this reasoning is alarming. So is the praise heaped upon *The Criminal Personality* by a variety of law enforcement and criminal justice practitioners. Why such praise for a book which is little more than its authors' clinical assessments of offenders institutionalized in a federal mental hospital? It blurs distinctions between types of criminals and fails to employ control groups or measures of rate reliability. As proof for their theory Yochelson and Samenow demand that patients admit that they have the criminal personality. This may not sound like a very objective approach to scientific research. It isn't. Although *The Criminal Personality* is presented in the jargon and technical terms of scientific research, its real appeal is to those who intuitively "know" that criminals are pathological people.

The Elusive Search for the Psychopath

A final theme in the literature of psychological pathology involves the recurrent search for people who are devoid of conscience and, thereby, detached from the moral fiber of society. At various times such people have been labeled as morally insane, psychopathic, or sociopathic. Current diagnostic manuals use the term *antisocial personality*. Estimates vary as to the number of people afflicted with the antisocial personality. Some suggest as high as 3 percent of the entire adult population, others only 20 percent of the adult prison population.[65]

Belief in the existence of psychopathic people is as old as psychiatry itself.[66] French reformer Philippe Pinel used the term *manie sans délire* ("mania without delusions") to challenge the notion that intellectual impairment is always a feature of mental disorders. People could be rational and clear-thinking but still mentally ill. Their illness could be of a moral rather than an intellectual nature. American psychiatrist Benjamin Rush employed the term *moral aliena-tion*, and English physician J. S. Prichard the term *moral insanity*, to connote a similar "disorder of affections and feelings." The term *psychopath* was first applied clinically in 1936 by Dr. Samuel Woodward, superintendent of the Massachusetts State Lunatic Hospital. Two years later Isaac Ray published a landmark treatise in which the psychopath was pictured as someone with no signs of mental disorder other than a history of wrongful acts for which he or she denied responsibility. In the twentieth century, some Freudian theorists suggested that sociopaths were "orally fixated," while other theorists located the origins of psychopathic impulsivity in early childhood trauma.

The publication of Hervey Cleckley's *The Mask of Sanity* marks the most comprehensive listing of the symptoms of the psychopathic, or sociopathic, disorder.[67] According to Cleckley, the antisocial sociopath is recognizable by the following checklist of symptoms:

1 Superficial charm and good intelligence.
2 Absence of delusions and other signs of irrational thinking.
3 Absence of nervousness and other psychoneurotic manifestations.
4 Unreliability.
5 Untruthfulness and insincerity.
6 Lack of remorse or shame.
7 Inadequately motivated anti-social behavior.
8 Poor judgment and failure to learn by experience.
9 Pathologic egocentricity and incapacity for love.
10 General poverty of major affective reactions.
11 Specific loss of insight.
12 Unresponsiveness in interpersonal behavior.
13 Fantastic and uninviting behavior, with drink and sometimes without.
14 Suicide rarely carried out.
15 Sex life impersonal, trivial, and poorly integrated.
16 Failure to follow any life plan.

Examine these symptoms carefully. They are not very precise. How does one diagnose superficial charm (symptom 1) as distinguished from nonsuperficial charm? Even if this is possible, don't the codes of normal politeness instruct us all in the daily exercise of superficial charm? What about symptoms 2, 3, and 14? Under most conditions the absence of delusions, the absence of nervousness, ad the failure to carry out suicide are not seen as negative. Why include them in this cluster of sociopathic symptoms? What exactly is "fantastic and uninviting behavior" (symptom 13)? How can one adequately measure insincerity (symptom 5) in a culture that promotes high-pressure salesmanship as a desirable business trait? What is an "impersonal" or "trivial" sex life (symptom 15)? Couldn't this categorize all those "hot and heavy" singles waiting in line for a "one-night stand"? The categories are simply too vague, too imprecise.

The empirical research on psychopathy is not much more precise. It generally fails to adequately distinguish the disease from the behaviors it is said to produce. Harrison Gough theorized that sociopaths never learned to empathize with the perspective of others.[68] Baker tested this idea by examining whether sociopathic inmates were less empathetic than their nonsociopathic cellmates.[69] The participating inmates were asked to complete questionnaires measuring their perceptions of themselves, their cellmates, and their cellmates' assessments of themselves and others. Sociopaths were found to be less able to see themselves through another's eyes. This may be true, but isn't it a criterion for classifying a person as a sociopath in the first place?

Such circular reasoning is unfortunately characteristic of other studies as well. Albrecht and Sarbin found sociopaths to be "poor tension binders,"[70] while McCord and McCord documented them as remorseless, guiltless, and loveless.[71] Robins followed a group of ninety-four patients diagnosed as childhood sociopaths to discover that thirty years later they rated high on measures of financial dependency, poor work history, multiple arrests, unsuccessful marriage, impulsiveness, vagrancy, and use of aliases.[72] This tells us little about sociopathy as a disease. All that Robins's data really say is that people who acted antisocially as children were likely to act that way as adults. With no additional evidence, why equate such actions with a sickness?

Contemporary Studies of Sociopathy

Recent studies have suggested that biological abnormality may lie behind the psychological abnormality of the sociopath. These studies are intriguing but also plagued by serious methodological drawbacks. Funkenstein opened the door to physiological studies of sociopathy in 1944 when he injected fifteen sociopathic prisoners with the drug epinephrine.[73] The diagnosed sociopaths (thirteen men and two women) were all violent offenders, referred for court examination to the Boston Psychopathic Hospital. When compared to a comparison group of psychotics and neurotics, they sustained a much higher (75 mm Hg) rise in systolic blood pressure without experienced discomfort.

What does this mean? In 1955 D. T. Lykken suggested the answer when he reported that "primary sociopaths" revealed a diminished galvanic skin response (GSR) when lying and a reduced capacity for learning when stressed.[74] The GSR was measured by attaching sensitive wires to the subject's skin. Learning was measured by the time it took a subject confronted with aversive stimuli (electric shocks) to solve a mazelike task. This suggested that sociopaths are "hypoaroused." This meant that sociopaths have a body chemistry that is understimulated. With higher than normal sensory intake thresholds, sociopaths were said to be less sensitive to environmental stimuli. In order to experience their environment, they would have to act out, or make things happen. This is to suggest that sociopathic behavior is explainable by biological abnormality.

Lykken's work was followed by Schachtner and Latane's study of fifteen sociopaths.[75] Sociopaths were shown to have marked learning improvement (when given electric shocks) after having been injected with the stimulant epinephrine. Controls did not. Nor did sociopaths when given a placebo. Later studies by Lippert and by Hare suggested that sociopaths manifested less GSR when exposed to threats and reacted more quickly than normals to situations of artificially generated stress.[76] At Ohio State University an inter-disciplinary team of researchers replicated elements of previous studies, discovering a difference between "simple" and "hostile" sociopaths.[77] Simple sociopaths (defined as nonaggressive) manifested the hypoarousal syndrome; hostile or violent sociopaths did not.

The psychobiological research described above promises a breakthrough in the chemical control of antisocial behavior. It is nonetheless plagued by a basic methodological flaw. How are subjects defined as sociopaths in these hypoarousal experiments? While use is made of the Cleckley scale and the MMPI, the single most important indicator is an anxiety scale developed by Lykken. Sociopaths are determined by extremely low levels of anxiety when confronted with so-called high-anxiety situations. They are then confronted with laboratory-generated anxiety arousers (electric shocks, etc.) and are found to behave more anxiously. Low-anxiety people are found to act with low anxiety. This is what differentiates them from "normals." Once again we are confronted with a disturbing circularity in pathological research methods. There is no doubt that low anxiety has a measurable biological correlate. Nor is there doubt that if you inject anxiety-producing drugs into low-anxiety people, you can make them more anxious. None of this proves that low-anxiety persons are carriers of a disease.

Two things stand out about psychobiological studies of sociopathy. The first concerns sampling procedure. Nonanxious or underaroused prisoners are classified as remorseless sociopaths. This is said to distinguish them from other sociopathic inmates. But what about the remorseless politician, police officer, or general who, with little anxiety, makes an unfulfillable promise, fires a deadly bullet, or releases a nuclear warhead? Although such people are not ordinarily labeled psychopathic, if measured by a Lykken scale or epi-nephrine experiments they may reveal a similar psychobiological profile. Such tests have not been performed. Thus it seems that the elusive search for the psychopath is, at least implicitly, a matter of political perception. Some people are subjects for psychobiological examinations. Others are not.

Another methodological problem with psychobiological studies involves the issue of causality. Sociopathic behavior may be correlated with under-arousal. This does not mean that it is biologically caused. Maybe it is behavior which causes biochemical differences. This happens with ulcers or with high blood pressure. Few would argue that ulcers or high blood pressure cause people to lead a fast-paced, high-stress life. Why leap into such reasoning in the case of sociopathy? The answer has much to do with the simplistic social and political attractiveness of pathological theorizing.

Identifying Pathological Deviance

Every breath you take
Every move you make
Every bond you break
Every step you take

I'll be watching you.

Sting[78]

The search for the causes and cures of pathological deviance is fueled by a faith in the power of positivistic science. Pathological theorists believe that valid knowledge is obtainable only through rigorous and quantifiable measurements of cause and effect. The true test of positivism lies in the scientist's ability to predict and control the way things occur in nature. Rational mastery over nature is its ultimate goal. This way of seeing the world is so deeply ingrained in modern consciousness that it is difficult to envision a time when positivist explanations were not applied to all that is human. Today the human sciences offer causal theories about almost everything we think, feel, and do. When The Police sing the lyrics of "Every Breath You Take" they could well be referring to the omnipresent explanatory eye of positivism. When paired with an image of deviance as sickness, the positivistic human sciences promise a medical-like explanation and a therapeutic cure for the disease of nonconformity.

In the preceding pages we have reviewed many positivistic studies of pathological deviance. Most of these research projects were flawed by serious conceptual and methodological problems. Studies of physiological pathology have traditionally been hampered by imprecise definitions of abnormality, poor sampling procedures, and inadequate control-group comparisons. Psychological studies have fared no better. According to a recent review of the clinical literature, assessments of psychological pathology are typically biased by such factors as the professional socialization of diagnostic experts, contextual variations in diagnostic practice, problems of class and cultural stereotyping, and definitional ambiguity in the formulation of psychiatric classifications.

Given the inadequacy of so much pathological research, it is important to ask why this perspective has for so long been blessed by the halo of positivist respectability. The answer is found in the complex historical conjuncture between the masterful promise of positivistic human science and that offered by a medicalized vision of nonconformity. By examining the historical dynamics of this conjuncture we may better appreciate how it is that patholog-ical research strategies have carried so much power.

The Positivistic Study of Deviance as Disease

Some Historical Considerations   It was no accident that from the begin-ning positivist explanations of human behavior were linked to pathological images of deviance. Both were linked historically to another phenomenon—the development of western capitalism. To understand these linkages, let us begin with capitalism and its relationship to human labor. Productive effi-ciency is a cornerstone of the capitalist economy. The more efficient that capitalists are in exercising rational control over both material and human resources, the greater will be their profit. This demand for efficiency pre-cludes the possibility that capitalists will maintain direct physical control over the work of each wage laborer. This would be too costly. Under capitalism the centralized management of labor cannot be secured efficiently by the threat-ening hand of the boss. This is replaced by the "invisible hand" of a more subtle and omnipresent form of control—the technology of inner discipline. According to Michel Foucault this new internal technology of human sub-jugation produces the rationally self-controlled worker needed by capital-ism.[79] It permits the capitalist system to accumulate a self-disciplined workforce in much the same way that individual capitalists accumulate a mass of raw materials or natural resources.

It is here that we discover an affinity between the disciplinary demands of capitalism and the promise of positivist human science. According to Jurgen Habermas, positivist human science has been wed, from the beginning, to a promise of technical control. Its aim is to make "possible the control of the social life processes . . . in a manner not unlike that in which material science becomes the power of technical control."[80] Foucault goes a step further in tracing the origins of the positivist approach to the disciplinary laboratories of the early nineteenth century—the state penitentiary and other institutions of "total control." Although classical control agents sentenced criminals to such places for rational punishment, within a century they were transformed into institutions for corrective treatment or rehabilitation. Why? According to Foucault this transformation is rooted in the technical control possibilities of prison itself.

Prisons capture the bodies and minds of those they incarcerate. Day and night inmates are surrounded by the ever-watchful, yet often invisible, eye of those who stand guard. For control purposes inmates are classified into various types, each of which reduces concrete people to abstract categories suggestive of different ways of thinking, feeling, or acting. This classification was a first step toward what Foucault refers to as "capturing the soul," or *persona,* of the deviant. Out of this classificatory project grows the explanatory focus of positivist behavioral science. Early prison classification programs, with their detailed case histories and institutional logs on each inmate, are interpreted as a major impetus for the predictive-control promise of the human sciences. It is a short step from comparative classificatory typologies to explanatory causal accounts. Foucault concludes that "the sciences of man . . . which have so delighted our 'humanity for over a century, have their technical matrix in the petty, malicious minutiae of the [penal] disciplines.'"[81]

The impetus for human science arose simultaneously in other classificatory projects of the nineteenth century—the endless examination procedures by which educational institutions categorize students, weeding out the less able and the troublesome, and the clinical "gaze" of modern medicine, which analytically freezes the humanity of its subject into a machinelike arrangement of anatomical parts. Such projects herald a new vision of what humans are and how they might best be controlled. Not only were humans classifiable into a variety of different types, but the types themselves were arranged along a graded continuum of normality. Some were pictured as better adapted to the competitive demands of modern capitalist society; others were abnormal and did not fit into what was viewed as the natural order of things.

It may be hard for us to appreciate the newness of this today. Since birth we have been so classified. From the moment we leave our mother's womb (and often long before) we are subject to a host of medical, psychological, and intellectual measurements: eye tests, teeth tests, blood tests, IQ tests, achievement tests, entrance and exit exams. Throughout our lives we are measured and remeasured, classified and reclassified. In the early nineteenth century, such naturalistic classification was as new as its effect was profound. Out of this classification grew the human sciences, an array of disciplined positivistic examinations of factors believed to differentiate normal types from people who were pathological.

Just as the great classificatory project of the nineteenth century gave birth to the human sciences, so did it provide an intellectual justification for new strategies of disciplinary control, strategies aimed at correcting, rehabilitating, or curing abnormal types and thereby converting them into an internally motivated supply of human labor. In other words, in searching for scientific accounts and cures for abnormality, the human sciences legitimize the power of the capitalist enterprise out of which they are born. This is because the positivistic human sciences are a means of exercising instrumental or disciplinary control over people. This is not to say that the human sciences exist exclusively within the domain of capitalist economy. They do not. They manifest an affinity with other modern "control-at-the-top" political economies as well. This is evident when considering the repressive uses of human science methods in the state-socialist societies of eastern Europe throughout much of the twentieth century. Behavioral scientists working in the (former) USSR contributed significantly to the development of positivist methods aimed at "normalizing" nonconforming behaviors. In this sense, many state-socialist regimes were more successful in temporarily shedding the market structure of capitalism than the technologies of human management pro-

moted by early capitalist development. With the return of capitalist economics to eastern Europe, the fate of positivism's promise of instrumental mastery
remains a question of great historical concern.

Positivism in Relation to Gender and Race   The instrumental promise of
positivism is also connected to gender-specific and racial hierarchies. Concerning gender, positivism's disembodied advocacy of contextless objectivity
and emotional distance is suggestive of its historical grounding in the minds
of predominantly male theorists. This is evident in the works of Auguste
Comte, the founder of positivism. A figure whose methodological edicts
inspired many studies of deviants as sick individuals, Comte was himself a
psychically and spiritually divided man. Indeed, a close examination of
Comte's texts reveals a wide-ranging set of social and sexual repressions that
haunt the organization of positivist thinking in general. As Comte himself
confesses in the preface to his 1851 *Systeme de Politique Positive,* the painful
mental labor that enabled his *manly ascension* to a positivist viewpoint came at
the cost of suppressing such so-called *feminine moral feelings* as love and
compassion for others. Comte viewed the cold silencing of tender emotions as
a natural and necessary phase in the emergence of positivist science.

Positivism's abstract embrace of an emotionally detached perspective resembles Susan Griffin's description of pornography.[82] For Griffin, pornography represents something more than a set of obscene writings and sexualized
images. It is a male-dominated culture's revenge against the natural world
which it both denies and fears. It is a cultural practice by which many men
distance themselves from the material reality of their own human-animal
interdependencies within nature. As a voyeur of pinned-up or pinned-down
images of women, the pornographer struggles to hold himself apart from the
world his eyes behold. The pornographer denies his own vulnerable participation in nature. In so doing, he projects distorted images of his own fragile
mortality upon the bodies of women, nonwhites, children, and others whom
he envisions as threats to the "purity" of his own masterful abstractions. As
such, the pornographer fashions sadistic images which silence the voices of
others as well as alternative, less masterful voices within himself. The positivist scientist may perform a similar operation. Like the pornographer, the
positivist appears to position himself *as if* outside nature and looking down
upon it. While the pornographer may employ sadistic methods to cut into his
victim's fantastically bound body, the positivist gazes upon the body of
nature set apart from himself and laid bare by his supposedly "naturalistic"
laws.

This chilling parallel between positivism and pornography is far from
coincidental. In Chapter 3, in discussing the emergence of classical thought, I
noted that the rise of a predominantly individualist viewpoint on deviance in
the eighteenth century was accompanied by the emergence of sadism as a
specifically modern male form of sexualized power. As modern cultural
forms, both the individualization of deviance and sadism repress a reflexive

recognition of interdependent human animality. In the name of a new and emotionally distanced scientific method, positivism may carry this repression a step further.

In representing humans as rational calculators of pleasure and pain the classical perspective signals a violent abstraction from the real social contradictions in which we—as gendered social animals—find ourselves struggling. In this sense, classical thought substitutes a *dispassionate virtual reality*, characterized by a rational model of cost/benefit analysis, for the *passionate actualities* of our lived historical existence. Sadistic pornographic fantasies promise something similar. Such fantasies virtually silence women by substituting dispassionate literary signs of male dominance and female submission for the passionate intensity of actual struggles between women and men. Nevertheless, by operating in a virtual rather than an actual sphere of relations, the objectifications produced by both eighteenth-century classical logic and literary pornography are nowhere near as effective as the subsequent emergence, in the nineteenth century, of forms of objectification which not only signal, but actually put into practice, the imagination of male-dominated flights from material interdependency into the purified abstractions of the positivist viewpoint.

During the heyday of classical theorizing, thinkers such as Beccaria and Bentham envisioned a world where the rational power of signs would deter potential wrongdoers from violating the law. Confined within the supposedly rationalized penal system imagined by Beccaria and Bentham, de Sade's pornographic vision of control carried classical thinking a step further. De Sade imagined a world where isolated humans would be forced into submission not by rational signs but by disciplinary machines that would bind and break into their minds and bodies. This represented a new phase of objectification at the crossroads between the virtual realities of pornographic fiction and the positivist actualities of emerging scientific practice. Here, what was once an abstract male fantasy promised to become a concrete form of social production, as the objectifying machines that populated de Sade's writings would go beyond the mere representational threat of pain. Like the technological offshoots of positivist medicine, these pornographic machines would press themselves upon the captured subjectivity of the individuals they sought to change, forcing them into submission or, worse yet, killing them off.

Still, for all its violence, de Sade's vision of objectification remains a literary one—a virtual realm of total control, fueled by the abstract power of words rather than the actualities of forceful physical intervention. It is in such contexts that positivist medicine may put into practice what classical reasoning and literary pornography only promise. Through surgery, pharmaceutical treatments, genetic manipulations, and other forms of therapeutic discipline, positivism goes beyond previous projections of control in that it literally makes over the body and/or the mind of the alleged deviant. In this respect, positivist approaches to deviance resemble pornography that is put into practice. They attempt to force nonconformers to submit to the masterful scientific objectifications of the scientists who study them.

This is not to equate positivism with the realization of a pornographic imagination but to point to disturbing parallels between these two nineteenth-century social forms. It is also to suggest that the positivist control agent, like someone who translates the virtual objectification of women in pornography into actual acts of violence against women, may be driven not merely by the pursuit of neutral knowledge but also by passions for abstract and disembodying forms of social power.

If positivism appears from its historical origins as gender divided, its suppression of approaches to knowledge that lie outside (or under the gun of) white western methodologies is no less important. In this sense, positivism's commitment to value neutrality and emotional disengagement place it at odds with many nonwhite or non-Eurocentric cultural traditions. This is particularly the case in a comparison of positivism with traditional African-American approaches to truth. Although it was driven underground during slavery, and later covered over by Christian imagery, within the African-American diaspora there exists a long tradition of ecstatic knowledge, methods of knowing which periodically shout, dance, or laugh away the "objective" cultural distance between a detached observer and the object an observer studies. This is documented in the sociological and fictional writings of Zora Neale Hurston. In her account of African-American church rituals, Hurston describes forms of ecstatic knowledge that are characteristic of Haitian voodoo and other African-derived approaches to truth.[83] These Afrocentric methods resemble pagan approaches to knowledge that were destroyed, along with the women "witches" who were said to be their guardians, at the historical threshold of white western modernity.

By denigrating methods of ecstatic wisdom, western institutions have paved an intellectual runway for the disembodied flight of white male and positivist efforts at instrumental world mastery. Thus it is not surprising that positivist studies of "pathological deviance" have often characterized blacks as organically weak or mentally inadequate to modern social norms. Thus, late-nineteenth-century pathological theorists, such as J. B. Andrews and J. F. Miller, sought explanations for high rates of "Negro insanity," by pointing to such factors as African-Americans' alleged inability to handle situations of "enlarged freedom" without an "excitement of emotions" or "nervous disorganization." Ignored by such research was the violent suppression of African cultural practices. Highlighted, instead, was the supposed constitutional inferiority of blacks. This positivist obliteration of racist social realities continued well into the twentieth century. In 1908 William F. Drewry presented a paper to the National Conference of Charities and Correction in which he concluded that insanity among blacks was attributable to "hereditary deficiencies and unchecked constitutional diseases and defects."[84] Four years later a scholarly presentation of the relationship between madness and blackness argued that it was the "simple nature of the blacks, their childlike essence, which did not permit them to function well in the complexities of the modern world and predisposed them to insanity."[85]

It is not simply that positivism transforms the historical effects of racist power hierarchies into matters of individual pathology. In presenting itself as an exclusive standard of scientific truth, positivism also denies and/or erases the material reality of alternative forms of knowledge. This is documented by Patricia Hill Collins, who suggests that the "objectivist" claims of positivism—emphasizing researcher distance, the absence of emotions, value neutrality, and adversarial debate—silence African-American women's knowledge. Rooted in Afrocentric struggles against oppression, African-American women approach knowledge in ways that put them at odds with positivism. Theirs is an "epistemology" which emphasizes concrete interactional experience, dialogical exchange, an ethic of caring, and a demand for personal accountability. Yet, within a scientific terrain dominated by white masculine viewpoints, theorists "trying to rearticulate a Black woman's standpoint" routinely "face potential rejection."[86]

The obliteration of alternative distinctive standpoints is an unfortunate legacy of positivist thought. Such exclusions are particularly evident in a consideration of the history of pathological theories of deviance.

SOCIAL CONTROL OF PATHOLOGICAL DEVIANCE

The pathological perspective is associated with a medical model of social control. Whether administered by physicians or by other "helping professionals," such as psychologists, nurses, and social workers, treatment is prescribed as a cure for virtually all types of nonconformity.[87] Since the late nineteenth century, therapeutic controls have been devised for everything from violent crime to alcoholism, drug addiction, homosexuality, and even obesity. This proliferation of control in the name of treatment is described by Nicholas Kittrie as the rise of the "therapeutic state."[88] In such a state medical solutions are mandated for nearly all human problems, while the legal principle of *parens patriae* (the duty of the state to help those who cannot help themselves) is used to justify treatment and often to force it upon nonconformists.

While many people view the therapeutic state as a progressive historical development, there are several antihumanitarian features in its program of professional helping. Chief among these is the unwarranted assumption that deviants have no real choice in behaving the way they do. Also of concern is the way in which therapeutic control agents pretend to separate moral judgments from scientifically informed treatment. Conrad and Schneider cite several examples: treatments proposed by Dr. Samuel Cartwright, a respected southern physician who coined the term *drapetomania* to describe a disease affecting only slaves, the symptoms of which involved attempts to escape the plantations of "lawful" white masters; the use of mechanical or surgical controls by Victorian physicians to cure masturbation; and the work of Soviet physicians who diagnosed political dissidents as mentally ill, as helpless victims of "paranoia with counterrevolutionary delusions."[89] Although these appear to be extreme examples, "they highlight the fact that all medical designations of deviance are influenced significantly by the moral order of society and thus cannot be considered morally neutral."[90]

Caught up in the humanitarian dream of creating a healthy society, theorists of pathology have rarely heeded such criticism. Most have lived to see their ideas translated into practical policies. Consider the therapeutic response to such crude theories as phrenology and atavism. As George Vold points out, "phrenologists were the *medicine men* of their day, lecturing for fees to an eager public, counseling and advising on public and private welfare."[91] Phrenology was also used as a control mechanism in public institutions. Between 1831 and 1904, all inmates at the Eastern State Penitentiary in Philadelphia were classified phrenologically according to the bumps on their criminal heads. Lombroso's ideas about atavism were put to similar use. Under the direction of Dr. Hamilton Wey, an American disciple of Lombroso's, delinquents at the New York State Reformatory at Elmira were classified according to the presence or absence of atavistic anomalies. Wey believed that such measurements would aid in the diagnosis and treatment of the "criminal class." As a corrective, Wey advocated a rigorous program of physical therapy and exercise. By such control strategies, Wey hoped, inferior bodies would be strengthened and biological propensities toward deviance overcome.

More drastic were control strategies derived from the early theories of feeblemindedness and heredity. During the early twentieth century these provided a "scientific" rationale for the repressive biological control efforts of the eugenics movement.

The Eugenics Movement: Putting Theories of Hereditary Pathology into Practice

What theories of hereditary deviance lacked in scientific rigor they made up for in popular appeal.[92] A good example is T. W. Shannon's 1916 handbook *Eugenics*.[93] Within its pages one finds allegedly scientific rules of proper etiquette, social ethics for unmarried persons, techniques of hygienic bathing, and warnings about the dangerous effects of "self-pollution" (masturbation) and overindulgence in the sexual act. Violations of these rules were said to alter the normal course of heredity and breed deviance. Masturbation and overindulgence were particularly troublesome. "Touching oneself" was said to produce glassy eyes which permanently recede deep into their sockets. Too much sex "lowered the whole moral and physical tone of the race"; destroyed human vitality; and led to the birth of "puny" or "scrawny" offspring, "many of whom in early life pass to untimely graves."[94]

Texts such as Shannon's may today seem outdated and humorous. These books, however, often contained humorless recommendations for "constructive" eugenic action. For instance, Charles R. Henderson's 1901 *Dependent, Defective and Delinquent Classes: And of Their Social Treatment* proposes that all so-called defective criminals be placed in airtight chambers to be eliminated with poisonous (but not unpleasant) gas.[95] Such medical solutions to deviance were taken seriously by the Nazi architects of the Holocaust. Indeed the Nazis rationalized their atrocities with positivistically framed arguments about racial purity and the necessity of genetic control.

In the United States, one of the most repressive consequences of eugenic thinking came in the form of laws permitting the involuntary sterilization or castration of deviants. According to Charles McCaghy, between 1907 and 1937 thirty-one states passed laws allowing sterilization without consent for the mentally ill, the mentally deficient, and epileptics.[96] As late as 1976 twenty-six states still permitted involuntary sterilization of the mentally ill. Twenty-four allowed sterilization of the retarded, while fourteen permitted the operation for epileptics. Eleven other states allowed the sterilization of "hereditary criminals." Seven others permitted such procedures to be involuntarily used to control sex offenders, degenerates, and "moral degenerates." The vague terminology of such laws is troubling. Consider an Oregon statute allowing sterilization for "all persons who are feebleminded, insane, epileptic, habitual criminals, incurable syphilitics, moral degenerates or sex perverts, and who are . . . or will likely become, a menace to society."

The laws mentioned above are based upon the unproven assumptions of pathological theorizing. They have sanctioned over 70,000 involuntary sterilizations in the United States alone.[97] In the last few years many of these statutes have been challenged by advocates for people whose deviance has placed them under the scalpel of the eugenic surgeon. Most may soon be declared unconstitutional violations of individual rights. Yet, sterilization efforts have recently spread to new areas of control. McCaghy describes a 1973 incident in which two children of a welfare mother were involuntarily sterilized in a Montgomery, Alabama, family-planning clinic.[98] The mother of two girls, one diagnosed as retarded, the other normal, yielded to a caseworker's insistence that she sign a form of parental consent. The woman did not understand that the operations were permanent. She had been told that welfare payments would be cut off if she refused consent. An investigation of this incident revealed eleven other instances in which involuntary sterilization had been forced upon clinic clients during the same year. Similar incidents have been documented in states in every region in the country. Rooted in faulty logic and shoddy science, such operations are the lurid and repressive offspring of pathological theorizing.

The Mental Hospital

A Short History of Institutional Treatment   Advocates of eugenic control hope to prevent the birth of future generations of deviants. Other medicalized control practices seek to rehabilitate or change the behaviors of existing deviants. Perhaps the most important of these has been the use of hospitalization as a mode of "curative control" for individuals afflicted by some form of mental disorder.

Beginning with the great confinement of the late seventeenth and eighteenth centuries, large numbers of psychologically disturbed people have been treated behind the locked doors of the mental hospital or lunatic asylum.[99] As late as the early nineteenth century, medical treatments for madness differed little from those which had been practiced by nonmedical specialists for centuries: dunking, bloodletting, purgation, starvation, restraint. From that time to the present the history of the mental hospital reads like the cyclic history of other pathological control strategies; periods of optimism are followed by periods of devastating disillusionment. By the mid-nineteenth century the antiquated cures listed above had been replaced by a regime of disciplined routine known as the "asylum cure." Overseen by so-called moral physicians, this therapeutic program of enforced orderliness promoted a "cult of curability" which was overturned by the shocking investigative reports of reformers such as Dorothea Dix later in the century. Not only were cures not taking place, but the alleged disciplinary routines of the asylum were little more than a cover for what in actuality were practices of harsh custodial control.

By the mid-twentieth century little had changed. Despite increased medical involvement and the exhortations of progressive reformers, the hospitals were still essentially warehouses for the mentally impaired. Physical terror at the hands of an overworked, undertrained, and poorly paid staff was a common, if guarded, secret of life within the state hospital. A few new technologies of control had become popular—electroconvulsive, or "shock," therapy and psychosurgery—but talk or insight therapies, such as psychoanalysis, were seldom used. These forms of psychotherapy were reserved for patients from the higher social classes and in private or outpatient care.[100] Even then there is virtually no evidence that medically supervised psychotherapy is an effective cure for madness. After a comprehensive review of the treatment literature, Schwitzgebel concludes that "the results of controlled follow-up studies . . . have been consistently negative. . . . Traditional forms of therapy have been living for many years on public faith . . . [that] treatment can in fact change behavior."[101]

The Psychopharmaceutical Revolution   In 1952 the mental hospital entered a new phase of optimism. In that year French researchers synthesized chlorpromazine, the first of the so-called psychotropic drugs. Two years later a giant pharmaceutical company, Smith, Kline and French, began an aggressive campaign to market this drug for psychiatric use in the United States. Sold under the name Thorazine, the drug was billed as an antipsychotic or a major tranquilizer. A special task force of fifty high-powered salespersons promised that the new chemical agent would soon revolutionize the treatment of mental illness. It did. The drug could be used to quell severe symptoms, restore order to unruly hospital wards, and permit medical personnel to get on with the business of serious psychotherapy.

Proponents of the pharmaceutical revolution could not speak highly enough of the benefits of the new medications. Fueled by the advertising and promotional activities of the multi-billion-dollar pharmaceutical industry, hospital administrators praised the tranquilizing effects of Thorazine and heralded the day when chemotherapy would permit outpatient care for severely disturbed patients. Critics pointed to the fact that drugs were used more to control and manage patients than to cure and ameliorate the causes of mental disturbance. Dangerous side effects were also noted. The heavy and long-term use of Thorazine frequently results in *tardive dyskinesia,* a disfiguring and disabling disorder of the central nervous system. This physician-induced condition has caused irreversible damage to thousands of medically tranquilized patients. Its symptoms include involuntary lip, tongue, hand, and finger movements, general bodily shaking, and distortions of speech, facial expression, and body posture.[102]

This might seem like a big price for patients to pay in order to be treated more professionally. It was and continues to be a big price, and thus the optimism surrounding the pharmaceutical revolution was short-lived. Rather than preparing patients for treatment, the widespread use of psychotropic drugs soon became a form of treatment. Chemotherapy became a substitute for psychotherapy. Within a decade medication was the only demonstrable form of treatment offered to the vast majority of publicly institutionalized mental patients.

Depopulating Mental Hospitals: The Impact of Litigation and Fiscal Crises The number of persons hospitalized in public mental institutions grew steadily until 1955, when the patient count nationwide reached 558,000. Therefore, there occurred a steady decline in the use of involuntary hospitalization as a mode of social control. By 1977 the inpatient count had dropped to 174,000.[103] Why this sudden decrease? The use of psychotropic drugs is commonly cited as the major reason. While this was undoubtedly a factor, the issue is considerably more complex. Two other factors were also of importance: a nationwide movement of right-to-treatment litigation on behalf of involuntarily hospitalized patients and the growing fiscal crisis of state government.

Right-to-treatment litigation contends that involuntarily confined mental patients have a constitutional right to be adequately treated in the least restrictive environment or to be released. By 1974 the principle was given constitutional standing in the landmark Alabama case of *Wyatt v. Stickney.* Following a hearing on conditions at Alabama's 5,000-patient Bryce Hospital, Federal District Court Judge Frank Johnson ruled, "There can be no legal (or moral) justification for the State of Alabama's failure to afford treatment . . . and adequate treatment from a medical standpoint . . . to the several thousand patients who have been civilly committed to Bryce for treatment purposes."[104] Johnson subsequently delineated three conditions for adequate treatment: (1) a humane psychological and physical environment, (2) qualified staff in adequate numbers, and (3) individualized treatment plans. These general conditions had to be accompanied by specific standards detailing everything from the required components of a treatment plan and a formula for determining adequate staff-patient ratios to the size and number of toilets and showers required for a humane environment.

The *Wyatt* decision and other patients'-rights rulings were the result of over a decade of hard-fought legal struggles on behalf of persons involuntarily committed to the dark wards and hallways of the nation's public mental hospitals.[105] Prompted by journalistic exposés, critical sociological research, and a series of successful patients'-rights litigations, the right-to-treatment movement represented a new optimism for those concerned with the medical cure of madness. Its effects include a dramatic reduction in the number of patients subject to involuntary hospitalization and the issuance of more stringent criteria for involuntary commitment. Psychiatric judgments that someone is dangerous are replacing previous criteria which permitted commitment for serious illness alone. Many states are also urging formerly involuntarily committed patients to switch their status to that of voluntary patients. By such strategies, states hope to reduce the incredible costs required to reshape outdated custodial institutions into humane and modern treatment centers.

The issue of costliness is an important one. According to sociologist Andrew Scull, it has been a prime mover for the depopulation of mental hospitals from the outset.[106] Scull presents evidence suggesting that the timing of depopulation closely parallels the growing fiscal crisis of state government. Burdened with expensive union contracts, old and costly-to-maintain state buildings and property, and inflation-struck decreases in actual tax revenues, state governments are said to be confronted by strong economic pressures to save money by deinstitutionalizing their control of deviant populations such as the "mentally ill." Such fiscal pressure rather than high-minded reform is, for Scull, the prime mover of hospital depopulation. Without denying the influence of right-to-treatment reformers, Scull's analysis reminds us of a more general affinity between principled reform and practical material circumstances. As mutually determinant historical events, each breaks ground for the influence of the other. Ideas about the need to depopulate mental hospitals coincide with material circumstances which promote fiscal savings and institutional cutbacks.

Public Mental Hospitals Today: An Uncertain Future   Changes produced by the right-to-treatment movement and the practical realities of fiscal cutbacks present uncertainties for the continued reliance on public mental institutions of treatment and control. States are seriously considering the possibility of getting out of the mental hospital "business" altogether. Proposals exist to contract for beds in private hospitals for the most severely disturbed of the state's patients. Other patients would have to seek medical assistance through normal, noninstitutional channels. The future of such proposals is unclear. What is not unclear is one highly negative consequence of hospital depopulation—the "dumping" of deinstitutionalized patients into communities that are ill prepared to receive them.

Where do previously institutionalized patients go after release? This question is of the utmost importance for the thousands of old and long-term patients pushed out of hospitals by new policies resulting from twin forces of litigation and fiscal crisis. One place these patients generally do not go to is the wide assortment of community health facilities opened nationwide during the 1960s. Although these federally funded centers were originally designed to care for the seriously mentally ill in locations closer to home, this goal was never realized. The new community mental health centers soon found themselves busy counseling family problems, school troubles, alcoholism, predelinquency, bad marriages, job losses and even the problems of aging. Community mental health centers greatly expanded the reach of medical controls without significantly affecting the care of patients who had already been institutionalized.

If not to community-based mental health facilities, where do the large mass of formerly hospitalized mental patients turn? Too often, the answer is nowhere. This is particularly a problem for the many deinstitutionalized patients, especially elderly patients, who have spent their entire adult lives within hospitals. Unable to properly care for themselves, they are released into communities ill prepared to handle them. This problem has been overlooked by many otherwise zealous reformers and buried beneath the budgets of state bureaucracies. States which have undertaken extensive depopulation have experienced enormous difficulties. The city of San Jose, for instance, had to deal with an unanticipated influx of nearly 2,000 ex-patients when nearby Agnews State Hospital emptied its wards. Many released patients became the welfare tenants of area business entrepreneurs who purchased abandoned houses and filled them with ex-patients.

The situation may be even more dramatic in New York, where the population of hospitalized patients decreased from 78,000 to 34,000 during the mid-1970s. Private nursing homes, welfare hotels, and old-age homes were overburdened with the new releases. In New York City alone, about 25 percent of the estimated 100,000 residents of welfare homes are considered to be "severely mentally dysfunctional." Most of these persons are ex-patients of state hospitals. The assembly of newly released patients in places like Long Beach, a town on the south shore of Long Island, is even more critical. Long Beach has 34,000 residents, thirty-one hotels, and 712 so-called walkers (a name given by townspeople to ex-mental patients). According to one report, "The walkers . . . get their name because they are often seen wandering aimlessly on the city's two-mile boardwalk. Most of them are old, most are schizophrenic, most are on phenothiazines or other medication, and all of them are on welfare."[107] The situation at Long Beach is not unique. To rectify such problems some legal advocates have asked courts to consider the right to proper posthospital care as an element of the right to treatment. Without such a remedy the future lives of former patients may be worse than their years of confinement. With this in mind, I close this short history of mental hospitals, a history in which optimism about cures has recurrently been upstaged by the harsh reality of custodial control, a history in which effective treatment has rarely been realized.

THE PATHOLOGICAL PERSPECTIVE TODAY

Despite its long legacy of failure the pathological perspective is still very much alive. Indeed, reborn pathological theorizing often commands the favor of governmental agencies committed to fighting crime and nonconformity. This has been particularly evident from the late 1970s to the present, as economic turmoil and international instability have prompted a new birth of conservative thought and action. Programs of social reform, many of which were poorly administered or inadequately funded, were shelved in favor of a new wave of sociobiological publications and renewed government sponsorship of "basic" causal research on deviance.

This trend was presaged at the 1978 meetings of the prestigious American Society of Criminology (ASC) when approximately half the papers presented concerned biological approaches to criminal behavior. This "pathological" tone was set by ASC president C. Ray Jeffery. Known previously for his studies of environmental factors related to crime, Jeffery had become a born-again pathologist. In addressing the convention he stated:

> We must move beyond . . . measurements of environmental impact. . . . We must develop the capacity for tracing painful stimulus into the organism to the associational and motivational areas of the brain and then to the motor centers and to behavior. Between the stimulus and the response is the great big black box. . . . It is here that we will find the questions we should be asking.[108]

Jeffery's allusion to "the great big black box" places him in the company of Lombroso and a long line of pathological theorists who locate deviance within the physiology of nonconformists. In his book *Biology and Crime*, Jeffery laments the "historical misfortune" by which sociology "captured" the study of crime, deviance, and social control during the 1920s.[109] Arguing that social science is rooted in biology, Jeffery beseeches students of deviance to attend to such allegedly urgent issues as the relationship between low intelligence and delinquency. He speculates about the possibility that protein deficiency may be the true biological culprit behind much nonconformity.

Jeffery is not alone in reviving interest in the pathological perspective. At the 1977 meetings of the American Sociological Association Donald Cressey urged researchers to return to solid "hard-science" research, such as that exemplified by Max G. Schlapp and Edward H. Smith's 1928 book *The New*

Criminology.[110] This supposedly model study claims that criminality is caused by glandular disturbances resulting from chemical imbalances in the blood and lymph nodes of a criminal's mother during pregnancy. It advocates an assortment of pathological controls, including compulsive treatment for all defectives, euthanasia for uncurables, sterilization, and the mandatory registration of delinquents.

Other theorists advocate a synthesis of pathological and social factors. In their 1977 *Biosocial Bases of Criminal Behavior,* Mednick and Christiansen present data suggesting that, while lower-class crime may be overwhelmingly determined by socioeconomic conditions, genetic factors are relatively great in the middle classes.[111] This conclusion is drawn from a variety of supposedly environmentally controlled studies of Danish twins and adoptees. Unfortunately, environmental pressures were measured largely in socioeconomic deprivation. Neglected were factors more likely to affect middle-class persons, such as intrafamily conflict, adolescent alienation, boredom, and socially nurtured meaninglessness. Had such variables been included, researchers would probably have discovered strong but different environmental pressures.

In a 1979 essay entitled "Biosociology and Crime" Harold Kelly also calls for a pooling of biochemical and social research.[112] He suggests that hypoglycemia (an insufficiency in blood glucose levels) may aggravate and perpetuate criminal behavior, while cerebral allergies (the existence of which is disputed by most reputable medical authorities) may cause fatigue, nervousness, irritability, or even perceptual distortions and thus lead to deviant behavior. The proposed cure for such conditions is "biochemical change." Kelly urges sociologists to take an unbiased look at some of the newer findings of biochemical research. The political implications of such a position are thinly veiled. In Kelly's words, "As the biochemical causes are found and treated most all citizens would see the goals and means and rewards and punishments provided by advanced capitalist societies to be sufficient for them to conform."[113]

Lest one think that Kelly's words are more science-fictional than real, it is important to note that many new forms of biomedical control are already in place. Several years ago the probation department of Cuyahoga Falls, Ohio, began to routinely screen offenders for hypoglycemia. Moreover, as Stuart Hills points out, the use of drugs as a means of control in American prisons is now commonplace. "Inmates who show 'disrespect for authority' or highly politicized inmates who harbor 'subversive beliefs' are considered particularly dangerous and sometimes become the research subjects of powerful psychopharmaceutical technology."[114]

Given the drastic character of many medical responses to alleged pathological deviance, it is important to recognize the relatively uncritical quality of the most prominent of recent "celebrations" of this perspective. None has received more attention than the lengthy review of pathological studies presented in James Q. Wilson and Richard J. Herrnstein's 1985 book, *Crime and*

Human Nature. For the most part, Wilson and Herrnstein examine many of the same studies reviewed in this chapter, but without considering criticisms regarding such key matters as the typically flawed methods and unexamined social contexts that haunt so much of the medical and biological research on deviance. Instead of honestly confronting a rather substantive body of critical scholarship, Wilson and Herrnstein argue simply that "many criminologists, most often trained as sociologists, are simply uneasy with biological and psychological explanations."[115] This is an uneasiness that Wilson and Herrnstein clearly do not share. Avoiding any direct engagement with their critics, they make such glib pronouncements as, "The average offender tends to be constitutionally distinctive though not extremely or abnormally so."[116]

An extremely influential work, *Crime and Human Nature* relies more on the skillful rhetoric of its authors than on a balanced consideration of the pathological research they review. Without denying environmental influences, Wilson and Herrnstein underscore the roles of "constitutional predispositions," "biological factors," and "psychopathologies of various sorts," contending that "it is the clear consensus of those most intimately acquainted with the data" that crime and delinquency are, in large measure, shaped by inherited pathologies," and that "it would be hard to find a serious contemporary student of these topics who denies a genetic contribution, and in many cases a substantial one."[117]

More problematic still are the recent "gene-based evolutionary" theories of researchers such as Lee Ellis. Espousing "universal standards of [moral] conduct" with regard to "aggressive and property offenses," Ellis's 1990 paper, "The Evolution of Violent Criminal Behavior and Its Nonlegal Equivalent," evokes the principle of "natural selection" to explain deviant acts ranging from theft to rape and child abuse. Arguing that females tend to discriminate against mating with males who are only "minimally capable of resource procurement," Ellis contends that "there is considerable evidence that forcible copulatory tactics could have evolved as part of male efforts to mate with large numbers of females, and female tendencies to resist any encounters that effectively usurp control over their choice of [genetically resourceful] sex partners.[118] Ellis focuses on alleged evolutionary biological factors affecting rape, without even minimally considering the idea that "forcible copulatory tactics" may have less to do with the "mating efforts" of males discriminated against by females than with efforts by males within patriarchal cultures to assert power over women by violence. This so-called genetic theory of rape, guided as it is by a search for pathological factors, virtually ignores a large body of feminist research on the relationship between rape and power, as well as cross-cultural data suggesting that sexual violence has much more to do with culturally specific gender roles than with alleged human instincts for resourceful mating.[119]

Hardly an advance over the evolutionary speculations of early pathologists, the writings of contemporary theorists such as Ellis remind us that the "cyclical optimism" of the pathological thinking continues today. As further evidence of this perspective's far-reaching influence, let us consider two of its more prominent applications: the medical control of hyperkinetic behavior in children and the use of psychosurgery.

Pathologizing Unruly Children: The Case of Hyperkinesis

Hyperkinesis is today perhaps the number-one childhood problem. Thousands of special clinics, special diagnostic measures, and special school programs have been established, and millions of federal, state, and local dollars are earmarked for its cure. Once a young child is found to have hyperkinesis, the treatment of choice is generally pharmaceutical intervention. The drug Ritalin (methylphenidate) is prescribed to alter the child's behavior. Yet, although categorized as a disease, hyperkinesis is primarily a form of social deviance. It is recognized not by its physiological properties but by the unruly behavior of children.

The behavioral manifestations of hyperkinesis are several: hyperactivity (excessive motor activity), short attention span, and restless or fidgety behavior. Also included are fluctuations in mood, clumsiness, impulsive and/or aggressive behavior, low tolerance for frustration, trouble with sleeping at the proper time or talking at the proper age, and the inability to sit still and obey the rules of the schoolhouse. Such things make for an unruly child. Children who behave or misbehave in such ways present obvious control problems for parents, teachers, and other guardians. From an adult perspective such behaviors are clearly unacceptable. But why is it that such unacceptable behaviors have come to be seen in terms of sickness? Once they were signs of the bad child. Now they are symptoms of a disease. Why? This question was posed by sociologist Peter Conrad.[120] The answers he discovered are disturbing. They cast doubt on the physiological origins of a behavior problem that is commonly treated (or controlled) by drugs.

Conrad suggests that the equation of unruly child behavior with the disease of hyperkinesis may be more social than clinical in origin. Medical researchers never actually discovered an organic defect which causes hyperactive behavior. What was discovered was that certain drugs could change or reduce unruly behavior. Inferences regarding organic deficiency as the cause of unruliness were arrived at retrospectively. In other words, since chemicals were capable of changing unruly behavior, it was reasoned that chemical deficiencies must have caused the behavior in the first place. By such logic theorists converted what would otherwise be a social problem into a problem for medical control.

The diagnosis of hyperkinesis is a relatively recent phenomenon. Thirty years ago it was unknown. Troublesome children were simply troublesome children. In the last decade knowledge of the disease has caught on. How did this change come about? According to Conrad, the period of time from the mid-1950s to the early 1970s was ripe for such a discovery. Socially there had emerged within organized medicine a burgeoning interest in child mental health. The pediatric subspecialties within organized medicine were looking for new childhood diseases to combat. Many traditional organic diseases had already come under medical control. Pediatric know-how, particularly the administration of various drugs as preventatives for such diseases as small-pox, diphtheria, and polio, had made youth a more medically secure time of life. This presented mixed blessings for pediatric specialists. While successful they were aware that prestige within the medical profession was awarded commensurate with the dangerousness of the diseases being fought. Pediatric specialists were thus on the lookout for new dangerous diseases. The psychiatric problems of children was one area which attracted their attention.

Two developments in pharmacology commanded the interest of child-hood-disease investigators. The first derived from Charles Bradly's 1937 observation that amphetamines altered the behavior of children with behavior or learning problems. Amphetamines increased conformity and achievement scores. A related development involved the synthesis of the drug Ritalen in the mid-1950s. Ritalen had many of the same stimulant qualities as amphetamines, but was said to have fewer negative side effects. In 1961 the Federal Drug Administration approved the use of Ritalen for children. This paved the way for the medicalized control of unruly childhood behavior through drugs. But the fact that drugs alter behavior does not mean that such behavior is essentially chemical in origin. Marijuana may make someone laugh. Cocaine may enhance exhilarated action. Few, however, would argue that the lack of laughter or exhilaration is the result of a pathological deficiency of the chemicals in marijuana or cocaine. Such logic would be viewed as highly suspect. Yet a very similar logic is employed in calling hyperkinesis a disease or pathology. What gives legitimacy to such a retrospective logic within medicine?

According to Conrad, the second major factor contributing to the discovery of hyperkinesis was the pharmaceutical revolution in the mental health field. By the early 1960s the treatment of mental patients with drugs had become an established fact. In the 1950s it was discovered that a variety of psychoactive drugs would alter the symptoms of psychotic and other severely disturbed patients. The success of drugs in controlling such persons was cited as evidence that mental disorders may be physiological in origin. At least the use of such drugs reinforced the notion that the proper treatment of mental disorders was medical. Since pediatric specialists were scrutinizing the psychiatric problems of children for new diseases to combat, the fact that drugs had become available which controlled such problems reinforced the movement toward seeing nonacute childhood behavior problems as a disease. In discovering hyperkinesis this is exactly what happened.

The social factors mentioned above were not the only variables contributing to the discovery of hyperkinesis. Conrad also mentions political factors, such as the lobbying efforts of such influential groups as the Association for Children with Learning Disabilities, and the dominance of medical interests on a government committee established to investigate the use of drugs to treat childhood behavior problems. The most important factor, however, may have been economic. Major drug companies instituted a massive, high-intensity, and highly financed advertising campaign aimed at convincing physicians that hyperkinesis was a real disease and that it was treatable by drugs. As Conrad and his colleague Joseph Schneider point out:

> The pharmaceutical companies spent a great amount of time and money promoting stimulant medications for this new disorder. After the middle 1960s it is nearly impossible to read a medical journal or the free "throw away" magazines without seeing some elaborate advertising for either Ritalen or Dexedrine. These advertisements explain the utility of treating hyperkinesis . . . and urge the physician to diagnose and treat hyperkinetic children. . . . They often advise physicians that "the hyperkinetic syndrome exists" as a "distinct medical entity" and that the "syndrome is readily diagnosed through patient histories and psychometric testing." . . . These same firms also supply sophisticated packets of "diagnostic and treatment information, . . . pay for professional conferences on the subject, and support research in the identification and treatment of the disorder.[121]

The drug companies were well rewarded for their high-pressure advertising. Reports suggest that one company, CIBA, reaped $13 million in profits on Ritalen in 1971 alone. Sales of Ritalen represented 15 percent of its total gross profits during that twelve-month period. While drug companies lined their pockets, medical professionals expanded their interests in the domain of social controls. Hyperkinesis emerged as yet another speculative category of pathological deviance.

The Surgical Control of Human Behavior

Historical Background Psychosurgery is brain surgery aimed at changing human behavior. The first known psychosurgeries were performed by Dr. Gottlieb Burckhardt on six patients at an insane asylum in Prefargier, Switzerland, in 1890.[122] The patients involved were described as both dangerous and psychotic. Burckhardt removed a small section of each patient's brain. Despite his alleged success in rendering the patients harmless to themselves and others, Burckhardt's operations were soon halted by the ethical criticisms of his fellow medical practitioners.

In 1935 psychosurgery was reborn under the scalpel of António Moniz.[123] Moniz, a Portuguese physician, is credited with performing the first prefrontal lobotomy. With his associate Almeida Lima, he cut away portions of the frontal lobes of twenty long-term mental patients who had been unaffected by a battery of other psychiatric treatments. Moniz claimed success in fifteen of his twenty operations. Unfortunately, one of his "successful" patients would later pump five bullets into the renowned physician.

Moniz's efforts did not go unnoticed. In 1949 he was awarded the Nobel Prize. In the year following, his surgical techniques were carried to America by Walter Freeman and James Watts. These surgeons modified Moniz's approach by inserting an ice pick-like tool through the eye socket. Freeman, working at George Washington University in the District of Columbia, conducted 4,000 such surgeries. By the early 1950s, 50,000 lobotomies had been performed in the United States alone, many upon military personnel returning from World War II with allegedly severe mental problems.[124] All were conducted to control disruptive human behaviors.

Advocates of psychosurgery make strong claims about the desirability of the operation for individual patients and for society. Negative outcomes are downplayed or pictured as the exception. The Freeman and Watts lobotomy technique was heralded as relatively safe in that its mortality rate was a mere 1.7 percent.[125] But don't lobotomies turn people into vegetables? Some did. The specter of an empty-eyed Jack Nicholson playing the part of the lobotomized McMurphy in *One Flew Over the Cuckoo's Nest* is hard to forget. A more common side effect is for patients to lose the imaginative dimensions of human consciousness. Lobotomies are consistently followed by a dramatic reduction in the ability to fantasize, abstract, or think creatively. While not a total vegetable, the typical lobotomized patient loses some of the more distinctive features of human cognition.

During the 1950s a number of journalistic exposés revealed something of the darker side of psychosurgery. Stories of failure and of horrible side effects came to the public's attention. Questions about the kinds of people selected for the operation were raised. The official position was that the operation was reserved for last-ditch cases, particularly patients with a potential for violence. Critics remained unconvinced. Consider one of Walter Freeman's most well-known success stories. The person operated upon was a Peeping Tom.[126] His crime was spying on the private lives of others. Such behavior is surely a social nuisance. It may even be frightening. But is its prevention worth the risks of psychosurgery? Freeman thought so. His operation was termed a success. After surgery the man never peeped around the backs of houses again. Unrestrained by previous inhibitions, he would confidently approach houses and peer through their front windows.

During the mid-1950s the use of lobotomies dropped drastically. Most observers believe that the introduction of psychotropic drugs made it easier to control difficult inmates without the use of a surgeon's scalpel. Nonetheless, testimony presented before Senator Edward Kennedy's U.S. Senate Subcommittee on Health revealed that nearly 600 lobotomies were being performed annually as late as 1973. Of greater significance is the "new wave" of psychosurgical techniques introduced in the late 1960s and early 1970s. Using ultrasonic beams and electrodes, proponents of these new behavior-modifying operations attempt to distinguish themselves from those who performed lobotomies. These new anatomical interventions are said to be more effective, more precise, and less dangerous.

The New Wave of Psychosurgery   The new wave of psychosurgical techniques is generally directed at several subcortical structures of the "old" paleomammalian brain or the limbic system. The limbic lobe forms a ring around the human brain stem and is believed to play a key role in the regulation of emotions, aggression, and sexual behavior. Of particular concern are the hypothalamus, a connector between the brain stem and the surrounding limbic system, and the amygdala, a limbic structure related to the hypothalamus's functioning. Also important is the thalamus, or cingulate portions of the cerebral cortex. Abnormal functioning in these interconnected structures is believed to be associated with displays of emotional rage and physical aggression.

This conclusion is drawn from a variety of experiments on nonhuman animals. In such experiments sham rage can be induced in otherwise quiet animals and attack behavior can be stimulated or reduced by interfering with the hypothalamus or related structures. The new wave of psychosurgery is modeled upon such experiments.

New psychosurgical techniques are said to be less messy and less "hit-or-miss" than lobotomies. Neurosurgeon H. Thomas Ballentine, one of a small number of surgeons currently performing such operations in Massachusetts, recently described the procedures involved in a cingulotomy.[127] Two small holes are drilled just above the hairline on either side of the head. Hollow needles about 2½ inches long are inserted. Through these a current of air is followed by intense heat. This destroys about a forefinger of nerve tissue on either side. Ballentine has performed over 250 such operations during some fifteen years of psychosurgery.

How successful and how safe are such procedures? Advocates present them as relatively sure and safe mechanisms for normalizing some of society's most intractable and fearful deviants. Critics, including some prominent physicians, have strong reservations. They contend that psychosurgical operations are nothing but experiments. It is known that changing brain tissue changes brain functioning. It is not known whether the behavior problems originate in the brain tissues which are operated upon. According to George J. Amos, director of the Boston University Center for Law and Health Science, psychosurgeons operate without really knowing what they are doing.[128] Another critic, psychiatrist Peter Breggin, points to dangers in the surgical procedure. According to Breggin, "the procedure is not even experimental, it's simply dangerous and mutilative. We know enough about . . . the brain to know that any mutilation or destruction of the normal tissue will lead to brain damage and dysfunction.[129]

Two of the strongest proponents of psychosurgery are Dr. Vernon H. Mark and Dr. Frank R. Ervin, authors of *Violence and the Brain*.[130] In 1973 Mark and Ervin's federally funded research project at Harvard University was halted by negative publicity and public protest. Mark and Ervin attempt to justify psychosurgery by citing evidence from studies of the brain chemistry of nonhuman animals suggesting a link between aggressive behavior and abnormalities in the structure and/or functioning of the brain. Regarding humans, they argue that psychosurgery constrains aggression and should thus be applied to a violence-prone population suffering from the so-called dyscontrol syndrome. How valid are these contentions?

Regarding animal studies, it is true that repeated research has shown that emotional rage and aggressive behavior can be modulated by altering the electrical activity of regions of the brain, particularly the hypothalamus.[131] The most famous of such studies was conducted at Yale University in the laboratories of Jose Delgado. Delgado and his associates implanted sensitive radio receivers in the brains of cats, monkeys, and other species. By artificially activating parts of the hypothalamus and other parts of the limbic system, Delgado was able to create variations in what he observed to be aggressive behavior. In one of his more dramatic experiments, the behavior of a charging bull was halted in the process of attack. In research with rhesus monkeys, however, electrical stimulation could not get animals to violate fixed hierarchies of social deference. Low-ranking monkeys, even if electronically stimulated, would not attack monkeys of a higher dominance. Thus it appears that, even under controlled conditions, aggressive acts are as dependent upon environmental stimuli as upon electronic brain stimulation.

Other researchers implanted chemical tubes in the hypothalamus to produce behavioral changes.[132] Experimental animals were divided into two groups. Naturally aggressive rats were, for instance, separated from their passive counterparts. Chemicals which either activated or deactivated the hypothalamus were then injected into each group. Passive rats were converted into aggressive rats. "Killer rats" became docile. The chemical effects wore off after several hours, and the animals returned to their previous patterns of behavior.

What can one reasonably conclude about human behavior from such animal studies? There is little doubt that altering the electrical chemistry of the nonhuman brain is associated with changes in aggressive behavior.[133] This does not mean that aggressive behavior is caused by electrical or chemical changes per se. Aggression may be triggered by physiological change, but what triggers physiological change itself? It is reasonable to suggest that environmental cues ordinarily trigger the physiological changes which are associated with displays of aggression. Animals, after all, normally act aggressive only in relation to certain environmental stimuli. There is no pathology involved. The monkeys and rats in most experiments, even those which acted naturally aggressive prior to experimental intervention, were normal and not sick or pathological. Despite this fact, biomedical researchers make reference to such things as "yet undetected lesions" of "present, but not yet observed pathologies." This is strange language for supposedly hard-nosed positivistic scientists. Why speculate about undetected lesions? It seems as if researchers are convinced that pathology must be present if aggression is observed. Using similar logic, surgeons such as Mark and Ervin make giant leaps from data derived in animal studies to arguments about the physiological basis of human violence.

There are no studies of the biology of human violence comparable to the experiments performed on nonhuman animals. Nonetheless, Mark and Ervin point to known similarities between nonhuman primate and human brains and to instances in which observable brain pathology is associated with altered behaviors. A clear example is epilepsy. Lesions in the brains of epileptics produce periodic fits in which persons may temporarily lose control of their psychomotor functioning. Yet, despite the dramatic appearance of some severe epileptic fits, there is no evidence that epileptics act more aggressively toward others before, during, or after a seizure. Popular mythology aside, epileptics are no more violence-prone than anyone else. On the other hand, there have been a few rare instances in which episodic explosions of ragelike human behavior have been linked to documented damage to key areas of the limbic system. Such documented instances are rare and hardly a typical profile of human violence. Nonetheless, Mark and Ervin boldly leap beyond the evidence. They follow the inferential logic of some animal researchers in suggesting that brain pathology may lie behind a wide range of human violence.

Mark and Ervin offer a profile of potentially violent people as targets for psychosurgery. The people described by this profile are hypothetically carriers of a severely damaged limbic system, ready to erupt into violence at the slightest provocation. They are said to be victims of the dyscontrol syndrome, the combined symptoms of which make them candidates for neurological social control. These symptoms include: (1) a history of physical assaults, especially against women and children; (2) intoxication (even with small amounts of alcohol) which is frequently associated with displays of aggression; (3) impulsive sexual behavior, often leading to sexual assault; and (4) a history of accidents, particularly automobile accidents.

Implicit in the above profile is an image of pathology or sickness. Is there another interpretation? The history of assaults, intoxication, impulsive or aggressive sexuality, and accidents may also bring to mind an image of the angry, frustrated lower-class male. Indeed, contemporary profiles of criminal violence suggest that lower-class males are by far disproportionately over-represented in the ranks of those who commit acts of overt physical harm. Such persons are constantly bombarded with the "all-American" message that to be male is to be powerful. At the same time they are daily denied equal access to legitimate nonviolent channels of social power. Their search for power is deflected from the public to the private realms of social life. In physical violence, drinking, and sexual aggression, lower-class males play out a masculine "power game." Others, with greater economic, political, or social resources, might play out this game at the office, the convention, or the country club. The constricted power of lower-class males is steeped in danger. Anger is present on the surface of many private social encounters. The line between deliberate action and fatalistic accident may be frequently blurred. Conditions such as these increase the probability that lower-class males will use violence as a means to power. They suggest a social link between violence and power. Isn't this a reasonable nonpathological interpretation of the so-called dyscontrol syndrome? Why leap to ambiguous inferences of brain pathology based upon "as yet unobserved" abnormalities?

In a paper published in the prestigious *Journal of the American Medical Association*, Mark, Ervin, and a colleague, W. H. Sweet, respond to the "social conditions" objection to the dyscontrol profile. Yet, as clever pathological theorists, they transform questions about slum conditions into hypotheses for neurological investigation. On the trail of a physiological basis for urban violence, they reduce the political implications of urban rioting to speculation about the pathological brains of the rioters. Their mission is to "pinpoint, diagnose, and treat those with low violence thresholds." Thus they argue that "if slum conditions alone determined and initiated riots, why are the vast majority of slum dwellers able to resist the temptations of unrestrained violence?" Is there something peculiar, ask these psychosurgeons, about the violent slum dweller that differentiates him from his peaceful neighbor?[134]

As pathological theorists, Mark and Ervin view violence as a public health problem. They propose "early warning tests" to detect citizens with low thresholds for impulsive violence. But how effective is their program of surgical control? Mark and Ervin report on a number of successful cases. The most well known is now recognized as a major failure. The case involved Leonard A. Kille, an engineer in his thirties. Following a head injury Kille developed a form of psychomotor epilepsy and would occasionally exhibit outbursts of violent rage. Kille became a patient of Mark and Ervin and consented to undergo a bilateral amygdalotomy. Six years later Kille had become permanently incapacitated. His psychomotor coordination was reduced to vegetablelike status. His memory was severely impaired, and he suffered repeated hospitalizations and delusions. His violent explosions had increased. Acting on his behalf, Kille's mother brought suit against Mark and Ervin for $2 million in damages. In the spring of 1979, the surgeons were absolved of legal responsibility, not because they had refuted the sad facts of Kille's impairment but because the patient had given his prior consent to the dangerous operation.

Not all psychosurgery cases end so badly. Two recent studies on Boston-area psychosurgery patients did not find the same record of long-term impairment. Nor did they find significantly positive behavioral changes.[135] Yet both discovered that patients' intelligence, as measured by IQ tests and such things as card-sorting tasks, sank for about a four-month period after surgery, but returned to its previous level thereafter. Boston University researchers compared twenty-seven surgical patients with a small control group of persons with relatively similar symptoms who were not operated upon. The surgical patients demonstrating the greatest improvement were those whose initial complaints were more physical than behavioral—people who had experienced severe head pain. Once this physical-pain-only group was removed from the sample, surgical patients showed no more improvement than controls. Thirty percent of both groups showed some improvement.[136] Such evidence does little to convince me that surgery is an effective therapeutic tool. Its appeal is, if anything, more politically attractive than scientifically proven.

The Future of Psychosurgery   The future of psychosurgery remains uncertain. Its controversial and often dangerous record has created a climate of relative caution among government officials charged with its regulation. The National Commission for the Protection of Human Subjects of Biomedical and Behavioral Research recently issued a set of standards by which such operations may be permitted. According to the commission, psychosurgery may be allowed (1) if it is effective, (2) if it serves the advancement of science, (3) if the patient has been chosen for the right reasons (i.e., for his or her own good), and (4) if there is informed consent.[137] Several of these criteria are themselves quite controversial. What determines effectiveness? Can the operation ever really be considered effective if those who perform it don't even know why it does what it does? The issue of informed consent has been equally problematic. In the landmark case of *Kaimowitz v. the Department of Mental Health*, a Michigan court ruled that the operation could not be performed upon patients who had been involuntarily hospitalized. Involuntary commitment was seen as limiting a person's ability to make a free and fully consenting choice.

While legal restrictions have limited the spread of psychosurgery, they have not limited the imagination of pathological theorists. Some propose bold new biotechnical controls which go beyond the frontiers of current surgical practice. In *Physical Control of the Mind: Toward a Psychocivilized Society*, a pioneer psychosurgical researcher, Jose Delgado, calls for the formation of powerful national agencies (following the model of the National Aeronautics and Space Administration) and a full-scale media campaign to promote a program of neurobiological control.[138] Garage doors and television sets are already activated by remote-control radio transmitters. Why not regions of the brain? Two-way radio systems could be implanted in the brain. These would permit society to monitor and control the neurological activity of deviants. According to Delgado, "Neuronal activity related to behavioral disturbances . . . could be recognized in order to trigger stimulation of specific inhibitory structures."[139] The possibilities are both limitless and horrifying. Who will make what decisions to "inhibit" which kinds of behaviors? At the far extremes of the pathological perspective we are confronted with the total-control potential of positivistic science. This potential is not far from being realized. Our readiness for it is another matter.

ASSESSMENT OF THE PATHOLOGICAL PERSPECTIVE

Reducing Social Trouble to Individual Sickness

Only in the most limited sense is any historical event or problem like an illness. It is invariably an encouragement to simplify what is complex.

Susan Sontag[140]

Much of what has been written about the pathological perspective in this chapter has not been positive. The pathological perspective promises much but has delivered little. It claims to be rigorously scientific but has been wrought with poor methodological procedures. It hails the principles of curative treatment but often practices the politics of repressive intervention. This is not to say that there are no beneficial aspects to this perspective. What follows is a brief comparison of the advantages and disadvantages of pathological theorizing.

Advantages of the Medical Model

Perhaps the strongest feature of the pathological perspective is its emphasis on naturalistic causation. By locating deviance in the materiality of the body and mind, the pathological perspective introduces complexities ignored by earlier demonic and classical viewpoints. Other positive aspects of this perspective are outlined by Conrad and Schneider in their book *Deviance and Medicalization*.[141] These beneficial dimensions of the pathological approach include its humanitarian intent, its seemingly eternal optimism, and its flexibility. Also important are the social advantages of the sick role for deviants who comply with the therapeutic prescriptions of rehabilitation specialists. Indeed, pathologically defined rule breakers are able to avoid blame and shun responsibility so long as they behave like good patients, desirous of being cured of their nonconformity.

Disadvantages of Pathologizing Deviance

The liabilities of pathological theorizing outweigh its strengths. These weaknesses are also examined by Conrad and Schneider. Of particular concern is the manner in which the perspective's highly individualistic and overly deterministic medical imagery denigrate both human choice and its sociohistorical context. Life is rarely a matter of free choice, but neither is it usually totally determined.[142] Somewhere between freedom and determination we find ourselves struggling within history. Pathological theorizing misses this point. The pathological perspective also gives the false impression that the lives of "deviants" are more determined than those of "normal" people. Some of the other drawbacks to the logic of a medicalized viewpoint are described below.

The Mask of False Neutrality   False neutrality is a major failing of this perspective. There is nothing neutral about viewing deviants as sick. Prior to drawing head measurements, conducting chromosome tests, or administering psychological exams, the pathological researcher has made a moral judgment that deviant subjects have acted wrongly. While, in principle, the pathological perspective concerns itself with neutral-sounding references to "syndromes" and "disease types," in practice these are little more than code words for moral judgments about the undesirability of certain forms of behavior.

Domination by Experts   Once troublesome behaviors are defined as sick, their resolution is taken from the hands of ordinary people and turned over to medical experts, whose professional careers are staked on the premise that deviance is a problem of aberrant or abnormal individuals. No wonder the game of pursuing pathological traces is played from one losing season to the next. The expert control of deviance is a multi-billion-dollar business. The experts who have cornered the medical control market have little interest in depathologizing this ballgame.

This is not to suggest that those who professionally profit from the medicalized control of deviance do so in ways that are intentionally self-serving. It is more that they may become caught up in institutionally supported ways of thinking and thus become blinded to the insights of other perspectives. This was particularly evident in a study I once conducted of the diagnostic work of psychiatric professionals who were charged with predicting dangerousness on the part of their patients.[143] In case after case these experts would reduce the complexities and contradictions of their patients' daily lives to nothing but the narrowest categories of individualized pathology. Often such clinical reductions seemed extraordinarily naive. Thus, when a lower-class male responded to a question about what he might do if someone called him an obscene name by stating that it would depend on whether the name caller was a man or a woman, the psychiatric experts read his response as indicative of "ambivalence toward women" rather than as a class-based mode of making distinctions relating to gender. But does this mean that the experts involved were deliberately trying to avoid questions of economic equality? No. It is more likely that their expert schooling in individualistic theories of causation literally prevented them from imagining other ways of making sense of such situations.

All this becomes even more complicated when medical experts are bombarded by advertising campaigns, such as those conducted by the big pharmaceutical companies, attempting to persuade them that personal problems are truly biochemical problems and that drug therapy is the only reliable way to control deviance. The college students with whom I work, who are not exposed to such high-pressure sales pitches and have also not been professionally socialized into exclusively individualistic approaches to deviance, often perceive nonconformity in more complex ways than the so-called experts. This is not because my students know more about deviance than the experts but because their viewpoints are less institutionally constrained. In this sense, it is important that the opinions of trained experts be tempered by being brought into contact with the thoughts and perspectives of people who are less committed to specific disciplinary frameworks.

Individualizing Social Problems   Pathological theorizing also errs by individualizing complex social problems. Nothing would be deviant if nobody was bothered by certain types of nonconformity. This obvious sociological fact is usually ignored by the pathological perspective. It sidesteps the complex network of social forces which push and pull people toward certain types of behavior. The rich and often troubling complexity of life is reduced to biochemical or psychological formulations. We are, of course, biochemical and psychological beings. But we are never just that. Our biochemistry and psychology are always in interaction with those of our fellow social animals. By reducing theoretical explanations to psychophysiology the pathological perspective is untrue to the complexity of human life itself.

The tendency of the pathological perspective to reduce complex social troubles to matters of personal sickness is particularly evident in a consideration of recent medical theories about homelessness. Despite considerable evidence that homelessness is the result of unequal access to real estate and the distribution of wealth, there exists a powerful psychiatric myth that some form of mental illness lies behind the plight of people who do not have housing. Are homeless people infected with some pathological tendency to wander? Is homelessness a psychological disease? Using a rigorous combination of criteria, including records of prior mental hospitalizations, ethnographic observations of a sample of 164 homeless people in Austin, Texas, and homeless persons' psychological assessments of each other, David Snow and his associates estimate the prevalence of serious "mental illness" among the homeless as between 10 and 15 percent.[144] Since homelessness is itself a source of great personal stress, such rates hardly support the thesis that homelessness is nothing but a form of personal pathology. As David Snow, Susan Baker, and Leon Anderson remark, "the situations in which homeless people live constitute, in a very real sense, . . . 'insane contexts,' thus increasing the prospect that adaptation to them may be read as insanity. So long as contextual adaptive behaviors are confused with truly symptomatic behaviors, assessments of the incidence of mental illness on the streets will be fraught with error and . . . skewed toward overdiagnosis."[145]

Ignoring the Politics of Deviance   Pathological thinking also ignores the essential politicality of all nonconformity. Deviance and its control are always matters of power and politics. Blinded by its commitment to positivist rationality, pathological theorizing depoliticalizes deviance. Dissidents are chemically controlled, not because they are politically troublesome, but because they are believed to be mentally disturbed. Illegal drug users are forced into treatment, not because their escape into pleasure threatens an instrumental, achievement-oriented society, but because they are thought of as sick. Child abusers are treated psychiatrically, not because their actions constitute patriarchal family violence, but because they are imagined to be abnormal.

I do not mean to romanticize deviants as self-conscious rebels. Most deviants are not. Nonetheless, the story of deviance is always a story of resistance to power, regardless of whether the deviant be an alcoholic struggling with the fermented demons of unattainable power, an angry teenager who finds power in gang-related activities, or a trained terrorist who takes up a rifle to change the world. To effectively address the problem of deviance, we must attend to its political dimensions. This the pathological perspective avoids doing. It denies that nonconformity is shaped by anything but the abnormal body or mind.

Examples of the depoliticalization of deviance involve the medicalized treatment of various "female maladies," such as hysteria, panic or anxiety disorders, and eating disorders. Why are such behaviors viewed as diseases rather than as symptoms of the patriarchal violence engulfing women? When first diagnosed by Jean Martin Charcot in the late nineteenth century, hysteria was characterized by spectacular displays of nervousness; occasional paralysis; fainting; and seizures involving passionate mimicry, erotic posturing, exaggerated contortions, and the convulsive arching back of the body. Although Charcot interpreted such dramatic behaviors as a form of illness, these strange "symptoms" resemble the ritual performances of sorceresses and other female pagan healers prior to the modern period. In pagan societies the healing power of women was widely revered. Yet, by the time their "hysteria" became a focus for male medical research, the social status of women was far different. Viewed in this way, it is possible to read the gestures of the hysteric as remnants of a form of female power, now shorn of its prestige and believability.[146]

In Charcot's lecture hall, a huge amphitheater at Salpetriere clinic in Paris, hysterics performed their symptoms almost on cue. Under hypnosis and the eye of Charcot's camera, fascinated male physicians and medical students were informed that hysterics suffered from a hereditary trait, not unlike epilepsy. This peculiar illness, Charcot explained, was concentrated in sexual zones of the female body. The ovarian region was said to be a singularly sensitive hysterogenic zone.[147]

Charcot's theatrical demonstrations made a great impression on Sigmund Freud, who became convinced that hysteria was a true disease. Freud's subsequent writings on this topic were more complex and more contradictory than his earlier writings. In 1895, Freud and Josef Breuer published *Studies on Hysteria*, a series of case studies detailing their clinical observations of this "illness."[148] They portrayed hysterics as highly intelligent young women whose illnesses were connected to the boring enclosures of female life within Victorian society. This was particularly evident in the case of Bertha Pappenheim (or Anna O. as she became known in the coded annals of psychoanalysis). Bertha, a twenty-two-year-old, found herself stifled by the moral demands of an Orthodox Jewish family. Suffering a loss for words, this young hysteric remained silent about her experience until encouraged by Breuer to free-associate. Pappenheim spat out a plethora of fantastic stories, disturbing remembrances, and fantasies. These Breuer interpreted as the psychic by-products of "an unemployed surplus of mental liveliness and energy."[149]

Does this mean that hysteria is not merely an illness but a kind of covert protest against the silencing of women by a patriarchal culture? Both "Freud and Breuer saw the repetitive domestic routines, including needlework, knitting, playing scales, and sickbed nursing, to which bright [middle class] women were frequently confined, as the causes of hysterical sickness."[150] Later on, however, Freud presented a much less politicized interpretation of hysteria. In "Fragments of an Analysis of a Case of Hysteria," Freud provided ample evidence that a hysterical patient whom he called Dora was also the victim of a vicious patriarchal family drama. As a teenager, Dora had been offered as sexual barter to Herr K., a friend of her father's. In exchange, Herr K. was to quietly consent to an affair Dora's father was having with his wife. Rather than analyzing Dora's hysterical outbursts as symptomatic of a not-so-subtle game of male power, Freud elected to individualize the roots of her "sickness" as the effects of repressed childhood memories, masturbatory fantasies, incestuous desires, and lesbian or bisexual longings. When this happened, Dora took flight from Freud's psychoanalytic couch, dismissing the "father of psychoanalysis" as but a servant whose theoretical approach had become too self-limiting.

A related flight from the medicalization of problems facing women is found in the writings of Jackie Orr. Orr's research focuses on the psychiatric control of panic or anxiety disorders in the 1980s and 1990s. First named as a mental disorder in the 1980 revision of the *Diagnostic and Statistical Manual of Mental Disorders* (DSM III) in 1980, panic disorder resembles hysteria, if in a more contemporary guise. Typically manifested in the form of an intense and fearful "attack," panic is diagnosed by the presence of four or more of the following symptoms: shortness of breath or smothering sensations, choking, rapid heart palpitations, chest pain, sweating, dizziness, nausea, depersonalization or derealization, numbness, hot flashes or chills, trembling, fear of dying, and fear of going crazy.

For pharmaceutical companies such as the Upjohn Corporation, sponsor of the Worldwide Panic Project, involving over 2,000 "research subjects" in fifteen countries, the medicalized control of panic is today a big business. Sometimes this involves selling the pathological perspective itself. Consider Upjohn's recent advertising campaign on behalf of its highly addictive drug Xanex. Xanex is a leading seller among antianxiety pharmaceuticals and the only drug currently approved by the Federal Food and Drug Administration for the treatment of panic. As a means of marketing both panic disorder and its drugs, in the early 1990s Upjohn began sending free video news releases (VNRs) to local television stations. Although resembling documentary footage, the VNRs were, in reality, carefully packaged corporate promotions. Television stations were encouraged to broadcast clips from these pre-recorded VNRs as part of their own news programs. When watching the remixed VNRs, viewers may have thought they were seeing reports on the latest in mental health research. In truth, they were watching slick promotions for pharmaceutical solutions to panicky social and political problems.

Current estimates of panic disorder suggest that approximately 80 percent of the people who suffer from this supposed "disease" are women. Why is the experience of panic more prevalent among women than men? In addressing this issue, Orr moves beyond depoliticalized medical imagery. What happens, she asks, when "certain forms of dis-ease, and especially those categorized as 'mental dis-orders,'" are "(re)constructed by a feminist gaze attentive to the complex possibilities of resistance within intricate fields of power?"[151] With this question in mind, Orr examines the anxiety-inducing position of women in a high-tech society ruled by male-centered values, patriarchal economic processes, and the omnipresent depiction of women's bodies as commodities to be exchanged by men. In this more complex sociological framework, panic disorder appears to be less a symptom of individual illness than a social sickness engendered by heterosexist structures of power.

Pathological interpretations of eating disorders also tend to depoliticalize the contradictory relationship between contemporary women and food. *Anorexia* and *bulimia*, the focus of a growing body of research, are typically described as illnesses; but if this is a helpful way of talking about such behaviors, perhaps, like panic disorder, they are sicknesses caused by a society that literally feeds off women's bodies, just as it feeds us all with images of unrealistically thin and "picture-perfect" female models. In this sense, whether one "is inclined to relate [anorexia] to the enormous emphasis that Fashion places on slimness"[152] or to make symbolic connections between willful acts of depriving oneself of food within a culture that stereotypically pictures women as food to be consumed by men,[153] one thing is clear: anorexia is no simple pathology of the diseased individual. It seems politically wiser to read anorexia, like the cyclical binges and purges of bulimia, as symptomatic of an "obsessive resistance" to the subordination of women's bodies within a society dominated by men.[154]

Obscuring Judgments of Evil   A final problem with the pathological perspective is the way in which it diverts questions about what is evil and what is good. Issues of moral accountability are blurred within a technocratic framework devoid of reference to right and wrong. As Conrad and Schneider point out, "There is little gained by deploying a medical vocabulary of motives. It only hinders us from comprehending the human element in the decisions we make, the social structures we create, and the actions we take."[155] As an example, they point to medicalized explanations which reduce the violent actions of persons such as Hitler to clinical profiles of psychological disturbance. Imagine portraying the horrors of the Holocaust, the pain of slavery, or racist abuses of police power in such a fashion. By pathologizing "bad actors" we are all spared the responsibility of having created social contexts which nurture wrongdoing. If this is not evil, what is?

Concluding Comments on Pathological Theorizing

In summary, pathological theorizing has multiple weaknesses. It has not proved itself in the laboratories of rigorous positivistic science, nor does it adequately address matters of human responsibility. Furthermore, while cloaking itself in the false neutrality of expert medical control, it reduces complex social and political problems to a simplistic pursuit of technocratic solutions. Moreover, insomuch as the image of pathology impairs society's ability to confront questions of good and evil, one wonders whether there is something evil about this perspective itself.

In spite of all these problems, the pathological perspective remains perhaps the single most accepted theory of deviance. About this we can say for certain that as long as our image of deviance remains hospitalized within the positivist asylum of medicalized theorizing, we shall forever be denied a full vision of deviance and social control as aspects of the practical struggle of people together in history. In order to escape the institutional confines of this individualistic perspective, we now turn in Chapter 5 to a variety of sociological interpretations.

NOTES

1 Peter Conrad and Joseph Schneider, *Deviance and Medicalization*, Mosby, St. Louis, Mo., 1980, p. 1.
2 Jackie Orr, "Panic Diary: (Re)Constructing a Partial Politics and Poetics of Dis-Ease," in Gale Miller and James A. Holstein, *Reconsidering Social Constructionism*, JAI Press, Greenwich, Conn., 1993, p. 452.
3 Aihwa Ong, *Spirits of Resistance and Capitalist Discipline: Factory Women in Malaysia*, State University of New York Press, Albany, 1987, p. 204.
4 Aihwa Ong, "The Production of Possession: Spirits and the Multinational Corporation in Malaysia," *American Ethnologist*, vol. 15, no. 1, 1988, p. 36.
5 Aihwa Ong, *Spirits of Resistance*, p. 207.
6 Ong, "The Production of Possession," p. 38.
7 Ibid., p. 40.
8 Cesare Lombroso, *L'Uomo Delinquente*, Hoepli, Milan, 1876. See also Cesare Lombroso, *The Female Offender*, Unwin, London, 1895.
9 Conrad and Schneider, *Deviance and Medicalization*, pp. 39–40.
10 Stephen Schafer, *Theories in Criminology*, Random House, New York, 1969, p. 113.
11 George B. Vold, *Theoretical Criminology*, 2d ed., prepared by Thomas J. Bernard, Oxford University Press, New York, 1979, pp. 52–53.
12 Sybil Leek, *Phrenology*, Macmillan, New York, 1970.
13 Conrad and Schneider, *Deviance and Medicalization*, p. 49.
14 Ibid.
15 Charles Darwin, *The Descent of Man*, John Murray, London, 1871.
16 Gideon Fishman, "Positivism and NeoLombrosianism," in C. Ronald Huff and Israel Barak (eds.), *The Mad, the Bad and the Different*, Lexington Books, Heath, Lexington, Mass., 1981, p. 15.

17 Auguste Comte, as quoted in Lewis A. Coser, *Masters of Sociological Thought: Ideas in Historical and Social Context*, 2d ed., Harcourt Brace Jovanovich, New York, 1977, p. 7.
18 Charles Goring, *The English Convict*, H.M. Stationery Office, London, 1913.
19 Ernest A. Hooton, *The American Criminal: An Anthropological Study*, Harvard, Cambridge, Mass., 1939.
20 Robert K. Merton and M. F. Ashley Montague, "Crime and the Anthropologist," *American Anthropologist*, vol. 42, August 1940, pp. 384–408.
21 William H. Sheldon, *Varieties of Delinquent Youth: An Introduction to Constitutional Psychiatry*, Harper, New York, 1949.
22 Ernst Kretschmer, *Physique and Character*, W. J. H. Sprott (trans.), Kegan Paul, Trench, Trubner, London, 1925.
23 Edwin H. Sutherland, "Critique of Sheldon's *Varieties of Delinquent Youth*," *American Sociological Review*, vol. 18, 1951, pp. 142–148.
24 Sheldon Glueck and Eleanor Glueck, *Physique and Delinquency*, Harper, New York, 1956.
25 Goring, *The English Convict*.
26 Robert L. Dugdale, *The Jukes: A Study in Crime, Pauperism, and Heredity*, Putnam, New York, 1877.
27 Samuel Hopkins Adams, "The Jukes Myth," *Saturday Review*, vol. 14, Apr. 2, 1955.
28 Henry H. Goddard, *The Kallikak Family: A Study in the Heredity of Feeble-Mindedness*, Macmillan, New York, 1912.
29 Henry H. Goddard, *Feeble-Mindedness: Its Causes and Consequences*, Macmillan, New York, 1914. See also Henry H. Goddard, "Feeblemindedness and Delinquency," *Journal of Psycho-Asthenics*, vol. 25, 1921, pp. 168–176.
30 Carl Murchinson, *Criminal Intelligence*, Clark University Press, Worcester, Mass., 1926.
31 For a summary critique of the posited relationship between intelligence and criminality, see Daniel Glaser, *Crime in Our Changing Society*, Holt, Rinehart & Winston, New York, 1978, pp. 136–137.
32 Johannes Lange, *Verbrechen als Schicksal*, George Thieme, Leipzig, 1929. English translation by Charlotte Haldane, as *Crime and Destiny*, Boni, New York, 1930.
33 A. M. Legras, *Psychose en Criminaliteit bei Tweelingen*, Kremink, Utrecht, 1932; Heinrich Kranz, *Lebensschicksale Kriminelle Zwillinge*, Springer, Berlin, 1936.
34 Karl O. Christiansen, "Threshold of Tolerance in Various Population Groups Illustrated by Results from Danish Criminologic Twin Study," in A. V. S. deReuck and R. Porter (eds.), *The Mentally Abnormal Offender*, Little, Brown, Boston, 1968, pp. 107–116; Karl O. Christiansen, "Seriousness of Criminality and Concordance among Danish Twins," in Roger Hood (ed.), *Crime, Criminology and Public Policy*, Free Press, New York, 1974.
35 Ernest R. Mowrer, "Some Factors in the Affectional Adjustment of Twins," *American Sociological Review*, vol. 16, August 1954, pp. 468–471.
36 Fini Schulsinger, "Psychopathy: Heredity and Environment," *International Journal of Mental Health*, vol. 1, 1972, pp. 190–206.
37 Raymond R. Crowe, "The Adopted Offspring of Women Criminal Offenders," *Archives of General Psychiatry*, vol. 27, November 1972, pp. 600–603.
38 Barry Hutchings and Sarnoff A. Mednick, "Criminality in Adoptees and Their Adoptive and Biological Parents," in Sarnoff Mednick and Karl O. Christiansen

(eds.), *Biosocial Bases of Criminal Behavior,* Gardner Press, New York, 1977, pp. 127–241.

39 P. A. Jacobs, M. Bruton, M. M. Melville, et al., "Aggressive Behavior, Mental Subnormality and the XYY Male," *Nature,* vol. 208, December 1965, pp. 1351–1352.

40 See Richard S. Fox, "The XYY Offender: A Modern Myth?" *Journal of Criminal Law, Criminology and Police Science,* vol. 62, March 1971, pp. 59–73.

41 National Institute of Mental Health, *Report on the XYY Chromosomal Abnormality,* PHS Publication no. 2103, NIMH, Rockville, Md., 1970.

42 Theodore R. Sarbin and Jeffery E. Miller, "Demonism Revisited: The XYY Chromosomal Anomaly," *Issues in Criminology,* vol. 5, no. 2, summer 1970, pp. 199–207.

43 Raffaele Garofalo, *Criminology,* Little, Brown, Boston, 1914.

44 Franz Alexander and William Healy, *Roots of Crime,* Knopf, New York, 1935.

45 Sigmund Freud, *The Standard Edition of the Complete Psychological Works of Sigmund Freud,* Hogarth, London, 1963, vol. 19, p. 51. See also David Abrahamson, *The Psychology of Crime,* Columbia, New York, 1960; and Walter Bromberg, *Crime and the Mind: A Psychiatric Analysis of Crime and Punishment,* Macmillan, New York, 1965.

46 August Aichhorn, *Wayward Youth,* Viking, New York, 1963.

47 T. Bowlby, *Child Care and the Growth of Love,* Penguin, Baltimore, 1953.

48 A. M. Johnson and S. A. Szurek, "The Genesis of Antisocial Acting Out in Children and Adults," *Psychoanalytic Quarterly,* vol. 21, 1952, pp. 674–683.

49 Sigmund Freud, "Femininity," in *New Introductory Lectures on Psychoanalysis,* James Strachey (trans.), W. W. Norton, New York, 1965, p. 125.

50 Ibid., pp. 116, 125.

51 Ibid., p. 125.

52 Ibid., p. 116.

53 Elizabeth R. Moberly, *Psychogenesis: The Early Development of Gender Identity,* Routledge and Kegan Paul, London, 1983, p. 84.

54 Sandor S. Feldman, "On Homosexuality," in S. Lorand and M. Balint (eds.), *Perversions: Psychodynamics and Therapy,* Random House, New York, 1956, pp. 74–75.

55 See, for instance, Jacqueline Rose, "Feminism and the Psychic" in *Sexuality in the Field of Vision,* Verso, London, 1986, pp. 1–23.

56 See, for instance, Juliet Mitchell, *Psychoanalysis and Feminism,* Vintage, New York, 1974, and "Introduction" to *Feminine Sexuality: Jacques Lacan and the Ecole Freudienne,* W. W. Norton, New York, 1985, pp. 1–26; Luce Irigaray, *Speculum of the Other Woman,* Gillian C. Gill (trans.), Cornell University Press, Ithaca, N.Y., 1985; Judith Butler, *Gender Troubles: Feminism and the Subversion of Identity,* Routledge, New York, 1990; Jane Gallop, *The Daughter's Seduction: Feminism and Psychoanalysis,* Cornell University Press, Ithaca, N.Y., 1982; and Jonathan Dollimore, *Sexual Dissidence: Augustine to Wilde, Freud to Foucault,* Oxford University Press, New York, 1991.

57 Dollimore, *Sexual Dissidence,* p. 176.

58 Jan Hankin, "A Sociological Critique of Psychiatric Theories of Crime," unpublished paper cited in Marshall B. Clinard and Robert F. Meir (eds.), *Sociology of Deviant Behavior,* 5th ed., Holt, Rinehart & Winston, New York, 1979, p. 98.

59 See Karl F. Scheussler and Donald R. Cressey, "Personality Characteristics of

Criminals," *American Journal of Sociology*, vol. 55, March 1950, pp. 483–484; Gordon Waldo and Simon Dinitz, "Personality Attributes of the Criminal: An Analysis of Research Studies," *Journal of Research in Crime and Delinquency*, vol. 4, July 1967, pp. 185–202.

60 Hans J. Eysenck, *Crime and Personality*, Houghton Mifflin, Boston, 1964.

61 M. P. Feldman, *Criminal Behavior: A Psychological Analysis*, Wiley, New York, 1977.

62 Michael T. Nietzel, *Crime and Its Modification: A Social Learning Perspective*, Pergamon, New York, 1979, p. 89.

63 Samuel Yochelson and Stanton Samenow, *The Criminal Personality*, Aronson, New York, 1976.

64 Ibid., p. viii.

65 Simon Dinitz, "Chronically Abnormal Offenders," in John Conrad and Simon Dinitz (eds.), *For Fear of Each Other*, D.C. Heath, Lexington Books, Lexington, Mass., 1977, p. 22.

66 Sydney Maughs, "A Concept of Psychopathy and Psychopathic Personality: Its Evaluation and Historical Development," *Journal of Criminal Psychopathology*, vol. 2, April 1940, pp. 465–499.

67 Hervey Cleckley, *The Mask of Sanity*, 4th ed., Mosby, St. Louis, 1964.

68 Harrison Gough, "A Sociological Theory of Psychopathy," *American Journal of Sociology*, vol. 53, March 1948, pp. 359–366.

69 B. Baker's unpublished work is summarized in Theodore R. Sarbin, "Role Theory," in Gardner Lindzey (ed.), *Handbook of Social Psychology*, Addison-Wesley, Cambridge, Mass., 1954, p. 246.

70 R. Albrecht and T. R. Sarbin's unpublished work is summarized in Sarbin, "Role Theory," p. 246.

71 William McCord and Joan McCord, *Psychopathy and Delinquency*, Grune & Stratton, New York, 1956.

72 Lee Robins, *Deviant Children Grow Up*, Williams & Williams, Baltimore, 1966.

73 D. H. Funkenstein, M. Greenblatt, and H. C. Solomon, "Psychophysiological Study of Mentally Ill Patients," *American Journal of Psychiatry*, vol. 106, 1949, pp. 359–366.

74 D. T. Lykken, "A Study of Anxiety in the Sociopathic Personality," Ph.D. dissertation, University of Minnesota, Minneapolis, 1955 (University Microfilms, Ann Arbor, no. 55–944).

75 Stanley Schachter and Bibb Latane, "Crime, Cognition and the Autonomic Nervous System," in David Levine (ed.), *Nebraska Symposium of Motivation*, University of Nebraska Press, Lincoln, 1964, pp. 271–274.

76 W. W. Lippert, "The Electrodermal System of the Sociopath," Ph.D. dissertation, University of Cincinnati, 1965 (University Microfilms, Ann Arbor, no. 65–12,921); R. D. Hare, "Psychopathy, Autonomic Functioning, and the Orienting Response," *Journal of Abnormal Psychology*, vol. 73, suppl. 1968, pp. 1–24.

77 H. E. Allen, L. A. Lindner, H. Goldman, and S. Dinitz, "The Social and Biomedical Correlates of Sociopathy," *Criminologica*, vol. 6, 1969, pp. 68–75, and "Hostile and Simple Sociopaths: An Empirical Typology, *Criminology*, vol. 9, 1971, pp. 27–47; H. Goldman, L. A. Linder, S. Dinitz, and H. E. Allen, "The Simple Sociopath: Physiologic and Sociologic Characteristics," *Biological Psychiatry*, vol. 3, 1971, pp. 77–83.

78. Sting, "Every Breath You Take," from the album *Synchronicity* by The Police. A&M Records Inc., Hollywood, Calif., 1983.
79. Michel Foucault, *Discipline and Punish,* Alan Sheridan (trans.), Pantheon, New York, pp. 220–221.
80. Jurgen Habermas, "Knowledge and Interest," in D. Emmet and A. MacIntyre (eds.), *Sociological Theory and Philosophical Analysis,* Macmillan, New York, 1970, J. Shapiro (trans.), Beacon Press, Boston, 1971.
81. Foucault, *Discipline and Punish,* p. 226.
82. Susan Griffin, *Pornography and Silence: Culture's Revenge against Nature,* Harper and Row, New York, 1981.
83. Zora Neale Hurston, *The Sanctified Church,* Turtle Island, Berkeley, Calif., 1983.
84. For a description of this study, see Henry M. Hurd, ed., *The Institutional Care of the Insane in the United States and Canada,* Johns Hopkins University Press, Baltimore, Md., 1916, as cited in Sander L. Gilman, *Difference and Pathology: Stereotypes of Sexuality, Race, and Madness,* Cornell University Press, Ithaca, N.Y., 1985, p. 140.
85. Gilman, *Difference and Pathology,* p. 140.
86. Patricia Hill Collins, *Black Feminist Thought: Knowledge, Consciousness and the Politics of Empowerment,* Unwin Hyman, Boston, 1990, p. 204.
87. Malcolm Spector, "Beyond Crime: Seven Methods to Control Troublesome Rascals," in H. Lawrence Ross (ed.), *Law and Deviance,* Sage, Beverly Hills, Calif., 1981, p. 138.
88. Nicholas Kittrie, *The Right to Be Different: Deviance and Enforced Therapy,* Johns Hopkins, Baltimore, Md., 1971.
89. Conrad and Schneider, *Deviance and Medicalization,* p. 35.
90. Ibid.
91. Vold, *Theoretical Criminology,* p. 54.
92. This description of the eugenics movement is indebted to the excellent overview of this pathological control strategy in Charles H. McCaghy, *Deviant Behavior: Crime, Conflict and Interest Groups,* Macmillan, New York, 1976, pp. 19–21. For a more recent discussion of developments in moleculer genetics as these pertain to social control policies, see Troy Duster, *Backdoor to Genetics,* Routledge, New York, 1990.
93. T. W. Shannon, *Eugenics,* Mullikin, Marietta, Ohio, 1916.
94. Ibid., p. 160.
95. Charles R. Henderson, *Dependent, Defective, and Delinquent Classes: And of Their Social Treatment,* Heath, Boston, 1901, as discussed in McCaghy, *Deviant Behavior,* p. 20.
96. McCaghy, *Deviant Behavior,* p. 21.
97. Ibid.
98. Ibid.
99. Michel Foucault, *Madness and Civilization,* Pantheon, New York, 1965.
100. August B. Hollingshead and Frederick C. Redlich, *Social Class and Mental Illness,* Wiley, New York, 1958.
101. Ralph K. Schwitzgebel, "The Right to Effective Mental Treatment," *California Law Review,* vol. 3, May 1974, pp. 943, 948.
102. Stuart L. Hills, *Demystifying Social Deviance,* McGraw-Hill, New York, 1980, p. 125.

103 Conrad and Schneider, *Deviance and Medicalization,* pp. 62–63. Data on inpatients of state and county mental hospitals by courtesy of U.S. Department of Health, Education and Welfare, National Institutes of Mental Health.

104 *Wyatt v. Stickney,* 325 F. Supp. 781–785 (1974)

105 See Stephen J. Pfohl, *Right to Treatment Litigation: Judicial Intervention into Mental Health Policy,* Ohio Division of Mental Health, Columbus, 1975.

106 Andrew T. Scull, *Decarceration: Community Treatment and the Deviant—A Radical View,* Prentice-Hall, Englewood Cliffs, N.J., 1977.

107 *Medical World News,* Apr. 11, 1974, p. 47.

108 C. Ray Jeffery, "Punishment and Deterrence: A Psychobiological Statement," paper presented to annual meeting of American Society of Criminology, Dallas, November 1978, p. 19.

109 C. Ray Jeffery (ed.), *Biology and Crime,* Sage, Beverly Hills, Calif., 1979, p. 7.

110 Max G. Schlapp and Edward H. Smith, *The New Criminology: A Consideration of the Chemical Causation of Abnormal Behavior,* Boni & Liveright, New York, 1928.

111 Sarnoff Mednick and Karl O. Christiansen, *Biosocial Bases of Criminal Behavior,* Gardner Press, New York, 1977.

112 Harold E. Kelly, "Biosociology and Crime," in C. Ray Jeffery (ed.), *Biology and Crime,* Sage, Beverly Hills, Calif., 1979, pp. 93–94.

113 Ibid., p. 98.

114 Hills, *Demystifying Social Deviance,* pp. 126–127.

115 James Q. Wilson and Richard J. Herrnstein, *Crime and Human Nature,* Simon and Schuster, New York, 1985, p. 80.

116 Ibid., pp. 102–103.

117 Ibid., p. 209.

118 Lee Ellis, "The Evolution of Violent Criminal Behavior and its Nonlegal Equivalent," in Lee Ellis and Harry Hoffman (eds.), *Crime in Biological, Social and Moral Contexts,* Praeger, New York, 1990, pp. 71–72.

119 While Ellis's theories are typified by biological assumptions divorced from careful methodological scrutiny, a more careful assessment of both the promise and liabilities of contemporary pathological theorizing is found in Diana H. Fishbein, "Biological Perspectives in Criminology," *Criminology,* vol. 28, 1990, pp. 27–72.

120 Peter Conrad, *Identifying Hyperactive Children: The Medicalization of Deviant Behavior,* Heath, Lexington, Mass., 1976.

121 Conrad and Schneider, *Deviance and Medicalization,* pp. 159–160.

122 Richard Moran, "Medicine and Crime: The Search for the Born Criminal and the Medical Control of Criminality," in Conrad and Schneider, *Deviance and Medicalization,* pp. 224–226.

123 S. Chorover, "Big Brother and Psychotechnology," *Psychology Today,* vol. 7, October 1973, pp. 43–54; S. Chorover, "Psychosurgery: A Neuropsychological Perspective," *Boston University Law Review,* vol. 74, March 1974, pp. 231–248.

124 Moran, "Medicine and Crime," p. 224; see also McCaghy, *Deviant Behavior,* pp. 27–31.

125 Moran, "Medicine and Crime," p. 224.

126 Lee Edson, "The Psyche and the Surgeon," *New York Times Magazine,* Sept. 30, 1973, p. 79.

127 Ballentine's description is found in Joel Greenberg, "Altering Behavior with Brain Surgery," *New England Magazine, Boston Sunday Globe,* Jan. 1, 1978, pp. 6–12.

128 George J. Amos, as quoted in Greenberg, "Altering Behavior . . . ," p. 8.

129 Peter R. Breggin, as quoted in Greenberg, "Altering Behavior . . . ," p. 8.

130 Vernon Mark and Frank Ervin, *Violence and the Brain*, Harper & Row, New York, 1970.

131 For an overview of this research, see Harold Goldman, "The Limits of Clockwork: The Neurobiology of Violent Behavior," in J. Conrad and S. Dinitz (eds.), *In Fear of Each Other*, D.C. Heath, Lexington, Mass., 1977, pp. 43–76; and Saleem-Shah and Loren H. Roth, "Biological and Psychophysiological Factors in Criminality," in Daniel Glaser (ed.), *Handbook of Criminology*, Rand McNally, Chicago, 1974, pp. 101–173.

132 D. E. Smith, M. B. King, and B. G. Hoebel, "Lateral Hypothalamic Control of Killing: Evidence for a Cholinoceptive Mechanism," *Science*, vol. 167, 1970, pp. 900 ff.

133 W. W. Roberts and H. O. Kiess, "Motivational Properties of Hypothalamic Aggression in Cats," *Journal of Comparative and Physiological Psychology*, vol. 58, 1964, pp. 187 ff.; C. H. Woodworth, "Attack Elicited in Rats by Electrical Stimulation of the Lateral Hypothalamus," *Physiology and Behavior*, vol. 6, 1971, pp. 6 ff.; B. H. Turner, "Sensorimotor Syndrome Produced by Lesions of the Amygdala and Lateral Hypothalamus," *Journal of Comparative and Physiological Psychology*, vol. 82, 1973, pp. 82 ff.

134 V. H. Mark, W. H. Sweet, and F. R. Ervin, "Role of Brain Disease in Riots and Urban Violence," *Journal of the American Medical Association*, vol. 201, 1967, p. 895.

135 These two studies, conducted by researchers Corkin at Massachusetts Institute of Technology and Mirsky and Orzack at Boston University, are summarized in Greenberg, "Altering Behavior . . . ," pp. 6–12.

136 Ibid.

137 Samuel I. Shuman, *Psychosurgery and the Medical Control of Violence*, Wayne State University Press, Detroit, 1977.

138 Jose Delgado, *Physical Control of the Mind: Toward a Psychocivilized Society*, Harper and Row, New York, 1969, p. 259.

139 Ibid., p. 200.

140 Susan Sontag, *Illness as Metaphor*, Farrar, Straus, & Giroux, New York, 1978, p. 85.

141 Conrad and Schneider, *Deviance and Medicalization*, pp. 246–248.

142 Ibid., pp. 248–252.

143 See, for instance, Stephen Pfohl, *Predicting Dangerousness: the Social Construction of Psychiatric Reality*, D.C. Heath, Lexington Books, Lexington, Mass., 1978, and also "Deciding on Dangerousness: Predictions of Violence as Social Control," in Tony Platt and Paul Takagi (eds.), *Punishment and Penal Discipline: Essays on the Prison and Prisoners' Movement*, Crime and Social Justice Associates, Berkeley, Calif., 1980, pp. 129–141. See also Robert J. Menzies, *Survival of the Sanest: Order and Disorder in a Pretrial Psychiatric Clinic*, University of Toronto Press, Toronto, 1989.

144 David A. Snow, Susan G. Baker, Leon Anderson, and Michael Martin, "The Myth of Pervasive Mental Illness among the Homeless," *Social Problems*, vol. 33, 1986, pp. 407–423. The rather strict ethnographic criteria of measurement used by Snow et al. has been criticized by James Wright. Wright's own estimate of mental illness among a nineteen-city sample of Health Care for the Homeless patients selected by trained health care workers is closer to one-third. Although Wright's samples are large in size and geographically dispersed, his estimates are, in all likelihood, inflated by the acceptance of but a single criterion as an indicator of "true" mental illness. Biases were probably generated by using a sample composed of already physically ill patients, including persons making repeated visits to the same health care center. In addition, the judgments were rendered by health care providers, who previous studies indicate are likely to be low on diagnostic reliability but high on falsely positive estimates. For a critical exchange on methodologies shaping the best estimate of mental illness among the homeless, see James Wright, "The Mentally Ill Homeless: What Is Myth and What Is Fact?" *Social Problems,* vol. 35, no. 2, April 1985, pp. 182–191; and David A. Snow, Susan G. Baker, and Leon Anderson, "On the Precariousness of Measuring Insanity in Insane Contexts," *Social Problems,* vol. 35, no. 2, April 1988, pp. 192–196.

145 Snow, Baker, and Anderson, "On the Precariousness of Measuring Insanity . . . ," p. 195.

146 For an elaboration of this thesis, see Hélène Cixous and Catherine Clement, *The Newly Born Woman,* Betsy Wing (trans.), University of Minnesota Press, Minneapolis, 1986.

147 For a critical feminist reading of Charcot's so-called discoveries, see Elaine Showalter, *The Female Malady: Women, Madness and English Culture 1830–1980,* Pantheon Books, New York, 1985, pp. 145–164. See also Robert Romanyshyn, *Technology as Symptom and Dream,* Routledge, New York, 1989, pp. 163–170.

148 Sigmund Freud and Josef Breuer, *Studies on Hysteria,* Avon Books, New York, 1966.

149 For additional materials on the celebrated "Anna O." case, see Dora Edinger, *Bertha Pappenheim—Freud's Anna O.,* Congregation Solel, Highland Park, Ill., 1968; Lucy Freedman, *The Story of Anna O.,* Walker, New York, 1972; and Max Rosenbaum and Melvin Muroff (eds.), *Anna O.: Fourteen Contemporary Reinterpretations,* Free Press, New York, 1984.

150 Showalter, *The Female Malady,* p. 158; see also Diane Hunter, "Hysteria, Psychoanalysis, and Feminism: The Case of Anna O.," *Feminist Studies,* vol. 9, 1983, pp. 465–488.

151 Orr, "Panic Diary," p. 10. See also Jackie Orr, "Theory on the Market: Panic, Incorporated," *Social Problems,* vol. 37, no. 4, November 1990, pp. 460–484.

152 Hilde Bruch, *The Golden Cage: The Enigma of Anorexia Nervosa,* Harvard University Press, Cambridge, Mass., 1978, p. viii.

153 Elspeth Probyn, "The Anorexic Body," in Arthur and Marilouise Kroker, *Body Invaders: Panic Sex in America,* St. Martin's Press, New York, 1987, pp. 201–211.

154 For a critical analysis of "eating disorders" as symptomatic resistances to male cultural domination, see Kim Chernin, *The Obsession: Reflections on the Tyranny of Slenderness,* Harper and Row, New York, 1981.

155 Conrad and Schneider, *Deviance and Medicalization,* p. 252.

Adrift Chicago   By Joseph LaMantia and Stephen Pfohl

THE SOCIAL DISORGANIZATION PERSPECTIVE: Rapid Change and Normative Breakdown in the Slums of Chicago

With the growth of great cities, with the vast division of labor which has come in with machine industry, and with movement and change that have come about with the multiplication of the means of transportation and communication, the old forms of social control represented by the family, the neighborhood, and the local community have been undermined and their influence greatly diminished. The process by which the authority and influence of an earlier culture and system of social control is undermined and eventually destroyed is . . . social disorganization.

Robert E. Park, Ernest V. Burgess, and Roderick D. McKenzie[1]

INTRODUCTION

Over the Edge is a movie about middle-class teenagers who are literally out of control. Its fictitious setting is a half-completed "condo community" named New Granada, Colorado. Don't be surprised if you have never seen or heard of this movie. Although it was completed in 1979, its distributor (Warner Brothers) has largely withheld this explosive motion picture from a national viewing audience. It didn't play in New York until January 1982, and then only to a limited audience at two midtown theaters. Why this select and confined distribution? It is not because *Over the Edge* is a film that fails. Where it has been viewed, the film has drawn good crowds and sensational critical reviews. This perhaps is its problem. It succeeds in engaging viewers in a story that somebody is scared to let teenagers see—a story of teenagers cut loose from the moral norms and internalized social controls of conventional society.

In the movie's final scenes, the teenagers of New Granada go on a rampage, terrorizing their parents and trashing their school. Worried that the film may ignite similar episodes of teenage violence, distributors have kept a heavy lid on *Over the Edge*. According to director Jonathan Kaplan, the film was "delivered . . . at the time *Boulevard Nights* and *The Warriors* [which caused a few disturbances] were in general release. The theater owners in the suburbs were scared. They said, 'We don't want a picture where kids are going to tear up the sixplexes.' "[2]

The teenagers in *Over the Edge* are the offspring of a fast-paced, rapidly changing society. They are all new immigrants to an instantaneously erected "high-tech" community, a community of flat, tasteful dwellings with manicured lawns, sliding glass patio doors, and wood-beamed ceilings. The teenagers of New Granada have been moved there by parents who hope to escape the dirt, pressures, and tensions of city living. Inadvertently, however, the adults of New Granada recreate the alienating atmosphere of the world from which they sought refuge. The moral gulf which separates them from their children is dug deep by the rush of rapid social change. In one of the film's most telling scenes, a prospective business investor, horror-stricken by the deviant antics of the town's young people, tells the town's mayor, "You have turned your kids into what you were trying to get away from."

The neatly packaged world which New Granada's parents have arranged for their children produces a generation of lost souls. It is one change too many. Raised on color TV and stereophonic rock music, the kids retreat with their headphones and smoke dope while their parents mix drinks with complaints and worry about what has gone wrong. The parents don't understand. How could they? They have moved, the kids were moved. They have produced and procured technologies for a better world. The kids have become technological junkies, dependent on the electricity of ever more sensational stimulation. The parents have sought to protect their young from what they perceived as the cold anonymity of urban living. The kids have once again been subjected to massive changes beyond their control—now transplanted into a barren and boring array of backyards and bedrooms.

The kids of New Granada are the victims of socially institutionalized rootlessness. Like their real-life counterparts, the teenagers of Foster City, California, upon whom screenwriters Tim Hunter and Charlie Haas constructed their story, they react deviantly to the onset of rootlessness. In the words of film critic David Denby, they are "privileged nihilists, often stoned or smashed, growing up in a vacuum; their friendship for one another and a shared loathing for New Granada are the only values they've got. . . .The kids are cut off, sequestered in their instant 'community.'"[3]

The parents had hoped that New Granada would be a comfortable, organized place in which their children could grow into respectable adults. By the kids, New Granada is experienced as a disorganized nightmare. Everything has changed too fast. Everything is new. There is little continuity between life today and life yesterday, and virtually no continuity between the aspirations and expectations of their parents and those of their peers. As Denby points out, "Even a big city slum neighborhood has its traditions, its places to hang out, but the elders of New Granada are so eager to protect their investments that they send the cops to hassle the kids whenever they gather."[4] In the film this idea is painted in the recurrent visual imagery of kids wandering along the side of the road, kids passing by the speeding cars of their parents racing off to complete plans for a brighter future, kids by the side of a road going nowhere.

The rapid and uncontrolled changes to which New Granada's teenagers are exposed pushes them in the direction of deviance. Their lives seem disorganized and disorderly until they come together in a climactic celebration of rebellion. They vandalize. They riot. They strike out at the symbols of their parents' mortality. In so doing, the deviant teenagers appear, at least for an instant, to regain control over a world which ordinarily races ahead of them. How accurate is this cinematic portrayal of teenagers going over the edge? Is deviance actually associated with socially produced disorganization and lack of control? Are such events necessarily triggered by the forces of rapid change? In order to answer these questions, let us consider the writings of theorists associated with the social disorganization perspective.

THEORETICAL IMAGES

The social disorganization perspective emerged in the writings and research of sociologists at the University of Chicago during the 1920s. The early proponents of this perspective are often referred to as the "Chicago school." By emphasizing social causation, as opposed to rational choice or illness, the Chicago school departed from the individualistic focus of classical and pathological theorizing. Moreover, in demanding that sociological theory be tied to a rigorous scientific investigation of social life, Chicago's disorganization theorists separated themselves from a previous generation of speculative, sentimental, and reform-oriented social pathologists.

Disorganization theorists developed a model of naturalistic social causation. Deviance was viewed as a natural by-product of rapid social change. High rates of nonconformity occurred when too much change in too short a time disrupted the normative order of society. The disorganization perspective views society as a collectivity of people bound together by a set of interrelated rules or norms. Norms are guidelines for action. They inform us how we are to act, toward whom, where, and when. Norms are accompanied by values. Values justify norms and provide believable reasons as to why we should conform.

The Chicago theorists ask us to imagine the well-organized society. In such a society we find people who have internalized the norms which surround them: people who paradoxically have surrounded themselves from the inside out; people who act as their own watchtowers of control; people who are like gyroscopes; people whose internal mechanisms of self-balance are first set in motion and then continuously affected by the push and pull of forces external to their spin down the straight and narrow path of conformity. In this well-organized society the actions of people would be well coordinated because each person is bound within the same web of social norms. Having internalized these norms, people value the rules which control them.

This description of the well-organized society might imply that the Chicago theorists longed for the good old days of small-town America. This was not the case. The members of the Chicago school were not sentimental about the days of yesteryear. They were a breed of hard-nosed social scientists who refused to view social change in moralistic terms. Change was pictured as a natural social phenomenon. Change was as natural as normative social organization itself. While rapid change may temporarily fracture the normative organization of society, the Chicago theorists viewed this as but one phase in an ongoing process of social reorganization. Disorganization was a step toward reorganization.

The Chicago theorists thus viewed reorganization as the sociological step-child of disorganization. Prior to reorganization, society would experience an interim period of competition, competition between different and perhaps conflicting normative frameworks. Normative competition, conflict, or dissensus is a key characteristic of social disorganization. One of its by-products is an increase in the incidence of deviant behavior. The reason is simple. The normative web of society has been stripped of its power to control people. People are set free of normative constraints. Like an off-centered gyroscope, they tilt and turn into a dizzy path of unpredictability and nonconformity. Anything goes. An increasing number of people drift from conformity into deviance.

This is the kernel of the so-called Chicago perspective. Rapid changes damage the organized society's web of normative controls. This results in social disorganization. Normative consensus is replaced by normative dissensus. Disorganization has two kinds of by-products. One is long-term. It involves movement in the direction of normative reorganization. The second is more immediate or short-term. It involves movement in the direction of deviance.

What kinds of rapid change produce a shift from normative organization to disorganization and back again? Early disorganization theory focused on changes that were apparent in American society during the 1920s: changes in the areas of technological development, organization, and immigration. Its study of these matters involved two interrelated developments: (1) outlining the conceptual dynamics of social disorganization, and (2) studying the ecological or social-spatial dimensions of disorganization. The first development is best exemplified in the writings of W. I. Thomas and Florian Znaniecki; the second in the work of Robert Park, Ernest Burgess, and their students. Before considering the specific writings of these Chicago theorists, let us step back and view the origins of the Chicago school within its particular sociohistorical context.

The 1920s and the University of Chicago: A Time and Place for the Study of Social Disorganization

To appreciate the theoretical image of social disorganization it is helpful to locate its development within a particular time—the 1920s—and at a particular place—the University of Chicago. The 1920s were particularly important for the development of sociology in the United States. In the aftermath of the tragic events of World War I, sociologists were confronted with the task of rethinking optimistic assumptions about the inevitability of progress and the increasing rationality of the human social world. They were also challenged by the omnipresent manifestations of unprecedented social change and by demands from the emerging middle class of managerial professionals for factual knowledge with which to technically and efficiently direct the course of change. These challenges came to be concentrated at the University of Chicago, where sociologists found themselves visibly surrounded by the most pronounced changes in the social landscape of the United States and by financial and political support from the business elite of the nation and the city. In responding to these challenges, the Chicago sociologists produced a new theoretical image related to the nature and control of social problems: the image of social disorganization.

A Time for Social Disorganization: The Aftermath of World War I and the Professional Management of Rapid Social Change

Before World War I, U.S. sociology had not differentiated itself from speculative social philosophy. Although claiming the cloak of science, most early U.S. sociologists remained dressed in the ethical armor of progressive social reform. Their commitment to the scientific character of sociology was largely a commitment to a form of evolutionary theorizing in which the rational development of society was speculatively deduced as a kind of natural law. Science was viewed as a progressive feature of this natural human evolution, a guide for the rational human conquest of nature.

According to Albian Small, one of the "founding fathers" of U.S. sociology, the pre-World War I generation of sociologists was characterized by four general assumptions: (1) a belief that the purpose of sociology was to deduce "natural laws" of social existence; (2) a commitment to evolutionary theorizing, accompanied by faith in the inevitability of progress; (3) advocacy of social reform as a means of accelerating progressive social evolution; and (4) an emphasis on the individual and on motivated individual behavior as the core building blocks of social theory.[5] These assumptions provided great optimism. By speculatively deducing natural laws of social evolution, sociologists believed they would hasten the inevitable coming of rational reform and social betterment.

The shadows of World War I dimmed this optimistic viewpoint. The bloody trenches of Europe stood in stark contrast to sociological images of rational progress. Faith in the benign promise of scientific guidance was shattered by the awareness that the technological offspring of science had become the tools of ruthless and irrational destruction. For many European social theorists, the horrific spectacle of the "Great War" also engendered radical forms of cultural criticism. Among these was surrealism, a politically engaged movement of writers, artists, and researchers who were repulsed by the overly instrumental character of modern social life. Surrealists rejected positivist approaches to social science, arguing that such methods were complicit with the violence of western economic, cultural, and even sexual hierarchies.

In France, dissident surrealists, such as Georges Bataille and Michel Leiris, experimented with radical forms of research that sought to disturb positivist discipline and open social science to questions ignored by mainstream methods. Surrealists argued that mainstream research reduced the complexities of social life to predefined categories of western logic. In order to counter such reductionism, surrealists introduced poetic research strategies aimed at subverting the taken-for-granted character of western claims to objectivity. In so doing, surrealists pointed to the fact that social science writing was itself a form of (fictive) cultural production. This led to a *dialogue* with traditions canonically excluded by most modern forms of knowledge, as dissident surrealists sought to display the partial character of even their own claims to objectivity.[6] In this way, sociological surrealists hoped to interject heterogeneity into the production of social science itself. This was a political as well as a sociological project. In the years following World War I, it involved efforts to break out of "science's deep slumber" and engender a dialogue with "external data, foreign to lived experience."[7] Without such dialogue, surrealist sociologists believed that "nothing really new will have taken place and interpretations [will remain] unacceptable from the start."[8]

U.S. sociologists were also shaken by the events of the war. As Roscoe and Gisela Hinkle point out:

> The war severely shook the intellectuals' faith in progress. Many sociologists concurred with other intellectuals in concluding that man is not essentially rational. . . . Sociologists thus became pessimistic about progressive improvements which had heretofore been regarded as the inevitable products of man's rationality.[9]

For sociologists in the United States, the chilling disillusionment of World War I was short-lived, but many European theorists would continue for decades to question the supposed neutrality of positivist approaches to social science. This was true both of dissident French surrealists and of radical German scholars associated with "the Frankfurt School of critical theory."[10] Both challenged the value-free posture of positivism and sought to formulate historically specific and politically committed alternatives to modern social science inquiry. In the United States, however, momentary pessimism was followed by efforts to reformulate the positivist character of sociology and to propose new approaches to social control.[11] In this sense, postwar U.S.

sociology was marked by a new optimism, an optimism which contrasted sharply with the previous faith in the inevitability of progress, but an optimism nonetheless.

In reformulating the basis of its scientific identity, postwar U.S. sociology came to view faith in the inevitability of progress as incorrect. The events of the war had proved this position untenable. Irrationality loomed large as a feature of life itself. This, however, was no reason to abandon the scientific study of social life. For postwar sociologists, the naive theories of the preceding generation were viewed as lacking scientific rigor. "Natural laws" deduced before the war were now seen as more speculative than factual. Postwar sociologists proposed a different starting point for sociological theorizing. Sociology was to begin, not with speculation, but with the careful observation and measurement of social life—with inductive inquiry or rigorous empirical study. This was the basis for U.S. sociology's postwar optimism. It assumed that a precise empirical investigation of social life would yield both an explanation and a pragmatic program by which to control social chaos and irrationality.

The postwar transformation of U.S. sociology was far-reaching. Speculative assumptions about natural social laws were replaced by rigorous empirical inquiry. Belief in the progressive character of evolution was abandoned. Where once sociology had been equated with partisan progressive reform, now sociologists pledged allegiance to the principles of scientific neutrality. An analytic focus on individuals receded in favor of increased attention to society as a force in its own right. Each of these changes contributed greatly to the emergence of the social disorganization perspective.

Why the optimism of postwar sociology in the United States? Part of the answer lies in the fact that the United States emerged victorious from an awful war fought at a great distance. Unlike Europe, the heartland of the U.S. remained unravaged by the deadly tools of twentieth-century war. U.S. political power and economic influence multiplied without blood being spilt upon the country's own soil. Yet this answer is partial at best. The old optimism about the inevitability of progress was put to rest in the United States as well as in Europe. The new optimism of U.S. sociology was rooted in something different. It is better understood by a conjuncture of two factors: a decade of unprecedented social change and the managerial response of an emerging professional class of technical problem solvers to problems brought about by such change. At the center of this conjuncture were the University of Chicago sociologists, themselves members of this new professional class, who aimed to battle social change with the conceptual weapons of a new theoretical perspective—the theory of social disorganization.

A Decade of Rapid Change

Rapid social change was a central feature of the U.S. landscape in the 1920s. The U.S. economy was thrown into full gear by the war. This resulted in several developments which drastically altered the lifestyles and the work styles of U.S. citizens. Long strides were made toward the increased mechanization or technologicalization of both industrial and agricultural production. Demands for large-scale and efficient production were bolstered by major technological advances in the fields of communication and transportation. These developments propelled business organizations toward greater centralization, combination, and control of industrial effort. By 1923, for instance, the heyday of the small independent producer was largely past. Although only 4 percent of all U.S. businesses hired more than 250 workers, these companies had become the employers of well over half the entire industrial labor force.[12] This movement toward centralized control is described by James T. Carey as a "trend toward national integrative structures."[13] This trend was accompanied by a similar growth in centralized governmental regulatory agencies.

Changes such as these produced additional changes as well. Change, as the Chicago theorists would note, led to further change. The increased mechanization of agriculture produced agricultural unemployment. This resulted in a drift of farm workers to cities. There they joined large populations of foreign-born workers, an increasing number of women workers who had entered the industrial labor force during the war, and black workers who had migrated from the south to the urban industrial centers of the north and the west. By 1930, the black urban population in northern and western states was 2,228,000, nearly twice what it had been a decade earlier.[14] During the same decade, as the number of people living in rural areas shrank by 12 million, the nation's urban population increased by more than 14 million. Cities of more than 1 million persons had approximately 5 million more residents.[15] Many were immigrants. By 1930, one-third of all U.S. whites were foreign-born. Most of them were located in urban areas.[16]

The changes associated with increased technologicalization, immigration, and urbanization were compounded by massive occupational and organizational changes in U.S. industry. The increased centralization of industrial effort resulted in expansion of the administrative, managerial, and clerical sectors. The aggregate number of professional, technical, and managerial employees doubled between 1910 and 1930, increasing from 6,599,000 to 12,546,000. This proportional increase far outdistanced the more modest expansion of the working-class, or direct-production, occupational sector, which grew from 19,730,000 to 25,813,000 during the same period.[17]

Such changes did not affect all U.S citizens equally. This was particularly the case for the working class, persons described as blue-collar or wage laborers. The working class was affected negatively by significant increases in mechanized production and growth in the middle class of white-collar professionals and salaried employees. This "unevenness of prosperity" is documented by James Carey, who points to ground lost by the growing number of urban, immigrant, and blue-collar workers and by small farmers and farm laborers affected by massive mechanization and technological unemployment. Accordingly, while "increasing shares went to receivers at the top, . . . working men and women could not purchase what they produced."[18]

The Tension of Change: Social Reactions to Technologicalization, Immigration, and Urbanization

The differential impact of change in the 1920s was accompanied by considerable tension, fear, and anxiety. There was, however, little visible protest by the people who were affected most adversely by change—the displaced rural laborers, immigrants, and minorities concentrated in urban areas, each competing against the other for wage positions, and each affected negatively by postwar overproducing, mechanization, and the growing dominance of salaried white-collar workers. In contrast to the decades which went before, the 1920s was marked by a relative absence of organized labor strikes and violent collective outbursts, such as riots.[19]

Why so little dissent during the 1920s? In part, the answer lies in the relative success of harsh governmental repressions instituted during and after World War I. Viewing the war as benefiting capitalists at the top but not the average worker, progressive sectors of U.S. labor questioned its supposedly noble purpose. This gave the government an opportunity to crush the most radical of labor unions, the International Workers of the World (IWW, or "Wobblies"). In September 1917, federal agents made simultaneous raids on forty-eight IWW labor halls nationwide, seizing both official documents and informal correspondence. Soon thereafter, 165 Wobblies were charged with conspiring to hinder the draft and other "anti-American" activities; 101 Wobblies went on trial in April 1918. Although the union envisioned the trial as an opportunity to tell "the true story" of the oppressive conditions facing U.S. factory workers, all defendants were found guilty. Fifteen union leaders were sentenced to twenty years in prison, and 33 others given ten-year terms. Others were given shorter sentences, while the union as a whole was fined a total of $2,500,000. The most progressive wing of U.S. labor was thus broken before the war even ended.

After the war, the government acted quickly to suppress further dissent. In late 1919 and early 1920, still waving the flag of wartime patriotism, and spurred on by the explosion of a bomb in front of the home of Attorney General Mitchell Palmer, Palmer's men arrested and deported thousands of immigrant workers. In January 1920, 4,000 persons were "rounded up all over the country, held in seclusion for long periods of time, brought into secret hearings, and ordered deported."[20] In Boston, where Justice Department officials raided union halls and private homes, arresting over 600 persons, anarchists Nicola Sacco and Bartolomeo Vanzetti were made to face spurious charges for their alleged participation in a shoe factory holdup, and were sentenced to death and executed.

War-related patriotism also drove progressive thinkers out of university classrooms. At Columbia University, Charles Beard, whose "mild radicalism" involved little more than the suggestion that U.S. history was guided by a series of economic conflicts, resigned after a humiliating inquisition carried out by the school's board of trustees. Three years later he was forced from his position as director of the New York Bureau of Municipal Research when the Carnegie Foundation made it known that this agency would be denied funding as long as Beard remained. Progressive women scholars "who had established footholds in the women's colleges were also among the casualties. At Wellesley, Katherine Coman and Emily Balch had created a respected social science program with strong reformist leanings before the war. Always under careful watch for her political views, Balch was forced out of Wellesley when she became a pacifist during the war, and the social science program was virtually closed down for a decade."[21] The message was clear: in the United States of the 1920s, dissent was equated with disloyalty and met by a policy of "zero tolerance."

In addition to governmental repression, dissent also appeared to be fragmented by the emergence of mass society. Displaced persons, thrown together in urban anonymity, were further disadvantaged by their social context. Although people were crowded together in close physical proximity, the anonymity of urban life created a social distance, inhibiting them from identifying with each other. Social troubles were perceived in collective rather than individualistic terms, accentuating the sense of anonymity.

In summary, the people whose material destinies were the most directly and the most negatively affected by the rapid changes of the 1920s (displaced agricultural and industrial laborers, immigrants, and the urban poor) were involved in little collective social protest against the new mass society which engulfed them. This was not the case for another large segment of the U.S. population, those who clung to the cultural ideals of white, Protestant, small-town America. This group was also threatened by the increased centralization and technologicalization of social and economic life, by urbanization, and by what its members perceived as the strange and alien influx of immigrants.[22] This group reacted to the tensions of change with what may be described as the politics of nativism. *Nativism* is a term used to describe several strands of collective social action, each directed toward returning the United States to the good old days in which white, Protestant, small-town interests reigned supreme. The nativist reaction involved "hostility toward particular minority groups, especially radicals and recent immigrants, fanatical patriotism, and conviction that internal enemies who seriously threaten national security must be eliminated."[23]

The appeal of nativism has not vanished from the U.S. landscape. In more recent years groups such as the Ku Klux Klan and certain of the far-right supporters of Presidents Ronald Reagan and George Bush have emphasized similar themes. During the 1920s nativism manifested itself in a number of collective social movements. Notable among these were successful campaigns to restrict immigration and prohibit the manufacture and distribution of alcohol. Although Prohibition proved impossible to strictly enforce and was later repealed, the research of sociologist Joseph Gusfield suggests that it was first and foremost a symbolic victory for those who favored the old, conservative, and small-town ideals of a United States that was rapidly changing.[24] Other examples of nativism include the so-called Red Scare of 1920, a wave of fear and repression directed against people suspected of being Communists; the ban on the teaching of evolution in the public schools;[25] and the rapid growth and terrorist actions of the Ku Klux Klan.[26]

The Professional Management of Change: The Liberal Response

Nativism represented the reaction of groups whose previous dominance had been eroded by the changing economic, political, and social landscape of the United States in the 1920s. What was the reaction of groups whose power was enhanced by these changes? Two groups are particularly important in this regard: the owners emerging at the top and the professional managers ascending to powerful professional positions in the managerial middle.

A small number of individuals, families, or business associates came to control and dominate the ownership of the U.S. corporate economy following its period of centralization and consolidated combination during the 1920s. According to data recently reviewed by sociologist Maurice Zeitlin, "if we count up what the richest 1 percent of the population own, we find that they have a seventh of all the real estate in the country, more than half the corporate stock, and almost all the true assets."[27] Moreover, when considering only the richest of the corporate rich, one discovers that this "tiny owning class at the tip of the top, barely more than 1/20th of 1 percent of American adults, has a fifth of all the corporate stock."[28] But what about the other four-fifths? Because stock ownership is widely dispersed among members of both the middle class and the upper class, it is sometimes argued that the real ownership of the U.S. economy resides with the millions of people who possess small shares of huge corporations. In practical terms, the opposite is the case. As Zeitlin points out: "Precisely because the number of shareholders is so large and their holdings typically so minute compared to the few biggest shareholders in a large corporation, it may not take more than 1 or 2 percent of a company's stock to control it."[29]

In addition to the people who disproportionately controlled economic ownership, a second group emerged from the 1920s with increased power and influence—professionals occupying positions in the managerial middle. As suggested previously, increases in technological complexity and the centralized bureaucratic expansion of the workforce demanded a new form of specialized managerial expertise. Professional managers of all sorts came to fill positions in the middle and upper echelons of corporate life. This has prompted some students of economic organization to posit the advent of a managerial revolution. By this they mean that the ownership of corporations became separated from the day-to-day control over operations. This appears to be both true and untrue.

It is untrue insomuch as the upper echelons of management are continuously hired and fired by corporate boards or directorates which remain controlled by a small number of elite stockholders. On the other hand, professional managers bring to the economic organization a distinctive approach to the problems of human labor coordination. This approach involves a rational plan for the "scientific management" of human labor and a plan calculated to maximize both efficiency and profit." Since the 1920s, the day-to-day control of corporate business operations has increasingly been characterized by such professionally planned coordination. Yet, the fate of any particular managerial strategy remains dependent on whether or not it advances the profit margin of corporate owners. In this sense, the interests of managers and owners are relatively indistinguishable. According to Zeitlin, "Whatever their so-called professional motivations or power urges, their technocratic teamwork and bureaucratic mentality, managers' decisions on how to organize production and sales have to be measured against the bottom line: They dare not imperil corporate profit."[30]

Joined in the common pursuit of efficiently coordinated profit making, corporate owners and managerial professionals came to share a common view regarding solutions to the problems of rapid change. Each was desirous of a stable social climate in which to conduct business. Although they too saw rapid change as a threat to stability, the owners and managers, unlike the nativists, had no romantic dreams of going backward in time. How could they? The rapid social change that had led to the developments feared by the nativists had created their own positions of power in the first place. They were the true beneficiaries of rapid technologicalization, urbanization, and immigration.

Technologicalization permitted work to be more efficient and centrally controlled. Urbanization permitted industry to draw upon a concentrated workforce and to expedite systems of transportation, communication, and mass marketing. Immigration assured a large pool of laborers competing against each other for relatively low wages. But these were short-term gains. Over the long haul, such immediate advantages were likely to produce future liabilities. In the urban United States this is exactly what was happening. Cities became characterized by high rates of personal property crime, mental illness, alcoholism, divorce, and prostitution. For corporate owners and managers, such matters were omens of impending instability which demanded a new form of professional-technical problem solving. This they would obtain from the theoretical labor of the University of Chicago sociologists.

The Birth of Chicago Sociology: The Concept of Disorganization as a Liberal Tool for the Professional Management of Change

Having rejected the call of nativism, those who controlled the centralized corporate economy became advocates of a new form of problem solving. Social problems should be managed with the same professional detachment and technical efficiency as the business organization itself. During the 1920s this viewpoint resulted in a powerful coalition of business, governmental, and professional problem solving and the birth of a new U.S. political philosophy—liberalism. Unlike the reactionary nativists and the morally exultant progressivists of an earlier era, liberals accepted both the naturalness of social problems and their professionally managed resolution. Social problems were stripped of their moral and political character. Liberals did not view social problems as the bad deeds of people, but as the manageable by-products of such natural occurrences as rapid social change. While the management of programs of social adjustment might be carried out by public servants and government officials, a central tenet of liberalism was that the diagnosis and planned solution of social problems were the responsibilities of specialized professional problem solvers. With this in mind, let us return to our consideration of the sociologists at the University of Chicago in the 1920s.

The Chicago school and its theory of deviance as social disorganization is a classic example of the early liberal imagination. Chicago theorists produced a professional sociological diagnosis and solution for the instability resulting from social change. Their work found support among the business elite, in particular the philanthropic concerns of the Rockefellers. The Rockefellers had, after all, been instrumental in the founding and ongoing funding of the University of Chicago. The work of the Chicago sociologists was also connected to the public policy initiatives of the Chicago business community and to the intervention strategies of a new generation of salaried government problem solvers (welfare workers, youth workers, urban problem specialists, etc.). As James Carey suggests, "The Chicago sociologists responded 'both' to the concerns of this new salaried professional class" and "to the business-dominated urban society taking shape in the 1920's. . . . They did this by cooperating with certain elements within the business and welfare communities in an effort to alter the more undesirable features of urban institutional life."[31]

The theory of social disorganization helped propel the University of Chicago's department of sociology to a position of dominance within the discipline. As Roscoe and Gisela Hinkle point out, "during the period between the end of World War I and the Depression . . . the research, theorization, and graduate instruction at the University of Chicago gave its Department of Sociology an unprecedented preeminence."[32] In part, this was because disorganization theory was highly responsive to the post-World War I demands that sociology be grounded in the concreteness of inductive empirical research. Disorganization theorizing was from its onset a theory built upon the bedrock of empirical data—firsthand observations and detailed statistical analyses. No less important was the theory's responsiveness to the new managerial style of social problem solving in the United States. By viewing change as a natural social phenomenon, sociologists undermined the political positions of both the conservative right and the radical left of the new liberal managerial middle class.

In one grand sweep of sociological imagery, the Chicago theorists dismissed both the sentimental longings of the nativists and the structural critique of the radicals. By conceiving the negative consequences of rapid change as a deviant reaction of the naturally disorganized, rather than as discontented reaction of the structurally or historically disadvantaged, the Chicago school contributed to a depoliticalized image of social problems. This depoliticalization was viewed favorably both by the business community and by government problem-solving professionals. These groups had a clear stake in distinguishing between what they saw as social problems and what they saw as political problems. Social problems were viewed as naturally caused and technically correctable. Political problems were seen as the result of competing ideologies and resulted in little more than bitter partisan dispute. Yet, beneath this effort to distinguish the social from the political, there lay a deeper commitment to the fundamental structures of the existing social order.

The close and compatible relationship between the theoretical perspective of the Chicago school and demands for an apolitical scientific analysis of social problems during the rapidly changing 1920s is better understood by considering certain characteristics of Chicago as a city, of the University of Chicago as an institution, and of the Chicago sociologists as a social group. As a city, Chicago surrounded its sociologists with ever-present reminders of the massive changes that were occurring within U.S. society. The importance of this environmental inducement to study change was observed by Chicago sociologist Robert E. L. Faris, who describes the "vigorous city" of Chicago as a "supporting atmosphere" in which "the sociologists . . . were to find encouragement to dig and discover in amounts not customary in the gentler academic atmospheres where ivy sometimes grew faster than knowledge."[33]

As for the University of Chicago itself, a number of factors contributed to the early formulation of its unique brand of sociology. Foremost among these was the philanthropic backing which provided a stable financial base for its theoretical work, its research, and its application of knowledge to public problem solving. Foremost among its philanthropic supporters was John D. Rockefeller, whose corporate fortunes provided a total of $35 million to the university's funding. So too was the university supported by substantial gifts from Chicago-area donors who provided generous matches for the huge Rockefeller bequests.

There are numerous interpretations of the motives of wealthy philanthropists for donating to an institution of higher education. Some theorists emphasize the idea of stewardship—the belief by wealthy persons that they have a moral obligation to further the betterment of society. Others stress the lucrative tax breaks afforded by such donations. Still others emphasize the symbolic advantages of legitimating the equation of being wealthy with being good or the desire to direct the course and content of intellectual activity. All these things may have been a factor. Of greatest significance, however, may have been the simple fact that corporate giants like Rockefeller perceived the development of first-rate educational institutions as an essential element in producing the professional specialities and technical know-how needed to solve problems and provide the social stability necessary for the continued advance of profitable business. Nonetheless, corporate donations were often accompanied by directives as to how certain funds were to be spent. In the area of sociology this meant support for research aimed at the administrative or managerial control of the by-products of rapid change. Here one discovers a powerful coincidence between the theoretical concerns of the Chicago sociologists and the financial support of the business elite. In the words of James Carey, "The major impact of philanthropical support seems to have been . . . a more specific focus on urban problems which could be solved administratively."[34]

In addition to the financial backing of the wealthy philanthropists, the openness of university administrators to innovative ideas and approaches to research, the university's commitment to providing professional contributions to the management of public life, and the exposure of key members of the sociology department's senior faculty to the disciplined research model characteristic of German universities were important factors favoring the emergence of a new perspective on theory and research. Also important were the stable links with members of Chicago's local business and governmental elite. All of these things operated as institutional supporters for the development of a theoretical vision emphasizing both the naturalness and the solvability of problems related to rapid technologicalization, urbanization, and immigration.

A final factor contributing to the formulation of the kind of theory that was produced at the University of Chicago involves the social backgrounds of the Chicago sociologists themselves. Carey's recent study of this matter suggests that Chicago sociologists in the period from 1918 to the depression came from considerably different backgrounds than the founding generation of previous social scientists in the years before World War I.[35] The Chicagoans were far more heterogeneous, less religiously oriented, more urban, and more politically liberal. This means that the Chicago sociologists were similar to members of the emergent U.S. middle class of managers and professionals. No wonder they found congeniality with the problem-solving strategies of this class. They were part of it.

In short, the Chicago sociologists were much like the other new liberals. They were part of the emerging class of managerial and professional problem solvers who were attempting to guide social change toward stability. When professionals sought to manage and control such social problems as crime, mental disorders, family breakdown, and alcoholism, Chicago sociologists "stood by to help; they came from the same stratum as the new professionals and gave qualified acceptance to their views of what constituted problems." What kind of help did the Chicago sociologists offer? It came in the theoretical form of and had the control possibilities associated with their perspective on social disorganization. With this in mind, let us examine how the Chicago theorists first conceptualized the dynamics of disorganization and later employed socioecological models to study its differential impact.

The Dynamics of Disorganization: The Legacy of W. I. Thomas and Florian Znaniecki

The basic theoretical image of social disorganization was initially formulated by University of Chicago sociologist W. I. Thomas. Thomas was a dedicated reformer as well as an important and influential scholar. His advanced political ideas, flamboyant appearance, and bohemian lifestyle also made him a controversial figure at the university. In the summer of 1915, Thomas drew the ire of many of his conservative colleagues "when he addressed the Women's Equal Suffrage Association in Chicago and spoke in favor of enlarging access to birth control, removal of the legal status of 'illegitimate birth', and the right of unmarried women to bear children."[36] Thomas's intellectual accomplishments were many. They ranged from detailed ethnographic research to social psychological theory and the study of social disorganization. Yet, in 1918, Thomas was expelled from his faculty position in what sociologist Lewis Coser describes as "one of the most shameful chapters in the history of American Universities."[37] The impetus for Thomas's dramatic expulsion involved allegations by the FBI and the conservative *Chicago Tribune* that Thomas had violated the Mann Act, a federal statute outlawing the transportation of young women across state lines for "immoral purposes."

After examining the facts of the case, it appears that Thomas's real crime involved implications that he had had an affair with the wife of a U.S. Army officer who was away on duty in France. Formal legal charges, dubious as they were, were dropped. Professor Thomas was nonetheless dismissed by the university's president, Henry Pratt. Why? Given the University of Chicago's general reputation as a center for liberal or progressive thought, one wonders about the real issues behind the Thomas case. Why had the FBI been involved, in the first place? This question remains unanswered even today. There are, however, clues regarding the overreaching arm of federal law-enforcement officials. As Lewis Coser remarks, "it has been suggested that Thomas's wife was under surveillance for her pacifist activities and that the F.B.I. might have thought it expedient to discredit the husband so as to humiliate the wife."[38]

Although Thomas was forced to leave the University of Chicago, his ideas remained. His initial conceptualization of the problem of disorganization was a seed which germinated into a full-blown sociological perspective during the 1920s. The most succinct statement of this perspective is found in the classic study conducted by Thomas and his colleague Florian Znaniecki, *The Polish Peasant in Europe and America*.[39] According to Thomas and Znaniecki, social disorganization was to be defined "as a decrease of the influence of existing social rules of behavior upon individual members of the group."[40] Thomas and Znaniecki discovered just such a decrease in the lives of rural Polish peasants who had migrated to large U.S. cities in the early twentieth century. By analyzing the thematic content of letters, diaries, and other personal documents of Polish immigrants, Thomas and Znaniecki produced a detailed sociological story regarding the manner in which rapid social change dissipates the impact of social norms.

The Polish Peasant in Europe and America is a story of the disruptive forces accompanying immigration, of the disorientation of life caused by the rapid transportation of rural people with a different cultural tradition into the midst of the industrializing U.S. city. It is a story of social disorganization. In document after document, Thomas and Znaniecki discover evidence of the inability of immigrant families to exert social control over their members. The ways of the "old world" do not work in the "new world." Nor is it easy for immigrants to quickly assimilate the norms and standards of their new social environment. Immigrants are described as living in a world devoid of secure normative standards, as dwelling in a world of social disorganization. Without strong normative standards, immigrants develop an attitude that can best be described as a belief that "anything goes." This attitude facilitates a drift into deviance, a drift into delinquency, divorce, mental disorder, and the other forms of unruly behavior studied by the Chicago school.

Thomas and Znaniecki's depiction of social disorganization had a great influence on other sociologists working at the University of Chicago at the time. This is particularly evident in the writings of Robert Park. Park, a journalist and a humanitarian activist, had studied social philosophy and social science in Germany. His efforts to improve race relations in the United States attracted the attention of W. I. Thomas, who, in 1914, was instrumental in bringing Park into the sociology department at Chicago. While at Chicago, Park embarked upon a detailed study of changes in the U.S. social landscape, particularly changes associated with urbanization. In making sociological sense of these changes, Park drew heavily on the disorganizational framework introduced by Thomas. As Park stated, "The process by which the authority and influence of an earlier culture and system of social control is undermined and eventually destroyed is described by Thomas. . . . We are living in such a period of . . . social disorganization."[41]

The Ecology of Disorganization: The Legacy of Park and Burgess

Robert Park did more than simply adopt the basic conception of social disorganization proposed by W. I. Thomas. With his colleague Ernest Burgess, Park introduced an ecological model for the study of disorganization that is today the hallmark of the Chicago school's perspective on deviance. Ecology refers to the study of spatial relations between various species of living organisms. In attempting an ecological analysis of human society, Park and Burgess borrowed concepts from the field of plant ecology. Plant ecologists use the term *symbiosis* to denote the interdependent character of plants within a natural community of plants and other organisms. The life of each affects and is affected by all others within the superorganic community as a whole.

The image of symbiotic relationships between organisms within a superorganism had a certain attraction for Park. As an urban journalist, Park had observed the complex network of interrelated human parts that make up the life of the city. Viewing human social life in this fashion, Park made direct use of the terminology of plant ecologists. In *Human Communities,* he stated that "the urban community turns out to be something more than a mere congeries of peoples and institutions. . . . Its component elements, institutions, and persons are so intimately bound up that the whole tends to assume the character of . . . a superorganism."[42]

Ecologists assume a symbiotic interdependence of organisms within a given geographical community. They describe dangers in the activity of an ecological community in terms of a fourfold process involving (1) invasion by a competing species, (2) conflict for dominance between species, (3) the accommodation of weaker species to other species that demonstrate their dominance, and (4) assimilation of a new order of symbiosis based upon the accommodative outcomes of the previous three stages. Think, for instance, of the invasion of a pine forest by a competing species of oak tree. Conflict will occur. For a while the symbiotic organization of the forest will be in disarray. Eventually, the more powerful oaks will emerge as dominant. Pine trees will literally be uprooted. They will accommodate the oaks by replanting themselves in the soil of some adjacent area of the forest, where their own invasion must be accommodated by another, less deeply rooted, foliage, such as broom sedge. The new and old members of the previous pine forest will now be assimilated into a new symbiotic order based upon the dominance of oaks. The ecological community of the forest has thus been transformed.

Park and Burgess viewed change in human communities in a similar fashion. This had a particular importance for the study of deviance. The normative order of the well-organized community was viewed as a kind of social symbiosis which was disrupted by the invasion of some competing basis for social order. The forces of change that swept the U.S. landscape of the 1920s—rapid technologicalization, urbanization, immigration, and the like—were conceptualized as forces of invasion. Each was said to produce conflict for dominance within symbiotically interdependent human communities. This was another way of visualizing the process of social disorganization described by Thomas and Znaniecki. Throughout the stage of conflict for dominance, symbiotic coordination was lacking. The community lost its superorganic control over component parts. In human terms, the breakdown of normative structure represented a breakdown in social control. Deviance was widespread. It would remain at high levels until the processes of accommodation and assimilation were complete, until society became symbiotically reorganized around a new dominant form of normative order.

Using the ecological imagery of invasion, conflict, accommodation, and assimilation, Chicago sociologists attempted to identify "natural areas" of high or low deviance. High-deviance areas were spatially the most susceptible to the competitive invasion of the forces of rapid change. Low-deviance areas were least susceptible. In order to test this notion, social ecologists mapped out the "natural" physical spaces of the city into a ring of five concentric zones. Each zone possessed a unique population with a unique organizational style. The inhabitants of each zone possessed qualities, interests,

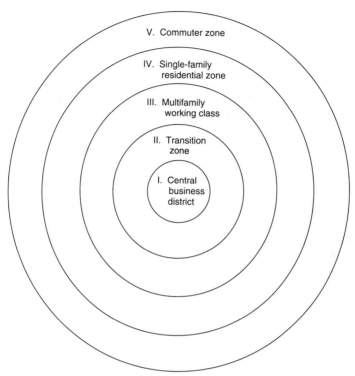

FIGURE 5-1
Concentric zones of deviance: The Park-Burgess model of natural urban areas. Ecological maps resembling that depicted above often accompany Chicago researchers' analysis of deviance. Rates of officially recorded deviance were typically highest in Zone II (transition zone) where forces of social change originating in Zone I (the central business district) were said to have the greatest impact. Rates decreased progressively through Zones III, IV, and V.

and cultural characteristics that were similar to each other but different from those of the inhabitants of other zones. Each zone, in other words, was organized or disorganized by virtue of a varying symbiotic relationship between its component parts and its organic whole.

The concentric zones mapped by Chicago theorists are displayed in Figure 5-1. At the center of the five urban zones was the central business district. This was literally the heart of the city, its center of organic power, the core of business, technology, and industry. This powerful zone was conceived as the dynamic force behind city life, as the focus of the primary energies of urbaniz- ation, as the source of urban social change. At the outer reaches of the city was the commuter zone. Here lived the wealthy commuters, whose spatial, social, and economic resources provided them with some buffer of stability against the forces of urbanization located in the central business district (Zone I). Zone III (a working-class neighborhood, characterized by the omnipresent arrangement of two- and three-family flats) and Zone IV (the old city neighborhood of one-family houses) were more affected, but spatially somewhat removed from the forces of social change located in the outwardly expanding central business district.

The zone most affected by change was the area into which the growing central business district constantly pushed. This was Zone II, the transition zone of most social disorganization and resultant deviance. At the very edge of the constantly expanding central business district, ecological theorists observed light industry, warehouses, and "hobohemia," a place of rootless people, vagabonds, and street bums. Immediately beyond lay the interstitial, or transition, zone. In plain language—a slum. In this natural area, the battle of competition-dominance was being fought. Its residents were the losers. Disorganized by rapid change, they were said to experience the highest rates of such measured deviance as delinquency, school truancy, adult crime, serious mental illness, prostitution, gambling, suicide, and taxi-dance halls (barlike establishments for the isolated and lonely). Each of these types of deviance was statistically measured by Chicago researchers. The prevalence of each decreased with increased ecological distance from the urban center of rapid change.

The Natural Areas of Deviance: Socioecological Studies of Disorganizational Deviance

The Chicago school emphasized the importance of maintaining a close connection between theory and empirical research. Let us briefly examine two areas in which their socioecological model was applied to the study of deviance—studies relating to the disorganizational causes of juvenile delinquency and mental disorders.

The Social Ecology of Delinquency: The Shaw and McKay Tradition
Clifford Shaw and Henry McKay were sociological researchers employed by a state-supported child-guidance clinic in Chicago—the Institute for Juvenile Research.[43] Although not formally affiliated with the University of Chicago, Shaw and McKay were greatly influenced by their close association with Ernest Burgess, who, with several students and other university faculty, maintained ongoing ties to a program of delinquency-prevention projects sponsored by the institute.

In 1929, Shaw, McKay, and their colleagues published *Delinquency Areas*, a classic work in the social disorganization study of delinquency. This report was based on the analysis of 55,998 juvenile court records compiled in the city of Chicago over a period of approximately thirty years.[44] In subsequent years, Shaw and McKay extended their analysis of the ecological distribution of delinquency to cities in other parts of the nation.[45] The findings of their research are supportive of the central tenets of disorganization theorizing. In mapping delinquency rates throughout the various zones of a city, Shaw and McKay discovered (1) that there was an uneven spatial distribution of the incidence of delinquency; (2) that the highest rates of delinquency occurred in the natural areas closest to the expanding central business district, and that rates decreased proportionately with distance from the center; (3) that certain ecological areas (slums or transition zones) were consistently characterized by the highest rates of delinquency, regardless of the changing ethnic composition of residents; and (4) that the areas highest in delinquency were also highest in a number of assumed indicators of social disorganization (e.g., demographic instability, high percentage of foreign-born residents, high percentage of nonwhites, low percentage of home ownership, high percentage of families on relief, and low median income).

Shaw and McKay interpreted their findings in accordance with the basic imagery of disorganization theory. The uneven spatial distribution of delinquency was explained by the fact that "in the areas of low rates of delinquents there is . . . uniformity, consistency, and universality of conventional values. . . . Whereas, in the high-rate areas, systems of competing and conflicting moral values have developed."[46] Similar logic explained the increased rates of delinquency for persons living in natural areas closest to the city's changing center. There "change involves the introduction of a new population with different institutions and practices" such that "institutional disruption and role discontinuity are to be expected."[47] For transition-zone adolescents, the problem may be doubly acute. They are in both a time (adolescence) when and a space (the slum) where "disorganization accompanying rapid change may be virtually complete."[48] Thus, children living in such communities are exposed to a variety of contradictory standards and forms of behavior rather than to a relatively consistent and conventional pattern."[49]

The pioneering research of Shaw and McKay prompted several subsequent studies of the social ecology of delinquency. In 1954, Bernard Lander examined the spatial distribution of 8,464 delinquency petitions filed in Baltimore, Maryland.[50] After analyzing rates of delinquency across 155 Baltimore census tracts, he concluded that high delinquency was associated with measures related to both lower-class standing and high social disorganization.

Shaw and McKay had also discovered that class was related to the delinquency distribution. As early as 1942, they reported that high-delinquency areas were also "low income areas, where there is the greatest deprivation and frustration." Why was this the case? Shaw and McKay proposed an answer that departs from the normative-breakdown focus of most disorganization theorizing. "Crime," they suggested, "may be regarded as one of the means employed by people to acquire . . . the economic and social values generally idealized in our culture, which persons in other circumstances acquire by conventional means."[51] In general, however, Shaw and McKay placed a greater emphasis on the role of disorganization factors. Although the deprivations of class might increase a person's motives for committing a crime, the causal factors with which they were most concerned were the disorganization forces which freed the individual from the scrutiny and control of conventional society.

Like Shaw and McKay, Lander emphasizes social disorganization rather than social class. Lander discovered that high-delinquency areas were characterized by overcrowding, low rents, low levels of owner occupancy, and low levels of education. The crux of his theory, however, is related to the racial composition of high-delinquency areas. If status deprivation increases delinquency, then one might reason that the areas with the highest percentage of nonwhite residents would also be highest in delinquency. To be nonwhite in America is, after all, to be in a position of status deprivation. Given the long history of racial discrimination, one can at least make a reasonable sociological argument along these lines. Lander's data do not support this interpretation. The rate of delinquency increases as the percentage of nonwhites increases from 0 to 50 percent. It decreases as the nonwhite percentage increases from 50 to 100 percent. To Lander this means that disorganization, as indicated by the "invasion" of communities by new culture groups (the 0 to 50 percent nonwhite condition), is what causes high delinquency. The 50 to 100 percent condition is associated with lower rates of delinquency because the changing ecological community has entered into a process of normative reorganization, or accommodation-assimilation. Lander attempts to buttress this controversial interpretation by suggesting that such factors as low percentage of owner-occupants and high percentage of renters are also indicators of disorganization—that they are better indicators of transience than of disadvantage.

In 1959, David Bordua published the results of research which attempted to replicate Lander's study in Detroit, Michigan.[52] The results were less favorable to a disorganization perspective. Bordua found the same relationships between lower-class, or status-deprivation, factors and high delinquency, but no evidence for the mixed racial area–disorganization interpretation. Bordua's study included an additional measure of social disorganization—the ratio of unattached individuals to intact families. This he found related to delinquency. The areas that had the highest ratios of unattached persons were also the areas with the highest rates of delinquency.

In 1964, Roland Chilton published a study which attempted to resolve the inconsistencies between the findings of Lander and Bordua.[53] After reanalyzing the earlier findings and presenting new data from Indianapolis, Chilton found no clear evidence favoring a disorganization interpretation. The only consistent data favoring the disorganization thesis involve percentage of home ownership. The percentage of nonwhites was not a significant factor. Nor were there consistent findings regarding such factors as proportion of unmarried men, high levels of residential mobility, or high numbers of persons per household (each of which had been used as an indicator of disorganization). Research in this area has advanced little beyond the conclusions drawn by Chilton. Inferences about the disorganization causes of delinquency remain ambiguous.

Psychoses in the Transition Zone: Social Disorganization and Mental Disorders   Chicago sociologists H. Warren Dunham and Robert E. L. Faris mapped the ecological distribution of public hospitalization for serious mental disorders.[54] In general, their findings supported a social disorganization interpretation. Rates of hospitalization were highest for residents of the transition zone and decreased proportionately to distance from the central business district. This pattern was applicable, however, only for schizophrenia, the diagnosed disorder which represented most of the cases. Schizophrenia is characteristically described as one of two disorders which compose the psychoses, the most serious category of mental illness. Schizophrenia is generally diagnosed as a severe distortion of reality accompanied by aural and/or visual hallucinations, and/or delusions (illusionary thoughts of self-perceptions not shared by others). According to Dunham and Faris, the ecological distribution of schizophrenia resembles that of social disorganization. Their research was heralded as an important breakthrough in the study of the social causation of psychiatric problems. According to Faris and Dunham, "The highest rates for schizophrenia are in hobohemia, the rooming-house, and foreign-born communities close to the center of the city . . . as these communities represent areas of some disorganization due to their close proximity to the steel factories.[55]

Manic-depressive psychosis did not fit the classic pattern of social disorganization. Manic-depressive psychosis is characterized by severe and uncontrollable mood swings, from giddy excitation to a deep and apathetic state of dejection. The Chicago data discovered that this form of mental disorder was distributed somewhat randomly throughout all zones of the city. Dunham speculated that this finding might be the result of a systematic error or bias on the part of psychiatric diagnosticians—i.e., that psychiatrists do not "see" this disorder when diagnosing persons from disorganized areas because they perceive them as more likely to be schizophrenic. He was also open to the possibility that social factors may play less of a causative role in the generation of manic depression than in the development of schizophrenia—that "there is a certain justification for asserting the priority of hereditary and constitutional factors."[56]

The research by Dunham and Faris was a landmark in the sociological study of mental disorders. Yet, within a short time medically oriented critics raised an important question about their disorganization thesis. Why assume that disorganization caused schizophrenia? Wasn't it equally possible that seriously disturbed schizophrenics drifted into disorganized areas because they could not cope with life in the city's more organized zones?

Faris and Dunham sought to answer this criticism (the so-called downward-drift hypothesis) by obtaining data on the residential patterns of the fathers of hospitalized schizophrenics. They found no evidence of downward drift. The parents of schizophrenics lived basically in the same ecological areas as their offspring. The downward-drift hypothesis was examined again in other studies in New Haven, Connecticut, Hagerstown, Maryland, and Buffalo, New York, and was found lacking there as well.[57]

A more damaging critique is not as easily dismissed. This criticism applies not only to Dunham and Faris but to social disorganization research in general. The point is that studies in this tradition typically fail to separate social disorganization from organized social disadvantage, social stratification, and lower-class status. I shall return to this critique in the closing section of this chapter.

The Theoretical Imagery of Disorganization: A Summary Comment

The social disorganization perspective departs from the individualistic focus of previous theorizing by emphasizing factors associated with the social causation of deviance—rapid social change resulting in a breakdown in normative social control. The social-ecological approach permitted disorganization researchers to study the natural areas of the city in which these causative factors were most powerful. Chicago theorists also obtained firsthand accounts from the people who were most affected by the forces of change and disorganization. I conclude my discussion of the theoretical imagery of disorganization with an excerpt from one such account: Clifford Shaw's *The Jack Roller*.[58] Shaw presents a detailed life history of a young man lured into delinquency by the forces of disorganization. In the following passage, Shaw describes the causal impact of the disorganized transition zone. The concluding reference to West Madison Street's exclusive "Four Hundred" is an allusion to the corporate offices located in Chicago's central business district, the nucleus of change and the primary source of social disorganization.

> The lures and the irresistible call drew me on like a magnet and I was always helpless before them. I was like a canoe on a storm-swept sea, buffeted here and there, helpless and frail. I had about as much chance of controlling my desires as of braving the storm. But here I mingled with bums and derelicts like myself, and people did not stare at my rags and misery. Here I felt at home, for "misery loves company." So, I drifted on with the rest of the human driftwood carried on by the current of W. Madison Street's exclusive "Four Hundred" or more.[59]

IDENTIFYING DISORGANIZATIONAL DEVIANCE

The study of social disorganization by University of Chicago sociologists combined two different traditions of social research. The first tradition emphasized efforts to objectively measure external factors and conditions which were believed to affect the organization or disorganization of society. Chicago researchers employed this tradition to develop statistical maps of natural areas within the city. These maps were said to reveal the spatial or ecological origins and consequences of social disorganization. The second Chicago research tradition emphasized the subjective side of social life. It sought to explore the meaning of social life as experienced by people themselves. It involved such things as in-depth interviews, firsthand observations, and the recording of life histories.

The willingness to combine external-objective and internal-subjective approaches to the study of social life was a definite strength of the early Chicago studies. Today these two different research traditions often represent points of irreconcilable division among sociologists. Some researchers adhere almost dogmatically to the external-objective tradition. They argue that social research must be quantitative or statistical if it is to be scientific. Zealous adherents to the internal-subjective tradition argue the opposite. Sociologists committed to qualitative or field methods often contend that it is necessary to first understand the meaning of human action before attempting to explain patterns or structures of action.

This division over the proper methods of social research is as old as the discipline of sociology itself. Since the early part of the nineteenth century, students of society have debated whether sociology should aspire to the status of a natural science or whether its distinctive subject matter (reflective human beings who create, maintain, and change social institutions in history) requires a special form of investigation. In nineteenth-century Europe this question prompted social theorists like Wilhelm Dilthey to argue for the formation of a distinctively human science (*Geisteswissenschaften*) based on the principles of subjective understanding, as opposed to natural science (*Naturwissenschaften*), which stressed the formulation of objective causal laws.[60]

In the United States this methodological debate surfaced dramatically in the period following World War I. Although sociologists of both methodological persuasions stressed the need for rigorous empirical research, lines were drawn between those who advocated quantitative approaches and those who advocated qualitative approaches.[61] These antagonisms were dissolved by the early Chicago researchers, who combined both traditions. The result was a detailed body of empirical literature that is broad in quantitative scope and deep in qualitative description.

The methodological eclecticism of the early Chicago researchers was nurtured by the complementary theoretical insights of W. I. Thomas and Robert Park. Thomas reminded students of the importance of considering the way that people define their own social situations. Park stressed the importance of external societal constraints in shaping the situations in which people found themselves. For Park, spatial or ecological factors were of greatest importance. Yet, despite the difference in theoretical emphasis, Thomas and Park were close and mutually respectful colleagues who, in Thomas's words, "enjoyed a very long and profitable association."[62] Exposure to Thomas and Park provided members of the Chicago school with a sense that a full scientific study of social disorganization required a look at both its external-objective and its internal-subjective dimensions. As such, the empirical investigation of deviance by the Chicago sociologists represented a pioneering effort in the areas of both sociological statistics and field research.

Sociological Statistics on Disorganization

Social disorganization researchers charted the distribution of many types of deviance across the landscape of urban America. Using statistics drawn from the official records of the police, the criminal courts, hospitals, mental institutions, and other public agencies, they methodically plotted the known presence of deviant populations throughout the various zones of the city. These data provided empirical support for theoretical claims regarding the impact of "naturally" disorganized areas in producing high rates of deviance.

An excellent illustration of the Chicago researchers' use of sociological statistics is found in the quantitative studies of delinquency conducted by Clifford Shaw and Henry McKay.[63] Shaw and McKay employed three different types of statistical mapping techniques: spot maps, rate maps, and zone maps. Spot maps pinpointed the residential patterns of juvenile offenders in accordance with their level of involvement in the criminal justice system. Hence maps depicting the residential concentration of arrested offenders could be compared with maps for convicted offenders, and so forth. Rate maps were used to show the percentage of the entire juvenile population involved in this or that stage of the criminal justice system. This second form of map was constructed for 140 separate square-mile areas. When compared to spot maps, rate maps suggested that the areas with the highest percentage of delinquency were not necessarily those with the highest numbers of delinquents. The reason for this involved the fact that certain high-rate areas had smaller absolute numbers of juvenile residents. Yet when it was a third form of map—the zone map—the pattern most distinctively associated with the disorganization perspective was revealed. Zone maps depicted distance from the central city, i.e., distance from the believed nucleus of urban change. Spot and rate maps suggested considerable variation in the distribution and rate of delinquency from one specific area to the next. Nonetheless, zone maps depicted a general concentration of youth crimes in zones closest to the central business district.

Field Research into Social Disorganization

The field studies of the early Chicago researchers complemented their statistical investigations. Some researchers, such as Clifford Shaw, contributed as much to the qualitative exploration of deviant life as to the quantitative mapping of rates of deviation. Notable among the early field studies were Shaw's *The Jack Roller* and his collaborative contributions to *The Natural History of a Delinquent Career* and *Brothers in Crime*.[64] Other field-research portraits of deviant life under the sway of social disorganization include *The Unadjusted Girl*,W. I. Thomas's intimate examination of the life of a prostitute; *The Hobo: The Sociology of the Homeless Man* by Nels Anderson; *The Ghetto* by Louis Wirth, *Gold Coast and Slum* by Harvey W. Zorbaugh, and *The Taxi-Dance Hall: A Sociological Study of Commercialized Recreation and City Life* by Paul G. Cressey.[65]

Howard Becker compares the scientific enterprise to a mosaic.[66] Each piece adds a little to the understanding of the whole. This is a good metaphor for describing the way in which statistical and field reports on disorganization fed into and illuminated one another. As Clifford Shaw suggested, field data were used "not only as a means of making preliminary explorations" but as the basis of "hypotheses . . . tested by the comparative study of other detailed case histories and by the formal methods of statistical analysis.[67]

SOCIAL CONTROL OF DISORGANIZATIONAL DEVIANCE

Social control was a key concept in the early writings of the Chicago school. According to Robert Park, "social control was the central fact and the central problem of society." Yet, because of their self-defined mission of creating an objective social science, the Chicago theorists disclaimed interest in advocating a particular strategy of social control. The Chicago sociologists were, in other words, eager to dissociate themselves from the image of sociology as social reform. In the words of Park, "It is probably not the business of the universities to agitate reforms nor to attempt directly to influence public opinion in regard to current issues. To do this is to relax [their] critical attitude, lessen [their] authority in matters of fact."[68]

Despite this posture of scientific neutrality the social disorganization perspective spawned a distinctive approach to the problem of social control. What distinguishes its program of control from those discussed previously is its goal of treating society rather than treating individuals. This control strategy is intimately associated with the perspective's vision of the disorganized society as the principal cause of the deviance of its members. Disorganization theorists believed that it would be a major mistake to treat individuals in isolation from the societal roots of their disorganizational malaise. Consider the following remarks by Clifford Shaw and Henry McKay:

> Successful treatment of the problem of delinquency in large cities will entail the development of programs which seek to effect changes in the conditions of life in specific local communities and in whole sections of the city. Diagnosis and supervision of the individual offender will probably not be sufficient to achieve this end.[69]

Shaw and McKay suggest that effective control programs must restore normative stability within disorganized communities. In 1932 this strategy of social reorganization was put into practice with the founding of the Chicago Area Project. This public experiment in neighborhood reorganization was coordinated by the Institute for Juvenile Research, where Shaw and McKay worked as researchers. Utilizing twenty-two different neighborhood centers in six areas of the city, the Chicago Area Project operated continuously for twenty-five years until the death of Shaw in 1957.

The Chicago Area Project represented an effort to translate disorganization theorizing into a practical program of delinquency prevention. Local residents were placed in positions of key organizational decision making. Moreover, most staff were recruited from among the residents of so-called disorganized neighborhoods. In this sense, the organizational structure of the program was itself a vehicle for planned social reorganization. Under the leadership of neighborhood representatives the program sought to prevent delinquency by

two broad strategies. The first involved coordinating the community resources of a wide variety of otherwise fragmented and even competing
groups. Efforts were made to solicit the joint efforts of schools, churches,
labor unions, industrial and business interests, clubs, and other local groups
in organizing to collectively combat community problems. The second project
strategy involved sponsoring a host of specific youth-activity programs. It
was hoped that organized participation in such programs would reduce
currents of social disorganization and that potentially deviant youths would
be given a lifeline back to the normative shores of the well-organized society.

Three types of youth-activity programs operated under the auspices of the
Chicago Area Project. The first was specifically geared toward the reduction
of criminal or delinquent behavior. It included such things as sending field
workers out to become involved with and to counsel members of neighborhood youth groups, aiding youths who had been placed in training schools
for delinquents and who were preparing for parole, and assisting police
officers and court personnel in developing special youth-oriented program-
ming. Two other types of project activities related more indirectly to the
prevention of delinquency. The first involved a host of general neighborhood-
improvement programs. These involved such things as upgrading health and
sanitation conditions and strengthening education, law enforcement, environmental conservation, and traffic safety. The second focused on expanding
recreational resources. Summer camps were opened. Church basements,
storefronts, and unused spaces in police stations were employed to provide
youths with constructive recreational alternatives to life on the street. When
considered as a whole, the central objectives of these diverse programs were,
as Terrence Morris points out, "to develop a positive interest by the inhabitants in their own welfare, to establish democratic bodies of local citizens who
would enable the whole community to become aware of its problems and to
attempt their solution by common action."[70]

How successful were the activities of the Chicago Area Project in realizing
its goals of community reorganization and delinquency prevention? Sympathetic commentators such as Martin Haskell and Lewis Yablonsky have
praised its organizational efforts and have suggested that "in all probability
delinquency was reduced."[71] Such praise may be based more on faith than on
concrete data. The practical accomplishments of the Chicago Area Project
were, unfortunately, never thoroughly and systematically evaluated.[72] As
Allen Liska points out, "The Chicagoans were more concerned with imple-
menting the policy implications of their theory and research than [with]
evaluating the success of their programs."[73]

A somewhat similar project in Boston was evaluated by Walter Miller.
Miller's analysis of Boston's "total-community delinquency control project"
provides clues to the strengths and weaknesses of control strategies based
upon the disorganization perspective.[74] Miller examined the impact of the
Boston reorganization project over a three-year period. His findings were

mixed. On one hand, he discovered that the project succeeded in promoting close ties between community organizers and local youth gangs and in organizing many gangs into more conventional, clublike associations. The Boston total-community project also increased recreational outlets and access to educational and occupational opportunities, fostered greater citizen involvement in local community programs, and stimulated higher levels of interagency cooperation. Regarding the prevention of delinquency the project was much less successful. It had only a "negligible impact."[75] Miller's assessment draws heavily upon the field reports that were recorded daily by the project's outreach workers. Workers were asked to classify the behavior of youths with whom they had contact. Behavior was classified as moral or immoral (as judged by the conventional moral standards of society) and as legal or illegal. Miller assumed that success in reducing delinquency would be reflected in trends recorded by the outreach workers. As the community became more organized, the behavior of youths should hypothetically become more moral and more legal.

This failed to happen. The ratio of moral to immoral conduct remained constant throughout the project's duration. There was, however, a slight decrease in the classification of known illegal acts. This improvement was, unfortunately, counterbalanced by an increase in the number of major or serious illegal acts committed. Thus the project as a whole appeared to do little to reduce the general level of delinquency, particularly serious delinquency. This finding was corroborated by another type of data—statistics on court appearances recorded before, during, and after the term of the project. Miller compared the court appearances of boys with project contact with a control group of similar boys not involved in the project. No measurable differences were found.

Miller's evaluation of the Boston project does not speak well for the practical utility of the preventive social control program suggested by disorganization theory. Gains were made in general community reorganization but not in the reduction of delinquency. Does this mean that the Chicago theorists were incorrect? This is the conclusion reached by critic Terrence Morris, who declares that disorganization and deviance may both be products of yet another factor—structured social inequality.[76] From Morris's point of view, efforts at neighborhood reorganization that do not address this deeper structural factor are doomed to fail. At best they treat symptoms of the deeper problem of inequality while "leaving the malady untouched." We will return to this issue later. For now it is sufficient to note the general nature of control efforts derived from disorganization theorizing. Following the lead of the Chicago sociologists, programs such as the Chicago Area Project and Boston's total-community project sought to put into practice what the perspective preached—that deviance can best be controlled by controlling the disorganizational impact of rapid social change. Although its practical efficacy has not been confirmed by sound evaluation data, this strategy of control represents a major departure from the individualistically oriented control models: the redemptive, the punitive, and the therapeutic, suggested, respectively, by demonic, classical, and pathological theorizing.

THE SOCIAL DISORGANIZATION PERSPECTIVE TODAY

Historical Background

As described above, the social disorganization perspective arose during the 1920s in the scholarly writings and empirical research of the Chicago school. In subsequent decades this perspective exerted an enormous influence on the study and control of deviant behavior in America. For a period of time social disorganization became the dominant theoretical imagery for thinking about such matters. As Don Gibbons points out, "During the 1950's, a generation of undergraduate students was introduced to formulations that attributed a variety of socially undesirable behavior . . . to social disorganization."[77]

A short time later the social disorganization perspective began to lose its powerful grip on the sociological imagination. In part this was because of the criticisms which I will discuss in the closing pages of this chapter. In part it was because of the emergence of alternative formulations of the deviance problem: the functionalist, anomie, and learning perspectives discussed in subsequent chapters. In part it was because of the waning influence of the University of Chicago as "the" center for U.S. sociology. Following the death of several of its key founding figures in the late 1930s, the unprecedented dominance of the Chicago school passed eastward to the elite universities of the Atlantic seaboard.[78] Thus, the gradual decrease in use of disorganizational imagery to explain deviance is due, in part, to intellectual and organizational changes within the field of sociology itself.

While this is undoubtedly true, it may also be the case that the decline in disorganization thinking reflects a change in American social life in general. The decline in disorganization theorizing was paralleled by a decline in the rate of uncontrolled industrialization, urbanization, and immigration. Laws have greatly reduced the levels of immigration, while for many, urbanization and industrialization have become routine features of everyday life. As a result, "social disorganization theory may be less applicable to contemporary America than to a bygone era."[79]

Disorganizational Deviance in Developing Countries

Despite its decline in dominance the social disorganization perspective continues to influence contemporary studies of deviance. One area of research in which disorganizational imagery has shown a particular vitality involves the study of deviance in developing countries. In such settings one might suspect the metaphor of disorganization to still be applicable because within developing nations the processes of industrialization and urbanization are still in their early and potentially most disruptive stages. Recent work by S. Kirson Weinberg on the problem of juvenile delinquency in Accra, Ghana,[80] and by Marshall Clinard and Daniel Abbott on property crime in Kampala, Uganda,[81] illustrates the use of the disorganization framework in the cross-cultural study of deviance in developing nations.

Weinberg's research tests Shaw and McKay's theories about the ecological distribution of disorganizational deviance. Although Weinberg's work lacks the rigor of the statistical mapping techniques used by the Chicago researchers, his descriptive ethnographic data point toward similar conclusions. Areas with high delinquency were high in social disorganization. Delinquent youths were concentrated in areas where families had migrated from northern rural settings into urban slums characterized by physical deterioration, high rates of adult crime, alcoholism, poverty, unskilled labor, poor education, disintegration of traditional family structures, and a decline of social control. In such places as contemporary Accra, youths are said to be exposed to "processes of susceptibility to delinquency" similar to those previously discovered in Chicago.[82] Traditional mechanisms of tribal social control were broken by the rapid process of urbanization and industrial change. The tight web of tribal values and norms was torn asunder. Integrated tribes were transformed into disintegrated ethnic groups. The bonds of social control were loosened, and with this loosening, Weinberg notes, there was an increase in delinquent behavior.[83]

Clinard and Abbott were concerned with similar questions of social disintegration. They gathered perceptual and official-indicator data on the extent of property crime in two slum areas of Kampala. The two slums were similar when considered in terms of their deteriorated physical conditions. Yet, in terms of property crime the two communities were radically different. The first, Kiseruji, was high in property crime. The second, Namuwongo, was low. Why? The answer, according to Clinard and Abbott, is found in differences in the degree of normative social organization between the two communities. Clinard and Abbott employed the Liberson technique, a means of estimating the tribal homogeneity or heterogeneity of each community, and a series of interviews with community members to document and explore the nature of such differences. Following the logic of social disorganization, Clinard and Abbott sought to discover whether the higher crime rates of the Kiseruji slum were associated with such indicators of normative breakdown as lesser degrees of tribal homogeneity, lower levels of communicative integration, less family stability, and higher residential mobility.

Clinard and Abbott's findings reflect positively on the social disorganization perspective. Both communities were very poor and living under conditions of social disadvantage. For this reason Clinard and Abbott ruled out differences in economic conditions as a factor accounting for differences in the level of property crime. Significant differences were found, however, in areas of normative social organization. The low-crime Namuwongo slum was discovered to be more homogeneous, in terms of both population mix and shared tribal customs. When compared to the high-crime Kiseruji community, Namuwongo was also characterized by a lower rate of residential change and higher rates of intimate communication and visiting between nonfamilial residents; greater family stability; and more participation in community organizations, including religious organizations. Clinard and Abbott reasoned that the low-crime community was thus better organized to exercise normative control over its members. Higher property crime in the less-organized slum was thus seen as a function of its weaker web of normative social control.

Other Contemporary Uses of Disorganizational Imagery

In addition to studies of deviance in developing countries the disorganization perspective continues to influence research conducted within modern western societies. One important example is found in Marshall Clinard's *Cities with Little Crime: The Case of Switzerland*.[84]

Switzerland represents an exception to the observation that high rates of crime follow high rates of industrialization and urbanization. Clinard measured Swiss crime by a variety of indicators: studies of public concern over crime; official crime rates; crime victimization surveys; insurance rates for burglary, theft, and auto theft; and the extent of crime as reported in the newspapers.[85] When controlled for a high level of affluence, a characteristic which Swiss society shares with such countries as Sweden, the United States, and the Federal Republic of Germany, the problem of crime was seen as far lower in Switzerland. The contrast with Sweden is most instructive. Switzerland and Sweden rank numbers one and two respectively in terms of per capita affluence. Both are also high in industrialization and urbanization. Nonetheless, the Swiss have far lower crime rates. Why? Clinard suggests an explanation which falls, in large part, within the theoretical scope of the social disorganization perspective.

The Swiss, a people with multiple languages and ethnic communities, appear far more heterogeneous than the Swedes. According to Clinard, "In sharp contrast to the Swiss diversity, Swedes are remarkably homogeneous." Swedes possess a unitary language, a state religion (on paper if not in practice), and a common cultural heritage. If heterogeneity were equated with disorganization one would expect the Swiss to rank higher in crime. Yet the opposite is true. The Swiss, for all their diversity, have lower crime rates than the homogeneous Swedes."[86] This Clinard explains by reference to three general social factors which promote the tight normative organization of Swiss society: (1) the slow development of urbanization, (2) a tradition of political decentralization and local responsibility; and (3) a tradition of age integration.

Switzerland is today highly urbanized. A great percentage of its citizenry live in metropolitan areas. Nonetheless, as a process urbanization has been gradual rather than sudden and disruptive. Its spread has been dispersed across several moderate-sized cities (Zurich, Basel, and Geneva) rather than concentrated, as in the case of Sweden, in one superurban area (Stockholm). Although Switzerland is heterogeneous as a nation, migration to particular Swiss cities has been relatively homogeneous. Different waves of linguistically and ethnically similar migrants have gradually followed one another into the same urban areas. This buffered the disruptive impact of rapid rural-to-urban population change. As a result, Switzerland was spared the radical disjuncture between the rural and the urban, a disjuncture characteristic of urbanization in other western nations, including Sweden. From a social disorganization point of view this is significant. Switzerland became urbanized but not normatively disrupted. According to Clinard, "even after years of residence in large cities, most persons still think of 'home' as their traditional canton. . . . A large proportion of urban inhabitants have never broken in spirit with the soil or the rugged mountain lands of their ancestors."[87]

The gradual urbanization of Switzerland may have minimized disorganization. Also important may be the long Swiss tradition of political decentralization. Clinard points out that the Swiss distrust the delegation of much responsibility to the national, or federal, level of government. Swiss society is characterized by its high levels of citizen participation in localized democratic rule and by an almost "ingrained faith in mutual help and solidarity."[88] Its nearly 6 million people are politically subdivided into twenty-five semi-autonomous cantons and half-cantons. Each canton is largely governed by its own legislature and controls its own educational institutions, its courts, and its police. Cantons are, in turn, divided into some 3,000 communes, smaller political units which handle the collection of taxes, the maintenance of public buildings, the selection of teachers, and the administration of elections and relief funds. This decentralization contrasts sharply with Sweden's large, centralized, impersonal federal bureaucracies. Sweden's bureaucracies ensure material welfare but contribute little to a feeling of direct, interpersonal social control. Individuals may feel, instead, that their lives are governed by vast, impersonal forces beyond their immediate and direct experience.

The opposite is said about Switzerland. High levels of direct participation in decentralized government are said to instill a widespread feeling among the Swiss "that they are their own masters."[89] Such widespread political participation nurtures a deep sense of involvement in the affairs of others. When combined with observations about high levels of age integration within Swiss society, Clinard's analysis suggests that reciprocal involvement and mutual responsibility strengthen the normative web of Switzerland—closing the door upon disruptive social disorganization and resultant high levels of deviance. As Clinard points out, "in Switzerland everyone is his own policeman."[90]

Clinard's account of the low Swiss crime rate is by no means the only recent study to apply social disorganizational imagery to the study of deviance in western society. Michalowski's study of vehicular homicide can also be interpreted within the general boundaries of the disorganization framework.[91] Michalowski discovered that people held responsible for automobile fatalities tended to come from ecological zones traditionally associated with disorganization. Such people had also been bombarded with such disorganizing experiences as recent marital trouble, loss of employment, emotional turmoil, and/or alcohol abuse. Sollenberger has also invoked disorganizational imagery to account for the traditionally low incidence of violent crime in tightly knit, family-oriented Chinese-American communities.[92] Extremely low divorce rates, positive attitudes toward spouses, strong beliefs in the moral authority of the family, high aspirations for children, and clear normative prohibitions against aggressiveness were said to combine in producing organized social controls against fighting and physical assault.

Contemporary Control Theory: A Social-Psychological Extension of the Disorganization Model

According to the basic logic of the disorganization perspective, social disorganization is likely to be followed by personal disorganization. A breakdown in normative controls increases the likelihood that individuals will experience a similar breakdown in moral constraints in their everyday behavior. Why? Disorganization theorists point, at least implicitly, in the direction of socialization. Socialization, the process through which one generation of people passes its beliefs, values, and normative constraints to another, is disrupted by social disorganization. The power of traditional beliefs, values, and norms is dissipated by a disorganized moral climate in which "anything goes." At the individual level this means that many people will fail to develop the self-censoring consciences which are said to regulate behavior in the well-organized society. Simply stated, disorganization theorists assume that (1) the presence of normative chaos results in disrupted socialization, and (2) disrupted socialization results in weakened internal normative constraint.

The first part of the chain linking disorganization, disrupted socialization, and deviance was documented in such early disorganization research efforts as Thomas and Znaniecki's *The Polish Peasant in Europe and America.* There an analysis of the letters and autobiographical reflections of recent immigrants revealed a stark picture of the inability of one generation to successfully socialize its young. A more precise formulation of the second part of the chain, the part linking disrupted socialization with the actual occurrence of deviant behavior, awaited the development of contemporary control theory. Control theory, as prefigured in the work of Walter Reckless, another member of the Chicago school, and refined in recent years by Travis Hirschi, examines factors associated with the production of social conformity. Control theory and disorganization theory are commonly concerned with processes which lessen the likelihood that people will be normatively constrained. For this reason control theory may be read as a social-psychological extension of the concerns of the Chicago school.[93] While early Chicagoans examined the deterioration of normative constraints, control theorists have focused on the manner in which this deterioration results in nonconformity or deviance. Control theorists make explicit something left implicit in most disorganizational theorizing—the link between disrupted or inadequately constraining socialization and the likelihood of acting deviantly.

Reckless's Version of Control Theory: The Principle of Containment

Walter Reckless was one of the first generation of graduate students to study sociology at the University of Chicago. A student of Park, Reckless was also a skilled firsthand observer of life in a city beset by the forces of social disorganization. He defrayed some of the cost of his education by playing the fiddle in a cafe reputedly controlled by the mobster Al Capone. In such settings Reckless noted that while the general processes of social disorganization may have unhinged the normative constraints of many persons, many others were never drawn into a life of deviance. To Reckless this meant that social-structural factors, such as social disorganization, were mediated by social-psychological factors surrounding the process of socialization. Reckless conceived of these factors as those of *inner containment* and *outer containment.*

For Reckless, inner containment consists largely of such factors as "self-control, good self-concept, ego strength, well-developed superego, high frustration tolerance, high resistance to diversions, high sense of responsibility, goal orientation, ability to find substitute satisfactions, tension-reducing rationalizations, and so on."[94] Such inner constraints or containments, once produced in the process of socialization, were said to isolate an individual from pushes or pulls in the direction of deviance or nonconformity. Such inner containment factors existed, however, in a kind of dynamic tension with the relative presence or absence of a host of outer containment factors. According to Reckless the forces of outer containment represent a "structural buffer in the person's immediate social world."[95] When strong this buffer reinforces the control power of inner containment. When weak it chips away at the forces of inner containment. According to Reckless, the buffer of outer containment includes such things as a consistent presentation of moral values; institutional support for belief in and realization of internalized norms, goals, and expectations; clear social delineation of roles, rules, and responsibilities; the effective operation of supervision and discipline; the availability of safety valves for letting off steam in a nondeviant fashion; and the opportunity for acceptance, identity, and belongingness.

During periods of high social disorganization a variety of external containment factors would, by definition, be lacking. Thus Reckless's theory of containment accounts, at least in principle, for resultant social-psychological strains in the direction of nonconformity. Nonetheless, Reckless contends that strong inner containment factors may still shield people from the lure of deviance.[96] According to containment theory the study of deviance must always consider the relative strengths and dynamic interplay between two generic forces of control—inner and outer supports for conformity.

Hirschi's Control Therapy: Failure of the Social Bond

Reckless's containment theory examines the ways people become insulated from pressures to deviate. Travis Hirschi's theory is presented in his 1969 book, *Causes of Delinquency*.[97] It focuses on the social bonds which tie people to the normative web of conventional society. Like the disorganization perspective as a whole, Hirschi's theory locates the cause of delinquency or deviance in the processes which set people free from the bonds of normative constraint. According to Hirschi, "delinquent acts result when an individual's bond to society is weak or broken."[98] Unlike most disorganization theorists, Hirschi attempts to specify several dimensions of the social bonding process which, when underdeveloped or disrupted, increase the likelihood of deviant behavior.

For Hirschi, social bonding has both inner and outer dimensions. Its inner dimension is characterized by socialization into a set of conventional beliefs about how one should act, toward whom, where, and when. A similarity in beliefs is said to induce a similarity in behavior. Thus, socialization into a society's conventional belief system is a central feature of bonding or social control. Conventional beliefs, however, are not always followed by conventional action. Sometimes, the push or pull of external forces may lead individuals to act in a manner inconsistent with or in contradiction to their internalized beliefs. Imagine yourself a teenager who honestly believes that shoplifting is wrong. In most instances, this might mean that you would not even consider shoplifting. Yet, on a particular evening, affected by the exhortations of peers to prove that you are one of the gang, angry with your parents for treating you like a child, bolstered by the intoxication of camaraderie and booze, feeling that you have nothing to lose, isn't it possible that your beliefs will take a backseat to the immediacy of your desires for acceptance and adventure? This possibility prompts Hirschi to consider several outer dimensions of social bonding which, like the internalization of conventional beliefs, operate as social-psychological controls against the likelihood of deviant behavior.

The outer dimensions of social bonding are described in terms of attachment, commitment, and involvement. *Attachment* refers to the strength of a person's ties to others, particularly to other persons who conform to society's normative standards. For Hirschi, relational ties to one's parents and conventional peers are the most emphasized sources of attachment. Strongly attached people are pictured as very sensitive to the opinions of others. They have a great investment in achieving or maintaining the respect of those with whom they associate. If someone's associates are conventionally oriented, then the greater the attachment to them, the less likely a person is to deviate from conventionality.

Commitment refers to the degree to which a person is tied to conventional ways of behaving by virtue of the social rewards obtained by acting in accordance with the prevailing norms. The logic of commitment is this: the more people gain by acting conventionally, the more they stand to lose by deviating, and thus the less likely they are to break from the prevailing norms. Consider the professor who is also a homosexual. In which situation is the professor more likely to be public about her or his personal sexual preferences: a situation in which she or he is currently being reviewed for tenure at a small, rural, conservative Southern Baptist college or a situation in which she or he already has the guarantee of tenure at a large, urban, liberally oriented university in the San Francisco Bay area? According to the logic of commitment, the answer is obvious. The professor would have much more to lose in the first situation than the second. Hence, she or he is more likely to play it straight in the first situation, and more likely to come straightforwardly out of the closet in the second.[99]

Involvement, the third of Hirschi's outer dimensions of social bonding, refers to the proportion of a person's time engaged in the pursuit of conventionality. The logic here is that if a great percentage of someone's time (and perhaps energy as well) is taken up by "appointments, deadlines, working hours," etc., then there is little time left over for potential deviance. This, perhaps, is what those who direct seminaries or administer boarding schools mean by the old saying, "A busy mind is a pure mind." By totally scheduling the lives of their young residents, by filling even periods of "free time" with mandatory participation in supervised athletics, rectors and headmasters have long sought to curb thoughts of sex and other supposed lures toward deviance.

Taken as a whole, Hirschi's fourfold analysis of inner and outer bonding mechanisms represents a social-psychological consideration of forces which control or constrain persons to stay within the straight and narrow boundaries of the established normative order. According to disorganization theorizing, rapid social change destroys the control power of the normative order. Hirschi's depiction of the bonding process permits us to imagine more concretely how this happens. Change disrupts one or more of the components of bonding, weakening or suspending the power of internalized beliefs and/or external attachments, commitments, and involvements.

In order to obtain a systematic measure of the adequacy of his theory, Hirschi presented self-administered questionnaires to a sample of approximately 1,300 Richmond, California, boys in grades 6 through 12. He asked them to report on delinquent activities which they had been involved in, and he sought to determine their levels of social bonding. To determine the degree to which youths were attached to conventional associations, he asked about their attachment to parents, peers, and school officials. Students were presented with such questions as "Would you like to be the kind of person your father is?" To determine commitment to a system rewarding conformity, he asked about the importance students placed upon getting good grades. To determine involvement in conventional, or deviance-precluding, activities, he obtained information on time spent in various school-oriented projects. The conventionality of internalized beliefs was measured by questions assessing such things as respect for the law or the police.

In general, Hirschi's research findings support the central positions of his control theory. Although most of the delinquency reported by youths was of a minor nature, Hirschi's data suggest that high levels of attachment, commitment, involvement, and belief are related to a low level of delinquency. Consider the question regarding a youth's desire to be like his father. For boys who "would like to be like their father in every way," 64 percent reported a low level of delinquency. This was the case for only 41 percent of those who did not want to be like their fathers. Hirschi's analysis of other measures of social bonding reveals a similar pattern. These findings were, with one notable exception, confirmed in research conducted by Michael Hindelang a few years later.[100] Hindelang's measures of delinquency and bonding were similar to Hirschi's. His sample was composed of boys and girls in a rural east coast location. His results were consistent with Hirschi's except with regard to attachment. Hirschi's data suggest that as parental, peer, and school attachments increase, levels of delinquency decrease. Hindelang did not find evidence of this pattern. Perhaps the reason lies in the fact that neither researcher had reliable data about the actual conventionality of the persons to whom the youths had the most attachment. If people are greatly attached to unconventional persons, they may be influenced in the direction of deviance rather than conventionality. This is suggested in Hirschi's data and in other studies that examine the impact of delinquent peers on the likelihood of becoming delinquent.[101]

In summary, Hirschi's control theory may be viewed as a promising social-psychological extension of basic themes involved in the disorganization perspective. The disorganization perspective locates the causes of deviant behavior in the disruption of society's normative order. Hirschi's control theory locates the realms of immediate social and psychological experience where norms actually come into play. If the disorganization perspective is correct in asserting that disrupted norms increase the likelihood of deviant behavior, then this societal-level increase should be mirrored at the level of individual social-psychological experience. Empirical support for Hirschi's theory suggests that this is the case. Thus, control theory represents further evidence of the continued importance of disorganization theorizing.

ASSESSMENT OF THE DISORGANIZATION PERSPECTIVE

The disorganization perspective is a thoroughly social viewpoint on the study of deviance and social control. It transcends many of the individualistic limitations and biases of previous perspectives. This is its primary strength. In the period of rapid social changes following World War I, the disorganization perspective permitted U.S. sociologists to shed previous illusions about the inevitability of rational progress without pessimistic disillusionment about the usefulness of social science. The disorganization perspective rejected both speculative evolutionary theorizing about and romantic attachment to the ideals of white, Protestant, small-town America. It did so, moreover, without abandoning faith in the belief that the careful study of social life is helpful in constructing a more humane and knowledgeable approach to the problems of living. These conclusions are reflected in the Chicago school's twin commitments to disciplined empirical research and liberal social policy formation. As James Carey points out:

> The disorganization perspective had a broad . . . appeal to . . . sociologists, because it was more complex than the evolutionary view. It did not automatically assume the superiority of American ways and it allowed for a more penetrating analysis of probable outcomes of meetings between diverse peoples. It seemed better suited to the realities of a complex, differential society.[102]

Another strength of the disorganization perspective is that it asks us to imagine that deviants are people like ourselves. They are in no way spiritually cursed, rationally miscalculative, or pathologically defective. The factor that separates deviants from anyone else is an unfortunate spatial location in the natural ecology of a changing society. Deviants, argues the perspective, are disproportionately exposed to the disruptive forces of rapid social change. Nondeviants suddenly confronted with the same disruptive forces would find themselves pulled similarly toward nonconformity.

Despite its strengths, there are serious weaknesses in the formulation and application of disorganization theorizing. Four important criticisms are noted below. A consideration of each reminds us that this perspective has serious blind spots as well as interesting areas of illumination.

Inadequate Operationalization of the Concept of Disorganization

In testing the key components of a theoretical perspective, researchers must be careful to precisely and consistently operationalize their concepts so that measurements adequately reflect ideas suggested by the theory itself. Despite a consistent emphasis on relating theory to research, disorganization researchers were not always careful in operationalizing conceptual measurements. Problems in this area assumed one of two forms. Sometimes, researchers failed to justify why a particular indicator of disorganization was taken as a measure of normative breakdown. Consider several of the indicators of disorganization used in studies of delinquency. Measures such as a high proportion of working women, a high proportion of unmarried men, and a high number of persons per household have all been used to indicate the presence of disorganization. Why? Why should we assume that working women are more disorganized than nonworking women, or that unmarried men or large households are overtaken by normative breakdown? Such things have been used as indirect measurements of normative disorganization, and yet we are not told exactly how or why. Perhaps they do reflect normative chaos. On the other hand, they may indicate little more than a researcher's own prejudice or bias.

A second problem in the measurement of disorganization was that statistics on deviance were themselves occasionally used as indicators of disorganization. This is troublesome because disorganization is then said to cause deviance. Can something be both an indicator and a cause of the same thing? Logically, the answer is no. Unfortunately, disorganization researchers were not always logically consistent. Consider the following statement by Chicago researchers Robert E. L. Faris and H. Warren Dunham. In explaining high rates of deviance among second- and third-generation immigrants, Faris and Dunham offer the following analysis:

> A type of disorganizing factor operates among the members of the second and third generations. The very high delinquency rate among the second-generation children has been shown by Shaw. This disorganization can be shown to develop from the nature of the child's social situation.[103]

In this passage Faris and Dunham appear to see the high delinquency rate as something which was both an example of disorganization and something caused by disorganization. Such confusion was unfortunately all too common in social disorganization research.

Confusion of Disorganization and Differential Organization

Disorganization theorists (like most scientists) are disproportionately male, middle-class, and white. Often their sociological journeys do not take them beyond the constraints of their backgrounds. Many of them fail to appreciate the ways that people from other class, cultural, or ethnic backgrounds organize their worlds. Differences in organization may thus be confused with the presence of disorganization. Despite sympathy for various groups of immigrants and others vulnerable to the disruptive forces of rapid social change, researchers working within the social disorganization tradition have too often interpreted the cultures of others through the distortive lenses of their own viewpoints.

An important instance of such confusion involved the so-called Moynihan Report.[104] This report (*The Negro Family: The Case for National Action*) was prepared for President Lyndon Johnson in 1965 by Daniel Patrick Moynihan, then assistant secretary of labor and White House adviser. The basis for a compassionate stance on race relations by Johnson, the report was nonetheless mired in the biases of disorganization theorizing. High rates of black crime, delinquency, and other forms of deviance were explained by the social disorganization of the black family. Originating in slavery and reinforced by the latter-day forces of rapid urbanization and unemployment, the family structure of blacks was said to be the opposite of that of whites. Higher rates of fatherless homes, divorce, separation, and marital desertion, the reverse of traditional (white) husband-wife roles, and greater vulnerability to economic and criminal victimization were said to have disrupted the organization of lower-class black family life. The resulting lack of normative controls fostered deviance and made the problem cyclical, passed on from generation to generation.

Since the time that the Moynihan Report was first issued, it has become the subject of considerable debate and criticism.[105] One wave of criticism questioned the equation of female-headed households with disorganization.[106] Wasn't this historical development within the black family an organized, highly adaptive response to the systematic removal of black males, initially through slavery and later through a social discriminatory economy, the welfare rules of which penalized families with low-income male household heads?

A later wave of criticism questioned the empirical accuracy of the lack of adult male presence.[107] Subsequent research suggested that males were more involved, even if not officially married into the family, than previously estimated. The lower-class black family was differently organized rather than disorganized. Bound by a singular ethnocentric view of what constitutes proper organization, researchers were blind to this important distinction. Confusion of this kind is a liability of much disorganization theorizing.

Neglect of Organized, "Respectable" Deviance

The types of deviance discovered in the transition zone (street crime, delinquency, mental illness, drug addiction, etc.) were generally "disrespectable" in character. But what of such acts as embezzlement, deceitful advertising, the abuse of governmental power, and corporate price fixing? These kinds of deviance are typically performed by "respectable" persons. Individuals who commit such acts are more likely to reside in the protected commuter zone than in the troubled transition zone. How has disorganization theory dealt with these forms of deviance? The answer is simple. It hasn't. The disorganization perspective has been biased in its consideration of disrespectable over respectable deviance. This bias limits its utility as a general explanation of deviance.

Relative Inattention to Social Stratification

The emphasis on deviance as a natural by-product of rapid social change has led critics to suggest that the disorganization perspective fails to consider the potential causative influence of structured differences in social power and social class. Such structured differences are referred to by sociologists as "social stratification." Research by the Chicago school discovered the highest rates of officially recorded deviance in the so-called transition zone. This ecological region was said to be most disorganized by social change. Deviance was its unfortunate by-product. Its residents were conceived of as victims of change. Perhaps. But isn't it just as plausible to suggest that its residents were victims of a highly unequal system of social stratification?

By describing slum dwellers as disorganized, the disorganization perspective neglects the fact that they are also poor. Slums are the product of an unequal distribution of material resources. Yet, disorganization theorists talk about slums as if they were somehow natural, rather than socially created. The central business zone is talked about as the natural center of change. It is also the socially structured location of powerful and privileged economic forces which exploit as well as disorganize. People are said to engage in deviance because social disorganization has robbed them of norms and constraints. Neglected is the possibility that people deviate because social stratification has robbed them of human resources and a sense of dignity.

Isn't it possible that poor people may experience higher rates of what the society officially defines as deviant, not because they lack organized normative constraints, but because they are frustrated, angry, or seeking escape from the oppression of a stratified social existence? The social disorganization perspective is relatively inattentive to such matters. Disturbing political questions about the unequal organization of our whole society are bypassed in favor of questions about the disproportionate disorganization of specific ecological sectors.

Whatever the benefits of the disorganization metaphor, its disadvantages for the socially and economically powerless are significant. What the Chicago theorists describe as natural ecological conflict is really an unequal human struggle over the control of urban space. This is documented by John Rex and Robert Moore, whose study of ecological conflict in a British city modifies the disorganization format by including differences in political power as a central determinant of the outcomes of competition for spatial dominance.[108] This is also a central theme in David Downes's *The Delinquent Solution*[109] and in Terrence Morris's *The Criminal Area*.[110] These British researchers do not counter the Chicago school's observation that common crimes and deviance are concentrated in slums and zones of ecological transition. What differs is the interpretation of such findings. Whereas the Chicago tradition blurred the natural forces of disorganization, critical British researchers have defined disorganization as a historical by-product of social domination by the powerful.

Not all the Chicago researchers ignored the issue of social stratification. The later work of Clifford Shaw and Henry McKay, for instance, gave increasing emphasis to structural factors related to unequal social position. As Harold Firestone observes, Shaw and McKay shifted from "an emphasis upon the 'push' factors . . . represented by . . . social disorganization" toward "the 'pull' factors represented by access to an illegitimate opportunity structure."[111] A similar observation is made by Albert J. Reiss, who suggests

that "one of the great contributions of Shaw and McKay is . . . that delinquency is endemic in certain neighborhoods and that the problem of becoming delinquent is greater for persons in lower than higher income status
groups."[112]

Firestone and Reiss are correct. The later work of Shaw and McKay moves
beyond the confines of disorganization theorizing by recognizing that "the
struggle for space in the city is not independent of the struggle for power,
prestige and material well-being in society as a whole."[113] With this in mind,
we too shall move beyond the disorganization perspective and examine
several other sociological viewpoints on deviance and its control.

NOTES

1 Robert E. Park, Ernest V. Burgess, and Roderick D. McKenzie, *The City*, University of Chicago Press, Chicago, 1967, pp. 106–107.
2 Jonathan Kaplan, as quoted in David Denby, "Mondo Condo," *New York*, Jan.
   18, 1982, p. 62.
3 Ibid.
4 Ibid.
5 Albian Small, "Points of Agreement among Sociologists," *Publications of the
   American Sociological Society*, vol. I, 1907, pp. 55–71.
6 For an overview of surrealist ethnographic practice, see James Clifford, "On
   Ethnographic Surrealism," in James Clifford, *The Predicament of Culture: Twentieth
   Century Ethnography, Literature and Art*, Harvard University Press, Cambridge,
   Mass., 1988, pp. 146–147. For a discussion of the political subversion of "self-
   evidency" in the writings of Bataille, Leiris, and others, see Allan Stoekl, *Politics,
   Writing, Mutilation: the Cases of Bataille, Blanchot, Roussel, Leiris and Ponge*, University of Minnesota Press, Minneapolis, 1985.
7 Georges Bataille, "Attraction and Repulsion II: Social Structure," in Denis Hollier
   (ed.), *The College of Sociology 1937–39*, Betsy Wing (trans.), University of Minnesota Press, Minneapolis, 1988, pp. 114–115.
8 Ibid., p. 115.
9 Roscoe C. Hinkle, Jr., and Gisela J. Hinkle, *The Development of Modern Sociology:
   Its Nature and Growth in the United States*, Random House, New York, 1954, p. 21.
10 For a comparison between French surrealist ethnography and Frankfurt critical
   theory, see Annette Michelson, "Heterology and the Critique of Instrumental
   Reason," *October*, vol. 37, spring 1986, pp. 11–127.
11 For an excellent overview of this process, see Dorothy Ross, *The Origins of
   American Social Science*, Cambridge University Press, New York, 1991.
12 James T. Carey, *Sociology and Public Affairs: The Chicago School*, Sage, Beverly Hills,
   Calif., 1975, p. 29. See also E. F. Gay and L. Wolman, "Trends in Economic
   Organizations," in *President's Research Committee on Social Trends*, McGraw-Hill,
   New York, 1933, pp. 218–267.
13 Carey, *Sociology and Public Affairs*, p. 29.
14 Ibid., p. 19.
15 Ibid., pp. 19–20. See also R. D. McKenzie, "The Rise of Metropolitan Communities," in *President's Research Committee on Social Trends*, McGraw-Hill, New York,
   1933, pp. 443–496.

16 Carey, *Sociology and Public Affairs*, p. 20.

17 R. G. Hurlin and M. B. Givens, "Shifting Occupational Patterns," in *President's Research Committee on Social Trends*, p. 299.

18 Carey, *Sociology and Public Affairs*, p. 16.

19 Ibid., pp. 23–27. One notable exception involves the Wall Street bombing of 1920. Yet, as Carey (p. 26) suggests, this act of protest "was apparently the work of a small group of anarchists." See also S. Cohen, "A Study in Nativism: The American Red Scare of 1919–1920," *Political Science Quarterly*, vol. 79, March 1964, pp. 52–75. For analysis of labor during this period, see I. Berstein, *The Lean Years: Workers in an Unbalanced Society*, Houghton Mifflin, Boston, 1960.

20 Howard Zinn, *A People's History of the United States*, Harper Collins Publishers, 1980, p. 366.

21 Ross, *The Origins of American Social Science*, pp. 235–236.

22 W. E. Leuchtenberg, *The Perils of Prosperity, 1914–1932*, University of Chicago Press, Chicago, 1958.

23 Carey, *Sociology and Public Affairs*, p. 24.

24 Joseph Gusfield, *Symbolic Crusade: Status Politics and the American Temperance Movement*, University of Illinois Press, Urbana, 1963.

25 M. Gordon, *Assimilation in American Life*, Oxford University Press, New York, 1964.

26 R. D. Brown, "The American Vigilante Tradition," in H. D. Graham and T. R. Gurr (eds.), *Violence in America: Historical and Comparative Perspectives*, Praeger, New York, 1969; see also D. M. Chalmers, *Hooded Americanism*, Doubleday, Garden City, N.Y., 1965.

27 Maurice Zeitlin, "Who Owns America?" in Richard Quinney (ed.), *Capitalist Society*, Dorsey, Homewood, Ill., 1979, p. 60.

28 Ibid.

29 Ibid., p. 65.

30 Ibid., p. 66.

31 Carey, *Sociology and Public Affairs*, pp. 41, 43.

32 Hinkle and Hinkle, *The Development of Modern Sociology*, p. 18.

33 Robert E. L. Faris, *Chicago Sociology: 1920–1932*, Chandler, San Francisco, 1967, p. 7.

34 Carey, *Sociology and Public Affairs*, p. 64.

35 Ibid., p. 49.

36 Ross, *The Origins of American Social Science*, p. 309.

37 Lewis A. Coser, *Masters of Sociological Thought: Ideas in Historical and Social Context*, 2d ed., Harcourt, Brace, Jovanovich, New York, 1977, p. 535.

38 Ibid.

39 W. I. Thomas and Florian Znaniecki, *The Polish Peasant in Europe and America*, Gorham Press, Boston, 1920.

40 W. I. Thomas and Florian Znaniecki, "The Concept of Social Disorganization," in S. H. Traub and C. B. Little (eds.), *Theories of Deviance*, Peacock, Itasca, Ill., 1975, p. 35.

41 Park, Burgess, and McKenzie, *The City*, p. 107.

42 Robert E. Park, *Human Communities*, Free Press, Glencoe, Ill., 1952, p. 118.

43 For a summary description of the work of Shaw and McKay, see Don C. Gibbons, *The Criminological Enterprise*, Prentice-Hall, Englewood Cliffs, N.J., 1979, pp. 40–46.

The Criminological Enterprise, Prentice-Hall, Englewood Cliffs, N.J., 1979, pp. 40–46.

44 Clifford R. Shaw, Frederick M. Forgaugh, Henry D. McKay, and Leonard S. Cottreel, *Delinquency Areas*, University of Chicago Press, Chicago, 1929.

45 Clifford R. Shaw and Henry D. McKay, *Juvenile Delinquency and Urban Areas: A Study of Rates of Delinquency in Relation to Differential Characteristics of Local Communities in American Cities*, University of Chicago Press, Chicago, 1969.

46 Clifford R. Shaw and Henry D. McKay, "Juvenile Delinquency and Urban Areas," in Leon Radzinowitz and Marvin E. Wolfgang (eds.), *Crime and Justice*, Basic Books, New York, 1971, vol. I, p. 411.

47 Shaw and McKay, "Juvenile Delinquency and Urban Areas," p. 382.

48 Ibid.

49 Ibid., p. 412.

50 Bernard Lander, *Towards an Understanding of Juvenile Delinquency*, Columbia, New York, 1954.

51 Shaw and McKay, "Juvenile Delinquency and Urban Areas," p. 418.

52 David J. Bordua, "Juvenile Delinquency and Anomie: An Attempt at Replication," *Social Problems*, vol. 6, winter 1959, pp. 230–238.

53 Roland J. Chilton, "Continuity in Delinquency Area Research: A Comparison of Studies for Baltimore, Detroit and Indianapolis," *American Sociological Review*, vol. 29, February 1964, pp. 11–83.

54 Robert E. L. Faris and H. Warren Dunham, *Mental Disorders in Urban Areas*, University of Chicago Press, Chicago, 1939.

55 Ibid., p. 95.

56 Ibid., p. 101.

57 See, for instance, August B. Hollingshead and Frederick C. Redlich, "Social Stratification and Schizophrenia," *American Sociological Review*, vol. 19, 1954, pp. 302–306; R. Lapouse et al., "The Drift Hypothesis and Socioeconomic Differentials in Schizophrenia," *American Journal of Public Health*, vol. 46, 1956, pp. 978–986; John A. Clausen and Melvin L. Kahn, "Relation of Schizophrenia to the Social Structure of a Small City," in Benjamin Pasomanick (ed.), *Epidemiology of Mental Disorder*, American Association for the Advancement of Science Publication 60, Washington, D.C., 1959, pp. 69–85.

58 Clifford R. Shaw, *The Jack Roller: A Delinquent Boy's Own Story*, University of Chicago Press, Chicago, 1930.

59 Ibid., p. 93.

60 H. A. Hodge, *Wilhelm Dilthey: An Introduction*, Routledge & Kegan Paul, London, 1944; See also Wilhelm Dilthey, "On the Special Character of the Human Sciences," in Marcello Truzzi (ed.), *Verstehen: Subjective Understanding in the Social Sciences*, Addison-Wesley, Reading, Mass., 1974, pp. 8–17.

61 Hinkle and Hinkle, *The Development of Modern Sociology*, p. 24.

62 Coser, *Masters of Sociological Thought*, p. 554.

63 Shaw and McKay, "Juvenile Delinquency and Urban Areas."

64 Shaw, *The Jack Roller*; Clifford Shaw and Maurice Moore, *The Natural History of a Delinquent Career*, University of Chicago Press, Chicago, 1931; Clifford Shaw and James F. McDonald, *Brothers in Crime*, University of Chicago Press, Chicago, 1938.

65 W. I. Thomas, *The Unadjusted Girl*, Little, Brown, Boston, 1923; Nels Anderson, *The Hobo: The Sociology of the Homeless Man*, University of Chicago Press, Chicago, 1923; Harvey W. Zorbaugh, *Gold Coast and Slum*, University of Chicago Press, Chicago, 1929; Louis Wirth, *Ghetto*, University of Chicago Press, Chicago, 1928; Paul G. Cressey, *The Taxi-Dance Hall: A Sociological Study of Commercialized Recreation and City Life*, University of Chicago Press, Chicago, 1932.

66 Howard Becker, "Introduction," in Shaw, *The Jack Roller*, p. viii.

67 Shaw, *The Jack Roller*, p. 19.

68 Robert E. Park, *Selected Papers*, Ralph E. Turner (ed.), University of Chicago Press, Chicago, 1967, p. xi.

69 Shaw and McKay, "Juvenile Delinquency and Urban Areas," p. 4.

70 Terrence Morris, *The Criminal Area*, Humanities Press, New York, 1966, p. 83.

71 Martin R. Haskell and Lewis Yablonsky, *Juvenile Delinquency*, Rand McNally, Chicago, 1974, p. 423.

72 George Vold, *Theoretical Criminology*, 2d ed., prepared by Thomas J. Bernard, Oxford, New York, 1979, p. 197.

73 Allen E. Liska, *Perspective on Deviance*, Prentice-Hall, Englewood Cliffs, N.J., 1981, p. 80.

74 Walter B. Miller, "The Impact of a 'Total-Community' Delinquency Control Project," *Social Problems*, vol. 10, fall 1962, pp. 168–191.

75 Ibid., p. 187.

76 Morris, *The Criminal Area*, p. 84.

77 Don C. Gibbons, *The Criminological Enterprise: Theories and Perspectives*, Prentice-Hall, Englewood Cliffs., N.J., 1979, p. 45.

78 Hinkle and Hinkle, *The Development of Modern Sociology*, pp. 44–70; Carey, *Sociology and Public Affairs*, p. 119.

79 Liska, *Perspectives on Deviance*, p. 83.

80 S. Kirson Weinberg, "Shaw-McKay Theories of Delinquency in Cross-Cultural Context," in James F. Short (ed.), *Delinquency, Crime and Society*, University of Chicago Press, Chicago, 1976, pp. 167–185.

81 Marshall B. Clinard and Daniel J. Abbott, "Community Organization and Property Crime: A Comparative Study of Social Control in the Slums of an African City," in James F. Short (ed.), *Delinquency, Crime and Society*, University of Chicago Press, Chicago, 1976, pp. 186–206.

82 Weinberg, "Shaw-McKay Theories of Delinquency . . . ," pp. 173, 169, 177.

83 Ibid., p. 173.

84 Marshall B. Clinard, *Cities with Little Crime: The Case of Switzerland*, Cambridge University Press, Cambridge, 1978.

85 Ibid., pp. 12–82.

86 Ibid., p. 10.

87 Ibid., p. 106.

88 Ibid., p. 111.

89 Ibid., p. 81.

90 Ibid., pp. 112–113.

91 Raymond Michalowski, "The Social and Criminal Patterns of Urban Traffic Fatalities," *British Journal of Criminology*, vol. 17, no. 2, April 1977, pp. 126–140.

92 R. T. Sollenberger, "Why Chinatown's Children Are Not Delinquent," *Transaction*, vol. 5, September 1968, p. 3.

93 The link between control theory and disorganization was first suggested by Gary Jensen, in a thoughtful review of an earlier version of this book.

94 Walter C. Reckless, *The Crime Problem*, 5th ed., Prentice-Hall, Englewood Cliffs, N.J., 1973, pp. 55–56.

95 Ibid.

96 A partial test of Reckless's idea is found in the good self-concept as containment research by Reckless and his associates at Ohio State University. See, for instance, Walter C. Reckless, Simon Dinitz, and Ellen Murray, "Self Concept as an Insulator against Delinquency," *American Sociological Review*, vol. 21, December 1956, pp. 744–756; Walter Reckless, Simon Dinitz, and Barbara Kay, "The Self-Component in Potential Delinquency and Potential Non-Delinquency," *American Sociological Review*, vol. 22, October 1957, pp. 566–570; Frank R. Scarpitti, Ellen Murray, Simon Dinitz, and Walter C. Reckless, "The 'Good Boy' in a High Delinquency Area: Four Years Later," *American Sociological Review*, vol. 25, August 1960, pp. 555–558; and Walter C. Reckless and Simon Dinitz, "Pioneering with Self-Concept as a Vulnerability Factor in Delinquency," *Journal of Criminal Law, Criminology and Police Science*, vol. 58, December 1967, p. 517.

    For criticism of this research, see Clarence Schrag, *Crime and Justice: American Style*, National Institutes of Mental Health, Rockville, Md., 1971, p. 88; Michael Schwartz and Sandra S. Tangri, "A Note on Self-Concept as an Insulator against Delinquency," *American Sociological Review*, vol. 30, December 1965, pp. 922–926; Sandra S. Tangri and Michael Schwartz, "Delinquency Research and the Self Concept Variable," *Journal of Criminal Law, Criminology and Police Science*, vol. 58, June 1967, pp. 182–190; James Orcutt, "Self Concept and Insulation against Delinquency: Some Critical Notes," *Sociological Quarterly*, vol. 2, summer 1970, pp. 381–390.

97 Travis Hirschi, *Causes of Delinquency*, University of California Press, Berkeley, 1969.

98 Ibid., p. 16.

99 Ibid., p. 22. An edited composite of excerpts from several confidential biographical essays written for a course in deviant behavior at a large midwestern university during the mid-1970s.

100 Michael T. Hindelang, "Causes of Delinquency: A Partial Replication and Extension," *Social Problems*, vol. 20, spring 1973, pp. 471–487.

101 Eric Linden and James C. Hackler, "Affective Ties and Delinquency," *Pacific Sociological Review*, vol. 16, January 1973, pp. 27–46; Rand Conger, "Social Control and Social Learning Models of Delinquency: A Synthesis," *Criminology*, vol. 14, May 1976, pp. 17–40.

102 Carey, *Sociology and Public Affairs*, p. 119.

103 Robert E. L. Faris and H. Warren Dunham, *Mental Disorders in Urban Areas*, University of Chicago Press, Chicago, 1939, pp. 8–9.

104 For an overview of this issue, see Ritchie P. Lowry, *Social Problems: A Critical Analysis of Theories and Public Policy*, D. C. Heath, Lexington, Mass., 1974, pp. 164–167.

105 Lee Rainwater and William L. Yancey, *The Moynihan Report and the Politics of Controversy*, M.I.T. Press, Cambridge, Mass., 1967.

106 Lawrence Rosen, "Matriarchy and Lower Class Negro Male Delinquency," *Social Problems*, vol. 17, fall 1969, pp. 175–189; Lee Rainwater and William L. Yancey,

"Black Families and the White House," *Transaction,* vol. 3, July/August 1966, pp. 6–11, 48–53.

107 Reynolds Farley and Albert I. Hermalin, "Family Stability: A Comparison of Trends between Blacks and Whites," *American Sociological Review,* vol. 36, February 1971, pp. 1–17.

108 John Rex and Robert Moore, *Race, Community and Conflict: A Study in Sparkbrook,* Oxford University Press, London, 1967.

109 David Downes, *The Delinquent Solution,* Routledge & Kegan Paul, London, 1966.

110 Terrence Morris, *The Criminal Area,* Humanities Press, New York, 1966.

111 Harold Firestone, "The Delinquent and Society: The Shaw and McKay Tradition," in James F. Short (ed.), *Delinquency, Crime and Society,* University of Chicago Press, Chicago, 1976, p. 33.

112 Albert J. Reiss, Jr., "Settling the Frontiers of a Pioneer in American Criminology: Henry McKay," in Short (ed.), *Delinquency, Crime and Society,* p. 71.

113 Ian Taylor, Paul Walton, and Jock Young, *The New Criminology: For a Social Theory of Deviance,* Harper & Row, New York, 1973, p. 119.

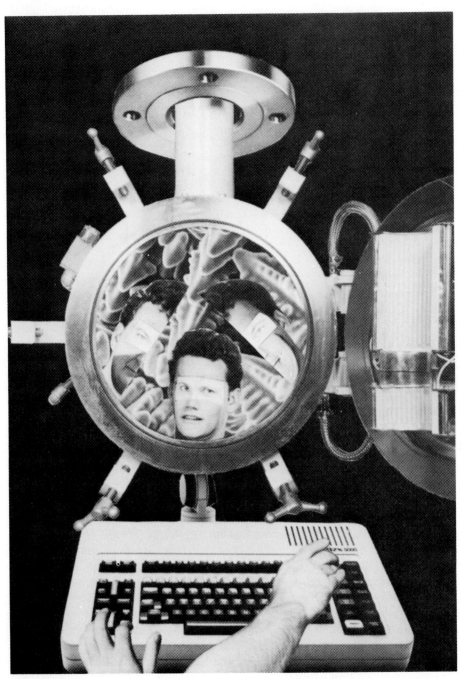

The Social Machine. It turns me on. By Joseph LaMantia and Stephen Pfohl

CHAPTER 6

THE FUNCTIONALIST PERSPECTIVE:
Cybernetics, Negative Feedback, and the Benefits of Deviance

Crime is . . . necessary; it is bound up with the fundamental conditions of all social life, and by that very fact it is useful.

Émile Durkheim[1]

Societies somehow "need" their quotas of deviants and function in such a way as to keep them intact.

Kai T. Erikson[2]

INTRODUCTION

On stage an image of a woman in chains appears within a mirror. The woman's wrists are bound and her muslin dress is torn, exposing her breasts. The woman is an actress playing the part of a prostitute playing the part of The Thief. In front of the woman stands a tall muscular man stripped to the waist. A whip hangs from the man's belt. This man is The Executioner. Another man crawls belly to the floor clothed in the robe of a judge. This man, playing the part of a man with sufficient economic means to play the part of The Judge, crawls toward the woman playing the part of a prostitute playing the part of The Thief. She shrinks from the man's approach, then orders The Judge to lick her foot. Thereafter, a strange dialogue occurs. The Thief is informed that to ensure a proper balance of social order she must both confess her crimes and submit to the beating The Executioner will deliver upon legal commands from The Judge.

The Judge, The Executioner, and The Thief, this "fine trio," are characters in Jean Genet's play *The Balcony*. Each appears to be functionally interdependent upon the others. Even The Thief, although clearly scripted as a deviant, seems capable of contributing to the social order. The Judge cannot be a judge unless The Thief embraces her role as a thief, and The Executioner mirrors The Judge's every word. "Ah! ah!" says The Judge to The Executioner, "your pleasure depends on me. You like to thrash, eh? I'm pleased with you, Executioner! Masterly mountain of meat, hunk of beef that's set in motion at a word from me! Mirror that glorifies me!" And to The Thief, The Judge remarks, "Look here: you've got to be a model thief if I'm to be a model judge. If you're a fake thief, I become a fake judge. Is that clear?"[3]

"Oh, yes, my Lord," responds The Thief. Everything is clear, as clear as the functionalist perspective on deviance and social control. Unlike other theoretical perspectives, functionalism views deviance as contributing to, rather than threatening, a given order of roles, rules, and regulations. In this sense, social order is said to feed off social deviance, as The Judge and The Executioner feed parasitically off the scripted actions of The Thief.

"My being a judge is an emanation of Your being a thief," says the legal officer to the deviant. "You need only refuse—but you'd better not!—need only refuse to be who you are—what you are, therefore who you are—for me to cease to be . . . to vanish, evaporate. Burst. Volatized. Denied. Hence: good born of. . . . What then? What then? But you won't refuse, will you? You won't refuse to be a thief? That would be wicked. It would be criminal. You'd deprive me of being!"[4]

Genet's play theatrically displays something at the core of funtionalist logic—an assumption that, in actuality, even the aspects of society which appear most unruly contribute to the reproduction of orderly social relations. By providing a kind of "negative feedback," deviance, like the woman playing the part of a prostitute playing the role of The Thief, helps society to secure its lawful boundaries and strengthen its adaptability to changing environmental circumstances. Nevertheless, unlike Genet's play, which critically reveals the violence by which people are recruited into roles demanding their unjust subordination, functionalist theory appears to be guided by an abstractly optimistic viewpoint. Functionalism envisions society as a "goal-directed" system that informs its members about how they must behave if the system itself is to be reproduced. In this, functionalism converges with cybernetics—a theoretical viewpoint which depicts society as a goal-directed mechanism that deploys information to command needed energetic actions. For cybernetics, energetic social actions, including deviant actions, are interpreted as coded instances of feedback which help a particular social system to stay on course. In this way, society is said to depend upon crime, delinquency, political dissent, and other forms of deviant feedback, in much the same manner as The Judge, in Genet's play, depends upon the woman actress playing the prostitute playing The Thief.

THEORETICAL IMAGES

The functionalist perspective on deviance is unique in that it emphasizes the positive contributions of deviance. Something is defined as functional if it has positive consequences for the organization of society as a whole. If its consequences are negative it is dysfunctional. Deviance is said to be functional because it strengthens the bonds of an existing social order. This view of deviance as constructive originates in the late-nineteenth-century writings of the French social theorist Émile Durkheim.

Durkheim: Searching for the Moral Integration of Social Organisms

Durkheim, who in 1887 taught the first French university course in sociology, was preoccupied with the problems of social modernity, with the normative disintegration generated by the transition from a simple to a complex society. In the years following World War II, Durkheim's provocative ideas were incorporated into the cybernetic theories of U.S. sociologist Talcott Parsons. Parsons was, without a doubt, the most influential sociologist in the postwar United States. Whether or not we agree with Parsons's vision of society as a functionally interrelated system, one thing is clear: Parsons's thinking stamped itself upon an entire generation of social theorists, selectively filtering how most North American sociologists would interpret Durkheim. Durkheim's theses will be examined in the next several pages, while Parsons's ideas about deviance and its cybernetic control will be discussed in subsequent sections of this chapter.

Durkheim's concern with the moral crisis of his age led him to view sociology as a scientific solution for social disruption. Religious belief and philosophical speculation were seen as no longer capable of providing a sense of collective social order. The basis of a new modern order would await the lawlike findings of scientific sociology. For Durkheim, sociology was first and foremost a science of morals. As Lewis Coser points out:

> Durkheim . . . wanted to devote himself to a discipline that would contribute to the clarification of the great moral questions that agitate the age, as well as to practical guidance of the affairs of contemporary society. . . . What he considered imperative was to construct a scientific sociological system, not as an end in itself, but as a means for the moral direction of society.[5]

As a "moral scientist" Durkheim attempted to identify the necessary or normal features of any healthy functioning society. He also sought to analyze the conditions under which the normative could be restored in societies endangered by the pathology of disintegration. According to Durkheim a pathological society was one in which norms were paradoxically either too strong or too weak. When they were too strong, society would be overly conformist, unable to flexibly adapt to changing environmental circumstances. When they were too weak, it would be too loosely defined and its members too weakly joined to accomplish basic tasks needed to assure its own survival. Durkheim's analysis of the pathological "looseness" of modern society is examined in the discussion of the anomie perspective in Chapter 7. This chapter explores Durkheim's view of deviance as normal.

Deviance as Normal: Contributions to Moral Integration

In *The Rules of the Sociological Method* Durkheim argued that a social phenomenon was normal if it was both universal and necessary. By *universal*, Durkheim meant that something must be present in all, or the majority of all, societies of the same type. By *necessary*, he meant that it represented a determining condition, i.e., that it was needed for the continued existence of society. If both criteria were met, something could be deemed normal. Such was the case with crime or deviance, an aspect of social life that Durkheim viewed as universally present and as the product of certain determining conditions which necessitated its existence. This is the essence of Durkheim's view of deviance as functional. It was an omnipresent feature of social life necessary for the existence of a stable social order. In Durkheim's own words:

> Crime is present not only in the majority of societies of one particular species but in all societies of all types. There is no society that is not confronted with the problem of criminality. . . . [This] is not to say merely that it is an inevitable, although regrettable phenomenon, due to the incorrigible wickedness of men; it is to affirm that it is a factor in public health, an integral part of all healthy societies.[6]

According to Durkheim and other functionalists, deviance contributes to social order in several ways: by setting moral boundaries, strengthening in-group solidarity, allowing for adaptive innovation, and reducing internal societal tensions.

Boundary-Setting Function The boundary-setting function of deviance was first discussed by Durkheim in *The Rules of the Sociological Method*. Deviance was said to help define the moral boundaries which distinguish between right and wrong. In sanctioning the deviant, society informs its members of the type of person they cannot become and still live "normally" within its boundaries. It symbolizes what we are to avoid and reminds us of the sanctions we face if we stray beyond established normative conventions. Such boundary marking enables us to know what is expected of us. We are provided with a kind of moral map to guide us in the dos and don'ts of everyday social life.

For Durkheim the boundary-setting functions of deviance had a certain elasticity. Even if a society was extremely conformist, deviance would not disappear. It would merely be redefined in narrower terms. What had previously been acceptable may not be condemned. The boundaries would be drawn more tightly. As an example, Durkheim asks us to "image a society of saints, a perfect cloister of exemplary individuals. Crimes, properly so called, will be there unknown: but faults which appear venial to the layman will create there the same scandal that the ordinary offense does in ordinary consciousness."[7] Thus while specific forms of deviance may vary, some forms must exist in every society. Without deviance there will be no moral boundaries, and without such boundaries there can be no society.

Group Solidarity Function   In addition to setting boundaries, deviance may also bring society together against a common enemy. It may increase group solidarity for members united in collective opposition to the normative threats of nonconformity. To wage war against deviant "outsiders" may thus strengthen the social bonds of nondeviant "insiders."

Although noted by Durkheim, the group function of deviance is nowhere better expressed than in the writings of the early U.S. sociologist and philosopher George Herbert Mead. In "The Psychology of Punitive Justice," Mead states that "the revulsions against criminality reveal themselves in a sense of solidarity within the group . . . [which] inhibits tendencies to criminal acts in the citizen himself."[8]

Innovation Functions   The functionalist perspective also recognizes that overly rigid boundaries may limit a society's adaptability. Imagine that a particular society had become extremely successful in controlling and creating conformity. On one hand, such a society may appear to be very strong. On the other hand, it may be weakened in its capacity to flexibly adapt to an ever-changing external environment. It might become locked into outdated traditions and be unable to adjust to the new, and thereby it would stagnate or wither away. Innovative deviance encourages society to revise its rules in response to new environmental problems. In Durkheim's words:

> Where crime exists, collective sentiments are sufficiently flexible to take on a new form, and crime sometimes helps to determine the form they will take. How many times, indeed, it is only an anticipation of future morality—a step toward what will be.[9]

Deviance may help society to adapt by challenging the foundation of old and outdated rules. The deviant rule-breaker of today may be an innovator of new rules tomorrow. Durkheim cites the example of Socrates. Although Socrates was condemned as a deviant thinker in his own day, his ideas later came to constitute a new basis for conformity. More recently, Martin Luther King, Jr., exemplifies the deviant as an innovator. King clearly deviated from the social boundaries established by a racist and segregated society. He deliberately broke laws which he considered to be morally objectionable, laws that subordinated blacks to whites. In doing so he paid the price of being deviant. He was harassed, arrested, and beaten by "normal" citizens and even by some who were empowered to guard the "acceptable" social boundaries. Yet, through the deviance of Martin Luther King and his followers the boundaries of race relations in the United States came to be partially altered. The acceptable social rules he once opposed are now themselves illegal. His deviant actions paved the way for a subsequent redefinition of normative social boundaries.

Tension-Reduction Function   Deviance may also be useful by functioning as a safety valve for strains within society itself. Society sometimes projects its own problems onto the shoulders of some deviant group. Minorities, for instance, may be blamed for tensions produced by society as a whole. By scapegoating its own problems on witches, hippies, Jews, Communists, welfare recipients, or homosexuals, society may temporarily drain off some of its own self-produced contradictions and tensions.

The tension-reduction idea also recognizes that a bit of deviance may drain off some of the tensions that people accumulate in their day-to-day attempts to conform to the announced rules of society's game. In previous times a socially sanctioned "feast of fools" was a common part of the calendar year. On such a day people were permitted to deviate from the routine restraints of conformist living, to let off steam.[10] One wonders if "getting crazy" on weekends and "fooling around" at the annual professional convention are not modern-day counterparts to such ritually scheduled times for letting off steam.

Latent Functions   Besides identifying the positive consequences of deviance, functionalist theorists distinguish the consequences which are recognized and intended from those which are not. Recognized and intended consequences are referred to as "manifest functions." Unrecognized and unintended contributions are called "latent functions." Deviance is usually seen as manifestly dysfunctional. It is controlled because society recognizes its disintegrating consequences. Nonetheless it may at the same time have latent functions. For this reason certain acts may be manifestly condemned but latently permitted.

The distinction between manifest and latent functions is attributed to the sociologist Robert K. Merton.[11] Merton applied this distinction in analyzing the corrupt big-city political machine. Manifestly, the lawless practices of the machine were dysfunctional to a society ordered by the rule of law. Latently, the machine helped to create order by integrating people who were integrative and by meeting the needs of marginal urban subgroups, such as immigrant or ethnic minorities. As an efficient provider of extralegal services, it maximized the political privileges of "underdogs" and "topdogs" alike. As an intermediary in the plight of the urban needy, the machine was functionally superior to the slow and impersonal workings of the official government bureaucracy.

Another example of the latent functions of deviance is found in Kingsley Davis's study of prostitution.[12] Although Davis makes certain assumptions which today we would probably recognize as sexist, his work illustrates the ease with which functionalist theorists can find positive consequences for just about anything. Prostitution is said to have manifest dysfunctions for a society which normatively confines legitimate sexual relationships to married heterosexual couples. The married couple is said to express the combined sexual goals of reproduction and sentimental attachment. The prostitute, who exchanges sex for money, defies both of these goals and is thus manifestly condemned and subject to criminal sanctioning.

Although prostitution is manifestly condemned, it is rarely shut off entirely. Prostitutes (and only recently their customers) are periodically rounded up and cycled through short periods of imprisonment. They are not once and for all eliminated. In fact, observes Davis, this oldest of professions has existed throughout most of human history. Why? Latently it must be playing some important function, contributing some needed social service. Davis locates its contribution by examining what he assumes is a higher male need for sexual adventure or experimentation. Although today most sexually knowledgeable men and women would regard this premise as absurd, at the time Davis did his work the assumption was probably culturally widespread. Following this premise one could reasonably foresee certain structural tensions arising within the marriage dyad. Greater sexual needs would constantly push the male outside the coupled unit. If he directed his sexual energies toward another "eligible" female, sex might soon be infused with love and the male would be caught between loves (the eternal triangle and all that). This division of affections would inevitably produce high rates of marital conflict, divorce, and assumed societal instability. But what if a male's excessive sexual need was to be met by a "noneligible" female, one who exchanged sex not for love but for money? Sentimental attachments would not be formed. Male sexual drives could be expressed without getting connected with love. Sex with a prostitute would thus provide a useful contribution to social order. Latently prostitution would protect the emotional bonds which preserved marriages and at the same time would permit men to realize their supposedly greater sexual needs. By such functionalist logic, Davis "discovered" the latent functions of prostitution.

Beginning in the 1960s, major changes in sexual attitudes, behaviors, and understandings have occurred, such that we are increasingly aware that males and females display equal degrees of sexual interest. Given this new awareness, let us speculatively extend the functionalist narrative outlined above. Is it possible that a recognition of equalitarian needs for sexual adventure or experimentation accounted for an increase in "swinging," another manifestly deviant sexual activity, while at the same time promoting a decrease in the need for prostitution? Swinging, or "mate swapping," gained much attention in the late 1960s and early 1970s.[13] These terms refer to the highly organized way in which some modern spouses permit their mates to pursue sexual relations outside marriage without threatening the marriage. What distinguishes swinging from other forms of extramarital sexual involvement is that husbands and wives who swing generally agree to have sexual relations with other persons, couples, or groups at the same time and place. Swingers might, for instance, go together to a private club or party where it is understood that at some point in the evening they will be permitted and encouraged to have free and impersonal sex with others.

Couples typically find out about or are recruited into swinging in one of several ways. Some may be attracted to experimenting with mate swapping by learning about swinging clubs or bars. Others may learn about swinging from experienced couples who pass the word or invite friends to join them in the pursuit of carefully controlled nonmonogynous and nonmonandrous sexual pleasure. Still others may read of this deviance in one of a variety of swinger magazines, or by simply perusing the personal ad sections in many "respectable" publications.

Is it possible that the impersonal sexual exchanges engaged in through swinging are a functional equivalent of the latent consequences of prostitution outlined by Davis? Social scientists who have studied swinging contend that it permits participants to release sexual fantasies for an evening or a weekend without damaging the sentimental bond of marriage. In an article subtitled "The Family that Swings Together Clings Together," Diane Denfield and Michael Gordon report that swinging may actually prolong marriage.[14] Romantic involvements are taboo among most swingers in much the same manner as between prostitutes and their customers. According to the suggestive logic of functionalist analysis, both types of deviance may be viewed as latently positive for society as a whole.

IDENTIFYING FUNCTIONAL DEVIANCE

There is no one research strategy that is the exclusive property of functionalist theory. Nonetheless, most functionalist interpretations of deviance are based upon a relatively common set of analytic assumptions. These constrain researchers to see nonconformity in a particular way. Functional analysis begins with the assumption that deviance must be studied in terms of its relationship to society as a whole. Functionalist theorists view society as a system of interrelated parts or structures. Each part is to be examined for its relationship to others and to the operation of the entire system. Each part is to be analyzed for the way it contributes to or detracts from the integrated survival of the system. This image of social life as a system of interrelated parts is present in Durkheim's choice of an organic metaphor to describe the workings of society.

In contemporary sociological theory the functional interrelationship of systemic parts is a central concern in the highly influential writings of sociologist Talcott Parsons. For Parsons, functional analysis involves "relating all problems explicitly and systematically to the total system."[15] His book *The Social System* includes a detailed catalog of the functional contributions of all major parts of the system to the system.[16] Parsons's work is considered in greater detail in my subsequent discussion of the social control of functional deviance. At present it is sufficient to ask how Durkheim, Parsons, and other functionalist theorists sought to document claims regarding the positive contributions of deviance.

According to Durkheim, for functional analysis to be properly scientific, it must separate the study of what causes a particular social phenomenon from an examination of its consequences. For the study of deviance this meant that observations regarding its universal presence were to be analytically distinct from those considering its cause or determining conditions. For Durkheim this rule was stronger in principle than in practice. Durkheim's "analyses of actual phenomena . . . lapsed into assertions that the need for integration caused a particular event."[17] This resulted in the twin problems of *tautology* (circular reasoning) and *false teleology* (the assertion that things like deviance happen in order to realize the goals of the system, without specifying how exactly the system causes these functional activities to arise in the first place).

The problems of tautology and false teleology sound very abstract. They nonetheless create very concrete and practical problems for the truth claims of functional analysis. Consider tautology. To suggest that deviance is functional for society because it can be found (universally) in every society represents a kind of circular logic. Because it exists it must be functional! If it were not functional it would not exist! Such reasoning catches us in a circle of word games. It tells us very little about the specific reasons that deviance is found in all societies. Durkheim was aware of this problem. He argued that the functionality of deviance cannot be determined solely by the criteria of universality. In order to know whether deviance is truly functional, we are asked to consider a second criterion—the criterion of determining conditions.

What exactly are these determining conditions? What exactly causes deviance to come into being and be sustained as a continuing phenomenon within all societies? On this issue Durkheim is unfortunately vague. His answer seems to slip into the region of false teleology. In *The Rules of the Sociological Method*, Durkheim cautions functionalist researchers to avoid this problem. False teleology, he argues, arises when researchers assume that social phenomena come into being because society needs them to survive. This assumption confuses the study of cause with that of function. Society may need deviance. Yet, as Durkheim points out, "The need we have of things cannot give them existence."[18] This is not to say that once some needed thing comes into being it will not be reciprocally supported by the very society which needed it in the first place. As Anthony Giddens remarks, Durkheim's attempt to avoid false teleology by separating the study of cause form the study of functional consequences did not prevent him from positing a reciprocal relation between these two things.[19] According to Durkheim, "The effect can doubtless not exist without its cause; but the latter, in turn, needs its effect. It is from the cause that the effect draws its energy; but it also restores it to the cause on occasion, and consequently it cannot disappear without the cause showing the effects of its disappearance."[20]

For Durkheim the effects of deviance are to secure integrated social stability while allowing for flexible adaptive change. These are its primary functional contributions. These effects are what makes deviance normal. But what actually causes deviance, and how do its effects "on occasion" restore energy to its cause? If you as a reader think such matters to be vague and highly abstract, you are not incorrect. Durkheim provides us with very little concrete information about the actual causes of normal deviance or about the ways its effects reinforce these causes. We are left, instead, with a series of statements which pair the existence of deviance with its functional contributions. Crime or deviance, states Durkheim, "is a factor in public health, an integral part of all healthy societies. . . . [I]t is bound up with the fundamental conditions of all social life, and by that very fact it is useful, because these conditions of which it is a part are themselves indispensable to . . . normal evolution."[21]

Durkheim warns us not to equate the functions of deviance with goal-like end-states which are said to cause their own realization. Yet by pairing the existence of deviance with its functional contributions Durkheim provides just such an equation. At other points Durkheim moves even closer to suggesting that functional needs operate (teleologically) as goals which set in motion certain processes which guarantee goal fulfillment. In discussing the possibility that society could curb all crime or deviance, Durkheim suggests that "the very cause which would thus dry up the sources of criminality would immediately open up new ones. Indeed, for the collective sentiments which are protected by the penal law . . . to take hold of the public conscience . . . they must acquire an intensity greater than that which they had hitherto had."[22] Here Durkheim comes dangerously close to false teleology. What causes greater intensity in the penal sanctioning of deviance? Its cause becomes equated with its functional consequence—the collective sentiments it produces. Why? We are left, at least implicitly, with the idea that a need for social integration operates as a goal or an end-state which paradoxically produces the deviance which produces it. Here Durkheim tilts heavily in the direction of false teleology. He tells us virtually nothing about the original causes of deviance or about the process of reciprocal causation in which functional effects feed back upon that which caused them. Despite intentions to the contrary, Durkheim's functional analysis remains trapped in a mire of confusing tautologies and unwarranted teleological reasoning. After reading what Durkheim has to say about the functional contributions of deviance, one is left with the distinct sense that deviance exists because it is brought into being to fulfill the purposes or goals of society as an organic system.

Few theorists have fared better than Durkheim in overcoming the problems of tautology and false teleology. These problems seem endemic to functional analysis. Nonetheless, one recent theorist, Robert K. Merton, has provided a methodological guide designed to eliminate many of the shortcomings of previous functionalist theorizing.[23] According to Merton, functionalist researchers must avoid all assumptions regarding (1) the harmonious integration of all parts of a social system, (2) the relationship between the existence of a social phenomenon and the belief that it must contribute to the maintenance of the social whole, and (3) the idea that genuine societal needs can only be served by the structural unit which appears to positively or functionally contribute to the fulfillment of such needs in the present. There can, in other words, be various alternative structural paths for fulfilling even the most basic of society's needs.

Merton's suggestions have important implications for the study of deviance. By not assuming the harmonious integration of all parts of the system, Merton paves the way for functionalists to consider the possibility that deviance may be functional for some people (i.e., the ones who benefit the most from the way that social life is organized at the present time) but dysfunctional for others (i.e., the people who benefit least from the existing system, particularly the ones who are condemned, punished, or ostracized as deviants). By not assuming that because a particular pattern of social interaction exists it must be functional, Merton directs attention to the "net balance" of positive and negative consequences. This provides a corrective for an otherwise one-sided emphasis on positive contributions. Also to be considered is the possibility of both manifest (recognized and intended) and latent (unrecognized and unintended) functions. Recall the previous discussion of the manifest and latent consequences of prostitution and the corrupt political machine. Moreover, by not assuming that there is only one structural alternative for fulfilling a particular social need, Merton asks us to explicitly compare alternative means for fulfilling that same need.

Why, for instance, does our society rely so heavily on correcting the deviant rather than on changing the societal conditions out of which deviance grows or generating efforts to reconcile offenders and the offended? These strategies represent divergent alternatives to the problem of nonconformity. A more traditional (and more tautological and falsely teleological) functionalism might simply assume that the present state of things exists because it contributes positively to the entire society. Merton's functional analysis is more careful. Once it has identified the dominant alternative employed to control deviance, it seeks to locate its causal origins. It does this not by identifying its contributions to society as a whole, but by examining its relationship to a host of other socially structured economic, political, and cultural alternatives. Merton's program of functional analysis is designed for researchers who wish to explain the causes of particular forms of deviance and social control and to assess the net balance of their positive and negative consequences. According to Merton a proper functionalist analysis must follow five steps.

1 *Provide a specific description of the form of deviance or social control being studied.* How are activities structured or patterned between specific actors or groups or organizations under investigation? The researcher is instructed to describe as precisely as possible the dominant pattern of interaction followed by the social units under analysis.

2 *Indicate the range and type of alternatives excluded by the dominant pattern of deviance or social control.* This methodological prescription is aimed at directing researchers' attention to what Merton calls the "structural context" in which a particular pattern of deviance or social control emerged. Consider the topic of

child abuse. Why, for instance, are more lower-class parents officially discovered as abusers than middle- and upper-class parents? Why is it so common for abusers to report that they too had been abused as children? Why when laws were passed to control child abuse was preference given to control strategies based upon therapeutic treatment rather than corrective punishment? By exploring such questions Merton hoped that researchers would derive clues as to both the causes and the functional (or dysfunctional) consequences of observed interaction patterns.

3 *Assess the meaning of the deviant or social control activity for those involved.* What does deviance or control work mean subjectively to those who engage in it? By asking this question Merton hoped that functional analysts would arrive at some insights into the manifest or intended consequences of a particular activity. Once again, consider the matter of child abuse. Why is it that so many abusive parents state that they did nothing to "really" hurt their child? What does the administration of brutal punishment actually mean to a parent who beats his or her child? On the social control side of the problem, how is it that child abuse means so much to the large army of medical practitioners who today fight against it, while before the 1960s, when child abuse was first discovered as a major social problem, most doctors saw some unexplained physical trauma as the cause of mysterious childhood bruises, broken bones, and lacerations?

4 *Discern the motives for conforming to or deviating from a particular dominant interaction pattern.* Here Merton refers the research to the social-psychological needs served or not served by conforming to or deviating from a particular action pattern. In this search Merton hoped to further uncover clues to the consequences which certain deviant or control practices create for actors in a given society. What does acting in a certain fashion do for people? By asking this question Merton's functionalism seeks to connect the individual deviant or controller to structured patterns in society at large.

5 *Describe patterns not recognized by participants but which appear to have consequences for either the particular individuals involved and/or other patterns or regularities in the wider social context.* The aim here is to examine potentially latent consequences of deviance or control work which, even if they escape the attention of actors involved, may affect the activities being studied by affecting other activities in related sectors of society.

The five principles for functional analysis outlined by Merton are today considered to be the most comprehensive guidelines for this approach to social research and theory building. In principle they avoid the circular and falsely teleological problems encountered by Durkheim and other early functionalists. In practice the application of these principles may be considerably elusive. This is particularly true regarding the notion of latent consequences. Consider Merton's analysis of the latent positive functions of the corrupt big-city political machine. Merton states:

> Proceeding from the functional view . . . we should ordinarily (not invariably) expect persistent social patterns and social structures to perform positive functions

which are at the time not fulfilled by other patterns and structures; the thought occurs that perhaps this publicly maligned organization is, under present conditions, satisfying basic latent functions.[24]

Despite his warnings against assuming a relationship between persisting patterns and contributing functions, Merton starts out with (almost) just such an assumption. The phrase "not invariably" may spare Merton the charge of being technically tautological. Yet, the "thought" which occurs to him that the "maligned organization" may be "satisfying latent functions" appears to represent a serious lapse into false teleological reasoning. Does the machine really operate to fulfill societal needs? Was this happening even if nobody intended it to happen? Was this happening even if nobody, until Merton, recognized that it was happening? How easy it is for even the most careful of functional theorists to see systemic needs behind every act of deviance. Perhaps functional deviance can never fully escape the dual trap of tautology and false teleology.

SOCIAL CONTROL OF FUNCTIONAL DEVIANCE

Following Durkheim the functionalist perspective recognizes the positive, or functional, contributions of deviance. Some deviance is good for the system. But what about a lot of deviance? Isn't deviance dysfunctional as well? Durkheim thought so. His statements about the usefulness of deviance were prefaced by the qualification that it must not exceed a certain level. Excess deviance was seen as pathological rather than normal. According to Durkheim, "This excess is . . . undoubtedly morbid in nature. What is normal . . . is the existence of criminality, provided that it attains and does not exceed . . . a certain level."[25]

The problems of excess deviance are of great concern to modern functionalists such as Talcott Parsons. Until his death in 1979, Parsons was the foremost functionalist theorist in sociology. Like Durkheim, Parsons considered society as a "thing in itself." The healthy society was equated with the stable society. The social activities of its members would be highly coordinated as interrelated parts of an organic system. By such coordination the social system fulfilled its basic needs.

What are the basic needs of society? According to Parsons, there are four functional prerequisites for the survival of any social system.[26] These include: (1) *adaptation* to the external environment; (2) *integration* of all of the system's parts, such that the values, roles, interests, and motives of its members contribute to the orderly operation of society as a whole; (3) *goal attainment*, or the coordinated, cooperative achievement of collective social objectives; and (4) *pattern maintenance–tension reduction* (also referred to as "latency"), the ongoing recruitment of individuals into the patterned social roles needed to keep the system functioning and mechanisms to reduce the systemic strains of conformity.

Parsons suggests that basic social institutions arise to fulfill the needs outlined above. Social institutions are defined as relatively stable patterns of interaction between actors whose roles in the system are governed by an internalized set of norms or expectations. Basic institutions rise up to meet each of the basic societal needs or functional requisites. Economic institutions develop relatively stable ways of adapting to society's external physical and human environment, to natural resources and the demands of other social systems. By providing a system of commonly shared beliefs and values the institution of religion was said to play a central role in integration. Political institutions contribute to setting and realizing societywide goals. Educational institutions teach people necessary social roles. Education thus functions as an institution of pattern maintenance. The family, in both teaching and supporting its members in doing their part, also serves a pattern-maintenance function. So too can it act as an institution of tension reduction. After a hard day's work, family members return home, where they are often permitted to blow off the steam accumulated in conforming to prescribed institutional norms. When tensions become too great, people may deviate. When this happens other tension-reduction institutions are mobilized to back up the family. Such social control institutions range from institutions which use therapy to return actors to their expected roles to institutions which use coercion to enforce conformity.

Parsons's vision of social life as an equilibrium-producing machine is highly mechanistic. It likens the exchange between individual parts of the system to the cybernetic exchange between parts of a self-regulating machine. A core (if implicit) feature of scientific social management since World War II, cybernetics represents a kind of "guiding light" or "climate of belief" behind contemporary capitalist culture. With cybernetics, human actions are emptied of their historical meaning. Specific acts and gestures are then abstractly transcoded as if they were timeless and interchangeable units of energy and information. This input/output approach to the "human factor" is a major feature of speculative capitalist economics. It is also a central aspect of functionalist theory. Strains or tensions within one part of the social machine, between parts, or between one system and another are said to produce adjustive reactions by which the system restabilizes itself. This is how functionalism views deviance. Deviance is pictured as both generating its own control and renewing the system's equilibrium. For cybernetic theorists such as Parsons, deviance is like the overheating of a part within a machine containing a built-in "cool-out component." When the temperature rises above a certain safety point, an automatic sprinkler is activated to reduce the heat. Deviance is like the heat. Social control is like the automatic sprinkling component.

For Parsons and other modern functionalists, the heat of excessive deviance is cooled by four mechanisms of social control: socialization, profit, persuasion, and (when all else fails) coercion.[27] If socialization were totally successful, no other mechanism would be needed. Socialization teaches people to internalize the patterned roles necessary for achieving ordered social equilibrium. When socialization is imperfect, profit and persuasion arise as additional mechanisms to secure conformity. Profit reinforces equilibrium-producing behaviors. It teaches us that we get payoffs when we conform and punishment when we don't. Payoffs can range from such things as obtaining a good grade or a top salary to getting the desired smile from a person we value. Punishment can run the same wide gamut.

In singling out persuasion as the third mechanism of control, Parsons suggests that people organize their lives as much by symbols as by practical rewards. Sometimes persuasion attempts to correct an existing pattern of deviance. The minister delivering a sermon to sinners and the psychiatrist exhorting patients to gain insight into their psychological deviance are using persuasion as a corrective. Other forms of persuasion aim at preventing deviance. Think of television advertising. This form of persuasion may induce us to adopt a certain look, feel, or way of acting that is compatible with the dominant economic (adaptive), political (goal attainment), religious (integrative), and family-educational (pattern maintenance–tension reduction) institutions of our day.

Socialization, profit, and persuasion are together said to contribute to social control by providing, reinforcing, and legitimizing lines of conformity. When socialization is imperfect, when profit is lacking, when persuasion is weak, the likelihood of deviance increases. Members become alienated from society. They become lost within the machine—dysfunctional parts which endanger the system's equilibrium. Such alienation may be active or passive and could involve either a direct rejection of conformity or an indirect avoidance of doing the "responsible" thing. Active rejection is associated with hostile or aggressive deviance. Passive rejection involves withdrawal, perhaps into a world of "madness." An active and compulsive avoidance of responsibility is illustrated by the career of the hobo. On the other hand, the alcoholic and the drug abuser may represent a more passive form of responsibility avoidance. Modern functionalism views all these types of deviance as examples of the failure of socialization, profit, and persuasion. If unchecked they pave a destructive path of disequilibrium. To limit this disequilibrium, society must institute a fourth mechanism of control—coercion.

For functionalists, coercion is society's trump card in the game of social control. Its concern with curtailing the forces of disorder underscores the need and legitimacy of coercive state power. According to functionalists the state must exercise its prerogative to constrain nonconformists, even if by violence.

THE FUNCTIONALIST PERSPECTIVE TODAY

Although the origins of functionalist theory are commonly traced to Durkheim, it was under the guidance of the cybernetic-like thinking of Talcott Parsons that functionalism emerged as the dominant perspective in American sociology during the 1950s. Its preeminence continued until the mid-1960s, when a variety of competing perspectives arose, challenging its grip on the sociological imagination. Before considering examples of the empirical application of functionalist imagery, I shall locate the rise of functionalism within its contemporary historical context.

The Great Depression and World War II: A Crisis in U.S. Order and the Rise of Functionalist Cybernetics

The dominance of functionalism during the 1950s had led commentators to associate this perspective with a time of economic prosperity and perceived political stability. Parsons's image of society as a self-adjusting system is seen as but an abstraction of the naive optimism of that decade. This depiction of functionalism misses an important point—that Parsons's theoretical project was largely accomplished in the decade preceding the 1950s. To miss this point is to overlook the relationship between functionalism and what Alvin Gouldner has referred to as "the general crisis of the American middle-class."[28] It is also to ignore the role of wartime thinking as a contributing factor to Parsons's extension of functionalist theory in the direction of cybernetics.

According to Gouldner, this crisis was occasioned by the great depression of the 1930s. To fully appreciate Gouldner's thesis, it is necessary to recall the sociological optimism of the Chicago school a decade earlier. As suggested in the preceding chapter, its optimism was based on several interrelated assumptions: (1) that disruptive social disorganization was a temporary by-product of rapid social change, (2) that temporary disorganization was but a phase in the natural course of social reorganization, and (3) that reorganization could be efficiently facilitated by empirically informed professional problem solving.

Each of these assumptions was upended by the depression. The depression, in other words, undermined sociologists' confidence in their ability to rationally control social problems.

The depression triggered problems which could not be explained as the by-products of rapid change, problems which presented deeper images of disorder, problems which challenged the fundamental structure of the U.S. economy. During the 1920s, sociologists, like other members of the expanding U.S. middle class, viewed the economy as strong, resilient, and adaptive. This view was proved wrong by the economic collapse of the next decade. As Gouldner points out: "In the 1930's, the economic system had broken down. It could no longer produce the massive daily gratification that helped hold middle-class society together and foster commitment to its values."[29] Moreover, it rendered "the previous American tradition of the study of isolated social problems" as "manifestly incompetent to deal with social strains that obviously ramified through all institutions and social strata."[30]

The depression crystalized a general mood of unease which had hung like an ominous storm cloud over the European and American middle classes since the end of World War I. Other events contributing to this mood included the war itself, with its irrational images of the dark side of human nature, the Russian Revolution and the resulting political struggle between east and west, and the rise of fascism in Italy and Germany, which "signaled that the European middle class's anxieties had become a panic that undermined social and political stability."[31] For a time, the geographic isolation of the United States may have spared its middle class the acute anxiety experienced by Europeans. During the depression this changed. Residents of the United States were drawn into an international crisis that simultaneously threatened the middle class in capitalist countries worldwide.

Existing U.S. sociological theory was unable to fully comprehend the international crisis described by Gouldner. Its emphasis on piecemeal technical problem solving rendered it unable to deal with the more fundamental structural problems posed by the international collapse of the capitalist economy. What other theoretical alternatives presented themselves? Marxism was one alternative debated in European intellectual circles. In the United States, however, Marxism had not yet emerged as a serious intellectual tradition within the U.S. university.[32] Its proposals for overturning the capitalist economic system were alien to most of the middle-class sociologists whose investment in that system had increased so dramatically in the years following World War I. Where then would U.S. sociology turn? The answer is found in the theoretical appeal of Parsonian functionalism.

Parsons's cybernetic description of society as a self-maintaining homeostatic system offered an image of social order that was relatively independent of questions related to economic order. Economic institutions were seen as counterbalanced by other institutions—the state, the family, the church, etc. Parsons described the stabilizing exchanges between the various parts of the system in a highly abstract language removed from the everyday realities of concrete economic crisis. For many critics this has meant that Parsons's abstract functionalism was devoid of relevance for U.S. life. Gouldner disagrees. Although Parsons wrote little about practical social problems—delinquency, family instability, poverty, etc.—his extremely abstract notion of a self-preserving social system is interpreted as the basis of the essential relevance of functionalism for the crisis-embattled U.S. middle class. Parsons's emphasis on orderly equilibrium provided a conceptual escape from a world engulfed by economic and social disorder. It allowed sociologists to make peace with the existing order on the assumption that society would work things out in time. It offered a new optimism based, not upon anything observable, but upon abstract generalities. As Gouldner points out, "He one-sidedly emphasized the adaptability of the status quo, considering the ways in which it was open to change rather than the manner in which its own characteristics were inducing the disorder and resisting adaptation to it."[33]

Gouldner provides a biographical account of Parsons's conservative optimism. Born in 1902, the son of a Congregational minister in central Ohio, Parsons was too young to have directly experienced the horrors of World War I. Completing his graduate education during the prosperous 1920s, Parsons had settled into marriage and a comfortable faculty position at Harvard University two years before the stock market crash in 1929. Financially secure, Harvard was little affected by the economic crisis of the thirties. Moreover, unlike the University of Chicago during the 1920s, Harvard was an elite institution with a long tradition of detachment from the problems of its surrounding community.

This is not to suggest that functionalist sociologists, such as Parsons, played no role in shaping public policy. With Kenneth Clark, Parsons edited *The American Negro,* a 1966 collection of essays calling for a pluralistic solution to racial divisions within the United States.[34] More problematic was Parsons's involvement in certain "covert" cold war operations. In the years following World War II, Parsons worked "under cover" with U.S. Army Intelligence and the State Department. As a "secret agent," the noted sociologist helped gather data on the Soviet Union by recruiting Russian-born Nazi collaborators, including a social scientist wanted as a "war criminal."[35] Nevertheless, within Harvard's ivy-covered halls, Parsons's optimistic view of society as a self-adjusting social system was transmitted to an entire generation of influential sociologists. Under Parsons's guidance the dominant center for North American sociology shifted from Chicago to the Atlantic coast.

During his tenure at Harvard, Parsons was also a leading sociological proponent of cybernetics. As a scientific world view, cybernetics rose to prominence during World War II. In conjunction with early analog computers, cybernetics was envisioned as a "scientific" means by which to more efficiently coordinate the actions of human operators with new high-tech weapons of war—anti-aircraft guns, navigation devices, and precision bombing equipment. According to Norbert Weiner of the Massachusetts Institute of Technology (MIT), who coined the phrase, *cybernetics* refers to the unified study of control and communication in animals and machines. Each was viewed as a source of feedback for the other, just as units of energy were said to (analogously) feed back into units of information, and the reverse. This viewpoint was attractive to Parsons, who, throughout his career, maintained an interest in translating the latest developments in biology into theories of social and economic equilibrium.[36]

Cybernetic thinking today permeates the most powerful sectors of capitalism, as entire "nations, their economies, their peoples, their responses, their land, can be simulated and displayed" as nothing but "inputs" and "outputs" of information exchanging with energy.[37] From a cybernetic viewpoint, even "deviance" may be viewed as something positive, a temporary instance of "negative feedback," triggering adjustive responses within the social system as a whole. Masked in the neutral-sounding language of "management information systems" (MISs), and materially linked to a vast array of hardware and software "information technologies," cybernetics is a dominant ideological force (or belief system) behind contemporary capitalist institutions. Like capitalism's most flexible features, cybernetics is also an offshoot of the white-male-guided industrialization of modern warfare. This was evident in the language of W. Ross Ashby, an early theorist and popularizer of cybernetic discourse, when he announced:

> The inborn characteristics of living organisms are simply the strategies that have been found satisfactory over centuries of competition and built into the young animal so as to be ready for use at the first demand. Just as so many players have found "P-Q4" a good way of opening a game of chess, so many species found "growth teeth" to be a good way of opening the Battle of Life.[38]

If this sounds a bit like the Spencerian rhetoric of "survival of the fittest," it should be no surprise if you are familiar with the writings of Talcott Parsons. Parsons's "cybernetic functionalism" combines Spencer's evolutionary viewpoint with ideas about adjustive feedback drawn from twentieth-century biology. Parsons used the term "cybernetic hierarchy of control" to describe the orderly adjustment of social systems, a process whereby "informational/energetic interchanges among action systems provide the potential for change within or between action systems. One source of change may be excesses in either information or energy in the exchange among action systems. In turn, these excesses alter the informational or energetic outputs across systems and within any system. . . . Another source of change comes from an insufficient supply of either energy or information, again causing external and internal readjustments in the structure of action systems."[39] If this image of social change seems both overly abstract and inattentive to questions about the historical role of social power, perhaps this is because Parsons defines power as merely the "capacity of a social system to mobilize resources to attain collective goals."[40] This ignores the effects of social hierarchies and the struggles of people oppressed by unequal power. Such thorny issues are smoothed over by the machinelike metaphors of cybernetic theory.

In tracing his own interest in cybernetics, Parsons posits the influence of various "systems-oriented" biological theorists. Of particular significance are the teachings of Harvard biochemist L. J. Henderson. During the great depression, Henderson's "seminars" on the Italian social theorist Vilfredo Pareto underscored the role of "living systems" in the organization of all social forms. These influential gatherings were attended by a variety of well-known thinkers, including Parsons, sociobiologist E. O. Wilson, sociologists George Homans and Robert K. Merton, and anthropologist Clyde Kluckholm. "Henderson stressed the importance of Pareto's model of a social system and the notion of equilibrium in his teaching although it is also true that the Harvard physiologist's support for the Italian intellectual's ideas was connected to his anti-Marxist elitism. Henderson was an extreme conservative in his political views and saw Pareto's theory as many others with his opinions saw it—as the one social/economic theory which could counterpose Marxism in accounting for the depression."[41]

For Henderson, as for Parsons and others who would soon develop an enthusiasm for cybernetics, Pareto's theories heralded "the commencement of a new era in the history of thought."[42] They also presaged a dissolving of boundaries between sociology, biology, and economics. Moreover, as Lewis Coser points out: "That the America of the depression proved receptive to Pareto's thought is not surprising. . . . His work appealed to two major strains in the climate of opinion of the thirties: belief in the saving authority of science and loss of belief in the authority of tradition. His positivism appealed in an intellectual climate in which only the claims of science still stood unchallenged, and his debunking stance was congenial to intellectuals whose moorings had been severely shaken ever since the bottom dropped out of the stock market in 1929. [As a theorist of self-adjusting systems,] Pareto was largely read as a kind of bourgeois answer to Marx."[43]

Parsons also acknowledged the importance of the annual Conference on Systems Theory which was held in Chicago from 1952 to 1957, and particularly the role of insect biologist Alfred Emerson, who persuaded the functionalist sociologist of the importance of "the then just emerging conceptions of cybernetic control."[44] According to the cybernetic model, human energy is regulated by informational feedback, as both energy and information are pictured as systemically commanding each other. This is an assumption shared by cybernetics, functionalist theories of deviance, and contemporary capitalist economics. Each of these "systems" assumes a self-regulating interchange between information and energy. Each is also based on a related disavowal of lived historical contradictions. By positing an ideal state of self-adjusting equilibrium, these forms of systems logic deny the reality of conflictual social processes that elevate certain forms of scientific reasoning at the expense of others.

As a militaristic daydream of total or totalitarian control, the cybernetic fantasy of a self-sustaining system is nothing new. Nevertheless, by the 1950s, such a functionalist world view had come to dominate mainstream North American sociology. Just as functionalism's conservative optimism represented a safe professional response to the crisis of the great depression, its widespread acceptance is associated with the triumphant emergence of the United States from the depression during and after World War II. The U.S. system's cybernetic-like adjustment was linked to the New Deal economic policies of the Roosevelt administration. In purely functionalist terminology, political institutions had provided an adjustive balance for strains arising within economic institutions. Indeed, the U.S. "system" seemed stronger than ever. As Gouldner points out, "During the war and after it, prosperity returned; at least for the middle-class, American society was reknit by affluence and by war-induced solidarity. The working class and its unions became increasingly integrated into the society; the sense of an imminent threat to public order disappeared."[45] But lest you become overly enchanted by the seductive logic of cybernetic functionalism, I must point out that it is at once ironic and revealing that the popularity of this perspective was conditioned not by smooth societal self-regulation but by violent social conflict.

Sociology after World War II: Temporary Images of Prosperity and the Reign of Functionalism

During World War II, many sociologists worked for the federal government, conducting research on such matters as the social organization of command, the training of recruits, and the origins of combat fatigue. The U.S. triumph in the war was, moreover, accompanied by the triumph of professional sociology as a science. In the years following the war the abstract generality of functionalism provided sociology with an identity as a science of high-level conceptualization, and even predictive ability. After all, hadn't functionalist theorizing prefigured the return to economic prosperity which manifested itself in the United States during the postwar years? This apparent functionalist strength was more illusionary than real. It disguised as much as it revealed. In describing U.S. society as a system of interdependent parts, it ignored (or was incapable of seeing) deeper cleavages in the economic, racial, and sexual organization of the United States itself. The rose-colored glasses of functionalist optimism were seemingly tinted by the conservatism of the people who benefited most from the way in which stability was currently arranged—the people at the top of the social, political, and economic order, whom critical sociologist C. Wright Mills designated as the "power elite." For more than a decade the rose-colored glasses of functionalism belonged to the power elite, and so, perhaps, did most sociologists of the time.[46]

The surfacing of suppressed racial and political tensions during the 1960s destroyed the dominance of functionalist theory. Arguing that society was better described as a coordination of conflictual interests, many sociologists abandoned ideas about self-regulating systemic equilibrium. Yet, despite its limitations, the functionalist approach has shed light on certain aspects of deviance previously shadowed by darkness. Presented below are overviews of two of the more influential studies derived from the functionalist framework. The thoughtful questions raised by these projects remind those of us who are critical of functionalism of the age-old maxim "Don't throw the baby out with the bathwater."

Dentler and Erikson's Analysis of the Functions of Deviance in Groups In their study, Dentler and Erikson depict the positive consequences of deviance for the organization of ten Quaker work projects and for basic trainees in the U.S. Army.[47] They employed a variety of field-research techniques to examine the consequences of deviance in each case. The specific goals of the two groups were, of course, different. While the army sought to train competent combatants, the Quakers hoped to induce "conformity with norms of tolerance, pacifism, democratic group relations and related social attitudes."[48] Nonetheless, data gathered on both groups were said to illustrate three functionalist propositions:

1 Groups tend to induce, sustain, and permit deviant behavior.
2 Deviant behavior functions in inducing groups to maintain group equilibrium.

3 Groups will resist any trend toward alienation of a member whose behavior is deviant.

In each Quaker group a deviant recurrently emerged who acted, dressed, and talked differently from other members. The existence of such deviants provided the group with someone whose irritable oddness became the target of other members' tolerance and care. Groups went out of their way to adjust to and not alienate or exclude such functional deviants. This process of adjustment symbolized dominant group values, such as tolerance, and enhanced members' solidarity. According to Dentler and Erikson, the groups with "more extremely deviant members" were actually the ones which achieved the highest equilibrium or intensity in social relationships.[49]

Similar things happened in the basic-trainee situation. Each high-stress boot-camp group produced a clumsy, bumbling deviant. This "helpless," "soft," and "offbeat" person contributed to group unity in an interesting way. Remember that army life, particularly in basic training, is tightly structured, authoritarian, hard, and traditionally "masculine." The soft helplessness of deviant trainees "introduced emotional qualities which the population—lacking women and younger persons—could not otherwise afford." As such, the deviant was seen as functional in reducing tensions and maintaining group equilibrium. Although manifestly a low producer and a potential handicap, latently the deviant contributes something that nondeviant members cannot. Thus, according to Dentler and Erikson, "the group neither exerts strong pressures on him to conform nor attempts to expel him from the squad. Instead, he is typically given a wide license to deviate."[50]

Such research on the functions of deviance in groups opens our eyes to another side of nonconformity. Do groups really produce deviants to meet their own needs? The description of the bumbling boot-camp deviant may seem familiar to those who have shared a house, a dormitory floor, or a long-term work situation with a small group of people. Isn't it often true that someone in such groups becomes singled out as deviant? Arlene Kaplan Daniels and Richard Daniels wrote about this in a fascinating article on the social role of the "career fool." Such deviants were said to "appear in small, rather tightly knit social worlds" and to provide others with "a feeling of comfortable superiority and confidence," and "vicarious satisfaction . . . that not everyone is broken or 'processed' by the system."[51] This unorthodox way of seeing deviance is a good illustration of the functionalist perspective. For a wider, society-level view, we shall examine Kai Erikson's historical study of deviance in seventeenth-century Massachusetts.

The Wayward Puritans: Moral Boundaries and the Constancy of Social Control By examining court records and other historical documents, Erikson attempted to reconstruct the role of deviance among the Puritans of the Massachusetts Bay Colony.[52] He draws three conclusions supportive of the functionalist perspective. The first concerns the establishment of moral boundaries. In keeping with Durkheim, Erikson observes that "each time the community moves to censure some act of deviation, it sharpens the authority of the violated norm and restates where the boundaries of the group are located."[53]

In addition to establishing moral boundaries, the nature of the acts declared to be deviant is reflective of the dominant values of society at a particular time. For the Puritans, a constant concern with heresy and witchcraft revealed not only the "shape of the devil," but also the shape of the community's focal values. Erikson documents this point by noting that the specific content of Puritan crimes varied with changes in the nature of the threats to the community's religious purity. Accordingly, "it is not surprising that deviant behavior should appear in a community at exactly those points where it is most feared. Men who fear witches soon find themselves surrounded by them; men who become jealous of private property soon encounter eager thieves."[54]

Does the fear of deviance create deviance, or does deviance create fear? Erikson never really answers this question, although he admits that the affinity between these two things "has been a continuous source of wonder in human affairs."[55] He observes, however, that over a period of thirty years the volume of persons charged with deviance remained remarkably constant. This suggests that deviance may be produced by society in proportion to its capacity for social control. Nonetheless, while the volume of criminals remained relatively constant, the number of action convictions changed during difficult time periods. Conviction rates increased in times when the dominant religious values of the Puritans came under threat. During such "crime waves" the community was called upon to reaffirm its moral boundaries.

Despite periodic fluctuations of conviction rates, the observed constancy of an offender population is taken as evidence that society generates something like "quotas" of functionally needed deviants.[56] The so-called Quaker invasion, which may have induced higher levels of general religious conformity, is suggestive of this point. Even at the height of this moral revival, the "pool" of deviants remained constant. As such, Erikson offers a general functionalist observation that *society channels certain of its members into relatively fixed careers in deviance.*[57]

Erikson's analysis may raise more questions than it answers. Historians have questioned the adequacy of his use of official documents.[58] Sociologists have asked questions about the comparability of the small, tightly knit, authoritarian Puritan society and the large, amorphous, and multivalued world of today. Others have wondered whether the volume of deviance isn't better explained by the self-serving organizational activities of control agents themselves. Nonetheless, *Wayward Puritans* stands as an imaginative and provocative piece of research that raises significant questions about a society's functional need for deviance.

ASSESSMENT OF THE FUNCTIONALIST PERSPECTIVE

The genius of the functionalist perspective is that it transports the concept of deviance away from its nearly exclusive identification with the dark and shadowy. In "lightening up" the study of deviance the functionalist perspective sensitizes us to its more positive consequences. In contributing to social boundaries, group solidarity, and tension reduction, deviance helps to order rather than disorder the social system. In its innovative dimensions deviance may contribute to social vitality by challenging outdated ways of doing things.

Despite its advantages, there are decided disadvantages built into the logic of functionalist thinking. These include (1) an overly mechanistic view of social life as a social system, (2) the circularity of functional analysis, and (3) the conservative bias of functional analysis.

An Overly Mechanistic Image of Society: Cybernetic Reasoning and the Specter of False Teleology

From the cybernetic viewpoint of the functionalist perspective, the social system creates and regulates its own needs. By such adjustments the system is said to defend itself against all threats to its borders. Such militaristic logic is very neat on paper, but where in everyday life do we find such a perfectly self-regulating system? It is the contradictory actions of people that create and control deviance, not some impersonal social machine.

As a poetic metaphor, the idea of a social system is quite interesting. When we are stuck on the freeway at eight o'clock on a weekday morning, in line at the supermarket, or waiting to register for class, life may seem to be controlled by some giant computer which regulates our needs and modulates our tensions. Indeed, as the military-guided logic of cybernetic reasoning extends to virtually all aspects of our culture, the omnipresent appeal of systems metaphors is difficult to deny. Surrounded by wide-ranging informational technologies, from Sony Walkmen to portable telephones, answering machines, fax machines, video recorders, and even talking cars, many of us may experience the world as if it were actually regulated by digitally screened telecommunicative feedback.[59] In truth, things are less rational and less orderly. Freeways, weekday mornings, supermarkets, and class registration procedures are not created by a disembodied cybernetic system. They are sociological effects of often contradictory human actions in history. If social life seems more systemlike than spontaneous, more impersonal than personal, more constraining than creative, it is because we (or those of us who have the power to do so) have made it that way. Like Dr. Frankenstein, we have allowed our creations to become more masterful than ourselves. We should be wary of the oversimplification and overmechanization of human life inherent in the functionalist perspective.[60]

We have previously noted the relationship between functional analysis and the problem of false teleology. With regard to the study of deviance, a proposition is falsely teleological if it asserts that nonconformity comes about to realize the goals of the system, without specifying exactly how the system causes this to happen. The reason that cybernetic-minded functionalists find it so difficult to escape the specter of false teleology involves their reliance on the overly mechanistic metaphor of the social system. This metaphor suggests that deviance exists because it fulfills the goals of the system. The system metaphor traps functionalists into describing society in these terms. Once within this conceptual trap, functionalists fail to distinguish between a society of real people struggling in history and a "cybernetic machine" which stabilizes itself by molding people into well-oiled parts. Social life may seem like a cybernetic system with nearly everything feeding back into everything else. That is not to say that social life is a cybernetic system. It is not. Social life is guided less by the goal-directed imperatives of self-regulation than by contradictory historical forces that give certain things the defensive halo of appearing *as if* undoubtedly real, while making other things (or ways of doing things) appear deviant. Influenced by the defensive logic of militarism, the functionalist perspective is set up to miss this point.

The Circularity of Functional Analysis: The Specter of Tautology

Following Durkheim, the functionalists note the universal presence of crime and deviance, and describe the ways that they contribute to social order. As suggested previously, there is a kind of circular reasoning at work here. If something exists, then, by the typical logic of functional analysis, it must be contributing to the health of the whole society. With enough imagination one can find a positive function for anything. Child abuse may contribute to population control. Bank robberies may promote a more rational system of computerized monetary allocations. Arson can rid society of old buildings which occupy valuable space and waste energy.

The circular nature of much functional analysis is nowhere more evident than in Herbert Gans's analysis of the functions of poverty.[61] Gans suggests that poverty, despite all the bad press it gets from "bleeding-heart" liberals, can be viewed as a positive and necessary feature of social life. Gans offers us a laundry list of the fifteen "latent functions" of poverty. Among other things, it provides a constant market for spoiled or defective commodities, and it ensures that there will be needy people available to do the distasteful but necessary social "dirty work," a guaranteed surplus of people ready to assume jobs with low wages and poor working conditions. Gans also observes that poverty provides needed employment opportunities for helping professionals and those trained in the control of social disorder, and offers the opportunity for the nonpoor to vicariously participate in the poor's stereotypically uninhibited sexuality. The crux of Gans's satirical analysis involves a description of the contribution of poverty to political stability. Poverty is associated with a fatalistic view of life and with low interest in voting. Since poor people vote less, the political system is free to ignore them. Imagine what would happen if this were not the case. Thank heavens for poverty! If the poor participated fully in the political process, they would almost certainly demand a basic redistribution of jobs and incomes, "and would thus generate further political conflict between the haves and have-nots."[62]

When stretched to its imaginative limits the circular logic of functionalism can identify the positive consequences of virtually any aspect of social life. Gans's list of the useful contributions of poverty is a clear illustration. Yet, this analysis tells us nothing about the historical conditions that bring about or perpetuate poverty or about the concrete experiences of those subject to impoverishment. The same is true regarding the supposed positive functions of deviance. The circular logic of functionalism has a self-fulfilling character. By emphasizing benefits to the system as a whole, functionalism generally ignores the importance of historical circumstances and personal meanings.

The Conservative Bias of Functional Analysis

In addition to its mechanistic and circular features the functionalist perspective is also plagued by a certain conservative bias. In documenting positive contributions, the perspective fails to ask whether deviance might be more positive for some than for others. The arrested criminal might serve as a moral boundary marker or as a scored target for solidarity, but is being arrested functional for the deviant? Martin Luther King's acts of courageous political deviance may have been innovative from the viewpoint of the 1990s, but were his long nights in jail during the 1960s functional for him and his family?

Some people benefit more from deviance and/or its control than others. Who gains the most, and who loses the most? This question is alien to the conservative logic of functionalism. From the functionalist point of view the whole system benefits. Assuming the functionalists are correct, shouldn't we then ask who within the system benefits most? As a social system Nazi Germany may have benefited from the mass deviantizing of Jews. It would be absurd, however, to argue that all German citizens, including Jews, benefited equally from the Holocaust. When confronted with such issues the functionalist perspective reveals its fundamental conservatism. The system's benefits are recited without exploring who controls the system. Deviance may be functional. Yet in an unequal society its functions will not be equally distributed.

NOTES

1 Émile Durkheim, *The Rules of the Sociological Method*, translated by Sarah A. Solovay and John H. Muller and edited by Sir George E. G. Carlin, Macmillan, New York, 1964, p. 70.
2 Kai T. Erikson, *Wayward Puritans: A Study in the Sociology of Deviance*, Wiley, New York, 1966, p. 181.

3 The dialogue here being analyzed is from Jean Genet, *The Balcony*, Bernard Frecht-man (trans.), Grove Press, New York, 1966, p. 18.

4 Ibid., p. 19.

5 Lewis A. Coser, "Some Functions of Deviant Behavior and Normative Flexibility," *American Journal of Sociology*, vol. 69, September 1962, pp. 172–182, reprinted in M. Lefton, L. K. Skipper, Jr., and C. H. McCaghy (eds.), *Approaches to Deviance*, Appleton-Century-Crofts, New York, 1968, p. 286.

6 Durkheim, *The Rules of the Sociological Method*, p. 67.

7 Ibid., p. 71.

8 George Herbert Mead, "The Psychology of Punitive Justice," *American Journal of Sociology*, vol. 23, 1918, p. 586.

9 Durkheim, *The Rules of the Sociological Method*, p. 71.

10 See, for instance, Roger Caillois, *Man and the Sacred*, Meyer Barash (trans.), Free Press, New York, 1959; and Richard Stivers, *Evil in Modern Myth and Ritual*, University of Georgia Press, Athens, 1982, pp. 37–44.

11 Robert K. Merton, *Social Theory and Social Structure*, Free Press, New York, 1957, 1968.

12 Kingsley Davis, "Prostitution," in R. K. Merton and R. Nisbet (eds.), *Contemporary Social Problems*, 3d ed., Harcourt, Brace Jovanovich, New York, 1971.

13 For research on swinging, see Gilbert D. Bartell, *Group Sex*, Wyden, New York, 1971; Gilbert D. Bartell, "Group Sex among the Mid-Americans," *Journal of Sex Research*, vol. 6, 1970, pp. 113–130; James R. Smith and Lynn G. Smith, "Co-Marital Sex and the Sexual Freedom Movement," *Journal of Sex Research*, vol. 6, 1970, pp. 131–142; Charles and Rebecca Palson, "Swinging Wedlock," *Society*, vol. 9, 1972, pp. 28–37; and Mary Lindenstein Walshak, "The Emergence of Middle-Class Deviant Subcultures: The Case of Swingers," *Social Problems*, vol. 18, 1971, pp. 488–495.

14 Diane Denfield and Michael Gordon, "The Sociology of Mate Swapping: Or the Family that Swings Together Clings Together," *Journal of Sex Research*, vol. 6, 1970, pp. 85–100.

15 Talcott Parsons, *Essays in Sociological Theory*, Free Press, New York, 1949, p. 217.

16 Talcott Parsons, *The Social System*, Free Press, New York, 1951.

17 Jonathan Turner, *The Structure of Sociological Theory*, 2d ed., Dorsey, Homewood, Ill., 1978, p. 19.

18 Durkheim, *The Rules of the Sociological Method*, p. 90.

19 Anthony Giddens, *Capitalism and Modern Social Theory: An Analysis of the Writings of Marx, Durkheim and Max Weber*, Cambridge University Press, Cambridge, 1971, p. 91.

20 Durkheim, *The Rules of the Sociological Method*, pp. 95–96.

21 Ibid., p. 67, 70.

22 Ibid., p. 67.

23 Merton, *Social Theory and Social Structure*.

24 Ibid., p. 127.

25 Durkheim, *The Rules of the Sociological Method*, p. 66.

26 See Talcott Parsons, Robert F. Bales, and Edward A. Shils, *Working Papers in the Theory of Action*, Free Press, Glencoe, Ill., 1953; and Talcott Parsons and Neil L. Smelser, *Economy and Society*, Free Press, New York, 1956.

27 Parsons, *The Social System*. For a summary analysis of Parsons's conception of social control, see Nanette J. Davis, *Sociological Constructions of Deviance*, 2d ed., Brown,

Dubuque, Iowa, 1980, pp. 91–97; S. N. Eisenstadt, "Societal Goals, Systemic Needs, Social Interaction and Individual Behavior: Some Tentative Explanations," in H. Turk and R. L. Simpson (eds.), *Institutions and Social Exchange: The Sociologies of Talcott Parsons and George C. Homans,* Bobbs-Merrill, Indianapolis, 1971, pp. 36–55; Jonathan Turner, *The Structure of Sociological Theory,* 3d ed., Dorsey, Homewood, Ill., 1982, pp. 48–49.

28 Alvin W. Gouldner, *The Coming Crisis of Western Sociology,* Basic Books, New York, 1970, pp. 144–148.

29 Ibid., p. 141.

30 Ibid., p. 177.

31 Ibid., p. 25.

32 Patrick J. Gurney, "Historical Origins of Ideological Denial: The Case of Marx in American Sociology," *American Sociologist,* vol. 16, 1981, pp. 196–201.

33 Gouldner, *The Coming Crisis,* p. 147.

34 Talcott Parsons and Kenneth Clark (eds.), *The American Negro,* Houghton Mifflin Co., Boston, 1966.

35 See, for instance, Jon Wiener, "Talcott Parsons's Role: Bringing Nazi Sympathizers to the U.S.," *The Nation,* March 6, 1989, cover page and pp. 306–309.

36 Talcott Parsons, "A Paradigm for the Analysis of Social Systems," in Peter Hamilton (ed.), *Readings from Talcott Parsons,* Tavistock, London, 1985, pp. 172, 176.

37 Sol Yurik, *Behold Metatron, the Recording Angel,* Semiotext (e), New York, 1985, pp. 3–4.

38 W. Ross Ashby, as quoted in Donna Haraway, "The High Cost of Information in Post-War Evolutionary Biology: Ergonomics, Semiotics and Sociology of Communicative Systems," *The Philosophy Forum,* vol. XIII, nos. 2–3, winter-spring, 1981–1982, p. 249. Haraway's work is particularly important in tracing the patriarchal and military origins of cybernetic thinking. See also Donna J. Haraway, *Simians, Cyborgs and Women: the Reinvention of Nature,* Routledge, New York, 1991; and Les Levidow and Kevin Robins (eds.), *Cyborg Worlds: the Military Information Society,* Free Association Books, London, 1989.

39 Jonathan Turner, *The Structure of Sociological Theory,* 5th ed., Wadsworth, Belmont, Calif., 1991, p. 67.

40 Talcott Parsons, *Social Theory and Modern Society,* The Free Press, New York, 1967, p. 225.

41 Peter Hamilton, *Talcott Parsons,* Tavistock, London, 1983, pp. 59–60.

42 Lawrence J. Henderson, as quoted in Lewis A. Coser, *Masters of Sociological Thought,* 2d ed., Harcourt, Brace Jovanovich, New York, 1977, p. 422.

43 Coser, *Masters of Sociological Thought,* p. 423.

44 Talcott Parsons, "On Building Social Systems Theory," *Daedalus,* fall 1970, p. 831.

45 Gouldner, *The Coming Crisis,* p. 142.

46 C. Wright Mills, *The Power Elite,* Oxford University Press, New York, 1956.

47 Robert A. Dentler and Kai T. Erikson, "The Function of Deviance in Groups," *Social Problems,* vol. 7, fall 1959, pp. 98–107.

48 Ibid., p. 102.

49 Ibid., p. 104.

50 Ibid., p. 105.

51 Arlene K. Daniels and Richard R. Daniels, "The Social Role of the Career Fool," *Psychiatry,* vol. 27, August 1964, pp. 219–229, reprinted in M. Lefton, J. F. Skipper, Jr., and C. H. McCaghy, *Approaches to Deviance,* Appleton-Century-Crofts, New York, 1968, pp. 308, 309.

52 Erikson, *Wayward Puritans.*

53 Ibid., p. 13.

54 Ibid., p. 22.

55 Ibid.

56 Ibid., pp. 163–181.

57 Ibid., p. 181.

58 See, for instance, Ann Nelson and Hart Nelson, "Problems in the Application of a Sociological Method to Historical Data: A Case Example," *American Sociologist,* May 1969, pp. 149–151. See also John B. Williamson, David A. Karp, John R. Dalphin, and Paul S. Gray, *The Research Craft,* 2d ed., Little, Brown, Boston, 1982, pp. 239–259.

59 For an excellent, if disturbing, overview of the infiltration of everyday life by the militaristic logic of informational technologies, see Les Levidow and Kevin Robins (eds.), *Cyborg Worlds: The Military Information Society,* London, Free Association Books, 1989.

60 Nanette J. Davis, *Sociological Constructions of Deviance,* 2d ed., W. C. Brown Publishers, Dubuque, Iowa, 1980, pp. 110–111.

61 Herbert Gans, "The Positive Function of Poverty," *American Journal of Sociology,* vol. 78, September 1972, pp. 275–289.

62 Ibid., p. 283.

Suicidal Walkman   By Joseph LaMantia and Stephen Pfohl

CHAPTER 7

THE ANOMIE PERSPECTIVE:
Normlessness, Inequality, and Deviant Aspirations

To pursue a goal which is by definition unattainable is to condemn oneself to a state of perpetual unhappiness.

Émile Durkheim[1]

Frustration and thwarted aspiration lead to the search for avenues of escape from a culturally induced intolerable situation.

Robert K. Merton[2]

INTRODUCTION

During the spring of 1977 I experienced my worst day as a college teacher. I discovered a mass outbreak of cheating on the midterm exam for my course in criminology. As a young lecturer I was teaching without the help of teaching assistants. This meant that I'd have to grade nearly 200 midterms on my own. The thought was staggering. I had always distrusted multiple-choice tests. Although they are easy to grade, I thought them better indicators of test-taking ability than of sociological reasoning. Despite what I am about to tell you, I still believe this.

Another problem with multiple-choice tests is that they systematically discriminate against many lower-class, minority students and others denied the advantages of "college prep" curriculums and resourceful educational environments. These facts present no great sociological mystery. They are well known to even the most casual observer. Since they were well known to me also, I experienced a dilemma that was both practical and ethical. Practically, I couldn't imagine how I could grade 200 non-multiple-choice exams. Ethically I was worried about penalizing students who didn't read as well or quickly, who were less adept at coping with in-class exam pressure, or who simply required more time to do their best. My solution was to offer an out-of-class multiple-choice exam. This provided students with an extended period of time and was to be completed according to the honor system. Students were to pick up the exam from the department secretary, go to a quiet setting, answer all questions without using notes (just like an in-class exam), and return the exam before the day's end. With this solution, my troubles began.

It didn't take long for me to realize that things had gone wrong. The exams were available to students at 9:00 a.m. At 9:30 a student appeared at my door in tears. Everybody was cheating, the student reported. The student was correct. I soon learned that cheating was occurring everywhere—from private dorm rooms to the public corridors of the library. Students were apparently even cheating while gulping down "Big Macs" at the campus McDonald's. But why? How could I have been so naive, the frustrated student complained. Nobody gives an honor-system exam these days. Nobody knew what to do. Nobody knew what the rules were. If you didn't cheat and others did, then you'd be penalized. Everyone knows that teachers mark on a curve, and so, no matter how hard you studied, if others cheated harder, you'd be penalized. Hence, you'd better cheat, too, if you wanted to come out of this chaotic situation with a decent grade. All of this made good sociological sense, at least from the anomie perspective on deviance.

There are two related versions of the anomie perspective. The first, developed by Émile Durkheim, sees deviance as the result of a state of normlessness in which nobody knows the rules. The second version of anomie theory is more complicated. It defines anomie as a discrepancy between socially engendered goals and the availability of legitimate means to achieve such goals. Both versions apply to the cheating incident. By offering an honor-system exam, I had introduced a type of normlessness into an otherwise orderly academic world. Ordinarily exams were tightly proctored. Teachers even had multiple versions of the same exam printed with the questions in different sequences so as to penalize those who copied from other students' computerized answer sheets. Given the routine nature of such drastic control policies, my use of the honor system may have generated a situation in which few knew what was expected. The honor system may also have produced a strain between established goals (i.e., getting a good grade) and legitimate means to achieve goals (i.e., not cheating when one knows that others are cheating).

This brings us to the conclusion of this disconcerting tale of "anomic cheating." Since I had no means of knowing who cheated, I announced that everyone would be assigned an A, but that course grades would be determined by a curve combining the midterm and final exam grades. This meant that in actuality the grades would be determined by the final. An exception was made for students who had studied, done well without cheating, and were willing to defend their knowledge in a short oral exam. On the final, students were asked to write an essay using theoretical perspectives to explain the high rate of cheating on the midterm. A great number of students drew upon the imagery of the anomie perspective to explain this deviant episode. In examining this perspective, perhaps we shall learn why.

THEORETICAL IMAGES

At the heart of the anomie perspective is the notion that deviance arises as a result of unfulfilled human aspirations. There are two distinct traditions within this perspective. Each conceives of aspirations and their lack of fulfillment in slightly different terms. The first tradition is rooted in the late-nineteenth-century work of Émile Durkheim; the second in the mid-twentieth-century writings of Robert K. Merton. While the two traditions are related, they are sufficiently distinct to merit our separate consideration.

Durkheim: Anomie as Normlessness

Durkheim used the term *anomie* to describe a state of normlessness. A society beset by anomie was said to lack the regulatory constraints necessary for the adequate social control of its members. As such, the concept of anomie resembles the idea of social disorganization envisioned by the theorists of the Chicago school. Anomie and social disorganization are both seen as consequences of social change. Both are also characterized by a kind of normative chaos.

There are, however, several important differences between the concepts of social disorganization and anomie. Social disorganization was typically presented as a spatial or socioecological problem affecting the particular parts or zones of a society most exposed to the forces of rapid change. On the other hand, anomie was conceived more as a temporal problem affecting the entirety of a given society. Anomie was a discrete problem, a historically specific problem of societies in transition from the traditional to the modern world. Social disorganization, however, was a problem for all societies at all periods of time, an ongoing problem characterized by change, disruption, and reorganization. Thus the consequences and control implications of anomie and disorganization were conceived differently. In terms of consequences, Durkheim suggested that anomie unleashed an instinctually based form of human greed, the pursuit of unlimited aspirations. Social disorganization produced a search for reorganization, sometimes through involvement in deviance. Regarding social control strategies, while disorganizational theorists supported efforts to "patch up" or restore the normative organization of particular zones or sectors of society, Durkheim saw the need for a massive, societywide reorganization of the normative structure.

Durkheim's View of Human Nature: Normatively Controlled Greed

In attempting to understand the origins and consequences of Durkheim's conception of anomie, it is necessary to consider two things: Durkheim's view of human nature and his perceptions of the social context in which he lived. Durkheim's conception of human nature was extremely ambivalent, even contradictory. Durkheim asserted that there is no human nature (as he knew it) without society. Individuals had no existence apart from society. What people thought, how they perceived the world, how they conceived of their relationship to the world—all these things were shaped by participation in society. This commitment to the primacy of society over the individual is found in many of Durkheim's writings but is nowhere stronger than in his book *The Elementary Forms of the Religious Life*.[3]

Elsewhere Durkheim seems to allow for a set of human propensities, a kind of human nature that exists prior to society. These propensities, or natural tendencies, could not, however, be realized outside society. They are almost described as the reason or basis for society. In his work *Suicide*, for instance, Durkheim suggests that our human nature is characterized by an "inextinguishable thirst"; that our capacity for desire and feeling is in itself an insatiable and bottomless abyss. For this reason human nature can never be simply "in itself." It would demand too much. By themselves our needs or desires (seemingly rooted in our psychobiological capabilities) would be too great. Somehow, our inextinguishable thirst, our unlimited capacity for desire, must be curbed or regulated. It is to provide this proportion, to regulate our otherwise insatiable aspirations, that society apparently comes into being. According to Durkheim:

> Human nature is substantially the same among all men. . . . It is not human nature which can assign the variable limits necessary to our needs. They are thus unlimited so far as they depend on the individual alone. Irrespective of any external regulatory force, our capacity for feeling is in itself an insatiable and bottomless abyss. . . . [S]ociety alone can play this moderating role; for it is the only moral power superior to the individual, the authority of which he accepts. It alone has the power necessary to stipulate laws and to set the point beyond which the passions must not go.[4]

I will not here try to reconcile Durkheim's ambivalence as to the existence of a human nature independent of society. Perhaps it is enough to say that while Durkheim believed that humans possess an unlimited appetite of aspirations or desire, he also argued that it is society which arouses specific aspirations. What is clear in both instances is that aspirations cannot be infinitely filled. Desired social resources are finite. Everyone cannot have everything. There must be limits. These limits, since not internally generated, must come from society. They must be perceived as fair. They must be perceived as moral. When they aren't, there will be trouble. Too much unregulated desire! Too few resources with which to fulfill limitless desires! The lack of moral norms constraining human aspirations! Anomie! This was what Durkheim saw around him; the crisis of modern society and the basis for his understanding of anomic deviance. In *Suicide* Durkheim described this crisis in the following manner:

Religion has lost most of its power. And government, instead of regulating economic life, has become its tool and servant. . . . [I]ndustry, instead of being still regarded as a means to an end transcending itself, has become the supreme end of individuals and societies alike. Thereupon the appetites thus excited have become freed of any limiting authority.[5]

The Transition from Traditional to Modern Society: The Social Context of Durkheim's Analysis

We have already considered Durkheim's contribution to the functionalist theory of deviance. It was Durkheim who argued that deviance was a normal and necessary social phenomenon which contributed to the order of a given society. That functionalist viewpoint was in keeping with Durkheim's analysis of the interrelationships of the parts or structures of society at any given point in time. Durkheim, however, was not exclusively concerned with society at any given point in time. He was also concerned with society at a particular point in time—his own time, a time characterized by the transition from the traditional to the modern world. Durkheim described this transition as a shift in the basic normative patterns around which societies are organized. In his own terms this involved a shift from the patterns of *mechanical solidarity* to those of *organic solidarity*. The specific meanings of these terms will be spelled out later. For now it is enough to note that the problems presented by the transition from simple, traditional forms of society to complex, modern forms were problems which occupied the entirety of Durkheim's career as a social theorist. They were problems which were filled with danger. They were problems which shaped Durkheim's conception of anomie and its relationship to deviant behavior.

Durkheim's analysis of the dangers involved in the transition from traditional society to modern society was undoubtedly related to his own biographical location within history.[6] He was born into a highly traditional society and spent his adult life in an intellectual wrestling match with a society undergoing the pains of modernization. He was born in 1858, the son of a rabbi in the eastern French province of Lorraine. The Jews who lived in that region of France belonged to the Ashkenazic branch of Judaism. The Ashkenazim had remained relatively isolated from the whole of French society since their migration from Germany into the eastern French provinces of Alsace and Lorraine during the sixteenth century. For years most members of the community spoke entirely in Yiddish and Hebrew, maintaining a traditional Jewish cultural identity which insulated them from the forces of modernization sweeping the French nation as a whole. In this sense the Ashkenazim differed greatly from the Sephardic Jews of southwestern France. Although they had lived in France for about the same length of time as their Ashkenazic brethren, the Sephardic Jews (who had fled religious persecution in Spain and Portugal) had taken far greater steps toward assimilation into the modernizing mainstream of the nation. The Ashkenazim, however, retained their traditional forms of social organization long after the revolution had emancipated Jews and granted them French citizenship in the early nineteenth century.

Although reared within the traditional world of the Ashkenazic community, Durkheim was also exposed to the rigors of a demanding secular French education. Attending the school of his hometown, the Collège d'Épinal, Durkheim was soon recognized as a brilliant student and was the recipient of numerous honors and awards. In the process Durkheim developed what Coser describes metaphorically as an intense romance with the principles and politics of the secular French republic.[7] In pursuit of this romance he left Épinal to attend one of France's outstanding secondary schools, the Lycée Louis-le-Grand in Paris. From there he proceeded to the prestigious École Normale Supérieure and entered deeply into dialogue with the intellectual elite of French society. In other words, within the course of a lifetime Durkheim made the transition which French society as a whole took several centuries to make—the transition from traditional to modern social life. Hence, through the journey which was his own life, Durkheim became acutely aware of the consequences of massive social transformation. His description of these consequences is concentrated in his analysis of anomie.

Anomie, Deviance, and the Study of Suicide

Durkheim's analysis of the relationship between anomie and deviance is concentrated in his analysis of suicide. His book *Suicide* was first published in Paris in 1897. The culmination of nearly ten years of research and reflection, *Suicide* is a classic example of the use of a sociological perspective to explain human problems. In many ways *Suicide* provided Durkheim with a concrete example by which to demonstrate the explanatory potential of sociology. Although suicide is commonly thought of as a very private act, Durkheim persuasively argued that changes in the rate of suicide could not be explained adequately by the individualistic sciences of psychology and biology. Fluctuations in the rates of suicide within and between societies were explained, instead, by the way that societies are structured.

Durkheim's work on suicide represents what might be considered the intellectual "culmination of the moral statistics tradition" begun in Europe during the eighteenth century.[8] This tradition involved the collection of different kinds of statistics on such things as economic, geographic, racial, and even climatic factors and their relationship to a wide variety of such contemporary "moral" problems as insanity, crime, and suicide. Durkheim carefully examined the available statistical data on patterns of suicide and produced a thoroughly sociological account by which to explain variations in the suicide rate. In 1889 he published his first article on the topic. His thoughts on the matter were expanded during the course of a full year's lecture course on suicide which he taught during the 1889–1890 academic year. During the next seven years he collected statistics and with the assistance of his nephew Marcel Mauss developed the theoretical groundwork for his 1897 book.

Despite the intellectual challenge presented by using available statistics to demonstrate the utility of the perspective and methods of the new science of sociology, Durkheim's analysis of suicide was prompted by concerns that were as deeply personal as they were professional. Once again we see the intersection of historical biography and explanatory vision in the formulation of social theory. For Durkheim suicide was but a symptom of the growing social malaise of a society in transition, of his own thoughts of suicide. By wrestling with the problem of suicide Durkheim was in actuality wrestling with what he perceived as the dissolution of normative constraints in European society as a whole. Thus, as Steven Lukes suggests in his intellectual biography of Durkheim, "the study of suicide offered a means of approaching 'the causes of the general malaise currently being undergone by European societies,' since it was 'one of the forms through which the collective malady . . . is transmitted.'"[9] For Durkheim the matter was more personal. Durkheim was affected greatly by the suicide of Victor Hommay, his friend and colleague at the École. Convinced that more than psychological factors were involved in Hommay's death, Durkheim was moved to explore the sociological grounds for suicide. As Lukes points out, Hommay's death "influenced not only his [Durkheim's] interest in suicide but also his explanation of it."[10]

Durkheim's primary explanation of the comparatively high rates of suicide in the modernizing industrial nations of western Europe involved his conception of the deviance-producing potential of anomie. In addition to anomie, however, Durkheim outlined three other forms of social organization which induced high rates of suicide: *egoism, altruism,* and *fatalism.* In contrast to the normlessness of anomie, these other social forms represented instances in which the normative or moral order encourages its members to take their own lives. For Durkheim, "moral order" was described as an external force which constrained human passion and desire. The moral order is symbolized in ritualistic expressions of what Durkheim referred to as the "collective conscience." By this Durkheim meant that individual morality is first shaped by ritualized participation in the collective morality or conscience of the society as a whole. In egoistic, altruistic, and fatalistic societies, rituals of collective moral order are said to increase the likelihood of suicide. Before turning to a specific analysis of anomie, I shall briefly consider the way that social structures produce suicide in the three other suicide-prone moral orders discussed by Durkheim.

Suicide in Egoistic, Altruistic, and Fatalistic Societies

The first form of morally induced suicide was labeled egoistic. Here the collective conscience of a given society paradoxically contains the seeds of its own destruction. The moral order contains ideas which encourage a radical separation between individuals and the social group. Durkheim viewed the moral orders of Protestantism and of western intellectual society as constraining individuals in such a paradoxical fashion. Each gives birth to a type of dangerous individualism by socially providing a moral vision of people as responsible for their own actions—Protestantism by stressing the individual's direct, unmediated relationship to God, and intellectualism by stressing the rule of individual reason over the traditions of the social group.

Durkheim noted a similar focus on egoistic individualism in the normative order surrounding unattached or single persons as opposed to that governing the married couple. Married people are bound by normative rules which tie them into a system of regulated interaction. Single persons were said to lack such ties and the socially controlling constraints which come with them. Such exaggerated individualism raises the probability of suicide. The person constrained by this morality of individual responsibility was seen to be especially vulnerable to suicide. In times of trouble or error the moral individualist has no community to turn to for support. The problem of egoistic suicide is generated not by the lack of authoritative moral norms but by the presence of norms oddly encouraging individual freedom from norms.

Durkheim's second form of morally induced suicide is less complicated. It is found in societies in which the collective conscience is so binding that there is virtually no distinction between the individual and the group. The individual literally lives for the group. His or her own personality is but a reflection of the collective personality of the group. All members are as one. As such the individual is willing to give his or her life for the life of the group. Examples of such "altruistic suicide" are typically found in extremely close-knit societies. For years the Japanese rite of hara-kiri has been used by sociology teachers as an example of what Durkheim meant by altruistic suicide. A dramatic illustration is the seventeenth-century story of the forty-seven Ronin. When their master was insulted, these legendary Samurai warriors followed his example by collectively taking their own lives after assassinating the palace official who had offended their leader's honor. Following their collective moral code, the forty-seven warriors killed themselves out of closeness to, rather than distance from, society.

A more contemporary example of hara-kiri is found during World War II. Bound by a code of collective identification with the life of their nation, Japanese pilots willingly crashed their planes into the decks of American carriers. Although they would die as individuals, they valued their individual lives less than the collective life of the nation. An even more current example is that of Jonestown. In that bizarre community in Guyana, hundreds of followers of the Reverend Jim Jones apparently took their own lives so that they might journey together to the promised land. Mesmerized by Jones's hypnotic preaching, the Jonestown faithful drank poison and went to their deaths in a classic instance of what Durkheim referred to as "altruistic suicide."

In addition to egoistic and altruistic suicide Durkheim made brief reference to "fatalistic suicide." Although relatively unelaborated in his own writings, this type of suicide was socially induced by the hopelessness structured into the regulatory frameworks of slave societies. Durkheim offered it as a sociological account of high suicide rates among enslaved populations. Under slavery, Durkheim apparently believed, human aspirations may be totally crushed rather than channeled into the pursuit of individual responsibility (as in the egoistic society) or into sacrifices for the collective good (as in the altruistic society). Those who live in slavery are devoid of aspirations and dominated by a sense of fatalism—a sense that their actions cannot change their state in life—and thus slavery, according to Durkheim, is yet another socially structured route toward high rates of suicide.

Anomic Suicide: The Rise and Fall of Economic Aspirations

The egoistic, altruistic, and fatalistic forms of suicide were each encouraged by the normative structures of certain societies. But what happens when the normative structure of a society is weak or disrupted? This is what Durkheim meant by anomie, a social condition which also produces high rates of suicide and, by implication, other forms of deviant behavior as well. Why? To understand the full meaning of anomie we must return to Durkheim's notion of the collective conscience. Recall that it is the collective conscience, the normative force of society, which shields individuals from the "inextinguishable thirst," from the "bottomless abyss" of unlimited aspiration. When something disrupts the normative structure, the thirst of aspirations emerges as again insatiable. This is said to happen during periods of severe economic crisis or sudden prosperity and growth. During economic crisis "something like a declassification occurs which suddenly casts certain individuals into a lower state than their previous one."[11] The rewards that people have come to expect as the just deserts of their positions in society are no longer forthcoming. A new and unaccustomed order of morality, or readjusted expectations, must be learned. This is difficult and cannot be achieved overnight. In the meantime, people continue to cling to old aspirations, nurtured by the now irrelevant norms of precrisis society. This only makes things more painful. The old norms do not fit the new situation. According to Durkheim, people "are not adjusted to the condition forced on them, and its very prospect is intolerable."[12] Such a state of anomie increases the likelihood of suicide by heightening "the suffering which detaches [people] from a reduced state of existence even before they have made a trial of it."[13]

Anomie resulting from economic disaster might be used to explain increases in the suicide rate during depressions. The image of people leaping out of Wall Street windows was a familiar accompaniment of the onset of economic collapse during the 1930s. Durkheim claims that sudden turns toward prosperity also create anomie and result in high rates of suicide. The "unknown limits" of economic growth disrupt norms which had kept aspirations in check. "Appetites, not being controlled by a public opinion, become disoriented, no longer recognizing the limits proper to them."[14] Sudden prosperity destroys the authority of traditional norms. Passionate desires escalate without constraint. The sky appears to be the limit. But it is not. Social and economic resources are always finite in character. It is the illusion of anomie which prevents people from realizing this.

Everyone cannot have everything. Unchecked by a regulative morality, the awareness is lacking. Competition and aspirations spiral together; spiral until they crash into the empty abyss of unfulfillment. The race for unlimited aspirations is described as a race for an unobtainable goal, a race offering "no other pleasure but that of the race itself."[15] Competition becomes both more violent and more painful. In Durkheim's words: "Effort grows, just when it becomes less productive. How could the desire to live not be weakened under such conditions?"[16]

Long-Term Anomie: A Problem of Modern Times

Anomie would be destructive enough if limited to short periods of economic crisis or rapid prosperity. In Durkheim's opinion the problem was much greater. Anomie was becoming a chronic, if tragic, condition in the modern world. Durkheim viewed society's turn into the twentieth century as the passage of an entire century in which economic progress consisted largely in the freeing of industrial relations from all social and moral constraints.

In previous times the normative powers of religion, of the state, and of occupational groups had imposed constraints on the economic order. The force of religion impacted on both workers and masters, the poor and the rich. The poor had been provided with an otherworldly vision of compensation in the next world for suffering in this. The rich had been constrained by a belief that worldly interests are but a part of the human lot, a part not to be pursued without rule or restraint. Moreover, the subordination of the economy to the temporal power of the state and the regulation of the salary structure by occupational guilds were seen as additional constraints on the rise of human economic aspirations.

These restraints were losing their force. Here Durkheim made his important distinction between restraints governing simple, relatively undifferentiated traditional societies and those needed to restrain complex, highly specialized, modern societies. Members of simple societies generally approach each other as whole persons and engage in very similar social and economic activities. Simple societies were constituted by a group of people whose whole lives were relatively visible to one another and who were tightly joined by what Durkheim called the repressive norms of *mechanical solidarity*. Individual uniqueness was repressed in favor of collective oneness. One set of diffuse norms mechanically governed society as a whole. Think of the small tribe or town, bound together in face-to-face interaction under the constraining rituals of commonly held religious beliefs. Think also of the mechanical solidarity of the Ashkenazic Jews of eastern France. It was in this community that Durkheim spent his early years. Undoubtedly his experiences with the traditional bonds of the Ashkenazim provided the great French sociologist with a vivid image of a traditional society under attack by the forces of modernization.

Simple societies were on the decline. Massive increases in the volume and density of human populations had made social life more complex. The personal quality of simple society was being replaced by anonymity, the similarity of roles by a highly specialized division of labor roles. The common religious beliefs and rituals which promoted solidarity were losing their power. New rules and regulations were needed. These were to be based, not on the mechanical repression of difference but on the rational "restitutive" regulation of variety. Science, not religion, would guide the construction of this new order of morality. Yet the rules of the new order, the rules of what Durkheim called *organic solidarity*, were slow in coming. What was visible to the classical French sociologist was the lack of order, the lack of morality. The old, normative "mechanical" order was disappearing more quickly than the new "organic" order was emerging. As a result society was thrown into a state of anomic deregulation. Suicide and, by implication, other forms of deviance were on the rise.

The decline of commonly held religious constraints on the economic activity of complex societies hastened a state of anomie. So did the ascendance of the unfettered pursuit of economic prosperity over the previous constraints of governmental and occupational-group regulation. These developments combined to sanctify economic and industrial success at the expense of all other aspects of human life. In Durkheim's mind, economic achievement had "become the supreme end of individuals and societies alike. Thereupon the appetites thus excited have become freed of any limiting authority. By sanctifying them, so to speak, this apotheosis of well-being has placed them above all human law. Their restraint seems like a sort of sacrilege."[17] Anomie had become the unholy fruit of unrestrained economic activity. People were unable to fulfill unrealistic economic goals, yet the lack of constraining norms failed to prevent them from trying; failed to prevent them from jumping into the abyss of disillusionment; failed to prevent them from becoming subject to those social forces which promote suicide and other forms of self-destructive deviance.

Robert K. Merton: Inequality in Opportunities to Conform

Durkheim's theory of anomic suicide grew out of the influential French sociologist's interpretation of the crisis of early-twentieth-century European society. Robert K. Merton's extension of the anomie perspective into a formal theory of deviance grew out of Merton's interpretation of the crisis of mid-twentieth-century America. For Merton the American crisis was conceived of as a structured disparity between promises of achievable prosperity and real-life opportunities to realize those promises. Unfulfilled aspirations were still a central concern. Normlessness was not. In his 1938 essay "Social Structure and Anomie" Merton pictured anomie as a socially structured contradiction between normative aspirations and the lack of available means for legitimately attaining valued cultural goals.

Robert Merton was born on July 5, 1910, in the slums of South Philadelphia, the child of immigrants from eastern Europe. According to his own recollections the slum was a lively, noisy place where he joined in the zesty, if largely ceremonial, gang warfare between groups of streetcorner boys.[18] Much as Durkheim's early life in the traditional Jewish community of eastern France may have contributed to his vision of anomie, so was Merton's reformulation of this concept probably influenced by his childhood in the slum. Intellectually gifted, Merton achieved a way out of the slum by obtaining a scholarship to Temple University. Four years later he was awarded a fellowship to pursue graduate studies at Harvard. Such opportunities are, however, far rarer than is implied by the American promise of prosperity for anyone who tries hard. Most of Merton's slum neighbors did not fare so well. The reason had little to do with their motives and a lot to do with their lack of socially structured opportunities for successfully pursuing the American dream. In spite of his own success, this was a lesson of slum life which Merton never forgot.

Merton's theory examines the relationship between two aspects of social life: cultural goals and socially available means of goal attainment. Unlike Durkheim, Merton makes no assumptions regarding the unlimited nature of human aspirations for individuals unrestrained by societal norms. The reverse is more the case. Norms induce certain aspirations. Aspirations are cultural artifacts. They are learned in the family, in the school, in the church, in listening to and watching the media, in the whole cultural life of society. American culture teaches people the aspiration of success. Become rich! Become powerful! Become prestigious! Everybody can do it. Any child can become president. Everyone should try. These aspects of the great American dream are seen by Merton as the aspirations or culturally induced goals of American society. The probability of deviance increases when the "anybody can do it" aspirations of American society are confronted with the "not everybody has an equal chance" opportunity structure of the same society. Durkheim argued that desired resources are finite. Merton expanded this argument by suggesting that they are unequally obtainable as well. Everyone is exposed to the goals of success. Only a few are provided with the legitimate means needed to be successful. Imagine a society in which everyone learned and accepted the same goals and was provided with an equal opportunity to achieve those goals. There would be far less deviance. Everyone would desire and could achieve the same social goals. Conformity would be the normal product of such an equal society. Merton did not view American society in such ideal terms. Merton saw the obvious disjuncture between American goals and means. Not everyone could achieve the widely accepted goals of wealth, power, and prestige. For many the American dream was a lie. Deviance was the normal product of such an unequal society.

TABLE 7-1
MERTON'S TYPOLOGY OF INDIVIDUAL ADAPTATION TO ANOMIE*

	Culturally given goals or aspirations	Institutionally available means of goal attainment
I. Conformity	+	+
II. Innovation	+	−
III. Ritualism	−	+
IV. Retreatism	−	−
V. Rebellion	±	±

* This modified representation of Merton's typology is based upon the depiction of these modes of adaptation in Robert K. Merton, "Social Structure and Anomie," *American Sociological Review*, vol. 3, October 1938, pp. 672–682.

Merton's analysis of deviance reveals a set of adaptations to the socially structured contradiction between cultural goals and available means of goal attainment (see Table 7-1). Each adaptation contrasts with the path of conformity. The conformist is one whose experience in society leads to the acceptance of both culturally prescribed goals and the socially legitimate means for reaching those goals. He or she accepts the goals and plays by the rules because they work. The "right" family background, attendance at the "right" schools, placement in the "right" firm, promotion at the "right" times, etc., convince the conformist that the rules of society are "right." There is no need to deviate. According to Merton the path of conformity is the most common adaptation to socially structured goals and means. If this were not so, "the stability and continuity of society could not be maintained."[19]

While Merton believed conformity to be the most common type of goal-means adaptation, it was not the only path. The inequality of American life was said to produce structural pressures toward deviations along four other paths. The first of these was the path of *innovation*. This was the path of persons who accepted the dominant cultural goal of success, but whose experience in a stratified society led them to reject legitimate avenues of goal attainment. The legitimate channels (e.g., hard work, patience, and waiting one's turn) simply proved unsuccessful. Think of youngsters in the ghetto or of the slum gangs that were part of Merton's youth. The door of success is not as open for these persons as it is for the Ivy League sons of the wealthy. The call to success may, however, be just as strong. One has only to watch a half-hour of television to be "turned on" to the get-ahead, be-successful, look-good, "drive-a-good-car" goals of American society. What happens when people accept goals but later discover that they are unreachable by the lawful rules of the society's game? Put simply, washing dishes provides little access to major channels of wealth, power, and prestige. How is the contradiction to be resolved?

One way to resolve the contradiction presented above is through *innovation*. Merton uses this term to refer to the "creative" use of illegitimate means to obtain valued legitimate ends. He states that, "Given the American stigmatization of manual labor . . . , and the absence of realistic opportunities for advancement beyond this level, the result is a marked tendency toward deviant behavior."[20] For persons systematically deprived of access to avenues of success, how can the "honest" job of dishwashing compete with the easy money obtained through dishonest behavior? For persons systematically denied access to other, more promising avenues of legitimate success, it is not hard to understand why the prospect of years of washing dishes often pales in comparison to the easy money, quick power, and instant status promised by a life of crime. This is the logic of Merton's analysis. Innovative deviance is a normal outgrowth of having accepted cultural goals without having been provided with the opportunity to legitimately achieve those goals. Relatively ineffectual legitimate means are rejected. Promising illegitimate means are explored. Innovation occurs. Deviance occurs. The criminal career of former Chicago gang boss Al Capone is cited by Merton as the prototype of this important deviant adaptation. According to Merton: "Capone represents the triumph of amoral intelligence over morally proscribed 'failure,' when channels of vertical mobility are closed or narrowed in *a society which places a high premium on economic affluence and social ascent for all its members.*"[21] This aspect of Merton's analysis seems particularly applicable to such innovative deviant organizations as inner-city drug gangs. Cut off from legal access to more acceptable channels of economic prosperity, gangs which market drugs such as crack and cocaine may mimic rather than reject the entrepreneurial logic of contemporary capitalism.

A second, less frequently discussed, deviant adaptation is what Merton calls *ritualism*. Here goals are rejected but legitimate means are accepted. One does not really believe in the goals, does not really care about becoming number one, has little desire to get to the top. Yet, one plays by the rules anyway. Think of the middle-level corporate bureaucrat, government worker, or tenured college professor who really doesn't care about getting further ahead. Such a person may play the game, put in the appropriate time, work the nine-to-five shift. Yet he or she cares little for advancement and perhaps desires only to get through the day without making waves and then to go home and get stoned. We all know someone who plays the part without really believing in it. Although difficult to spot from a distance, ritualists are the second type of deviants identified by Merton's analysis.

One recent and important example of ritualism involves what corporate executives refer to as the negligent sabotage of the assembly line by careless or uncommitted workers. Indeed the American economy abounds with reports of workers who put in their time but care little for the products of the companies they work for. Why? Merton's conception of ritualism provides a sociological answer. Workers may get what they can from an economic system upon which they must depend for survival but may have little structural incentive for truly committing themselves to the goals of a company whose success shows little evidence of trickling down to the employees who actually operate it. Put in your time. Check in on time. Punch out when the hour comes. A relatively unstudied form of ritualistic deviance, negligent sabotage looms large within the American economy. It affects companies and affects all of us who, like the driver of an unsafely made automobile, experience the anomic impact of a systemic disparity between nurtured goals and offered means.

Retreatism is the third of Merton's deviant adaptations. This involves a lack of attachment to either goals or means. One neither accepts the success values nor acts in conformity with the acceptable way of doing things. One retreats from both the conventional goals and the conventional means. In this category Merton lumps together the "adaptive activities of psychotics, artists, pariahs, outcasts, vagrants, tramps, chronic drunkards and drug addicts."[22] The social experience of such persons has led them to be the "true aliens." They have excluded themselves from both shared values and shared activities. They are the dropouts, according to Merton. They "can be included as members of society . . . only in a fictional sense. . . . People . . . in the society but not of it."[23] Retreatists escape from, or drop out of, major societal goals and normative activities.

Merton's final category of adaptation is reserved for those who not only drop out but actively seek to replace old goals and normative activities with new ones. This is the adaptation of *rebellion*. The terrorist or revolutionary best exemplifies this category. These rebels may use illegitimate means (e.g., civil disobedience, sabotage, assassination, kidnapping, or hijacking). Their goal cannot be defined in the terms of the present culture. It is their intention to replace one set of cultural standards with another. The illegitimate activities of the rebel should not be confused with those of the innovator. The gangster who kidnaps for money and the Red Brigade member who kidnaps to destroy the system are quite different. The first uses illegitimate means to obtain the dominant get-rich goals of society. The latter seeks to *replace* the dominant goals and means with "something better." He or she rejects established goals and means in order to hasten the birth of a new set of norms, a new standard for aspirations and acceptable action.

This last of Merton's adaptations is directed toward what might be called the "political deviant." Like the other adaptations, rebellion is viewed as the normal product of a contradictory and stratified structuring of society's goals and means. Deviance is explained by the manner in which society strains people, rather than by the way people strain society.

Extending Merton's Theory of Anomie: The Contributions of Parsons and Dubin

Merton's provocative thesis has generated a number of extensions, reformulations, and modifications. In 1951 Talcott Parsons extended Merton's notion of strain between culturally nurtured goals and institutionally available means to include strains at the interpersonal and individual level.[24] Parsons argued that, in addition to the anomic structural strains described by Merton, deviance can also be generated by strains involving such things as the inability to reconcile one's own expectations with the expectations of others or by strains produced by the failure to make institutionally prescribed object attachments, such as socially appropriate romantic involvements with members of the opposite sex. Another extension of Merton's ideas was proposed by Robert Dubin in 1959.[25] Dubin attempted to reformulate Merton's original five categories of deviant adaptation by subdividing the notion of institutionally available means of goal attainment into norms about how one should act and behavioral descriptions about how people actually act. While this distinction permitted a more specific analysis of a variety of adaptational options, Merton himself believed that Dubin's complex formulation shifted attention away from the core theoretical imagery of anomie theory—that a systemic disjuncture between goals and the means necessary to achieve those goals produces a strain in the direction of deviant behavior.[26]

Richard Cloward: Differential Opportunity for Illegitimate Means

Two other modifications of Merton's work have been heralded as significantly advancing the anomie perspective. These involve the contributions of Richard Cloward and Albert Cohen. Cloward accepted Merton's basic assumptions about the deviance-producing strain generated by differential access to systemically nurtured societal goals. Indeed, Cloward's study of deviance produced by blocked access to culturally encouraged aspirations within a military prison is among the earliest empirical applications of Merton's perspective.[27] Yet, for Cloward, opportunities to deviate successfully were also seen as differentially available. In other words, blocked access to the legitimate means of goal attainment should not be equated with open access to the means of deviation. In his 1959 article "Illegitimate Means, Anomie, and Deviant Behavior," Cloward asserts that access to illegitimate means can be blocked as well.[28] In so arguing Cloward provides a sociological dynamic missing in Merton's category of retreatism. Why should persons retreat rather than innovate in their deviant adaptations? The answer, according to Cloward, is found in the idea of "double failure." According to Cloward, retreatists may be persons who fail or are denied access to both legitimate and illegitimate channels of goal attainment. In Cloward's words, "If illegitimate means are unavailable, if efforts at innovation fail, then retreatist adaptations may be the consequence, and the 'escape' mechanism chosen by the defeated individual may perhaps be all the more deviant because of his 'double failure.'"[29]

Cloward and Ohlin: Subculture Opportunities for Deviance Attention to the differential availability of illegitimate means of goal attainment was elaborated by Cloward and his colleague Lloyd Ohlin in their 1960 book

Delinquency and Opportunity.[30] This book is dedicated to Robert Merton and to Edwin Sutherland, whose learning perspective on deviance is discussed in Chapter 8. Cloward and Ohlin's work attempts to synthesize key elements of Merton's anomie thesis with Sutherland's theory that deviance is learned in everyday social interaction with others. One need not describe Sutherland's theory in detail to outline the basic tenets of Cloward and Ohlin's position. In the first place, Cloward and Ohlin firmly adopt Merton's position in locating the fundamental sociological cause of strains toward deviance in blocked opportunities to achieve socially valued goals. Cloward and Ohlin are concerned with the "position discontent" of persons faced "with limitations on legitimate avenues of access to conventional goals."[31] While they argue that such position discontent produces frustration and a search for alternative means of fulfilling one's aspirations, Cloward and Ohlin maintain that "pressures that lead to deviant patterns do not necessarily determine the particular pattern of deviance that results."[32] At this point they turn to Sutherland's proposition that deviance is learned in interaction with others in order to explain the particular dynamics by which one form of adjustment to frustration is selected instead of others.

In exploring the formation of delinquent subculture, Cloward and Ohlin introduce an analytic approach that can be applied to other forms of deviance as well. They view subcultures as collective social adjustments to the strains of blocked opportunity. Within subcultures people learn to adjust to the frustrations of position discontent in a particular fashion. The manner in which this occurs is, however, not evenly distributed throughout society. Cloward and Ohlin argue that, like channels of legitimate opportunity, the opportunities for particular kinds of subcultural adjustments, and hence particular types of deviant behavior, are unequally distributed. Their study of juvenile delinquency identifies three general forms of subcultural involvement: the *criminal* subculture, the *conflict* subculture, and the *retreatist* subculture. The general source of societal strain is the same for all three—anomie produced by blocked legitimate opportunities. What varies is the specific channel for deviant adaptation.

Criminal subcultures are available to youths raised in specialized social environments—environments which integrate offenders at various age levels and connect conventional and illegitimate values. Youths who reside in such environments and who experience blocked legitimate opportunity channels are nonetheless offered the illegitimate opportunity of an orderly introduction into a world of profitable deviant adaptations. Their delinquency will be organized, disciplined, rational, and respectful of the deviant or organized criminal authority structure. Think of alienated youths who learn their delinquency within an environment dominated by professional or organized criminals. This is the kind of environment envisioned by Cloward and Ohlin in discussing the differential opportunities to deviate offered by criminal subcultures. In such environments youths may adjust to the strains of anomie by becoming apprentices in highly organized deviant activities.

The second type of adaptation environment discussed by Cloward and Ohlin is that of the conflict subculture. There is little age integration between alienated persons and a minimum of convergence between conventional and deviant values. In such environments one is less apt to learn deviance as an instrumentally successful means of obtaining socially valued rewards and more likely to see it as "a way of expressing pent-up angers and frustrations."[33] In such environments there is little opportunity for an orderly apprenticeship into crime as a successful form of business. Adult criminals in such environments are largely unskilled, unsuccessful, and disorganized. Youths within such environments "are deprived not only of conventional opportunity but also of criminal routes to 'big money.'"[34] The collective conflict-subculture adjustment most typical of such neighborhoods is the expressively violent juvenile gang.

The third of Cloward and Ohlin's collective adaptations to position discontent on the part of juveniles is the retreatist subculture. Here Cloward and Ohlin reformulate Merton's notion concerning the meaning of retreatism. Merton describes this adaptation in terms of persons who, unable to reach culturally valued goals through legitimate channels, are unable to employ illegitimate means because of internalized prohibitions. This may be the case for some retreatists. Yet, in commenting on youthful drug addicts, Cloward and Ohlin are quick to point out that "the great majority" of such retreatists "had a history of delinquency before becoming addicted."[35] At this point they introject Cloward's thesis regarding the link between retreatism and double failure. What they describe as the retreatist subculture is really more of a collection of dropouts from the two previously described subcultural adaptations. It is a collectivity of persons who have doubly failed in both legitimate and illegitimate channels. In summary, Cloward and Ohlin state:

> Whether the sequence of adaptations is from criminal to retreatist or from conflict to retreatist, we suggest that limitations on legitimate and illegitimate opportunity combine to produce intense pressures toward retreatist behavior. When both systems of means are simultaneously restricted, it is not strange that some persons become detached from the social structure, abandoning cultural goals and efforts to achieve them by any means.[36]

Albert Cohen: Subculture Adjustments to Frustration

Albert Cohen has been viewed as simultaneously a critic and an advocate of Merton's anomie perspective. As a critic he argued that while Merton's theory was a "sociologically sophisticated and highly plausible . . . explanation" of utilitarian, or instrumentality-oriented, forms of deviance, it failed to account for nonutilitarian or expressive forms, such as that described by Cohen in his book *Delinquent Boys: The Culture of the Gang*.[37] Moreover, in a 1965 article subtitled "Anomie Theory and Beyond" Cohen argues that Merton's formulation is "too atomistic" and that it places undue emphasis on the discontinuity of the deviant act.[38]

In using the term *atomistic* Cohen means that Merton's discussion of deviant adaptations is too individualistic. It presents an image of the isolated person confronted by the strain of blocked opportunity. In contrast, Cohen argues that the way a person experiences strain and selects one or another mode of deviant adaptation is highly dependent upon his or her interpersonal associations, upon his or her social reference group.[39] In stating that Merton's theory reflects a false discontinuity between acts of conformity and deviance Cohen is suggesting something similar. According to Cohen, Merton "treats the deviant act as though it were an abrupt change of state, a leap from a state of strain or anomie to a state of deviance."[40] Is involvement in deviance really such a discontinuous jump? For Cohen the answer is no. Cohen views the entrance into modes of deviant adaptation as a more gradual, step-by-step process, a process in which people constantly define and redefine their situations in relation to the actions and responses of others.[41]

Two things are particularly important about Cohen's criticisms of Merton's theory. First, Cohen's ideas represent concrete suggestions for improving and strengthening the anomie perspective. Second, Merton acknowledged the insightfulness of Cohen's suggestions and incorporated a discussion of the mediating role of group interactional process into subsequent revisions of anomie theory. In 1964 Merton pointed out that, except for his first formulation, in which preoccupation with structural variables "usurped" a discussion of interaction process, all his subsequent presentations of anomie theory have included an emphasis upon reference groups and the importance of social interaction in shaping the adaptational alternatives selected by persons confronted with the strains of anomie.[42] Merton argues that his revised theoretical presentations actually consolidate the anomie perspective with the interactional learning model presented by Edwin Sutherland, one of Cohen's teachers.[43] Thus Merton asserts that there is nothing "integral to the theory of SS and A [social structure and anomie] . . . which requires it to be atomistic and individualistic" in the manner suggested by Cohen.[44]

In responding to Cohen's constructive critique Merton actually advances upon previous formulations of the anomie perspective and incorporates several of Cohen's concerns as his own. He argues that a key concept in Cohen's analysis of delinquent subcultures implicitly contains an important connection to anomie theory. The bulk of Cohen's analysis involves a depiction of the "short-run hedonism" of the delinquent subculture as a collective reaction-formation against the unreachable yet valued status of middle-class culture. For Cohen the irrational, malicious and unaccountable delinquent subculture offers lower-class boys a means of solving the status-frustration problem generated by the denial of access to the world of the middle class. Merton does not take issue with Cohen on these points. Nor does he contest

Cohen's account of the self-perpetuating character of existing delinquent subcultures. Indeed, once operative, delinquent subcultures may well provide the frustration-relieving rewards needed to sustain members' involvement, as well as recruit and instruct new members into nonutilitarian, malicious, and negativistic ways of delinquency.

But what of the origins of delinquent subcultures in the first place? Here Merton (and most other readers) sees great similarity between Cohen's analysis and his own. While much of Cohen's work is concerned with the interactional dynamics by which youths collectively recognize the delinquent subculture as a solution to their status-frustration problems, he is quite explicit about the structural contradictions or strains which generate status-frustration in the first place. In Cohen's own words, "The delinquent subculture . . . is a way of adjustment [to] status problems: certain children are denied status in respectable society because they cannot meet the criteria of the respectable status system."[45] Why can't they meet these criteria? Cohen proceeds at length to outline the structurally generated blocks to lower-class youths' ability to realize culturally desired goals. These include class differentials in the organization of child-rearing and parental aspirations which make it more likely that lower-class youths will fail in school and the world of work and thereby experience an exaggerated sense of status-frustration, making them particularly vulnerable to the solution offered by the delinquent subculture: a collective rejection of middle-class aspirations that they were structurally unable to obtain in the first place.[46] Without formally using the term *anomie*, Cohen thus appears to make an argument that is highly compatible with Merton's use of this concept. In this sense, Cohen's work, like that of Cloward and Ohlin, represents a valuable extension of the line of sociological reasoning introduced by Émile Durkheim and reformulated by Robert K. Merton.

IDENTIFYING ANOMIC DEVIANCE

In the period following World War II, the United States was alive with a renewed faith in the positive power of science. American scientific know-how had, after all, ended the war. In the postwar years it was up to science to likewise conquer the natural and social problems of a more peaceable time and to preserve the world for the American way of life. This naive revival of faith in the scientific enterprise is somewhat bizarre, given that this country's greatest scientific achievement during the war was the nuclear holocaust of thousands of people in Hiroshima and Nagasaki. Perhaps the horrific nature of this scientific accomplishment was simply too staggering for Americans to grasp. In any event, the postwar years were filled with a new scientific commitment to the ever more destructive technologies of defense, as well as the conquest of outer space, bodily disease, and such diverse social problems as poverty, crime, drug addiction, and mental disorders.

The research methods used by social scientists associated with the anomie perspective have generally reflected the professional-technical interests of the post-World War II liberal welfare state. For the most part, anomie researchers used the quantifiable tools of survey research (fixed questionnaires and coded interviews) or data drawn from official statistics. These tools produced statistical measures of anomie and its relationship to deviance. By adopting such quantifiable research instruments sociologists dressed themselves in the authoritative garb of "hard science" and thereby managed to obtain a piece of the profitable pie of scientific problem solving.

Unfortunately, this commitment to a hard-science method of social research distracted most anomie researchers from the insights which were potentially available from other, less quantifiable forms of investigation. In particular, most anomie research was lacking in a historical perspective on the origins of the social structures being studied and in the rich experiential viewpoint provided by field studies. Indeed, a comprehensive inventory of eighty-six studies of anomie published between 1941 and 1964 indicates that only four included the use of historical methods, while only nine employed field-observation or participatory techniques. On the other hand, sixty studies used the quantitative tools of the survey (questionnaire and interview methods), and another fifteen involved the analysis of official statistics.[47] This is not to suggest that anomie research failed to provide a variety of useful insights into the contradictory relationship between social structure and deviant behavior. It is simply to point out that the vast percentage of such studies operated within the narrow confines of the professional-technical research model which came to dominate American sociology in the mid-twentieth century. For the most part, this model systematically neglected the historical development of specific social-structural arrangements and the concrete human experiences of persons said to be caught up in such structures.

Specific Measures of Anomie

Within the general confines of the professional-technical research tradition described above, investigators developed several well-known measures of anomie. In the following paragraphs, I will describe three of the most commonly discussed measurement techniques. The first presents itself as an objective measure of normlessness within a given community. The second and third represent attempts to quantitatively assess the subjective experience of anomie at the individual level.

One of the best-known and most commonly cited objective indicators of anomie was developed by Bernard Lander in his study of 8,464 cases of delinquency in Baltimore, Maryland, between 1939 and 1942.[48] The substantive results in Lander's work have been discussed previously, as they provide data related to certain themes of the social disorganization perspective. With regard to anomie, Lander devised a three-factor cluster index which included official data on the rate of delinquency, a measurement of the percentage of nonwhite population within a particular geographical area, and the percentage of homes which were owner-occupied. According to Lander, these things were indicative of normlessness within a given community insomuch as they were believed to reflect "the breakdown or weakening of the regulatory structure of society."[49] While delinquency was taken as direct evidence of the lack of normative regulation, a large percentage of nonwhites in a previously white area was considered to be an indicator of the transitory or unstable nature of a particular neighborhood. Lack of home ownership was taken as a measure of family instability, another indicator of normlessness.

In analyzing these factors, Lander found high rates of delinquency to be related both to low percentage of home ownership and to high rates of nonwhite population (until this measure reached 50 percent, after which the rate decreased in proportion to an increasing percentage of nonwhites). Lander's findings have been challenged by researchers such as Roland Chilton, who has underscored the importance of economic as well as anomic factors in relationship to delinquency.[50] Nonetheless, Lander's methods have been commented upon positively by Merton, who characterized them as "a symptomatic advance" toward "a measure of anomie, as an objective condition of life."[51]

Subjective measures of anomie have generally taken one of two directions—the use of the five-item scale developed by Leo Srole in 1956 [52] or some variation of what might best be described as a measure of position discontent. The Srole scale attempts to identify the experience of anomia, or an individual's sense of being dislocated within the world of social structure. It does so by posing five questions. These seek to tap a person's sense regarding whether (1) community leaders are indifferent to his or her needs; (2) little can be accomplished in a society which is basically unpredictable and lacking order; (3) life goals are receding rather than being realized; (4) life holds little meaning and small prospect for one's children; and (5) one cannot count on associates for social and psychological support.

Do the questions posed by Srole really tap into the concept of anomie as developed by Durkheim and/or modified by Merton? According to Dorothy Meier and Wendell Bell, Srole's scale can be better described as an index of such things as despair, hopelessness, and discouragement.[53] Other researchers point to a certain imprecision in differentiating anomie from the more generic concept of alienation. As Gwynn Nettler points out, although "alienation and anomie are undoubtedly correlated; at least it is difficult to conceive of any notable degree of anomie that would not result in alienation . . . this seems a poor reason for confusing the two."[54] Robert Merton, however, viewed Srole's scale of anomia in somewhat different terms.[55] Merton recognized that Srole's instrument measured anomia as a subjective condition of individuals (a concept closer to the psychological meaning of alienation than Merton's own formulation of anomie as a structural disjuncture between socially promoted goals and socially approved means of goal attainment). Nonetheless, Merton argued that when aggregated, the Srole scale could provide an effective measure of the means-ends discrepancy within the society at large. In other words, by combining individual measures of anomia into an aggregate measure, one "would then constitute an index of anomie for the given social unit under investigation."[56] For Merton, this procedure offered the distinct advantage of "combining indices of anomie (of social systems) with indices of (individual) anomia" and thereby of testing the hypothesis that individuals with like degrees of anomia "are more apt to engage in deviant behavior, the higher the degree of anomie in the social system."[57]

A second subjective measure of anomie, a measure of position discontent, attempts to obtain an index of the degree of pressure toward deviant behavior that is exerted by one's aspirations. Following the lead of Merton and the subsequent extension of his theory by Cloward and Ohlin, and by Cohen, the position-discontent measure seeks to identify discrepancies between a person's socially nurtured aspirations and his or her socially positioned expectancy to fulfill those aspirations. Such a measure was used by James Short and his associates in a series of studies of delinquency in Chicago.[58] Through the use of interviews, Short obtained measures of discrepancies between occupational aspirations and expectations, as well as information on discrepancies between a father's actual occupation (a somewhat more objective measure) and the aspirations and expectations of boys studied. Using these measures of anomie, Short compared gang boys with nongang boys from the same neighborhoods as well as with middle-class boys from other neighborhoods. Black and white subsamples were also obtained for each category so as to assess the differences between the socially positioned aspirations and expectations of youths in a society in which race makes a difference.

A Concluding Comment on Anomie Research: The Use of Official Statistics on Deviance

While anomie has commonly been measured by one of the objective or subjective measures discussed above, the measurement of deviance by anomie researchers has generally involved the use of official government statistics. This introduces a certain bias into the research process. Official data cannot be equated with valid and reliable scientific data. They are collected by and for the use of public agencies. At one end of the reporting process they include commonsense stereotypical perceptions by police and various diagnostic agents about who is likely to be seen as deviant. Such things as location of residence, appearance, demeanor, race, gender, social class, and the timing and context of the official judgment all play a part. In the middle of the record-keeping process are organizational factors affecting the quantity and style of official data production. These include such things as pressure from above or below, the style of management, the availability of clerical help, and the reward structure within the social control agency. On the other hand, a number of overtly political factors also contribute to official reports. What will the public think? How will the presentation of data affect future funding? All these factors make the exclusive use of official data a poor vehicle for assessing deviance.

Dependence upon official statistics to define deviants is not limited to the anomie perspective. Indeed most researchers associated with the social disorganization and functionalist perspectives chart the distribution of deviance in a similar fashion. Yet, because of the critical potential of anomie theory, its nearly exclusive reliance on official data by anomie theorists is particularly disturbing. Why? Given their awareness of the systemic nature of structured social inequality, why should Merton and his students by satisfied with the inequality of the data on deviance that find their way into the public record? Perhaps the answer is to be found in what I have referred to as the professional-technical posture of post-World War II government-sponsored social science research. While Merton himself opposed the abandonment of social science problem formulation to the demands or needs of state bureaucracies, it is today evident that the bulk of social science research accepted official definitions of what and who was deviant. Definitions of problems followed the money. The question for most liberal social scientists was to explain the troublesome deviance of the lower class. Research in the anomie tradition generally followed suit.

SOCIAL CONTROL OF ANOMIC DEVIANCE

Control strategies associated with the anomie perspective aim at changing the structures of society as a whole. Different structural changes are recommended by each of the perspective's two dominant theoretical strands. For the Durkheimian strand social control is said to begin with the reconstruction of the normative, or moral, structure of society. There is a certain contemporary ring to this call for moral reconstruction. Recall my discussion in Chapter 2 of the rise of the Moral Majority and other groups preaching a revival of Christian morality. When I presented an early draft of the chapter to a postdoctoral seminar on the sociology of social control at Yale University, one of the participants commented upon what he perceived to be a great similarity between the chapter's opening quotation by the Reverend Jerry Falwell's and Durkheim's descriptions of anomie and the need for moral reconstruction. Indeed, Falwell and Durkheim offer related diagnoses of the moral malaise affecting the modern world. They part ways, however, regarding what to do about this malaise. Falwell wants us to return to the fundamentalist religious values of yesteryear. Durkheim beckons us toward the establishment of a new civic or secular moral order. For Durkheim, religion was viewed as the basis for moral order in the previous days of traditional *mechanical* society. Modern *organic* society must construct a new secular base for civic morality.

Durkheim: Constructing a Secular Moral Order
for Modern Society

Durkheim's call for establishing a new secular moral order took two general forms. The first involved his proposal for the formation of occupational associations which would provide experiential ties for increasingly specialized workers in the highly rational modern economy. In traditional or mechanical society workers performed more similar economic tasks and were in this sense linked together in the rituals of everyday labor. In modern organic society a highly specialized division of the labor force separated workers from each other and thereby inhibited the development of common moral perspectives on life and its organization. By proposing the development of modern occupational associations Durkheim envisioned the development of socially organized "nodal points" where workers in varying occupational positions could come together and forge a common perspective.[59]

Durkheim was, unfortunately, never very specific about the exact nature of his proposed occupational associations. They would not be equated with trade unions, which Durkheim saw as creating a permanent conflict between workers and employers. Nor were they a revival of the medieval guild, an organization regulating the economic activities of a particular craft or trade. They would be wide in scope and more interested in the general social structure than either of these forms. They would mediate political relations between individuals and the centralized state and resolve conflicts within and between local groups. Such occupational associations would also be involved in a wide range of educational and recreational activities. They would be "close enough to the individual for him to be able to rely directly upon [them], and durable enough to be able to give him a perspective."[60]

The second general area for moral reconstruction was education. Durkheim was an active adviser to the Ministry of Education in France during the period of the Third Republic. In that capacity Durkheim argued that it was the moral duty of social scientists to use their knowledge to guide public affairs along an enlightened course.[61] The course Durkheim had in mind was one informed by the scientific findings of sociology. In this sense, sociology was for Durkheim the functional equivalent of what religion had been in the past—a means of making sense of the world and of morally orienting oneself toward future action.

In his book *The Rules of the Sociological Method* Durkheim stated that "the future is already written for him who knows how to read it."[62] And how better can one read the future than by the disciplined study of sociology? Durkheim believed that sociology would foster a new form of secular morality based upon a rational comprehension of social facts. In France, where Durkheim's influence was enormous, sociology was introduced as a key element in the curriculum of the *écoles normales,* institutions which prepared future generations of primary and secondary school teachers. By 1914, the Durkheimian perspective had become a standard feature of elementary school courses in civic morality throughout France.[63]

Merton: Reducing Aspirations or Increasing Opportunities

For Merton the social control of anomic deviance took a different form. It was directed at efforts to eliminate the strain between societal goals and differentially available means. In principle this could be achieved in one of two ways. First, society could be resocialized to accept the "reality" that not all persons were meant to achieve the same goals. This would reinforce, rather than eliminate, the present class system. It would introduce the ideology of caste, eradicating any sentiments favoring the "myth" that all people were to have equal access to societal resources. The poor were meant to be indigent and the rich wealthy! Without aspirations which could not be met there would be little tension between goals and means, no structural inducement toward deviance.

The classic sociological example of a society organized without structured conflict over unmet aspirations is that of traditional India. Guided by religious principles, traditional Indian society was organized into distinct castes. Some castes were highly privileged. Others were less advantaged. At the bottom was a caste of "untouchables," truly the lowest of the low. According to traditional Indian beliefs, all this inequality was supernaturally ordained. Nobody aspired to more. One's caste was one's fate for life. It could not be changed. Mobility between caste groupings was unthinkable. In such a fatalistic system one would expect few of the structural strains toward deviance suggested by Merton's analysis.

As attractive as it may be for those at the top of society, it would be difficult to effectively establish a caste-system ideology within American society. For too many years too many people have spent too much time trying to convert the "noble lie" about equality in America into some semblance of truth.

The second control strategy flowing from Merton's formulation demands far more of the same. Smash the lie about equality of means and replace it with a genuine system of equal access for all! The realization of current affirmative-action, equal-opportunity, antiracism, and antisexism strategies would be in keeping with this aspect of the anomie perspective. By removing barriers to equal access to societal goals, one might hope to eliminate contradictions with the U.S. social structure. Deviance would thus be reduced because people would have been given an equal opportunity to conform.

In the early 1960s Merton's ideas about anomie were translated into an applied program of social reform. This was particularly the case for the portions of Merton's work embodied in Richard Cloward and Lloyd Ohlin's thesis regarding the relationship between delinquency and the opportunity structures of society. At the time that they were completing their book *Delinquency and Opportunity*, Cloward and Ohlin worked closely with staff members of the Henry Street Settlement in New York City's Lower East Side. The result was a sociologically informed program of "action research" referred to as "Mobilization for Youth." Plans for this program called for a massive assault on the socially structured obstacles to success for youths in a predominantly nonwhite sixty-seven-square-block area of Manhattan. In essence, Mobilization for Youth was directed at the following objectives:

1 to increase the employment ability of youths from low-income families,
2 to improve and make more accessible training and work preparation facilities,
3 to help young people achieve employment goals equal to their capacities,
4 to increase employment opportunities for the area's youth, and
5 to help minority-group youngsters overcome discrimination in hiring.[64]

To meet the above-stated objectives, Mobilization for Youth proposed a series of programmatic interventions designed not only to deliver specialized educational, vocational, and youth-worker services, but also to assist residents of lower-income neighborhoods in developing effective strategies of community organization. These things, it was hoped, would in turn reduce delinquency and other related forms of deviance (alcoholism, drug addiction, etc.). Mobilization for Youth was a far-reaching program of theoretically based social experimentation, an attempt to systematically blend sociology with social reform.[65] In the early 1960s this blend resonated well with the liberal domestic politics of President John F. Kennedy. Soon after his 1961 inauguration, Kennedy voiced a long-standing family commitment to the problems of youth by appointing a high-level presidential commission on juvenile delinquency. David Hackett, the executive director of this group (the President's Committee on Juvenile Delinquency and Youth Crime), was briefed on the central tenets of anomie theory by officers of the philanthropic Ford Foundation. Cloward and Ohlin were consultants to the Ford Foundation. Hackett soon recognized an affinity between their ideas and the Kennedy administration's promise of a New Frontier of equal opportunity.

Ohlin, a professor at Harvard, was invited to join the committee in devising a new battle plan to combat delinquency. Fresh with ideas about the proposed Mobilization for Youth, Ohlin helped shape the course of federal legislation authorizing the expenditure of $10 million over the course of three years. This legislation called for coordinated community action to alter the opportunity structures constraining the integration of low-income youths into the mainstream of American society. Its preamble reads like a passage from Cloward and Ohlin's book on this topic.[66]

New York City's Mobilization for Youth was among the first programs to receive federal funds under the new legislation. This program was, after all, something of a blueprint for the legislative package as a whole. On May 31, 1962, Mobilization for Youth was blessed by a formal White House garden ceremony and awarded a three-year grant of $12.5 million. Additional funds were provided by the Ford Foundation and by New York City. Ideas originating in the sociological writings of a former street-gang member from South Philadelphia (Merton) were now officially sanctioned as those of the U.S. government. These ideas had been well received in academic circles. How well did they fare when put into practice on New York's Lower East Side?

Mobilization for Youth was a precursor of seventeen similar programs established during the early 1960s.[67] How successful were such programs? If measured by a specific reduction in delinquency, they generated few positive outcomes. Why? The general consensus among thoughtful observers is that such programs were doomed to failure because they were at once too radical and not radical enough.

Programs based on the Mobilization blueprint were generally too radical for those who had originally commissioned them. This was especially the case for their community-organization components. Recall that a key aspect of Mobilization for Youth involved efforts to "organize the afflicted—to overturn the status quo and replace it with a higher level of stability, without delinquents, alcoholism or drug addiction."[68] Some participants may have become too serious in realizing this goal. Lower-income citizens actually began using federal funds to strategically oppose a wide range of systemic blocks to equal opportunity. Mobilization efforts supported rent strikes, public demonstrations, and legal action on behalf of welfare clients. Participants began to collect data on patterns of discrimination and housing code violations by landlords.

Theoretically these political developments should be judged as evidence of the project's success. Poor people were using the tools of the system to make the system more responsive to their goals and aspirations. This was not how those who were already part of the system saw it. Within a short time participants in Mobilization for Youth were being described by the *New York Daily News* as "Commies and Commie sympathizers."

It was not long before Mobilization, a child of the government, became harassed and thereafter abandoned by its fearful parent. The Federal Bureau of Investigation conducted investigations of key community organizers. Project files were confiscated. The use of federal and local funds was questioned and eventually denied.[69] Similar dismantling was occurring in Washington. The presidential committee which had promoted the Mobilization concept was allowed to wither away. This committee had always encountered resistance from entrenched bureaucratic interests within the federal government. Yet, as LaMar Empey points out, when complaints and charges of radicalism reached the legislative halls of the Capitol, "influential members of Congress made it clear that the mandate of the President's Committee was to reduce delinquency, not to reform urban society or try out sociological theories on American youths."[70] But what was it that was so radical about Mobilization for Youth? What could be more American than trying to incorporate all people into the opportunity structure of the society as a whole? The answer is provided by Richard Quinney, who suggests that what was most fearful about Mobilization for Youth was its potential for becoming a "widespread movement among the poor."[71] According to Quinney, "to provide the poor with services and assistance from above has been the traditional way of doing things; it is regarded as subversive when the poor attempt to change the social pattern of their poverty."[72]

Rife with controversy, Mobilization for Youth soon dissolved into the unequal American opportunity structure which it had been designed to challenge. Its challenge was short-lived. Its last days were full of conflict, not only between participants and opponents but also between staff and those who were to benefit from staff efforts.[73] Within a few years the program had become little more than a reminder of the turbulent 1960s in which it was conceived. There has been little in the way of serious assessment of its actual effect on the rate of delinquency. Perhaps its vision was simply never radical enough. The practical power of the sociological reformers proved no match for the strong political and economic interests of those threatened by a fundamental restructuring of the American opportunity system. With this in mind it is easy to understand why Mobilization for Youth was sentenced to death before attempting its crime. The reason is simple. In the words of Allen Liska, "changing social conditions means changing the lives of those in power, and they resist."[74]

THE ANOMIE PERSPECTIVE TODAY

The anomie perspective has had enormous influence on contemporary thinking about deviance and social control. In his book *Sociology since Mid-Century* Randall Collins observes that anomie "was the dominant theory in the area of deviance from the early 1950s until about 1970."[75] According to Collins, Merton's essay "Social Structure and Anomie" is the "most cited paper in all of sociology."[76] A similar point was made by Albert Cohen. Writing in 1965, Cohen noted that "'anomie theory' . . . has been the most influential single formulation in the sociology of deviance in the last 25 years."[77] No small credit for this should go to Cohen himself. In considering the fact that Merton's essay sat dormant for about fifteen years after its first publication in 1938, Collins suggests the possibility that its importance became widely recognized only after Cohen's critique. Collins asks that we consider the possibility that "it was really Albert K. Cohen who made Merton famous in this area, and not vice versa."[78] In this regard, one should also note the role of Richard Cloward and Lloyd Ohlin in attracting attention to the anomie framework. A recent survey of literature on crime and delinquency discovered that Cloward and Ohlin's book *Delinquency and Opportunity* was one of the two most cited publications in the field of criminology.[79]

The writings of Cohen and of Cloward and Ohlin undoubtedly contributed to the widespread recognition of Merton's anomie formulation, but they do not account for its general acceptance by sociologists of deviance through most of the 1950s and 1960s. Was the available empirical evidence so convincing that the theory could not be denied? Hardly! Although a fairly large number of studies drew upon the conceptual imagery of anomie, few provided a direct test of Merton's position. According to Don Gibbons and Joseph Jones, "anomie propositions have been employed most commonly as a high-level explanatory metaphor, with no real attempt to assess their theoretical utility."[80] Relatively few of the papers citing Merton provide a test of his theory. Even fewer present contradictory evidence. Most simply reference Merton's formulation as part of a review of the literature or as support for their own theoretical positions.

Why was the anomie perspective so widely accepted despite a lack of clear empirical support for its central concepts? According to Marshall Clinard, the widespread endorsement of anomie theory reflects a "common tendency in sociology to accept intriguing and well-formulated theories in advance of adequate empirical support."[81] What accounts for this tendency? The most plausible sociological answer is that the vision offered by an untested but commonly accepted theory shares an affinity with the more general, commonsensical vision of scholars at the time. Indeed this was clearly the case with anomie theorizing. This becomes evident when one considers the historical situation of U.S. sociology in the years following World War II. During the postwar years nearly all walks of American society were affected by what is today commonly known as the "rise of the modern welfare state." This term refers to the spiderlike involvement of government bureaucracies in the organization of everyday life. Most historians mark the New Deal, or the massive entrance of the federal government into the social and economic life of the nation during the 1930s depression, as a significant step in the direction of the modern welfare state. During World War II the influence of government grew larger, and it stayed large after the war's completion. In the years following the war millions of Americans came to believe in the necessity and efficacy of the government's involvement in, and regulation of matters related to, nearly all human social problems. Put into practice this belief led to an enormous expansion of governmental agencies. This expansion was so great that by the early 1970s opposition to the long reach of governmental bureaucracy had become a major political battle cry.

In what ways did the rise of the welfare state affect the discipline of sociology? The answer to this question provides significant clues as to why the anomie perspective was adopted so readily by sociologists during the 1950s. The growth of the welfare state led to a growth in professional sociology. As Alvin Gouldner points out, "The social sciences increasingly became a well financed technological basis for the Welfare State's effort to solve the problems of its industrial society."[82] In one three-year period in the early 1960s federal spending on social science research rose approximately 70 percent. In 1962 the federal government invested $118 million in such research. In 1964 it spent $200 million.[83] This large-scale government financing of sociological research was accompanied by a demand for applied, or useful, programs of research. It also altered what was demanded from sociological theory. Theory must be made to fit the practical needs of bureaucratic problem solvers because along with government money comes the expectation "that the social sciences will help administrators to design and operate national policies, welfare apparatus, urban settlements, and even industrial establishments."[84]

The demand for usable, applied sociological theory presented certain dilemmas for sociologists of the 1950s and early 1960s. In the first place, U.S. sociology remained generally within the conceptual grip of functionalist theorizing. As suggested in the preceding chapter, functionalism provided sociology with an optimistic viewpoint on how problems such as deviance could be viewed as actually contributing to the vitality of the social system as a whole. Yet, since functionalism could easily identify a manifest or latently positive consequence of almost anything, it offered little of the "system-fixing" utility demanded by government funding agencies.

Sociologists could, of course, abandon their theoretical concerns when turning their eyes toward applied matters. Many did. This led to a kind of schizoid division between sociological theory and research, to the gulf between what sociological critic C. Wright Mills described as the vacuous realm of "grand theory" and the administratively oriented practice of "abstracted empiricism."[85] It also led to the danger that sociologists would be co-opted by those who paid them, or as Nanette Davis states, that they would be "drafted as common intellectual laborers, capable of fulfilling technical tasks, but unable to understand . . . the direction and form of dominant institutions."[86]

How could sociologists escape the dilemmas outlined above? How could they respond to demands for applied theorizing while retaining the intellectual heritage of sociology? The work of Robert K. Merton provided a solution. Merton argued for a theory of the "middle range." Such a theory would retain functionalism's concern for the interrelationship of parts within the structure of the system as a whole. At the same time it would be pitched at a low enough level of abstraction so as to be translated into empirical research and concrete policy analysis. Middle-range theory was an ideal solution for sociologists at work in the welfare state. It would be theoretically abstract enough for them to maintain their identity as detached scholars. It would be practically concrete enough for them to maintain attachments to the business of problem solving and to reap the financial and political benefits associated with government-sponsored research.

One area of sociological specialization to particularly benefit from Merton's concept of middle-range theory was that involving the study of deviance. Merton's theory of social structure and anomie was the middle-range theory par excellence. It was commonly viewed as both theoretically sophisticated and practically useful. It excited both the sociological imagination and that of the bureaucratic welfare-state reformer. It had another advantage as well. It could be viewed as critical of certain elements in the existing social structure without being read as critical of the system as a whole. In this sense Merton's theory of anomie was basically an "all-American" theory. As Randall Collins suggests, "the great American creed of social mobility occupies the center of the stage, and lack of mobility opportunities (not the more fundamental structure of inequalities of distribution) is the villain of this structural drama."[87] It was this quality more than any other which may have enhanced the marketability of the anomie perspective during the 1950s. Having said this, let us examine the legacy of anomie as it was translated into a practical program of sociological research.

Empirical Studies of Anomic Deviance

Numerous empirical studies have employed concepts related to anomie. Studies of mental disorders have sought to document the relationship between rising rates of schizophrenia and "breakdown in [the] controlling and regularity functions" of the social system as a whole.[88] Studies of drug use and addiction have also drawn upon the anomie framework. Of particular importance are studies clarifying the applicability of Merton's category of retreatism. Are drug users actually persons who are blocked in the use of both legitimate and illegitimate means? Merton argued that such persons were externally constrained in the use of legitimate means. At the same time, they were said to be denied illegitimate means by the tight internal moral constraints of conscience. Cloward and Ohlin disagreed. They viewed drug users not as doubly blocked escapists but as double failures. They were persons who had unsuccessfully explored both illegitimate and legitimate avenues of goal attainment before dropping out into a retreatist subculture. This interpretation is challenged by data presented by researchers Daniel Glaser[89] and Michael Lewis.[90] In separate studies Glaser and Lewis conclude that lower-class drug addicts do not really drop out of the innovative-means or illegitimate-means category. To support their expensive habits, addicts commonly work hard within the employment structure of the criminal world. Nor is the initial choice of drugs an exclusively retreatist endeavor. As Alfred Lindesmith and John Simon suggest, the differential availability of drugs within different neighborhoods may be as much or more of a factor in determining drug use than are strains toward retreatism.[91]

In addition to studies of mental disorders and drug use, a considerable body of anomie-related research has accumulated on the topic of suicide.

Indeed some of the most significant studies of the problem have been guided by the theoretical imagery of anomie. Of particular importance are the 1954 work of Henry and Short,[92] the 1969 research of Ronald Maris,[93] and the investigations of Jack Gibbs and Walter Martin.[94] In varying ways each of these studies attempts to document the relationship between the absence of normative constraint or social integration and the presence of high rates of suicide.

Also important is the large body of delinquency research which draws upon the analytic framework of anomie. For a comprehensive review of this research see LaMar Empey's *American Delinquency*.[95] Of particular relevance is Empey's consideration of the relationship between socially structured strain and juvenile lawbreaking. This crucial area of anomie research may also be the most confusing. It is crucial because strain is typically viewed as the causal link between a contradictory social structure and concrete instances of deviance. It is confusing because this concept has rarely been measured in precise terms. Most delinquency research simply assumes that strain must be present when youths report such things as a low likelihood that they will graduate from school. Unfortunately there have been few direct measures of strain itself. Thus, according to Empey, "we do not really know whether . . . assumptions [regarding the presence of strain] are true."[96] This lack of knowledge has yielded the center stage of delinquency research to studies of aspiration levels, such as that conducted by Travis Hirschi. Hirschi found that juveniles with high aspirations were less likely to be deviant than those with lower aspirations. From this he concluded that "frustrated occupational ambitions . . . cannot be an important cause of delinquency."[97]

Empey entertains the possibility that Hirschi might be correct. He also explores the suggestion that youthful frustration may arise from something other than a failure to realize long-term occupational aspirations. Reference is made to a variety of studies suggesting that for many students, particularly those who do not present themselves in terms of a set of preformulated aspirational goals, school itself may be a frustrating experience.[98] Anomie strain, in other words, may be "created not by frustration of deeply held conventional goals, but by the interaction of students who lack such goals with teachers and principals who think they ought to have them."[99] Hirschi argues somewhat differently. Seemingly determined to turn the anomie argument inside out, Hirschi contends that those who get in trouble in school are neither disproportionately lower-class nor teacher-frustrated. They are simply those with a minimal commitment to the legitimate means of success, those who are little motivated toward hard work, deferral of gratification, and long-range planning. Hirschi views such troublesome youths as poorly or inadequately controlled.

Maybe, but what is the root cause of this out-of-controlness? In Chapter 6 we considered the specifics of Hirschi's own control theory. This focuses upon the immediate interactional context in which people acquire internal constraints and come under the normative control of others. The anomie perspective asks that we relocate individuals, and their internal and interactional constraints, within the wider world of social structure. Failing to find a relationship between class position and strains toward delinquency, Hirschi retreats to the level of individual and interactional analysis. This retreat should not be taken as evidence of the insufficiency of the anomie perspective. Perhaps it is a structured denial of a sense of control over one's own destiny that frustrates youth and not class position or school experience alone. In our society self-control is an aspiration for nearly all males. Nonetheless in the mundane and often boring routines of everyday life, few of us find that we are actually in control of our own social, political, or economic destinies. What a horrific awareness—anomie in its most extreme form. Perhaps most nondelinquents have simply been protected from this awareness by a variety of things which distract them from this fundamental lack of control—concern with interpersonal relations, looking good, having a car that works, getting to the job on time—things which Hirschi might view as elements of control, but which a more radical version of anomie theory might see as illusions of control. Delinquents, on the other hand, through some combination of structural position and life experience, might more clearly see and act toward the social world as it "really" is—as out of control. I do not in any way mean to romanticize the delinquent. My point is simply to suggest one of the many as yet unexplored possibilities for the study of anomic strain.

ASSESSMENT OF THE ANOMIE PERSPECTIVE

Aspirations to deviate are rooted in the structural contradictions of society. This is the essential message of the anomie perspective. It is an important message, one that has had an enormous impact on the sociological study of deviance in the mid-twentieth century. It is also the message of two enormously important sociologists, Durkheim and Merton, scholars who have oriented and reoriented social science inquiry toward the analysis of the systemic interrelationship between parts within the structure of society as a whole.

This is not to say that most sociologists have come to agree upon the specifics of Durkheim's or Merton's analysis. Each has been the subject of major and sustained criticism. Yet, despite a variety of specific critiques, the general theoretical thrust of both Durkheim's and Merton's formulation has endured.

Specific Criticisms of Durkheim and Merton

Durkheim's work on anomic suicide has been the subject of numerous critical essays. Whitney Pope, for instance, points to several specific weaknesses in Durkheim's formulation.[100] According to Pope, Durkheim's conception of the causal link between normative deregulation and suicide is vague and occasionally contradictory. In developing his explanation Durkheim refers to such diverse matters as a structurally induced discrepancy between aspirations and means, stress created by the collapse of external standards, meaninglessness resulting from a breakdown in social constraints, and even social irresponsibility generated by moral deregulation. Pope argues that this inconsistency prevented Durkheim from developing a coherent explanation of the dynamics of anomic suicide. Pope also quarrels with Durkheim's interpretation of his statistical data. After reanalyzing many of the statistics used by Durkheim, Pope argues that empirical support for Durkheim's thesis is less conclusive than once believed. Instances are noted in which cases that don't fit are either ignored or inadequately explained.[101]

Merton's work has also been criticized on numerous grounds. Marshall Clinard lists eleven areas in which Merton's thesis has been faulted by contemporary sociologists.[102] Many of these criticisms have been discussed earlier in this chapter. Some have been incorporated into subsequent revisions of Merton's theory. This is the case, for instance, with Cohen's criticisms regarding the overly atomistic and falsely discontinuous aspects of the theory of social structure and anomie. Other criticisms have taken issue with the implication that the highest rates of deviance occur among the lower classes. The structural position of lower-class persons might make them more susceptible to the opportunities offered by certain deviant adaptations. The same, however, might be said of middle-class managers and upper-class owners of highly competitive corporations. Aren't such persons also exposed to powerful strains to use any available means to achieve the great American dream of being number one? The failure of Merton and his students to systematically consider anomic deviation by the more privileged social classes may be associated with what we have previously referred to as the theory's responsiveness to the prepackaged problem-solving demands of the U.S. welfare state, and with its users' unfortunate reliance upon the analysis of official statistics. Other criticisms are directed toward what is left out of Merton's theory—attention to the intervening impact of being labeled deviant and the failure to consider anomie in societies where social position is fixed or ascribed, as opposed to societies in which aspirations for upward mobility are culturally reinforced.

Enduring Theoretical Concerns: The General Importance of Durkheim and Merton

The general theoretical message of the anomie perspective has weathered the storm of numerous specific criticisms. The ideas presented by Durkheim and Merton have become part of the theoretical core of the contemporary sociological imagination. In this sense, both sociologists realized their own theoretical goals. Each was concerned more with presenting a general conceptual orientation than with laying out a series of precisely testable propositions. This, for Durkheim, was the proper role of sociological theory for a science "still in the stage of system building." In his preface to *Suicide,* Durkheim notes a preference for "brilliant generalities," as opposed to casting a more focused "light upon a limited portion of the . . . field."[103] Merton viewed his own theoretical project in similar terms. According to Merton the goal of sociological theory is to provide "general orientations toward data, suggesting types of variables which theorists must . . . take into account, rather than clearly formulated, verifiable statements of relationships."[104] This is a good description of what Durkheim's and Merton's theories accomplished. On these terms their work can only be judged successful.

Durkheim's and Merton's conceptual concerns converge at a general point of theoretical orientation. High rates of deviance are said to be structurally encouraged by contradictory developments in the organization of society. If you ask a sociologist how to deal with the problem of deviant people, don't be surprised if the answer suggests that you must first deal with the problem of social structure. This is the basic point made by most sociologists today.

According to theoretical commentator Robert Bierstadt, the point is simply this: "It is not wayward personalities but ordinary social structures that motivate behavior that is labeled deviant."[105]

Concluding Comments: Limitations of the Anomie Perspective

The attempt to link deviant behavior to the contradictory organization of social structure is clearly a strength of the anomie perspective. Nonetheless, in closing my discussion of anomie I will point to two general problems with the use of social-structure concepts by anomie theorists. The first involves an overly exaggerated sense of the unity of social structure. The second suggests an area in which structural analysis is not extended far enough.

Exaggerated Structural Unity   Anomie theory overly exaggerates, or re-ifies, the idea of a unitary structure for society as a whole. Merton paints a picture of a unitary U.S. society bound together in a common cultural com-mitment to the goals of the great American dream. But is U.S. culture really as homogeneous as Merton suggests? Merton's position is challenged by those who view society as a collection of interrelated but frequently competitive subgroups or subcultures, each with a relatively distinct set of cultural goals. Merton is undoubtedly correct that the entirety of U.S. society is bombarded by the mass mediation of cultural values. Indeed the U.S. household without a television set or two is a rarity. Nonetheless, the specific impact of mass mediation may itself be mediated by a plurality of diverse ethnic, regional, gender, class, age, and neighborhood reference groups.

Critics of the unitary-culture thesis, such as Edwin Lemert, contend that American society might better be described in terms of value pluralism.[106] Lemert suggests that what appears to be unitary in U.S. culture is, in actu-ality, the result of the efforts of dominant groups to extend their own values in such a way as "to become a basis for normative regulation of ethnic or religious populations having divergent values."[107] Lemert envisions society as a collective of subgroups competing with unequal resources for the prize of cultural dominance. Other critics view subcultures as arising out of or in reaction to the cultural categories of dominant groups. This is the way Cohen explained what he perceived to be the anti-middle-class values of the delin-quent culture. The subculture of delinquent boys was described as a collective reaction formation against the values and goals of a parent culture which systematically denied access to those with lower-class backgrounds. In some-what different fashion Walter Miller described the entirety of lower-class culture as founded upon values differentiating it from other groups in society. Miller viewed the lower-class subculture as providing a basis by which disad-vantaged groups might adjust to the realities of class society. At the same time, focal concerns of lower-class culture (trouble, toughness, smartness, excitement, fate, and autonomy) constantly pitted the lower class against the dominant institutions of the wider society. This contradictory and somewhat paradoxical characteristic of subcultures has led sociologist Milton Yinger to the development of the idea of *contracultures*. Of related interest is the recent use of the term *subculture* by Dick Hebdige and other British scholars.[108] In studying the coded meaning of the contemporary punk subculture, Hebdige suggests that subcultural styles represent a forceful, if often unrecognized, rejection of the cultural dominance, or *hegemony*, of those in structured positions of power.

Each of the above-mentioned subcultural approaches rejects assumptions regarding the cultural unity of society as a whole. So do recent studies of the deviance and criminality of women. Theorists like Eileen Leonard point out that women in the United States have been presented with goals quite dissimilar from those presented to men.[109] In contrast to the success-oriented male version of the American dream, "The goal that women are traditionally socialized to desire . . . is marriage and a family; the accepted means is to secure the romantic love of a man through courtship."[110] Leonard criticizes Merton's formulation for failing to recognize this basic division of U.S. culture in terms of gender. But what if Merton's theory was reformulated so as to apply to the deviance of women culturally indoctrinated into the goals of wifehood and family raising? Leonard reformulates anomie theory in such a way. Her revision of Merton's theory offers a partial explanation for traditional differences between the crime rates of men and women. Women, argues Leonard, have had relatively easy access to the goals of marriage and the family. For this reason, she suggests, they may not have been subject to the same anomic strains toward crime as men, who have been exposed to the less achievable goals of economic dominance. In Leonard's words, "Women have very low aspirations and their goals are extremely accessible."[111]

The same logic may be used to explain the notable rise in women's crime rates in recent years. According to Leonard, "Emancipation has increased somewhat, and certain women are now aiming to achieve financial success. . . . Challenging traditional restrictions and expectations can lead to anomie and, hence, to an increase in female crime."[112] All this appears to support the general utility of Merton's theory, once it is reformulated to account for the differential organization of aspirations by gender. Nonetheless the specific value of the theory diminishes when it comes to analyzing the criminal adaptations available to marriage-oriented women in traditional society. Once again we have a case in which anomie theory is useful as a general orientation but inadequate as a specific theory.

Extending Anomie to a Critique of the Political-Economic Structure   Anomie theory is frequently read as a critique of the structural organization of contemporary society. Alvin Gouldner, for instance, notes an affinity between Merton's theory and Marxist analysis. Both, at least implicitly, point to contradictions inherent in the social structure of capitalist societies. Capitalism presents a contradictory message to people who labor under its economic constraints. On one hand, it promises a free market of opportunity in which those who work hard can rise as far as their abilities permit. At the same time, capitalism systematically limits access to decisions affecting the allocation and distribution of economic resources to those who control what Marx referred to as *the means of production* in society.[113] Thus a fundamental contradiction is built into the political-economic structure of capitalism. Capitalism promises something for all which can be achieved only by some. According to Gouldner, a tacit recognition of this contradiction of capitalism is a major element of Merton's theory."[114]

British criminologists Ian Taylor, Paul Walton, and Jock Young agree with Gouldner's assessment. They describe Merton as a "cautious rebel" who "stand[s] outside the system and make[s] criticisms, which, if taken to their logical conclusion, would necessitate radical social change."[115] Having made this point, they criticize Merton for never fully realizing the logic of his own position. Merton settled for a critique of the lack of equal opportunity and for a reformist strategy aimed at expanding access to the American dream. Merton failed to recognize that full and equal access to the political and economic resources of society is prohibited by the structural organization of capitalism itself. This point is made somewhat poetically by Laurie Taylor, who likens Merton's model of society to that of individuals playing an electronic game rigged so that only some players are consistently rewarded. "But in the analysis nobody appeared to ask who put the game there in the first place. Criticism . . . is confined to changing the pay-out sequences so that the deprived can get a better deal."[116]

How might Merton's analysis better realize its full critical potential? What remains tacit or implicit in Merton's work must be made explicit. The political-economic structure of capitalism must be seen as a basic source of the contradictions which produce high rates of deviance. To resolve these contradictions, and thereby structurally curtail deviance, capitalism must be replaced by a system of economic relations in which everyone would be guaranteed not simply access to wage labor, but equal access to the means by which production is organized and its benefits distributed. In practical terms this means some form of participatory economic democracy or democratic socialism. According to certain of Merton's critics, this is the logical implication of anomie theory. Partial reforms within the system are not enough. The system is itself the problem. Workers may obtain greater access to employment or procure higher wages for their labor, yet they will still be systematically denied access to the means by which economic activities and economic payoffs are socially structured. Those who control the production process will continue to reap unequal benefits at the expense of those whom they employ. As such, unequal access to culturally desired goals and high rates of deviance will continue as well. Efforts to structurally reduce the systematic character of anomic deviance must go beyond the liberal orientation of the perspective as traditionally formulated.

The challenge of going beyond limited economic reforms to a critique of capitalism as a whole is important. At the same time, it is crucial to recognize that capitalist societies are today undergoing major structural changes. Such transformations may *dissolve* rather than *resolve* the contradictions of structured economic inequality, and thereby reinforce capitalist hierarchies. This is the picture of "postmodern" capitalism painted by critics such as Jean Baudrillard and Arthur Kroker. By saturating daily life with fascinating media images, new and technology-driven forms of capitalism appear to blur experiential differences between real social contradictions and imaginary cultural obsessions. Here we enter a world in which it becomes increasingly difficult to distinguish between authentic human experience and the corporate packaging of simulated memories, preprocessed pseudo events, and video-generated mood swings. This is a world in which what is most valued is broken down into dense and fast-moving bytes of information, a world of "virtual experience." This is the New World Order, ruled as much by commodified images from TV, radio, portable "sound systems," computer screens, and shopping malls as by discriminatory bank lending policies, systematic unemployment, and police bullets. Within this "postmodern scene," capitalist culture begins to shift from the potentially explosive condition of *anomie* to the more absorbent or implosive condition of *anomaly*.[117]

What happens to the experience of structured social contradiction (or anomie) when power no longer appears to vertically suppress one class beneath another? What happens when contradictions are not repressed but made so excessively visible that they prove almost blinding? What is the fate of anomie theory when power cynically blurs differences between insiders and outsiders, without giving away any of the economic, racial, or sexual privileges that one group holds over/against others? Here, we enter a world of postmodern capitalism, ruled less by meaningful cultural commitments than by a nihilistic play between what fascinates and what is fearful. One disturbing indicator of such nihilism is the widespread feeling among relatively privileged white men that they themselves are victims of the "affirmative actions" which benefit those whom the privileged exploit—women, nonwhites, and the economically disenfranchised. In other words, despite "real" evidence of a continuing structural gulf between the aspirations and the means available to attain such aspirations, between the rich and the poor, between men and women, and between whites and nonwhites, many privileged white men today experience the "virtual reality" of themselves as downtrodden "minorities." How can this be? I shall return to questions raised by the (possible) emergence of such postmodern cultural tendencies in Chapter 11. But for now, let us turn from the structural concerns of anomie theory to the more concrete interpersonal concerns of the social-learning perspective.

NOTES

1 Émile Durkheim, *Suicide*, John A. Spaulding and George Simpson (trans.), Free Press, New York, 1952, p. 248.

2 Robert K. Merton, "Social Structure and Anomie," *American Sociological Review*, vol. 3, 1938, p. 680.

3 Émile Durkheim, *The Elementary Forms of the Religious Life*, Joseph W. Swain (trans.), Free Press, New York, 1965.

4 Durkheim, *Suicide*, p. 247.

5 Ibid., p. 255.

6 For greater detail on Durkheim's biography and on the social context in which he wrote, see Lewis Coser, *Masters of Sociological Thought*, Harcourt, Brace, Jovanovich, New York, 1971, pp. 129–174.

7 Ibid., p. 162.

8 For a discussion of Durkheim's relationship to the moral statisticians of France, Belgium, Germany, and Italy, see Steven Lukes, *Émile Durkheim, His Life and Work: A Historical and Critical Study*, Penguin, Middlesex, England, 1971, pp. 191–192.

9 Ibid., p. 193.

10 Ibid., p. 190.

11 Durkheim, *Suicide*, p. 252.

12 Ibid.

13 Ibid.

14 Ibid., p. 253.

15 Ibid.

16 Ibid.

17 Ibid., p. 255.

18 For additional biographical information on Merton, see Morton Hunt, "A Biographical Profile of Robert K. Merton," *New Yorker*, Jan. 28, 1961.

19 Robert K. Merton, *Social Theory and Social Structure*, Free Press, New York, 1957, p. 141.

20 Ibid., p. 145.

21 Ibid., p. 146.

22 Ibid., p. 153.

23 Ibid.

24 Talcott Parsons, *The Social System*, Free Press, New York, 1951. For a discussion of Parsons's work as it applies to the theory of anomie, see Marshall B. Clinard, "The Theoretical Implications of Anomie and Deviant Behavior," in Marshall B. Clinard (ed.), *Anomie and Deviant Behavior*, Free Press, New York, 1964, pp. 23–24.

25 Robert Dubin, "Deviant Behavior and Social Structure: Continuities in Social Theory," *American Sociological Review*, vol. 24, April 1959, pp. 147–164.

26 Robert K. Merton, "Social Conformity, Deviation and Opportunity Structures: A Comment on the Contributions of Dubin and Cloward," *American Sociological Review*, vol. 24, April 1959. Merton also criticizes Dubin for confusing the notion of normative constraint with attitudes toward norms, and for producing a theory related more to options for conformity than to strains toward deviation.

27 Richard A. Cloward, "Social Control in the Prison," *Theoretical Studies of the Social Organization of the Prison*, Bulletin no. 15, Social Science Research Council, New York, March 1960, pp. 20–48, esp. 28–35.

28 Richard A. Cloward, "Illegitimate Means, Anomie, and Deviant Behavior," *American Sociological Review*, vol. 24, April 1959, pp. 164–176.

29 Ibid., p. 168.

30 Richard A. Cloward and Lloyd E. Ohlin, *Delinquency and Opportunity: A Theory of Delinquent Gangs*, Free Press, New York, 1960.

31 Ibid., pp. 82, 86.

32 Ibid., p. 40.

33 Ibid., p. 175.
34 Ibid., p. 180.
35 Ibid., p. 186.
36 Ibid.
37 Albert J. Cohen, *Delinquent Boys: The Culture of the Gang*, Free Press, New York, 1955.
38 Albert J. Cohen, "The Sociology of the Deviant Act: Anomie Theory and Beyond," *American Sociological Review*, vol. 30, February 1965, pp. 5–14.
39 Ibid., p. 6.
40 Ibid., p. 8.
41 In stressing the importance of the interaction process in the development of deviance, Cohen reflects the influence of learning-perspective theorist Edwin Sutherland. Cohen was one of Sutherland's students. Sutherland's work is discussed in detail in Chapter 8.
42 Robert K. Merton, "Anomie, Anomia and Social Interaction," in Clinard, *Anomie and Deviant Behavior*, pp. 213–242.
43 Ibid., p. 231. In this article Merton cites his statements at a May 1955 conference on the sociology and psychiatry of delinquency, published verbatim as part of the conference record, as evidence that he was concerned with interaction long before Cohen's published criticisms. See Robert K. Merton in *New Perspectives for Research on Juvenile Delinquency*, Helen L. Widmer and Ruth Kotinsky (eds.), GPO, Washington, D.C., 1956, pp. 37–38.
44 Ibid., p. 234. Merton was here responding to an earlier version of Albert Cohen's criticism which was included in Cohen's paper "Towards a Theory of Deviant Behavior: Continuities Considered," presented at the annual meeting of the American Sociological Association, 1963.
45 Cohen, *Delinquent Boys*, p. 121.
46 See particularly ibid., pp. 73–119.
47 Stephen Cole and Harriet Zuckerman, "Inventory of Empirical and Theoretical Studies of Anomie," in Clinard, *Anomie and Deviant Behavior*, pp. 243–289.
48 Bernard Lander, *Towards an Understanding of Juvenile Delinquency*, Columbia, New York, 1954.
49 Ibid., p. 65.
50 Roland J. Chilton, "Continuity in Delinquency Area Research: A Comparison of Studies for Baltimore, Detroit, and Indianapolis," *American Sociological Review*, vol. 29, February 1964, pp. 71–83.
51 Robert K. Merton, *Social Theory and Social Structure*, rev. ed., Free Press, New York, 1957, p. 165.
52 Leo Srole, "Social Integration and Certain Corollaries: An Exploratory Study," *American Sociological Review*, vol. 21, December 1956, pp. 709–716.
53 Dorothy L. Meier and Wendell Bell, "Anomia and Differential Access to the Achievement of Life Goals," *American Sociological Review*, vol. 24, April 1959, pp. 189–208.
54 Gwynn Nettler, "A Measure of Alienation," *American Sociological Review*, vol. 22, December 1957, p. 672. For a related discussion, see also Melvin Seeman, "On the Meaning of Alienation," *American Sociological Review*, vol. 24, December 1959, pp. 783–791.
55 Merton, "Anomie, Anomia, and Social Interaction," pp. 212–242.
56 Ibid., p. 229.

57 Ibid.
58 James F. Short, "Gang Delinquency and Anomie," in Clinard, *Anomie and Deviant Behavior,* pp. 98–127.
59 Anthony Giddens, *Capitalism and Modern Social Theory: An Analysis of the Writings of Marx, Durkheim and Max Weber,* Cambridge University Press, Cambridge, 1971, p. 103.
60 Émile Durkheim, "La famille conjugale," as excerpted and translated in Giddens, *Capitalism and Modern Social Theory, p. 103.*
61 Émile Durkheim, *Education and Society,* Free Press, New York, 1956.
62 Émile Durkheim, *The Rules of the Sociological Method,* Macmillan, London, 1964, p. 368.
63 Coser, *Masters of Sociological Thought,* p. 163. LaMar T. Empey, *American Delinquency: Its Meaning and Construction,* rev. ed., Dorsey, Homewood, Ill., 1982, p. 24.
64 *Action on the Lower East Side,* Program Report: July 1962–January 1964. Mobilization for Youth, New York, 1964, excerpted in Richard Quinney, *Criminology: Analysis and Critique of Crime in America,* Little, Brown, Boston, 1975, p. 246.
65 For detailed discussion of Mobilization for Youth, see James F. Short, Jr., "The Natural History of an Applied Theory: Differential Opportunity and Mobilization for Youth," in N. J. Demerath, III, et al. (eds.), *Social Policy and Sociology,* Academic Press, New York, 1975, pp. 193–210. See also LaMar T. Empey, *American Delinquency,* rev. ed., Dorsey, Homewood, Ill., 1982, pp. 193–210.
66 Peter Marris and Martin Reen, *Dilemmas of Social Reform,* 2d ed., Aldine, Chicago, 1973, p. 22.
67 Frances Fox Piven and Richard Cloward, *Regulating the Poor: The Functions of Public Welfare,* Vintage, New York, 1971, p. 290.
68 Murray Kempton, "When You Mobilize the Poor," *New Republic,* Dec. 5, 1964, p. 12, excerpted in Richard Quinney, *Criminology,* 2d ed., Little, Brown, Boston, 1979, p. 368.
69 Ibid.
70 Empey, *American Delinquency,* p. 209.
71 Quinney, *Criminology,* p. 369.
72 Ibid., p. 368.
73 Robert Arnold, "Mobilization for Youth: Patchwork or Solution?" *Dissertation,* vol. 11, summer 1964, pp. 347–354.
74 Allen E. Liska, *Perspectives on Deviance,* Prentice-Hall, Englewood Cliffs, N.J., 1981, p. 52.
75 Randall Collins, *Sociology since Mid-Century: Essays in Theory Cumulation,* Academic Press, New York, 1981, p. 299. Collins credits (without citation) the work of Stephen Cole as the basis for his remarks about the dominance of Merton's contribution.
76 Ibid.
77 Cohen, "The Sociology of the Deviant Act," p. 5.
78 Collins, *Sociology since Mid-Century,* p. 299.
79 James Q. Wilson, *Thinking about Crime,* Vintage Books, New York, 1975, p. 48.
80 Don C. Gibbons and Joseph F. Jones, *The Study of Deviance: Perspectives and Problems,* Prentice-Hall, Englewood Cliffs, N.J., 1975, p. 92.
81 Clinard, "The Theoretical Implications of Anomie and Deviant Behavior," p. 55.

82 Alvin W. Gouldner, *The Coming Crisis of Western Sociology*, Basic Books, New York, 1970, p. 345.

83 Ibid.

84 Ibid., p. 343.

85 C. Wright Mills, *The Sociological Imagination*, Oxford University Press, New York, 1959.

86 Nanette J. Davis, *Sociological Constructions of Deviance*, Brown, Dubuque, Iowa, 1980, p. 148.

87 Collins, *Sociology since Mid-Century*, p. 299.

88 H. Warren Dunham, "Anomie and Mental Disorder," in Clinard, *Anomie and Deviant Behavior*, p. 149.

89 Daniel Glaser, Bernard Lander and William Abbott, "Opiate Addiction and Non-Addicted Siblings in a Slum Area," *Social Problems*, vol. 18, spring 1971, pp. 510–521.

90 Michael Lewis, "Structural Deviance and Normative Conformity—the 'Hustle' and the 'Gang,'" in Daniel Glaser (ed.), *Crime in the City*, Harper and Row, New York, 1970.

91 Alfred R. Lindesmith and John H. Simon, "Anomie and Drug Addiction," in Clinard, *Anomie and Deviant Behavior*, pp. 158–188.

92 Andrew Henry and James F. Short, *Suicide and Homicide*, Free Press, Glencoe, Ill., 1954.

93 Ronald W. Maris, *Social Forces in Urban Suicide*, Dorsey, Homewood, Ill., 1969.

94 Jack P. Gibbs and Walter T. Martin, "A Theory of Status Integration and Its Relationship to Suicide," *American Sociological Review*, vol. 23, April 1958, pp. 140–147. See also Jack P. Gibbs and Walter T. Martin, *Status Integration and Suicide*, University of Oregon Press, Eugene, 1964.

95 Empey, *American Delinquency*, pp. 245–254.

96 Ibid., p. 247.

97 Travis Hirschi, *Causes of Delinquency*, University of California Press, Los Angeles, 1969, pp. 182–183.

98 Delbert S. Elliot and Harwin Voss, *Delinquent and Dropout*, Heath, Lexington, Mass., 1974; Dean E. Freese, "Delinquency, Social Class and the Schools," *Sociology and Social Research*, vol. 57, July 1973, pp. 443–459; Kenneth Polk and Walter E. Schaefer (eds.), *School and Delinquency*, Prentice-Hall, Englewood Cliffs, N.J., 1972.

99 Empey, *American Delinquency*, p. 248.

100 Whitney Pope, *Durkheim's "Suicide": A Classic Reanalyzed*, University of Chicago Press, Chicago, 1976.

101 Liska, *Perspectives on Deviance*, pp. 42–47.

102 Clinard, "The Theoretical Implications of Anomie and Deviant Behavior," pp. 55–56.

103 Durkheim, *Suicide*, p. 35.

104 Merton, *Social Theory and Social Structure*, p. 47.

105 Robert Bierstadt, *American Sociological Theory: A Critical History*, Academic Press, New York, 1981, p. 461.

106 Edwin M. Lemert, "Social Structure, Social Control and Deviation," in Clinard, *Anomie and Deviant Behavior*, pp. 57–97.

107 Ibid., p. 64.
108 For some fascinating studies on the rise of British youth subcultures, see Dick Hebdige, *Subculture: The Meaning of Style*, Methuen, London, 1979; Stuart Hall and Tony Jefferson, *Resistance through Rituals*, Hutchinson, London, 1975; and Paul E. Willis, *Profane Culture*, Routledge & Kegan Paul, London, 1978.
109 Eileen B. Leonard, *Women, Crime and Society: A Critique of Criminology Theory*, Kongman, New York, 1982.
110 Ibid., p. 58.
111 Ibid., p. 59.
112 Ibid., p. 60.
113 Karl Marx, *Capital*, Lawrence & Wishart, London, 1970.
114 Gouldner, *The Coming Crisis of Western Sociology*, p. 426.
115 Ian Taylor, Paul Walton, and Jock Young, *The New Criminology: For a Social Theory of Deviance*, Harper & Row, New York, 1973, p. 101.
116 Laurie Taylor, *Deviance and Society*, Michael Joseph, London, 1971, p. 148.
117 For the distinction between anomie and anomaly, see Jean Baudrillard, *Fatal Strategies*, Philip Beitchman and W. G. J. Niesluchowski (trans.), Semiotext(e), New York, 1990. For a discussion of the implications of Baudrillard's work on the cynical dissolution of contradictory experiences with advancing capitalism, see Arthur Kroker, "Baudrillard's Marx," in Arthur Kroker and David Cook, *The Postmodern Scene: Excremental Culture and Hyper-Aesthetics*, St. Martin's Press, New York, 1986, pp. 170–188.

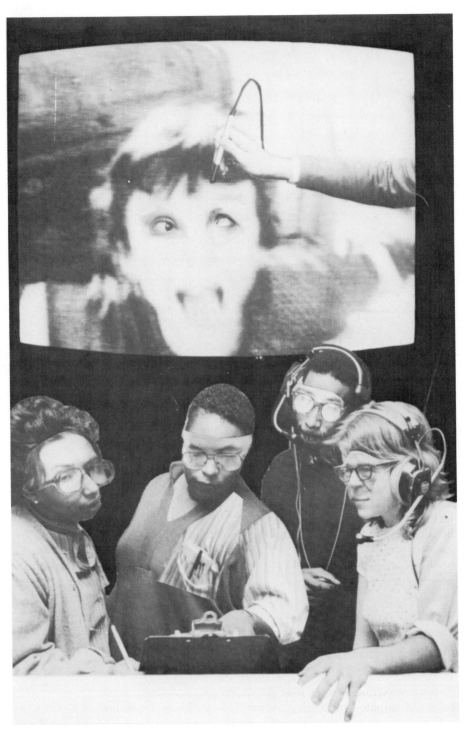

Enforced Imitation   By Joseph LaMantia and Stephen Pfohl

CHAPTER 8

THE LEARNING PERSPECTIVE: Acquiring Deviance in Association with Others

All the important acts of social life are carried out under the domination of examples. . . . One kills or does not kill, because of imitation.

Gabriel Tarde[1]

When persons become criminal they do so because of contacts with criminal patterns and also because of isolation from anti-criminal patterns.

Edwin Sutherland and Donald R. Cressey[2]

INTRODUCTION

Jack Henry Abbott was in prison when he wrote *In the Belly of the Beast*.[3] This book depicts the brutal manner in which prison teaches people who they are—criminals deserving the torturous experience that is incarceration. His book helped Jack Henry Abbott get out of prison. Its convincing narration and penetrating insight gained him a reputation as a skilled author and a rehabilitated inmate. Abbott was praised in the high circles of New York's literary elite and was soon granted an early parole by state officials.

Months after being rehabilitated and released, Abbott became engaged in a verbal dispute with a New York City waiter. It was late at night. Abbott wanted to use the restaurant's men's room. The waiter informed him there was none. The two stepped outside. Accounts vary about what happened next. Some witnesses say that the waiter was escorting Abbott outside so that he could urinate in the alley. According to Abbott, it seemed as if the waiter was going to attack him. Abbott reacted as one might in prison; he had a knife and used it. Charged with the waiter's death, Abbott disputed not so much facts of the case as their interpretation. He claimed that he acted as he did because he had learned to act that way. Most of Jack Henry Abbott's learning occurred throughout a lifetime of imprisonment in an assortment of juvenile and adult institutions. Because of this, Abbott claimed that the state of New York, rather than himself as an individual, should be held responsible for his act of violence. Abbott's claim was a sociological one. He argued that the process of social learning, a process over which he had little personal control, was the real culprit in his act of deviance. His claim echoed in the theoretical imagery of the learning perspective.

THEORETICAL IMAGES

The central theme in this perspective is simply that deviance is a form of learned behavior. In this regard learning deviance is essentially no different from learning to tie one's shoes, learning to like modern art, or learning to be a sociologist. The learning perspective is a sociological perspective. Yet, unlike the disorganization, functionalist, and anomie perspectives, the learning perspective does not view society as a whole as the cause of deviance. Society is considered an abstraction. What really counts is the collective activity of its members. What is society aside from people? The learning perspective answers this question by turning its attention to people and what they do together. Rather than look at the social system as a whole, the learning perspective views deviance as arising in the diverse ways in which people learn through interacting with each other in everyday life.

Gabriel Tarde and the Imitation of Deviance

One of the earliest formulations of a learning perspective on deviance is discovered in the writings of the French social theorist Gabriel Tarde (1843–1904). Tarde, a critic of Durkheim's conception of society as a "thing in itself," directed attention to the social processes whereby forms of behavior and ways of thinking and feeling are passed on from group to group and person to person. His was a theory of "imitation and suggestion." The origins of deviance were pictured as very similar to the origins of fads and fashions. Each was a socially learned acquisition, governed by what Tarde referred to as the "three laws of imitation." These included (1) the law of close contact, (2) the law of imitation of superiors by inferiors, and (3) the law of insertion.

By the law of close contact, Tarde meant simply that people have a greater tendency to imitate the fashions and customs of those with whom they have the most contact. Thus, if I were regularly surrounded by people involved in a world of deviant behaviors, ideas, and/or lifestyles, I would be more likely to imitate these people than I would others with whom I had little association. Direct contact with deviance was believed to foster more deviance.

What about indirect contact? Think of a world (such as our own) in which many of our contacts with people, their actions, and their beliefs are mediated by mass communications. Tarde's writing anticipated such a world of indirect imitation. He believed that the media played a central role in the proliferation of such nineteenth-century "epidemics of deviance" as the rise in mutilations of women, the practice of women disfiguring the faces of male lovers, and the rash of "Jack the Ripper"-type murders. In Tarde's own words, "infectious epidemics spread with air or wind; epidemics of crime follow the telegraph."[4] If only Tarde had known of the coming of television. Surely his law of close contact is relevant to the current debate over whether violence and other forms of deviance are learned from models displayed by the mass media.

Tarde's second law suggests that superiors, or persons of higher social status, are more commonly the imitated than the imitators. Perhaps people follow the model of high-status others in hopes that their imitative behavior will procure some of the rewards associated with being of a "superior" class. In any event, Tarde's ideas have a particular relevance in our own age of visibly "high-class" deviance. Does post-Watergate knowledge of the deviance of "superior" persons, such as high governmental officials and corporate executives, increase the likelihood of deviance by us all? Tarde's law of imitation of superiors suggests that possibility.

The law of insertion, Tarde's third law, refers to the power inherent in newness or novelty. New "fashions" were said to replace old "customs." When two mutually exclusive ways of doing something come into conflict, Tarde believed that the newer one would ordinarily win out. The replacement of the knife by the gun as a weapon of deviant destruction was cited as an example of this process.

Tarde's three laws are rather loose and have been criticized for being overly simplistic and for neglecting a host of other physical, psychological, social, political, and economic factors related to deviance. Some of the dynamics of these laws were never specifically laid out. Why, for instance, was newness more attractive than established custom? Is the disruption of routine itself alluring? Are we more likely to accept new forms of doing things if they do old things better? Tarde was not clear about such issues. Nonetheless, his ideas about the imitative origins of deviance opened the door for an interpretation of deviance as learned behavior. Tarde rejected biological explanations as well as explanations which viewed society as independent of the activities of its members. He planted the theoretical seeds of a perspective which would later come to fruition in Edwin Sutherland's theory of a differential association. Note the importance placed upon associative imitation in the following excerpt from Tarde's *Penal Philosophy*.

> The majority of murderers and notorious thieves [begin] as children who have been abandoned, and the true seminary of crime must be sought for upon each public square and/or each crossroad of our town, whether they be small or large, in those

flocks of pillaging street urchins, who like bands of sparrows, associate together, at first for marauding, and then for theft, because of a lack of education and food in their homes.[5]

Sutherland's Theory of Differential Association

Edwin H. Sutherland's theory of differential association was first formally presented in the third edition of his textbook *Principles of Criminology* in 1939. Key concepts of this learning theory of crime or deviance were present in the 1934 version of the same text. There, Sutherland hypothesized that "any person can be trained to adopt and follow" a pattern of criminal behavior.[6] At that time, however, Sutherland was more interested in explaining variations in the rate of crime between different groups in society than in articulating a general thesis regarding the sociobiographical or sociogenetic origins of criminal behavior. Sutherland had been trained in the tradition of the Chicago school and spent much of his early sociological career modifying central aspects of the social disorganization perspective. For Sutherland, differences in the rates of crime between groups in the same society could better be explained by the principle of differential social organization than by the idea that crime-prone groups were disorganized.

By "differential social organization," Sutherland referred to the fact that modern society, at least since the time of the industrial revolution, had become divided into a variety of ethnic and normative subcultures. Guided by a common belief in individualism, the pursuit of monetary wealth, and ever greater social mobility, subcultures competed with each other for a slice of society's pie. Access to this pie was not, however, distributed equally. Some culture groups had greater access than others. These groups possessed not only differential access to valued social resources but the ability to define norms and cultural standards and to impose them upon others. For Sutherland this differential access to social resources and dominant social norms offered an explanation of differential rates of deviant behavior.

Sutherland's idea of differential social organization made extensive use of the concept of culture conflict, a concept that was elaborated by his colleague Thorsten Sellin.[7] Indeed, Sutherland went so far as to argue that in the differentially organized society, the criminal law operates as "a device of one party in conflict with another."[8] Sutherland's ideas also foreshadowed the theoretical imagery of opportunity conflict contained in Robert K. Merton's theory of anomie. The work of Sellin and Merton is discussed elsewhere in this book. At present let us turn to the manner in which Sutherland's focus on differential social organization was later dwarfed by his concern with differential association.

Sutherland's initial concerns were with expanding the conceptual boundaries of the Chicago school. He did this by relating the differential organization of society to differential rates of crime between subgroups or subcultures within society. Sutherland recalls his own surprise when, in 1935, Henry D.

McKay made reference to his distinctive "theory of criminal behavior."[9] What was this theory? McKay pointed to a section of Sutherland's 1934 textbook *Principles of Criminology,* in which he had paired the concept of culture conflict with the suggestion that a lack of harmonious social influences may lead individuals to be trained into a pattern of criminal behavior. McKay's comments alerted Sutherland to his own implicit social-psychological emphasis on the process of learning. Indeed, according to Sutherland's own recollections, he would shortly conclude "that learning, interaction, and communication were the processes around which a theory of criminal behavior should be developed."[10]

By 1937, Sutherland had explicitly incorporated the systematic learning of crime as a central theme in his case study *The Professional Thief.*[11] In tracing the criminal career of "Chic Conwell," Sutherland outlined the social-learning process that was said to be essential to a professional thief's acquisition of the proper norms, values, and techniques of the criminal trade. According to Sutherland, "Tutelage by professional thieves is essential for the development of skills, attitudes, codes, and connections, which are required in professional theft."[12]

In *The Professional Thief,* Sutherland likened the learning of crime to the learning of any other "group way of life." In 1939, he combined this emphasis on learning with his previous concerns relating to differential group organization. In his first formal statement of the theory of differential association, Sutherland proposed that while "systematic criminal behavior is determined in a process of association with those who commit crimes, cultural conflict is the underlying cause of this differential association."[13] By this formulation, Sutherland tried to address both the specific causes of criminal behavior and variations in the rates of crime between groups exposed to the forces of differential social organization. The theory generated considerable comment, debate, and criticism. Was it necessary for persons to directly associate with criminals in order to learn criminal behavior? Although Sutherland had indicated that "the chance that a person will participate in systematic criminal behavior is determined roughly by the frequency and consistency of his contacts with the patterns of criminal behavior," critics such as Richard Korn and Lloyd McCorkle claimed that Sutherland's 1939 theory represent little more than a thesis proposing "contamination by exposure, without specifically delineating the learning process by which certain frequencies and consistencies of exposure lead to actual criminal behavior."[14]

Responding both to criticism and to the evolving nature of his own concerns, Sutherland thoroughly reformulated the theory of differential association in preparation for the 1947 edition of *Principles of Criminology.* The 1947 version has remained essentially unchanged in subsequent editions of the text authored by Sutherland and his student and colleague, Donald Cressey. The 1947 presentation of the theory is important both because it is more specific about the dynamics of the criminal learning process and because it separates Sutherland's model of the social-psychological causes of deviance from his social-structural account of variations in the crime rate. In other words, it separates the theory of differential association from that of differential social organization. These two theories were related but operated at different levels of analysis. As Sutherland and Cressey state the matter, "Differential social organization . . . should explain the crime rate, while 'differential association' should explain the criminal behavior of a person. The two explanations must be consistent with each other."[15]

The theory of differential association, as formulated in 1947, was intended as a comprehensive explanation of criminal behavior. It is considered applicable to a wide range of noncriminal deviance as well. The theory is based upon two core assumptions: (1) that deviance occurs when people define a certain human situation as an appropriate occasion for violating social norms or criminal laws and (2) that definitions of the situation are acquired through an individual's history of past experience, particularly in terms of past associations with others. As such, the theory emphasizes the social-psychological processes whereby people produce subjective definitions of their situation in life. It deemphasizes social-structural factors which operate as objective constraints upon the types of associations which an individual is most likely to encounter. This is not to say that Sutherland was unconcerned with structural factors. Throughout his career he maintained a consistent interest in the manner in which the structural outgrowths of differential social organization exposed different groups of people to different associational ties. The point is simply that Sutherland argued that in considering the social-psychological processes which cause individual deviance "it is not necessary . . . to explain why a person has the associations he has."[16] What is necessary is to examine the normal learning process whereby a person comes to define a particular social situation as more or less appropriate for deviant behavior.

Learning deviance involves learning to (1) define certain situations as the appropriate occasions for deviant behavior, (2) master the techniques of successful deviant activity, and (3) acquire motives, drives, attitudes, and rationalizations which justify violations of norms and/or laws. According to the theory of differential association, these three things are learned principally in the process of communicative interaction with others, within intimate personal groups. The crucial step in learning deviance occurs when people acquire an excess of definitions favorable to deviance over definitions unfavorable to deviance. Acting deviant then becomes probable. This is the essence of differential association: an imbalance in the interactional forces for and against favoring the path of nonconformity. When what one learns from others about deviating or conforming is weighted in the direction of deviating, it is probable that one will engage in deviant behavior. But how probable? The answer is said to depend on the frequency, duration, priority, and intensity of one's associations with those who define deviance positively or negatively. Each of these things is mentioned by Sutherland, who developed the following nine propositions to summarize his theory:

1 Criminal [deviant] behavior is learned.

2 Criminal [deviant] behavior is learned in interaction with other persons in a process of communication.

3 The principal part of the learning of criminal [deviant] behavior occurs within intimate personal groups.

4 When criminal [deviant] behavior is learned, the learning includes (a) techniques of committing the crime, which are sometimes very complicated, sometimes very simple; (b) the specific direction of motives, drives, rationalizations, and attitudes.

5 The specific direction of motives and drives is learned from definitions of the legal codes [conventional norms] as favorable or unfavorable.

6 A person becomes delinquent because of an excess of definitions favorable to violation of law [conventional norms] over definitions unfavorable to violation of law [unconventional norms].

7 Differential associations may vary in frequency, duration, priority and intensity.

8 The process of learning criminal [deviant] behavior by association with criminal and anti-criminal [deviant and antideviant] patterns involves all of the mechanisms that are involved in any other learning.

9 While criminal [deviant] behavior is an expression of general needs and values, it is not explained by those general needs and values since non-criminal [nondeviant] behavior is an expression of the same needs and values.[17]

The frequency, duration, priority, and intensity of prodeviant and antideviant associations are difficult to measure. Ideally, each of these factors could be converted into a precise mathematical formula. The likelihood of deviant behavior could then be determined by calculating the difference between favorable and unfavorable associations. Yet, as Sutherland recognized, "The development of such a formula would be extremely difficult." One short but highly intense involvement with a very high priority prodeviant friend might overshadow hundreds of long-term but less significant antideviant associations. How can such things as priority and intensity be adequately measured? What is commonplace for the widely experienced person may be extraordinarily intense for the naive person. Although the importance of associations is obviously influenced by such factors, the factors themselves are difficult to reliably measure in any standardized fashion.

The Legacy of Differential Association Sutherland's theory of differential association normalized our understanding of deviance. It allowed us to imagine that, given an exposure to strong interpersonal forces favoring nonconformity, we could be as deviant as any of our fellow human beings. The differential association idea contributed to the notion that deviants were normal people overly exposed to a learning process which equated being normal with what others saw as being deviant. Its image of deviance as learned behavior has become the most widely accepted modern perspective on deviance.

Sutherland's theory prompted a number of research efforts aimed at testing key elements of the process of differential association. In 1957, James Short reported on a study of adolescents (126 boys and 50 girls) housed in a training school for youths. After obtaining self-reported measures of delinquency (e.g., asking youths about whether they had stolen things of small, medium, and large value; driven without a license; used narcotics; defied parental authority; etc.), Short attempted to obtain information on the frequency, duration, priority, and intensity of their prodelinquent associations. To obtain a measure of frequency, Short asked the following question: "Think of friends you have associated with most often. Were (or are) any of them juvenile delinquents?" Similar questions were asked regarding friends known for the longest time (duration), the first friends remembered (priority), and best friends (intensity). Although Short acknowledged that his research represented an "extremely limited application of a very broadly conceived concept,"[18] his data suggest a moderately strong relationship between exposure to delinquents and delinquent behavior.

Of related concern was a study by Albert J. Reiss, Jr., and A. Lewis Rhodes.[19] Short had used youths' assessments of other youths as his measure of the delinquency of one's associates. Reiss and Rhodes obtained measures of the actual delinquent behavior of 299 boys and each boy's two best friends. These researchers discovered that close friendships were "closely correlated with delinquency" but less so with specific patterns of delinquency of the same type as those of one's friends. Reiss and Rhodes also concluded that correlations with the same type of delinquent patterns, although greater than chance, "were well below what one expected from the learning hypothesis in differential association theory." Nor were the correlations independent of social class. Thus, the work of Reiss and Rhodes provides a general but qualified support for differential association theory as a whole. Their findings are similar to a variety of other studies[20] which, as summarized by social-learning theorist Ronald Akers, suggest that "while not all research directed toward testing the theory has supported it, on balance, the empirical evidence accumulated thus far supports the importance in deviant behavior of associations in primary groups such as families and peers."[21]

Despite its generally favorable reception, differential association theory has not lacked its critics. For instance, Sheldon Glueck has charged that Sutherland's original theory was too vague to be adequately tested, since it is practically impossible to quantitatively assess the enormous number of prodeviant and antideviant definitions to which someone is exposed.[22] Glueck also argued that differential association was inapplicable to certain forms of deviance which persons learn to perform on their own (e.g., lying, taking things that belong to another, fighting, and sex play) and that Sutherland's theory ignored the role of various physiological or psychological factors which allegedly predispose one to define things in a prodeviant way. Another critic, David Matza, has commented upon the "overly deterministic" imagery in

Sutherland's formulation. Matza contends that the theory of differential associations ignores the role of human choice in human action. According to Matza, "Sutherland nearly made his subject a captive of the milieu . . . a creature of affiliational circumstances. . . . Sutherland's subject was a creature, but he was half a man."[23] Other critics have raised questions about the necessity of firsthand, intimate associations with prodeviant people.[24] Is direct contact a necessary stage in the learning of deviance?

Criticism has indicated the need for caution but has not curtailed the importance of the differential association theme. After a thorough review of the logical structure and empirical testability of the theory, Melvin DeFleur and Richard Quinney[25] conclude that while all but one of the theory's propositions are logically consistent,[26] its high level of abstraction makes it nearly impossible to test the theory as a whole in a strictly empirical fashion. Nonetheless, DeFleur and Quinney observe that the theory has generated a large number of more specific hypotheses capable of being operationally measured and empirically examined.

Modifying the Image of Differential Association

The theory of differential association has also generated several important modifications which extend and strengthen the applicability of the learning perspective. Major modifications include Glaser's principle of differential identification, Sykes and Matza's and later Douglas's consideration of the problem of neutralizing conventional morality, and Burgess and Akers's reformulation according to the operant principles of modern social-learning theory.

Differential Identification   Is direct intimate contact with prodeviant people necessary for deviant learning? This question has been raised since the initial exposition of the theory of differential association. Certainly people are socialized indirectly by the media and more distant reference groups. Daniel Glaser had this in mind when he suggested reformulating the idea of differential association in terms of differential identification.[27] We may identify with Clint Eastwood, James Bond, or "the Fonz" without ever associating directly with any of these real or fictitious characters. The identification may affect us, our definitions about the world, and our actions within it. According to Glaser this identification, rather than interpersonal association per se, is at the heart of deviant learning.

Learning Techniques of Neutralization   This modification of differential association picks up on Sutherland's suggestion that one of the things learned in learning deviance is a set of rationalizations which protect one against the moral claims of the conventional world. Sykes and Matza's contribution to the learning perspective is also less deterministic than most. It recognizes that deviants live in, and often in-between, worlds of conformity and nonconformity. Deviants are affected by both. They are not strictly determined by either. What Sykes and Matza refer to as techniques of neutralization are verbal or linguistic strategies "chosen" by deviants to reconcile one world to the other.

Neutralizing rhetorics or vocabularies are developed by deviants who together use them to ward off the normative attacks of the social world, to make the constraints of conventional social control inoperative, and to free up the deviant for further deviant action. Sykes and Matza list five such typical neutralizing techniques.[28] These include:

1 *Denial of responsibility.* With this technique the deviant declares, "I didn't mean it!" The social scientist's view of what causes deviance is applied to and by oneself. What one ends up with is a "billiard ball" concept of the self, pushed and pulled by uncontrolled social forces. One here imagines the delinquents in the play *West Side Story* humorously singing about how they are unfortunate products of society. In many ways, this is a modern expression of "the devil made me do it" theme.

2 *Denial of injury.* "I didn't hurt anybody." With this neutralization, deviants admit that they chose to do something, but not something which was really harmful. Car theft becomes simply an act of borrowing. Stealing probably helps those who have insurance.

3 *Denial of victim.* "They had it coming!" Here, deviants accept responsibility for the act and for the resultant harm, but suggest that the victims are really the rightful targets for retaliation or retribution. They are not really victims. Often this neutralization has a Robin Hood flavor. "We ripped off the store. But everybody knows that the store itself is a 'rip-off.'" "The minority group kids we beat up had no right to be in our neighborhood." "The homosexuals we frightened on the train had it coming." Language games of this kind contribute to the rationalization of deviant actions.

4 *Condemning the condemners.* "Everybody's picking on me!" With this verbal defense, deviants attack those who would point their finger at them. "Everyone knows the police are corrupt." "The government is more violent than we are." "Teachers are biased and unfair." "Parents are hypocrites." Agents of social control are ridiculed, their moral power undermined.

5 *Appeal to higher loyalties.* "I didn't do it for myself!" Deviance is admitted, but its motive is unselfish. The act was done in order to help one's friends, family, gang, or holy and/or political causes. Higher loyalties excuse lower acts.

Sykes and Matza's work is important because it reminds us that deviants must regularly deal with moral challenges from members of the straight world. Yet for sociologists such as Jack Douglas, the positing of rhetorical vocabularies of denial may be seen as too rationalistic or too cognitive. While not denying the value of such cognitive constructs, Douglas argues that in everyday social life, feelings often operate independently of and even more powerfully than thoughts.[29] Verbal rationalizations may commonly be used to connect rule breakers with the world of conventional people. Nevertheless, their value dissipates greatly when deviants are confronted with the feeling that their comforting cognitive fictions are not shared by members of the straight world. When this happens, the clever vocabularies of neutralization may do little to cover a deviant's deep feeling of shame.[30] Something else is needed. Successful deviants need to learn strategies of self-deception or self-seduction in order to master their feelings of shame. If such feelings cannot be hidden or evaded, then at least they may be managed through such emotionally charged protection strategies as "aggressive countermoralism" or "counterpride displays." In this sense, Douglas's discussion of the deviant's self-deceptive or manipulative management of feelings represents an important counterpoint to the cognitive defense strategies outlined by Sykes and Matza. Both represent useful extensions of key components of Sutherland's original theory.

Modern Social-Learning Theory: The Principle of Differential Reinforcement

What makes one association or identification more influential (e.g., of higher priority or more intensity) than others? This question has been recurrently raised by critics of Sutherland's theory of differential association. This criticism has arisen, in part, because of the open-ended nature of Sutherland's own conception of learning. Recall that in his 1947 formulation, Sutherland stated only that "the process of learning criminal behavior . . . involves all of the mechanisms that are involved in any other learning." In certain ways, the vagueness of Sutherland's statement was an advantage. Since its initial formulation, major advances have occurred in the social and psychological study of learning. By the early 1960s, these advances led Donald Cressey to suggest that critics should stop complaining about the vagueness of Sutherland's propositions and get on with the business of completing the differential association project by drawing upon developments in modern social-learning theory. In Cressey's words, "It is one thing to criticize the theory for failure to specify the learning process accurately and another to specify which aspects of the learning process should be included and in what ways."[31]

In the mid-1960s, sociological students of crime and deviance responded to Cressey's challenge by suggesting ways in which Sutherland's theory could be enhanced by insights derived from contemporary studies on learning, particularly those which made use of the principles of behavioral or operant psychology. In 1965 C. Ray Jeffery outlined the basis for such a revision of Sutherland's work.[32] A thorough behaviorist reformulation of differential association would, however, await the 1966 publication of Robert Burgess and Ronald Akers's article "A Differential Association: Reinforcement Theory of Criminal Behavior."[33]

Burgess and Akers begin their reformulation of Sutherland's theory with an explanation of the basic principles of operant psychology. They point to an important difference between operant psychology and respondent psychology. Respondent psychology is associated with the work of the Russian psychologist Ivan Pavlov and is commonly formulated in terms of a stimulus-response model of learning. The hungry dog is presented with an image of food (stimulus), and it salivates (response). The sound of a bell is paired with the sight of food; the bell gradually takes on the salivation-producing effects of the food itself. It becomes a conditioned stimulus, such that the bell itself may bring about the behavioral response even without the presence of food. The stimulus-response model of respondent psychology is not used by Burgess and Akers. They look, instead, to the principles of operant psychology. Operant psychology, the study of operant behaviors, was originally associated with the learning theories of B. F. Skinner. It may be thought of as a response-stimulus-response, or r-s-r, model of learning. According to the operant model, behavior at one point in time (the initial response) produces an environment effect or consequence (stimulus), which influences the likelihood of similar behavior in the future (the subsequent response).

The basic principles of operant learning theory are relatively simple. They are used to explain the behavior of human as well as nonhuman organisms. All behaviors, whether mental, emotional, or physical, are said to be shaped or governed by the consequences they produce. Some acts lead to consequences (stimuli) which humans experience as positive, pleasurable, or desirable. These acts are reinforced and are thus likely to be repeated in a similar fashion. This happens in one of two ways: by *positive reinforcement*, in which something good happens as a result of one's actions (e.g., one is given praise, a kiss, or a piece of cake), or by *negative reinforcement*, in which something bad is removed or avoided (e.g., one is spared the anticipated scolding or let out of the boring class early). Other acts produce negative, painful, or undesirable consequences. These acts are punished and are thus not likely to be repeated in a similar fashion. Once again, this happens in one of two ways: by *positive punishment*, in which something bad happens (e.g., one is spanked, reprimanded, or humiliated), or by *negative punishment*, in which something good is taken away (e.g., one is denied the affection of a valued person, prohibited from watching a favorite television show, or whatever). In abbreviated form, this is the essence of operant theory. We repeat behaviors which have in the past produced reinforcement. We shy away from behaviors which have produced punishment.

When applied to the learning of deviant behavior, operant theory transforms the concepts of differential association into a sequence of differentially reinforced and punished social experiences. Why is it that we associate more or with great intensity with prodeviant others? Why do we define and rationalize certain occasions in terms of a preference for deviance instead of conformity? According to Burgess and Akers's operant reformulation, it is because either (1) those behaviors have been reinforced in the past or (2) they have come to be associated with certain discriminative stimuli which provide cues that reinforcement is forthcoming (e.g., the teacher's smile, which the student associates with a good grade). Following the logic of these operant principles, Ronald Akers has recently presented the following statement of his and Burgess's reformulation of differential association in terms of differential reinforcement.

1 Deviant behavior is learned according to the principles of operant conditioning.

2 Deviant behavior is learned both in nonsocial situations that are reinforcing or discriminating and through that social interaction in which the behavior of other persons is reinforcing or discriminating for such behavior.

3 The principal part of the learning of deviant behavior occurs in those groups which comprise or control the individual's major source of reinforcements.

4 The learning of deviant behavior occurs in those groups which comprise or control the individual's major source of reinforcements.

5 The learning of deviant behavior, including specific techniques, attitudes, and avoidance procedures, is a function of the effective and available reinforcers and the existing reinforcement centerpieces.

6 The probability that a person will commit deviant behavior is increased in the presence of normative statements, definitions, and verbalizations which, in the process of differential reinforcement of such behavior over conforming behavior, have acquired discriminative value.

7 The strength of deviant behavior is a direct function of the amount, frequency, and probability of its reinforcement. The modalities of association with deviant patterns are important, insofar as they affect the source, amount, and scheduling of reinforcement.[34]

Burgess and Akers's perspective offers a way of measuring the balance between the prodeviant and antideviant forces of learning. Akers's text *Deviant Behavior: A Social Learning Approach* creatively applies this rather simple perspective to an entire range of deviant behaviors from murder to homosexuality to white-collar crime. In each instance, he outlines a general pattern of social reinforcement which provides the basis for involvement in deviant behavior. Undoubtedly, there is a great deal of merit to this approach. Who would doubt that our future definitions, feelings, and actions are influenced by the consequences of our present actions? If my students respond positively to the way that I explain the theory of differential association, surely I will be likely to explain it in a similar fashion in the future. The same goes for punching my spouse, picking your pocket, creating an artificial gas shortage, or forging a check.

Another advantage of Burgess and Akers's differential-reinforcement perspective is its interdisciplinary focus. Burgess and Akers present a social-psychological framework which bridges the fields of sociology and psychology. Social psychology refers to the study of individuals in a social context. Social psychologists trained within departments of sociology are likely to have been exposed to the tenets of a perspective known as symbolic interactionism. Psychologically trained social psychologists are more likely to have been influenced by some version of operant behaviorism or modern social-learning theory. Following the lead of social philosopher George Herbert Mead, symbolic interactionism emphasizes the dynamic adjustment of humans acting together in anticipation of the reactions of others. For symbolic interactionists, the way we define ourselves, our world, and appropriate lines of action in the world depends upon our grasp of the viewpoint of others toward ourselves. The process by which people imagine and adjust the viewpoint of others is referred to as "taking the role of others." Through this process of interpretive interaction, particularly with the significant others who are closest and/or most important to us, we come to define social reality in a particular way.

Given these assumptions about the nature of social life, it is easy to see why many sociologists saw the imagery of symbolic interaction as highly compatible with Sutherland's theory of differential association.

Key components of Sutherland's formulation are clearly amenable to an interactionist framework, i.e., that people will define situations in a prodeviant manner if the balance of their frequent, high-priority, intense, and long-term interactional associations provide definitions favoring deviance. These interpretive or "mentalistic" components of Sutherland's theory are rejected by strict behaviorists. According to hard-core behavioral psychologists, the scientific analysis of behavior must confine itself to the relationship between overt behavioral responses and directly observable external stimuli. Such rigid behaviorism is an extremely limited framework which unfortunately ignores the rich and important terrain of the human mind and heart.

To Burgess and Akers's credit, their behaviorist reformulation of the idea of differential association is not of the rigid Skinnerian variety described above. Burgess and Akers's work is more closely associated with the "soft behaviorism" of psychologists such as Julian Rotter,[35] Albert Bandura and Richard Walters,[36] Leonard Ullmann and Leonard Krasner,[37] and Arthur and Carolyn Staats.[38] These theorists emphasize the importance of reinforcement and punishment, while also recognizing the role of cognitive processes (e.g., self-reinforcement, anticipations of reinforcement, and vicarious or imitative reinforcement). If raising one's arm is amenable to behavioral analysis, why couldn't raising one's expectations be studied as well? If being painfully punished for acting in a certain way is likely to affect my future actions, why shouldn't watching another being painfully punished have a similar effect? If the electric light bulb on the stove acts as a discriminative stimulus which indicates that touching the burner will hurt, why shouldn't the conceptual light bulb in my mind be afforded the same respect? For Burgess and Akers these things are both permitted and important for a thorough social-learning-theory analysis. This applies even to the imaginative self's conversation about the anticipated reaction of others that is so central to the symbolic interactionist framework. This conversation, its form and content, this process of defining social reality in interaction with others, can be viewed as a set of behaviors (albeit less observable than arm or leg movements) governed by the same reinforcement contingencies affecting any other set of behaviors. This is the crux of Burgess and Akers's interdisciplinary focus. It joins key sociological concepts with concepts employed by less rigid versions of psychological behaviorism. Akers points out that the concept of verbalization in his and Burgess's differential-reinforcement model "is taken more from the meaning of *definition* in the original Sutherland theory than from the way verbal behavior is treated in . . . [rigid] behavior theory. . . . Insofar as it is implied that one may apply these definitions to his own behavior in a sort of conversation with himself or to protect his self concept, it is congruent with . . . symbolic interactionism."[39]

Burgess and Akers's reformulation promises greater researchable precision and the strengths of an interdisciplinary focus. Nonetheless, the theory of differential reinforcement does not escape other problems associated with the learning perspective. Reinforcements and punishments may seem more amenable to tight measurement than such vague concepts as intensity and priority. But how exactly does one measure the quantity of reinforcement provided by a lifetime of complex prodeviant and antideviant associations? In actuality, differential reinforcement may offer little more than a new set of hard-to-measure imagery. With this in mind, let us examine the various research strategies employed by advocates of the learning perspective.

IDENTIFYING LEARNED DEVIANCE

From a learning perspective, it is not enough to isolate deviants in terms of some individualistic legal infraction (the classical approach) or abnormal characteristic (the pathological approach). Nor is it sufficient to aggregate deviants in terms of some abstract social condition (the disorganizational, functionalist, and anomic approaches). To study deviance one must identify the deviant as a person with a specific biographical history of social experiences and interpersonal associations and a favoring engagement in unconventional or rule-breaking behavior. As Ronald Akers suggests, the goal of this approach is "to spell out a typical process or processes through which the person progresses from conforming to deviant behavior—a 'natural history' of becoming a homosexual, an addict, an alcoholic, and so on."[40]

Official statistics do not provide the biographical and associative information necessary to identify factors related to the learning of deviance. As a result, learning theorists have relied on in-depth interviews, observations, and self-reports to describe and analyze the deviant learning process. From these multiple sources of data, learning theorists generally develop a profile of the deviant behavior system.

Sutherland provided a model for this behavior-systems approach in his 1937 study *The Professional Thief.* In-depth interviews with "Chic Conwell" provided information on the biographical or career stages involved in learning highly skilled criminality, the network of associations through which thieves learn the techniques, deviance-confirming attitudes, and rationalizations of their trade, and the social context which affects the success and duration of their work.

The behavioral system of the thief is not the same as that of the violent criminal, the corporate defrauder, or the prostitute. Learning theorists have provided behavioral-system descriptions of these and numerous other deviant types. Recurrent differences and/or similarities have been observed between the biographical or career stages, associative patterns, and social-psychological contexts of varying deviant activities. In general, learning theorists have examined the comparative differences and similarities between various deviant behavior systems by using one or more of the following analytic techniques: (1) typological classification, (2) analytic induction, and (3) reinforcement contingency analysis.

Typological Classification

Typologies are means of classifying differences and similarities between comparable analytic units. By categorically arranging factors associated with the learned acquisition of deviance, deviant-systems typologies permit an understanding of the social development of nonconforming behavior. The biographical road to one type of deviance can be catalogued and compared with the avenue to another type and to the path of conformity as well. According to Don Gibbons, an early proponent of the typological approach to the study of criminal behavior, typologies are "a way of gaining a more detailed and accurate group of causal processes."[41] Gibbons used a "role-career" typology to classify the biographical backgrounds of criminal offenders into four broad categories: social-class origins, family-background patterns, peer-group associations, and contacts with defining or control agencies. Another typology, proposed by Daniel Glaser, relates crime and criminals by intersecting "offense descriptive factors," such as those which separate personal from property crime and predatory from nonpredatory offenses, with "career commitment factors" associated with such things as repeat offending and criminal-group contacts.[42] Yet another typology, developed by Marshall Clinard and Richard Quinney, examined criminal-behavior systems according to four additional dimensions: (1) the career stages of the offender, (2) group or associative support for criminal activity, (3) the correspondence between criminal and legitimate behavior patterns, and (4) the social reaction to criminality.[43] These factors were used to analyze the recurrent, regular, or typical behavioral system associated with different kinds of crime. These include violent personal crime (murder, assault, rape, etc.), occasional property crime (shoplifting, check forgery, vandalism, etc.), occupational crime (embezzlement, fraud, false advertising, fee-splitting, etc.), conventional property crime (burglary and larceny), political crime (treason, espionage, sabotage, terrorism, etc.), public-order crime (prostitution, gambling, drug addiction, homosexuality, etc.), organized crime (racketeering, organized drug traffic, gambling, prostitution, etc.), and professional crime (confidence games, professional thievery, pickpocketing, etc.).

For the student of learned deviance, typologies offer a convenient mechanism for sorting out and examining factors related to the development of prodeviant behaviors, attitudes, and rationalizations. Typological analysis has also been viewed as a first step toward a sociologically informed policy of social control. As Nanette Davis points out, "the typological approach attempted to identify homogeneous patterns of deviant conduct. The notion was that once behavior was sociologically ordered, causal, diagnostic, and treatment propositions could follow."[44] The central problem with typological analysis, however, is that there is little one-to-one correspondence between the abstract types proposed by sociologists and the complexities of real-life deviant behavior. This is recognized by Don Gibbons, whose recent survey of the behavioral and role-career diversity of criminal offenders suggests that while "some lawbreakers closely resemble the sketches of 'naive check forgers,' 'semi-professional property criminals,' or 'aggressive rapists' that appear in offender typologies . . . a much larger number . . . defy classification in some distinct type category."[45] Thus, while typological analysis has been used extensively by students of crime and deviance, it is today recognized as an oversimplified categorization of the complex world of deviant learning, unlearning, and relearning.

Analytic Induction

Most typological analyses begin with a listing of general factors which sociologists believe to be related to the learned development of deviant behavior. Individual cases are then examined in terms of their relationship to these general factors. Analytic induction reverses the process. It constructs a theory of deviant learning from the ground up. As such, analytic induction involves two steps: (1) the detailed study of individual cases in order to produce generalizations applicable to all cases and (2) the use of negative cases (cases which don't fit the typically proposed pattern) to modify or reject generalizations.

The best-known example of the analytic-induction strategy is, perhaps, Alfred Lindesmith's study of opiate addiction.[46] Lindesmith was forced to revise his original thesis suggesting that addiction was produced by a self-conscious use of drugs to the point where physical withdrawal symptoms would occur in their absence. The basis for his revision was a negative case involving one nonaddicted physician who had knowingly taken opiates to the withdrawal level. Lindesmith ended up by suggesting that the self-conscious use of drugs to eliminate withdrawal was the crucial factor in addiction. This proposition was again subsequently modified by data providing a wider description of the biography, associations, and context of the street addict than originally available to Lindesmith. Analytic induction is extremely rigorous.

Most researchers rely more on a general-tendency typology. Analytic induction provides a detailed analysis of the developmental stages, interactional patterns, and environmental contingencies which constitute the core of the learning perspective.

Reinforcement Contingency Analysis

This research strategy is associated with modern social-learning theory. It examines the specific arrangements of reinforcing and punishing stimuli by which operant theorists explain the development and maintenance of deviant behavior. Ideally, this approach requires an experimental framework to sort out the differential impacts of varying forms of reinforcement and punishment. Indeed, all the basic principles of operant psychology were derived from tightly controlled laboratory experiments. Most of these studied the behavioral learning processes of nonhuman animals.

Some studies of deviance have attempted to transport an experimental model from the psychologist's laboratory to the lab of everyday learning. Examples are found in the social-psychological study of aggressive behavior. In Brown and Elliot's study of the behavioral control of aggression in nursery school, teachers were instructed to ignore all examples of aggressive behavior and simultaneously to reward cooperative behavior with generous doses of praise and attention.[47] Researchers made behavioral notations of classroom behavior for a period of two weeks. A significant decrease in the level of classroom aggression was observed. In another experiment by Parke, Ewall, and Slaby, increased aggressive behavioral displays were associated with increases in the social reinforcement of aggressive verbalizations.[48] Male college students were differentially reinforced for saying words that were aggressive, neutral, or helpful. The same students were subsequently presented with the opportunity to deliver electric shocks to other individuals. Those who had been previously reinforced for aggressive talk delivered the strongest shocks. Those who had been reinforced for neutral verbalization administered intermediate levels of shock, while those reinforced for helpful talk provided the lowest levels of shock.

Experiments such as those described above aid social psychologists in understanding basic processes through which deviant behaviors may be acquired. More difficult is an operant behavioral analysis of complex patterns of deviance which have been learned over many years. How are operant theorists to retrospectively reconstruct this intricate patterning of reinforcement and punishment? The solution to this problem is neither easy nor clear. Research typically begins with data collected for some other purpose. Behavioral researchers then retrospectively examine this existing data for indirect evidence of patterns of differential reinforcement.

Examples of this retrospective approach to the study of differential reinforcement include Linda Anderson's analysis of the learning of marijuana use [49] and Rand Conger's study of peer and parental reinforcement for delinquen-cy.[50] These studies reconstructed operant patterns from a behaviorist reading of available interview and questionnaire data. Anderson concluded that both formal and informal sanctions impact on the likelihood of marijuana use. The people most apt to smoke were those who perceived little legal risk, whose friends approved of and/or smoked marijuana themselves, and whose par-ents did not show active disapproval. Along similar lines, Conger found evidence suggesting that the individuals who report the highest involvement in delinquency are the ones who experience both positive reinforcement for such behavior and low social support for behaving conventionally.

The frequent use of retrospective reconstructions has produced criticism regarding the tautological or circular nature of operant theorizing. Behavioral sociologists Burgess and Akers admit that this criticism would be valid if learning formulations asserted simply that a certain stimulus strengthens deviant behavior *because* it is reinforcing. According to Burgess and Akers, careful operant analysis avoids such a circular statement. It awaits the results of a direct test of whether or not something is reinforcing: "Observe the frequency of a selected behavior, then make a stimulus event contingent upon it and observe any change in frequency. If there is a change in frequen-cy, we may classify the stimulus as reinforcing to the individual under the stated conditions."[51]

The nontautological test proposed by Burgess and Akers is, unfortunately, more applicable to the tightly controlled experiment than to a retrospective reading of reinforcement contingencies into past biographical reports. In the 1977 revision of *Deviant Behavior: A Social Learning Approach*, Akers recognizes this problem. He recognizes that, for nonexperimental analyses, the solution that he and Burgess originally proposed "may not be satisfactory."[52] Akers instructs researchers to precisely describe and document the "sources, con-tent and impact of differential reinforcement; . . . imitation, and other behav-ioral processes," so as to construct "a typical learning history . . . which shows how a person first emerges in the behavior and then progresses to more habitual or stable patterns."[53]

SOCIAL CONTROL OF LEARNED DEVIANCE

According to the learning perspective, deviance may be controlled either by the *preventive learning* of proconventional attitudes and behaviors or by the *corrective unlearning* of unconventionality. Preventive learning is a broad con-cept that includes the entirety of a person's social experience. It encompasses all that is referred to by the term *socialization*. It involves all our direct in-terpersonal contacts with others (i.e., the way we are influenced by parents, peers, teachers, and others) and even indirect contacts with people who enter our lives through television and other mass media. When religious organiza-tions or parent groups present demands for less violence on TV, they are advocating a strategy of preventive learning. Proponents of summer employment or supervised recreation programs for youths may also have a preventive learning concept in mind. It is often hoped that giving youths something constructive to do will cause them to learn the values of responsible citizenship and shun deviant involvements.

Corrective learning strategies are ordinarily more focused. Corrective learning control programs attempt to influence the imitation process by providing positive, or antideviant, role models; to alter the differentiation association process by surrounding a deviant with a group of persons who define deviance in an unfavorable way; or to shape the operant learning process by the use of behavior-modification strategies. Each of these approaches is briefly described below.

Imitative Control: Providing Models of Conventionality

A social worker, counselor, or other "helping professional" will often express satisfaction with the feeling that he or she has been an influential positive role model for but a single client. Youth-serving programs such as Big Brothers and Big Sisters are based on a belief that the young participants will benefit from imitating influential adults. Control programs which employ detached youth or gang workers to reach out to kids in trouble operate with a similar philosophy. Youth workers are commonly selected because they embody a number of positive, prosocial, or conventional characteristics and are believed to be people with whom troubled youths will easily identify.

Despite their commonsensical appeal, there is little evidence that role-model control programs actually reduce deviance. Gene Kassebaum has reviewed programs of this type in the area of juvenile delinquency.[54] Drawing upon the evaluative research of Malcolm Klein and others, Kassebaum contends that such programs may inadvertently encourage more deviance than they prevent. A 1979 report by the federal Office of Juvenile Justice and Delinquency Prevention arrives at a similar conclusion. According to the authors of the report, "From the standpoint of differential association theory, workers' efforts to introduce 'definitions unfavorable to violation of the law' had the unintended side effects of increasing the frequency and intensity of interaction within the gang."[55]

This unanticipated prodeviant learning effect is illustrated by a role-model youth-worker program which operated in the city of Boston between 1954 and 1957. The program involved extensive contact between youth workers and gang members. Yet, when compared to a control-group sample of gangs not exposed to this treatment, youth-worker gangs showed a greater increase in the recorded incidence of serious criminal offenses.[56] Why? According to Kassebaum, the attention afforded gang members by role-model youth workers increased the gang's sense of group cohesion and resulted in increased interaction among gang members. This may have resulted both in increased group pressure to deviate and in a greater visibility of the gang to the suspicious eye of law enforcers. Thus, a program originally intended to reduce delinquency may have had the opposite effect. This points to the difficulty of trying to reduce deviance through an overly simple imitative-learning approach. Imitation may affect the unlearning of deviance, but its impact is always complicated and sometimes confounded by other factors related to learning.

Group Unlearning: Altering Differential Association

A second form of corrective unlearning involves exposing deviants to strong group pressures toward conventionality. Sometimes this is done by professional agents of rehabilitative control. Most typically this involves removing offenders from previous prodeviant associations and providing them with a new source of group support for going straight. As Walter Reckless points out, "most knowledgeable probation workers, parole workers, and institutional staff are . . . helping the juvenile or adult offender . . . internalize new models of behavior [and] working on social ties, anchors, supportive relationships, limits and alternative opportunities."[57]

Professional control agents may use residential settings or intensive group therapy to develop proconventional differential associations. Similar control strategies have been employed by self-help groups of deviants who wish to aid one another in returning to conventionality. Alcoholics Anonymous (AA), Recovery Inc. (a support group for persons confronted with mental problems), and Synanon (a self-help drug-addiction rehabilitation organization) are examples of such groups. Members of AA receive strong group support in exchange for testimonial-like admissions to being alcoholics. The typical AA meeting is a weekly event. It begins when one member stands up and declares that he or she is an alcoholic. After telling a personal story of being "down and out," the confessed alcoholic then proceeds to delineate the wonders of AA and the benefits of the supportive understanding that only alcoholics can provide for each other if they are to avoid future deviation. Members exhort one another to stay in each other's company as often as possible and to regularly check in with members struggling to stay off the bottle.

All this suggests that the principle of reverse differential association is a key part of the strategy of AA. In essence, AA provides the deviant drinker with a new set of associations, the intensity, duration, frequency, and priority of which are intended to aid in the unlearning of unconventional behavior. A similar concept is advanced by Recovery Inc., a group founded by Dr. Abraham Law to aid persons afflicted with mental problems to develop the will to be well. According to Law, the initial strategy was to encourage members to "meet frequently and regularly in classes and at parties; they get together in family gatherings and consort socially; they form sewing clubs, bowling parties, and dancing teams; many of them spend evenings or Sundays together, dining or visiting theaters and amusement places."[58]

In recent years Law has somewhat reversed himself about the benefits of Recovery Inc. members spending an inordinate amount of time in each other's presence. Concerned that members would learn to "normally" interact only with one another, Law has sought to limit the time that participants share together.[59] Synanon does somewhat the opposite.

Unlike AA and Recovery Inc., Synanon is a total learning environment. Within its self-contained boundaries, drug addicts are taught to kick their habits. Synanon is a nearly complete, if unintended, application of the differential association perspective. Members initially share a common residence in which everyone lives, eats, works, plays, and participates in daily group discussions together. In subsequent stages of the Synanon program, members obtain employment outside the house and eventually graduate to life on the outside. According to Rita Volkman and Donald Cressey, Synanon is structured upon (1) the addicts' willingness to suppress individual desires in order to become completely assimilated into a group dedicated to "hating" drug addiction, (2) maximization of family-style cohesion of members engaged in continuous joint activity, (3) an exchange of valuable social status for staying off drugs and developing anti-drug-use attitudes, and (4) emphasis on total dissociation from former drug- and criminal-culture acquaintances.[60]

The most dramatic part of Synanon may be its daily group sessions in which members attempt to trigger raw feelings and thereby produce a cathartic release from drugs. Such sessions often involve what is referred to as the "haircut," a method of attack therapy in which members are challenged to tell the truth, the whole truth, and nothing but the truth. In actuality, such therapy is aimed at altering a member's truth by altering his or her direct interpersonal associations. People are pushed to renounce the former truths of drug addiction and to accept the present truth of a drug-free existence. Each person "must be willing to give up all ambitions, desires and social interactions that might prevent the group from assimilating him completely."[61] Those who resist are subjected to intense ridicule, emotional denunciations, and tests of organizational loyalty, such as having their hair shaved off, giving up all their money, or severing all ties to their families.

How successful are Synanon's strident efforts to alter the differential associations of its members? Volkman and Cressey sought to answer this question by obtaining information on 372 members. Twenty-nine percent were classified as being off drugs. More significantly, of 215 members who had participated for at least one month, the drug-free percentage rose to 48. For those in Synanon for three months, 66 percent were off drugs, while 86 percent of those in the program for seven months were similarly nonusers. This suggests that the longer one is exposed to intense, frequent, and high-priority antidrug associations, the more likely she or he will learn to kick the drug habit. On the other hand, it should be remembered that Synanon is a highly selective program. It accepts only people who are willing to make a total commitment to the group process. It has a very high rate of attrition by members during the first few months of involvement. According to Volkman and Cressey, of 263 members admitted during a three-year period, 72 percent dropped out, with 90 percent of the dropouts occurring during the first three months. For this reason, Synanon's success with long-term members may reflect more about the power of strong motivational investment than about the general benefits of proconventional group learning. Nonetheless, Synanon stands as an important example of the practical use of differential-association-like thinking in the area of planned correctional unlearning.

Behavior Modification: Modern Social Learning Theory as Social Control

Operant psychology is commonly presented as a theory of how learning occurs. According to sociologist Richard Emerson, it is more correct to view operant psychology as a theory of behavior control.[62] This is nowhere more evident than in the correctional uses of operant psychology to modify deviant behaviors in the direction of conformity.

As opposed to more traditional forms of psychotherapeutic intervention, behavior modification does not concern itself with a person's inner thoughts or feelings or with such things as helping someone gain insight into the deep but hidden causes of deviance. Behavior modification is instead directed toward manipulating the various ways in which socially organized reinforcements and punishments exercise control over an individual's actions.

In the late 1950s and early 1960s, operant psychologists paved the way for the widespread use of behavior-modification techniques by reporting upon a number of successful cases in which manipulations of the learning environment resulted in dramatic reductions in deviant behavior.[63] In 1960, for instance, Isaacs, Thomas, and Goldiamond reported that they had drastically improved the behavior of a 40-year-old male who was diagnosed as a catatonic schizophrenic.[64] The modification technique they used is referred to as *successive approximation*. Existing behavior is reshaped by successively reinforcing elements which are in the desired direction and extinguishing those which are not. In the case of the catatonic schizophrenic, psychologists were working with someone who had remained mute and relatively motionless throughout the course of his nineteen-year hospitalization. He had been all but abandoned as an incurable case. Behavior-modification specialists observed, however, that the sight of a stick of gum produced eye movement on the part of the patient. Using gum as a reinforcer, they carefully introduced a succession of learned responses which began with the eyes and in stages included facial movement, the mouth, lips, vocalizations, word utterances, and eventually, the restoration of verbal behavior.

In the first two weeks of their work, the behavioral psychologists held a stick of gum before the patient's face. They waited until the patient moved his eyes toward the gum. When this happened, he was given the gum. By the end of the second week, the patient's eyes moved toward the gum as soon as it was presented. During the third and fourth weeks the psychologists waited for the patient's lips to move before reinforcing him with the gum. During the fifth and sixth weeks, they waited until he actually said, "Say gum, gum." Giving the gum was made contingent upon the patient's increased vocalizations. Eventually he began to talk.

Other dramatic breakthroughs in the control of deviant behaviors were reported at approximately the same time. Williams published findings suggesting the progressive reduction of childhood tantrums.[65] Allyon and Michael discussed techniques used to "extinguish" violent outbursts and to promote positive behaviors, such as patient self-feeding.[66] Each case was different, but the general approaches were similar: systematically evaluate the contingencies of reinforcement and punishment in order to manipulatively produce successive approximations of the desired response. This is illustrated in the following excerpt from the instructions given by behavioral psychologists Allyon and Michael to a nurse attempting to treat a psychotic patient. The patient's eating habits had so deteriorated that she had to be spoon-fed in bed each day. Note the behavioral prescriptions set forth in the modification plan:

> Continue spoon feeding the patient; but from now on, do it in such a careless way that the patient will have a few drops of food fall on her dress. . . . As the patient likes having her clothes clean, she will have to choose between feeding herself and keeping her clothes on her, or being fed by others and risk getting her clothes soiled. Whenever she eats on her own, be sure to stay with her for a while . . . talking to her, or simply being seated with her. We do this to reinforce eating on her own.[67]

The number of clinical cases reporting the successful use of behavior-modification techniques grew steadily during the 1960s. Many of these are presented or reviewed in such volumes as J. J. Eysenck's *Experiments in Behavior Therapy*,[68] L. P. Ullmann and L. Krasner's *Case Studies in Behavior Modification*,[69] J. A. Wolpe, A. Salter, and L. J. Regina's *The Conditioning Therapies*,[70] and A. Bandura's *Principles of Behavior Modification*.[71] Although these early studies often involved but a single case, many dealt with serious disorders unable to be treated by other intervention strategies. In 1969, behavioral researchers Ullman and Krasner posed the following question, "If what has been done with a smile, a head nod, and a grunt is fact, what can be done with stronger and continuing reinforcing stimuli?"[72] The therapeutic and/or control possibilities of behavior modification loomed large. By the 1970s, a great number of behavior-modification programs were being used in mental health, mental retardation, and correctional facilities and in nonresidential programs concerned with the treatment of various forms of sexual deviance, alcohol and drug abuse, and other forms of nonconventionality. Two prominent examples of such control efforts include the use of *token economies* and *aversive conditioning*.

Token Economics   A common application of behavior modification in the fields of mental health and criminal justice involves the use of token economies. In such programs, persons who demonstrate compliance with the rules or goals of a particular institution are reinforced by being given a token which can be exchanged for certain institutional privileges (e.g., smoking, a pass to leave the premises, or the opportunity to attend a movie) or commodities (e.g., candy, an extra soda, or a pack of cigarettes). Inmates typically receive tokens when they do such things as be on time, be courteous, be cooperative, be well groomed, and, most particularly, be obedient. When they fail to do such things they may be penalized or punished by having a certain number of tokens taken away.

Examples of token economies include programs implemented at the Walter Reed Hospital in Washington, D.C.; the Draper Correctional Center in Elmora, Alabama; the Medical Center for Federal Prisoners in Springfield, Missouri; and the Patuxent Institution in Jessup, Maryland.[73] At the Walter Reed Hospital, soldiers with character or behavior disorders were provided with token points for such nondeviant activities as fulfillment of military assignments, attendance at educational classes, or dressing in appropriate attire.[74] Points could be exchanged for such privileges as obtaining a semiprivate room, free coffee, or access to recreational activities. At the Draper prison, points were deposited to inmate "token checking accounts." Checks could be written for television watching, being away from the cellblock, or purchases at the prison commissary. Points were awarded when inmates contributed to the custodial management of the prison—e.g., making their beds, getting out of bed on time, being physically presentable, cleaning their living area, etc.[75]

The START program in Missouri was considerably more controversial. This Special Treatment and Rehabilitative Training Program required inmates to pass through eight distinct levels of behavioral competence. Designed for hard-core and hard-to-manage inmates, the various levels of the START program were arranged so that graduation to each successive level meant both higher levels of behavioral control and higher levels of available reinforcing privileges. Critics, however, argued that the participants in the START program were selected because they were among the handful of inmates who had managed to maintain a sense of individuality, leadership, and independence, and that the real goals of START were to force strong-willed inmate leaders into submission. The behavioral goals reinforced by the START system included such things as performing assignments "without needing persuasion" and accepting assignments "without bickering." Representatives of the American Civil Liberties Union and other observers have charged that START was little more than a program of coerced compliance, designed to eliminate dissent and cloaked in the guise of scientifically proven behavioral therapy.[76]

The Patuxent Institution in Maryland was the home for another highly controversial behavior-modification program. There, inmates diagnosed as compulsively criminal or dangerously antisocial were given an indeterminate sentence. They were held within one of the institution's four-level behavioral-incentive systems until they were assessed to be under proper behavioral control and thereby cured. As in the START program, Patuxent's incentive levels involved the progressive attainment of greater personal autonomy and privileges in exchange for increased behavioral compliance. Inmates could also be demoted in level for a number of vaguely defined behavioral infractions, such as displays of inappropriate attitudes. Each demotion was viewed as a negative reinforcer. One such negative reinforcer involved confinement in the "hole" (an isolated, bare, and dark segregation cell). The behaviorally minded staff referred to this as a "negative reinforcement unit." In 1971, a federal judge outlawed Patuxent's ill-governed use of this behavior-modification technique.

Token economy programs treat the deviant like a rat in a psychologist's box. Like the rat who finds its way through the maze, the captured deviant is reinforced when she or he acts in conformity with an established regime of social control. When the deviant fails or refuses to conform, punishment is delivered. Candy, cigarettes, or television privileges are denied. Extra work assignments or time in isolation may be meted out. The objective is to reshape the behavior of nonconformers toward compliance.

Despite their popularity, token economy programs share a common conceptual and practical flaw. They fail to realize that outside the walls of a particular social-control institution, candy bars and television privileges may not be very powerful reinforcements. Indeed, there is virtually no evidence documenting a long-term pattern of conformity following a behaviorally modified deviant's graduation from a token economy program. In part, this may be because very little sound evaluative research has been conducted about the effects of such programs. As psychologist Michael Nietzel points out, "Evaluations of institutional behavior modification have yet to reveal a single instance in which an adequate non-treatment control group has been included.[77] On the other hand, there are good social and psychological reasons to suspect that such a program will, at best, have a very short-term impact on a deviant's life. Once released from a token economy, a person may be reexposed to the reinforcers and punishers that gave shape to his or her deviation in the first place. Thus, most token economies represent little more than systematic efforts to instill order among deviants during the term of their containment. Other behavior-modification programs make claims that are more powerful. Of particular concern are various programs of aversive therapy.

Aversive Therapy Programs   If you have read Anthony Burgess's novel *A Clockwork Orange* or seen Stanley Kubrick's film version of this story of futuristic deviance and social control, you will undoubtedly recall the behavioral reconditioning of "young Alex." Alex, whose escapades of sexual violence had led him to incarceration, was offered a way out. He would be released if he first agreed to undergo a program of reconditioning. Strapped to a chair, Alex was presented with a mixture of violent and sexual stimuli, each paired with excruciating electrical shocks and physical pain. Thereafter, Alex avoided all violent and sexual urges. When confronted with violent or sexual stimuli, he would convulse with pain.

The reconditioning depicted in *A Clockwork Orange* is not distant fiction. It is but a dramatic example of certain forms of aversive therapy that are today used to reshape the behavior of deviants. Some of these therapies have been directed toward drug addicts. Electric shocks and nausea-inducing chemicals are used to convert the experience of drug use from one of pleasure to one of pain. Several related techniques have been applied to the behavior control of sexual deviants. Most of these control strategies have been used on voluntary subjects whose sexual offense was of a nonviolent nature (e.g., public exhibitionism, voyeurism or "peeping Tomism," and fetishes associated with arousal toward socially inappropriate objects for sexual attraction). In recent years aversive techniques have also been used to alter the behavior of violent offenders, such as rapists.

Aversive therapy directed at sexual deviants typically attempts to reduce sexual arousal associated with deviant stimuli by pairing the presentation of such stimuli with electrical shock or chemically induced pain. An offender may be shown sexually stimulating films or pictures. The person may be encouraged to masturbate, but sometimes offenders are simply asked to fantasize or imagine deviant sexual acts. Subsequent presentations of the prohibited act are accompanied by painful punishments. This continues until arousal levels associated with deviant stimuli are significantly reduced.

Many programs using such aversive techniques attempt to simultaneously recondition arousal to more appropriate sexual objects through similar procedures which induce masturbatory pleasure rather than pain. In 1976, for instance, Forgione reported upon the aversive reconditioning of two pedophiles (persons who engage in sexual activities with children). Photos were taken of the two clients engaging in sex with two life-size child mannequins. These images, which produced high levels of arousal on the part of the patients to whom they were shown, were subsequently paired with painful aversive stimuli. Sexually explicit photos of heterosexual couples and provocative adult females were interspersed with the deviant photographic images. The clients were able to avoid shocks by verbally rejecting the deviant photos within three seconds of their initial display. After thorough exposure to this program of behavior modification, the two patients were followed up for periods of two and three years, respectively. According to Forgione, this follow-up revealed a total absence of their previous child-molesting behaviors as well as general improvement in the areas of interpersonal and adult heterosexual communication.

Most information on the use of aversive therapy comes from a small number of successful case studies with nonresidentially treated deviants. Aversive techniques have also been used upon persons involuntarily confined within state institutions. In 1970, Reimringer, Morgan, and Bramwell reported upon the use of a chemical-based aversion technique to alter the behavior of troublesome patients at California's Atascadero State Hospital.[78] This "therapy" was used upon ninety patients described by staff as manifesting "persistent physical or verbal violence, deviant sexual behavior and lack of cooperation and involvement with the individual treatment prescribed by the patient's ward team."[79] In order to quell uncooperative behavior, staff injected intravenous doses of succinylcholine, a chemical producing paralysis of the diaphragm and suppression of breathing. The experience is terrifying. Those who receive such injections feel as if they are drawing their last breath. Overcome by this fearful physical sensation, patients were admonished to discontinue their unacceptable behaviors and to act more constructively.

As measured by frequency of "acting out" over the next three months, the Atascadero program was declared a success. Sixty-eight percent of the patients were classified as having improved. Nonetheless, professional and ethical criticism of this program resulted in its eventual termination. Its proponents argued that it was helpful in treating patients unresponsive to more traditional forms of hospital therapy (e.g., restraint, isolation, and the use of tranquilizing drugs). Opponents argued that it resembled torture more than treatment and that practitioners had failed to obtain the informed consent of those whom they allegedly were helping to unlearn deviance.[80]

The Atascadero project is not an isolated example of the use of aversive therapy within institutions. In recent years, reports have described the deployment of aversive procedures at Vacaville, a California medical-correctional institution, the California Institute for Women, the Wisconsin State Penitentiary, the Iowa Security Medical Facility, the Connecticut Correctional Institution, and several branches of the Ontario Regional Penitentiaries.[81] Unlike the Atascadero project, several of these programs made greater efforts to obtain permission from those who were subjected to rigorous aversive regimes of behavior modification. Yet, like the Atascadero project, they represent vivid examples of the dramatic conversion of the learning perspective from paper to practice. Ralph Schwitzgebel, an expert on the use of behavior modification, has recently alluded to the control potential of what he calls "behavioral engineering" or "behavioral instrumentation." In describing the use of various electronic devices used to modify behavior, Schwitzgebel cites studies in which animals have been reconditioned to alter their heart rates, intestinal and stomach contractions, brain waves, and even urine formation. The potential for control over human behavior is both staggering and frightening. Schwitzgebel himself has suggested the use of electronic surveillance apparatus as an alternative to incarceration. Wired with specialized monitoring devices, deviants could be watched and then shockingly jolted should their actions depart from those programmed by high-tech specialists in behavior modification.[82]

From minor to major forms of behavior modification, the learning perspective is associated with a posture of practical social control. New technologies for altering behavior raise the potential for such control. They also raise the frightening specter of mass behavioral manipulation. Indeed, the power of the state to socially control deviants has increased dramatically with recent advances within the learning perspective.

THE LEARNING PERSPECTIVE TODAY

The learning perspective is today a major perspective on deviant behavior. Its importance is reflected in the diversity of its contemporary research applications. These are too numerous to list in their entirety. Instead, I shall review four general themes addressed by these projects and provide illustrative examples of each. These include analyses of the *stages, content, modes,* and *social context* of learned deviance.

The Stages of Learned Deviance

Learning theorists often use the metaphor of a career to depict the development of deviant behavior. Just as career development entails various stages, so too do people pass through a sequence of steps on the road to becoming deviant. As Paul Higgins and Richard Butler point out, "One does not go from being square to being hip overnight. Instead, there is likely to be a gradual progression from one activity to another."[83]

Barbara Sherman Heyl's study of the stages of becoming a professional madam is a good illustration.[84] A madam is a combined business manager and hostess for a house of prostitution. According to Heyl, a woman passes through four distinct stages en route to this deviant role. Learning at each stage is analyzed according to five dimensions: (1) an assessment of interactional partners (the relative balance between a woman's "square" and "in the racket" associates); (2) employment (the world in which a women works—straight or deviant); (3) perception of prostitution (a woman's cognitive and ethical images of this oldest of professions); (4) normative conceptions of sexuality (a woman's sense of the dos and don'ts of permissible sexual expression); and (5) the timing of the sexual encounters (the frequency and degree of predictability of a woman's actual sexual behavior).

As the future madam passes through successive stages of involvement in prostitution, Heyl notes, there are changes in the several dimensions of the learning process.

The initial stage is that of "willing to try." It is typically associated with three influential subjective predispositions. The first of these involves a strong feeling of dissatisfaction or tension regarding one's present situation in life. Perhaps a woman feels trapped in a boring, low-paying job, is experiencing great stress in her domestic life, or is alone and isolated in a strange city. The second concerns a woman's gradual perception that prostitution represents a way out of her personal and/or economic malaise. The third occurs when a woman comes to view herself as capable of providing men with the sexual satisfaction required by prostitution. These things are nurtured by and nurture her associations with persons "in the racket" until she is "willing to try." At that point a woman may advance to the novice stage. Novices have continued contacts with persons already in the racket. Through such people they are presented with the opportunity to "turn tricks." After such initial experiences the fledgling prostitute is provided with assistance in learning to interpret her work positively, i.e., in beginning to reformulate her own sense of sexuality and realize that she can make good money in the business.

The third and fourth stages of becoming a madam involve processes of additional learning. In the stage in which a woman graduates from novice to professional she receives additional training in the behavioral skills, attitudes, and rationalizations appropriate to the business of exchanging sex for money. She is also encouraged to compartmentalize her sex life, to separate nonemotional or impersonal sex on the job from personal sex with her pimp or lover. In a final stage of learning the professional becomes a madam. Heyl describes the sponsorship and learning of administrative skills required by this phase of an entrepreneurial prostitute's career. In essence the prostitute learns to advance from a line staff position to one of management. Only then does she become madam of the house.

Another example of the sequential development of learned deviance is Lawrence Sherman's analysis of the six stages of the "moral career of the corrupt policeman."[85] Sherman describes the process through which a new police officer becomes a "grafter" (someone who accepts bribes). The key determinant of the strength of this process is the extent to which grafting is already a part of normal police work. Where grafting is a regular feature of daily work, there is great peer pressure to accept small favors, or "perks." These usually involve little more than free coffee and meals from restaurants along an officer's beat. Yet in accepting perks the officer also learns to make minor adjustments in his or her on-the-job morality. Receiving perks is the initial step along a career continuum of corruption. According to Sherman it is but the first step "up a ladder of increasing self-perceived social harm . . . , neutralizing any moral objections to the (crime-specific) graft at each rung of the ladder—each stage of the moral career."[86]

The officer who accepts a perk soon enters a second stage in the grafting career. Here the officer is confronted with a bar owner operating after hours who offers a drink. The decision to drink while ignoring the clock once again "redefines the policeman's self."[87]

The officer learns to adjust self-concepts and moral notions to justify his or her actual behavior. Subsequent steps in learning to be corrupted include accepting the *regulatory bribe* (money handed over along with the license of a stopped motorist, or cash forked over by the construction contractor for overlooking materials illegally obstructing a sidewalk), the *gambling payoff* (for passing over local betting operations), *prostitution graft*, and eventually *narcotics money* (earned for inattention to drug dealing). Like Heyl's description of the career phases of becoming a madam, Sherman's analysis of the sequential development of police corruption exemplifies the cumulative nature of the stages of deviant learning. Each stage prepares the emerging deviant for continued and deeper involvement in the underworld of rule breaking.

The Content of Learning

This second theme in contemporary studies of learned deviance elaborates Sutherland's notion that the development of deviant behavior involves the acquisition of prodeviant attitudes and guilt-neutralizing rationalizations as well as the "how-to-do-it" techniques of the deviant trade or activity. Howard Becker's study of learning to become a marijuana smoker during the 1950s represents a classic example of this approach.[88] During the 1950s marijuana smoking was considerably more of an underground phenomenon than it is today. In many ways, however, Becker's learning model is still applicable to the process through which new users are exposed to the ritualized pleasures of "getting high." According to Becker a person must first overcome any previous feelings about the negative effects or the immoral images of smoking. This is typically done in association with good friends or positively perceived associates who help the novice learn that smoking can be fun, that nothing bad will happen, that one is not likely to get caught, that people do not become slaves to the drug, and that it is possible to manage or fake the appearance of normality even when high. Equally important is learning the proper techniques of smoking and to perceive and enjoy the effect of pot. This, contends Becker, is no automatic process. His research points out that careful observation, imitation, and direct instruction are often necessary for the new user to cue into the proper techniques of smoking and to sense and enjoy the physical effects of the drug in a pleasurable manner.

Another important study related to the content of learned deviance is Gilbert Geis's examination of the corporate criminality of electrical equipment company officials involved in the price-fixing and price-rigging conspiracy of 1961.[89] The conspirators were forty-five reputable executives from twenty-nine major companies, including General Electric, Westinghouse, Allis-Chalmers, ITE, and Federal Pacific. They engaged in an elaborate plot to eliminate the competitive nature of open bidding for lucrative government contracts. The means used by these supposedly respectable executives appeared to have been borrowed from the scenario of a gangster film or some far-out spy movie. They developed a specialized language (their own peculiar argot) and a set of secret operating procedures designed to outwit government inspectors and deceive the public. Attendance at conspiratorial meetings was recorded by means of "Christmas card lists," while the meetings themselves were code-named "choir practices."

How was it that top business officials came to act in a manner more commonly associated with the slick criminal or the sleazy con artist? According to Geis, external business and control conditions were an important factor. When market conditions were unstable and the policies of government enforcers weak, business price-fixing flourished. These factors in themselves do not explain the development of shrewd criminal activity by people within the corporate world.[90] In search of a more specific explanation, Geis follows the lead of Edwin Sutherland's own 1949 pioneering investigation, *"White Collar Crime,"* in pointing to "learning and associational patterns as important elements in the genesis of the violations."[91] In the complex of informal associations within the corporation, executives learned that significant personal and professional rewards were available for those willing to risk breaking the law.

According to Geis, the offenders also learned to neutralize or rationalize their behavior in a manner in keeping with their image as "law-abiding, decent, respectable persons."[92] This was accomplished by a process of informal learning in which executives arrived at self-definitions of their behavior as not really criminal. Consider the following statement of one corporate official as reported by Geis.

> Illegal? Yes, but not criminal. I didn't find that out until I read the indictment. . . . I assumed that criminal action meant damaging someone, and we did not do that. . . . I thought that we were more or less working on a survival basis in order to keep our plant and our employees.[93]

Modes of Learning Deviance

Studies of socially acquired deviance have also focused on different modes in which the techniques, attitudes, and rationalizations of rule breaking are acquired. While certain forms of deviance are acquired through direct, almost formal instruction or coaching, others are more loosely picked up by hanging around a deviant scene. Still others are learned through indirect imitation.

Formal Instruction   Examples of the formal-instruction route to deviance include David Maurer's description of learning to become a professional thief[94] and separate analyses by James H. Bryan[95] and Barbara Sherman Heyl[96] of the formal apprenticeship provided for novice prostitutes. Maurer's work resembles Sutherland's earlier analysis of the tutelage of thieves by thieves. Maurer describes the complicated and often lengthy period of instruction and testing used by such diverse professionals as con artists, pickpockets, and safecracking specialists in introducing a select few new members into their ranks.

Both Bryan and Heyl report upon formal procedures used to instruct novice prostitutes about the tricks of their trade. Heyl describes one "house" in which a madam specializes in "turning out" new professionals. Novices are instructed in the physical, verbal, and business skills necessary for the successful management of a deviant career. Physical training includes instruction in various sexual positions, specialized or kinky tricks, and techniques of self-defense. More difficult is the teaching of proper techniques of hustling. As Heyl points out, a new "girl" must be taught to "be mentally alert and sensitive to the clients response" and to "maintain a steady pattern of verbal coaxing, during which her tone of voice may be more important than her actual words."[97]

Informal Learning   This second mode is exemplified by Robert Prus and C. R. D. Sharper's depiction of learning the trade of road hustling.[98] Professional road hustlers are masters of the deceptive card or dice game. Like other professional deviants, they occasionally take on apprentices. Novice hustlers are taught techniques of larceny, strategies for interacting with coworkers in a nonexploitive manner, and ways to "make the nut," hints for minimizing expenses on the road.

While hustling requires such learning, it does not usually involve formal instruction. Experienced professionals tend to select novices familiar with the general attitudes and techniques required in the trade. Crews do not see the tutelage of newcomers as a central responsibility. Thus, "much of the learning comes about either . . . by 'hanging around' practicing hustlers, or through being criticized in post-facto 'coaching.'"[99]

Indirect-Imitative Learning   Other forms of deviance may be learned by imitating behavior presented in the media or in some other type of indirect communication. This is the case for embezzlers, employees who steal secretly from their companies. Donald Cressey describes the typical embezzler as a person in a position of financial trust who views a secret trust violation as a way out of a financial problem that cannot be shared with others.[100] The embezzler develops a "vocabulary of adjustment" to rationalize theft in such terms as: "I am just borrowing the money; I will pay it back soon," or "It is only fair that I get something more. I'm certainly not getting paid what I'm worth."

How do people learn to become self-justified embezzlers? Unlike corporate criminals, who conspire to fix prices or deceive the public, embezzlers do not ordinarily share associative ties with fellow deviants. This is not to say that their deviance is unlearned. Cressey points to indirect sources by which embezzlers learn their "secret solution" and its accompanying rationalizations. People learn of the practical potential of embezzlement in the mass media, from company folklore about employee dishonesty, and from a company's policy of bonding its "trusted" employees.[101] Business culture is, moreover, filled with rationalizations for illicit action. As Cressey points out, employees do not invent new rationalizations for each trust violation, but depend instead upon a "culture" in which such verbalizations are present.[102]

Additional evidence for the indirect learning of deviance is found in studies on the impact of televised violence. In 1972 a report of a special commission of the surgeon general of the United States reviewed all existing correlational, laboratory-experimental, and field-experimental research on this topic.[103] The vast majority of these studies found consistent, if not always strong, evidence that watching aggression on television or in films is positively associated with the likelihood of acting aggressively.

Context of Learning

Research has also produced knowledge regarding the varying social contexts in which deviant behaviors may be acquired. Some contexts openly encourage deviance. The prototype of such manifestly supportive contexts is the so-called deviant subculture. Subcultural theories have been advanced as accounting for a wide range of deviance, including such divergent activities as violent behavior, illegal drug use, public nudity, homosexuality, and juvenile delinquency.

One illuminating account of the role of subcultures in fostering deviance is Martin Weinberg's study of the management of moral respectability by the managers and members of a nudist camp.[104] Weinberg observes that to become a nudist one must relearn moral meanings associated with public heterosexual nudity. In addition to learning about the positive healthful benefits of nudity, nudists must also learn that nudity and sexuality are unrelated, and that there is nothing shameful about public nakedness. These new moral meanings violate widely held social beliefs. Hence, the nudist subculture involves a careful process of adult resocialization in which members learn to protect themselves from the moral accusations of others.

Weinberg's research combines participatory field work with data gathered from interviews and questionnaires. It describes strategies used by the nudist subculture to reeducate its members into nudist morality. One important strategy involves precautions regarding who can enter a nudist camp. Most camps prohibit or discourage "singles." Another typical screening device involves an elaborate procedure for certifying the respectability of prospective members. Some camps require letters of reference regarding an applicant's moral character. Equally important are in-the-camp norms of interpersonal conduct. These include such prohibitions as no staring, no sex talk, no body contact, no alcoholic beverages, no unauthorized photo taking, no accentuation of the body, and no "unnatural" attempts at covering the body. These strictly enforced rules aid the nudist subculture in resocializing members into its "new system of moral meanings."[105]

Other group-learning contexts are not as manifest. Lewis Yablonsky uses the term *near-group* to describe associative contexts where deviance may be encouraged but not in the explicit manner of an all-encompassing subculture.[106] Yablonski describes juvenile gangs are near-groups. In such loose contexts deviant social learning is characterized by diffuse role definitions, limited cohesion, impermanence, minimal consensus about norms, shifting membership, disturbed leadership, and a limited definition of membership expectations. The near-group concept is applicable to a variety of other deviant learning contexts.[107] Think of the informal association of people who occasionally "toot" cocaine together. Deviant learning may occur, but probably not in the elaborate manner suggested by the term *subculture*.

At the other extreme of the learning continuum are contexts in which interactional associations may latently encourage deviance. This may happen independently of the intent or awareness of the parties involved. Two examples come to mind. The first is Ronald Akers's description of the social reinforcement of self-destructive behavior.[108] Akers reviews a variety of studies of extremely self-injurious behavior on the part of emotionally disturbed and/or retarded children.[109] He concludes that *"social attention* commonly follows and subsequently reinforces the self-mutilating behavior."[110]

Another example of latent social support for deviance is found in the in-depth case studies of severe schizophrenia by psychiatrist R. D. Laing and his associates.[111] Laing discovered that the immediate "communicative nexus" of the schizophrenic (his or her network of significant social relationships) contains strong but contradictory social forces, pulling the person in different directions at the same time. The schizophrenic is trapped within what anthropologist Gregory Bateson describes as the "double bind" of intimate interpersonal communications.[112] If the person acts one way, he or she is rewarded by one of the conflicting parties but punished by the other. If the person acts in a manner pleasing to the other party, the opposite occurs. How can one escape this double bind? One way, suggests Laing, is to learn the language of madness, to act in a fashion that will get one classified as a schizophrenic. For Laing, the term *mental illness* unfortunately disguises the fact that schizophrenic behavior may be a rationally learned response to a contradictory and excruciatingly painful social situation. By acting in a schizophrenic manner, by existentially leaping into the dark reality of madness, one escapes the contradictory demands of the double bind. One cannot, after all, be held responsible if one is sick. Thus schizophrenics may be said to escape the dilemma of contradictory social expectations by learning to sleep under the safe covers of sickness.

ASSESSMENT OF THE LEARNING PERSPECTIVE

From its early inception in Tarde's three laws of imitation, the learning perspective has exerted an enormous impact on the study of deviance and social control. The learning perspective normalizes our images of deviance. It presents the deviant as a fellow human being. Deviance is no longer far away. It is neither an abnormal condition nor the product of abstract social forces. It is concrete. It is the product of learning to be in the world in a particular way, learning with and from others about how to define, feel, and act within a world which we create together.

Despite its widespread appeal, not all versions of the learning perspective have gained equal acceptance. This is evident when one compares Sutherland's theory of differential association with Burgess and Akers's subsequent reformulation. According to Clinard and Meir, "In spite of its shortcomings, no other theory of deviance has generated such a favorable long-term acceptance as . . . differential association theory."[113] On the other hand, Rand Conger has commented upon the relative neglect of Burgess and Akers's work in sociological circles.

According to Conger several things account for sociologists' general disregard of Burgess and Akers's operant social-learning model.[114] Many of Burgess and Akers's propositions are borrowed from another discipline—psychology. This may have retarded the acceptance of the differential-reinforcement framework. Of greater importance may be the highly abstract nature of early operant formulations.

Another factor related to the lack of interest in reinforcement theory was the rise of the societal-reaction perspective. As Conger points out, at the time when Burgess and Akers's work was first introduced, many sociologists had begun to shift their attention from the study of causation to an analysis of the deviant labeling process. The social-historical reasons for this will be discussed in Chapter 9. For now it is enough to note that in the 1980s, interest in causal explanations returned to center stage. Basic causation research is again a top priority for government funding. Liberal reforms associated with the societal-reaction perspective were intended to reduce harsh and ineffective control policies. Such reforms, however, did little to alter the basic social conditions out of which deviance arises. In the economically bad times of the 1980s and early 1990s, liberal efforts aimed at humanizing control policies were replaced by conservative rhetoric and policies again directed at deterring, containing, or rehabilitating the deviant. This conservative mood rekindled interest in the learning perspective. Indeed, in a speech on priorities for criminal justice policy, Warren Burger, former Chief Justice of the United States Supreme Court, called for a renewed emphasis on rehabilitative strategies which would teach convicted criminals "respect for self, respect for others, accountability for conduct, appreciation of the value of work, of thought, of family," and for a program by which offenders would literally "learn the way out of prison."[115]

Concluding Comments: Four Reservations about the Scope and Uses of the Learning Perspective

Renewed interest in the learning perspective leads me to conclude this section with four general reservations. These focus on its tendency to be overly deterministic, its inattention to matters pertaining to unconscious repressions, its underdevelopment of concerns related to gendered and multicultural models of learning, and its relative neglect of questions related to the social origins of deviant categories. While significant, these reservations do not counter the advantages of including some model of learning in any comprehensive analysis of deviance. Each simply cautions against an overemphasis on learning as traditionally conceived.

Overly Deterministic Learning   Critics such as Ian Taylor, Paul Walton, and Jock Young argue that "human choice is not adequately stressed and the resulting behavior appears to be totally determined."[116] A similar conclusion is arrived at in Short and Strodtbeck's study of delinquent gangs. Short and Strodtbeck suggest that youths are neither blindly driven nor irrationally lured into subcultures of deviance. Potential deviants enter into subcultural associations only after assessing the gains and losses, benefits and risks. Deviants, in other words, understand the risks entailed by nonconformity.

Short and Strodtbeck argue that youths enter delinquent subcultures believing that the advantages of achieving high status within the deviant group outweigh the disadvantages of getting caught.[117] Their assessment of risks is aleatory. It is dependent upon unforeseen contingencies. Much can go wrong. There is no way of assuring successful deviance, of reaping its benefits without paying the price of social control. For this reason Short and Strodtbeck describe their theory as one of aleatory risks.

Once someone is involved in the delinquent gang, the subculture may reinforce his or her confidence in the rationality of the choice for deviance. Short and Strodtbeck's theory thus modifies rather than rejects the central tenets of the learning perspective. Subcultures are said to reinforce deviant options in two ways: by emphasizing the low probability of unforeseen negative sanctions and by promising high status to those who remain members. Again the emphasis is on rational choice. Persons choose to enter and remain within deviant subcultures because these are perceived as efficient avenues for obtaining status, respect, and relative success.

Short and Strodtbeck's work inserts the concept of rational choice into the learning perspective. David Matza takes the issue one step further. He suggests that deviance, like any other human behavior, can best be understood as partly chosen and partly determined. Matza's work has been referred to as "soft determinism." Matza's image of the deviant is of a person who drifts in and out of conventional society.[118] Matza's image of drift suggests that persons do not once and for all enter into a deviant subculture but rather, join loosely together in a process of mutual support. Neutralization techniques arise as verbal strategies which provide distance from the hold of conventional norms and values. The drift toward deviance is supported, moreover, by a "subterranean" American tradition favoring excitement, risk, and adventure. Matza suggests that below the surface of conventional life is a set of attitudes and values favoring nonconventionality. Thematized in literature, art, and the mass media, this desire for adventuresome risk taking is a present, if ordinarily suppressed, element of American life. When deviants tap into this subterranean tradition they are revealing another face of the dominant culture. Deviants are thus less unconventional than they may seem. The realization of this reinforces the drift into deviance.

Matza offers an open-ended rather than a deterministic vision of the deviant learning process. Through interaction with others, someone prepares for rule breaking by learning to neutralize guilt and explore the realm of subterranean value convergence, thus becoming a potential deviant. Then this person is hit by an unforeseen crisis. Things seem desperate. He or she is beset by a mood of fatalism and the sense that things are out of control. In an attempt to regain control, he or she may experiment with deviance. The whole process is described by Matza as a drift toward deviance. If the experiment with deviant action proves successful, i.e., if it helps the person regain a sense of control, then he or she is likely to continue to choose to deviate. This is Matza's image of how deviance is learned. It involves a combination of choice and determination, of being desirous and being socially propelled.

Matza's alternative to an overly deterministic learning theory is elaborated by Edwin Pfuhl.[119] Pfuhl stresses the importance of *biographical affinity* for becoming deviant. This refers to a constellation of prodeviant associations, rationalizations, opportunities, meanings, and self-concept. Nonetheless, Pfuhl contends that even a very strong biographical affinity is but a general condition favoring deviance. Biographical affinities encourage but do not determine deviant action. In the final analysis, deviance remains a choice, an act of human willingness.

Willingness, however, is not to be confused with free will. Willingness is an openness to deviance. It exists only in a situated context of immediate social experience. In such contexts the assessment of alternative courses of action is partially shaped by a history of prior learning. Thus, for Pfuhl, as for Matza, and for Short and Strodtbeck, while it may be technically incorrect to state that deviance is learned, it is correct to state that people learn that deviance is possible, permissible, rationalizable, and even valued within a particular social context.

Ignoring the Role of Unconscious Repressions

While learning theory offers numerous insights into the way that deviance is acquired and reinforced, it has generally underemphasized the role of unconscious social processes in shaping nonconformity. Here, the lessons of the learning perspective might be expanded by broadening its scope to include various sociological uses of psychoanalysis. Indeed, one of the most important theoretical contributions of psychoanalysis is its suggestion that nothing is ever learned without other things being (at least temporarily) repressed from conscious memory. Learning, in other words, involves not just the positive acquisition of self-definitions, behavioral techniques, and motives but also the unconscious repression of other possible ways of acting.

Repressed from conscious cultural recognition, excluded social possibilities often return in a disguised or distorted form. Consider, for instance, the so-called epidemic of hysteria among women factory workers in Malaysia, which was discussed in the introduction to Chapter 4. While this hysteria was classified as a form of sickness by medical control agents, isn't it possible to think more sociologically about this phenomenon as the return of repressed social conflicts between men and women, as well as between Malay society and the transnational corporations which were exploiting its work force? In learning new economic roles that furthered their cultural disempowerment, were the "possessed" Malay workers also learning to function as something like unconscious signs of social "dis-ease" and political contradiction?

Related questions might be raised about the sociological significance of *hysteria, panic disorder,* and the *eating disorders* discussed in the closing pages of Chapter 4. Although commonly thought of as forms of psychiatric illness affecting women more than men, don't such behaviors also signify the masked historical return of struggles for power that are socially repressed in learning the codes of modern patriarchy? And what of the typically militaristic character of the learned behavior of both "street-wise" male delinquents and high-level corporate and government criminals? In what ways do such deviants act out competitive forms of "male bonding" that are symptomatic of unconscious cultural prohibitions against more intimate forms of contact between men? This is an important question to raise within a society such as our own, a society that routinely deviantizes homosexuality while valorizing the homosocial power of some men over other men and over virtually all women. Unfortunately, such questions have been ignored by most modern learning theorists.

Inattention to Gendered and Multicultural Models of Learning

Recent research on cultural differences affecting various styles of learning are also important to the study of deviance. Carol Gilligan's claim to have uncovered differences in the moral reasoning of women in comparison to that of men represents a case in point.[120] Gilligan's research refutes psychologist Lawrence Kohlberg's claim that women display a moral logic that is less "mature" than that of men.[121] Gilligan examined the hypothetical responses of twenty-nine middle-class white women faced with a decision concerning abortion, and a comparison of the responses of eight boys and eight girls in response to a fictive "moral dilemma." Her findings suggest that women (as a social group) have learned to approach morality in a more caring and relational manner than men. While the limited character of the sample and the failure to examine issues pertaining to social class and ethnicity have led to criticism of Gilligan's supposedly "universal" findings, her suggestion that learning may be mediated by gender is important and needs to be included within studies of socially acquired deviance.

A more adequate formulation of this concern involves what feminist and multicultural scholars today call "standpoint theory." Standpoint theory recognizes the partiality rather than the universality of all forms of knowledge. The most objective forms of knowledge are those that recognize that historical and cultural contexts are mediating features of all valid claims to truth. As Patricia Hill Collins observes, "Each group speaks from its own standpoint and shares its own partial, situated knowledge. Because each group perceives its own truth as partial, its knowledge is unfinished."[122] To respond seriously to the ongoing challenge of standpoint theory, learning theorists must recognize the partial and provisional confines of their own learned (if scholarly) standpoints. But for this to happen, learning theorists must first unlearn the apparent "universality" of certain of the most dominant models of learning.

Relative Inattention to the Social Learning of Deviant Categories The learning perspective does little to clarify why it is that certain types of behavior are thought of as deviant. In this sense, the general acceptance given to Sutherland's theory of differential association submerged or buried the more critical elements of his previous differential-organization ideas. The learning perspective is largely social-psychological. It ignores or downplays the role of conflicting social interests in producing a particular order of conformity (favoring those with greatest power) and in controlling the non-conformity of the relatively powerless individuals and groups with little stake in that order. Sutherland's early observations concerning the relationship between law and cultural conflict become lost in the flurry of attention generated by his model of the mechanisms of deviant learning.

Why has Sutherland's learning theory received far greater attention than the more critical focus of his earlier thought? The answer may lie in the fact that most men and women who have studied deviance have shared, at least implicitly, the official government position on what acts and which people were really deviant.

In the years following World War II social scientists came to play an increasingly important role in the social control process. Accepting government money for research, researchers commonly accepted the government's definition of deviance as well.

In abstract terms questions raised by the government about deviance were different from those asked by social scientists. The government wanted to know what caused people to deviate so that deviance could be stopped. Social scientists wanted to know such things as whether differential-association theory was testable. In concrete terms, however, the questions were the same. Social science research provided information on how to best control deviants. The ultimate test of social science explanations was whether they offered workable programs of social control. Herein lies the preference for the learning perspective. The government could use it in an attempt to change deviants into conformists. All that had to be done was to alter the learning environment of the nonconformist.

Had social scientists placed an equal emphasis on differential organization, the task of providing social control solutions would have been more complex and more precarious. The structural environment of societal interests, rather than the learning environment of particular deviants, would have had to be changed. Social scientists would have been asking the government itself to change. Unfortunately such recommendations have little payoff in government-sponsored research contracts. The proposals of learning theorists fared much better. Perhaps this was because such theorists offered little challenge to society's official position on deviance.

Compliance with official definitions of deviance may be less of an inherent problem with the learning perspective than a problem with the way the perspective has been used in practice. This point is made by Conger. He argues that the same learning principles that are used to explain deviance might be used to account for particular policies of control.[123] While this is undoubtedly true, there has been little systematic use of the perspective toward this end. Maybe most theorists and researchers have simply learned to see deviance in the same way that it is seen by those charged with its control. Social scientists are, after all, generally middle-class, generally white, generally male, generally sheltered from social indignities. Perhaps these advantages provide social scientists with a biographical affinity for identifying the problem of deviance in the same way as those who pay them—the government and their universities.

Like the deviants they study, researchers may also learn to associate themselves with the path of greatest reinforcement. In any event, until the emergence of the societal reaction and conflict perspectives during the 1960s, social science research did little to challenge and a lot to support official definitions of deviance. Deviance remained a problem of deviants. The nearly exclusive social-psychological focus of the learning perspective guaranteed that this would happen.

NOTES

1 Gabriel Tarde, *Penal Philosophy*, Little, Brown, Boston, 1912, p. 322.
2 Edwin H. Sutherland and Donald R. Cressey, *Principles of Criminology*, 10th ed., Lippincott, Philadelphia, 1978, p. 81.
3 Jack Henry Abbott, *In the Belly of the Beast: Letters from Prison*, Vintage, New York, 1981.
4 Tarde, *Penal Philosophy*.
5 Ibid., p. 340.
6 Edwin H. Sutherland, *Principles of Criminology*, Lippincott, Philadelphia, 1934, p. 51.
7 Thorsten Sellin, *Culture Conflict and Crime*, Social Science Research Council, 1938. According to Don C. Gibbons, Sutherland worked with Sellin on this monograph even though he did not share in its authorship. See Don C. Gibbons, *The Criminological Enterprise*, Prentice-Hall, Englewood Cliffs, N.J., 1979, pp. 47–48.
8 Albert Cohen, Alfred Lindesmith, and Karl Schuessler (eds.), *The Sutherland Papers*, Indiana University Press, Bloomington, 1956, p. 103.
9 Edwin H. Sutherland, "Development of the Theory," in Cohen, Lindesmith, and Schuessler, *The Sutherland Papers*, pp. 14–15.
10 Ibid., p. 19.
11 Edwin H. Sutherland, *The Professional Thief*, University of Chicago Press, Chicago, 1937.
12 Ibid., pp. v–vi.
13 Edwin H. Sutherland, *Principles of Criminology*, 3d ed., Lippincott, Philadelphia,

1939, pp. 4, 7. This edition of *Principles of Criminology* was subsequently reprinted as a War Department Educational Manual (EM 266) by the United States Armed Forces Institute. Its practical utility to the government is suggested by Sutherland, who states that "criminology is concerned with the immediate application of knowledge to programs of social control of crime. . . . If practical programs wait until theoretical knowledge is complete, they will wait for eternity, for theoretical knowledge is increased most significantly in the efforts at social control" (pp. 1–2).

14 Richard R. Korn and Lloyd W. McCorkle, *Criminology and Penology*, Holt, Rinehart & Winston, New York, 1959, pp. 298–301.

15 Sutherland and Cressey, *Principles of Criminology*, 10th ed., p. 83.

16 Ibid., p. 82.

17 Ibid., pp. 80–82.

18 James F. Short, Jr., "Differential Association as a Hypothesis: Problems of Empirical Testing," *Social Problems*, vol. 8, summer 1960, pp. 14–25.

19 Albert J. Reiss Jr., and A. Lewis Rhodes, "An Empirical Test of Differential Association Theory," *Journal of Research in Crime and Delinquency*, vol. 1, January 1964, pp. 5–18.

20 See also Donald Cressey, *Other People's Money*, Free Press, Glencoe, Ill., 1953; John C. Ball, "Delinquent and Non-Delinquent Attitudes toward the Prevalence of Stealing," *Journal of Criminal Law, Criminology and Police Science*, vol. 48, September-October 1957, pp. 259–274; Harwin Voss, "Differential Association and Reported Delinquent Behavior: A Replication," *Social Problems*, vol. 12, summer 1964, pp. 28–85; Marvin D. Krohn, "An Investigation of the Effect of Parental and Peer Association on Marijuana Use: An Empirical Test of Differential Association Theory," in Marc Riedel and Terrence P. Thornbery (eds.), *Crime and Delinquency: Dimensions of Deviance*, Praeger, New York, 1979, pp. 75–89; Gary F. Jensen, "Parents, Peers and Delinquent Action: A Test of the Differential Association Perspective," *American Journal of Sociology*, vol. 78, November 1972, pp. 63–72; Steven Burkett and Eric L. Jensen, "Conventional Ties, Peer Influence, and the Fear of Apprehension: A Study of Adolescent Marijuana Use," *Sociological Quarterly*, vol. 16, autumn 1975, pp. 522–533.

21 Ronald L. Akers, *Deviant Behavior: A Social Learning Approach*, 2d ed., Wadsworth, Belmont, Calif., 1977, p. 56.

22 Sheldon Glueck, "Theory and Fact in Criminology: A Criticism of Differential Association," *British Journal of Delinquency*, vol. 7, October 1956, pp. 92–109.

23 David Matza, *Becoming Deviant*, Prentice-Hall, Englewood Cliffs, N.J., 1969, p. 107.

24 Daniel Glaser, "Criminality Theories and Behavioral Images," *American Journal of Sociology*, vol. 61, March 1956, pp. 433–444.

25 Melvin L. DeFleur and Richard Quinney, "A Reformulation of Sutherland's Differential Association Theory and a Strategy of Empirical Verification," *Journal of Research in Crime and Delinquency*, vol. 3, January 1966, pp. 1–22.

26 Ibid. The authors reformulate Sutherland's sixth proposition regarding an excess of procriminal or prodeviant definition to read as follows: "Overt criminal behavior has as its necessary and sufficient conditions a set of criminal motivations, attitudes, and techniques, the learning of which takes place when there is exposure to criminal norms in excess of exposure to corresponding anti-criminal norms during symbolic interaction in primary groups." p. 20.

27 Glaser, "Criminality Theories and Behavioral Images," pp. 433–444.

28 Gresham M. Sykes and David Matza, "Techniques of Neutralization: A Theory of Delinquency," *American Sociological Review*, vol. 22, December 1957, pp. 664–670.

29 Jack D. Douglas, "Existential Sociology," in Jack D. Douglas and John M. Johnson (eds.), *Existential Sociology*, Cambridge University Press, Cambridge, 1977, p. 27.

30 Jack D. Douglas, "Shame and Deceit in Creative Deviance," in Edward Sagarin (ed.), *Deviance and Social Change*, Sage, Beverly Hills, Calif., 1977, pp. 59–86.

31 Donald R. Cressey, "Epidemiology and Individual Conduct: A Case from Criminology," *Pacific Sociological Review*, vol. 3, fall 1960, p. 54.

32 C. Ray Jeffery, "Criminal Behavioral and Learning Theory," *Journal of Criminal Law, Criminology and Police Science*, vol. 56, September 1965, pp. 294–300.

33 Robert L. Burgess and Ronald L. Akers, "A Differential Association: Reinforcement Theory of Criminal Behavior," *Social Problems*, vol. 14, no. 2, fall 1966, pp. 128–147.

34 Akers, *Deviant Behavior*, pp. 42–43.

35 Julian Rotter, *Social Learning and Clinical Psychology*, Prentice-Hall, Englewood Cliffs, N.J., 1954.

36 Albert Bandura and Richard H. Walters, *Social Learning and Personality Development*, Holt, Rinehart & Winston, New York, 1963.

37 Leonard P. Ullmann and Leonard Krasner, *A Psychological Approach to Abnormal Behavior*, Prentice-Hall, Englewood Cliffs., N.J., 1969.

38 Arthur W. Staats and Carolyn K. Staats, *Complex Human Behavior: A Systematic Extension of Learning Principles*, Holt, Rinehart & Winston, New York, 1963.

39 Akers, *Deviant Behavior*, p. 62.

40 Ibid., p. 60.

41 Don C. Gibbons, *Society, Crime and Criminal Behavior*, 4th ed., Prentice-Hall, Englewood Cliffs, N.J., 1982, p. 233.

42 Daniel Glaser, *Adult Crime and Social Policy*, Prentice-Hall, Englewood Cliffs, N.J., 1972.

43 Marshall B. Clinard and Richard Quinney, *Criminal Behavior Systems*, 2d ed., Holt, Rinehart & Winston, New York, 1973.

44 Nanette Davis, *Sociological Construction of Deviance*, Brown, Dubuque, Iowa, 1980, p. 171.

45 Gibbons, *Society, Crime and Criminal Behavior*, p. 232.

46 Alfred R. Lindesmith, "A Sociological Theory of Drug Addiction," *American Journal of Sociology*, vol. 43, January 1938, pp. 593–613.

47 P. Brown and R. Elliot, "Control of Aggression in Nursery School Class," *Journal of Experimental Child Psychology*, vol. 2, 1965, pp. 103–107.

48 R. Parke, W. Ewall, and R. Slaby, "Hostile and Helpful Verbalization as Regulators of Non-Verbal Aggression," *Journal of Personality and Social Psychology*, vol. 23, 1972, pp. 243–248.

49 Linda S. Anderson, "The Impact of Formal and Informal Sanctions on Marijuana Use," M. A. thesis, Florida State University, as described in Akers, *Deviant Behavior*, pp. 56–57.

50 Rand Conger, "Social Control and Social Learning Models of Delinquency: A Synthesis," *Criminology*, vol. 14, May 1976, pp. 17–40.

51 Robert L. Burgess and Ronald L. Akers, "A Differential Association-Reinforcement Theory of Criminal Behavior," in Robert L. Burgess and Don Bushell, Jr. (eds.), *Behavioral Sociology: The Experimental Analysis of Social Process*, Columbia, New York, 1969, p. 299.

52. Akers, *Deviant Behavior*, p. 55.

53 Ibid., pp. 58, 60.

54 Gene Kassebaum, *Delinquency and Social Policy*, Prentice-Hall, Englewood Cliffs, N.J., 1974.

55 Grant Johnson, Tom Bird, and Judith Warren Little, *Delinquency Prevention: Theories and Strategies*, prepared for the Office of Juvenile Justice and Delinquency Prevention, Department of Justice, Washington, D.C., April 1979, p. 28.

56 Ibid., p. 78.

57 Walter Reckless, *The Crime Problem*, 5th ed., Appleton-Century-Crofts, New York, 1973, p. 57.

58 Abraham A. Law, *Mental Health through Will-Training*, Christopher, Boston, 1950, p. 15.

59 John Lofland, *Deviance and Identity*, Prentice-Hall, Englewood Cliffs, N.J., 1969, p. 238.

60 Rita Volkman and Donald R. Cressey, "Differential Association and the Rehabilitation of Drug Addicts," *American Journal of Sociology*, vol. 69, 1963, pp. 129–142.

61 Ibid., p. 132.

62 Richard M. Emerson, "Operant Psychology and Exchange Theory," in Robert L. Burgess and Don Bushell, Jr. (eds.), *Behavioral Sociology: The Experimental Analysis of Social Process*, Columbia, New York, 1969, p. 386.

63 For an extended discussion of pioneering efforts in behavior modification, see Staats and Staats, *Complex Human Behavior*, pp. 488–511.

64 W. Isaacs, J. Thomas, and I. Goldiamond, "Application of Operant Conditioning to Reinstate Verbal Behavior in Psychotics," *Journal of Speech and Hearing Disorders*, vol. 25, 1960, pp. 8–12.

65 C. D. Williams, "The Elimination of Tantrum Behavior by Extinction Procedures," *Journal of Abnormal and Social Psychology*, vol. 59, 1959, p. 269.

66 T. Allyon and J. Michael, "The Psychiatric Nurse as Behavioral Engineer," *Journal of Experimental Analysis of Behavior*," vol. 29, 1959, pp. 323–334.

67 Ibid., pp. 330–331.

68 J. J. Eysenck (ed.), *Experiments in Behavior Therapy: Reading in Modern Methods of Treatment of Mental Disorders Derived from Learning Theory*, Macmillan, Pergamon, New York, 1964.

69 Leonard P. Ullmann and Leonard Krasner (eds.), *Case Studies in Behavior Modification*, Holt, Rinehart & Winston, New York, 1965. See also Leonard Krasner and Leonard Ullmann (ed.), *Research in Behavior Modification*, Holt, Rinehart & Winston, New York, 1965.

70 Joseph A. Wolpe, Andrew Salter, and L. J. Regina (eds.), *The Conditioning Therapies*, Holt, Rinehart & Winston, New York, 1964.

71 Albert Bandura, *Principles of Behavior Modification*, Holt, Rinehart & Winston, New York, 1969.

72 Ullmann and Krasner, *A Psychological Approach to Abnormal Behavior*, p. 408.

73 For a comprehensive review and analysis of these programs, see Michael T. Nietzel, *Crime and Its Modification: A Social Learning Perspective*, Pergamon, New York, 1979, pp. 121–141.

74 J. J. Boren and A. D. Colman, "Some Experiments on Reinforcement Principles within a Psychiatric Ward for Delinquent Soldiers," *Journal of Applied Behavioral Analysis*, vol. 3, 1979, pp. 29–38.

75 M. A. Milan and J. M. McKee, "Behavior Modification: Principles and Applications in Corrections," in Daniel Glaser (ed.), *Handbook of Criminology*, Rand McNally, Chicago, 1974.

76 R. E. Kennedy, "Behavioral Modification in Prisons," in W. E. Craighead, A. E. Kazden, and M. H. Mahoney (eds.), *Behavior Modification: Principles, Issues and Applications*, Houghton-Mifflin, Boston, 1976.

77 Nietzel, *Crime and Its Modification*, p. 228.

78 M. J. Reimringer, S. Morgan, and P. Bramwell, "Succinylcholine as a Modifier of Acting and Behavior," *Clinical Medicine*, July 1970, pp. 28–29.

79 Ibid.

80 R. Space, "Conditioning and Other Technologies Used to 'Treat?' 'Rehabilitate?' 'Demolish?' Prisoners and Mental Patients," *Southern California Law Review*, vol. 85, 1972, pp. 616–684.

81 Nietzel, *Crime and Its Modification*, pp. 141–146.

82 R. K. Schwitzgebel, "Electronic Alternatives to Prison," *Lex et Science*, vol. 5, no. 3, 1968, pp. 99–104.

83 Paul C. Higgins and Richard R. Butler, *Understanding Deviance*, McGraw-Hill, New York, 1982, p. 182.

84 Barbara Sherman Heyl, *The Madam as Entrepreneur: Career Management in House Prostitution*, Transaction, New Brunswick, N.J., 1979.

85 Lawrence Sherman, *Police Corruption*, Doubleday, New York, 1974.

86 Lawrence Sherman, "The Subculture of Police Corruption," in Earl Rubington and Martin S. Weinberg (eds.), *Deviance: The Interactionist Perspective*, 4th ed., Macmillan, New York, 1981, p. 323.

87 Ibid.

88 Howard S. Becker, *Outsiders: Studies in the Sociology of Deviance*, Free Press, New York, 1963, pp. 41–58.

89 Gilbert Geis, "White Collar Crime: The Heavy Electrical Equipment Anti-Trust Cases of 1961," in Gilbert Geis and Robert F. Meir (eds.), *White Collar Crime*, rev. ed., Free Press, New York, 1977.

90 Edwin H. Sutherland, *White Collar Crime*, Holt, Rinehart & Winston, New York, 1949.

91 Gilbert Geis, "White Collar Crime: The Heavy Electrical Equipment Anti-Trust Cases of 1961," in Marshall B. Clinard and Richard Quinney (eds.), *Criminal Behavior Systems: A Typology*. Holt, Rinehart & Winston, New York, 1967, p. 150.

92 Ibid.

93 Ibid., p. 144.

94 David W. Maurer, *Whiz Mob: A Correlation of the Technical Argot of Pick-Pockets with Their Behavior*, College and University Press, New Haven, Conn., 1964.

95 James H. Bryan, "Apprentices in Prostitution," *Social Problems*, vol. 12, winter 1965, pp. 287–299.

96 Barbara Sherman Heyl, "The Madam as Teacher: The Training of House Prostitutes," in Delos H. Kelly (ed.), *Deviant Behavior: Readings in the Sociology of Deviance*, St. Martin's, New York, 1979.

97 Ibid., p. 514.

98 Robert C. Prus and C. R. D. Sharper, *Road Hustler*, Lexington Books, D.C. Heath, Lexington, Mass., 1977.

99 Robert C. Prus and C. R. D. Sharper, "Road Hustlers," in Earl Rubington and Martin S. Weinberg (eds.), *Deviance: The Interactionist Perspective*, 4th ed., Macmillan, New York, 1981, p. 327.

100 Donald R. Cressey, *Other People's Money: A Study in the Social Psychology of Embezzlement,* Free Press, New York, 1953.

101 For an extended discussion of these adjustive vocabulary practices, see ibid., pp. 93–138.

102 Ibid., p. 137.

103 Surgeon General's Scientific Advisory Committee on Television and Social Behavior, *Television and Growing Up: The Impact of Televised Violence,* Department of Health, Education and Welfare, Washington, D.C., 1972.

104 Martin S. Weinberg, "The Nudist Management of Respectability," in Earl Rubington and Martin S. Weinberg (eds.), *Deviance: The Interactionist Perspective,* 4th ed., Macmillan, New York, 1981, pp. 336–345. See also Martin S. Weinberg, "Becoming a Nudist," *Psychiatry,* vol. 29, February 1966, pp. 15–24.

105 Weinberg, "The Nudist Management of Respectability," p. 345.

106 Lewis Yablonsky, "The Delinquent Gang as a Near-Group," *Social Problems,* vol. 7, no. 2, fall 1959, pp. 108–117.

107 J. L. Simmons, *Deviants,* Boyd & Fraser, San Francisco, 1969, p. 115.

108 Akers, *Deviant Behavior,* pp. 297–304.

109 See, for instance, B. G. Tate and G. S. Baroff, "Aversive Control of Self-Injurious Behavior in a Psychotic Boy," *Behavior Research and Therapy,* vol. 4, 1966, pp. 281–287; I. O. Lovaas and J. Q. Simmons, "Manipulation of Self-Destruction in Three Retarded Children," *Journal of Applied Behavioral Analysis,* vol. 2, fall 1969, pp. 143–157; and I. O. Lovaas, G. Freitag, V. Gold, and I. Kassorla, "Experimental Studies in Childhood Schizophrenia, I: Analysis of Self-Destructive Behavior," *Journal of Experimental Child Psychology,* vol. 2, 1968, pp. 67–84.

110 Akers, *Deviant Behavior,* pp. 298–299.

111 See R. D. Laing, *The Divided Self,* Penguin, Baltimore, 1965 (originally published in 1960); and R. D. Laing and A. Esterson, *Sanity, Madness and the Family,* Basic Books, New York, 1964.

112 G. Bateson, D. D. Jackson, J. Haley, and J. Weakland, "Toward a Theory of Schizophrenia," *Behavioral Science,* vol. 1, 1956, pp. 251–264.

113 Marshall B. Clinard and Robert F. Meir, *Sociology of Deviant Behavior,* 5th ed., Holt, Rinehart & Winston, New York, 1979, p. 92.

114 Rand D. Conger, "From Social Learning to Criminal Behavior," in Marvin D. Krohn and Ronald L. Akers (eds.), *Crime, Law and Sanctions: Theoretical Perspectives,* Sage, Beverly Hills, Calif., 1978, pp. 91–104.

115 Warren Burger, "The Perspective of the Chief Justice of the U.S. Supreme Court," speech at the annual conference of the American Bar Association, Feb. 8, 1981, Houston, Texas, as printed in *Crime and Social Justice,* vol. 15, summer 1981, p. 46.

116 Ian Taylor, Paul Walton, and Jock Young, *The New Criminology: For a Theory of Deviance,* Harper & Row, New York, 1973, p. 132.

117 James F. Short and Fred L. Strodtbeck, *Group Process and Gang Delinquency,* University of Chicago Press, Chicago, 1965.

118 Matza, *Becoming Deviant.*

119 Edwin H. Pfuhl, Jr., *The Deviance Process,* Van Nostrand, New York, 1980, pp. 55–79.

120 Carol Gilligan, *In a Different Voice: Psychological Theory and Women's Development,* Harvard University Press, Cambridge, Mass., 1982.

121 Other critiques of Kohlberg's analysis, while debunking his claims concerning the greater "maturity" of men, do not find the same male/female differences inferred by Gilligan. See, for instance, Lawrence Walker, "Sex Differences in the Development of Moral Reasoning: A Critical Review," *Child Development*, vol. 55, 1982, pp. 667–691; and Catherine Greeno and Eleanor Maccoby, "How Different Is the Different Voice?" *Signs*, vol. 11, no. 2, 1986, pp. 310–316. For an overview of related issues, see Cynthia Fuchs Epstein, "It's All in the Mind: Personality and Social Structure," in Laura Kramer (ed.), *The Sociology of Gender*, St. Martin's Press, New York, 1991, pp. 84–104.

122 Patricia Hill Collins, *Black Feminist Thought: Knowledge, Consciousness and the Politics of Empowerment*, Unwin Hyman, Boston, 1990, p. 236.

123 Conger, "From Social Learning to Criminal Behavior," pp. 91–104.

Behind the Words   By Joseph LaMantia and Stephen Pfohl

CHAPTER 9

THE SOCIETAL REACTION PERSPECTIVE:
Labeling and the Social Construction of Deviance

Deviance, like beauty, is in the eyes of the beholder. There is nothing inherently deviant in any human act, something is deviant only because some people have been successful in labelling it so.

J. L. Simmons[1]

INTRODUCTION

Deviance does not exist independently of the negative reaction of people who condemn it. Behaviors are never weird, bad, sick, or deviant in themselves. They are deviant only because someone or some group responds to them in this fashion. This is the essence of the societal reaction perspective. In the words of reaction theorist Howard S. Becker, "Deviance is not a quality of the act the person commits, but rather a consequence of the application of rules and sanctions to an 'offender.' The deviant is one to whom the label has successfully been applied; deviant behavior is behavior that people so label."[2]

Throughout the course of my graduate studies in sociology I was becoming familiar with the major theoretical concerns of the societal reaction perspective. It made great sense to me that the study of social deviance should include an analysis of the processes by which certain types of behavior become viewed as unacceptable and by which certain types of people are made subject to corrective or rehabilitative machinery of social control. During the oral portion of my Ph.D. examination I was challenged to defend this perspective. One of my examiners asked whether the theoretical claims of the societal reaction viewpoint were not somewhat exaggerated. I was asked about the existence of certain types of behavior which were naturally deviant in any society. What about homicide? Isn't homicide deviant regardless of how anybody reacts to it? My answer was no.

Homicide is a way of categorizing the act of killing, such that taking another's life is viewed as totally reprehensible and devoid of any redeeming social justification. Some types of killing are categorized as homicide. Others are not. What differs is not the behavior but the manner in which reactions to that behavior are socially organized. The behavior is essentially the same: killing a police officer or killing by a police officer; stabbing an old lady in the back or stabbing the unsuspecting wartime enemy; a black slave shooting a white master or a white master lynching a black slave; being run over by a drunken driver or slowly dying of a painful cancer caused by a polluting factor. Each is a type of killing. Some are labeled homicide. Others are excused, justified, or viewed, as in the case of dangerous industrial pollution, as environmental risks, necessary for the health of our economy if not our bodies. The form and content of what is seen as homicide thus varies with social context and circumstance. This is hardly the characteristic of something which can be considered to be naturally or universally deviant.

"Well," continued the examining professor, "what about hyperkinesis? Certainly the problems caused by hyperkinetic children cause a universal disturbance in any culture." Again I disagreed. I suggested that the professor's perspective was colored by the way that our society views unruly and hyperactive children. I asked that he consider how similar behaviors are interpreted by the inhabitants of several South Sea island communities. There, behaviors which we associate with hyperkinesis are revered with a halo of religious sanctity. As the examiner paused to consider my answer for an infinitely long second, I felt the panic of skating on the thin ice of a potentially deviant intellectual response. I awaited the examining committee's reaction. To my relief, a second examiner, an anthropologist who had studied island communities, agreed with my interpretation. He cited other examples of things which we may consider naturally deviant but which peoples in other places or other times would not.

"All right," replied the original examiner, "Is there anything that is universal about deviance?" I answered that what is universal is not a matter of content or substance but of process—the process by which definitions of acts and persons as deviant are socially generated and applied. A concern with the dynamics of this process differentiates the societal reaction perspective from other theoretical vantage points on deviance. This point is made by John Kituse, who states that "the distinctive character of the societal reaction perspective . . . leads . . . to a consideration of how deviants come to be differentiated by imputations made about them by others, how these imputations activate systems of social control, and how these control activities become legitimated as institution responses to deviance."[3]

THEORETICAL IMAGES

The theoretical study of societal reactions to deviance has been carried out under different names—labeling theory, the interactionist perspective, and the social constructionist perspective. In general, societal reaction theorists

have pursued three interrelated concerns: (1) the social-historical development of deviant labels, (2) the application of labels to certain types of people
in specific times and places, and (3) the symbolic and practical consequences
of the labeling process.

Although it was not until the 1960s that the societal reaction perspective
emerged as a major theoretical tradition, its intellectual origins may be traced
to a 1918 essay by social philosopher George Herbert Mead. In "The Psychology of Punitive Justice," Mead likened the majesty of criminal labeling to
"that of the angel with the fiery sword at the gate who can cut one off from
the world to which he belongs."[4] The labeling process, in other words, sets
boundaries between those who are acceptable and those who are condemned, between insiders and outsiders, between conventional people and
deviants. Mead's essay points to the positive contributions of labeling in
awakening the consciences of law-abiding citizens and in strengthening the
cohesiveness of society as a whole. In this sense, Mead's ideas resemble those
of the functionalist theorists discussed in Chapter 6. Yet, unlike the functionalists, Mead was less concerned with the systemic consequences of deviance than with the interactional ritual through which labels were applied. In
1938 Frank Tannenbaum used the term *tagging* to describe a similar process.[5]
According to Tannenbaum, the stigma accompanying the deviant label may
drive people deeply into the realm of nonconformity.

The Emergence of the Societal Reaction Perspective during the 1960s

The early ideas of Mead and Tannenbaum were elaborated by Edwin Lemert
in his 1951 book *Social Pathology*.[6] Lemert's book took issue with the way that
deviance was defined by theorists working within the pathological, disorganizational, functionalist, anomie, and learning traditions. These perspectives took the existence of deviance for granted. For Lemert this was a
mistake. The other perspectives failed to consider how something or some
people came to be defined as deviant in the first place. So also did they fail to
examine the impact of labeling on persons processed as deviants. Rather than
accepting conventional definitions of deviance, Lemert argued that deviance
should be seen as "behavior which is effectively disapproved of in social
interaction."[7] The social dynamics and consequences of such disapproval
were presented as important topics for sociological investigation.

Lemert's ideas waited a full decade before blossoming into a major new
sociological perspective. During the early 1960s this perspective "took off" in
the writings of Howard S. Becker, John Kituse, Erving Goffman, Kai Erikson,
and others. In the fall of 1962 a series of articles using the societal reaction
framework first appeared in a special issue of the journal *Social Problems*. A
year later many of the same papers were reissued in the pages of *The Other
Side*, a book edited by Howard Becker. The importance of Becker's contribu-

tion cannot be overstated. As Don Gibbons points out, while "Lemert's book was a dozen years ahead of its time . . . Becker's volume quickly became one of the critical works to which many others paid homage."[8]

What was it about the early 1960s that made sociologists in the United States particularly ripe for the societal reaction viewpoint? The answer to this question involves some reference to the massive social and political struggles which rocked college campuses nationwide. During the late 1950s and early 1960s, college students (and even some of their professors) had begun to join with African-American civil rights advocates and later with anti-Vietnam War activists in demanding a more humane and just social order. This brought the label of deviance closer to home. Sociologists soon found their students, children, friends, spouses, and even themselves being tear-gassed, arrested, spied upon, stigmatized, and bullied like "common deviants." The target of social control had shifted from burglars and dope addicts to political activists and disenchanted young people.

Riots in the ghettos of urban America. Imprisonment for young men who refused to participate in what they believed was an unjust war. Criminal status for people who preferred to use marijuana rather than alcohol. These things contributed not only to the development of a youthful counterculture and the rise of political militancy, but also to a new viewpoint on social deviance. Understanding deviance meant first understanding why people react against certain forms of behavior. It required that one study the activities of social control agents as well as the behavior of labeled deviants.

When the police broke into the Chicago apartment of members of the Black Panther party and opened fire on its residents, violent death was referred to as "justifiable homicide." When an angry black youth returned fire, it was murder. When a skilled politician talked of an ever-present Communist conspiracy, he was considered realistic. Political activists who alleged that their phones were being tapped were labeled paranoid. Men who drove their tailor-suited bodies into heart attacks, ulcers, and high blood pressure were viewed as dedicated. Women who wanted equal pay for equal work were pictured as psychological misfits. Awareness of such contradictions led reaction theorists to question the relationship between the labelers and those who are labeled as deviant.

With the societal reaction perspective came what Howard Becker referred to as an "unconventional sentimentality." Becker noted the tendency of reaction theorists to "fall into deep sympathy with the people we are studying, so that while the rest of society views them as unfit . . ., we believe that they are at least as good as anyone else, more sinned against than sinning."[9] By challenging conventional stereotypes about deviance and laying the blame for much of the deviance problem upon the doorstep of respectable control agents, societal reaction theorists participated in the growing mood of rebellion and social critique which was gathering momentum during the early 1960s. According to Nanette Davis, this liberal response resembled that of an earlier generation of social turmoil. "Like some intellectuals in the 1930s who identified with the oppressed working class, labelers took on the deviant's plight as their own."[10] A similar point is made by Edwin Lemert, who traces the development of the societal reaction perspective to a growing awareness of the "powerlessness of individuals" before the ever-widening control machinery of the "welfare state," the "administrative state," the "garrison state," and the "military industrial combine."[11]

Spatial Influences on the Societal Reaction Viewpoint

The societal reaction perspective was a product not only of the times but also of particular places. Two places were of importance: the University of Chicago and the west coast. "The vast majority of the [early] labelling proponents received their graduate training" in the sociology department of the University of Chicago.[12] There they were exposed to the so-called Chicago school of symbolic interaction, a sociological theory stressing the importance of the real or imagined reactions of others upon how we act and how we conceive of ourselves. This perspective would play a critical role in early formulations of reaction perspective.

At Chicago societal reaction theorists were also trained in the methods of participatory field research. Under the guidance of Everett Hughes they came in direct contact with deviants and control agents. As a result, their research was not mediated by the official viewpoint of government statistics. Through contact with those whom they studied they achieved a certain empathy and often sympathy for people who otherwise might have remained little more than numbers on a long sheet of anonymously coded computerized data. Such field work was often accompanied by an interest in liberal social reform. According to Everett Hughes, it was undertaken by people "who believed that social facts well presented would point the way to reform."[13] During the 1960s, such field work also nurtured what Alvin Gouldner once referred to as the "hip style" of early reaction theorists and their attraction to the deviant underlife of American cities. According to Gouldner, "This group of Chicagoans finds itself at home in the world of the hip [and] prefers the off beat to the familiar, the vivid ethnographic detail to the dull taxonomy, the seriously expressive to dry analysis, naturalistic observation to formal questionnaires."[14]

The other place which proved particularly fertile for societal reaction theorizing was the U.S. west coast. In California, a host of Chicago-trained sociologists of deviance found academic jobs. For this reason early reaction theorists were for a time referred to both as "neo-Chicagoans" and as the "west coast school." These designations served to contrast their studies of deviance with the etiological, or causal, research of the so-called eastern establishment. According to Edwin Lemert, "The western-looking deviance sociologists . . . focused their work on the consequences of the moral order and social control, seeking to show how categories of deviance are invoked and applied to individuals and groups."[15]

What was it about California universities which encouraged the development of the societal reaction viewpoint? Of foremost importance was the fact that during the early 1960s the California university and state college system was rapidly expanding. In response to major increases in population, resulting from westward migration and the postwar baby boom, California's colleges hired many new faculty members. This provided room for new young scholars with fresh ideas. Also important was the fact that higher education in California was by and large public education. It was cheap and attracted an array of students from far more widely varying backgrounds than those accepted within the costly gates of elite eastern universities. This meant that California professors would more quickly be confronted with students of varied class and color, students whose concerns would not easily be addressed by more traditional theoretical and research frameworks. Also important was the failure of conservative functionalist theorizing to dominate west coast sociology. The dominance of functionalism in eastern sociology was discussed in Chapter 6. Suffice it to say that the zenith of functionalism was passing just as California sociology was expanding during the early 1960s. This permitted a plurality of new ways of envisioning the social world to rise up more quickly in the west than in the east.

Another factor contributing to the rise of reaction theorizing in the west was the political turmoil which beset California campuses throughout the 1960s. Just as expansion opened the gates of the university to new and sometimes radical viewpoints, the state government was being captured by conservatives led by a former movie star and spokesperson for the General Electric Company. When Ronald Reagan assumed the governorship in Sacramento he immediately set about fulfilling one of his most important campaign promises—to stem the spread of unorthodox and radical thinking at state universities. Assisted by a notoriously conservative board of regents Reagan delivered on many of his promises. California campuses soon became hotbeds of conflict and controversy. Students claimed that they were denied the rights to think, speak, and act freely. Professors charged that a "correct" political viewpoint had subtly become a criterion for tenure. New conservative policies of academic social control had come to campuses, and with them a new breed of deviants. Teachers and students were targeted for public labeling and harsh sanctions. Thus, for many sociologists on the west coast the societal reaction perspective was born as much out of personal as out of intellectual concern. As social unrest spread nationwide, so did this new perspective.

Theoretical Foundations of the Societal Reaction Perspective: The Influence of Interpretive Sociology

Societal reaction theorists work within the interpretive sociological tradition. Following the lead of the classical German sociologist Max Weber, interpretive sociology emphasizes the importance of *subjective meaning* in the social organization of everyday life.[16] Three variants of interpretive sociology were particularly influential: symbolic interactionism, phenomenological sociology, and ethnomethodology.

Symbolic Interactionism   This perspective traces its origins to the writings of University of Chicago philosopher George Herbert Mead. Mead's work emphasized the interpretive adjustment of humans to the real or imagined reactions of others. The phrase *symbolic interaction* was coined by Mead's student, Herbert Blumer. According to Blumer, "The term 'symbolic interaction' refers to the fact that human beings interpret or 'define' each other's actions instead of merely reacting to each other's actions."[17]

For symbolic interactionists society is processual—a dynamic alignment of people, each acting in relation to how she or he interprets the actions of others. Interactionists also view the self in processual terms. The self is described as a "moving communication process," a dynamic series of "self-indications" by which people interpretively take the viewpoint of others toward themselves. Of particular influence is the viewpoint of significant others, people whose importance contributes greatly to the way we define ourselves and decide upon appropriate lines of action.

The definitional and processual emphasis of symbolic interactionism permeates the societal reaction perspective. Their influence is particularly evident in the way in which reaction theorists conceive of such matters as *labeling*, the *sequential model of deviance*, *master status*, *secondary deviance*, and *stigma*.

Labeling: Interactional and Historical Concerns   Labeling refers to "the process by which deviants are defined by the rest of society."[18] Reaction theorists such as Howard Becker contend that we cannot assume a given act to be deviant "simply because it is commonly regarded as so. Instead, we look to the process by which the common definition arises . . . the process of labeling."[19]

Becker's concerns with the labeling process are pitched at two levels: (1) the concrete interaction between the labelers and potential targets for labeling and (2) the historical construction of labels themselves. The first level concerns what goes on between control agents and others such that deviant labels are applied, withheld, or avoided. Becker's work questions the adequacy of official definitions of deviance. Some people act in a manner which is defined as deviant; they get caught and are labeled. Others may not act in such a fashion but are falsely labeled anyway. Still others may do it and get away with it unlabeled. Becker refers to such persons as "secret deviants." These several types of interactional possibilities are displayed in Table 9-1.

The labeling process may be either formal or informal. In formal terms, imagine a police officer late at night on a darkened street. She has just received word that a burglar is nearby. She turns the corner and sees a figure in an alley. Will she apprehend the person? Will a formal deviant label be applied? Think of all the social contingencies which might affect the officer's

TABLE 9-1
TYPES OF DEVIANT BEHAVIOR

	Obedient behavior	Rule-breaking behavior
Perceived as deviant	Falsely accused	Pure deviant
Not perceived as deviant	Conforming	Secret deviant

Source: Adapted from Howard S. Becker, *Outsiders: Studies in the Sociology of Deviance,* Free Press, New York, 1963, p. 20.

actions: the person's gender, size, color, age, mode of dress, way of walking, manner of speech. Also of importance might be pressures from the department to make more arrests, the presence of witnesses, or the kind of neighborhood and whether the suspect is perceived as the type of person who would normally be found in such a place. The interaction of all these factors is important to an analysis of the formal labeling process.

Similar factors are applicable to informal labeling. This is illustrated in an early societal reaction study in which John Kituse examined how college students label others as homosexual.[20] Kituse discovered that imputations of homosexuality reveal as much about informal labelers as about the people being labeled. People who acted similarly were reacted to differently by different labelers under different circumstances. Labeling occurred, in other words, independently of the actual speech, interests, dating patterns, or sexual relations of those categorized as homosexual.

But why has something like homosexuality acquired the label of deviance in the first place? Where in history do deviant labels come from? This is the second set of questions raised by Becker. In *The Other Side* he suggests that deviant labels arise as the result of the efforts of powerful "moral entrepreneurs." Moral entrepreneurs are persons or groups who lobby for the deviantization of certain types of behavior. One classic study of moral entrepreneurship is Becker's analysis of the origins of the Marijuana Stamp Tax Act of 1937, legislation which made it a criminal offense to smoke pot. The specific details of Becker's study are discussed later. At present it is enough to note that a concern with the historical development of deviant categories is an important aspect of the societal reaction perspective.

A Sequential Model of Deviance Deviance unfolds in time. The factors which influence its development do not all operate at the same time. Some factors may be more important in encouraging a person to experiment with nonconformity. Others are more influential in sustaining existing patterns of rule breaking. For these reasons Becker proposes a sequential model of deviance—"a model which takes into account the fact that patterns of behavior develop in orderly sequence."[21] Becker illustrates the importance of such a sequential model by pointing to the progressive stages involved in becoming a deviant drug user. Factors which may be significantly associated with drug use may affect some persons and not others. Why? The answer lies in the fact that unaffected persons may not (yet) have reached a stage in the development of deviance where such factors really count. According to Becker, variables such as personal alienation "will only produce drug use in people who are in a position to experiment because they participate in groups in which drugs are available; alienated people who do not have drugs available to them cannot begin experimentation and they cannot become users, no matter how alienated they are."[22]

Becker employs the metaphor of career development to explicate progressive stages in deviant involvement. Other societal reaction theorists, such as J. L. Simmons, analyze the sequential unfolding of deviance in terms of such phrases as (1) initial recruitment, (2) role imprisonment, and (3) entrance into sustaining deviant subcultures.[23] At each stage in the process potential deviants face a wide range of pushes and pulls, and choose (although not freely) to continue or discontinue their advance into nonconformity. According to John Lofland, such choices are influenced by a variety of situational factors (such as whom one associates with; one's immediate sociogeographical environment; the availability of the "hardware," or physical props, necessary for certain forms of deviant action; and individual capacities, such as self-esteem, technical skill, and self-concept), and by the more generic cultural and social-institution setting in which one is located.[24]

Sequential "career contingencies" include both objective facts of social structure and changes in the perspective, motivations, and desires of the individual.[25] Of particular importance are the reactions of others to deviant labeling. Other people may come to think and act toward the labeled deviant in a manner different from before. The life chances of a deviant may thus be drastically altered. He or she may be locked up, denied employment, or forced to hide. All this may lead to a new identity organized around the awareness of one's status as an outsider.

Even if one is not caught, the fear of being discovered might significantly change a person's life. Rule breakers must constantly be on their guard: classifying others as potential threats, controlling the kinds of communications they have about their activities, hiding traces of the deviant act.[26] Think of the teenager who smokes marijuana behind his or her parents' backs. Such people must be cautious about whom they associate with and what they say about what they were doing or whom they were with last night. In hiding the physical traces of their deviant act, they may go so far as to light incense, to use an eyewash to remove redness, or even to splash alcoholic beverages on their faces in order to provide a more acceptable excuse for being high. In any event the threat of being labeled is an important variable in the sequential development of deviance.

Deviance as a Master Status Almost everybody occupies multiple social positions or statuses. Such things as age, gender, occupation, race or ethnicity, educational background, religious preference, class, political affiliation, and even physical appearance tell us about who people are and how we can expect them to act. Some statuses may be more central than others. Race is a good example. Somebody may be tall, wealthy, personable, a Harvard graduate, married, the parent of three children, a successful lawyer, and also black. Yet, in a racially stratified society such as the United States, one status may stand out above all others—being black: "I met a black lawyer at the party." According to Everett Hughes, a status like race may operate as a *master status,* one which overshadows all others.[27]

Deviance may also operate as a master status. According to Hughes's student Howard Becker, "Possession of one deviant trait may have a generalized symbolic value, so that people automatically assume that its bearer possesses other undesirable traits allegedly associated with it."[28] Being gay has virtually nothing to do with being a banker. Nonetheless, as long as homosexuality continues to be labeled as deviant, it is likely that it, like race, will function as a master status: "I met a gay banker at the party." When deviance operates as a master status, labeled deviants may encounter severe interactional troubles in dealing with other people. They may even identify with the primacy of the deviant label in defining themselves. This can be troublesome.

Secondary Deviance   People may initially deviate for any number of reasons—biological, psychological, or sociological. Nonetheless, once one is caught and labeled, the reaction to deviance may itself cause further deviance. Labeling may amplify deviance. This point is made by Edwin Lemert, who differentiates between primary and secondary deviation. The former may be caused by anything; the latter by an individual's reactions to others' reactions. According to Lemert, "When a person begins to employ his deviant behavior or a role based upon it as a means of defense, attack, or adjustment to the overt and covert problems created by the consequent societal reaction to him, his deviation is secondary."[29]

Stigma   The writings of Erving Goffman liken social interaction to the performance of theatrical roles.[30] Like actors on a stage, people are said to carefully manage social cues which enable them to create and sustain an impression of who they are and what they are up to. Some people, however, are cast into roles which constrain their abilities to manage positive impressions of themselves. Such persons are stigmatized, the bearers of what Goffman describes as a "spoiled identity."[31]

Goffman parallels the stigmatized problems of labeled deviants to the plight of physically or mentally handicapped persons. He extends the scope of the societal reaction perspective to people who are negatively labeled for how they appear in addition to how they may act. The threat of stigmatization does not, however, eliminate a person's capacity for impression management. Stigmatized persons who are "wise" to their precarious social conditions may restrict themselves to the company of other stigmatized persons or to those sympathetic to their condition. In this way they restrict the flow of information about themselves to others whom they can trust. Whether or not they are successful in managing stigma, labeled deviants are confronted with social problems not faced by the straight world. This underscores a central theme of the societal reaction perspective—that a full sociological understanding of deviance requires attention to the interactive dynamics between people who condemn nonconformity and people who are condemned.

Phenomenological Sociology   Phenomenological sociology is the study of society as it appears within the consciousness of its members. Phenomenological sociologists suspend judgment about the objective reality of social life in order to describe social reality as it is constructed in the minds of those who experience it.[32] Many phenomenological sociologists trace their concerns to the writings of Alfred Schutz.[33] Schutz depicted the experience of everyday life as filtered through a set of categorical definitions or typifications about what the world is and how one should act within it. This stock of typical meanings and recipes for action provides people with a common sense about the nature of social reality, with a sense that the everyday social world can be taken for granted, that it exists independently of one's immediate experience of it, and that, for all practical purposes, others experience it in similar fashion.

Schutz's work provides a description of the structure of the everyday-life world as it is typically experienced by those who live within it. Where does this structure come from? How do we commonsensically come to know that a "real man" should act in a certain fashion, while a "real woman" should not? How do we know what is normal? How do we know what is deviant? One answer is presented by Schutz's students Peter Berger and Thomas Luckmann in their book *The Social Construction of Reality*.[34] Berger and Luckmann contend that, unlike other species of animals, we humans are not instinctually provided with a fixed and stable sense of social order. We must rely, instead, on our ability to use language to symbolically create an artificial world order. Once this occurs, the names we affix to things begin to take on a life of their own. We are trapped in the reality of our own words. We become prisoners of the symbols we create. We are in a position not unlike that of Victor Frankenstein in Mary Shelley's terrifying novel. The creature has come to rule the creator.

The process whereby humanly created symbols are experientially transformed into externally given social realities is described by Berger and Luckmann as *objectification*. Through socialization the reality of these symbols is brought within. They come to rule not by external force but by the internal constraints of conscience. They come to be experienced as natural realities. Forgotten is the fact these symbols were once nothing but an arbitrary way of naming something, derivatives of prior symbolic *externalization*. As institutionalized versions of social reality they operate as controls over what we experience as real. To deny their reality is to defy common sense and run the risk of being labeled deviant.

Ethnomethodology   Ethnomethodology extends the phenomenological perspective to the study of everyday social interaction. It is concerned with the methods which people use to accomplish a reasonable account of what is happening in social interaction and to provide a structure for the interaction itself. Unlike symbolic interactionists, ethnomethodologists do not assume that people actually share common symbolic meanings.[35] What they share is a ceaseless body of interpretive work which enables them to convince themselves and others that they share common meanings. Ethnomethodologists also differ from phenomenological sociologists who emphasize the manner in which people are socialized into a particular version of reality. For ethnomethodologists, social reality is far more fragile. It is organized, not by an internalized stock of meanings, but by the moment-to-moment creation and re-creation of the social world in interaction with others.[36]

More important are the differences between ethnomethodology and theoretical perspectives which assume the independent existence of social structure. For ethnomethodologists, social structure is never independent of the consciousness of the actors who experience its force. The sense that social life is governed by a predefined structure of meanings, roles, and rules is just that—a sense, a common sense. This makes social structure no less important. It simply relocates it within, rather than outside, the world of human thinking and doing, talking and acting, working and playing. Social structure, in other words, is viewed as a practical accomplishment rather than a determinant of our daily social existence. From the ethnomethodological vantage point, the structures of everyday life experience are never fully independent of the interpretive work which people do in order to make sense of a particular moment or place in social life. For this reason ethnomethodologists attend to the small, detailed, practical features of interpretive social interactions as keys to deeper mysteries of social structure and life in general.

Given its concern with the processes by which people construct believable, acceptable, or defendable accounts of what social life "really" is, it is not surprising that ethnomethodology has paid particular attention to the problems of deviance and social control. By categorizing certain behaviors as deviant we dramatize the recognizably "real" boundaries of social life itself. By interpretively "recognizing" that certain people are outside the accepted rules of society we pay homage to the reality of these rules and the social structure assumed to be behind them. Ethnomethodology addresses these matters by focusing on the practical interpretive work of people in constructing imputations about what is deviant and what is normal. Its theoretical contribution to the societal reaction perspective can best be understood by examining what are considered to be the three interrelated features of all practical interpretive work: indexicality, reflexivity, documentary interpretation.

Indexicality The term *indexicality* refers to the fact that all human interpretive work is bound to the context in which it occurs. The "reality" of deviance will be conceived very differently, depending on whether it is viewed from a police patrol car or from the backseat of a vehicle full of partying teenagers. The importance of indexicality to the labeling of deviance is suggested by David Sudnow's study of public defenders.[37] Sudnow describes an overcrowded court context in which public attorneys are pressured toward using commonsense stereotypes about who is and who isn't the "normal" criminal and who should be provided with a certain type of defense or plea bargaining. The stereotypical identification of "normal crimes" is linked to the practical demands of an overworked and understaffed public defender's office. Such contextual or indexical demands significantly influence the shape of societal reactions. Their importance is also observed in other ethnomethodological studies, including Aaron Cicourel's examination of juvenile justice decision making,[38] Richard McCleary's consideration of career contingencies affecting parole officers' production of "bad records for good reasons,"[39] and Arlene Kaplan Daniels's research into the use of psychiatry in the military.[40]

Reflexivity   Ethnomethodologists use the term *reflexivity* to express that paradoxical characteristic of human existence whereby objects exist only in relation to the interpretive meaning they have for the people who behold them. In other words, for all practical purposes, who you are is never independent of the way in which I construct and express my understanding of you. The key phrase here is "for all practical purposes." For some abstract philosophical purposes I may speculate about such things as your universal metaphysical essence. Ethnomethodologists care little about such abstract speculations. They are concerned with the mundane, practical ways in which people arrive at knowledge about things of this world. In this very practical sense, what I know about you as an object is always shaped by how I, as a subject, reflexively envision you. There is no pure objectivity, nor, for that matter, is there any pure subjectivity. Everything is impure. Everything is contaminated by everything else. Everything is in relationship to everything else. By the principle of indexicality I understand my interpretations of you to be bound by the social and material context in which we are related. Thus my grasp of you is never purely subjective. Yet, since I must make interpretive use of our context to arrive at a certain knowledge of you, it is also impossible for my knowledge to be purely objective. It is always the product of my own context-bound interpretive work. This I understand by the principle of reflexivity.

Reflexivity and indexicality are interrelated phenomena. Each conditions the other. What is reflexively constructed in one moment becomes indexically part of the context of my experience in the next. They are as altering moments in the hour that is life. The bright interpretive activities of reflexivity fold into the dark shadows of indexicality just as the day folds into dark, just as the experience of creating a world folds into the experience of being created by a world that is fixed and prestructured. Ethnomethodologists Hugh Mehan and Houston Wood liken the difference between reflexivity and indexicality to that between dawn and dusk.[41] At dawn I awaken; my eyes (reflexively) put all things in their place. At dusk I doze; my eyes (indexically) put things into context as things among other things, each in its place.

What does all of this talk about indexicality and reflexivity have to do with the labeling of deviants? The answer is plenty. The principles of indexicality and reflexivity constitute the interpretive core of the labeling process. They are present at each step of the labeling process, yet often pass unnoticed by most participants. The unnoticeable character of interpretive work is particularly evident in the production of deviant labels. The end product of successful imputational work is paradoxically to forget (or at least be inattentive to) the fact that such interpretive work was even involved. This reflexive disguising of the created character of deviance is observed by Melvin Pollner, who notes that "while a community creates deviance, it may simultaneously mask its creative work from itself."[42]

A good example of the unnoticed character of reflexive interpretive work is Lawrence Weider's study of the inmate code of the halfway house.[43] This code operates not as an abstract set of rules but as an interactionally generated solution to specific instances of tension. It permits inmates to call one another into question. The code is invoked to order a disorderly situation. According to Weider this code is reflexively invoked only when strategically useful. This is rarely noticed. The reflexive use of rules to give a sense of structure to life in the halfway house fades into its indexical shadows as soon as its work is complete.

The paradoxical character of unnoticed interpretive work is further illustrated in Harold Garfinkel's study of jury decision making.[44] Garfinkel notes that jurors commonly provide retrospective justifications for decisions which they have already made. They look backward in producing a quasi-legal rereading of the available evidence after having already decided upon a person's guilt or innocence. Once this is done jurors appear oblivious to the fact that they have engaged in such retrospective interpretation. They reorder their understandings so as to suggest that "fair deliberations" were guided by the same sound logic from the beginning—logic which was, in fact, after the fact. A similar hiding of the reflexive nature of the labeling process is shown in Sacks's analysis of the reality of suicide threats discovered during hot-line crisis conversations[45] and in Douglas's examination of official descriptions of suicide as cause of death.[46]

Documentary Interpretation Harold Garfinkel, the central figure in the development of ethnomethodology, uses the term *documentary interpretation* to refer to the way in which people infer meaningful action patterns from the appearance of simple behavioral stimuli. Appearances are treated as documents of something deeper, as expressions of underlying patterns or structures. According to Garfinkel, "Not only is the underlying pattern derived from its individual documentary evidences, but the individual documentary evidences, in their turn, are interpreted on the basis of 'what is known' about the underlying pattern. Each is used to elaborate the other."[47]

The method of documentary interpretation is used by people to make sense of other people. By documentary interpretation we know that the politician who shakes our hand outside the supermarket is doing what is expected and not exercising a hand fetish. But would we think the same of someone who was not a politician? Probably not. We see the politician as acting normally because we pair the appearance of handshaking with patterned expectations we have come to associate with the person's position (e.g., what you're supposed to do if you're a politician). We take for granted that appearances represent something deeper, that they tell us about who the person is and why the person is doing what he or she is doing. How shocked I would be if I discovered that the little man in the cafeteria with the mush-room-shaped white cap and the apron was stirring mud rather than vegeta-bles into my soup. Why? Because by his appearance I had documentarily interpreted him as a cook. Now I know him as a jokester or as a deviant in need of control.

The study of documentary interpretive practices has contributed much to the theoretical scope of the societal reaction perspective. Examples include Egon Bittner's description of the interpretive work employed by police offi-cers in documenting the presence of "real" troublemakers,[48] Robert Emer-son's analysis of how juvenile court personnel use a few pieces of surface information to construct elaborate biographical profiles of troublesome youths,[49] and Jacqueline Wiseman's consideration of the way control agents size up persons charged with public drunkenness.[50] Wiseman describes the manner in which such things as physical appearance, past performance, and social position are taken as indicators of the kind of person a particular offender is and how his or her case should be handled.

In each of the studies described above, the interpretive work of social control agents reduces complex and often contradictory social, political, and economic realities into a neatly packaged stereotype of the offender as a deviant individual. Similar findings were reported in my own ethno-methodological analysis of the way in which psychiatric professionals arrived at judgments regarding the potential dangerousness of patients confined within a hospital for the criminally insane.[51] Of particular importance was the way in which clinicians used past records to construct a theoretical view of a patient's problems in the present, the manner in which the conversational structure of clinical interviews was selectively managed in keeping with what diagnosticians already knew about their clients, and the influence of such things as the anticipation of the legal consequences of a particular diagnosis in shaping the form and substance of what was clinically said about patients. Also important was the omnipresent influence of power struggles between members of a diagnostic team and the strategies for diagnosticians to come off as a certain kind of expert professional, a "tough-minded shrink," a "human-itarian reformer," a "good guy," or whatever. Although none of these things were elements pertinent to the case of a patient being diagnosed, each contributed significantly to the interpretive imputation of a deviant label.

Societal Reactions and Power: A Note on Driving Force

Whether working within the theoretical traditions of symbolic interactionism, phenomenological sociology, or ethnomethodology, one concern remains constant for students of the societal reaction perspective—a concern with power as a driving force behind the labeling process. Differences in power translate into differences in the ability to label. In the words of Howard Becker, "The groups whose social position gives them weapons and power are best able to enforce their rules. Distinctions of age, sex, ethnicity, and class are all related to differences in power, which account for differences in the degree to which groups, so distinguished, can make rules for others."[52]

Although a concern with power is a central feature of the societal reaction perspective, this concern has sometimes been more implicit than explicit. For a time, many students of societal reaction were distracted from issues of power by a preoccupation with the interpretive microdynamics of the labeling process.[53] Some, however, were never so distracted. One example is John Lofland, who defines deviance as a "conflict game in which individuals or loosely organized small groups with little power are strongly feared by a well-organized, sizable minority or majority who have a large amount of power."[54] Another is Edwin M. Schur, whose book *The Politics of Deviance* is subtitled *Stigma Contests and the Uses of Power*.[55] Similar ideas are presented by Erich Goode, who likens labeling to a form of "linguistic armament,"[56] and by Peter Conrad and Joseph Schneider, who contend that the proper designation of deviance is "a political question . . . decided frequently through political contact."[57] With this in mind let us consider the manner in which reaction theorists study the problem of deviance.

IDENTIFYING SOCIETAL REACTION DEVIANCE

The societal reaction perspective has contributed significantly to the methods of deviance research. Its influence is particularly evident regarding (1) the critique of official statistics, (2) the definition of what should be considered deviant, and (3) the reflexive nature of the research process.

The Critique of Official Statistics

Much research on deviance involves an uncritical acceptance of official statistics on rule breakers and what they do. The societal reaction perspective questions the validity of research which relies exclusively on such official data. It suggests that the social production of official statistics may tell us more about the organizational concerns of control agencies than about the actions of deviants.[58] According to Edwin Schur, this means "that official statistics should be considered an object of investigation to be explained in their own right. Our primary interest should not be in what they might tell us about the causation of deviance, but rather in exploring the causation of the rates themselves."[59]

The societal reaction perspective encourages us to study the social construction of official statistics. Many students of societal reaction have done just that. The results of their research suggest that official accounts of deviance are influenced by such things as the perceptual biases of control agents, the situational dynamics of the labeling process, the differential visibility of potential deviant populations, the organizational characteristics of control bureaucracies, and the politicality of official data.

Perceptual Bias of Control Agents   The production and perpetuation of stereotypical perceptions of race, ethnicity, gender, social class, age, religion, and even physical appearance influence one's chances of being caught and officially labeled as a deviant. The influence of stereotypical perceptions is noted in such research as Aaron Cicourel's *The Social Organization of Juvenile Justice*. Cicourel spent two years as a participant-observer in police and proba-tion agencies in two cities. His detailed description of the manner in which control agents employ stereotypical notions of who is deviant unmasks the myth of objectivity surrounding official statistics. Boys whose deviant behav-ior may be relatively harmless, but whose social characteristics are stereo-typically associated with serious criminality, are often labeled more harshly than youths whose acts are more harmful, but whose social backgrounds are more respectable. The case of Smithfield is a good example. Smithfield was a young black male from a socioeconomic environment alien to that of the white middle-class control agents who sought to help him. According to Cicourel, "It is difficult for white, middle-income teachers, probation officers, policemen, therapists, students, and the like, to view . . . Smithfield in clini-cal terms, and make clinical imputations about the cause of his 'deviant' behavior, because [his] appearance . . . is itself a frightening experience for all of them."[60] Similar observations are made by Arnold S. Linsky, William Rushing, and William Wilde, each of whom presents data suggesting class and social-attribute bias in the official diagnosis of mental illness.[61]

Other studies documenting the influence of stereotypical perceptions in the construction of official data on deviance include Chambliss and Na-gasawa's comparison between the official arrest rates of white, black, and Japanese-American youths in Seattle, Washington.[62] Chambliss and Na-gasawa conclude that ethnic stereotypes lead police to overestimate the crimi-nal involvement of blacks and underestimate the involvement of Japanese-Americans. With regard to shoplifting, Mary Cameron also discovered a significant difference between the treatment of blacks and nonblacks who were caught and subsequently charged with larceny.[63] Approximately 11 per-cent of nonblacks were charged, compared to 58 percent of those appre-hended who were black. Along similar lines Jack Douglas notes that factors such as religious background, the presence or absence of supportive social relations, and the social status of the deceased impact upon whether a coroner perceives a death as a suicide.[64] Such biases distort the public record regarding the true population of typical deviants.

Situational Dynamics of Labeling   Whether something is officially re-corded as deviance also depends upon the dynamics of the situation in which labeling occurs. Irving Piliavin and Scott Briar, for instance, underscore the importance of demeanor in determining whether juvenile suspects will be apprehended by police.[65] Of youths who displayed a posture of polite cooperation, only 2 of 45 were arrested. Of youths with a noncooperative demeanor, 14 of 21 were apprehended. Noncooperative youths were those whose body movements, dress, facial expressions, and manner of talking suggested to police that they were "punks." They acted nonchalantly, wore leather jackets and/or soiled jeans, and displayed little remorse. Regardless of the seriousness of their actual behaviors they were far more likely to be officially categorized as deviant.

In *The Police and the Public* Albert Reiss points to another situational contingency affecting the likelihood of official labeling—the presence of a citizen complainant who demands that an arrest be made.[66] Police typically defer to such demands. Moreover, black citizens made such demands more commonly than whites. Hence, official arrest statistics were systematically distorted by a situational factor independent of the behavior of those labeled. A related distortion is noted by Temerlin regarding psychiatric labeling.[67] Temerlin presented the same videotape of a patient to different groups of diagnosticians. What differed was how the case was clinically explained. Some diagnosticians were provided with clinically favorable information; others with the opposite. This apparently made all the difference. Presented with exactly the same tape, different groups literally saw very different things. Those with a positive preview noted positive attributes. Those with prior negative information saw negative symptoms everywhere. Such are the situational dynamics of labeling—dynamics which when converted into official statistics distort and confuse the nature and extent of the deviance problem.

Differential Visibility This is another limit to the accuracy of official statistics. Some populations of people are more visible than others to the watchful eyes of control agents. "This is particularly the case for persons on welfare, ADC mothers, and others whose lives, as part of the price of obtaining public assistance, are subject to sometimes microscopic scrutiny."[68] The relative visibility of lower-class persons is just one aspect of the problem. Alienation generated by differential surveillance may also limit what lower-class persons voluntarily report about deviance. Lower-class citizens, and particularly lower-class black citizens, are, for instance, less likely to make such reports.

At the upper end of the social ladder, people may be more protected from deviant labels. It is big news when the child of a wealthy family is arrested. Bigger news still are a variety of poorly controlled deviant behaviors which only the privileged have a chance to commit. Corporate and so-called white-collar crimes cannot be committed by just anyone. Offenders must be in positions of trust or power to deviate in such "high-brow" fashion. Such crimes are, moreover, among the least reported, prosecuted, and punished. Thus, public knowledge about the extent of said deviance is distorted by the relative invisibility of the crimes of the privileged.

Organizational Characteristics   Official statistics on deviance are produced by bureaucratic organizations. They are influenced by the way work is organized and by internal and external sources of pressure. Consider James Q. Wilson's analysis of the organizational styles of police work in two cities.[69] In Western City the police department was organized around a highly centralized and legalistic enforcement of the law. The laws were enforced in an impersonal and professional manner by officers who were more middle-class, more educated, and more likely to follow universal standards than their Eastern City counterparts. Eastern City police were more decentralized and personal in their work. Locals themselves, they knew people in the areas they patrolled and were organized more to contain trouble than to make arrests. The opposite was true in Western City. Pressured by bureaucratic demands for conformity, "some [Western City] officers felt that their 'productivity' was being measured—number of arrests made, citations written, field contact reports filed, and suspicious persons checked."[70] As a result, Western City officers were more likely to handle such matters as juvenile crime in a more formal fashion. In the more bureaucratically pressurized Western City, officers were more likely to check IDs and question juveniles. This resulted in higher rates of officially recorded deviance—not because there was more deviance but because there was greater organizational demand to record deviance.

Sometimes the pressure to officially record deviance is differentially distributed within the same control bureaucracy. Thus, the "peacekeeping" work of officers patrolling skid row varies greatly from the arrest-producing activities of the narcotics squad.[71] While the former try to prevent trouble without burdening the department with the arrest of unsavory drunks, the latter depend upon arrest records as a measure of organizational performance. The same is true for detectives. Under pressure to clear unsolved crimes, such officers are often willing to make the "big case" by accepting the confession of a suspect for many offenses which in all likelihood he or she never committed. In this way police clear their books and fend off organizational pressure. In exchange, the big-case confessor is promised an easy time with the charges that can be proved. This, of course, distorts the construction of official records. Yet, as Jerome Skolnick observes, "If clearances are valued, then criminality becomes a commodity for exchange. Thus it is possible that in some cases defendants who confess to large numbers of crimes will tend to be shown more leniency."[72]

The Politicality of Official Statistics   Official statistics are not produced in a politically neutral context. They are produced by agencies with a stake in showing that they are doing a good job. The officials of such agencies are ordinarily responsible to elected politicians who campaign with promises to fight deviance. This may affect the social production of crime rates. As Richard Quinney points out, "Crime rates are . . . used to justify or instigate a multitude of political (including social and economic) interests. High crime rates are used by the police to rationalize the need for more personnel and equipment. . . . The police have an interest in maintaining both a high and a low rate of crime."[73]

Political pressure to show both high and low rates of crime was particularly acute during the Nixon administration's "war on crime" in the late 1960s. This encouraged police to invent a new statistic—one showing that crime was increasing but at a decreasing rate. Law-enforcement officials could thus have it both ways: they could show that they were making good use of the resources they had (the rate decreased) and that they needed new resources (crimes were still going up). Sometimes the distortion of official crime rates was more deliberate.[74] As Charles McCaghy has noted, "Departments may encourage police to deliberately downgrade for record purposes the seriousness of some offenses. Aggravated assault becomes simple assault; robbery becomes larceny. By such manipulations, departments can prove to the public that they are 'doing something' about crime."[75]

Defining Deviance

A second methodological contribution of the societal reaction perspective concerns the issue of what is to be considered deviant. Students of deviance have long argued over this issue. Some contend that deviance should be limited to those acts which are legally prohibited. Others maintain that deviance should be equated with behaviors which are normatively prohibited. Still others wish to define deviance as things which ought to be prohibited, even if they are not. The societal reaction position is clear: Do not start with any preconceived definition. Rely, instead, on definitions used by real people in particular historical contexts. This follows from the reaction perspective's assumption that deviance never exists independently of the interpretive work of the control agents who see it. If this is true, then the way that everyday people define deviance should be the starting point for sociologically informed research.

This concern with how everyday people define deviance has prompted many societal reaction researchers to employ field methods to study the labeling process. Whether being a participant-observer in a mental hospital, riding in the back seat of a police car, or hanging out in a gay bar, the researchers who have produced many of the most notable studies of societal reaction have used naturalistic field strategies. Yet, regardless of methodological strategy, societal reaction researchers share a common investigative edict—*begin with the interpretive perspective of those being studied.*[76]

The Reflexive Nature of Societal Reaction Research

Societal reaction researchers, like anyone else, are bound to the social context in which their studies occur. In interpreting the interpretations of others, researchers must rely on the same interpretive practices as everyday people. How, then, can they claim objectivity for their analyses?

The answer is not found by retreating to the scientific haven of survey analysis or fixed-choice questionnaires. These methods may be useful, but they also depend upon interpretive inferences and context-bound judgments about what is or isn't a meaningful answer to a prepackaged question. In constructing surveys or questionnaires, researchers must rely on essentially the same interpretive practices as field researchers. The difference is simply that they do all their interpreting before coming in contact with the people they study. Unfortunately, this means that many respondents are unable to "get into" or hear questions in the same way as those who made them up. This is because respondents, when asked to choose an answer, are likely to be involved in an entirely different set of interpretive relevancies than researchers. Maybe their dog died or they won the lottery or were robbed. These things, which might be noted by the field researcher, will unfortunately be missed by those conducting a survey. The use of such allegedly objective research instruments may thus present as many interpretive problems as those raised in the course of field work. The societal reaction perspective's answer is twofold. It acknowledges that objectivity is partial, at best. The task of the disciplined researcher is to approximate objectivity while providing a detailed account of the "natural history" of the research—a description of the social context and context-bound interpretive decisions that are an inherent feature of the research process. Two things help researchers to approximate objectivity. The first involves attempts to partially replicate a particular study. No two research projects are ever identical. But what happens if we try to repeat a particular investigation in some other context? Do we find something similar? If not, why not? By approaching research in such a comparative fashion, we may better understand and thus transcend the social factors which limit objectivity. This helps us to become more objective.

A second strategy used by reaction theorists to maximize objectivity is to display the verbal or nonverbal actions of the individuals who are being studied. The use of verbatim audio or visual transcripts permits the audience to partially join the researcher in interpreting the scene being analyzed. It provides data by which others may reject, modify, or accept a particular interpretive account. The advantages of such procedures are summarized by Aaron Cicourel, who advocates the "examination of verbatim materials to show how the researcher makes sense of the subject's remarks, while also involving features of the action scenes or past scenes felt to be relevant to the subject and the observer in deciding what is happening."[77]

SOCIAL CONTROL OF SOCIETAL REACTIONS TO DEVIANCE

Many societal reaction studies document the differential nature of social control. Control agents often discriminate between individuals of varying race, sex, age, ethnicity, gender, and social class. Indeed, much of the societal reaction literature may be read as an "exposé" of inequalities of control as dished out by official state agents and others. Because of this, reaction theorists are generally supportive of reforms which limit the discretionary power of control agents and guarantee the basic civil rights of all accused deviants. Two other programs of reform are supported as well: decriminalizing victimless crimes and deploying "least restrictive" control options.

Decriminalization of Victimless Crimes

The term *victimless crime* refers to a wide range of consensual social exchanges punished by the criminal law: abortion, gambling, deviance, drug use, selling sex, choosing alternative sexual orientations.[78] Although the term is used extensively in the literature of the societal reaction perspective, *victimless* may not best define this category of deviance. Indeed, some people see victimization as resulting from each of these moral offenses. Others do not.

Consider the issue of abortion. Today there is widespread disagreement about whether abortion violates the rights of an unborn fetus or whether its prohibition violates the rights of a woman to control her own body. Is there a true victim in the choice of a woman who is unready, unable, or unwilling to assume the responsibilities of parenthood to terminate pregnancy after two months? What about after three months or five? The answer varies with the person you ask. Even if one believes that there is a violation of rights, is the criminalization of abortion the best way to control against its occurrence?

Similar ambiguity exists with regard to other "moral," or "public order," offenses. Gambling and illegal drug use are said to detract from the industriousness of society, corrupt youths, and provide escapes from necessary social responsibilities. Other critics point to the way in which such deviance destabilizes lower-class and minority communities.[79] The same is said of prostitution and pornographic businesses. Antiprostitution forces also argue that areas dominated by "sex for sale" soon become havens for more predatory forms of crime, such as robbery or pickpocketing. Straight businesses and real estate values may be damaged by the porn movie houses, street hookers, or massage parlors down the block. Feminist groups stress the manner in which sexist and often violent pornography contributes to the victimization of women. The harm of alternative forms of sexual expression, such as homosexuality, is more difficult to document. Nonetheless, zealous religious groups commonly depict sexual relations between members of the same gender as a demonically inspired assault upon the kingdom of God on earth.

Regardless of whether such "moral offenses" have documentable victims, another question must be asked: Does making them illegal contribute to the good of society? The societal reaction perspective's answer to this question is an unambiguous no. It contends that the legal prohibition of consensual deviant exchanges amplifies rather than decreases the negative consequences of nonconformity. The negative effects of criminalization are seen as far worse than any possible positive gains. In support of this position, reaction theorists raise the following issues.[80]

Laws prohibiting consensual deviant exchanges are essentially unenforceable. Abortion does not cease to exist when it is made illegal. It is simply more costly and more dangerous as women are forced to obtain illegal abortions without the guarantee of medical safeguards. The same goes for gambling, illegal drug use, the sale of sex, and alternative forms of sexual relations. There are no unwilling participants in such deviant activities, unlike such predatory crimes as burglary, fraud, or assault. Moreover, since these exchanges generally occur in private, there is little that society can do to enforce prohibitions against such behavior, short of a policy of total surveillance, undercover espionage, and a thorough disregard for the sanctity of private life. There are, of course, self-proclaimed moralists who believe that the protection of their own versions of morality justify tactics of total control. Societal reaction theorists refuse to be counted among their number.

Laws prohibiting consensual deviant exchanges lead to discriminatory enforcement patterns. Some persons' private lives are less private than others'. The wealthy woman who desires to terminate a pregnancy will not have to rely upon the services of a known underground abortionist. She is able to afford the discreet services of a less visible, respectable physician. When a crackdown comes, her ability to obtain an abortion is not likely to be jeopardized in the same manner as that of her less privileged lower-class "sister." The same holds for the rich and famous addict as compared to the lower-class junkie, or for the high-priced and low-profile call girl, whose "favors" are purchased by wealthy executives, as compared to the lower-class street hooker. Thus the criminalization of consensual deviance invariably produces a pattern of discriminatory enforcement.

Laws prohibiting consensual deviant exchanges encourage deviant behavior on the part of social control agents. This is true regarding two aspects of law enforcement: the likelihood that control agents will (1) use illegal means to obtain evidence, and (2) be corrupted by people who do business in the market of desired but prohibited goods and services. In the first instance, control agents may find themselves under strong organizational pressures to bend the rules of proper legal procedure in order to enforce laws which are essentially unenforceable. Undercover agents may beat up on a lower-class junkie in order to obtain evidence on "Mr. Big." Police officers may physically harass homosexuals. Vice squad members may entrap or even assault prostitutes. To whom are such persons to complain? Who would believe them if they did? The illegal nature of their personal activities makes them relatively vulnerable to equally illegal activities of law enforcers.

Corruption is also a problem for the controllers of consensual deviance. Unseen by anyone but the deviants with whom they do business, police officials, judges, and politicians may find it very easy to line their wallets with funds obtained by looking the other way. Given public ambivalence about such matters, it is easy for corrupt officials to rationalize their behaviors. According to the highly publicized 1972 report of New York City's Knapp Commission, laws against gambling, narcotics, and prostitution were themselves major contributors to police corruption.[81]

Laws prohibiting consensual deviant exchanges may increase secondary deviance. The illegal status of heroin makes it extremely expensive to purchase. As such, the addict may have to resort to other illegal activities simply to obtain enough money to fight off the pains of withdrawal. In this sense, the criminalization of consensual deviance may lead to secondary deviance—deviance resulting from the labeling process itself. The addict may become a burglar or robber. So too may certain consensual deviants become victims of blackmail. Blackmail has historically represented a problem for many homosexuals, forced to pay large sums of money in order to prevent someone from making public the nature of their private sexual preference.

Laws prohibiting consensual deviant exchanges are extremely costly to enforce. The public pays an enormous economic price for attempts to enforce the prohibition of consensual deviance. Law-enforcement officials estimate that approximately 22 percent of all arrests during a given year are for moral offenses such as those being discussed.[82] The dollar total for the control work which produces those arrests is fantastic. The amount of money spent on marijuana busts alone is staggering. In California during 1972 the average arrest cost taxpayers approximately $1,340.[83] During 1977, 457,600 such arrests occurred nationwide.[84] At a figure of only $1,000 per arrest, that would drain the public of almost $500 million per annum.[85] Once California changed its drug laws by decriminalizing the possession of less than one ounce of marijuana, the state treasury saved more than $25 million per year.[86]

Law prohibiting consensual deviant exchanges support organized crime. Many criminal organizations are staked by profits reaped from the black-market sale of illegal goods and services. Revenues from gambling, prostitution, pornography, and the sale of illegal drugs constitute the economic backbone of organized criminal activity.

Laws prohibiting consensual deviant exchanges damage the public's respect for law. Efforts to enforce laws over which there is great public disagreement and little chance of success may instill a spirit of public cynicism toward law in general. How common it is to hear young people disdainfully comment upon a system of law which permits their parents to get high on booze but threatens to imprison them for smoking a joint.

Least Restrictive Control

A central theme in the societal reaction perspective is that social control can turn back upon itself when it is too severe. Severely labeled deviants may be propelled by circumstances or an altered self-concept toward further deviance. They may become imprisoned or encapsulated within a deviant role.

This is particularly the case for deviants closed in by walls of the "total institution"—the prison, the mental hospital, or some other environment of total control. According to Erving Goffman, such extreme settings of social control have four distinctive characteristics.

1 Everything in the life of an inmate takes place within the same place and under the everwatchful eye of a centralized institutional authority.

2 Everything that an inmate does is carried out in the immediate company of a large batch of other people, each of whom are treated alike and forced to enact the same routines.

3 All of an inmate's time is tightly scheduled by a body of rules and administrative order imposed by those in charge.

4 The entire system of enforced activities, time and space control, is purportedly organized around an overall rational plan of institutional goals—in the case of deviance, the goals of correction and/or treatment.[87]

In *Asylums* Goffman reports upon his research as a participant-observer on the staff of St. Elizabeth's mental hospital in Washington, D.C. Rather than rehabilitating deviants, this total institution contributed to the self-mortification and stigmatization of patients, reducing their chances of returning to the normal world. During the late 1960s and early 1970s the research of Goffman and other reaction theorists was used to support reform movements advocating deinstitutionalization and least restrictive policies of social control. Reformers hoped to curtail the stigmatizing and amplification of deviance by limiting the use of total institutions to those who were severely disturbed and dangerous.

Related policy developments were supported by societal reaction theorists in the fields of criminal justice and delinquency prevention. Edwin Schur's important *Radical Non-Intervention* is a case in point.[88] In 1967 the Presidential Commission on Law Enforcement and the Administration of Justice echoed the concerns of many labeling theorists by calling for efforts to divert offenders from the stigmatization of the courtroom. Youthful offenders, for instance, were targeted for counseling or community work rather than a formal hearing or trial. Such programs were far less costly than formal adjudication and possible incarceration. Estimates suggest that the cost of diversion is a tenth of that entailed by formal prosecution, and that the public might save as much as $1.5 billion per year by implementing such lesser-restrictive-option alternatives for minor offenses.

In sociological terms the results are less clear. Although some research suggests that diverted offenders may perceive themselves as less stigmatized, there is little evidence that such programs actually reduce future crime. Unfortunately most studies of this matter have been poorly constructed, using very small samples and less than ideal matches between persons assigned to diversion and those subject to more traditional crime-control measures. Nonetheless, the financial and perceptual advantages of diversion are significant enough to justify continued experimentation with efforts to control deviance in the least restrictive manner possible.

THE SOCIETAL REACTION PERSPECTIVE TODAY

The societal reaction perspective today exerts an enormous influence on the field of deviance and social control. Guided by an omnipresent concern for the relationship between control agents and the people who are labeled deviant, societal reaction researchers have pursued three general areas of inquiry: (1) the historical development of deviant labels, (2) the process by which labels are applied, and (3) the consequences of being labeled.

The Historical Development of Deviant Labels

The social history of deviant labels involves what Malcolm Spector and John Kituse refer to as the study of "claims-making" activity on the part of various groups within society. Groups with sufficient power are able to stake and defend their claims regarding what should be considered deviant. In the words of Spector and Kituse, "The theoretical problem is to account for how categories of deviance are produced, and how methods of social control and treatment are institutionally established."[89]

Numerous historical studies fall within the general historical concerns of the societal reaction perspective. Classic studies in this tradition include Joseph Gusfield's analysis of the class and cultural politics of the Women's Christian Temperance Union and its crusade to prohibit the sale of alcoholic beverages,[90] Kai Erikson's analysis of the construction and control of crime in the Massachusetts Bay Colony,[91] Anthony Platt's study of the "invention of delinquency" and the founding of the first juvenile court,[92] William Chambliss's investigations into the origins and use of vagrancy laws,[93] and Elliot Currie's examination of the social control of witches in Europe and Great Britain.[94] More recent studies include Joseph Schneider's analysis of the development of the medicalized concept of alcoholism,[95] Peter Conrad's account of the discovery of hyperkinesis,[96] Kathleen Tierney's consideration of the origins of the spouse-abuse movement, and Gerald Markle and Ronald Troyer's examination of the antismoking movement.[97] These are just a few of the growing number of sociological investigations into the developmental history of deviant labels.

In order to provide a familiarity with the kinds of historical questions raised by reaction research, I have selected two examples for further elaboration. The first is Howard Becker's classic analysis of the origins of the Marijuana Tax Act of 1937.[98] The description of Becker's research is accompanied by a discussion of related inquiries into the origins of U.S. drug laws in general. The second study considered in this section is my own analysis of the discovery of child abuse as a form of labeled deviance.[99] Both studies illustrate a central theme in the reaction perspective—that deviance never exists independently in the eyes of those who have a powerful interest in not seeing it.

The Marijuana Tax Act of 1937: U.S. Drug Laws and the Control Work of a Bureaucratic Agency To appreciate the historical origins of the antimarijuana laws of the 1930s one needs to first consider the criminalization of opiate use some twenty years earlier. The antiopiate and antimarijuana laws are connected by an important historical thread—the bureaucratic politics of the Federal Bureau of Narcotics and its predecessor, the Narcotics Division of the U.S. Treasury Department.

During the nineteenth century opiate use was permitted without legal sanction. The typical morphine addict was a white middle-class housewife. There was little interest in developing formal legal controls against the use of opiates by such persons. By the early twentieth century things had changed. Of particular importance was the growing fear of competition from Chinese laborers, a population equated in the public mind with opium use. This fostered a new view of opiate use as a social problem. Following an international conference on this problem, U.S. officials pledged tight legislative controls restricting the distribution of opiates to authorized medical prescriptions, which would be registered with federal authorities and for which a tax would be collected. These terms were set forth in the 1914 Harrison Stamp Act. The Narcotics Division of the U.S. Treasury was established to oversee its proper administration.

What happened next is the story of a social control agency redefining its mission and expanding its bureaucratic scope and power.[100] Once in existence, the Narcotics Division reached beyond the law in efforts to criminalize rather than regulate the use of opiates (including morphine and the recently synthesized heroin). Medical prescriptions to kill pain would be permitted, but the medical maintenance of addicts would not. Through a series of administrative decisions, accompanied by a well-orchestrated campaign against the moral depravity of addiction, the Narcotics Division effectively curtailed the ability of doctors to treat outpatient addicts by administering safe and regular doses of the drug. When doctors balked at this legal interference, they were harassed and arrested. In 1925 the aggressive control policies of the Narcotics Division were challenged in the case of *Lindner v. United States.* The position of doctors was technically and temporarily vindicated. The Supreme Court ruled that medical practitioners had the right to treat addicts as they deemed best.

The *Lindner* ruling did little to change the Narcotics Division's policies or politics. The division continued to harass physicians and arrest addicts. The powerful American Medical Association fell into line. In 1925 it passed a resolution condemning the ambulatory, or outpatient, maintenance of addicts. The Narcotics Division had won. Without technically changing the law it had effectively created a new category of deviants—persons who possessed opiates.

Through its successful campaign against opiate use the Narcotics Division had expanded its function from tax collector to police officer. So also had it enlarged its bureaucratic scope, prestige, and power. In 1930 it separated form the Treasury Department to become an independent agency, the Federal

Bureau of Narcotics. It is here that Becker begins his analysis of the Marijuana Tax Act of 1937. Once again we see a federal agency generating a campaign to condemn and control a form of deviant drug use—marijuana smoking. Led by Commissioner Harry J. Anslinger, the bureau launched a campaign which involved "cooperating in the development of state legislation affecting the use of marijuana, and providing facts and figures for journalistic accounts of the problem."[101]

The facts and figures presented by the bureau may today seem highly unscientific, even laughable. Despite many years and millions of dollars of research there is no reliable empirical evidence that marijuana endangers a person's health or welfare. Such are the findings of the recent National Commission of Marijuana and Drug Abuse, which concluded that "from what is now known about the effects of marijuana, its use at the present level does not constitute a major threat to public health."[102] The facts alleged by the Bureau of Narcotics during the 1930s were considerably more "creative." Using pseudo-scientific language the bureau suggested that marijuana led to everything from madness to murder. Sexual immorality, crime, and physical deterioration were all said to be common side effects. The 1937 film *Reefer Madness* was an outgrowth of this period of moral crusading. So were articles such as the one published in the *American Magazine* in which Commissioner Anslinger told the following tragic story of pot smoking.

> An entire family was murdered by a youthful [marijuana] addict in Florida. When officers arrived at the home they found the youth staggering about in a human slaughterhouse. With an ax he had killed his father, mother and two brothers, and a sister. He seemed to be in a daze. . . . He had no recollection of having committed the multiple crime. The officers knew him ordinarily as a sane, rather quiet young man; now he was pitifully crazed. They sought the reason. The boy said he had been in the habit of smoking something which youthful friends called "muggles," a childish name for marijuana.[103]

The propaganda campaign engineered by the Bureau of Narcotics inspired a rash of antimarijuana warnings everywhere. Illustrated posters in public trains and buses read: "BEWARE! This marijuana cigarette may be handed to you by the *friendly stranger*. It contains the Killer Drug Marijuana in which lurks MURDER! INSANITY! DEATH!"[104] A scientific-sounding pamphlet distributed by the International Narcotics Education Association referred to marijuana as a "narcotic poison," a "killer drug," the habitual use of which "always causes a very marked mental deterioration and sometimes causes insanity," and which "sometimes gives man the lust to kill unreasonably and without motive."[105]

The Federal Bureau of Narcotics supported antimarijuana legislation at both the federal and state levels. Such legislation was passed with ease. The 1937 Marijuana Federal Tax Act sailed through the halls of Congress virtually unopposed. As Becker points out, "Marijuana smokers, powerless, unorganized, and lacking publicly legitimate grounds for attack, sent no representatives to the hearings and their point of view found no place in the record. . . . The [moral] enterprise of the Bureau had produced new rules, whose subsequent enforcement would help to create a new class of out-siders—marijuana users."[106]

Becker's analysis of the entrepreneurial campaigning of the Federal Bureau of Narcotics was supplemented by subsequent research within the societal reaction tradition. Donald Dickson, for instance, has argued that the bureau's motives may have been more budgetary than moral; that cutbacks in the agency's funding prompted it to search for a new "dangerous" drug to fight so that it could preserve or expand its bureaucratic position.[107] Another interpretation is offered by David Musto, who points to a popular association between marijuana use and the unrestricted flow of Mexican migrant laborers into the American southwest.[108] This stereotypical link between Mexican immigrants and marijuana made the southwest particularly susceptible to horror stories about the evils of pot. There, tales of marijuana-induced rape, mayhem, and murder fed into economic anxieties and hateful ethnic stereo-types. Still another interpretation, by John Galliher and Allynn Walker, sug-gests that marijuana legislation was prompted by concerns which were more symbolic than practical, that the legislation provided symbolic assurance of the values of order and orderliness in a period of social and economic dis-order.[109] This interpretation has much contemporary relevance. Given the rather large body of evidence suggesting that pot smoking is relatively harm-less, why today is such behavior still labeled deviant? Perhaps its prohibition is more symbolic than practical. In any event the continued deviantization of marijuana use presents a challenge to students inspired by Becker's early formulation of the problem.

Discovering Child Abuse: The Professional Politics of Control Work on the origins of child-abuse laws (by Stephen Pfohl, of all people) has also contributed to an understanding of professional social control work and the creation of deviant categories.[110] It is startling to learn that there were no laws which prohibited child abuse until the early 1960s. Then in a few short years all fifty states "discovered" the problem and hurriedly passed legislation calling for its control. Why then? Violence against children is as old as the earliest of our nation's legal statutes. In actuality there were several attempts to draw attention to this problem during the nineteenth and early twentieth centuries. None, however, had the backing of groups powerful enough to break the legal hold that parents had over children. Rather than deviantizing violent parents, early efforts to fight child abuse generally resulted in the institutionalization of beaten children.

Medical professionals, who would seemingly be the most logical people to see and report the ravages of parental violence, were actually unaware of the problem until they were dragged into the arena by one of medicine's sub-specialties, pediatric radiology. At last a group of medical professionals were rewarded for seeing what other doctors had failed to see. Other medical professionals, even those who treated children directly, had simply not seen or perceived child abuse before it was "discovered" in the x-rays of the pediatric radiology researchers.

There were strong professional reasons why doctors had not seen violence against children. Medicine as a profession was dominated by a concern for totally controlling the consequences of its professional activities. To see something like child abuse was likely to subordinate medicine to the working interests of another profession—the law. Doctors would have to leave the hospitals they controlled to become accessories in the courtroom domain of lawyers. Furthermore, doctors perceived parents as their real clients. Parents, not children, paid the bills. Seeing abuse might create conflict for those hypothetically protected by the shadows of professional medical confidence. Likewise, child abuse was not something doctors had been trained to diagnose. Up until its discovery by the pediatric radiologists, doctors, most of whom were parents themselves, bypassed the psychological horror of child abuse and saw instead a wide range of unusual yet physiological problems. Where they could have seen evidence of deliberate beatings they saw unexplained bruisings and bone fractures. Their failure to see child abuse for what it was involved not bad motives but a socially organized lack of perception, a lack of perception that kept them from coming into conflict with their organized professional interests.

Pediatric radiologists broke through the perceptual barriers impeding doctors from seeing child abuse, not because they were more heroic, but because they had more to professionally gain than lose. Radiologists were near the bottom of the prestige rankings within medicine, but the discovery of child abuse allowed them to participate in the higher-status, life-or-death work of their more clinically oriented colleagues. Moreover, their indirect technical investigations and research mission to uncover new diagnoses may have freed radiologists from the restraints of psychological denial and confidentiality which inhibited the diagnostic vision of other medical professionals.

In a similar manner, the radiologists avoided the subordination of medical to legal interests by discovering, not a new form of criminal behavior, but a medical "syndrome." Following this medical model, child abuse would generally be treated rather than punished. Perpetrators would be viewed as sick rather than bad. Parents would be referred to medically styled clinics rather than legally structured prisons.

The lesson to be learned from all the medical maneuvering behind the discovery of child abuse is nothing less than a lesson in the omnipresent relationship between social control and social conflict. The discovery and control of something that today seems as consensually deviant as anything we can imagine awaited a moment in history in which it would be advanced with the professional interests of a group that (1) had the power to make deviant labels stick and (2) had something to gain by doing so. This is not to impute bad or cynical motives to the medical authorities who acted as agents of social control. Good or bad motives are not a central feature of the conflict perspective. What is central is the fact that control efforts arise when social interests are provided with an opportunity for advance or confronted with the need for defense. In the case of child abuse, social control advanced with the advance of powerful and defensible medical interests.

Application of Deviant Labels

This second body of societal reaction research concerns such matters as the conditions under which control agents successfully label others, as well as the social contingencies under which potential deviants resist or escape the labeling process.[111] Of the many studies on the social dynamics of the labeling process, none is more systematic than Thomas Scheff's work on the societal reaction to mental illness.[112] A detailed discussion of Scheff's work will permit us to appreciate the empirical character of one of the most important studies within the societal reaction tradition.

A Labeling Theory of Mental Illness: The Work of Thomas J. Scheff
Scheff defines *mental illness* as a type of *residual deviance*, a catchall category for a variety of behaviors which violate the rules of everyday social interaction. Such violations include inappropriate gestures and postures, and inappropriate ways of looking, talking, or positioning one's body in relation to other people. People who act in such a fashion may be thought of as odd. They may even be labeled as mentally ill, but not always. What determines whether this will happen? Scheff formulates nine propositions which guide the labeling process. The core of Scheff's theory is that, without labeling, most residual rule breaking will be ignored or denied and will pass away as a matter of transitory significance. It is labeling that fixes a residual rule breaker into a stereotypical career as a mentally ill person. This is underscored in Scheff's ninth proposition, which states that "labeling is the single most important cause of careers in residual deviance."[113]

But what causes labeling? According to Scheff, seven factors are important: the degree of rule breaking, the amount of rule breaking, the visibility of rule breaking, the power of the rule breaker, the social distance between the rule breaker and control agents, the tolerance level of a particular community, and the availability of alternative nondeviant roles. The first two variables, degree and amount of rule breaking, are characteristics of the individual being labeled. The last five are social factors which exist independently of an act of rule breaking. The logic of Scheff's thesis is this—that labeling may be regarded as the single most important cause of a career in residual deviance if the last five variables outweigh the influence of the first two. Social contingencies, in other words, are said to be more important than the bizarre behavior of the deviant.

Scheff tested his labeling theory in a two-phase study of psychiatric decision making. The initial phase (obtaining independent psychiatric ratings of candidates for involuntary commitment to a mental hospital) uncovered high levels of clinical uncertainty regarding the mental state of patients examined. Despite such uncertainty, Scheff observed 196 consecutive cases in which patients were committed anyway. From this Scheff inferred that there was a presumption of illness behind the work of psychiatric labelers.

Why do psychiatric examiners presume illness on the part of patients being considered for involuntary commitment? David Mechanic attributes this predisposition for medical labeling to the professional socialization of psychiatrists as physicians and to the pressing time constraints of hospital work.[114] Scheff identifies three additional factors—financial, ideological, and political. Paid on a per case basis, psychiatrists have a financial incentive to process cases quickly. Ideologically, several features of the so-called medical model reinforce the tendency to see illness. One is the belief that, like other diseases, mental illness will get progressively worse unless detected and treated. Another assumes that a finding of illness is not irreversible and that the results of a little treatment will be neutral at worst. Political considerations also encourage psychiatrists to be "safe rather than sorry." Of major concern is the fear of public censure for releasing patients who later act violently. Visions of newspaper headlines reading "Psychiatrist Released KILLER" must undoubtedly pass through a clinician's mind.

Each of the above factors contributed to labeling that was rapid and perfunctory. The formal court commitment hearings lasted an average of only 1.6 minutes. The consequence was that persons from marginal social backgrounds, who were subject to social isolation or family conflict, were placed in mental hospitals for a period of ninety days. According to Scheff, the reasons were typically more social than medical, influenced by more organizational contingencies surrounding labeling than by the behavior of those labeled.[115] Other studies of psychiatric labeling arrive at similar conclusions. Controlling for patient behavior such things as the preference of family members,[116] socioeconomic status,[117] whether or not a lawyer is present,[118] how patients rank on a host of nonclinical social attributes,[119] and diagnosticians' knowledge of prior labels have all been determined to have an impact.[120]

One particularly vivid example of the impact of prior labels is found in the work of psychologist David Rosenhan.[121] Rosenhan placed eight sane people (pseudo patients) in twelve different mental hospitals. To gain admission each reported a phony symptom of schizophrenia (hearing voices) during the course of a diagnostic interview. Thereafter the pseudo patients were instructed to act as they would in normal, everyday life. The pseudo patients were a varied group. Among them were three psychologists, a painter, a pediatrician, a housewife, and a psychiatrist. What did not vary was the reaction of hospital staff. Despite the fact that they acted normal, the pseudo patients remained hospitalized for an average of nineteen days. Their length of hospitalization ranged from seven to fifty-two days.

During the course of confinement the pseudo patients soon discovered that behaviors which might be ordinarily seen as normal were now interpreted by staff members in accordance with the manner in which they had been labeled. Routine frictions in interpersonal relationships were seen as deep-seated signs of personal instability. Boredom was interpreted as nervousness. A review of the nursing records for three of the pseudo patients revealed that even the writing of research notes was laden with negative clinical meaning. Note taking was recast in a pathological framework, as but a symptom of some deeper disturbance.

Interestingly enough, other patients did not read the behaviors of the pseudo patients in such a negative fashion. It was common for real patients to detect the pseudo patients or to suspect them of being undercover journalists or covert researchers. Caught on the other side of the official labeling process, staff members perceived no such thing. Even when eventually discharged, all but one of the pseudo patients retained the diagnosis of being schizophrenic, although their symptoms were said to be "in remission." Thus, as Rosenhan points out, "the data speak to the massive role of labeling in psychiatric assessment. Having once been labeled schizophrenic, there is nothing the pseudo patient can do to overcome the tag."[122]

The Consequences of Being Labeled

Societal reaction researchers follow the lead of Edwin Lemert in examining how labeling may amplify deviance or produce secondary deviation. Also of importance is Harold Garfinkel's depiction of the labeling process as a ceremony of social degradation, a process whereby a person's social identity is literally reconstituted as a lesser form of human being.[123]

One need not be publicly labeled to experience the identity transformation suggested by Garfinkel. Carol Warren and John Johnson suggest that groups such as homosexuals may engage in *symbolic labeling*, a process whereby people adopt culturally disseminated deviant stereotypes without actually being caught up in a cycle of public condemnation.[124] Warren's research within the gay community indicates that members commonly "defined themselves as essentially being homosexual, and tend[ed] to organize their lives around the fact of possessing this symbolic stigma."[125]

Whether one is labeled by others or by oneself, the consequences of labeling may be profound. In his study of the social control of public drunks, James Spradley reports upon drastic identity changes for persons labeled as "bums." Such persons are "cut off from former roles and identities, treated as objects to be manipulated, and coerced into being acutely aware of the new definitions of social interaction, space, time and identity which are part of the jail."[126] Related findings were presented by Robert Scott in analyzing the stigma of physical blindness[127] and by Charles Frazier in considering the case of "Ken," a young man from a small town who was "branded" a criminal.[128] Following the degradation ceremony of a public trial, virtually all of Ken's life was retrospectively read as indicative of deviance. Rejected by previous friends and associates, Ken began to reformulate his own definitions about life. "What the hell," states Ken in Frazier's narrative, "if I'm going to be named a criminal I might as well be one."

Sometimes the stigma of labeling extends to a person's close friends, associates, or relatives. Erving Goffman uses the term *courtesy stigma* to describe this phenomenon.[129] Merle Miller notes this with regard to the families of both convicted felons and gays.[130] Research by Yarrow, Schwartz, Murphy, and Deasy discovered something similar with reference to the spouses and offspring of hospitalized mental patients.[131] Birnbaum notes its effect on the families of the retarded.[132]

Quasi-Experimental Assessments of Labeling Consequences   Other researchers have used quasi-experimental measures to assess the consequences of labeling. Derek Phillips collected information on the likelihood that people will reject persons labeled as having a mental problem.[133] Phillips presented a set of hypothetical cases about people with behavioral problems to a sample of 300 married white females in a southern New England town. Each respondent was presented with exactly the same behavioral descriptions. What varied was whether people in the hypothetical cases sought no help or utilized the services of a member of the clergy, a physician, a psychiatrist, or a mental hospital. The more someone was perceived as obtaining help from an official mental health (labeling) source, the more likely he or she was to be rejected by the respondents.

Another study, by Loman and Larkin, presented college students with videotapes of a counseling session depicting another student's poor academic progress.[134] In one version of the tape, the student's problems were attributed to the impersonality of the school atmosphere. In another the student was labeled mentally ill. Characteristics of the client's behavior and his own self-accounts were also manipulated. Measures were taken to discover which factors were most influential in determining an audience's assessment of the troubled student's "social competence." What counted most was whether the person being observed was labeled as mentally ill. When this occurred viewers were significantly more likely to provide low assessments of the student's social competence.

Other research documents the *self-fulfilling* nature of certain deviant labels. An example is Delos Kelly's study of the consequences of having been labeled a "remedial-type" student in school.[135] Kelly combined a variety of data sources (observation, interviewing, the results of educational testing, etc.) to determine the basis for high school teachers' nomination of certain students for placement in a remedial-reading track. He discovered that a student's current performance and actual test scores were less important than the stigma of prior labels. Thus, "the label *remedial reader* can effectively be viewed as a *master status* such that, instead of considering present academic performance, some teachers appear to look, retrospectively, to a student's past history, and if the student has been involved with remedial reading, then such involvement increases his or her changes of being selected again."[136]

Labeling also affects a person's material life chances. This was demonstrated in a study by Schwartz and Skolnick of the impact of a criminal record on employment.[137] Introducing themselves as representatives of the employment agency, researchers presented prospective employers with the employment credentials of fictitious job applicants. The applicant credentials were identical except for one factor—whether or not the applicant had a past criminal record. Twenty-five prospective employers were presented with each of the following conditions: (1) information that the applicant had been sentenced for assault; (2) information that the applicant had been tried for assault but acquitted; (3) information that the applicant had been tried and acquitted, along with a letter from the judge affirming the person's innocence; and (4) no reference at all to past criminal involvement. Schwartz and Skolnick discovered that labeling made a difference in the likelihood that candidates would be considered for a job. For employers in the no-criminal-record condition, 36 percent indicated that they might use the person. Thereafter the percentage of positive responses shrunk in proportion to the severity of labeling. Twenty-four percent in condition 3, 12 percent in condition 2, and only 4 percent in condition 1 gave an affirmative answer. Similar findings were presented by W. Buikhuisen and P. H. Dijksterhuis, who presented companies in the Netherlands with employment applications varying only by reference to convictions for theft, drunk driving, or no criminality.[138] Findings revealed that 52 percent of the noncriminal group were reviewed positively, in comparison to 32 percent of the theft group and 26 percent of the drunk-driving group.

Labelers and the Expansion of the Deviance Problem: The Ironies of Social Control

To this point we have been considering the possibility that labeling may amplify the problems of deviance for those labeled—that it may alter their self-concepts and their positions in the material world, and may stabilize their careers in deviance. Labeling may also have unintended negative consequences for society as a whole. In a recent article entitled "Ironies of Social Control," Gary Marx makes this point by suggesting that through escalation, nonenforcement, and covert facilitation, control agents may create as much deviance as they curtail.[139]

Escalation   Marx uses this term to describe how control work may generate new forms of deviation. Police intervention into domestic disputes may, for instance, "up the ante" in family quarrels. It may make a big issue out of what was once a small disturbance. Police overreactions to collective disturbances may have a similar effect. History is filled with cases in which police intervention has fueled the fire of minor outbreaks into major riots. Another is the high-speed chase in which dramatic police action raises the risk that people, even innocent bystanders, may be hurt. What starts out as a traffic problem may escalate into a bloody incident of a much more serious nature.

Nonenforcement   This is a common by-product of control work. In order to be successful, police must frequently negotiate with underworld informants, trading information for the tacit permission to deviate. At other times police may look the other way so as not to see the illegal activities of vigilante-type groups whose general objectives mirror their own. In other instances, legal authorities may actually make use of the deviant skills of persons whose activities they supposedly oppose. Consider the symbiotic relationship between the CIA and members of organized-crime syndicates who combined forces to develop "executive action programs" directed at "eliminating the effectiveness" of certain foreign leaders. It is public record that the U.S. government contracted Mafia "hit men" to try to murder Cuban President Fidel Castro and Congo President Lumumba. Also important are instances in which authorities fail to take action to stop a crime until after the whole episode is complete. According to Marx, "This permits arrest quotas to be met and can lead to heavier charges, greater leverage in negotiations, better evidence, and a higher level of offender arrest."[140]

Covert Facilitation   By using deceptive law-enforcement tactics, control agents may intentionally encourage rule breaking. Critics of Operation ABSCAM (an undercover FBI program in which agents posing as Arab sheikhs offered bribes to government officials, including members of Congress) contend that it is an example of zealous legal authorities going "beyond the law" to encourage others to break the law. Officials caught "holding the money" in this so-called sting operation argued that they had been lured into deviance by undercover control agents and that they never would have committed such crimes on their own. Regardless of the merits of such claims, covert facilitation has for years been an element of control policies aimed at exposing the deviance of drug dealers, prostitutes, homosexuals, and political activists. The use of decoys, undercover infiltrators, and agents provocateurs (secret police agents who urge others to take the step into deviance) has long been recognized by less respectable rule breakers who are the common targets of such authorized deviousness. Public concern about this issue has appeared only after a few respectable officials have been caught in the web of such covert control work. Along with escalation and nonenforcement, covert facilitation may expand the problem which control work is supposed to solve. As suggested by Marx, "Each involves the possibility of deviance amplification and illustrates—from the labeling perspective . . . —the ironic insight that authorities often contribute to the deviance they set out to control."[141]

Collective Responses of Deviants to Deviant Labels

This final consequence of the labeling process generally takes one of two forms. The first involves the organization of deviant subcultures in which labeled or potentially labelable rule breakers find support or positive recognition for their nonconformity. Since deviant subcultures were discussed in Chapter 8, we shall here briefly examine a second form of collective reaction to labeling—the development of voluntary associations of deviants aimed at restoring respectability to those stigmatized. According to Edward Sagarin, author of *Odd Man In*,[142] a study of societies organized to promote a positive image of labeled deviants, voluntary associations of deviants are today on the rise. Their proliferation may be the result of several factors: the permissive anonymity of contemporary urban life; the civil rights movement and its concern for alleviating the problems of oppressed minorities; and the 1960s counterculture, with its challenge to the desirability of conventional standards and call for a greater tolerance of human diversity. Even the growth of a medical (or pathological) model of deviance, with its emphasis on helping rather than punishing deviants, may have contributed.

Not all voluntary associations of deviants have the same goals or operate in the same fashion. Some may seek to show that the moral meaning of certain forms of deviance is compatible with the existing social order. Others may seek to change the social order. Following the lead of Stanford Lyman, one might classify the goals of the first of these two types as *conformative* and the second as *alienative*.[143] The means selected by deviants to achieve these goals may likewise be divided into two analytic types: *expressive* and *instrumental*. Expressive groups tend to focus on the social, emotional, or recreational needs of their members, while instrumental groups are more practical in their efforts to restructure the shape of societal reactions. In combination these characteristics reflect the following types of voluntary deviant associations.

Conformative-Instrumental Groups   This type of deviant association includes groups which campaign to be included within the existing social order. The Gay Activist Alliance (GAA) is a good example. Founded in 1969, this organization is dedicated to working within the system so that gay people can be made part of the system. Through public information, political lobbying, and organized protest, the GAA endeavors to eliminate discrimination against gay people in such areas as employment and housing and to present a positive image of gays as respectable citizens.[144]

COYOTE (an acronym for the slogan "call-off-your-old-tired-ethics) is another example of a conformative-instrumental group. Its objective is to decriminalize prostitution. COYOTE claims a membership of over 3,500; publishes a newsletter, *Coyote Howls;* and together with several affiliate chapters, such as PONY (Prostitutes of New York) and ASP (Associated Seattle Prostitutes), promotes legislation permitting prostitutes to utilize the services of public defenders, fights discriminatory laws, and advocates prostitution as a legitimate business.[145] The National Organization for the Reform of Marijuana Laws (NORMAL) employs similar strategies in hopes of decriminalizing the possession and sale of pot. So does the National Stuttering Project, whose goals involve an end to employment discrimination against stutterers.

Conformative-Expressive Groups   Groups such as Weight Watchers and Alcoholics Anonymous fit within this second type. They encourage their members to see themselves not as deviants but as people with a problem that can be overcome. By attending weekly meetings and keeping in close contact, members assist each other in fitting back into the existing social order. Other conformative-expressive groups, such as Little People of America (a group of dwarfs and others of diminutive height), circulate information geared toward helping stigmatized persons develop normal competencies as well as helping normal people to feel at ease with people bearing a particular deviant stigma.

Alienative-Instrumental Groups   This type of association uses practical political means to change the system. One example is the Gay Liberation Front (GLF). Founded about a month after the "Stonewall Rebellion" of 1969, GLF is a self-consciously militant and politically radical organization. The Stonewall Inn was a small but well-known gay bar in Greenwich Village. Such places had long been subject to police harassment and intimidation—ritualized ceremonies of public humiliation. On June 27, 1969, things became different. Patrons of the Stonewall Inn fought back, hurling rocks and bottles and shouting "Gay Power": a new, aggressive, politically aware gay community was born. Unlike straightforward gay rights groups, such as the Gay Activist Alliance, the GLF was organized to liberate not just homosexuals, but oppressed peoples the world over.[146]

In recent years, activist groups, such as Queer Nation, have expanded the struggles of gays, lesbians, bisexuals, and others oppressed by the homophobic character of many contemporary institutions. Inspired, in part, by the successes of ACT UP (AIDS Coalition to Unleash Power), a militant organization aimed at countering ineffectual public responses to the AIDS epidemic, and by a documented rise in the rates of physical assaults against gays and lesbians, Queer Nation was born in June 1990. At that time over 1,200 self-proclaimed "queers" marched to take back the streets of New York City's East Village and West Village. A multicultural, polygendered, and direct-action organization, Queer Nation is dedicated to countering both homophobic violence and compulsive inequalities of heterosexist privilege. It is like other alienative-instrumental associations in that its provocative use of street theater, queer "kiss-ins," outrage, and parodic humor is aimed not only at influencing the inclusion of homosexuals within existing social institutions but also at uprooting the sexually oppressive character of these institutions themselves.

Alienative-Expressive Groups Certain deviant religious groups and "cults" of various sorts fall into this category. Rather than seeking to change the world, such groups offer their participants a change of worlds. They commonly attract and often consciously recruit people whose personal lives are in great disarray; people experiencing great trauma, confusion, or isolation; people who may feel deviant. Membership in groups such as the Unification Church (the "Moonies") or the People's Temple (the group which was led to its ceremonial death in Jonestown by the Reverend Jim Jones) has great appeal to people who see themselves as outsiders. Membership in a more traditional religious group might serve a similar purpose, providing expressive support for the alienative notion that the things of this world are meant to pass away.

Some voluntary associations of deviants do not fit clearly into any of the above types. Examples include groups of ex-mental patients and prisoners' rights organizations. These associations may be both instrumental and expressive, trying to change public policy while at the same time offering emotional and/or material support for persons released from public institutions. In any event, the study of voluntary associations is yet another part of the wider picture of deviance painted by scholars of the societal reaction perspective.

ASSESSMENT OF THE SOCIETAL REACTION PERSPECTIVE

The societal reaction perspective is one of the most important approaches to the study of deviance and social control. Substantively it reminds us that the study of deviance can never be fully detached from the study of social control work. It contends that behaviors are never deviant in themselves. Things are deviant only because they are viewed that way by people with enough power to make deviant labels stick. The tribal leader who hallucinates is viewed as a sacred visionary. The contemporary urban dweller who hallucinates is viewed as a psychotic. One is normal. The other is deviant. The behavior is the same. Its social meaning is different.

Methodologically, the societal reaction perspective offers an important lesson as well. Treat official statistics as a topic for research rather than as reliable data on deviance. Who gets classified as deviant? Why are classifications done the way they are? Who is missing from official classifications of deviants? Why? The societal reaction perspective makes the official production and recording of deviance as much a topic for investigation as the distribution of deviance within the population.

Despite its important substantive and methodological contributions, the societal reaction perspective has been the target of a number of criticisms. These fall into five general categories: (1) the causal critique, (2) the normative critique, (3) the empirical critique, (4) the situated knowledge critique, and (5) the structural critique.

The Causal Critique

Since its inception, critics have taken issue with the perspective's alleged theory that labeling is the true cause of deviant behavior. I use the term "alleged" because this criticism clearly misunderstands the theoretical thrust of the perspective itself. As presented by reaction theorist Howard Becker, the perspective is not intended as a causative theory per se, but as a "way of looking at a general area of human activity," a way of looking which expands the traditional scope of deviance research, so as to include a focus on the processes of social control and thereby undermine the "hidden power" of those who define nonconformity and attempt to contain nonconformists.[147]

Not all reaction theorists state the matter as succinctly as Becker. Perhaps unclarity on the part of some proponents has confused critics about the general intentions of this perspective. In actuality, the societal reaction perspective seeks to supplement, rather than replace, the causal insights of other theoretical frameworks. Why have so many critics missed this point? One reason is offered by Travis Hirschi. According to Hirschi:

> It is not easy for a traditional student . . . to approach labeling theory with an open mind. Labelling theorists are not kind to the traditional approach: they typically begin with a flat denial of the validity of most of the research the traditional approach has produced. Further, and perhaps worst of all, labelling theorists often appear with little effort to have won the battle. Students are enthralled: the journals begin to bulge with "critiques," "tests," "appreciative reviews," and all the other perquisites of theoretical victory.[148]

The major exception to the reaction perspective's disinterest in causative theories of deviance concerns the issue of secondary deviance. Even here, reaction theorists have not so much argued that labeling invariably causes further deviance as that labeling must always be considered a potential factor in the causation of subsequent deviance. In this sense, the societal reaction perspective is something which sensitizes us to issues ignored by other theories. Being labeled may indeed affect the future lives of deviants. Exactly how is an empirical question. Sometimes being labeled may box one into a deviant career. But not always. What are the consequences of labeling? Sensitization to this issue, rather than an assumption as to its causal significance, is the real strength of this perspective.

The Normative Critique

This critique is set forth by Jack Gibbs, who attempts to interject clarity at points where the idea of labeling stumbles into conceptual confusion.[149] One such point involves the topic of *secret deviance*, Becker's category for unlabeled acts which were nonetheless deviant. How did Becker know they were deviant if they were not labeled? According to Gibbs, Becker must have been using some set of normative standards. Norms thus precede labels. Hence, norms, not labels, should be the focus for a truly sociological study of deviance.

Gibbs uses two examples to buttress his argument. In the first he asks the reader to imagine two persons on the street. One is naked. The other is not. Need we wait to see how each is reacted to in order to decide which is the deviant? After all, won't one person be immediately seen as violating a rather clear set of societal norms? In his second example, Gibbs criticizes Becker's interpretation of a Trobriand marital dispute (reported by the anthropologist Malinowski) as an instance of the ambiguity of labeling theory. Becker suggests that although a man who has sexual relations with his mother's sister does something which is generally disapproved, his act does not become deviant until the woman's discarded lover returns and accuses (or labels) the violator. Why wait to focus on the accusal or labeling process, asks Gibbs. Hasn't the act already been evaluated as violating normative expectations? Implicitly, Malinowski, Becker, the discarded lover, and everyone else must have recognized that a norm was broken. If not, how did they recognize the accusal as an accusal? Preceding the labeling process there must have been a judgment that a norm was violated.

Gibbs's criticisms are helpful in delineating inconsistencies in the societal reaction perspective. Yet, his own formulation is no easy solution to the study of deviance. His preference for defining deviance by reference to norms confronts him with the problem of identifying the rules which spell out the dos and don'ts of normative behavior. The sociologist addressing this problem has but two solutions: to survey members of a social group about their expectations of others or to infer rules from observations of how members actually behave.

As solutions these two alternatives present further problems. Verbal statements offer no assurance that people actually do what they say they do. Moreover, as John Kituse points out, such "statements may not even be 'normative' in the sense that they urge that persons *ought* to behave as their statements specify, but simply represent what is said when people are asked about conduct in certain circumstances, an expression of an ideal that prescribes no sanctions when the norm is violated, set aside, or otherwise ignored."[150]

Inferring norms from behavior may be even more complicated. Many inferences may be drawn from any one observation. The sociologist is thus confronted with the task of constructing valid rules of inference. The problem is to decide upon a set of operational definitions which best represent the normative world as it really exists. This is no simple matter. Adequate and pertinent definitions entail a high degree of specificity regarding the questions of what conduct is prescribed or proscribed, by whom, for whom, in what situations, under what circumstances, assuming what degree of mental and social competence, etc. To date, sociologists have not been very successful in specifying all these variables for all or even most situations. Instead, "the common practice is for the sociologist to gloss over the methodological problems by relying, as a (presumed) member of the system being studied, on his or her own implicit and tacitly held understanding of the social norms."[151]

Such sociological glossing is troubling for two reasons. First, it ignores the fact that their own social backgrounds, training, and political ideologies hardly qualify sociologists as typical members of a cultural system being studied. As John Kituse points out, "Sociologists may find that members ignore, dismiss, and even applaud those acts that sociologists classify as unambiguously clear violations of the norm."[152] The second problem with sociological glossing is that it ignores the situated character of deviance. For instance, "the naked person on the street" example offered by Gibbs takes on an entirely different meaning when we realize that the street in question is in the middle of a nudist camp. Gibbs's question (Won't one person be immediately seen as violating a rather clear set of societal norms?) is presented in a different light. The evaluation of normativity becomes less immediate and more problematic. It is preceded by a process of definitional or interpretive work (i.e., by the work of societal reaction). It is this situated construction of deviance which is at the heart of societal reaction theorizing.

If norm violations are the products of actors' interpretive work and not mere behaviors, then to appreciate fully the problem of deviance the sociologist must attend not to a catalog of norms, but to the context-bound cataloging of actors themselves. This frees sociologists from the dilemma of trying to decide whether their definitions or those of the people they study are more appropriate operationalizations of norm violations. As Kituse points out, it is this focus on members' accounting practices, on the interactional, context-bound process of deviant attribution, which is offered as something *distinctive* or *new* by the societal reaction perspective.

The Empirical Critique

Empirical critiques of the societal reaction perspective have, for the most part, focused on two questions: (1) Do social variables account for a higher proportion of deviant labeling than behavioral variables? and (2) Are labeled persons more likely than nonlabeled persons to deviate more often or with greater seriousness in the future? In general, critics have either ignored or accepted the empirical insights of the perspective regarding the historical origins of deviant categories and the social dynamics of the labeling process. At issue are questions of a more quantitative nature: Do social factors account for more than half of all deviant labels? Do more than half of all labeled deviants deviate more after labeling?

The use of such questions as a definitive test of the societal reaction thesis does violence to the central theoretical concerns of the perspective as a whole. As suggested previously, the main contribution of reaction theorizing is to direct attention to the social dynamics and consequences of labeling, not to propose that more than half of something causes more than half of something else. When critics such as Charles R. Tittle state that "general studies of recidivism do not confirm labeling expectations that more than half [of those labeled] will be recidivists," it is not clear which reaction theorists are being rebuked.[153] Such critics present propositions which misrepresent the basic concerns of the reaction framework, discover that these propositions are not supported by quantitative data (taken mostly from official statistics), and thereby condemn the perspective for failing to prove what it never promised to prove in the first place. As Don Gibbons points out, it is as if straw men were set up and then attacked.[154]

An example of the "straw man" critique is Tittle's often-cited paper "Labelling and Crime: An Empirical Evaluation." Tittle provides an excellent guide to the methodological problems involved in testing the reaction perspective. With few exceptions, reaction research fails to meet such rigorous methodological standards as (1) holding constant actual rule breaking while measuring the relationship between labeling and social factors influencing labeling, and (2) comparing the magnitude of that relationship with that measured when social factors are held constant and the levels of actual rule breaking and labeling are associated. Nonetheless, when proposing his own test, Tittle is far less careful. He proposes a test which is alien to the perspective itself—a test of whether "the probability of being officially classified as a deviant is more heavily influenced by other variables, particularly social disadvantages, than by actual rule-breaking."[155]

Despite the inadequacy of Tittle's empirical standard, his review of the literature uncovers numerous studies which support the general reaction thesis. Thirteen out of seventeen studies suggest that social disadvantage has *some* effect on labeling. A similar pattern is noted for studies which assess the impact of labeling on future deviation. Thus, the vast majority of labeling studies suggest "that social disadvantage may have some effect on labeling and that labeling may have some influence in producing criminal behavior."[156]

A similar conclusion may be drawn regarding the labeling of mental illness. In response to critics such as Walter Gove,[157] reaction theorist Scheff reviews eighteen studies measuring the impact of social contingencies on labeling.[158] Thirteen present evidence favorable to the societal reaction perspective. Evidence favoring secondary deviation is somewhat weaker. Yet, as Ronald Farrell and Victoria Swigert point out, nearly all studies of stigma are weakened by a disregard for the role of *reference groups* in mediating the impact of labeling.[159] One exception is Farrell and James Nelson's study of gays confronted with the label of homosexuality.[160] Here reference groups were seen to have a decisive impact in determining the positive or negative effects of labeling. Had similar measures been included in studies of psychiatric labeling, we would today have a clearer empirical grasp of this type of societal reaction.

The Situated Knowledge Critique

Some of the most challenging research associated with the societal reaction perspective has focused on the historical construction of deviant labels. How is it that certain types of action are broadly recognized as "breaking the rules," while others are viewed as acceptable? This question seems as urgent as ever. Consider, for example, such categories as *sexual harassment* and *date rape*. In the early 1990s attention was focused upon these "controversial" forms of deviance by sensational media coverage of charges of sexual harassment brought by Law Professor Anita Hill against her former employer, and now U.S. Supreme Court Justice, Clarence Thomas, and by allegations by Patricia Bowman that she was raped while on a date with William Kennedy Smith. What constitutes sexual harassment? Why, until recently, have harassing behaviors existed as routine features of the patriarchal workplace? Why, moreover, do allegations of date rape continue to be ridiculed by many men?

Such questions are central to constructionist concerns. Constructionist theory points to historical struggles over the meaning of alleged deviant acts. In this sense, increasing public awareness of both sexual harassment and rape by acquaintances may be viewed as the result of hard-fought struggles by women to redefine the meaning of violent behaviors long justified by male-centered cultural norms.

According to Malcolm Spector and John Kituse's influential 1977 book, *Constructing Social Problems,* the goal of constructionist theory "is to account for how categories of social problems and deviance are produced and how methods of social control and treatment are institutionally established."[161] With this goal in mind, constructionist researchers (particularly those writing for the journal *Social Problems*) have studied efforts to influence public opinion, laws, and other social controls concerning what should be categorized as deviant.[162] Constructionist research on such matters has ranged from the study of deviant labeling of certain types of drug use (but not others) to cigarette smoking, mugging, racial and ethnic images, coffee drinking, alcohol abuse, child and spouse abuse, sudden infant death syndrome, professional medical deviance, homosexuality, panic disorder, missing children, menopause, midwifery, premenstrual syndrome (PMS), and AIDS.[163]

As important as constructionism has been in underscoring historical processes affecting the labeling of deviance, aspects of this perspective are today challenged by critics who raise questions about the situated character of constructionists' own theoretical accounts. One such critic is Donna Haraway. According to Haraway, the "temptations" of a "social constructionist" framework lie in its contention that "*all* . . . knowledge claims, most certainly and especially scientific ones" are to be "theorized as power moves, not moves towards truth."[164] While sympathetic to this "temptation," Haraway voices reservations about a perspective that seemingly offers no "objectively" defendable or "ethically scientific" position from which to question existing structures of power. For Haraway, radical constructionism represents "a terrifying view of the relationship of body and language for those of us who would still like to talk about reality with more confidence than we allow the Christian right's discussion of the Second Coming."[165] Without denying the situated character of all knowledge, something that links constructionism to feminism and other critical viewpoints, Haraway asks:

> [H]ow [can we] have simultaneously an account of radical historical contingency for all knowledge claims and knowing subjects, a critical practice for recognizing our own "semiotic technologies" for making meanings, and a no-nonsense commitment to faithful accounts of a "real" world, one that can be partially shared and friendly to earth-wide projects of finite freedom, adequate material abundance, modest meaning in suffering, and limited happiness[?][166]

Rather than simply opposing constructionism, Haraway supplements its theoretical claims with those of "feminist critical empiricism." This is a perspective which takes seriously the "embodied objectivity" or "experiential standpoint" of women and other disempowered groups. This is not because the standpoint of the oppressed is viewed as being without distortions. It is because the selective distortions forced upon women by patriarchy, as upon nonwhites by white racism, are social constructions that are themselves visibly affected by power. This is what gives the constructions of the oppressed their partial objectivity—an attentiveness (if in sometimes disguised or symptomatic ways) to the effects of power in shaping all claims to knowledge. This may be conveniently overlooked by the people who are most privileged by power. As such, the powerful are often less objective than those they oppress. In this sense, what Haraway describes as *situated objectivity* represents a reflexive form of historical knowledge. Framed by a recognition of its own historical limits, *situated objectivity* begins with an awareness of interdependence between power and knowledge. A methodological move away from all purely scientific "doctrines," the *situated knowledge critique* demands that constructionists be as reflexive about the contexts of their own theoretical activities as they are about the claims of the people they study. "The moral is simple: only partial perspective promises objective vision. This is an objective vision that initiates, rather than closes off, the problem of responsibility for the generativity of all . . . [epistemological] practices."[167]

The Structural Critique

This important criticism suggests that while reaction theorists have spent much time studying (micro) interactions between labeling and deviants, less time has been devoted to examining the relationship between control work and (macro) structural features of society as a whole. "It is not," as Taylor, Walton, and Young point out, "that structural analysis . . . is precluded in the social reaction perspective, but rather that it remains consistently underapplied."[168] A similar point is made by Alex Liazos, who suggests that reaction theory has been guided by a misplaced emphasis on lower- and middle-level agents of control to the exclusion of more basic questions related to the structural organization of power at the top of the social ladder.[169]

Why this misplaced emphasis, this relative inattention to structural questions? Some critics suggest that reaction theorists were unduly constrained by the microlevel theoretical insights of interpretive sociology. Others, such as Alvin Gouldner, suggest that reaction theory was hampered by "a liberal conception . . . that wins sympathy and tolerance for the deviant [but which] does not see deviance as deriving from the specific master institutions of this larger society, or as expressing an active opposition to them."[170] In recent years societal reaction theorists have begun to take this structural critique to heart. In increasing numbers, reaction theorists today reach beyond microlevel studies of labeling in order to explore the relationships between labeling and the social, political, and economic organization of society as a whole. As this happens, the concerns of the societal reaction perspective become more critical. With this in mind, I turn in Chapter 10 to my final theoretical image of deviance—an image of deviance as a power-reflexive feature of the struggle for such control.

NOTES

1 J. L. Simmons, *Deviants*, Boyd & Fraser, San Francisco, 1969, p. 4.

2 Howard S. Becker, *Outsiders: Studies in the Sociology of Deviance*, Free Press, New York, 1963, p. 9.

3 John Kituse, "The 'New Conception of Deviance' and Its Critics," in Walter Gove (ed.), *The Labeling of Deviance: Evaluating a Perspective*, Halstead, New York, 1975, p. 274.

4 George Herbert Mead, "The Psychology of Primitive Justice," *American Journal of Sociology*, vol. 23, 1918, pp. 577–602.

5 Frank Tannenbaum, *Crime and Community*, Ginn, New York, 1938, pp. 19–21.

6 Edwin M. Lemert, *Social Pathology*, McGraw-Hill, New York, 1951.

7 Ibid., p. 449.

8 Don C. Gibbons, *The Criminological Enterprise: Theories and Perspectives*, Prentice-Hall, Englewood Cliffs, N.J., 1979, p. 148.

9 Howard S. Becker, "Whose Side Are We On?" *Social Problems*, vol. 14, winter 1967, p. 240.

10 Nanette J. Davis, *Sociological Constructions of Deviance*, Brown, Dubuque, Iowa, 1980, p. 200.

11 Edwin M. Lemert, *Human Deviance, Social Problems and Social Control*, 2d ed., Prentice-Hall, Englewood Cliffs, N.J., 1972, pp. 16–17.

12 Joseph A. Kotarba, "Labelling Theory and Everyday Deviance," in Jack Douglas et al. (eds.), *Introduction to the Sociologies of Everyday Life*, Allyn & Bacon, Boston, 1980, p. 87.

13 Everett C. Hughes, "Introduction," in Richard Wright, *Black Metropolis: A Study of Negro Life in a Northern City*, Harcourt Brace, New York, 1962, p. xxxvii.

14 Alvin W. Gouldner, "Anti-Minotaur: The Myth of Value Free Sociology," *Social Problems*, vol. 9, 1962, p. 209.

15 Lemert, *Human Deviance, Social Problems and Social Control*, p. 15.

16 Max Weber, *The Methodology of the Social Sciences*, Free Press, New York, 1949.

17 Herbert Blumer, *Symbolic Interactivism*, Prentice-Hall, Englewood Cliffs, N.J., 1966, p. 148.

18 Howard S. Becker (ed.), *The Other Side: Perspectives on Deviance*, Free Press, New York, 1964, p. 2.

19 Ibid., pp. 2–3.

20 John Kituse, "Societal Reaction to Deviant Behavior," *Social Problems*, vol. 9, no. 3, winter 1962, pp. 247–256.

21 Becker, *Outsiders*, p. 23.

22 Ibid., pp. 23–24.

23 Simmons, *Deviants*, pp. 50–102.

24 John Lofland, *Deviance and Identity*, Prentice-Hall, Englewood Cliffs, N.J., 1969, pp. 30–31.

25 Becker, *Outsiders*, p. 24.

26 Simmons, *Deviants*, pp. 64–84.

27 Everett C. Hughes, "Dilemmas and Contradictions of Status," *American Journal of Sociology*, vol. 50, March 1975, pp. 353–359.

28 Becker, *Outsiders*, p. 33.

29 Lemert, *Social Pathology*, as excerpted in Stuart H. Traub and Craig B. Little, *Theories of Deviance*, Peacock, Itasca, Ill., 1975, p. 120.

30 Erving Goffman, *The Presentation of Self in Everyday Life*, Doubleday, Garden City, N.Y., 1959.

31 Erving Goffman, *Stigma: Notes on the Management of Spoiled Identity*, Prentice-Hall, Englewood Cliffs, N.J., 1963.

32 Following the lead of philosopher Edmund Husserl, phenomenological theorists refer to this suspension of judgment as "bracketing" or *epoche*. See, for instance, Edmund Husserl, "Phenomenology," in *Encyclopedia Britannica*, 14th ed., Encyclopedia Britannica Inc., Chicago, 1946, vol. 17, pp. 699–702.

33 Alfred Schutz, *Collective Papers 1: The Problems of Social Reality*, Maurice Natanson (ed.), Nijhoff, The Hague, 1962. Schutz's work represents a synthesis of the phenomenological concerns of philosopher Edmund Husserl and interpretive sociologist Max Weber.

34 Peter Berger and Thomas Luckmann, *The Social Construction of Reality*, Anchor Books, Doubleday, Garden City, N.Y., 1967.

35 For a comparison of ethnomethodology with symbolic interactions, see Don H. Zimmerman and D. Lawrence Weider, "Ethnomethodology and the Problem of Order: Comment on Denzin," in Jack Douglas (ed.), *Understanding Everyday Life*, Aldine, Chicago, 1970, pp. 285–298; see also Stephen J. Pfohl, "Social Role Analysis: The Ethnomethodological Critique," *Sociology and Social Research*, vol. 29, no. 3, April 1975, pp. 243–265.

36 For an ethnomethodological discussion of socialization in the development of interpretive competence, see Peter K. Manning, "Talking and Becoming: A World View of Organizational Socialization," in Jack Douglas (ed.), *Understanding Everyday Life*, Aldine, Chicago, 1970, pp. 239–256.

37 David Sudnow, "Normal Crimes," *Social Problems*, vol. 12, winter 1965, pp. 255–270.

38 Aaron V. Cicourel, *The Social Organization of Juvenile Justice*, Wiley, New York, 1969.

39 Richard McCleary, "How Parole Officers Use Records," *Social Problems*, vol. 24, June 1977, pp. 576–589.

40 Arlene Kaplan Daniels, "The Social Construction of Psychiatric Diagnosis," in H. P. Dreitzel (ed.), *New Sociology No. 2*, Macmillan, New York, 1970, pp. 182–205.

41 Hugh Mehan and Houston Wood, *The Reality of Ethnomethodology*, Wiley, New York, 1975.

42 Melvin Pollner, "Sociological and Commonsense Models of the Labeling Process," in Roy Turner (ed.), *Ethnomethodology*, Penguin, Middlesex, England, 1974, p. 39.

43 D. Lawrence Weider, "Telling the Code," in Turner (ed.), *Ethnomethodology*, pp. 144–172.

44 Harold Garfinkel, *Studies in Ethnomethodology*, Prentice-Hall, Englewood Cliffs, N.J., 1967, pp. 104–115.

45 Harvey Sacks, "On Initial Investigation of the Usability of Conversational Data for Doing Sociology," in David Sudnow (ed.), *Studies in Social Interaction*, Free Press, New York, 1972.

46 Jack D. Douglas, *The Social Meanings of Suicide*, Princeton University Press, Princeton, N.J., 1967.

47 Garfinkel, *Studies in Ethnomethodology*, p. 78.

48 Egon Bittner, "The Police on Skid-Row: A Study of Peace Keeping," *American Sociological Review*, vol. 32, 1969, pp. 669–715.

49 Robert M. Emerson, *Judging Delinquents: Context and Process in Juvenile Justice*, Aldine, Chicago, 1969.

50 Jacqueline P. Wiseman, *Stations of the Lost: The Treatment of Skid Row Alcoholics*, Prentice-Hall, Englewood Cliffs, N.J., 1970.

51 Stephen J. Pfohl, *Predicting Dangerousness: The Social Construction of Psychiatric Reality*, Lexington Books, D.C. Heath, Lexington, Mass., 1978.

52 Becker, *Outsiders*, p. 18.

53 Edwin M. Lemert, "Beyond Mead: The Societal Reduction to Deviance," *Social Problems*, vol. 21, April 1974, pp. 457–468.

54 Lofland, *Deviance and Identity*, p. 14.

55 Edwin M. Schur, *The Politics of Deviance: Stigma Contests and the Uses of Power*, Prentice-Hall, Englewood Cliff, N.J., 1980.

56 Erich Goode, "Marijuana and the Politics of Reality," *Journal of Health and Social Behavior*, vol. 10, September 1969, pp. 83–94.

57 Peter Conrad and Joseph W. Schneider, *Deviance and Medicalization: From Badness to Sickness*, Mosby, St. Louis, 1980, p. 26.

58 See, for instance, Garfinkel, *Studies in Ethnomethodology*, pp. 186–207; and John I. Kituse and Aaron V. Cicourel, "A Note on the Use of Official Statistics," *Social Problems*, vol. 11, fall 1963, pp. 131–139.

59 Edwin M. Schur, *Interpreting Deviance: A Sociological Approach*, Harper & Row, New York, 1979, p. 363.

60 Cicourel, *The Social Organization of Juvenile Justice*, p. 207.

61 Arnold S. Linsky, "Community Homogeneity and the Exclusion of the Mentally Ill: Rejection v. Consensus about Deviance," *Journal of Health and Social Behavior*, vol. 14, December 1970, pp. 304–311; William A. Rushing, "Legitimate, Transitional and Illegitimate Mental Patients in a Midwestern State," *American Journal of Sociology*, vol. 77, November 1971, pp. 511–526; William A. Wilde, "Decision-Making in a Psychiatric Screening Agency," *Journal of Health and Social Behavior*, vol. 9, September 1968, pp. 215–221; and Arnold S. Linsky, "Who Shall Be Excluded: The Influence of Personal Attributes in Community Reactions to the Mentally Ill," *Social Psychiatry*, vol. 5, July 1970, pp. 166–171.

62 William J. Chambliss and Richard H. Nagasawa, "On the Validity of Official Statistics: A Comparative Study of White, Black, and Japanese High-School Boys," *Journal of Research in Crime and Delinquency,* vol. 6, January 1969, pp. 71–77.

63 Mary O. Cameron, *The Booster and the Snitch: Department Store Shoplifting,* Free Press, New York, 1964, p. 136.

64 Douglas, *The Social Meanings of Suicide.*

65 Irving Piliavan and Scott Briar, "Police Encounters with Juveniles," *American Journal of Sociology,* vol. 70, 1964, pp. 206–214.

66 Albert Reiss, *The Police and the Public,* Yale, New Haven, 1971.

67 Maurice Temerlin, "Suggestion Effects in Psychiatric Diagnosis," *Journal of Mental Disease,* vol. 147, April 1968, pp. 349–353.

68 Edwin Pfuhl, *The Deviance Process,* Van Nostrand, New York, 1980, pp. 110–111.

69 James Q. Wilson, "Police Work in Two Cities," in E. Rubington and M. S. Weinberg (eds.), *Deviance: The Interactionist Perspective,* 4th ed., Macmillan, New York, pp. 169–177.

70 Ibid., p. 174.

71 Bittner, "The Police on Skid-Row."

72 Jerome Skolnick, *Justice without Trial,* 2d ed., Wiley, New York, 1975, pp. 176, 179–180.

73 Richard Quinney, *Criminology: Analysis and Critique of Crime in America,* Little, Brown, Boston, 1975, p. 23.

74 Michael E. Milakovich and Kurt Weis, "Politics and Measures of Success in the War on Crime," *Crime and Delinquency,* vol. 21, January 1975, pp. 1–10.

75 Charles H. McCaghy, *Crime in American Society,* Macmillan, New York, 1980, p. 38.

76 See, for instance, Michael Phillipson, *Understanding Crime and Deviance: A Sociological Introduction,* Aldine, Chicago, 1974.

77 Cicourel, *The Social Organization of Juvenile Justice,* p. 15.

78 See, for instance, Edwin M. Schur, *Crimes without Victims: Deviant Behavior and Public Policy,* Prentice-Hall, Englewood Cliffs, N.J., 1965.

79 John Helmer, *Drugs and Minority Oppression,* Seabury, New York, 1975.

80 For a more detailed discussion of these problems, see McCaghy, *Crime in American Society,* pp. 318–357.

81 *The Knapp Commission Report on Police Corruption,* Braziller, New York, 1972.

82 *Crime in the United States, Uniform Crime Reports, 1977,* Department of Justice, Washington, D.C., 1978, p. 172.

83 *Marijuana: A Study of State Policies and Penalties,* report prepared for the National Governors' Conference Center for Policy Research and Analysis, National Institute of Law Enforcement and Criminal Justice, Washington, D.C., 1977.

84 *Uniform Crime Reports, 1977,* p. 172.

85 McCaghy, *Crime in American Society,* p. 346.

86 *Marijuana: A Study of State Policies and Penalties,* p. 140.

87 Erving Goffman, *Asylums,* Anchor Books, Doubleday, New York, 1961.

88 Edwin Schur, *Radical Non-Intervention,* Prentice-Hall, Englewood Cliffs, N.J., 1973.

89 Malcolm Spector and John Kituse, *Constructing Social Problems,* Benjamin/Cummings, Menlo Park, Calif., 1977, p. 72.

90 Joseph R. Gusfield, *Symbolic Crusade,* University of Illinois Press, Urbana, 1963.

91 Kai Erikson, *Wayward Puritans*, Wiley, New York, 1966.

92 Anthony Platt, *The Child-Savers*, University of Chicago Press, Chicago, 1969.

93 William Chambliss, "A Sociological Analysis of the Law of Vagrancy," *Social Problems*, vol. 12, summer 1964, pp. 46–47.

94 Elliot Currie, "Crime without Criminals: Witchcraft and Its Control in Renaissance Europe," *Law and Society Review*, vol. 3, August 1968, pp. 7–32.

95 Joseph Schneider, "Deviant Drinking as Disease: Alcoholism as a Social Accomplishment," *Social Problems*, vol. 25, April 1978, pp. 361–372.

96 Peter Conrad, *Identifying Hyperactive Children: The Medicalization of Deviant Behavior*, D.C. Heath, Lexington, Mass., 1976.

97 Kathleen Tierney, "The Battered Women Movement and the Creation of the Wife Beating Problem," *Social Problems*, vol. 29, February 1982, pp. 207–220; Gerald E. Markle and Ronald J. Troyer, "Smoke Gets in Your Eyes: Cigarette Smoking as Deviant Behavior," *Social Problems*, vol. 26, June 1979, pp. 611–625; and Ronald J. Troyer and Gerald E. Markle, *Cigarettes: The Battle over Smoking*, Rutgers, New Brunswick, N.J., 1983.

98 Becker, *Outsiders*.

99 Stephen J. Pfohl, "The 'Discovery' of Child Abuse," *Social Problems*, vol. 24, February 1977, pp. 310–323.

100 For a sociohistorical account of this organized shift in social control policy, see Alfred R. Lindesmith, *The Addict and the Law*, Indiana University Press, Bloomington, 1965; Charles E. Reasons, "The Politics of Drugs: An Inquiry into the Sociology of Social Problems," *Sociological Quarterly*, vol. 15, summer 1974, pp. 381–404; and David F. Musto, *The American Disease: Origins of Narcotic Control*, Yale, New Haven, Conn., 1973.

101 Becker, *Outsiders*, p. 138.

102 *Marijuana: A Signal of Misunderstanding*, First Report of the National Commission on Marijuana and Drug Abuse, GPO, Washington, D.C., 1972, p. 90. See also *Drug Use in America: Problem in Perspective*, Second Report of the National Commission on Marijuana and Drug Abuse, GPO, Washington, D.C., 1972; *Marijuana and Health*, report to Congress from the Department of Health, Education and Welfare, GPO, Washington, D.C., 1976; and Lester Grinspoon, *Marijuana Reconsidered*, Harvard, Cambridge, Mass., 1971.

103 This July 1937 article is cited in Becker, *Outsiders*, p. 142.

104 Cited in Charles H. McCaghy, *Deviant Behavior: Crime, Conflict and Interest Groups*, Macmillan, New York, 1976, p. 299.

105 Allen Gellen and Maxwell Boas, *The Drug Beat*, McGraw-Hill, New York, 1969, pp. 24–26.

106 Becker, *Outsiders*, p. 145.

107 Donald T. Dickson, "Bureaucracy and Morality: An Organizational Perspective on a Moral Crusade," *Social Problems*, vol. 16, fall 1968, pp. 143–156. See also Charles E. Reasons, "The 'Dope' on the Bureau of Narcotics in Maintaining the Criminal Approach to the Drug Problem," in Charles E. Reasons (ed.), *The Criminologist: Crime and the Criminal*, Goodyear, Pacific Palisades, Calif., 1974, pp. 144–155.

108 Musto, *The American Disease*.

109 John F. Galliher and Allynn Walker, "The Puzzle of the Social Origins of the Marijuana Tax Act of 1937, *Social Problems*, vol. 24, February 1977, pp. 366–376.

110 Pfohl, "The 'Discovery' of Child Abuse."

111 See, for instance, Robert C. Prus, "Resisting Designations: An Extension of Attribution Theory into a Negotiated Context," *Sociological Inquiry*, vol. 45, 1974, pp. 3–14, and "Labelling Theory: A Reconceptualization and a Propositional Statement on Typing," *Sociological Focus*, vol. 8, January 1975, pp. 79–96.

112 Thomas Scheff, *Being Mentally Ill: A Sociological Theory*, Aldine, Chicago, 1966.

113 Ibid., pp. 92–93.

114 David Mechanic, "Some Factors in Identifying and Defining Mental Illness," in S. Spitzer and N. Denzin (eds.), *The Mental Patient: Studies in the Sociology of Deviance*, McGraw-Hill, New York, 1968, pp. 197–198.

115 Of related concern is Richard Hawkins and Gary Tiedman's ethnomethodological description of the manner in which organizational demands for efficiency, self-perpetuation, and accountability contribute to the style and content of labeling. See Richard Hawkins and Gary Tiedman, *The Creation of Deviance*, Merrill, Columbus, Ohio, 1975.

116 James R. Greenley, "The Psychiatric Patient's Family and the Length of Hospitalization," *Journal of Health and Social Behavior*, vol. 13, March 1972, pp. 25–37.

117 Linsky, "Community Homogeneity and the Exclusion of the Mentally Ill"; Rushing, "Legitimate, Transitional and Illegitimate Mental Patients."

118 Dennis R. Wegner and C. Richard Fletcher, "The Effect of Legal Counsel on Admissions to a State Mental Hospital: A Confrontation of Professions," *Journal of Health and Social Behavior*, vol. 10, June 1969, pp. 349–353.

119 Wilde, "Decision-Making in a Psychiatric Screening Agency."

120 Maurice K. Temerlin, "Suggestion Effects in Psychiatric Diagnosis," *Journal of Nervous and Mental Disease*, vol. 147, April 1968, pp. 349–353.

121 David L. Rosenhan, "On Being Sane in Insane Places," *Science*, vol. 179, January 1973, pp. 205–258.

122 Ibid., as reprinted in E. Rubington and M. S. Weinberg (eds.), *Deviance: The Interactionist Perspective*, 4th ed., Macmillan, New York, 1981, p. 230.

123 Harold Garfinkel, "Conditions of Successful Degradation Ceremonies," *American Journal of Sociology*, vol. 61, February 1956, pp. 420–424.

124 Carol Warren and John Johnson, "A Critique of Labeling Theory from the Phenomenological Perspective," in J. D. Douglas and R. Scott (eds.), *Theoretical Perspectives on Deviance*, Basic Books, New York, 1973.

125 Ibid., p. 77.

126 James P. Spradley, *You Owe Yourself a Drink: An Ethnography of Urban Nomads*, Little, Brown, Boston, 1979, p. 254.

127 Robert A. Scott, *The Making of Blind Men*, Russell Sage, New York, 1969.

128 Charles Frazier, *Theoretical Approaches to Deviance: An Evaluation*, Merrill, Columbus, Ohio, 1976.

129 Goffman, *Stigma*.

130 Merle Miller, "What It Means to Be Homosexual," *New York Times Magazine*, January 17, 1971, pp. 9 ff.

131 Marion Yarrow, Charlotte Schwartz, Harriet Murphy, and Leila Deasy, "The Psychological Meaning of Mental Illness in the Family," *Journal of Social Issues*, vol. 11, 1955, pp. 12–24.

132 Arnold Birnhaum, "On Managing Courtesy Stigma," *Journal of Health and Social Behavior*, vol. 11, September 1970, pp. 196–206.

133 Derek Phillips, "Rejection: A Possible Consequence of Seeking Help for Mental Disorders," *American Sociological Review*, vol. 28, December 1963, pp. 963–973.

134 Anthony L. Loman and William E. Larkin, "Rejection of the Mentally Ill: An Experiment in Labelling," *Sociological Quarterly*, vol. 17, autumn 1976, pp. 555–560.

135 Delos H. Kelly, "The Role of Teachers' Nominations in the Perpetuation of Deviant Adolescent Careers," in Delos H. Kelly (ed.), *Deviant Behavior*, St. Martin's, New York, 1979, pp. 322–333.

136 Ibid., p. 332.

137 Richard D. Schwartz and Jerome H. Skolnick, "Two Studies of Legal Stigma," in Becker, *The Other Side*, pp. 103–117.

138 W. Buikhuisen and P. H. Dijksterhuis, "Delinquency and Stigmatization," *British Journal of Criminology*, vol. 11, April 1971, p. 186.

139 Gary T. Marx, "Ironies of Social Control: Authorities as Contributors to Deviance through Escalation, Non-Enforcement, and Covert Facilitation," *Social Problems*, vol. 28, February 1981, pp. 221–246.

140 Ibid., pp. 230–231.

141 Ibid., p. 221.

142 Edward Sagarin, *Odd Man In: Societies of Deviants in America*, Quadrangle, Chicago, 1969.

143 Stanford Lyman, *The Asian in the West*, Western Studies Center, Desert Research Center, Reno/Las Vegas, Nev., 1970, p. 37.

144 D. Teal, *The Gay Militants*, Stein & Day, New York, 1971.

145 See, for instance, Maurica Anderson, "Hookers, Arise!" *Human Behavior*, January 1975, pp. 40–42.

146 For a more detailed discussion of these matters, see Conrad and Schneider, *Deviance and Medicalization*, pp. 199–204.

147 Howard S. Becker, "Labelling Theory Reconsidered," in Howard S. Becker, *Outsiders: Studies in the Sociology of Deviance*, rev. ed., Free Press, New York, 1973, pp. 177–208.

148 Travis Hirschi, "Labelling Theory and Juvenile Delinquency: An Assessment of the Evidence," in Gove, *The Labeling of Deviance*, p. 181.

149 Jack Gibbs, "Issues in Defining Deviant Behavior," in R. A. Scott and J. D. Douglas (eds.), *Theoretical Perspectives on Deviance*, Basic Books, New York, pp. 56–64.

150 Kituse, "The 'New Conception of Deviance' and Its Critics."

151 Ibid.

152 Ibid., p. 278.

153 Charles R. Tittle, "Labelling and Crime: An Empirical Evaluation," in Gove, *The Labeling of Deviance*, pp. 157–179.

154 Gibbons, *The Criminological Enterprise*, pp. 151–152.

155 Tittle, "Labelling and Crime."

156 Ibid., p. 175.

157 Walter Gove, "Societal Reaction Theory as an Explanation of Mental Illness: An Evaluation," *American Sociological Review*, vol. 35, October 1970, pp. 873–874.

158 Thomas J. Scheff, "The Labelling Theory of Mental Illness," *American Sociological Review*, vol. 30, June 1974, pp. 444–452.

159 Ronald A. Farrell and Victoria L. Swigert, *Deviance and Social Control*, Scott, Foresman, Glenview, Ill. 1982, pp 115–122.

160 Ronald A. Farrell and James F. Nelson, "A Causal Model of Secondary Deviance: The Case of Homosexuality," *Sociological Quarterly*, vol. 17, winter 1976, pp. 109–120.

161 Malcolm Spector and John Kituse, *Constructing Social Problems*, Benjamin/Cummings, Menlo Park, Calif., 1977, p. 72.

162 See, for instance, Armand L. Mauss, *Social Problems as Social Movements*, Lippincott, Philadelphia, 1975; Joseph R. Gusfield, *The Culture of Public Problems*, University of Chicago Press, Chicago, 1981; Joel Best, *Images of Deviance*, Aldine De Gruyter, New York, 1989. For a critical reconsideration of theoretical, methodological, and political issues pertaining to the social constructionist perspective, see *Social Problems*, vol. 32, no. 3, February 1985, which includes a paper by Steve Woolgar and Dorothy Pawluch, "Ontological Gerrymandering: The Anatomy of Social Problems Explanation," pp. 211–227, with critical responses by Stephen Pfohl, Joseph W. Schneider, and Lawrence W. Hazelrigg. See also James A. Holstein and Gale Millers (eds.), *Reconsidering Social Constructionism*, JAI, Greenwich, Conn., 1993.

163 See, for instance, Naomi Aronson, "Nutrition as a Social Problem: A Case Study of Entrepreneurial Strategy in Science," *Social Problems*, vol. 29, 1982, pp. 474–487; Richard A. Ball and Robert J. Lilly, "The Menace of Margarine: The Rise and Fall of a Social Problem," *Social Problems*, vol. 29, 1982, pp. 488–498; Joel Best, "Rhetoric in Claims-Making: Constructing the Missing Children Problem," *Social Problems*, vol. 43, 187, pp. 101–121; Robert L. Chauncey, "New Careers for Moral Entrepreneurs: Teenage Drinking," *Journal of Drug Issues*, vol. 10, 1980, pp. 48–70; Peter Conrad, "The Discovery of Hyperactive Children: Notes on the Medicalization of Deviant Behavior," *Social Problems*, vol. 23, 1975, pp. 512–521; Jonathan Dollimore, *Sexual Dissidence: Augustine to Wilde, Freud to Foucault*, Clarendon Press, Oxford, 1991; Steven C. Dubin, "Symbolic Slavery: Black Representations in Popular Culture," *Social Problems*, vol. 34, 1987, pp. 122–140; Juan Flores and George Yudice, "Living Borders/Buscando America: Languages of Latino Self-Formation," *Social Text*, vol. 24, 1990, pp. 57–85; David Greenberg, *The Construction of Homosexuality*, University of Chicago Press, Chicago, 1988; Edward Guerro, "AIDS as Monster in Science Fiction and Horror Films," *Journal of Popular Film and Television*, vol. 18, 1990, pp. 86–93; Joseph R. Gusfield, "Categories of Ownership and Responsibility in Social Issues: Alcohol Abuse and Automobile Use," *Journal of Drug Issues*, vol. 5, 1975, pp. 285–303; Stuart Hall, Chas Critcher, Tony Jefferson, John Clarke, and Brian Roberts, *Policing the Crisis: Mugging, the State, and Law and Order*, Macmillan, London, 1978; Michael P. Johnson and Karl Hufbauer, "Sudden Infant Death Syndrome as a Medical Research Problem since 1945," *Social Problems*, vol. 30, 1982, pp. 65–81; Donileen R. Loseke and Spencer E. Cahill, "The Social Construction of Deviance: Experts on Battered Women," *Social Problems*, vol. 31, 1984, pp. 296–310; Gerald E. Markle and Ronald J. Troyer, "Smoke Gets in Your Eyes: Cigarette Smoking as Deviant Behavior," *Social Problems*, vol. 26, 1979, pp. 611–623; Frances B. McCrea, "The Politics of Menopause: The 'Discovery' of a Deficiency Disease," *Social Problems*, vol. 31, 1983, pp. 111–123; Carol Klaperman Morrow, "Sick Doctors: The Social Construction of Professional Deviance," *Social Problems*, vol. 30, 1982, pp. 92–108; Elaine Neuhring and Gerald D. Markle, "Nicotine and Norms: the Reemergence of a Deviant Behavior," *Social Problems*, vol. 21, 1974, pp. 513–526; Jackie Orr, "Theory on the Market: Panic, Incorporating," *Social Problems*, vol. 37, 1990, pp. 460–484; Stephen Pfohl, "The 'Discovery' of Child Abuse," *Social Problems*, vol. 24, 1977, pp. 310–324; Michael Rogin, " 'Make My Day!': Spectacle as Amnesia in Imperial Politics," *Representations*, vol. 29, 1990, pp. 99–123; Barbara Katz Rothman, "Midwives in Transition:

The Structure of a Clinical Revolution," *Social Problems*, vol. 30, 1983, pp. 262–271; Joseph Schneider, "Deviant Drinking as a Disease: Alcoholism as a Social Accomplishment," *Social Problems*, vol. 25, 1978, pp. 361–372; Ronald J. Troyer and Gerald E. Markle, "Coffee Drinking: An Emergent Social Problem?" *Social Problems*, vol. 31, 1984; pp. 403–416; and Simon Watney, *Policing Desire: Pornography, AIDS and the Media*, University of Minnesota Press, Minneapolis, 1987.

164 Donna J. Haraway, "Situated Knowledges," in *Simians, Cyborgs and Women: The Reinvention of Nature*, Routledge, New York, 1991, pp. 185–201.

165 Ibid., p. 184.

166 Ibid., p. 187.

167 Ibid., p. 191.

168 Ian Taylor, Paul Walton, and Jock Young, *The New Criminology: For a Social Theory of Deviance*, Routledge & Kegan Paul, London, 1973, p. 167.

169 Alexander Liazos, "The Poverty of the Sociology of Deviance: Nuts, Sluts, and Perverts," *Social Problems*, vol. 20, summer 1972, pp. 103–120.

170 Alvin W. Gouldner, "The Sociologist as Partisan: Sociology and the Welfare State," *American Sociologist*, May 1968, p. 107.

Make-Over By Joseph LaMantia and Stephen Pfohl

10

CRITICAL PERSPECTIVES:
Toward a Power-Reflexive Deconstruction of Deviance and Difference

So you can see I have powers. I recommend these powers because they impart control. But they can also drive you insane. It is imperative to remember that . . . power lies in the words, the symbols, and not in the self. . . . I get into lots of trouble . . . for my frequent assertion that the boundary between the legal and the illegitimate is just a metaphysical scripting of negotiated power.

Patricia J. Williams[1]

Without critical thought we are bound to the only form of social life we know—that which currently exists. We are unable to choose a better life; our only activity is in further support of the system in which we are enslaved.

Richard Quinney[2]

INTRODUCTION

Several years ago I received a phone call from a reporter for *Time.* The reporter, a white male journalist with a cover story on his mind, was involved in researching the so-called War on Drugs. He wanted my opinion. He was particularly concerned with crack cocaine. Viewing me as an expert on "deviant behavior," he asked whether I favored stricter punishments or thought that treatment was the answer.

These were the only options the reporter wanted me to comment upon. Instead, as a sociologist concerned with the ways that power shapes both our desires and our moral perceptions, I tried to offer the journalist an alternative perspective. I suggested that an exclusive focus on either punishment or rehabilitation ignores the more complex and contradictory context of contemporary drug use. I was speaking about the mass marketing of both legal and illegal drugs as a solution to the widespread experience of powerlessness, social alienation, and personal anxiety.

The reporter expressed uncertainty about what I was saying: "Does that mean you favor treatment?" Treatment programs, I explained, attempt to help people to break the hold of various psychic and chemical addictions. This is important. This is also why it is disturbing to see treatment programs vastly underfunded in comparison with programs aimed at arresting and imprisoning persons involved with illegal drugs. Still, by themselves, neither programs of treatment nor stricter punishment are likely to alter the historical and social structural conditions that today make illegal drug use so appealing.

"What do you mean by historical and structural conditions?" asked the reporter. I was thinking about sociological concerns that lie at the core of *critical perspectives* on deviance and social control. I explained that if our society really wanted to reduce the abuse of illegal drugs then we would have to shift our focus from the sale and consumption of "controlled substances" to what makes the highs offered by such drugs so appealing. This is particularly important when considering the attraction of drugs, such as crack cocaine, to people living in blighted inner-city neighborhoods. For people trying to survive the oppressive constraints of relative economic powerlessness, racism, and sexualized terror, cocaine-induced feelings of self-control and bodily pleasure may provide short-term relief from the pains of everyday life. From one crack-induced high to another the agony of powerlessness may momentarily be abated.

Feel the power! Take the power! Let the power take you! Messages such as these blast away at the poor, the racially oppressed, and the sexually terrorized, who are denied access to legitimate structures of power. The feeling of power promised by illegal drugs may operate as a seductive lure to the relatively powerless. Moreover, in areas scarred by unemployment, and particularly where rates of unemployment for young black and Latino males may reach upward of 50 percent, it is no accident that the financial incentives offered by the marketing of crack are today at a premium. These are historical and structural conditions. Such conditions have everything to do with the everyday social realities of drug use.

Historical and structural conditions also have everything to do with social power and the ways that power affects our perceptions of the most appropriate ways to act. Nevertheless, the practical importance of such conditions is routinely ignored by officials who are charged with finding solutions to "the drug problem" in terms of either treatment or punishment. Thus, efforts aimed at reducing the social and personal costs of illegal drug use are doomed to failure. The reason is simple. Such problems are never purely individualistic. They are also problems of social justice—problems concerning how various psychic and material resources are made both scarce and legitimately more available to some groups than to others.

By aiming to change individuals without also changing the ways in which relations of power give form to individuals' experience, isolated strategies of treatment or punishment may perpetuate rather than reduce the problems they hope to solve. On the other hand, to incorporate questions concerning power and social justice into efforts aimed at reducing the problems of drug abuse (or, for that matter, any other form of social deviance) is to widen the scope for both studying and responding to nonconformity. This, I suggested to the reporter, is what I had in mind when referring to historical and structural conditions. To deal seriously with questions about historical power and structures of social inequality is to also widen society's political approach to deviance. It is not enough to demand that deviants change. It is also necessary to radically transform the ritual organization of power in society as a whole.

Much of what I was saying still seemed rather abstract to the *Time* journalist. To be more concrete, I pointed to well-documented (if under-publicized) evidence of the U.S. government's own complicity in the marketing of illegal cocaine. Indeed, following a congressional ban on funding to support the Contras in Nicaragua during the 1980s, secret agents within the U.S. government had cut deals with various South American cocaine cartels, guaranteeing the safe passage of illegal drugs into the U.S. in exchange for money and guns to arm "our" Contra allies. The Contras, although they were called "freedom fighters" by the Reagan and Bush administrations, were, in actuality, U.S.-paid terrorists. Their mission was to undermine the Sandinista government in Nicaragua, following that country's 1979 overthrow of the brutal U.S.-backed dictator, Anastasio Somoza. U.S. actions on behalf of the Contras—including the mining of Nicaragua's harbors by the Central Intelligence Agency (CIA)—had been declared illegal by the World Court in Geneva. In response to mounting criticism, both by the international community and by U.S. citizens, Congress voted to cut off Contra funding. Nevertheless, bent on bringing Nicaragua back in line with U.S. economic interests, the Reagan and Bush administrations continued to support the Contras through illegal means.

One of the means chosen was the international drug trade—a major source of economic survival for impoverished South American countries, such as Peru and Colombia, and a secret avenue by which the United States could continue to fund its campaign of terror against Nicaragua. The details of such high-level "government deviance" are recounted in such important studies as Peter Dale Scott and Jonathan Marshall's *Cocaine Politics: Drugs, Armies and the C.I.A. in Central America*.[3] The implications for the social control of drugs are enormous. In order to covertly advance its own illegal campaigns against resistive third world countries, the United States made alliances with criminals it labeled "narco-terrorists." This helped to increase the supply and lower the price of cocaine being imported into the United States.

This, I explained to the journalist from *Time*, is another way of making structural connections between individual drug use and the organization of power in society as a whole. At this point, I was speaking of historical connections between the structure of poverty in the third world (where illegal cocaine is produced) and impoverishment in the United States (on the part of the people who are most caught up in the marketing and consumption of cocaine). I asked the reporter whether any of this made sense. I wondered if he now understood why I felt it unwise to discuss issues pertaining to punishment or treatment without linking these to wider questions of power. An uncomfortable silence haunted the telephone wires that connected us.

After a time the journalist responded with yet another question. "This is all very interesting, Professor, but do you think there's anyone else in this country who shares your particular viewpoint? I mean, I've been talking to a lot of experts, but what you're saying seems quite different. Is there some-body else you could refer me to who might offer a related perspective?"

I gave the reporter the names of a few books and articles he might read. But not a word of our nearly forty-five-minute conversation made it into the special issue of his magazine. There was a lot about punishment and quite a bit about treatment, but virtually nothing connecting desires for drugs to contradictory historical structures of power. It was as if all we had talked about had disappeared into the transnational airwaves of power itself. And maybe it had?

I wonder if my words will affect you any differently. Perhaps, if you've journeyed with me this far in this text, you might make something more of my words than the reporter did. This is a hope offered by *critical theoretical perspectives on deviance and control*—a hope that together we may begin to make theoretical sense of the troubling and contradictory social conditions in which we find ourselves historically positioned in relation to others—and that out of such reflexive sense-making we may move toward the construction of more just and more generous forms of both power and knowledge.

THEORETICAL IMAGES

Critical perspectives on deviance and social control are rooted in both *theoretical* and *practical* concerns. *Theoretically*, critical perspectives attempt to make sense of the relationship between human struggles for power in history and the ritual construction, deconstruction, and reconstruction of normative social boundaries. *Practically*, people who engage in critical theorizing ally themselves with people who are committed to the uprooting of hierarchical social forms and the realization of social justice. This combination of theoretical and practical concerns leads critical theorists to examine the material and symbolic relationships between power, social control, and actions which resist control. How might we best imagine the relationship between particular forms of power and the historical organization of both social control and resistance? How do powerful rituals of control affect the human rights, dignity, and material well-being of all people? In what ways do control rituals favor the economic, sex or gender, and/or racialized interests of some people to the exclusion of others?[4] Such questions guide the sociological imaginations of critical theorists.

I am referring to critical perspectives in the plural. This is no accident. Critical perspectives are unlike other perspectives examined in this text in that there is no one definitive version of critical theorizing. This is true not only because critical theory is today still emerging as a major conceptual framework. Critical thinking about the relationship between social hierarchies and historically specific forms of knowledge has long haunted the most influential theories about deviance, theories whose more comfortable relations to power have earned them considerable privilege and prestige. Nor is it true simply because no one version of critical theory is capable of addressing the multiple and contradictory faces of hierarchical power. The lack of a single standard for critical theory is no loss for people who recognize that social justice is better realized by a reciprocal convergence of different social standpoints than by the unilateral imposition of one conceptual framework to the exclusion of others. By emphasizing the multiplicity of critical perspectives I mean also to underscore the awareness, on the part of critical theorists, that even our own theoretical frameworks must be understood as but partial elements of the contradictory scenes of power in which we too are struggling in history.

Critical perspectives continue to conduct a passionate dialogue with the multiple social worlds that we, as theorists, embody. Critical thought acknowledges itself as socially situated thought; its own form and content are forever partial, provisional, and reflexively open to ongoing historical modifications. Thus, while critical theorists may seek to rigorously conceptualize and relentlessly challenge the multiple faces of hierarchical power, they nevertheless approach the study of deviance and social control with the recognition that there is never one absolutely correct theoretical or political framework by which to regulate critical thought and practice. To act upon this awareness is no easy task. It demands reflexive self-critique, as well as a commitment to complex historical, cultural, and experiential sociological analysis.

The general concerns of critical theorizing should, by now, be relatively familiar to many of you as readers. They have guided much of what I have written in this text. In Chapter 1 the story of deviance and social control was pictured as a story of battle, a story of struggles to define what is socially viewed as "normal." In each subsequent chapter I have attempted to raise questions about the diverse ways in which theoretical images of deviance arise out of and feed upon the social organization of power at different points in history. In this chapter I will try to make the theoretical basis of these concerns more explicit.

Power and Knowledge Hierarchies and the Ritual Control of Deviance

Critical theories about deviance and social control arise from multiple historical roots. In this chapter I ask you to consider the particular importance of *Marxist, anarchist, feminist,* and *radical multicultural* standpoints in the construction of critical theory and practice. Each of these perspectives labors to both interpret and change the social dynamics of hierarchical power. Each also recognizes that power and knowledge (about the role of power in shaping deviance and social control) are mutually constitutive—that neither exists nor can exist independently of its relations to the other.

For Marxist scholars this means that it is impossible to imagine either power or knowledge separately from the way that each is mediated by the contradictory social relations through which we human animals secure the material and imaginary conditions of our economic survival. For anarchists, feminists, and multicultural critics, the material and imaginary character of such mediations is even more complex. Anarchists weave critical theoretical stories about how rituals of authority transform the situated character of historically constructed hierarchies into seemingly "natural" or "timeless" factual realities. Feminist and multicultural critics underscore the sexually differentiated and racially coded violence embodied within ritual pretensions to a universalistic viewpoint.

Each of these critical standpoints also directs attention to the way in which *hegemonic ritual interaction* constructs both *historically material* and *symbolic relations* between *power* and *knowledge*. *Power, knowledge, historical materiality, symbolic social controls,* and *hegemonic ritual interactions*: it is at the crossroads of these five concepts that critical perspectives typically stake their theoretical challenge. Before examining the historical context and multiple contributions of Marxism, anarchism, feminism, and radical multicultural perspectives to the development of critical thought, I will first present an overview of each of these critical theoretical concepts.

Power: The Transformative Character of Social Control   The word *power* is derived from the Latin verb *potere*, meaning "to be able." Power is the ability to make things happen. A dynamic characteristic of all productive human animal relations, power affects both people and what happens between people. Power gives our imaginary and material relations to others their ritual social forms. Power both enables and constrains us. It permits us to recognize and act toward each other in socially patterned ways. As Michel Foucault points out, this is what makes power a transformative social force.[5] Power sets into place and continually replaces the fields of force in which we find ourselves embodied with and/or against others. Though power is an omnipresent feature of social life, it is, nevertheless, structured differently in different times and places in history. Thus, while it is possible (and perhaps even critically necessary) to imagine relatively equal or reciprocal forms of power, such forms are far from the reality of the economically exploitative, authoritarian, racist, and heterosexist hierarchies in which most of us currently live.

Power affects the way we are attracted to certain forms of relations while being repulsed by others. Power opens the door for some types of social experiences while prohibiting or imprisoning others. As such, power is a contradictory (and often unequal) feature of all orderly social forms. Power is the aspect of our ritual relations to others that is capable of transforming fluid and open-ended possibilities into something we may perceive as solid, fixed, or objective. Power works through, upon, and between our bodies, ceaselessly constructing and reconstructing the boundaries and limits of what we experience as real. To experience power is to recognize the diverse ways in which our actions control (and are controlled by) our relations to others. In this way, the experience of power is a fundamental human experience. According to psychologist Rollo May, to experience power is to experience "Being" itself. It is to experience a basic feature of our human-animal nature—the ability to create or procreate, the ability to exercise one's being in relation to others.

In his book *Power and Innocence*, May examines what happens when something blocks the experience of power, when the ritual structure of human relations suppresses our "power to be."[6] When this occurs we tend to search for alternative means by which to affirm, assert, or even aggressively realize the experience of power. Sometimes even these alternative avenues of power are denied us. When this is the case we may resort to violence. Violence is thus a power-play, a final and dramatic gesture through which we assert control over a world which appears to escape our grasp.

May's perspective on the relationship between power, powerlessness, and violence helps us to understand the social meaning of violence in a world in which power is unevenly distributed. People who are ritually positioned so as to exercise unequal power may use violence or threats of violence to defend their own abilities to transform the world. Thus, powerful governments, organizations, and individuals may deploy violence against others who resist their efforts to construct particular versions of social reality. This is evident in such violent defenses of hierarchy as recent U.S. foreign policy aimed at countering movements for social justice in Central America and the Caribbean, the suppression of democratic resistance in Communist China, and the denial of basic civil liberties to Palestinians living in Israeli-occupied territories. The state-supported oppression of Irish citizens living under British military rule and the long-term domination of black South Africans by the white racist institutions of apartheid are other examples of the use of violence to defend established hierarchies.

By using violence, the people most privileged by power attempt to defend themselves against threats to their own hierarchical controls. In societies characterized by heterosexist, economic, and racist hierarchies, the presence or threat of violence may form a backdrop for even the most mundane relations between men and women, between straight people and "queers," between the rich and the impoverished, and between peoples divided by the cultural privileging of certain shades of skin color over others. Although the violence of hierarchical power is most dramatic when it is physical and overt, as in men's violence against women or in white police violence against racial minorities, it may also take forms in which it is subtler and easier to deny. Think, for instance, of the psychic violence felt daily by women subjected to the unwanted catcalls of men. Consider also the implicit violence in pictures of female bodies pinned up for male pornographic pleasure and in the presence of ritualized sexual harassment at school and at work.

Related forms of psychic violence may be felt by gays, lesbians, and bisexuals, whose "queer" erotic preferences are daily greeted by brutal forms of discrimination on the part of defensive straight people. And what about the psychic violence experienced by people who must bear the stigma of AIDS, poverty, or homelessness? Or that felt by American Indians, African-Americans, Asian-Americans, and Latinos? These peoples have been ritually bombarded during more than 500 years of North American history, which speaks of freedom while ignoring both the lack of freedom and the cultural accomplishments of Americans who are not white. Strengthened by a variety of feminist, "queer," multicultural, and class-based movements for social justice, critical theorists of deviance and social control have become deeply concerned about the psychically and even bodily sickening consequences of these subtle forms of hierarchical violence.

May's conception of the relationship between power and violence is applicable also to violence by the relatively powerless. Consider people who find few experiences of power in the public world of social, economic, and political life. The people I have in mind may be unemployed or may work in jobs which provide very low income and even less prestige. Experiencing little control over their public destinies, such people may concentrate their search for power in the private sphere, in relation to spouses, lovers, children, or other intimate acquaintances. In so doing, they may be placing too many eggs in the same basket. The problem is exacerbated by the fact that powerlessness in the public sphere generates additional stress in private life. Crowded living spaces, inadequate health care, and limited provisions for recreation or other sources of tension release may narrow publicly impoverished persons' options for private power. Small interpersonal tensions or relatively minor disagreements can quickly escalate into big challenges to such persons' sense of power. This is a structural liability when the search for power is concentrated in the sphere of private, interpersonal relationships. These relationships become overburdened with power. The result may be higher rates of interpersonal and family violence.

So far, I have been discussing May's ideas about power in relation to violence. May suggests that where we find the smoke of violence we are also likely to find the fire of a power struggle. But what about the more general categories of deviance and social control? Are these related to power in a similar way? Such is certainly the case with social control. After all, what is social control but the ability to make things happen in some ways but not others? Social control is always an exercise of power. Does this mean that social control is always an exercise of power by some people over others—a hierarchical exercise of power such that some have more at the expense of those who have less? If this be the case, then deviance is always a power struggle too, an effort to reassert or regain power in relation to controllers who limit one's access to power in the first place.

Conceived of in this fashion, deviance appears to be a strategy of resistance, a way of asserting lost power, a mode of reestablishing the ability to make things happen, to transform things according to one's will. Social control is the opposite. It is the labor of the powerful to keep the powerless in positions of relative disadvantage. Deviance and social control are thus the twin blades of a power struggle, each like a razor slashing into the other's ability to transform the world into its own image and likeness. Moreover, just as with other power struggles, the trump card of both sides in the battle of deviance and social control is violence—the use of violent force to curtail the behavior of those who trespass upon the other's claim to power!

This is a fairly dramatic way of looking at deviance. Is social control truly to be conceived of as a struggle to deviantize people whose thoughts, feelings, or actions challenge those in positions of greater power? This is a troubling question. If Rollo May is correct that power is a basic feature of all human action, then to answer such questions we must critically examine the very core of our human social existence. In struggling with others over power, we must ask whether it is inevitable that one side must triumph while the other is branded deviant. Or is it possible to exert power without exerting restrictive control over the power of others? Is it possible, in other words, to ritually structure power such that power relations may be more reciprocal than hierarchical, such that power struggles may be resolved by reconciliation rather than by conquest, such that power may be collectively shared instead of institutionally stratified? To ask such questions is to begin to approach the study of deviance and social control from a critical perspective.

Knowledge: The Historical Materiality of Symbolic Power   Critical perspectives propose that, in a society stratified by hierarchical power, the social control of deviance will be governed by the interests of those most privileged by power. To classify certain behaviors as deviant is to suppress the resistance of those who threaten such privilege. This is to produce a knowledge of the world that is thoroughly mediated by power. To partake of such knowledge is to actively reproduce hierarchy. The social construction of such knowledge is as important to a critical understanding of deviance as is the social construction of power. Knowledge and power: each operates as the flip side of the other.

Knowledge, however, is no simple servant of power. Knowledge is supplementary to power. It feeds back upon power in either of two distinct ways: it either amplifies or subverts power's most dominant effects. In the first instance, knowledge may itself become a form of power. It exerts itself. It stabilizes the field of social relations secured by power. When this happens, knowledge may take on a life of its own, magnifying the effects of power by acting to symbolically control the relations out of which power arose.

Knowledge may also subvert power. By channeling the flow of relations in some directions but not in others, power surrounds itself with what it excludes. In this sense, all relations of power are haunted relations, contradictory relations made uneasy by what they repress. Out of such hauntings, power may engender deviant forms of knowledge. These resist the smooth operation of power, as relations repressed by power return with a vengeance. Such subversive forms of knowledge often appear in disguise, hovering around power but in unspoken, unconscious, or intuitive ways. Think, for instance, of the ways by which women may know that they are oppressed by patriarchy, even if such knowledge is not clearly formulated or theoretically framed. Prior to putting such knowledge into words, women may simply "feel" that something is not quite right about the way that their male teachers, employers, or lovers act in their presence. Although such feelings may be dismissed by most men as "hysterical" and "deviant," they are, nevertheless, real sources of knowledge about how power works within and upon women's bodily relations to others.

In order for such subversive forms of knowledge to counter the reproduction of hierarchy, it is necessary that they be collectively recognized as truthful. An important contribution of feminism and other movements to social justice is the public authorization of knowledge that challenges hierarchy. Even when resistive forms of knowledge are not publicly acknowledged, they may still detour, jam up, or slow down the working of hierarchy. This happens whenever subversive knowledge assumes such subtle political shapes as sickness, emotional disturbance, tardiness, or ironic detachment.

Whether amplifying or subverting power, the relationship between knowledge and power operates at multiple experiential levels. At a *cognitive level*, knowledge may function to either rationalize or resist power. Think, for instance, of the ways in which traditional Christian knowledge often portrayed women as deviant "gateways" to the charms of the devil. As pointed out in Chapter 2, such cognitions served to rationalize the continuance of patriarchy. In a related way, the "hedonistic rationality" guiding the eighteenth-century cognitions of classical theorists (discussed in Chapter 3) channeled people's perceptions of deviance in such a way that calculated choice was seen behind every act of nonconformity. This vision arose to the exclusion of others. It blinded classical theorists to the contradictory social situations in which people made real-life choices to obey or break with existing social norms. In this sense, cognitive knowledge functions as a filtering device or a logical control mechanism affecting our perceptions of deviant acts and actors.

The reverse may occur in the case of resistive cognitions. For instance, once someone begins to interpret the world through the critical standpoint of feminism, a wide range of previously taken-for-granted social experiences may assume new political meanings. For instance, when men and women share the same classroom, who talks more frequently and with what tone of voice? Who typically interrupts whom? Who uses certain metaphors or figures of speech? How, moreover, do such everyday social events connect to the reproduction or change of traditional gender hierarchies?

Moral and bodily levels of knowledge operate in a related manner. In using the term *moral knowledge,* I refer to the evaluative feelings and emotional tones that surround our judgments of what is right and wrong. For example, in the heterosexist society in which we currently live, many persons feel that there is something morally wrong with gay, lesbian, and bisexual conduct, even though few come up with logical reasons by which to cognitively rationalize such judgmental emotions. When questioned, some will say that they simply "know in their hearts" that homosexual behaviors are wrong. Such "heart-felt" moral or evaluative knowledge is an important form of social control. So, too, might it be a form of resistance. Another example is the disgust that many poor people feel toward even the best-meant gestures of the rich. This disgust represents a significant—if relatively undertheorized—form of knowledge about power's most insidious effects.

Like cognitive knowledge, moral knowledge filters the world through relations of power. So do bodily forms of knowledge. By *bodily knowledge* I mean "truths" that manifest themselves through physical or carnal sensations. When confronted with behaviors they sense as deviant, people may experience a wide variety of physical states: agitation, rage, queasiness, or even sickened repulsion. In a racist society such as our own, persons sometimes feel physically disturbed by the sight of interracial couples, though they may find nothing cognitively or morally wrong with interracial dating. People who are acting in resistance to power also may recognize its operations in such bodily ways. Thus, an interracial couple out on a date may literally sense others' discomfort at a physical level, even when the people who are made uncomfortable by the couple's "deviance" offer cognitive or moral disclaimers. In this way, knowledge of power operates in bodily ways that are never exactly equal to cognitive and moral knowledges. Power and knowledge function simultaneously at all three levels when they are most controlling or most subversive.

To "know" that somebody is a deviant—regardless of whether that knowledge is cognitive, moral, or bodily—is to exercise power. This may result in the reproduction of social inequality. If the "haves" had to constantly use force to keep an upper hand over the "have-nots," life would be little more than a war between opposing interests. But what if those most privileged by power manage the production of social knowledge in such a way that the relatively powerless are perceived as the cause of their own troubles? In this case, efforts aimed at controlling the resistance of disadvantaged persons might appear natural or necessary. The likelihood of an overt state of war would be reduced. This, of course, is exactly what happens when those who resist power become known as deviant. The label of deviance depoliticizes the maintenance of social hierarchy.

Stereotypical knowledge of deviance, implying as it does a class of troubled or defective persons, can both hide and advance the interests of those in positions of power. As George Jackson, the militant African-American prison writer, stated shortly before his 1971 assassination in California's San Quentin Prison, "The textbooks on criminology like to advance the idea that prisoners are mentally defective. There is only the merest suggestion that the system is at fault."[7] The U.S. society in which Jackson lived was stamped unalterably by racism and by rigid structural divisions between rich and poor. Reflecting on his own life, Jackson realized that state control of knowledge about who and what is deviant is a complex political act.

Jackson's analysis challenges us to see knowledge about deviance as structurally related to the organization of power. This understanding is crucial to critical standpoints on deviance and social control. By reflexively politicalizing all forms of knowledge, critical perspectives hope to "denaturalize" the otherwise taken-for-granted character of its valuation and protection by the forces of control. In this way, critical perspectives contribute to the deconstruction of unequal arrangements of power and knowledge, and to the reconstruction of more just and reciprocal forms of social order. But what is it that sociologically connects power and knowledge? In addressing this question, critical theorists emphasize the historical materiality and the symbolic character of hegemonic ritual interactions.

Historical Materiality: The Economic Basis of Power and Knowledge
For critical theorists the way in which knowledge operates in conjunction with power is at once *historically material* and *symbolic*. By pointing to the historical materiality of knowledge I mean to connote the diverse ways in which our perceptions of deviance are both constrained and facilitated by our economic relations to others. Thus, the materiality of a slave's economic vantage point will give that person access to knowledge (as unwelcome and accursed as this knowledge may be) that lies outside the historical limits of what the slave's master might know, or even imagine knowing. As a more contemporary example, consider a complaint commonly voiced by women in discussing sexual harassment. According to many women, "Men just don't get it." Why? Are men less able to cognitively comprehend the deviant character of harassing behaviors? Or does men's occupation of more privileged relations to power literally—that is, physically and materially—shape our perceptions in ways that conflict with women's? This is a key issue for critical theorists. From the standpoint of critical theory, power and knowledge historically condition each other in the most material of ways.

Symbolic Social Controls: The Ritual Force of Language   For critical theorists, the inseparability of power and knowledge is also rooted in the symbolic character of our human-animal natures. We humans are a particularly precarious species of animals. Like other species, we must establish a certain measure of power in relation to our environments, simply to survive. As animals, we depend on orderly forms of social interaction to enable us to meet basic demands for food, shelter, sexual procreation, and so forth. But unlike other species, we do not find the necessary technologies for such stable orderings within our own bodies. We lack innate, instinctual, or biologically imprinted technologies for survival. In other words, our bodies are not structured so as to secure stable relations with our environment by biology alone. This puts us at a deficit in comparison to most other species of animals. We must find the power to establish relatively stable relations—the power to survive economically—in technology. This technology is not outside the human body but supplementary to it. It is a social power that works through our bodies without being either biologically determined or in transcendence of the flesh.

Fortunately, our bodies carry within them the possibilities for such a supplementary technology of power. This technology we call language. By virtue of a highly developed central nervous system, our bodies permit us to create through signs, images, and gestures. Through such symbolic or linguistic practices we classify and interpret the world around us. In so doing, we exercise the power of language. This form of power operates materially in history. Rooted in our bodily capabilities, the power of language is also historically situated. As such, language is a technology which enables us to historically compensate for what we lack in the biological realm alone. Through language, we act symbolically to reduce the chaos of experiential flux to relatively stable categories of cultural meaning. This is crucial for human-animal survival. Without the symbolic power of language we would not have a stable social environment. Language is also what makes symbolic knowledge a material sociological double of power. Power and knowledge are at all times economically and symbolically interconnected. Neither is ever present without the other.

By linking power and knowledge to the general economic and symbolic conditions of our survival as a species of animals, critical theorists interpret the social world in ways that are, at once, historical and material. This is to recognize that, as sign-making human animals, we are embodied beings. In a sense, we do not actually *have* bodies. Rather, we live *in* and *through* bodies, bodies that are economically mediated by the languages we use to describe them. We are, as it were, spirits in a material world.

Hegemonic Ritual Interactions: Constructing "Common Sense" Rituals are patterned social interactions that are material in their effects and symbolic in the ways in which they connect us to a mythic sense of social life as *ready-made* or already structured. By repetitively engaging in ritual, we produce the sensation that the world we experience is ordered in ways that are timeless and/or natural. This is untrue. The world we experience is artificially given to us by the material and symbolic power of ritual. By artfully engaging in ritual we produce *imaginary* solutions to *real* demands for social order. In this sense, rituals coordinate our material and symbolic relations, constructing cultural substitutes for what, in other animals, may be given by nature alone. Without the artificial or cultural power of rituals we would be at a loss for orderly ways of interacting with others. Even though powerful rituals are artificial (or socially constructed), they are no less effective than instinct in controlling our perceptions, our evaluations, and our interactions with others. Rituals may operate with such material and symbolic force that the imaginary solutions they represent appear *as if* they were natural or timeless. This is an important lesson in the study of social control.

Rituals, including the rituals that guide the construction of theories about deviance, connect us to senses of what things are and should be. This is what I mean by saying that rituals lead to mythic senses of the world. The successful enactment of ritual informs us about what is real and how we should act toward what is real. Rituals are social structuring practices—interactional devices that channel people's perceptions of the world. Rituals oppress just as they enable. They enact regimes of power just as they produce sensations of truth. Thus, when studying deviance, it is important to examine how rituals make certain things possible, while excluding others. As Peter McLaren observes:

> All of us are under ritual's sway; absolutely none of us stands outside of ritual's symbolic jurisdiction. In fact, humanity has no other option. . . .[T]o engage in ritual is, for men and women, a human necessity. We cannot divest ourselves of our ritual rhythms since they [operate at] the very core of our central nervous systems. The roots of ritual in any society are the distilled meanings embodied in rhythms and gestures. . . . Rituals suffuse our biogenetic, political, economic, artistic and educational life. To engage in ritual is to achieve . . . historical-cultural existence. . . . Our entire social structure has a pre-emotive dependence on ritual for transmitting the symbolic codes of the dominant culture.[8]

Rituals are situated at the sociological crossroads of biographical understanding and historical constraint. The successful performance of ritual draws us into cognitive, moral, and bodily relations to things that carry us beyond raw physical sensations of the world-in-flux. In this sense, ritual is a core feature of all social control processes. Rituals transform fluid social relations into fixed or stereotypical social categories. By engaging in ritualized interactions we come to recognize and feel toward certain ways of doing things *as if* they were natural or undeniably real. They are not, but ritual makes them seem that way. Ritual removes things from the specific historical context in which they are socially constructed and provides them with an aura of being realities unto themselves. At the same time, everything that lies outside the boundaries of ritual is made to appear *as if* it were unnatural or deviant. This is what gives rituals their power: a classificatory power, a power that blesses some forms of experience as normal, while condemning others as impure, improper, or wrong.

Ritual actions are also inherently political actions. Rituals politically channel our sensations of what is real and what is to be expected from what is real. In this sense, even the most personal of rituals are political events. When we dress a certain way, or eat specific foods, or repetitively perform particular forms of work, artistic, or sexual activity, we are engaging in ritual. Rituals of eating, dwelling, dressing, working, sexing, and so forth permeate the entirety of social existence. When heterosexual men in our capitalist society bite into the leg of a chicken instead of a human, claim objects as private rather than shared property, wear pants instead of a skirt, seek to maximize the profits of time invested in labor, and engage in erotic acts with women instead of roosters (or "Heaven forbid," other men), they enact rituals which partially control what they take for granted about themselves and others. Things are not this way simply because they are imagined to be this way. This is "really" the way things are and should be! Or, so such stereotypical men are informed by ritual. Of course, things need not be this way, but under the constraints of ritual, this is how they appear to be.

In breaking rituals we may become disoriented. Our orderly world may suddenly become unhinged. This is evidence of the power of rituals as forms of social control. Life without ritual is life in a meaningless void; life without fixed objects of perception or desire; life amid an ever-shifting array of free-floating forms, none experienced as more solid than the next. Without ritual, we may lose all of reality and be overwhelmed by anxiety.

Such panicky losses of reality are reported by sociologist Harold Garfinkel. During the mid-1960s, Garfinkel asked students to breach some of the subtle, everyday rituals that guide interactions with families, friends, and associates. For example: Engage someone in conversation, but act on the assumption that the other's words are guided by hidden motives. Interact with your parents as if you were a "polite stranger" who just happened to be boarding at your parents' home. Enter into conversation with friends but refuse to let anything pass, don't allow anything to be taken for granted. ("What do you mean, 'How am I feeling?' " "What do you mean, 'You had a flat tire'?") Even these simple breaches created great disturbances. As Garfinkel points out:

> [Most people] were stupefied. They vigorously sought to make the strange actions intelligible and to restore the situation to normal appearances. Reports were filled with accounts of astonishment, bewilderment, shock, anxiety, embarrassment, and anger.[9]

To break powerful rituals is to deviate from common sense. Such deviance led Garfinkel's students to recognize the cultural fragility of things they had previously taken for granted. For many, this was shocking. Like "culturally shaken" travelers suddenly finding themselves on foreign terrain, they had become separated from what had previously seemed meaningful. Many were terrified, experiencing anxieties not unlike those reported by naive or fearful users of hallucinogenic drugs. Indeed, the bewilderment of Garfinkel's students closely resemble the terror experienced by the unsuspecting subjects of CIA experiments with lysergic acid diethylamide (LSD) and other "controlled substances."[10] Such persons experienced a terrifying distance from the rituals governing routine social encounters. Such experiences also parallel the onset of madness. Indeed, without the support of ritual, we may lose all perspective and begin to feel we are beside ourselves, homeless and alone. This is the fate awaiting deviants in a society where strict conformity holds sway: to be cast abjectly beyond the ritually constructed boundaries of social reality. The point is this: what we experience as "real" is, at all times, mediated by the material and symbolic power of ritual.

For rituals to be most effective, people must feel that they are actively choosing to participate in such patterned social actions. Still, there are always situational filters that limit and/or amplify the freedom of people's choices. Ritual exists as but one element at the crossroads of the five interrelated critical concepts mentioned above. The force of ritual is never independent of the way that its experiential effects are filtered by power, knowledge, historical materiality, and symbolic controls. Together these several elements constitute something like a *ritual field of social forces,* in which each of these aspects of social control both affects and is affected by the others. Each, in other words, is decentered in relation to the others; each both facilitates and constrains the operation of the others.

This critical conception of ritual is related to Antonio Gramsci's use of the term *hegemony.* Gramsci was a Marxist theorist and social activist struggling to counter both economic oppression and the appeal of fascism in early-twentieth-century Italy. Of central concern to Gramsci was why members of the Italian working class often collaborated with, rather than resisted, social forces leading to their own disempowerment. Gramsci used the term *hegemony* to significantly modify orthodox Marxist thinking. For orthodox Marxists, the realm of culture was likened to an "ideological superstructure" resting upon a determinant "base" of economic reality. Like a railway car constrained by the rails upon which it runs, cultural rituals were said to be determined by the mode of economic production in which they were set. More about the terminology of Marxism later; for the moment, it is sufficient to point out that Gramsci's notions about hegemony (a concept he borrowed from Lenin) went a long way toward freeing critical Marxist thought from the narrowness of its "economically determinate" orthodoxy.[11]

Rather than viewing cultural rituals as ideological by-products of economic reality, Gramsci developed a notion of ideology as itself a material historical force. This force was contingent upon the ritual welding together of otherwise contradictory political, economic, and social realities. In this sense, hegemony might be understood as the ritual production of an always only apparent and forever contestable social consensus, a "moving equilibrium" between classes of people divided by unequal access to power.[12]

To link ritual to the concept of hegemony is to recognize that while power may occasionally operate by brute force or physical coercion, more often than not it works by seducing our consent. Hegemonic power draws us into imaginary spaces where things may seem "as if" natural.[13] In this way, hegemony limits our moral imagination and makes other ways of interpreting the world unthinkable.[14] This is a complex and more subtle way of thinking about power. Unlike "orthodox" Marxist thought, which theorizes ideology as forced upon people by their economic relations, the concept of hegemony suggests that domination often involves the active participation of the dominated. How does this happen? Why do those oppressed by hierarchical power sometimes or often actively comply with structures that constrain them?

Think, for instance, of the different rituals by which men and women fashion their bodies in contemporary society. Why is it that so many women, but not so many men, engage in elaborate and often painful rites of dieting or rituals of purging the body of all traces of food? Why do such rites of extreme self-discipline so often proceed to the point of sickness? Why do women bend, contort, or force their bodies into overly tight jeans, uncomfortably short skirts, painfully high heels, and other so-called feminine apparel? In what ways are such rites disempowering for women? Or empowering, but only on terms defined by men—terms that demand that women make over their bodies in keeping with the advertised fantasies of men?

Even though such rites of fashion ultimately disempower women, few are physically coerced into disciplining their bodies in such a manner. Nevertheless, whether women are seduced by the prospect of being granted male approval and economic support or whether they are terrorized by the prospect of being denied these benefits, a great many women do *in fact* ritually make themselves over in this way. Why? Approaching such questions from the standpoint of hegemony may help us to better understand the gender-specific dynamics of social control. But before further exploring this and other issues, let us first examine the historical context and the separate (if interrelated) contributions of Marxism, anarchism, feminism, and multicultural perspectives to the development of critical theorizing.

Historical Background: Questioning the Powers That Be

When colonial white society invades and occupies our territories, these are not called criminal acts. But when Native people stand up and resist, these acts are considered criminal. But these are not crimes. They are political acts in which our people stand up for their rights of self-determination, self-dignity, and self-respect against the cruel and oppressive might of another nation.

Leonard Peltier[15]

Crime existed only to the degree that the law cooperated with it. . . . [I]n the country's entire social, political and economic structure, the criminal, the law, and the politicians were actually inseparable partners.

Malcolm X[16]

The occurrence of crime is inevitable in a society in which wealth is distributed unequally. . . . [C]rime is at once a protest against society and a desire to partake in its exploitive content.

Angela Davis[17]

Critical perspectives on deviance and control did not simply emerge at a particular point in time. They exploded against the conflictual social landscape of the United States and western Europe during the late 1960s and early 1970s. Although critical theorizing was intellectually nurtured by the development of the societal reaction perspective and its efforts to demystify the process by which certain behaviors and people are labeled deviant,[18] its central impetus was far more concrete. It was rooted in the struggles of the oppressed to break free of the complex and historically interconnected rule of racist, sex- and gender-based, and economic hierarchies. One important site of such struggles was the "ivory towers" of colleges and universities, which were rapidly transformed into intellectual battlegrounds on which people attempted to discern the nature of a widespread and deeply felt political crisis.[19]

Struggles for Racial Justice   In the United States the crisis erupted both internally and externally. Internally it was inflamed by a lengthy history of racial, sexual, and economic oppression—the ignition of a long-smoldering fire by people who had been promised a piece of the American pie but who were, on every street corner and in every discriminatory workplace blocked from consuming it. At the forefront of this crisis were the passionate struggles of African-Americans for civil rights, social dignity, and economic justice. In emphasizing the historical centrality of African-American social movements, I do not mean to minimize the political and cultural struggles of other "racialized" peoples in the United States and in the rest of North America. The organized resistance of Mexican-Americans, American Indians, Puerto Ricans, Asian-Americans, and others condemned to second-class social status by virtue of being classified as "nonwhite" was and continues to be of significance in the development of critical theoretical perspectives. Nevertheless, during the 1960s the struggles of blacks captured the sociological imaginations of critical theorists in a particularly important way. As Michael Omi and Howard Winant observed, "By challenging existing patterns of race relations, the black movement created new political subjects; expanded the terrain of political struggle beyond "normal" politics; and inspired and galvanized a range of 'new' social movements—student, antiwar, feminist, gay, environmental, etc."[20]

In the years following World War II the struggles of African-Americans against racism and severe economic deprivation were intensified by the combined experience of rising expectations and relative deprivations. During the war many blacks ventured for the first time into social terrain that had previously been the exclusive domain of whites. In so doing they expanded their visions of who they were and who they could become. Whether in military service or in migration to the booming wartime economy of the industrial north, many blacks were exposed for the first time since the years following slavery to a wide range of new hopes and aspirations. They were encouraged to believe that they too could earn honored places in society and thus fulfill the American dream.

In the years following World War II the optimism of black Americans was quickly squashed. During the war the incomes of African-American workers had risen significantly. The wages of blacks grew from 41.4 percent of the wages of whites in 1939 to 54.3 percent in 1947. There, however, the advance halted. Modest gains in the postwar years were soon reversed as white males reclaimed positions of privilege in the peacetime economy. When both men's and women's wages are measured and when median family income is examined, the position of blacks is seen to have been no better in 1959 than it was in 1947.[21] During that same period the rapidly growing electronic mass media were beaming images of a happy and prosperous family life nationwide. For the impoverished family of color this added insult to injury. There was little in the well-to-do lives of Ozzie and Harriet Nelson, June and Ward Cleaver, and the rest of U.S. television's early popular families that resembled the actual experiences of struggling black families. There was much, however, to be envied.

Fueled by a combination of wartime optimism and the relative deprivations of postwar existence, North American blacks began a conflictual march toward social equality. The leaders in this movement included new activist organizations such as the Student Nonviolent Coordinating Committee (SNCC) and the Black Panther Party, along with progressive African-American Christian organizations and the Nation of Islam, each of which launched a renewed push for social justice. By the mid-1960s, the modesty of the gains that had been made in formal legal equality (e.g., hard-fought victories by blacks on such issues as the rights to vote, to choose their own seats on buses, and to urinate in integrated public rest rooms) left many young blacks with an angry sense of how far they still had to go. The noted African-American and Muslim leader Malcolm X spoke for many young blacks when he stated that "in the ghettoes the white man has built for us, he has forced us to riot to aspire to greater things, but to view everyday life as survival."[22] The anger associated with this awareness was like tinder awaiting a match. During the mid-1960s that match was lit by a series of glaring acts of police brutality.[23] The result was an outpouring of violent protest and rioting in the black ghettoes of the nation's largest cities. Following the 1968 murder of civil rights leader Martin Luther King, violent protests erupted no farther than ten blocks from the White House. For nearly a week federal troops occupied the nation's capital. Street corners were patrolled by faceless soldiers wearing gas masks and firing rifles at rebellious citizens. The image of these events as broadcast worldwide was of a nation divided against itself, indicating the presence of a serious crisis in the organization of power in the United States.

The Prisoners' Rights Movement   This image was enlarged by a subsequent wave of political protest from behind the bars of U.S. prisons. Impoverished inmates who had entered prison as legally defined victimizers soon came to radically redefine themselves as victims of a larger order of social oppression. They also became reflexive theorists of their subordinate position within a hierarchically organized power structure. They read widely the literatures of sociology, history, and political theory and organized themselves to challenge that structure from within its deepest confines. As Assata Shakur, a revolutionary African-American woman and self-defined "political prisoner," would comment, "They call us bandits, yet every time most Black people pick up our paychecks, we are being robbed. Every time we walk into a store in our neighborhood, we are being held up. Every time we pay our rent, the landlord sticks a gun in our ribs."[24]

The activism of prisoners soon resulted in a renewed wave of repressive control. Prisoners became "victims of politically inspired actions against them by the prison administrators and the parole boards . . . victims of politically inspired frame-ups within the prison."[25] Many who were involved in the struggle for prisoner rights met untimely deaths at the hands of state control agents. These included the over forty inmates and guards slaughtered by state police in quelling the rebellion at New York's Attica State Prison. Why were these politicized prisoners so feared by people in positions of power? The answer is simple. They had broken with the official interpretations of themselves as individual bad guys. They had connected their crimes and criminality to a struggle for power within society as a whole.[26]

Opposition to the Vietnam War   The political activism of African-Americans and prisoners was a major impetus for the development of critical perspectives on deviance and social control. The importance of these "domestic" crises was compounded by the resistance of various third world or "underdeveloped" nations—countries subject to colonial and/or imperialist domination by first world nations. For the United States this resistance was most dramatically embodied in the struggles of the Vietnamese and Indo-Chinese peoples against the U.S. claim to control the political and economic destiny of southeast Asia. During the early 1960s attention to the growing U.S. involvement in Vietnam was prompted by Buddhists who set themselves on fire before television cameras in order to protest what they saw as the imperialist actions of the American state. Buddhists who acted against the perceived immorality of U.S. military policy were soon joined by other progressive religious activists, many of whom had already been mobilized toward struggles for justice by the civil rights movement. Disregarding such protests, the U.S. government escalated its military involvement, so that by the late 1960s it had drafted hundreds of thousands of young men to fight a ground war in defense of a corrupt and unpopular but allegedly democratic regime in South Vietnam.

The result was intensified fighting abroad and the generation of a dramatic war of protest and resistance at home. In increasingly large numbers, U.S. citizens began to say no. Resistance to the war affected nearly all aspects of life in the United States—the family, the workplace, schools, and religious institutions. Many young men went to jail as draft resisters or fled the country to avoid the compulsory command to fight a war they considered both unnecessary and unjust. The mechanisms of official justice cranked out prison sentences for draft evaders and political protestors and embarked upon a nationwide campaign of illegal surveillance of citizens who were suspected of encouraging others to resist.

The result was increased political turmoil, particularly on college campuses, where male students received the privilege of temporary draft deferments and where both males and females were presented with opportunities to reflexively ask questions about the power structures that their advanced education was preparing them to join. White students were also confronted, often for the first time, by African-Americans, Latinos, American Indians, and others from disadvantaged backgrounds who challenged them with questions about racism; the genocidal roots of North American history; the exploitative role of U.S. military and economic interests in Central and South America, the Philippines, Puerto Rico, and the Caribbean; and such matters as affirmative action or reparation for past injustices. Other aspects of campus life reminded students of the war which awaited many of them after graduation—the presence on campus of the Reserve Officers' Training Corps (ROTC), on-campus recruiting by military and government intelligence agencies, and knowledge of university research involvement in producing the weapons of war. All this disrupted "business as usual" at the leading colleges and universities in the country; led to the emergence of a variety of "new left" political organizations such as Students for a Democratic Society (SDS); and prompted scholars to seek new answers to urgent questions that troubled students and divided the nation as a whole.

Struggles over racial equality and the Vietnam war deeply affected the organization of daily life and thought in U.S. institutions of higher education. The nation's universities, like the country as a whole, were plunged into a state of crisis. Old theories about the nature of social order no longer seemed so applicable. Fresh new ways of envisioning social life were demanded. Out of such demands grew a variety of critical perspectives on power, deviance, and control. Another factor contributing to the birth of these perspectives was the significant on-campus influence of what may be loosely described as a counterculture of middle-class youths. Like the African-American civil rights movement, the origins of this highly publicized challenge to the style and content of dominant North American values may be traced to social, political, and economic developments in the years following World War II.

Dreams of a Counterculture The postwar baby boom and the return to economic prosperity for whites created the material basis for the youthful counterculture. This was the heyday of *Fordism*, a historical phase of capitalist economic expansion in which corporate-controlled production became linked to cultural desires for seeming unlimited mass consumption. White middle-class young people remained in school longer, postponing the economic commitments of adulthood while becoming the target of a massive advertising campaign aimed at making them an independent class of consumers, purchasers of the symbols of youthful style (clothing, cars, rock music, and the like) with money extracted from their parents' newly found and quickly mortgaged affluence.[27] The emergence of an educated and leisurely youth culture meant that an unprecedented number of middle-class youths remained, for an extended period of time, uncommitted to the practical experiences of the dominant economic and political system.[28] At the same time, this new generation was bombarded in an equally unprecedented fashion by the dominant sociological message of the 1950s—that "America" was the land of the free and the home of the brave, any one of whom could make it to the top by fair play and hard work. This, after all, was the first truly mass-media generation, the children of the early years of television, rock music, and extended adolescent consumerism. The more they consumed, the more they were told how blessed they were to have been born into a plenitude of Coca-Cola, disposable plastic containers, good cars, record players, and sexy make-up, and to be spared the cruel injustices suffered by people who lived on the other side of the awful "iron curtain."

Encouraged to believe both in the profitable pursuit of their generation's uniqueness and in the validity of the American dream, the youth culture of the 1960s was ripe for disillusionment and rebellion. Youths were deeply affected by the jarring images of racial discrimination and the violent and imperialist nature of the U.S. war effort in Vietnam. These images violated the more noble image of a good and generous "America" that had been presented to these young people since their birth. Large segments of youth disengaged themselves stylistically from the mainstream of U.S. culture, sprouting long hair, identifying (psychically and physically) with the African-American rhythms of rock music, and disavowing the discipline of the adult work ethic and the war which symbolized its established "truths." In search of another truth, perhaps a truth that would resemble the innocence contained in previously cherished images of "America the Beautiful," members of the youth culture also experimented with consciousness-expanding and pleasure-inducing drugs; explored new avenues of sexual expression; questioned the possessive, patriarchal, and heterosexualized rituals of the nuclear family; and pursued the spiritual insights of a variety of eastern religions. More than occasionally they also challenged what they took to be the irrelevant or politically untenable theories of their teachers. Indeed, many college classrooms, particularly those in which the social sciences were taught, became hotbeds of dissent and disagreement. In dramatic instances, students would shout out in class, seize university offices, or walk out in protest.

The Repressive Face of Control   For many instructors this was a time of profound confusion, disillusionment, and retreat. For others it was a time of radicalization. While some instructors struck back at students with power, verbal rebukes, or punitive grading policies, others struck out into new conceptual terrain. This was the case for an emerging generation of critical sociologists. For such scholars, U.S. military action in Indochina and riots in the ghettos of the urban United States no longer appeared to be unrelated phenomena. The huge cadres of young blacks and poor whites who were drafted to fight and die in Asia shared a single attribute with their brothers and cousins who were overcrowding the cells of U.S. prisons. They were outside the power structure of the United States. So were members of the American Indian Movement; activists who were illegally spied upon, harassed, jailed, and disrupted by "law-enforcement" agents; and the nearly thirty members of the militant Black Panther Party who were killed by police bullets. So were the thousands of political dissidents who were brought to trial for protesting the injustices perpetrated by the U.S. military-industrial-political elite. The political struggles of such groups prompted sociological students of deviance to begin relating theoretical discourse to the discourse of social justice. Their initial message was simple—that deviance and its control must be studied as a political phenomenon, the meaning of which could be understood only by reference to the organization of power in society as a whole.

Within a short time these early lessons of critical thought were manifestly observable on college campuses. Radical professors and students were singled out for surveillance and control. Phones were tapped, and many people were spied upon. Many were beaten by police. Some instructors were denied tenure. For others, control was more lethal. In 1970 students at Jackson State College in Mississippi and Kent State University in Ohio were gunned down during protests.

The Economic Crisis Comes Home   With the eventual withdrawal of U.S. troops from Vietnam in 1973, relative calm returned to the campuses. The war, it seemed, had been the primary catalyst for intense university politicalization. While the deprivation of blacks and other minorities remained a major problem, it was swept beneath the rug of the late 1970s economic crisis which the war had, in part, precipitated. Unlike previous wars, the Vietnam involvement of the United States was not followed by a postwar boom. A defeated United States had dissipated many resources in nontransferable military spending. At the same time its industrial allies in Japan and West Germany had been tooling up for a new technological assault on the world's marketplace.

The slumping U.S. economy was caught off guard. Rather than upgrading their investment in industry, leading sectors of business and banking swallowed the lure of short-term profits and government deregulation by making the speculative buy-out and selling of companies a business in itself. The energy-intensive and oil-dependent U.S. economy was surprised as well by the rising power of the oil-producing nations. Unable to command Asia by military force, the United States was now also limited in its exertion of economic power. Resulting cycles of spiraling inflation, recession, and high unemployment have haunted the U.S. economy throughout the 1980s and into the 1990s. With these developments came a new conservative mood, a period of retrenchment during which many U.S. citizens forgot the lessons of our most recent history. Searching nostalgically for bygone dreams of national omnipotence, many such citizens ignored the continuing plight of others who had been subordinated by economic, racial, ethnic, gender, sexual, and age hierarchies. For many—but certainly not all—young people the romantic dreams of the counterculture were exchanged for anxieties about how to make it economically in a less prosperous world. Many who had participated in struggles for social justice a decade earlier were said to have grown up with a "big chill," trading in idealism for conventional careers and family life.

This is not to suggest that the dreams of just social change, engendered by the political and countercultural movements of the 1960s, have disappeared entirely. Indeed, bolstered, in part, by the moderate "liberal" rhetoric of the Clinton administration, images of fairness, social inclusion, and shared sacrifice are once again being evoked as the basis for social and economic policy. This may provide encouragement for critical scholars and activists, whose theoretical orientations have matured during the last two decades. Provoked, in large measure, by the civil rights and antiwar activism of the 1960s, the continuing development of critical perspectives owes much to feminism, gay, lesbian, and multicultural resistance to straight-white-male forms of power; to postcolonial struggles against exploitation of the third world; and to increased public awareness of the systemic nature of corporate and government wrongdoing.

The Challenge of Feminism   The influence of feminism is particularly important. While women's struggles for justice have long been a part of western history, many factors have led to the intensification of such struggles in recent years. These include the mass introduction of middle-class white women to the realities of nonhousehold labor during World War II; increased educational opportunities for women in the postwar years; and the involvement of women in the civil rights, antiwar, and countercultural movements of the 1960s. These events drew attention to the gendered character of both personal and political experience, leading feminists to declare that the *personal is political*. The war and postwar years also provided women with unprecedented independence, elevated aspirations, and firsthand knowledge of discrimination on the basis of both sex and gender. During this time, relatively privileged, white middle-class women also came into contact with feminists of color and women who were struggling to rid themselves of severe economic oppression.

Participation in various forms of social activism also provided women with the awareness that, even in supposed movements of liberation, male leadership and female followership remained an unwritten rule of the game.[29] Out of such contradictory experiences the contemporary women's movement was born. Throughout the 1970s and the 1980s feminism was growing as a dynamic social movement, favoring reciprocal relations of power and struggling with difficult questions, such as those pertaining to the politics of sexuality and relations between women of different classes and cultures. By the 1990s, feminism was able to draw upon several decades of theoretical and practical struggle, in expanding its critique of heterosexist hierarchies within virtually all major social institutions. This is not to say that women's struggles for sexual and economic justice have been uniformly successful. The harsh realities of unequal pay for equally hard work, disproportionate male control of public institutions, threats to abortion rights, the failure to pass a nationwide equal rights amendment (ERA), and the omnipresence of sexual harassment and rape are all indicative of the continuation of gendered hierarchies of power.

In challenging such hierarchies, the women's movement has propelled critical theorists to recognize that the second-class citizenship of women in society has been mirrored in the marginalization of women within social science. As Dorothy Smith points out, the male-oriented theoretical structure of social science had led to a "conceptual imperialism," by which images of women were mediated through men's eyes.[30] In the words of Marcia Millman and Rosabeth Kanter, "Feminist critiques have shown us how social science has been divided by models representing a world dominated by white males, and so our studies . . . have been limited by the particular interests, perspectives and experiences of that one group."[31] Mainstream sociological studies of crime, deviance, and social control were no exception. As Eileen Leonard suggests, "Theoretical criminology was constructed by men, about men. It is simply not up to the analytic task of explaining female patterns of crime [or deviance]."[32]

Refusing Compulsory Heterosexuality   Also important to the development of recent critical thought has been the militancy of gay men, lesbians, and bisexuals against the deviantization of physical intimacy between people of the same gender. An important historical marker for the rise of "queer" refusals of heterosexist hierarchies occurred on June 27, 1968, when riots broke out in New York City following a police raid of the Stonewall Inn, a gay bar in Greenwich Village. What was unique about this event was not the police harassment of gays. For decades this had been an all too common form of social control. What was different was that gays collectively fought back. At Stonewall, a racially mixed group of African-American, Latino, and white working-class gays refused to submit to police threats. Protestors tore up street signs and parking meters and imprisoned police officers within the bar they sought to invade. Thereafter, inspired by the struggles of other civil rights activists, gays, lesbians, and bisexuals began a several-decade-long campaign aimed both at securing equal rights and at questioning what it is about contemporary heterosexuality that makes so many straight people fearful of homosexuals.

By the late 1970s, numerous gay and lesbian political organizations had joined forces in attempting to overturn formal legal discriminations and the enforcement of "compulsory heterosexuality." While increasing the visibility and acceptance of gays and lesbians in a number of social arenas, "queer" struggles for justice today remain far short of the mark. Twenty-five U.S. states still have so-called sodomy laws, while only six states and 110 municipalities have passed legislation guaranteeing the legal rights of gays and lesbians. Moreover, following the televised spectacle of the "gay bashing" which occurred during the 1992 Republican presidential convention, voters in several states have been presented with referendums aimed at turning back the calendar on gay rights. Following a petition drive by a right-wing and conservative Christian group—the Oregon Citizens Alliance—a resolution appeared on the state's ballot that, if passed, would have voided applications of the state's "hate-crimes law" with regard to gays and lesbians and banned the phrase "sexual orientation" in all areas of the state code. Teachers throughout Oregon would have been required to instruct their students that homosexuality was a "perversion" on the order of pedophilia, sadism, and masochism, a form of behavior "to be discouraged and avoided." Although the Oregon bill was defeated, a less dramatic, but still highly restrictive antigay bill was approved in Colorado in the fall of 1992. The fear and controversy provoked by such homophobic initiatives is evidence of a deep-rooted heterosexism operating beneath the veneer of U.S. democracy.

Despite strong opposition, from the mid-1980s to the present, struggles on behalf of alternative sexualities have greatly escalated. In part, this is due to the enormity of the acquired immune deficiency syndrome (AIDS) epidemic and the early spread of the human immunodeficiency virus (HIV) among U.S. gay men. Also important has been an alarming increase in reported incidents of violence targeted against gays and lesbians. The gay rights movement is being led by such influential protest groups as Aids Coalition to Unleash Power (ACT-UP), a media-savvy organization dedicated to fighting AIDS, and Queer Nation, a militant social movement aimed at both affirming and defending alternative sexualities. The perspectives of gays, lesbians, and bisexuals are today a vital force in the construction of critical frameworks on deviance.

Postcolonial Struggles   Still another catalyst for the critical perspective came from outside the boundaries of western society. The 1970s was a decade marked by power struggles between less developed nations and their imperialist counterparts in the third world. In Africa the people of Mozambique, Angola, and Guinea-Bissau freed themselves from the bloodstained grip of Portuguese colonial rule. Revolution resulted in independence for Zimbabwe and began in Namibia, while South Africa became an armed camp, the last outpost of a tyrannical white minority in southern Africa. In the middle east, oil-producing nations leaped to power in the international marketplace, while the countries of Indochina struggled to redefine themselves in the wake of the U.S. defeat in Vietnam. South America and Central America were also ablaze with the dream of liberation. While a U.S.-backed coup overthrew the democratic reforms of the duly elected Chilean socialist president, Salvadore Allende, Sandinista freedom fighters in Nicaragua overcame nearly a half-century of harsh dictatorial rule by the brutal Somoza family. In El Salvador prominent officials of the Roman Catholic Church supported the efforts of rebels to establish a just society, free of class and foreign domination. Some, such as the beloved Archbishop of San Salvador, Oscar Romero—and, nearly a decade later, in 1989, four influential Jesuit priests at El Salvador's leading university—paid with their lives, as the U.S. government continued spending millions of dollars to reinforce the existing Salvadoran regime with its vicious death squads and friendly attitude toward U.S. business. These international developments raise serious questions for critical students of social control. No longer can theorists rest easily in the comforting bed of first world perspectives, ignorant of the violent relationship between transnational social controls and global struggles for power.[33]

Continuing Elite Deviance Critical perspectives were also nurtured by increased attention to deviance by the powerful. The annual cost of corporate crime in America alone totals over $40 billion.[34] In addition to the economic costs of corporate collusion, price-fixing, and fraud, consider the enormous physical costs of unsafe or unhealthy working conditions, as well as the costs incurred as a result of faulty or poorly tested production practices and industrial pollution. The human toll of such deviance is astronomical. Yet when compared to the social control of "less respectable" types of deviance, efforts to curtail such elite crimes are minimal. Laws are weak. Enforcement is rare and penalties are minor, when compared to corporate gains. Quite simply, crimes by the powerful have not been a priority for most U.S. law-enforcement officials. Indeed, on the same day in 1981 that President Ronald Reagan pledged an all-out fight against "street criminals," the *Wall Street Journal* reported the quiet dismantling of federal programs aimed at corporate, or white-collar, deviance. Thus, it should come as no surprise that the later years of the Reagan and Bush administrations were marked by such giant criminal conspiracies as the Iran-Contra affair, the $500 billion looting of the savings and loan industry, and high-level money-laundering operations provided by the Bank of Commerce and Credit International for clients that included the CIA and an assortment of illegal drug kingpins.

This relative inattention to corporate wrongdoing is nothing new to critical theorists. During the 1960s and 1970s critical theorists became well versed in the crimes of government itself: public corruption, domestic spying upon citizens, police violence, military torture, state-sponsored terrorism, warfare against civilians, and even collaboration with gangland criminals in the planned assassinations of foreign leaders. The Watergate scandal was only the tip of the iceberg of governmental deviance. Two decades later, one of the final official acts of President George Bush was to pardon a host of high-level officials who had been involved in a plot to subvert the U.S. constitution by illegally exchanging arms for hostages with Iran and covertly using monies obtained in such secret dealings to defy a congressional ban on funding for the Contra terrorists in Nicaragua. During his years as vice president and president, Bush denied knowledge of such crimes. Yet, within weeks of his leaving office, information became available which showed that Bush had repeatedly lied about his and former President Reagan's involvement in such troubling criminal conspiracies. The illegal activities of government officials, like those of corporate executives, have seldom been subject to serious control. In the words of critical sociologist C. Wright Mills, deviance on the part of the powerful remains shrouded by a veil of "high morality."[35]

During the early 1960s, Mills's provocative essays on America's "power elite" contributed significantly to the development of critical perspectives. Mills argued that power in America was controlled by an interlocking network of economic, political, military, and media interests. But just as power was hierarchically structured, so was it subtly deployed—so subtly, in fact, that many or most people failed to realize that, in our supposed democracy, the rule of raw power remained the norm. In Mills's words, "those who hold power have often come to exercise it in hidden ways: they have moved and are moving from authority to manipulation."[36] Mills vehemently criticized his sociological colleagues for not attending to the implications of such inequity. In 1962 Mills's efforts to develop a critical perspective were cut short by his untimely death, of a heart condition, at the age of 46.

Mills's call for critical study of the hierarchical dynamics of power would not be answered by sociologists of deviance until a decade later. Why? A likely answer is posed by Alex Liazos: sociologists had become inordinately distracted by "a fascination with 'nuts, sluts, and perverts'" and, as a result, paid "little attention . . . to the unethical, illegal, and destructive actions of powerful individuals, groups and institutions,"[37] With the development of critical perspectives, this was soon to change.

Pluralistic Conflict Theory: A Step in the Direction of Critical Thinking

From the conflict perspective, those who are in positions of power have the ability to determine what . . . and . . . who shall be identified and processed as deviant, criminal or delinquent.

C. Ronald Huff[38]

The critical perspective was not produced overnight. Prior to the emergence of a theoretical image relating deviance and its control to the power structures of society as a whole, numerous sociologists viewed deviantization as the result of pluralistic conflict. Pluralistic conflict theory assumes an ongoing struggle between a variety of social, religious, political, ethnic, and economic factions. To the winner go the spoils of criminal law, the power to decide on what is deviant and legally prohibited. The classic statement of this position is provided in George Vold's 1958 theory of group conflict.[39] Vold likened legislatively defined criminals to a minority group, losers in a social struggle for power. "On the surface, the offenses [of groups struggling for power] may seem to be the ordinary common-law ones involving persons and property, but on closer examination they often are revealed as the acts of good soldiers fighting for a cause and against the threat of enemy encroachment."[40]

Vold's pluralistic thesis complemented the early culture-conflict theories of Lewis Wirth and Thorsten Sellin. Wirth and Sellin described the process by which dominant groups impose a vision of cultural reality upon weaker groups, deviantizing the behaviors of those with less power. Particular attention was paid to the delinquency of the children of immigrants caught in a struggle between two cultures. According to Wirth, "One of the most convincing bits of evidence for the importance of the role played by culture conflict . . . is the frequency with which delinquents, far from exhibiting a sense of guilt, made the charge of hypocrisy toward official representatives of the social order such as teachers, judges, newspapers, and social workers with whom they came in contact."[41]

Sellin extended culture conflict to include the struggles which occur as societies become more complex, conflicts between different cultural groups sharing a proximate geographic border, and the struggles of groups which impose cultural realities through colonization.[42] By imposing cultural standards, imperialist powers are better able to exploit the aspirations and efforts of colonized subjects. Think, for instance, of the imposition of western law upon the indigenous cultures of Africa and Asia. Religious practices, family structures, and tribal rituals that did not fit the "civilized" outlook of European colonizers were overnight declared illegal and subjected to harsh, punitive control measures.

The Social Reality of Crime: Law, Order, and Power   Though pluralistic conflict theory was prefigured in the writings of Vold, Wirth, and Sellin, its full realization awaited the 1970 publication of Richard Quinney's influential *The Social Reality of Crime*.[43] For Quinney, the enactment and enforcement of criminal law were more than legal victories. They were victories in the struggle to control social reality. According to Quinney, "We end up with some realities rather than others for good reason—because someone has something to protect. . . . Realities are, then, the most subtle and insidious of our forms of social control. . . . The reality of crime that is constructed for all of us by those in a position of power is the reality we tend to accept as our own. . . . *This is the politics of reality*."[44]

Pluralistic conflict theory is particularly attentive to the law as a tool of power. Nowhere is this more evident than in the 1971 publication of William Chambliss and Robert Seidman's *Law, Order and Power*, a detailed study of the impact of power differentials upon the daily work of lawmakers, the police, prosecutors, defense attorneys, criminal and appellate court judges, and other members of the legal bureaucracy.[45] Chambliss and Seidman review a great number of studies on the law in action. They conclude that the conflict model provides the most useful framework for understanding the actual operation of legal institutions in a complex, stratified, and bureaucratic society. As such, "the law represents an institutionalized tool of those in power which functions to provide them with superior moral as well as coercive power in conflict."[46] The distinction between moral and coercive power is important. It is not brute force but a subtle organization of "normative pressures" which guides the career decisions of legal actors in accordance with the interests of the most powerful. Conflict may thus be both present and disguised. It may operate in the form of structurally routinized pressure as well as overt struggle.

Universal Conflict over Authority   A final theory of pluralistic conflict is presented in Austin Turk's 1969 *Criminality and the Legal Order*.[47] Turk argues that conflict is the inevitable result of universal divisions between those in authority and those subject to authority. Turk builds upon the general conflict theory of sociologist Ralf Dahrendorf, which proposes that "societies . . . are held together not by consensus but by constraint, not by universal agreement but by coercion of some by others."[48] Coercion, however, is not the most stable form of organizational control. Total coercion requires that the people in authority constantly expend their resources. A more stable order necessitates a balance between consensus and coercion. Thus, persons in authority would be able to "condition" their subjects to accept and live with existing authority relations, if not to actually celebrate their existence.

Despite efforts to condition subjects, authority relations are always in a state of dynamic tension. One strategy which those in authority may use to keep an upper hand is their ability to deviantize or criminalize resistive subjects. Turk's theory attempts to specify the conditions under which this strategy is likely to be employed. Such variables as the organizational sophistication of conflicting parties, degrees of agreement between upper-level and lower-level authorities, and the differential effectiveness, or "realism," of certain "conflict moves" are all said to impact upon the use of criminal law as a tool of power.

The Limitations of Pluralistic Conflict Theories   Pluralistic conflict theories were extremely influential and paved the way for a more historically and structurally informed critical perspective.[49] In particular, the conflict approach played a major role in the demystification of what had been the more generally accepted view that law was consensually created and implemented with "value-neutrality."

Despite its advantages, pluralistic theory fails to adequately examine the historically based structural context in which power struggles occur. This limitation has been recognized by several of its most important proponents. In 1973 Richard Quinney stated that his own *The Social Reality of Crime* was "merely another bourgeois academic exercise" which failed to realize the structural "dynamics and contradictions of concrete historical conditions and processes."[50] In search of a more thoroughly critical understanding, Quinney adopts the standpoint of Marxist social theory. A similar change is evident in the 1982 revision of William Chambliss and Robert Seidman's *Law, Order and Power*.[51]

Pluralistic conflict theory implies that the human struggle for power inevitably results in the universal triumph of the mighty and the perpetual deviantization of the powerless. This is nowhere more evident than in the writings of Austin Turk. Unlike Quinney, Chambliss, and Seidman, Turk has remained within the theoretical confines of a pluralist model. This is not to say that Turk's theorizing has remained static. His more recent pronouncements are more structurally informed than his earlier instrumentalist ideas.[52] Turk's structuralism, however, is highly abstract and ahistorical. Structures that separate superordinates from subordinates are pictured as invariant features of the human condition. While "new authorities can be expected to replace old ones," hierarchical structures remain a timeless feature of all social life.[53] "The assumption here is that there are limits to the human capacity to include others as 'we.'"[54] Turk regards all suggestions to the contrary as little more than "metaphysical hopes for some tremendous breakthrough to a utopian state of universal love."[55] The most we can hope for is a more mutually beneficial way of "containing, redirecting, deescalating, transforming or otherwise handling"[56] losses incurred in the inevitable conflict between the people within and the people outside authorized positions of hierarchically structured power.

Despite its analytic utility, Turk's theory is little more than a description of the way in which contemporary social life is hierarchically structured. Turk falsely equates the way things are with the way things naturally have to be. He fails to realize that social structures are historical creations. Structures do not exist naturally. They exist only as they are produced and reproduced by the concrete struggles of people in history. This awareness separates the critical perspective from the more limited confines of conflict theory. Critical theorists recognize that under certain historically structured conditions, power relations can be relations of reciprocity rather than relations of hierarchical domination.

The Imagination Guiding Critical Perspectives: A Reciprocal Structuring of Power

Reciprocal relations of power are based upon mutual respect, generosity, and forms of social exchange that enliven and mutually enrich all those who participate. Under conditions of reciprocal power, social control need not be a battle with winners and losers. Social control can be participatory rather than imposed. It can reconcile conflicting parties by dissolving the troubles which separate them rather than by restricting the options of those with least power. Thus, while deviance may always represent a power struggle, its control need not represent a process of one-sided domination, a division between winners and losers, a structural differentiation between powerful insiders and powerless outsiders.

Unfortunately, ritual conditions which foster power-reciprocal relations—mutual vulnerability, equal access to material resources, and a ritualized respect for cultural difference—are generally absent from the world in which we live. Our society is, instead, dominated by various hierarchies: hierarchies which position owners and managers over workers, developed nations over third world countries, men over women, whites over people of other colors, heterosexuals over gays and lesbians, and the old (but not too old) over the young. These hierarchical divisions are so deeply rooted in our culture that they are often taken for granted or seen as natural. Critical theorists, however, see nothing natural about such hierarchies. Hierarchies are the ritual legacy of the unjust exercise of power in history.

The historical structuring of hierarchical power is of great concern to critical theorists. So is the ritual reproduction of power. For it is through a diverse host of everyday rituals that we either reproduce or resist the hierarchical structures which have surrounded us since birth. In so doing, we either "naturalize" or challenge the continuance of controlling hierarchies.

As long as the ritual reproduction of hierarchy continues, there is little chance that deviance and social control will be more than an endless battle over who controls whom. We will remain trapped in a history which seemingly creates us more than we create it. Is it possible to find a way out? Is it possible to create history in a different and more just way? Is it possible to construct rituals which support greater reciprocity in relations of power and controls which are more participatory than imposed? How might we engage with each other in ways that are mutually empowering, rather than empowering some at the expense of others? Before constructing such new forms of relations, is it first necessary to critically deconstruct or reflexively display the ritual constraints under which we currently labor? And how might we do so without being driven to despair, madness, fear, and resentful aggression? These are among the most important questions posed by critical perspectives. In addressing these concerns, critical theorists draw extensively upon four interrelated theoretical traditions: Marxism, anarchism, feminism, and multicultural criticism.

A Political Economy of Deviance and Control: Marxist Critical Thought

The fathers of the present working-class were chastised for their enforced transformation into vagabonds and paupers. Legislation treated them as "voluntary" criminals, and . . . depended on their own good will to go on working under . . . old conditions that no longer existed.

Karl Marx[57]

The clearest indication of the unbounded contempt of the workers for the existing social order is the wholesale manner in which they break its laws. If the demoralization of the worker passes beyond a certain point then it is just as natural that he will turn into a criminal—as inevitably as water turns into steam at boiling point.

Friedrich Engels[58]

In discussing the concept of hegemony we have already become acquainted with an important theme in contemporary Marxist thought. In what follows I will introduce you to other aspects of Marxist theory as they pertain to the study of deviance and social control.

Marxist social theory is rooted in the nineteenth-century European writings and political activities of Karl Marx. Born on May 5, 1818, into a family of German Jews, Marx experienced firsthand the alienation of those who were structurally denied the power to shape their own economic, political, and social destinies. Although each of Marx's parents came from a long line of rabbis, his father, Heinrich, "conveniently" converted to Lutheranism in the year before his birth, to escape the stigma of anti-Semitism and thereby make an uneasy compromise with the hierarchical arrangement of power in his country. For the young Marx such compromise was increasingly uneasy. His native Germany was covered by a blanket of oppression. The 1830s and 1840s were periods of great intellectual and political despair. Marx lived in the European aftermath of the French Revolution, when the "Holy Alliance, established by the powers that had defeated Napoleon in order to repress the forces of libertarian revolution, of radicalism and the rights of man, seemed forever able to stifle even faintly liberal stirrings."[59] The Germany of Marx's young adulthood was particularly stifling. Prussian officials promised strict control over all dangerous ideas, surveillance of political agitators, and a close monitoring of life at the universities. Lacking a representative parliament and the rights of free speech, assembly, and even trial by jury, the German state also instituted censorship over all publications.

Efforts to critically understand and alter the oppressive character of hierarchically imposed social structures were of importance to Marx from a young age. As part of his secondary school examinations, the adolescent Marx wrote an essay entitled "Reflections of a Young Man on Choosing a Career." In that essay Marx articulated a principle which would guide his intellectual and practical activities for a lifetime. Simply stated: to fully realize the power of one's own being, one must encourage the reciprocal expression of power by others as well. In the words of the young Marx:

> The central principle which must guide us in the selection of a vocation is the welfare of humanity, our own perfection. One should not think that these two interests combat each other, that one must destroy the other. Rather, man's nature makes it possible for him to reach his fulfillment only by working for the perfection and welfare of his society. . . . History calls those the greatest men who ennobled themselves by working for the universal.[60]

Marx's concern with understanding and changing the social organization of unequal and unjust social relations led him beyond the boundaries of existing social theory. In particular it led him to confront both the idealist philosophy of thinkers such as Georg Hegel and the materialist interpretation of life espoused by theorists such as Ludwig Feuerbach. Hegel viewed human life as but a moment in the "dialectical" unfolding of Absolute Spirit, an evolutionarylike advance toward a state of perfect reason. Hegel's "dialectical" method underscored the critical role of contradictions and the synthetic resolution of contradictions as a driving force in human history. Nevertheless, within Hegel's philosophy as a whole, the ceaseless play of contradictory tensions and their negation served as but a catalyst for the self-realization of Absolute Spirit in its totality. Materialists, such as Feuerbach, opposed this view of human life as part of a progressive unfolding of rational spirit. Feuerbach viewed all things, including the things of Hegelian philosophy, as nothing but the effects of a struggle for material existence. What Hegel saw as Absolute Spirit Feuerbach saw as an illusion projected by the concrete organization of material forces. Stated simply, Feuerbach argued that spirit or thought proceeds from concrete material being, not being from thought.[61]

Marx borrowed extensively from both Hegel and Feuerbach in developing his own social theory. From Hegel he took the notion that human history proceeds according to a dialectical movement in which contradictions generate structural strains toward change or social transformation. Yet, unlike Hegel, Marx rejected the view that dialectical contradictions or structural strains originated in the realm of spirit, rational ideas, or thought. Here Marx is indebted to Feuerbach. Feuerbach's theories about the origins of all things in the concreteness of material existence aided Marx in turning Hegelian thought upside down. Synthesizing the insights of Hegel and Feuerbach, Marx produced a new theoretical viewpoint, arguing that the central force behind history was the social production of concrete economic relations. In this, Marx emphasized the importance of the dominant social forms by which we humans economically secure our material existence in the world. These social forms, which Marx called *modes of production*, were said to permeate all other aspects of human social life.

Marx's theorization of historical relations as relations of material economic production has been of great practical and theoretical importance. Practically Marx spent much of his life as a political activist struggling against the material inequalities of nineteenth-century capitalist economic relations. Theoretically he labored to demonstrate the historical and social basis for capitalism's systemic inequalities and to identify economic, political, and cultural contradictions which might (dialectically) undermine capitalist exploitation. At the core of Marx's thought lay two critical theses: (1) that the exploitive dynamics of capitalist society revolve around the theft of workers' "unpaid labor" by those who own and/or control the dominant modes of economic production; and (2) that, forced to sell their labor like so many commodities on the market, workers would assume a mystified view of themselves and their relations to others, as if these relations were "naturally" governed by the logic of calculative economic exchange. The first of these theses is commonly referred to as the theory of the *surplus value of labor*, while the second, a theoretical impetus for numerous studies of the "reification" (or hegemonic ritual freezing) of the materiality of lived historical relations into the ideality of seemingly "natural" facts, is known as the *fetishization of commodities*.

Marx died in 1883, long before the full realization of either his complex theoretical project or its practical political objectives. Nonetheless, over a century later and after the failed attempts to turn Marx's critical ideas into state-socialist dogma throughout the Soviet Union and eastern Europe, Marxist social theory continues to inspire critical thought and action. The rudimentary features of the Marxist image of deviance and social control are outlined below.

The Marxist Image of Deviance and Social Control   The Marxist image of deviance suggests that the historical organization of material existence is a primary factor in determining the style and content of social control. Following Marx, this perspective asserts that the foremost task of any society is to secure the conditions of its own material survival. To do this, society must have adequate physical or material resources, a sufficient population of workers, and a capable technology. All these things are necessary for the survival of the human group. They are not, however, in themselves sufficient. Material resources, human population, and technological know-how must be socially organized if they are to provide for a stable economic environment. Economic production is a ritual social art. It is structured by social relations. The way this ritual structuring occurs is what Marx referred to as the "mode of production." Central as it is to the very survival of the social group, the mode of production is said to influence all other social relations, be they legal, religious, sexual, or whatever. How the mode of production influences relations of social control is central to critical theories of deviance.

The Marxist interpretation of history stresses the impact of unequal economic life on the entirety of social life. In the earliest known forms of society, all capable workers were required to work productively together, just so that the group as a whole could survive. In this sense, all of society's members were equal workers. Each contributed as much as she or he could. Each shared equally in the productivity of the group as a whole. These simple, survival-oriented societies existed in what Marx called a state of "primitive communism," a term that has much in common with the "headless" or *acephalous* societies described by anarchist theorists and with the "matriarchal social formations" imagined both by feminist theorists and by Marx's friend and collaborator, Friedrich Engels.[62] Within such societies, trouble between individual members was also trouble for the group as a whole. In this sense, the burden of deviance and the responsibility for social control were truly a collective matter. All members lost and gained in proportion to the collective actions of others.

This equalitarian structuring of economic relations became somewhat fragile as more efficient technologies evolved. These freed the time of some persons to administer and live off the labor of others. Some humans exploited this technological advantage. Once this happened, once one class of persons gained the upper hand in controlling society's economic mode, the course of human history would change. Banished from ritual social relations, and often from historical memory as well, was the material recognition of a collectively shared human animal fate. No longer would social control arise from the needs of all and contribute to the good of everyone. Some classes of people, by virtue of greater structural control over economic relations, would now benefit more than others through the existing relations of social control. This unequal distribution of economic control was accompanied by the rise and bureaucratic proliferation of the institutions of centralized state authority. Operating to ensure a stability no longer guaranteed by the equal distribution of the benefits of socially shared work, state institutions worked hand in hand with institutions of hierarchical economic advantage. The economy thus became politicized as one class of human actors sought to ritually authorize and perpetuate its control over others.

From Marx's perspective this institutionalization of an unequal mode of production affected the entire network of human social relations. The division between those who controlled and those who were subject to the dominant economic mode drove a wedge through the experience of collective cooperation. People were placed in structured positions of competition, positions in which they would either benefit or lose from the ritual reproduction of existing economic relations. This structured conflict was not always consciously experienced by those it involved. In fact, according to Marx, social institutions such as religion and education produced theological and philosophical systems of thought which justified or at least blunted the experience of structured conflict. In this sense, Marx argued, dominant modes of both formal and everyday knowledge were subtly shaped by the economic mode of a particular historical period. As I have suggested previously, this aspect of Marx's thought was subsequently elaborated by Antonio Gramsci and other critical theorists of hegemonic social control.

From Marx's point of view social responses to human trouble and deviance were also rooted in structural economic divisions. Acts which threatened dominant economic relations were the acts that provoked the strongest controls. As such, the production and control of deviance was directly related to the prevalence of structured economic inequality.

In *The German Ideology* Karl Marx and Friedrich Engels wrote a social history of dominant economic modes of production through slave, feudal, and capitalist economies.[63] Each of these unequal structures created social divisions between those who controlled and those who were controlled by economic activity. An exploitative upper class was structurally differentiated from those it economically dominated: in slavery, through total domination; in feudalism, through the control of subsistence determined by the amount of production remaining after taxation levied on serfs by lords; and in capitalism, through the commodified control of wage labor. Approaches to deviance and social control were structured in a similar fashion. Thus, it is no accident that feudal law was primarily concerned with issues of land and tenure, while law in capitalist society is dominated by concerns with the rights of property owners. In either case, the primary targets of social control are those who resist, disrupt, or otherwise threaten the existence of structured economic inequality. This, at least, is the central thesis of Marxist theories of deviance. Thus, according to British critical theorists Taylor, Walton, and Young:

> A full-blown Marxist theory of deviance . . . would be concerned to develop explanations of the ways in which particular historical periods, characterized by particular sets of social relationships and means of production, give rise to attempts by the economically and politically powerful to order society in particular ways. It would ask . . . who makes the rules and why?[64]

Marx himself did little in the way of any formal analysis of deviance or crime. What writing he did on these matters suggests that both deviants and control agents are inextricably bound to a larger political-economic order of struggle. Accordingly, "Crime, i.e., the struggle of the isolated individual against the prevailing conditions, is not the result of pure arbitrariness. On the contrary, it depends on the same conditions as that of rule."[65] This does not mean that Marx romanticized criminals as self-conscious rebels. Marx's view of the lower-class lumpen proletariat criminals of his own day suggests that he often viewed such people as a demoralized and unproductive lot. Elsewhere Marx ironically pictured the criminal as a contributor to social productivity by creating jobs for the police and other control agents and by stimulating the invention of such property-protecting devices as the lock and the investigative microscope. Hence, Marx argued cynically, "The criminal produces not only crime but also criminal law; he produces the professor who delivers lectures on this criminal law, and even the inevitable text-book in which the professor presents his lectures as commodity for sale in the market. . . . The criminal therefore appears as one of those natural 'equilibrating forces' which open up a whole perspective of 'useful' operations."[66]

In both irony and biting social criticism Marx viewed crime and deviance as inseparable from the problems of the political economy. To reduce deviance one must first erase structural economic inequality. For Marx this implied structural transformation in the direction of socialism—the construction of democratic economic rituals in which the needs of all, rather than the demands of a few, would guide the mode of production. This vision also guides critical perspectives on crime and deviance. As Taylor, Walton, and Young point out, "the abolition of crime is synonymous with the abolition of a criminogenic system of domination and control."[67]

Applications of Marxist Imagery   One of the first systematic attempts to apply Marxist theory to the problems of deviance and crime is found in the work of the Dutch criminologist Willem Bonger (1876–1940).[68] Bonger was particularly concerned with the relationship between crime and industrial capitalist economics. On one hand, he theorized that lower-class criminal activity arose in response to the miserable social conditions that capital foisted upon those it economically exploited. On the other hand, Bonger suggested that the dominant cultural logic of capital, a logic of "egoism" and greed, itself promoted high rates of crime among those both advantaged and disadvantaged by capital.

Bonger was not the only early European Marxist to link crime to capitalist economic relations. K. G. Rakowsky, Filippo Turati, Bruno Battaglia, Napoleone Colezanni, Achille Loria, Alfred Niceforo, August Bebel, Paul Lafargue, and Joseph Van Kan each also theorized crime and its control through a Marxist framework. Of particular importance, however, was Georg Rusche and Otto Kirchheimer's study, *Punishment and Social Structure.* As members of the Frankfurt Institute of Social Research, Rusche and Kirchheimer documented changes in early capitalist labor markets as these related to changes in the form of punishment and social control.[69] When labor was in short supply and the bargaining capacity of the working class the strongest, the legally available forms of punishment appeared most humane. But when economic conditions worsened, so did the harshness of punishment. Prison conditions became more brutal and the death penalty was applied more widely. This Rusche and Kirchheimer explained by the principle of "less eligibility."[70] A doctrine rooted in seventeenth- and eighteenth-century legal theory, this principle suggested that for criminal sanctions to be effective, penal conditions must be worse than the actual living conditions of the poorest sectors of labor. Otherwise, the poor would have no motivation to sell their labor to capitalists who exploited them.

While Rusche and Kirchheimer drew parallels between socioeconomic conditions and the forms of penal discipline, Soviet legal scholar E. B. Pashukanis examined why it was that "deprivation of freedom for a definite period of time" had become the standard form of punishment in capitalist society. The answer is found in the ways that capitalism "commodifies" the experience of time. Capitalist culture converts the flow of human experience into marketable units of measured labor. As such, "the principle of equivalent requital," which guides decisions about the length of punishment, is "closely (though unconsciously) associated with the idea of . . . abstract human labor measured in terms of time."[71]

Despite these European explorations of the Marxist theory of deviance, in the United States the influence of Marxist thought would await the early 1970s. Key to the emergence of a North American Marxist perspective were the writings of Richard Quinney[72] and the publication of *Crime and Social Justice*, a journal of radical criminology edited by, among others, Tony Platt, Paul Takagi, and Marlene Dixon. Other early contributions to U.S. Marxist perspectives included Herman and Julia Schwendinger's analysis of the relationship between social justice and definitions of crime,[73] Paul Takagi's historical study of bourgeois penal reforms and the founding of the Walnut Street Jail in Philadelphia,[74] Jerome Hall's examination of the political-economic context of modern laws pertaining to larceny or theft,[75] Raymond Michalowski and Edward Bohlander's analysis of the relationship between ruling-class state power and hegemonic definitions of both crime and criminal justice,[76] Anthony Platt's study of the historical origins of the juvenile justice movement and call for the development of radical criminology,[77] and William Chambliss's analysis of the economic basis of vagrancy laws and his influential 1975 article "Toward a Political Economy of Crime."[78]

Within a short time the influence of Marxism was widespread. The Marxist approach was, however, nowhere more evident than in the work of Quinney. According to this most prolific Marxist criminologist of the 1970s, "The basic question in the Marxist analysis of crime in this: What is the meaning of crime in the development of capitalism?"[79]

Quinney's Marxist formulations begin in 1973 with the publication of two important essays: "Crime Control in Capitalist Society" and "There's a Lot of Us Folks Grateful to the Lone Ranger."[80] In the latter work Quinney traces his own biographical movement away from the naive mentality of the heroic individual do-gooder. For Quinney, the Lone Ranger myth, as an aspect of capitalist folklore, prevents us from recognizing the structural barriers which deny most people control over the historical conditions of their own existence. Marxist theory demands that such myths be abandoned in order to prepare for a more power-reciprocal form of social order. Toward this end Quinney produced a variety of Marxist critiques of crime, criminology, and crime control. The most succinct of these is the 1977 *Class, State and Crime,* in which Quinney connects the organization of state crime control apparatus to capitalist economics and theorizes the lawbreaking of both the powerful and the powerless in relation to the ceaseless struggle for advantage within capitalism itself.

More elaborate Marxist models were subsequently formulated by radical criminological theorists such as Steven Spitzer[81] and Raymond Michalowski. Spitzer suggests that potentially deviant "problem populations" arise from within the capitalist political economy in two ways: (1) through the fundamental contradictions of the capitalist economic modes (e.g., the creation of a surplus worker population whose lack of stake in the system increases the likelihood of social tensions) and (2) through the indirect contradictions produced by social control institutions (e.g., the rising expectations, critical awareness, or alienating disenchantments produced by mandatory public schooling). Spitzer also identifies factors which increase the likelihood that troublesome populations will be officially controlled as deviants. These include such things as the extensiveness and intensity of existing state control apparatus, the size and level of the threat presented by the "problem population," the effectiveness of informal civil controls (e.g., controls through the family, the church, or the media) as opposed to formal state controls, the availability and effectiveness of alternative types of official processing (e.g., the draft or public works projects) rather than deviant processing, the availability and effectiveness of parallel control structures (e.g., vigilante groups or private police agencies), and the social utility of problem populations (e.g., as tension drains or scapegoats).

Michalowski's work also directs attention to the "dynamic" relations between the capitalist economic mode; the hierarchical workings of state control; and the hegemonic character of various cognitive, emotional, and bodily ritual processes. Analyzing a far-ranging host of historical and contemporary forms of deviance, Michalowski concludes that "it is the political economy of a society in connection with its cultural history that determines the definition of what acts are adaptive, rebellious, or maladaptive." But here the term *political economy* is shorn of any strictly determinist implications. As Michalowski is careful to point out, "to understand the 'criminality' of any particular individual or group" requires a critical examination of the "objective" yet "dynamic" (that is interactive and forever contestable) connections between individual experience and the historically specific character of "material and social relations."[82] Thus:

> Many variables that criminologists have included in the study of crimes—poverty, social class membership, race, ethnicity, and education, for instance—are not static conditions or states. They are a manifestation of specific social and material relations. For instance, being black in America is not simply the condition of having darker skin. It is a set of social and material relations between black Americans and

white Americans that extends back to the time the first black slaves were brought to the American colonies from Africa. . . . Similarly, being poor means existing within and adapting to a set of material and social relations that provide others with greater access to wealth than oneself. Poverty in America is not simply a characteristic of the poor; it is the outcome of the particular material and social relations that characterize American capitalism.[83]

In conclusion, the Marxist approach locates deviance and control in recurrent historical struggles to control material existence. As a mode of critical thought, Marxism is also associated with strategic critical action. As Quinney points out, "the solutions proposed by Marxism are predicated on transforming society, on constructing socialist political and economic institutions."[84]

Deconstructing Hierarchical Authority: Anarchist Critical Thought

Any rule is tyranny. The duty of the individual is to accept no rule, to be the initiator of his own acts, to be responsible. Only if he does so will the society live, and change, and adapt, and survive. We are not subjects of a State founded upon law, but members of a society. . . . We are responsible to you and you to us.

Ursula K. LeGuin[85]

Anarchism alone of all the ISMs approaches that one type of form which alone can interest us today, that strange attractor, the shape of chaos—which one must have within oneself, if one is to give birth to a dancing star.

Hakim Bey[86]

The social stratification of material resources undoubtedly affects the control of deviance. Those in hierarchical positions of material advantage are structurally pitted against those whose unequally rewarded labor makes this advantage possible. This is a basic Marxist thesis. Anarchism adds another dimension to this critique of hierarchical power. Anarchists seek to dispel the mythic power of authority and to display the socially constructed character of all "legitimate" forms of social control. From an anarchist perspective, institutionalized authority—whether externally embodied in legal codes and governmental regulations or internally incorporated as an aspect of conscience or personal morality—always operates to cover over the ritually negotiated basis of social order. Institutions of authority tend to "naturalize" historically given arrangements, making culturally specific ways of doing things appear timeless or universal. Anarchism defies the naturalization of authority. Anarchist theory calls for a reorganization of everyday life, based upon the principles of direct action, mutual respect, and the reciprocal negotiation of social power.

Hierarchical State Authority: A Structural Obstacle to Reciprocity Anarchism is particularly critical of the rule of centralized state power. State societies are governed by rulers who are legally authorized to command and correct the behavior of others. Priests, patriarchs, presidents, and the police: these "authority figures" are scorned by anarchists. By institutionalizing rituals which glorify authority—patriotic celebrations, unquestioned obedience to bureaucratic rules, and the omnipresence of "cop" shows on television—many of us forget that the legitimacy of authority is rooted in our historical relations to one another, and not in the way things "naturally" are. In this sense, anarchism aims at dislodging not only hierarchical state authority but also authoritarian states of mind and emotion, which perpetuate inequality by enslaving our moral imaginings of power.

In Chapter 2 I discussed the historical transition from headless, or *acephalous,* social groups to early state societies, organized around centralized religious authority. Anthropologists distinguish between these early *proto-states,* with their relatively simple technology and division of labor, and *civil states,* constructed around centralized administrative bureaucracies. In the west, the study of what we call "ancient history" is marked by the birth of civil states in the societies of Persia, Greece, and Rome. These imperial social forms shared a dream of bringing the entire world under a single standard of judgment. Everyone was supposed to believe in and obey one universal form of law. Those who deviated were banished or made to suffer.

Following the fall of the Roman Empire, the centralized western state disappeared for a time. In its place there arose a decentralized network of localized political rule, economic interdependency, and pagan religious practices. Referred to by later historians as "the Dark Ages"—perhaps because medieval society was less "enlightened" by the rule of timeless authority than our own—this was also an era in which strict obedience to authority was periodically abolished. This occurred during times of festival, carnivalesque rites of disorder that turned traditional power relations upside down. Medieval festivals reminded their participants of the chaotic flux underlying all forms of authority. As ecstatic rituals of anarchy, festivals released people from everyday forms of morality and hurled waves of laughter at the solemnity of supposed "natural" laws. Especially targeted were the patriarchal laws of priests and kings. Festivals, in other words, ritually deconstructed the sanctified hold of authority itself.

Although playful, festivals were also anarchistic religious events. Participants felt themselves to be one with the sacredness of nature and no longer the servants of some higher or external spiritual authority. Medieval festivals also overturned the authority of stereotypical sex and gender hierarchies. In so doing, they erotically undermined "masculine" standards of cultural mastery, while celebrating the more wildly "feminine" charms of immersing oneself in spiraling cycles of birth, death, and rebirth.[87] Thus, it should come as no surprise that, when the interrelated forces of capitalist patriarchy, rational bureaucracy, and hierarchical church power joined together in reviving the reign of centralized state authority in early modern Europe, pagan festivals were one of the first targets of legal censure and control. Indeed, under the centralized rule of the modern state, the anarchistic wisdom of pagan life was driven underground—and there it remains today, displaced onto the sacrificial figures of various scapegoats, among them "mad" people, women, children, nonwesterners, and anarchists. Within the authoritative confines of modern state society, these heterogeneous groupings of people have long been stereotyped as being somewhat "primitive," "irrational," and less "civilized."

The cultural repression of (pagan) anarchistic sensibilities begins with western men's efforts to abolish "cyclical" interpretations of time during the early thirteenth century. Set against a historical backdrop of increasingly centralized church authority, the ascendancy of regional kingships, and the mortgaging of feudal estates in exchange for the financing of wars and religious crusades, the repression of medieval anarchy is also a story of modern Eurocentric assaults upon the festivals and other "feminine" forms of power-reciprocal social exchange. In 1209, for instance, the Council of Avignon proclaimed "that at all saints' vigils, there shall not, in the churches, be any theater dances, indecent entertainments, gatherings of singers, or worldly songs, such as incite the souls of listeners to sin."[88] This is a thinly disguised attack upon peasant rites of anarchy and the ways in which medieval festivals displayed a laughing indifference to such supposedly "fearful" matters as death. In the words of medieval scholar Mikhail Bakhtin:

> The acute awareness of victory over fear is an essential element of medieval laughter. This feeling is expressed in a number of characteristic medieval comic images. We always find in them the defeat of fear presented in droll and monstrous forms, the symbols of power and violence turned inside out, the comic images of death and bodies rent asunder. All that was terrifying becomes grotesque. . . . [O]ne of the indispensable accessories of carnival was the set called "hell," a cornucopia; the monster, death, becomes pregnant. Various deformities, such as protruding bellies, enormous noses, or humps are all symptoms of pregnancy or of provocative power. Victory over fear is not its abstract elimination; it is a simultaneous uncrowning and renewal, a gay transformation. Hell is burst and has poured forth abundance. . . . There can be nothing terrifying on earth, just as there can be nothing frightening in a mother's body, with the nipples that are made to suckle, with the genital organ and warm blood. . . . All unearthly objects were transformed into earth, the mother which swallows up in order to give birth to something larger that has been improved. . . . The earthly element of terror is the womb, the bodily grave, but it flowers with delight and a new life.[89]

Such carnivalesque reversals between tomb and womb bore all the ritual markings of both Mother Earth-focused paganism and anarchism. This did not pass unnoticed by hostile church authorities. In the thirteenth century, these men attributed the existence of such rites to the newly figured image of Satan. During this time, the church also instituted the "singular" cult of the Virgin Mary. As the "one and only" mother of God, Mary was offered as an authoritative substitute for traditional pagan images of Mother Earth goddesses. Thus, in 1212, the Council of Paris acted to deny "assemblies of women, for the purpose of dancing and singing, permission to enter cemeteries or sacred places, regardless of considerations of dress." Also rendered taboo were "nuns from heading processions, either within their own cloister or without, that circle churches and their chapels while singing and dancing, something we cannot allow even secular women to do."[90] The target may have been nothing less than the ecstatic "round dances," whose association with spiraling ("feminine" and anarchist) reversals, and the encircling of death within life, represented obvious challenges to the linearity of the "world without end" promulgated by the masterful (masculine) forces of church power.

The historical linkage between "feminine" and anarchistic subversions of authority is important. Both feminists and anarchists are critical of the "universalizing" control structures of modern legal codes. Indeed, as Lynne Farrow and other anarcha-feminists suggest, "Feminism practices what anarchism preaches"[91]—the ritual destruction of "all vestiges of the male-dominated power structure, the State itself—with its whole ancient and dismal apparatus of jails, armies, and armed robbery (taxation); with all its murder; with all of its grotesque and repressive legislation and military attempts, internal and external, to interfere with people's private lives and freely-chosen cooperative ventures."[92]

Despite these connections between anarchism and feminism, I am here less concerned with a precise history of the modern patriarchal state than with the implications of centralized state authority for the control of deviance. In state societies the ritualistic control of deviance is typically removed from the hands of persons most directly involved with situations of trouble or conflict. It is invested, instead, in the office of some lawfully ordained authority.

The consequences of this change are far-reaching. In state societies, strategies of interpersonal reconciliation are replaced by impersonal legal rituals. This permits those in positions of authority to lawfully exclude deviant persons or groups. Structural tensions which may have produced trouble are in this way systematically disguised. Why? The answer is simple: state societies, unlike their acephalous antecedents, are themselves structurally oriented toward the production of trouble. From their historical inception, state societies are stratified according to a hierarchy of authorized political control over social, sexual, and economic activity.[93] This division—between those who legitimately control and those who are subject to control—drives a wedge through the experience of the collective cooperation which was so prominent a feature of acephalous societies.

In state societies we are placed in structured positions of relentless competition with one another. We are positioned so as to either benefit or lose by the reproduction of existing relations of authority. Such competition is an unfortunate outgrowth of the state. It is also a recurrent source of trouble—a structural inducement to deviate from one's present position in life in order to advance hierarchically beyond others. As such, state societies promote hierarchical conflict and deviance.

This contradictory feature of state social control is not always consciously recognized. As suggested in my previous discussion of the notion of *hegemonic ritual interactions*, people are not kept in positions of hierarchical advantage and disadvantage by coercion alone. The stable patterning of stratified state power requires that structured differences in the ability to control one's destiny be justified, legitimized, or authorized by the ritual construction of a "common sense" that things are the way they "naturally" have to be and should be. This means that the hegemonic organization of hierarchical state power is as much a state of mind, emotions, and bodily rituals as it is the effect of visible institutions of authorized governmental coercion. As British theorist Stuart Hall remarks, this enables those occupying hegemonic positions of control to exercise "total social authority" over their subjects, not simply by the threat of coercion but by "winning and shaping consent so the power of the dominant classes appears both legitimate and natural."[94]

The hegemonic dimension of control in state society makes life inherently complex and fragile. Structured social inequality is the historical product of the way that life is organized in the image and likeness of centralized authority. This reality, however, must be constantly disguised by the appearance that all this is a natural state of affairs. If such inequities are to be reproduced without major outbreaks of trouble or resistive deviance, a variety of everyday control rituals must be enacted so as to connect people to a common sense that things could be no different. In the daily routines of family life and in attending school, watching television, hunting for a job, dressing stylishly, and making ourselves up to look and feel attractive, we citizens of state society ritually contribute to the reproduction of the very structures which imprison us—structures which authoritatively position us according to a naturalized hierarchy of power.

One type of ritual which often contributes to the naturalization of hierarchical control is religion. This need not be the case. In Chapter 2 I noted that religion can both awaken and dull people's sense of the social structuring of injustice. This led Marx to once comment on the opiatelike quality of certain forms of religious observance. A similar view is taken by Andrew Gill and Jon King of the political punk rock/art group Gang of 4. In the lyrics of the song "Muscle for Brains" we hear the following critique of religion as a ritual of hierarchical control:

Don't help me, I can save myself
If I'm incomplete don't fill the gaps.
Save me from the people who would save me from my sin
They got muscle for brains.

For reasons that are not mysterious
The weak are sent to the wall
They have reservations in heaven
Down there they are not so fashionable

For reasons that are not so mysterious
Morality's used as a tool
The poor are told to be contented
But in this life they've no chance at all.[95]

The fragility of hegemonic control rituals and the structural strains inherent in the hierarchical positioning of people in state societies mean that state societies must rely heavily upon reactive (rather than reconciliatory) strategies of control. This is because state societies are founded upon the structural bedrock of nonreciprocal power. Reconciliation requires deconstructive actions that defuse trouble. This cannot truly happen under the rule of a centralized state. To reconcile is to bring people who have been separated by conflict back together. The hierarchical separation of people is, however, a central element of the social structure of state societies. A true process of reconciliation would require reciprocal rituals of social deconstruction and the abolition of centralized state authority.

Rather than change the structures by which they are legitimately empowered, state rulers have acted historically to delegitimate nonconformers, to isolate and exclude the deviant. When accomplished in a "lawlike" manner, this exclusion creates the impression that deviants are the primary source of the trouble in which they find themselves. This is the ritual importance of formal law in state society. As it legally excludes the deviant, the law produces the appearance (or collective representation) that troublesome persons rather than troublesome social structures are to blame. This mystifies the social roots of trouble in a society that is structurally unequal. A critique of this mystification constitutes the core of anarchist theory.

The Anarchist Vision: A Restoration of Reciprocity   According to Emma Goldman and Max Baginsky, "Anarchism alone makes non-authoritarian organization of common interest possible, since it abolishes the existing antagonism between individuals and classes."[96] In this sense, anarchism is more than a theoretical perspective. It is a way of life: an attempt to embody a fluid politics of nondogmatic justice, reciprocal empowerment, and a periodic and playful uprooting of all repressed, frozen, or fascistic ways of thinking, feeling, and acting in relation to oneself and others.[97] This is a central theme in the writings of both classical social-anarchists, such as Pierre-Joseph Proudhon, Mikhail Bakunin, Peter Kropotkin, and Gustav Landauer, as well as contemporary feminists, Situationists, radical art activists, punks, schizoanalysts, pacifists, and others influenced by the "black and red" colors of anarchist resistance.[98] Question external and internal authority at every turn! And collectively transform rigid social structures into graceful dance steps, guided by mutual respect for difference, rather than by the reduction of diversity to authoritarian legal codes and homogeneous moral standards! These are among the core theoretical notions guiding anarchist social criticism. In May 1968, when Paris students sought an end to authoritarian educational practices, they scrawled a phrase on the walls of the Sorbonne, suggestive of the most radical of anarchist imaginings. It read: "A cop sleeps in every one of us, he must be killed."

Anarchist theorists of crime and deviance such as Larry Tifft and Dennis Sullivan offer a related vision of human order without law, without the state.[99] This is a vision of return, not to the past but to the possibility of reciprocal relations of power in the immediate present. Under the domination of the state, humans are said to progressively lose the ability to act directly in mutual aid and support, resistance, and reconciliation. In a state society, direct action is replaced by the mediation of bureaucratic rules, personal responsibility by the actions of rulers. The immediacy of natural struggles between individuals and groups of individuals is supplanted by rituals of indirect mediation "in the interests of the ruling few, to maintain hegemony, hierarchy and authority."[100]

For anarchist theorists there is nothing natural about the hierarchical mediation of human experience. Contemporary anarchist writings on crime, social control, and social deviance by Tifft, Sullivan, and Harold Pepinsky,[101] among others, suggest that reciprocal cooperation is a natural human possibility but that such cooperation is torn asunder, not merely by deviants but by the unnaturally repressive institutions of centralized authority and state law.

But what is the alternative posed by anarchism? The answer is suggested by Emma Goldman, the brilliant Russian immigrant whose dedication to anarchist theory and struggles for justice led her to be denounced as a dangerous criminal and a madwoman by no less lofty a representative of the "American" state than President Theodore Roosevelt. In her memoirs *Living My Life*, Goldman presents us with a succinct summary of the critical vision of anarchist theory.

> Anarchism asserts the possibility of an organization without discipline, fear, or punishment and without the pressure of poverty: a new social organism, which will make an end to the struggle for the means of existence—the savage struggle which undermines the finest qualities of man [and of woman] and ever widens the social abyss. In short, anarchism strives toward a social organization which will establish well-being for all.[102]

Countering Heterosexism: Feminist Critical Thought

[I]nquiry into the implications of a sociology for women from the discovery of a point of rupture in my/our experience as woman/women within the social forms of consciousness—the cultures or ideology of our society—in relation to the world known otherwise, the world directly felt, sensed, responded to. . . . Inquiry does not begin within the conceptual organization or relevances of the sociological discourse, but in actual experience as embedded in particular historical forms of social relations that determine that experience.

Dorothy E. Smith[103]

Patriarchal culture is a culture founded on sacrifice, crime, war. . . . [T]he issue is not one of elaborating a new theory of which would be the subject or the object, but of jamming the theoretical machinery itself, of suspending its pretensions to the production of a truth and a meaning that are excessively univocal.

Luce Irigaray[104]

The economic and state hierarchies that are the target of Marxist and anarchist criticism are not gender-neutral. Nor do they exist independently of a compulsory heterosexist imagination of bodily pleasures and desires. An insistent recognition of the role played by sex and gender hierarchies in the construction and control of deviance is a core feature of feminist critical thought. Why, until recently, have long-established forms of male power—rape, spouse abuse, sexual harassment, gender-based discrimination in the workplace, and the pornographic debasement of female sexuality—escaped the stigma of deviance? And why have relatively minor deviations on the part of women— deviations from male-defined standards of female sexuality, dress, and self-presentation—often led to harsh and exclusionary forms of social control? Such questions are of major concern to feminist critics of deviance.

Feminist perspectives on power and social control are as old as the violence of patriarchy. Following the emergence of various women's movements in the 1960s, today there exists a complex and demanding body of feminist theories that challenge the dominance of male-centered conceptions of social life. Feminism both questions the silence of traditional forms of theory on issues of concern to women and exposes male bias in the normative organization of social science itself. In this sense, feminism asks more of the social sciences than that they simply open themselves up to women's issues. In deconstructing the taken-for-granted character of male-governed scientific viewpoints, feminist critical thought seeks to understand the world from the power-reciprocal standpoints of women.

This is not to suggest that feminists are united in their critical outlooks. As Donna Haraway observes,

> It has become difficult to name one's feminism by a single adjective—or even to insist in every circumstance upon the noun. Consciousness of exclusion through naming is acute. Identities seem contradictory, partial, and strategic. With the hard-won recognition of their social and historical constitution, gender, race and class cannot provide the basis for belief in "essential" unity. . . . Gender, race, or class consciousness is an achievement forced on us by the terrible historical experience of the contradictory social realities of patriarchy, colonialism, and capitalism. . . . But there has also been a growing recognition of another response through coalition—affinity, not identity.[105]

Despite or perhaps as a result of such productive multiplicities, critical feminist perspectives today converge on the following themes: *theory from the standpoint of the oppressed, a politics of the gendered body, a reflexive politics of representation, collective social resistance,* and *identities-in-excess* of patriarchal constructs. Together these convergent standpoints call for a radical reconstruction of male-centered understandings of the difference between what's normative and what's deviant.

Theory from the Standpoint of the Oppressed   Feminist critical thought originates in women's experience of gendered social oppression. This provides feminists with a firsthand understanding of contradictions involved in gendered processes of social control. Unequal pay for equally hard work, widespread ignorance of the cultural contributions and social histories of women, the omnipresent threat of male violence, the devaluation of feminine and/or feminist social styles, and the "homosocial" character of the most prestigious economic and social institutions—these are but a few of the oppressions that women experience daily. Awareness of these experiences eludes most male social theorists. Why? What is it about men's social positionings that allows so many of us to ignore or remain unconscious of the sacrifices our privilege demands from women?

According to Dorothy Smith, men's theoretical viewpoints are typically characterized by "extralocal relations of ruling." This means that men are routinely spared an awareness of the costs involved in assuming a universalist perspective on the world. Less distracted by such supposedly "trivial" matters as cooking, cleaning the house, doing the laundry, and caring for children, men have long been able to take a bird's eye view of matters such as deviance and social control. This "ability" to see things from abstract theoretical heights, without having to grapple with the social conditions of power which make such abstractions possible, is a privileged aspect of male social control. Women are not so fortunate. "Women," remarks Smith, "are outside the extralocal relations of ruling, for the most part located in work processes that sustain it and are essential to its existence."[106] Cursed from the point of view of everyday life, the standpoint of the oppressed, nevertheless, encourages women (and others who are structurally disempowered) to never lose sight of the material exigencies of power that underlie all forms of knowledge.

A Politics of the Gendered Body   Western patriarchal hierarchies are frequently characterized by the motto "Mind over matter." In these hierarchies, men are typically pictured as mind, while women are coded as matter, body, or chaotic nature. Mind over matter. According to Susan Griffin, this involves a cultural depreciation of the physical and moral value of woman, nature, and the material world. It also involves an elevation of all that is abstract, disembodied, and pornographic. Rather than partaking of this masculine devaluation of nature, numerous feminists are today engaged in reclaiming the female body as a politicized site from which to refuse the *phallocentric* priorities of patriarchy. In the words of Gloria Anzaldúa:

> Even when our bodies have been battered by life, . . . languages . . . spoken from the body, by the body, are still laden with aspirations, are still coded in hope and *"un desarme ensangretado,"* a bloodied truce. By sending our voices, visuals, visions outward into the world, we alter the walls and make them a framework for new windows and doors. We transform the *posos, aperatures, barrancas, abismos* that we are forced to speak from. Only then can we make a home out of the cracks.[107]

Phallocentricism is a term used to indicate the way in which patriarchal culture erects spaces of "extralocal" mastery. These are cold spaces—spaces of abstract male power—spaces that distance men from the fragile and interdependent body of nature "herself." Men occupy such phallocentric spaces whenever we pretend to speak from a universal point of view—whenever we speak from the point of view of "man," without recognizing that this excludes, marginalizes, or silences the bodily specificity of women's cultural positions. In this sense, phallocentric perspectives are illusory perspectives. They hide or cover over the wounds patriarchy inflicts on both women and nature. In making claims to "pure" knowledge, phallocentric perspectives repress the reality of men's own bodily relations to others. In particular, they repress the fact that men's social existence is itself dependent upon what it takes from women—food, mothering, clean houses, maybe even sex. Critical feminist theory deconstructs such phallic pretensions, drawing attention to women's bodily experiences as sites of struggle against male disembodiment.

Feminist efforts to contest the male invasion of women's bodies recognize that all forms of knowledge are mediated by a knower's bodily relations to others. Unlike men, few women are permitted to forget this most basic of epistemological premises. Women are routinely called upon to give themselves bodily to men: as sex objects, as assistants in work, as persons who clean up things that are physically and emotionally messy. Such contradictory experiences may remind women of the primacy of bodily awareness in making theoretical sense of the world. As Trinh T. Minh-ha points out, to elevate the intellect over the senses lacks both conceptual rigor and material "continuity in the practice of theory."[108] Thus, to write from (and of) the body as a contestable site of power is, for many feminists, a matter of considerable theoretical and political importance. This is underscored by Hélène Cixous when she writes:

> Listen to a woman speak in a meeting: she doesn't "speak," she launches her trembling body into the air, she *lets* herself *go,* she flies, she passes completely into her voice, it's with her body that she vitally sustains the "logic" of her speech. . . . She exposes herself. In truth, she materially incarnates what she thinks, she signifies it with her body. In a way, she *inscribes* what it says.[109]

A Reflexive Politics of Representation Writing from the body is not without its dangers in patriarchal culture. Patriarchy typically represents "woman" in terms of a sexualized body that is at once idealized and scorned. When men refer to women by such terms as "bimbos," "babes," "chicks," and "bitches," they engage in powerful rituals of linguistic social control. Such terms representationally position women outside and beneath the social worlds of men. Women are likened to infants, animals, and "other" creatures that are controlled by men's languages. In struggling to counter this representational debasement of women, feminist theory does more than simply reverse the tables of hierarchical language. Feminist critiques of representation do not claim a space of disembodied linguistic purity. Feminists, instead, demand that humans assume collective social responsibility for the partial and provisional truths that language historically engenders.

For feminist critics of male-governed representational practices, even such concepts as sex and gender are said to be socially constructed. Hidden within such constructions are a host of ritual distinctions which favor the power of men over women.[110] Thus, words commonly associated with the "female" sex—emotionality, intuition, softness, and so forth—are often made to take a backseat in a world driven by the supposedly rational, detached, and hard-edged thinking of men.

In order to undermine the violence of patriarchal language, Judith Butler and other critics urge feminists to join with gay, lesbian, and bisexual theorists in challenging the hierarchical coherence of straight-white-male discourse. The "fictive" coherence of such discourse like the hegemonic representation of race within a racist society, conceals the ways that language operates in the construction of contradictory social hierarchies. As Butler points out, "The construction of coherence conceals the gender discontinuities that run rampant within heterosexual, bisexual, and gay and lesbian contexts."[111] This results in the production of a "regulatory ideal," a powerful form of "normative fiction" that poses as the "truth" of sex and gender. Although fictive, this alleged truth will appear "natural" to men who are trapped within the representational confines of heterosexist patriarchy.

Critical feminist thought radically questions seemingly "natural" distinctions between female and male and between heterosexual and homosexual identities. This exposes the arbitrary, if powerful, character of the "regulatory ideals" and what Gayatri Spivak refers to as the "hidden ethico-political agenda" of patriarchal culture.[112] It also exposes the *false universality* that lies behind most straight-white-male-dominated economies of language.

False universality is a core feature of phallocentric language. Such language claims to speak for both men and women, while actually representing only the typically defensive standpoint of heterosexual men. Critical feminists reject the false universality of heterosexist language, without claiming a new universality for the language of women and gays. This is to recognize that language selectively constructs, rather than neutrally reflects, the world of which it is a part. Language never simply describes the things it signifies. It draws attention to some things but not to others. Language is always selective. Critical feminist theorists both recognize and take responsibility for this creative side of language.

Rooted in women's experience of being artificially constrained by patriarchal representational practices, critical feminist approaches to language do not draw rigid lines between fact and fiction. Facts are viewed as but powerful forms of theoretical fiction. Thus, unlike phallocentric language theories, feminist theories do not yearn for untainted, value-neutral, and totally objective forms of language. As an alternative to the false universality of patriarchal language, power-reflexive feminists seek to situate or historically ground the languages they use to construct understandings of the social world. This creates a "crisis of representation" for the supposedly neutral languages of male-governed social science.

This "crisis of representation" may be theoretically and politically fruitful for critical feminist thought. As Avery Gordon suggests, "such a crisis . . . has led to an understanding that the practices of writing, analysis, and investigation, whether of social or literary texts, constitute . . . a cultural practice which organizes particular rituals of storytelling, at the center of which is the investigating subject. This epistemological and social rupture, rather than leading away from an analysis of social relations of power, leads directly to a very different agenda for asking how power operates."[113] This is not to abandon objective claims to truth but to reflexively situate feminist claims to objectivity within the lived material and historical exigencies in which they were brought into being.

Collective Social Resistance Feminist perspectives on deviance and social control originate in the convergent struggles of women against patriarchy. Its practitioners are not heroic individual theorists but participants in a social movement seeking justice for women. Feminist theorists are also often targets for male resentment and institutional discrimination. Consider the career of Mary Daly. Daly is a controversial and internationally renowned radical feminist scholar. Yet, to be granted tenure and promotion, Daly had to bring legal action against the university in which she was employed.

Years later and after the publication of many widely debated books and articles, Daly has still never been promoted to the rank of full professor. The reason given by university administrators is that Daly's writings lack the scholarly rigor necessary for promotion. One thing is for sure: Daly's writings refuse conformity with what she theorizes as "the sado-ritual syndrome" governing patriarchal forms of thought. As a powerful form of social control, the sado-ritual syndrome is characterized by its erasure of the standpoint of women; by a reversal of actual power hierarchies, such that women are blamed for their own victimization; by the construction of false polarities that privilege the so-called enlightenment of men over the dark and chaotic messiness of women; and by strategies of "divide and conquer" that block women from making alliances with each other. So as to overturn this violent syndrome, Daly advocates feminist constructions of new, wildly poetic, laughing and raging feminist languages—languages that both affirm women's freedom and offer a critical (utopian) vision of living interdependently within nature. Daly's feminist theoretical demands suffer much when forced into comparison with the predominantly male-defined categories of supposed "scholarly rigor," such as those espoused by administrators at the university where she teaches.

Daly is not alone in suffering from the closure of institutional doors to feminist critique. As Susan Faludi has demonstrated, ours is an age of both feminist gains and concerted male backlash.[114] Indeed, one of the central targets of recent conservative campaigns to stamp out "political correctness" in North American universities is the on-campus presence of strong women with strong voices and an equally strong commitment to overturning centuries of male bias in the social construction of curriculum, learning styles, and academic procedures.

This is not to suggest that the critical voices of women are as one. As Audre Lorde has poignantly remarked, "Within the women's movement . . . white women focus upon their oppression as women and ignore differences of race, sexual preference, class, and age. . . . As a tool of social control, women have been encouraged to recognize only one area of difference as legitimate, those differences which exist between women and men."[115] Related critiques of some feminists' blindness to racialized and class-based differences are prominent in the writings of bell hooks, Angela Davis, and the contributors to *This Bridge Called My Back: Writings by Radical Women of Color*, edited by the critical Chicana theorists Cherrie Moraga and Gloria Anzaldúa. In response to such criticism, there today appears a wide range of recognized differences within women's movements, as feminists of different colors, ethnicities, class backgrounds, sexual orientations, national origins, and ages each question the theoretical and political strategies of others.[116] This commitment to working with rather than suppressing differences among women makes the challenge of contemporary feminism more dynamic, more diverse, and more difficult. It also engenders what bell hooks describes as a "yearning" for "shared sensibilities which cross [without conflating] the boundaries of class, gender, and race" and which provide "fertile ground for the construction of empathy—ties that promote the recognition of common commitments, and serve as a base for solidarity and action."[117] It is in relation to such diverse sensibilities that feminist critical scholars today attempt both to theorize and to practically deconstruct the heterosexist organization of social control.

Identities-in-Excess One additional feature of critical feminist theory is the recognition that the daily experience of gendered social power lies forever in excess of the concepts used to construct and describe it. As Teresa de Lauretis comments, "Gender, like the real, is not only the effect of representation but also its excess: what remains outside discourse as a potential trauma which can rupture or destabilize, if not contained, any representation."[118] This points to the limits of all theoretical discourse: a reflexive recognition that words will inevitably fail to capture the rich complexity of historical social relations. It is also why many feminist theorists today make use of dreams, poetry, fictive narration, art, theater, and ritual. These performance methods of inquiry help to carry critical feminist theory beyond the traditional boundaries of academic theory per se. As Gloria Anzaldúa suggests, "acts of writing, painting, performing and filming are acts of deliberate and desperate determination to subvert the status quo. Creative acts are forms of political activism employing definite aesthetic strategies for resisting dominant cultural norms and are not merely aesthetic exercises."[119]

Feminist efforts to break with male intellectual practices make some forms of feminist theory more evocative than literal, and also more sensorially engaging. This may involve what Avital Ronell calls the force of feminist "intensities"[120] or what Toni Morrison pictures as the critical role of the imagination in making connections to truth.[121] Consider, for instance, the theoretically fictive writings of Monique Wittig and Kathy Acker. Each descends into a material collage of unsettling theoretical poetics. In *The Lesbian Body* Wittig conjures up a multiplicity of women's bodily relations to each other that defy straight-minded male anatomical classifications.[122] On the other hand, Acker's spiraling texts scream of male violence tattooed across the bodies of women. The female protagonist in Acker's rewriting of *Don Quixote* discovers that "BEING BORN INTO AND PART OF THE MALE WORLD, SHE HAD NO SPEECH OF HER OWN. ALL SHE COULD DO WAS READ MALE TEXTS WHICH WEREN'T HER."[123]

When feminist writers attempt to exceed the homogeneous confines of much male theoretical writing, they often encounter questions about the accessibility of their more imaginative theoretical texts. But since "clarity is always ideological and reality always adaptive," as Trinh T. Minh-ha points out, "such a demand for clear communication often proves to be nothing else but an intolerance for any language other than the one approved by the dominant ideology. At times obscured and at other times blatant, this inability and unwillingness to deal with the unfamiliar, or with a language different from one's own, is, in fact, a trait that intimately belongs to the man of coercive power."[124] To demands for clear communicative access, Luce Irigaray, whose critical texts exceed the normative boundaries between theory and fiction, responds as follows:

> No clear nor univocal statement can, in fact, dissolve the mortgage, this obstacle . . . being caught, trapped in the same reign of credit. It is as yet better to speak only through equivocations, allusions, innuendoes, parables. . . . Even if you are asked for some *pre'cisions* [precise details].[125]

Countering Racism: Radical Multicultural Thought

Somewhere, on the edge of consciousness, there is what I call a mythic norm, which each one of us within our hearts knows "that it is not me." In america, this norm is usually defined as white, thin, male, young, heterosexual, christian, financially secure. It is with this mythical norm that the trappings of power reside within this society. . . . There is a pretense to a homogeneity of experience . . . that does not in fact exist.

Audre Lorde[126]

Racism, the word nobody likes. Whites who don't want to confront Racism and who don't name themselves white recoil in horror from it, shun it like the plague. To mention the word in their company disrupts their comfortable complacency. To call a text or methodology under discussion in a classroom . . . "racist," or to call a white person on her or his Racism, is to let loose a stink bomb. Like a tenacious weed, Racism crips up everywhere—it has a strangle hold on everyone. It is cultivated and produced in families, churches, temples and state institutions.

Gloria Anzaldúa[127]

From 1492 to the present the western theoretical imagination has been haunted by a shadowy history of racism and imperial conquest. For the most part, a lack of reflexive engagement with the methodological significance of race as a social construct has limited the critical power of even the most well-meaning of theoretical perspectives. Today, in a world where hierarchical differences between "racialized" cultures are manifest almost everywhere—from Miami and the south Bronx to south central Los Angeles and from South Africa and Bosnia to the Israeli-occupied territories of Palestine, critical theory can no longer afford the hegemonic white standpoint that has long characterized its most dominant strands. Critical theory must both help to counter the continuing violence of racism and open its ears to the voices of cultural traditions long silenced by Eurocentric approaches to world history. These twin objectives constitute the core of radical multicultural forms of critical theory.[128]

White racist viewpoints have, throughout modern history, been nurtured by a variety of religious and scientific forms of knowledge. When western religious officials raised questions about whether new world Indians or Africans had "God-given" souls, they were doing far more than engaging in abstract theological debate.

> At stake were not only the prospects for conversion, but types of treatment to be accorded them. The expropriation of property, the denial of political rights, the introduction of slavery and other forms of coercive labor, as well as outright extermination, all presupposed a world view which distinguished Europeans—children of God, human beings, etc.—from "others." Such a world view was needed to explain why some should be "free" and others enslaved, why some had rights to land and property while others did not. Race, and the interpretation of racial difference, was a central factor in that world view.[129]

The western scientific imagination, and particularly nineteenth- and early twentieth-century "eugenics" perspectives on deviance, have also contributed substantively to a racist structuring of hegemonic rituals of power. (See Chapter 4.) Moreover, despite important sociological critiques of correlations between races, measures of intelligence, and rates of deviance, racist thinking has hardly disappeared from contemporary scientific theorizing. In 1969 Arthur Jensen replicated the most common errors of previous IQ studies in a much discussed article published in the *Harvard Education Review*, while well into the 1990s criminologists such as James Q. Wilson, Richard J. Herrnstein, and Lee Ellis continue to claim validity for studies positing the "constitutional" character of forms of criminality that are typically associated with "non-whites," without even minimally addressing sociological criticism of the methods underlying these studies.

A more common effect of twentieth-century social science has been the tendency to negate or minimize the influence of race on social relations. Under the guidance of Franz Boas, comparative anthropological studies of culture did much to counter racist theories about the supposed higher "evolutionary" status of Euro-Americans. Moreover, following the lead of Robert Park, a former assistant to Booker T. Washington, the influential "Negro" proponent of racial assimilation, the Chicago school blamed cyclical processes of "social disorganization" rather than race for higher rates of officially recorded deviance on the part of blacks and other "minorities."

Although countering the racist viewpoints of "nativists," disorganization theory fell short of analyzing racism as a historical form of power. Robert Park's "natural history" model viewed the disorganizational processes of invasion and conflict as leading eventually to the reorganizational processes of accommodation and assimilation. Such thinking ignores the significance of race as a historical factor affecting deviance and social control. The consequences of this theoretical erasure are considerable. Park's thought reduced race to the category of ethnicity and ethnicity to but a step on the road to assimilation.[130] As later elaborated in the "liberal" sociological writings of Louis Wirth, E. Franklin Frazer, Gunnar Myrdal, Arnold Rose, Nathan Glazer, and Daniel Moynihan, this aspect of Park's thought resulted in the notion of a "melting pot," an idealized conception of social reorganization that sidestepped critical historical questions about the "racialization" of power in the United States.

Recognizing the manifest failure of U.S. society to "assimilate" blacks as one "ethnic group" melting into others, other theoretical frameworks attempted to explain this gap between theory and the actualities of social inequality. Of particular importance were Marxist theories which emphasized the exploitation of African-Americans and other "minorities" as a surplus labor pool, as well as theories which emphasized the role of cultural and economic imperialism and nationalist struggles of resistance. While such factors are undoubtedly significant, both Marxist and nationalist perspectives tend to ignore the particularity of racism as a form of power. In contrast, radical multicultural theorists today emphasize: (1) *the historical materiality of racial formations as modalities of social control;* (2) *the role of theory in struggling against and healing the violence of racism;* (3) *the racialized standpoint of white culture;* and (4) *an affirmation of nonracialized cultural difference*

Racial Formations as Social Control   Like other critical perspectives, radical multicultural theories are rooted in the survival strategies and struggles of oppressed peoples. Such theories attempt to destabilize the hegemonic power of *racial formations,* a theoretical term used by Michael Omi and Howard Winant to denote "the process by which social, economic and political forces determine the content and importance of racial categories, and by which they are in turn shaped by racial meanings."[131] Here race is conceived as a *central axis* in the ritual mediation of people's perceptions and actions, a social force affecting everything from feelings of belonging or exclusion to senses of economic trust and political believability. As theorists such as Franz Fanon, Homi K. Bhabha, Hortense Spillers, and Timothy Maliqalim Simone point out, historical constructions of race create dense and often unconscious psychic force fields which "color-code" our fears and repulsions, as well as our desires and attractions.[132]

To view race as a social construct rather than a biological category is to attend to the material specificity of shifting racial categories at different points in history. Indeed, it was only after the freeing of black slaves during the U.S. Civil War that the term *white* came to encompass virtually all European ethnic groups. Prior to that time, many southern Europeans, as well as Jews and the Irish, were racially classified as *nonwhite.* Nevertheless, from the time of Columbus to the present, racialized rituals of social control have targeted nonwestern "peoples of color" for unequal treatment. Simply read the opening pages of Toni Morrison's *The Bluest Eye* and you will be confronted with harsh educational rituals of exclusion that many Euro-Americans have long taken for granted. Morrison evokes the thoroughly white character of traditional U.S. grammar school stories about Dick and Jane, their smiling and happy white parents, and their running dog Spot.[133] Morrison's black-on-white writings deconstruct such supposedly "innocent" tales while revealing the ways that racially inscribed "others" are condemned to an "unyielding . . . plot of black dirt."

Indeed, what is commonly referred to as "western enlightenment" is also a time of the violent racialization of cultural difference between westerners and "others," a time of enslavement, colonization, and genocide for peoples subordinated by modern forms of western social power. It is not that the west has entirely exterminated the once-thriving cultures of those it has racialized and racially subordinated. Like ghostly reminders of a largely unacknowledged history of continuing white violence, many of these cultures still haunt western culture. This, perhaps, accounts for the perverse fascination with which many westerners view those subordinated by racist social institutions. Thus, while often denied legitimate access to powerful social resources, Africans, Asians, Latinos, and "others" are often felt to exert an exotic or even erotic allure on the culture that excludes them. Why? Is it that those most cursed by the violence of racism are simultaneously given access to "secret" forms of knowledge repressed within the west? Ironically, why is it that those who benefit most from racism achieve these benefits only at the cost of repressing alternate forms of knowledge from their own lives, just as they oppress the lives of others?

The positive affirmation of racially marginalized cultures is a central strategy of critical multicultural theories. As the Chicana tejana writer and theorist Gloria Anzaldúa declares, having been historically denied access to hegemonic theoretical discourse "because we are often disqualified and excluded from it, because what passes for theory these days is forbidden territory for us, it is *vital* that we occupy theorizing space, that we not allow white men and women solely to occupy it. By bringing in our own approaches and methodologies, we transform that theorizing space."[134]

This is not to suggest that African-Americans, Latin-Americans, Asian-Americans, American Indians, and others who have been subordinated to the white racist forms of control can ever return to untainted "native" cultures. The material and psychic violence of racism makes this literally impossible, forcing some of those it oppresses "to acquire the ability, like a chameleon, to change color when the dangers are many and the options few."[135] As Franz Fanon poignantly declares, "Every colonized people—in other words, every people in whose soul an inferiority complex has been created by the death and burial of its local cultural originality—finds itself face to face with the language of the [conquering master]."[136] Moreover, as Henry Louis Gates, Jr., suggests, "the Enlightenment, racism . . . marched arm in arm to delimit black people in perhaps the most pernicious way of all: to claim that they were subhuman, that they were 'a different species.'"[137] Gates is critical of the so-called "equalitarian criticism" of even well-intentioned white scholars "whose claims to 'universal' somehow always end up lopping off our arms, legs, and pug noses, muffling the peculiar timbre of our voices, and trying to straighten our always already kinky hair." As an alternative, Gates urges African-Americans to ground their own perspectives within vernacular traditions of the diasporic culture in which they find themselves historically situated.

Related challenges are contained in the critical writings of various Caribbean, Latino, and South American authors[138] and in the political allegories of African and Asian writers. Consider the following passage from the Vietnamese writer and filmmaker Trinh T. Minh-ha. What Euro-American scholars typically designate as historical narrative makes a canonical distinction between fact and fiction. Those who refuse this division are normatively exiled to the "primitive" enclaves of prehistory. In a critical postcolonial gesture, Trinh T. Min-ha inverts this racialized distinction, demanding instead that questions of truth be linked with narratives of culturally specific power.

> Which truth? The question unavoidably arises. . . . Managing to identify with History, history (with small letter *h*) thus manages to oppose the factual to the fictional (turning a blind eye to the 'magicality' of its claims; the story-writer—the historian—to the story-teller. As long as the transformation, manipulations, or redistributions inherent to the collecting of events are overlooked, the division continues its course, as sure of its itinerary as it certainly dreams to be. Story-writing becomes history-writing, and history quickly sets itself apart, consigning story to the realm of the tale, legend, myth, fiction, literature. Then since fictional and factual have come to a point where they mutually exclude each other, fiction, not infrequently, means lies, and fact truth. DID IT REALLY HAPPEN? IS IT A TRUE STORY?[139]

Theoretical Practice as Struggle and Healing   The twin theoretical objectives of struggle and healing are important elements in transforming the often unconscious grip of racism, including racist social theory. While racism may damage the lives of whites, its most costly effects are exacted from the minds and bodies of those it most oppresses. As Gloria Anzaldúa comments, "[W]e who are oppressed by Racism internalize its deadly pollen along with the air we breathe. Make no mistake about it, the fruits of this deadly pollen are dysfunctional lifestyles which mutilate our physical bodies, stunt our intellects and make emotional wrecks of us. Racism sucks out the life blood from our bodies, our souls."[140]

As survivors of perilous racist networks of power, radical multicultural theorists often embrace passionate theoretical discourse to both analyze and heal the wounds of racism. In the words of Chela Sandoval, "We had each tasted the shards of 'difference' until they had carved up our sides; now we are asking ourselves what shapes our healing would take."[141] In combining resistance and healing, radical multiculturalism often makes use of poetic forms that open the language of theory to politicalized expressions of emotions that are typically censored by traditional Eurocentric perspectives. Thus, it is not uncommon to find radical multicultural analyses mixed with intense articulations of anger, rage, laughter, and love. This enables critical theory to do more than merely comment upon unequal social power. By mixing analytic rigor with emotional intensity, radical multicultural criticism may employ languages that nurture rather than suppress "the to and fro movement of life."[142] In this way, radical multiculturalism contributes to reflexive transformations that are both intensely personal and social at the same time.

Whiteness as a Racialized Formation   Most social science studies of race focus exclusively on the lives and experiences of nonwhites. Ignored is the racialized construction of whiteness as a cultural form. It is as if whites remain outside the network of the racial hierarchies that their own imperial histories have produced. Nonwhites are rarely so privileged. Excluded from full participation in the color-coded privileges of white society, nonwhites are condemned to live within the terms of a culture that denigrates their very existence. The "strange fruit" of this contradictory social situation presents nonwhites with the cursed gift of "second sight" or what W. E. B. Dubois refers to as *double-consciousness*. "It is a peculiar situation this double-consciousness, this sense of always looking at one's self through the eyes of others, of measuring one's soul by the tape of a world that looks on in amused contempt and pity. One ever feels this twoness—an American, a Negro; two souls, two thoughts, two unreconciled strivings; two warring ideals in one dark body, whose dogged strength alone keeps it torn asunder."[143]

Dubois and other critical scholars of color have provided reflexive historical accounts of the painful contradictions of colonized peoples living in a state of *diaspora*, in forced exile from their traditional cultures. But what of the racialized specificity of white culture? Mustn't critical scholarship also attend to "Whiteness" as a "politically constructed category parasitic on 'Blackness'" and other racialized social divisions?[144] This challenge to critical white scholars is issued by bell hooks when she notes, "one change that would be real cool would be the production of a discourse on race that interrogates whiteness. It would be just so interesting for all those white folks who are giving us their take on blackness to let us know what's going on with whiteness."[145]

How might white scholars best respond to this critical challenge? How might Euro-Americans reflexively retheorize the conceptual structures, emotional overtones, and evaluative actions engendered by historical participation in the construction and reconstruction of racialized social differences? W. E. B. Dubois's theories about the "double-consciousness" of African-Americans were written at approximately the same time that the Chicago School was writing up its studies of deviance. Yet, unlike Dubois, the Chicago School, with its ideas about natural processes of social disorganization, virtually whitewashes the historical specificity of racialized oppression in the United States. In what ways is this theoretical displacement connected to the predominantly Euro-American backgrounds of such "liberal" Chicago theorists as Robert Park and Ernest Burgess?

The issue here is not simply intentional white racism, but the often unconscious role played by racialized social formations in shaping social scientists' approaches to deviance. Radical multicultural perspectives demand that critical scholars concern themselves with such power-reflexive concerns, making the racializing crossroads between western history and white biographical experience part of the context of theory production itself.

Affirmation of Nonracialized Cultural Difference   In addition to struggling against racism, radical multiculturalism demands respect for cultural diversity. It yearns for the historical emergence of a nonracist society, in which cultural difference would be a source of mutual enrichment rather than hierarchy. *Race* is not a code word for biological difference. Race is a form of social classification, invented by Europeans in the process of constructing imperial hierarchies between their culture and others. To counter the force of racism is to denaturalize the violence of racialized categories. It is also "to hope for a future in which we can recognize differences without seizing them as levers in a struggle for power."[146]

Respect for cultural diversity cannot be willed into being. We must first struggle to rid ourselves of the racialized social structures within which we currently live. For radical multicultural theorists, this means that the strategic affirmation of racialized identity may be a necessary first step toward creating a social world where the hierarchical power of race might eventually lose its hold. This may involve a provisional affirmation of the racialized identities of African-Americans, American Indians, Latinos, Asian-Americans, Jews, and others marginalized by white European culture. But for radical multicultural theorists the provisional affirmation of "identity politics" is never an end in itself. What makes radical multiculturalism truly critical is its refusal to uncouple "identity politics" from a deconstructive "politics of difference," a politics that affirms diversity while undermining the stability of race as a category of hierarchical power. As Cornel West points out, the most distinctive features of this "new cultural politics of difference are to trash the monolithic and homogeneity in the name of diversity, multiplicity, and heterogeneity; to reject the abstract, general, and universal in light of the concrete, specific, and particular; and to historicize, and pluralize by highlighting the contingent, provisional, variable, tentative, shifting and changing" dimensions of lived cultural experience.[147] When joined with key aspects of Marxism, anarchism, and feminism, this aspect of radical multicultural analysis helps to guide the construction of critical theoretical practice.

NOTES

1 Patricia J. Williams, "A Rare Case Study of Muleheadedness and Men, or How to Try an Unruly Black Witch, with Excerpts from the Heretical Testimony of Four Women, Known to Be Hysterics, Speaking in Their Own Voices, as Translated for This Publication by Brothers Hatch, Simpson, Deconcini, and Specter," in Toni Morrison (ed.), *Race-ing, Justice, En-gendering Power: Essays on Anita Hill, Clarence Thomas, and the Construction of Social Reality*, Pantheon, New York, 1992, pp. 167–168, 169.

2 Richard Quinney, *Criminal Justice in America: A Critical Understanding*, Little, Brown, Boston, 1974, p. 16.

3 Peter Dale Scott and Jonathan Marshall, *Cocaine Politics: Drugs, Armies, and the C.I.A. in Central America*, University of California Press, Berkeley, Calif., 1991.

4 In referring to hierarchies based on both sex and gender I wish to direct attention to the ways in which western patriarchy imposes restrictions upon both women and men's erotic practices (i.e., taboos against homosexuality, bisexuality, non-monogamous sex, etc.) and upon women as a social group subordinated to men. Together, these represent two dimensions of *heterosexist* social control rituals.

5 Michel Foucault, "The Subject and Power," Afterword to Hubert L. Dreyfus and Paul Rabinow, *Michel Foucault: Beyond Structuralism and Hermeneutics*, University of Chicago Press, Chicago, 1982, pp. 208–226.

6 Rollo May, *Power and Innocence: A Search for the Source of Violence*, Norton, New York, 1972.

7 George Jackson, *Soledad Brother: The Prison Letters of George Jackson*, Coward, McCann and Geoghegan, 1970, as excerpted in Barry Krisberg (ed.), *Crime and Privilege*, Prentice-Hall, Englewood Cliffs, N.J., 1975.

8 Peter McLaren, *Schooling as a Ritual Behavior*, Routledge and Kegan Paul, London, 1986, pp. 34–35, 36.

9 Harold Garfinkel, *Studies in Ethnomethodology*, Prentice-Hall, Englewood Cliffs, N.J., 1967, p. 47.

10 John Marks, *The Search for the "Manchurian Candidate,"* Times Books, New York, 1979. See also Martin A. Lee and Bruce Shlain, *Acid Dreams: The Complete Social History of LSD*, Grove Weidenfeld, New York, 1985.

11 For an important study of the concept of hegemony within Marxist and post-Marxist social criticism, see Ernesto Laclau and Chantal Mouffe, *Hegemony and Socialist Strategy: Toward a Radical Democratic Politics*, Verso, London, 1985.

12 Antonio Gramsci, *Selections from the Prison Notebooks*, Quintin Hoare and Geoffrey Nowell Smith (trans.), Lawrence and Wishart, London, 1971). See also Antonio Gramsci, *Selections from Cultural Writings*, William Boelhower (trans.), Harvard University Press, Cambridge, Mass., 1985; Chantal Mouffe (ed.), *Gramsci and Marxist Theory*, Routledge and Kegan Paul, London, 1979; Walter L. Adamson, *Hegemony and Revolution: A Study of Antonio Gramsci's Political and Cultural Theory*, University of California Press, Berkeley, 1980.

13 The ritual character of hegemonic processes is also an aspect of the cultural Marxist theories of Roland Barthes and Louis Althusser. See, for instance, Roland Barthes, *Mythologies*, Paladin, London, 1993; Louis Althusser, "Ideology and Ideological State Apparatuses," in Ben Brewster (trans.), *Lenin and Philosophy and Other Essays*, Monthly Review Press, New York, 1971, pp. 127–186. For an extended discussion of the relations between ritual, hegemony, and social control,

see Stephen Pfohl, *Death at the Parasite Cafe: Social Science (Fictions) and the Post-modern*, St. Martin's Press, New York, 1992.

14 A related theorization of the relation between ritual and hegemony is found in the writings of Stuart Hall, Dick Hebdige, Angela McRobbie and other members of the Birmingham Center for Contemporary Culture Studies during the late 1970s. See, for instance, Stuart Hall, John Clarke, Tony Jefferson, and Brian Roberts (eds.), *Resistance through Rituals*, Hutchinson, London, 1976; Stuart Hall, Chas Critcher, Tony Jefferson, John Clarke, and Brian Roberts, *Policing the Crisis*, MacMillan, London, 1978; Dick Hebdige, *Subcultures: The Meaning of Style*, Methuen, London, 1979; Stuart Hall, Dorothy Hobson, Andrew Lowe, and Paul Willis, *Culture, Media, Language*, Hutchinson, London, 1980.

15 Leonard Peltier, "Statement to the Canadian Court, May 13, 1976," in Ward Churchill and J. J. Vander Wall (eds.), *Cages of Steel: The Politics of Imprisonment in the United States*, Maisonneuve Press, Washington, D.C., 1992, p. 270.

16 Malcolm X, *The Autobiography of Malcolm X*, with the assistance of Alex Haley, Grove Press, New York, 1964, p. 116.

17 Angela Y. Davis, "Political Prisoners, Prisons and Black Liberation," in Barry Krisberg (ed.), *Crime and Privilege*, Prentice-Hall, Englewood Cliffs, N.J., 1975, p. 94.

18 Raymond Michalowski, "Conflict, Radical, and Critical Approaches to Criminology," in Israel Barak-Glantz and C. Ronald Huff (eds.), *The Mad, the Bad, and the Different*, Heath, Lexington, Mass., 1981, p. 40.

19 See David O. Friedrichs, "Radical Criminology in the United States: An Interpretive Understanding," in James A. Inciardi (ed.), *Radical Criminology: The Coming Crisis*, Sage, Beverly Hills, Calif., 1980, pp. 35–36; Gresham M. Sykes, "The Rise of Critical Criminology," *Journal of Criminal Law and Criminology*, vol. 65, no. 2, June 1974, pp. 206–213; Anthony Platt, "Prospects for a Radical Criminology in the United States," *Crime and Social Justice*, vol. 1, spring-summer 1974, pp. 2–10.

20 Michael Omi and Howard Winant, *Racial Formations in the United States: From the 1960s to the 1980s*, Routledge, New York, 1986, p. 4.

21 U.S. Department of Labor Statistics, as analyzed by Michael Harrington, *The Other America: Poverty in the United States*, Penguin, Baltimore, Md., 1963, pp. 2–10.

22 Malcolm X, *The Autobiography of Malcolm X*, p. 90.

23 See, for instance, *The National Advisory Commission on Civil Disorders Report*, GPO, Washington, D.C., 1968.

24 Assata Shakur, as quoted in Nancy Kurshan, "Women and Imprisonment in the U.S.—History and Current Reality," in Churchill and Vander Wall, *Cages of Steel*, p. 331.

25 Bettina Aptheker, "The Social Functions of Prisons in the United States," in Angela Davis (ed.), *If They Came in the Morning*, New American Library, Signet, New York, 1971, pp. 58–59.

26 See also Isaac Balbus, *The Dialectics of Legal Repression*, Russell Sage, New York, 1973.

27 For an analysis of the relationship between the emergence of the youth counterculture and economically manufactured youthful leisure, see Simon Frith, *Sound Effects: Youth, Leisure and the Politics of Rock and Roll*, Pantheon, New York, 1981.

28 See, for instance, Kenneth Kenniston, *The Uncommitted*, Bell, New York, 1965.

29 For a consideration of the contradictory relation between the 1960s countercul-

ture, "the new left," and feminist politics, see Alice Echols, "We Gotta Get Out of This Place," *Socialist Review*, vol. 22, no. 2, April-June 1992, pp. 9–33.

30 Dorothy Smith, "Women's Perspective as a Radical Critique of Sociology," *Sociological Inquiry*, vol. 44, no. 1, 1973, pp. 7–13.

31 Marcia Millman and Rosabeth Moss Kanter, *Another Voice: Feminist Perspectives on Social Life and Social Science*, Doubleday, New York, 1975, p. viii.

32 Eileen B. Leonard, *Women, Crime and Society, A Critique of Criminological Theory*, Longman, New York, 1982, pp. xi–xii.

33 See William Chambliss and Robert Seidman, *Law, Order and Power*, 2d ed., Addison-Wesley, Reading, Mass., 1982, pp. 303–305.

34 John E. Conklin, *Illegal but Not Criminal: Business Crime in America*, Prentice-Hall, Englewood Cliffs, N.J., 1977.

35 C. Wright Mills, *The Power Elite*, Oxford University Press, New York, 1959, p. 343.

36 C. Wright Mills, *White Collar: The American Middle Classes*, Oxford University Press, New York, 1951, p. 110.

37 Alexander Liazos, "The Poverty of the Sociology of Deviance: Nuts, Sluts, and Perverts," *Social Problems*, vol. 20, summer 1972, p. 111.

38 C. Ronald Huff, "Conflict Theory in Criminology," in James A. Inciardi (ed.), *Radical Criminology: The Coming Crisis*, Sage, Beverly Hills, Calif., 1980, p. 75.

39 George Vold, *Theoretical Criminology*, Oxford University Press, New York, 1958.

40 George Vold, *Theoretical Criminology*, 2d ed., prepared by Thomas J. Bernard, Oxford University Press, New York, 1979, p. 242.

41 Lewis Wirth, "Culture, Conflict and Misconduct," *Social Forces*, June 1931, reprinted in R. Farfell and V. Swigert (eds.), *Social Deviance*, 2d ed., Lippincott, Philadelphia, 1978, p. 304.

42 Thorsten Sellin, *Culture, Conflict and Crime*, Bulletin 41, Social Science Research Council, Washington, D.C., 1938.

43 Richard Quinney, *The Social Reality of Crime*, Little, Brown, Boston, 1970.

44 Ibid., p. 304.

45 William Chambliss and Robert Seidman, *Law, Order and Power*, Addison-Wesley, Reading, Mass., 1971.

46 Ibid., p. 504.

47 Austin Turk, *Criminality and the Legal Order*, Rand McNally, Chicago, 1969.

48 Ralf Dahrendorf, "Out of Utopia: Toward a Reorientation of Sociological Analysis," *American Journal of Sociology*, vol. 64, September 1958, p. 127.

49 The influence of pluralistic conflict theory is evident in such texts as Stuart C. Hills, *Crime, Power and Morality*, Chandler, Scranton, Penn., 1971; Clayton A. Hartjen, *Crime and Criminalization*, Praeger, New York, 1974; Charles H. McCaghy, *Deviant Behavior: Crime, Conflict and Interest Groups*, Macmillan, New York, 1976; and Alex Thio, *Deviant Behavior*, Houghton Mifflin, Boston, 1978. Works which attempt to combine societal-reaction and pluralistic conflict models include John Lofland, *Deviance and Liberty*, Prentice-Hall, Englewood Cliffs, N.J., 1969; and Edwin M. Schur, *The Politics of Deviance: Stigma Contests and the Uses of Power*, Prentice-Hall, Englewood Cliffs, N.J., 1980.

50 Richard Quinney, "Feature Review Symposium on the New Criminology," *Sociological Quarterly*, vol. 14, Autumn 1973, pp. 589, 595.

51 William Chambliss and Robert Seidman, *Law, Order and Power*, 2d ed., Addison-Wesley, Reading, Mass., 1982, p. x.

52 See, for instance, Austin T. Turk and Ruth Ellen Grimes, "Legal and Social Scientific Views of Law and Deviance," in H. Lawrence Ross (ed.), *Law and Deviance*, Sage, Beverly Hills, Calif., 1980, p. 84.

53 Austin T. Turk, "Conceptions of the Demise of Law," in P. J. Brautigham and J. M. Kress (eds.), *Structure, Law and Power*, Sage, Beverly Hills, Calif., 1979, p. 24.

54 Austin T. Turk, "Analyzing Official Crime: For Nonpartisan Conflict Analyses in Criminology," in James A. Inciardi (ed.), *Radical Criminology: The Coming Crisis*, Sage, Beverly Hills, Calif., 1980, p. 84.

55 Ibid.

56 Ibid.

57 Karl Marx, *Capital: A Critique of Political Economy*, vol. 1, Friedrich Engels (ed.), Samuel Moore and Edward Aveling (trans.), Swan Sonnenscheen, London, 1887, as excerpted in David F. Greenberg (ed.), *Crime and Capitalism*, Mayfield, Palo Alto, Calif., 1981, p. 48.

58 Friedrich Engels, *The Condition of the Working Class in England*, W. O. Henderson and W. H. Chaloner (eds. and trans.), Basil Blackwell, Oxford, 1968, as excerpted in Greenberg, *Crime and Capitalism*, p. 48.

59 Lewis Coser, *Masters of Sociological Thought*, Harcourt Brace Jovanovich, New York, 1971, p. 76.

60 Karl Marx, from Lloyd D. Easton and Kurt H. Goddat (eds.), *The Writings of the Young Karl Marx on Philosophy and Society*, as excerpted in Anthony Giddens, *Capitalism and Modern Social Theory*, Cambridge University Press, London, 1971, p. 1.

61 For a discussion of Feuerbach's 1841 *Essence of Christianity*, see Sidney Hook, *From Hegel to Marx*, Reynal and Hitchcock, New York, 1936, p. 221.

62 Friedrich Engels, *The Origin of the Family, Private Property and the State*, International Publishers, New York, 1972.

63 Karl Marx and Friedrich Engels, *The German Ideology*, Lawrence and Wishart, London, 1965.

64 Ian Taylor, Paul Walton, and Jock Young, *The New Criminology: For a Social Theory of Deviance*, Harper, Colophon, New York, 1973, p. 220.

65 Marx and Engels, *The German Ideology*, p. 367.

66 Karl Marx, "Theories of Surplus Value," in Greenberg, *Crime and Capitalism*, pp. 52–53.

67 Taylor, Walton, and Young, *The New Criminology*, p. 214.

68 Wilhelm Bonger, *Criminality and Economic Conditions*, Little, Brown, Boston, 1916.

69 Georg Rusche and Otto Kirchheimer, *Punishment and Social Structure*, Columbia University Press, New York, 1939. For a discussion of this influential work, see Dario Melossi, "Punishment and Social Structure," in Tony Platt and Paul Takagi (eds.), *Punishment and Penal Discipline: Essays on the Prison and the Prisoners' Movement*, Crime and Social Justice Associates, Berkeley, Calif., 1980, pp. 17–27.

70 This thesis was first developed by Georg Rusche in 1933. See Georg Rusche, "Labor Market and Penal Sanction: Thoughts on the Sociology of Criminal Law," Gerda Dinwiddie (trans.), in Platt and Takagi, *Punishment and Penal Disicipline* pp. 10–16.

71 E. B. Pashukanis, *The General Theory of Law and Marxism*, as quoted in Dario Melossi, "Punishment and Social Structure," in Tony Platt and Paul Takagi (eds.), *Punishment and Penal Discipline: Essays on the Prison and Prisoners' Movement*, Crime

and Social Justice Associates, Berkeley, Calif., 1980, p. 19.

72 Richard Quinney's Marxist criminological writings include *Critique of Legal Order*, Little, Brown, Boston, 1973; *Criminal Justice in America: A Critical Understanding*, Little, Brown, Boston, 1974; with John Wildeman, *The Problem of Crime*, 2d ed., Harper and Row, New York, 1977; *Class, State and Crime: On the Theory and Practice of Criminal Justice*, McKay, New York, 1977; and *Criminology*, 2d ed., Little, Brown, Boston, 1979.

73 Herman Schwendinger and Julia Schwendinger, "Social Class and the Definitions of Crime," *Crime and Social Justice*, vol. 7, spring-summer 1977, pp. 4–13.

74 Paul Takagi, "The Walnut Street Jail: A Penal Reform to Centralize the Powers of the State," *Federal Probation*, vol. 39, December 1975, pp. 119–125.

75 Jerome Hall, *Theft, Law and Society*, Bobbs-Merrill, Indianapolis, 1952.

76 Raymond Michalowski and Edward Bohlander, "Repression and Criminal Justice in America," *Sociological Inquiry*, vol. 26, no. 2, 1976, p. 99.

77 Anthony Platt, *The Child Savers*, University of Chicago Press, Chicago, 1969; and "Prospects for a Radical Criminology in the United States," *Crime and Social Justice*, no. 1, spring-summer 1974, pp. 2–3.

78 William J. Chambliss, "A Sociological Analysis of the Law of Vagrancy," *Social Problems*, vol. 12, summer 1964, pp. 46–67; and "Toward a Political Economy of Crime," *Theory and Society*, vol. 2, summer 1975, pp. 150–170.

79 Quinney, *Criminology*, 2d ed., p. 399.

80 Richard Quinney, "Crime Control in Capitalist Society: A Critical Philosophy of Legal Order," *Issues in Criminology*, vol. 8, spring 1973, pp. 75–95; and "There's a Lot of Us Folks Grateful to the Lone Ranger: Some Notes on the Rise and Fall of American Criminology," *Insurgent Sociologist*, vol. 4, fall 1973, pp. 56–64.

81 Steven Spitzer, "Toward a Marxian Theory of Deviance," *Social Problems*, vol. 22, June 1975, pp. 641–651.

82 Raymond J. Michalowski, "A Critical Model for the Study of Crime," in Delos H. Kelly (ed.), *Criminal Behavior: Text and Readings in Criminology*, 2d ed., St. Martin's Press, New York, 1990, p. 196.

83 Ibid., pp. 196–197.

84 Quinney, *Criminology*, 2d ed., p. 26.

85 Ursula K. Leguin, *The Dispossessed*, Avon, New York, 1974, pp. 288, 310.

86 Hakim Bey, *T. A. Z.: The Temporary Autonomous Zone, Ontological Anarchy, Poetic Terrorism*, Autonomedia, New York, 1991, p. 89.

87 Here the terms *masculine* and *feminine* are not equated with the terms *male* and *female*. In pagan religious rituals both men and women were believed to participate, if in different ways, in the sacred life cycles of Mother Earth. In this sense, the strict equation of masculinity with males and femininity with females may be a historical outcome of the genocidal elimination of pagan social forms by modern (patriarchal) state authority.

88 Jacques Attalli, *Noise: The Political Economy of Music*, Brian Massumi (trans), University of Minnesota Press, Minneapolis, 1985, p. 22.

89 Mikhail Bakhtin, *Rabelais and His World*, Helene Iswolsky (trans.), Indiana University Press, Bloomington, 1984, pp. 88, 89, 90.

90 Attalli, *Noise*, p. 22.

91 Lynne Farrow, "Feminism as Anarchism," in Dark Star (eds.), *Quiet Rumours: An Anarcha-Feminist Anthology*, Aldgate Press, London, p. 11.

92 Siren, "Who We Are: An Anarcho-Feminist Manifesto," in Dark Star, *Quiet Rumours*, p. 4.

93 For an elaboration of this thesis, see Stephen J. Pfohl, "Labeling Criminals," in H. Lawrence Ross (ed.), *Law and Deviance*, Sage, Beverly Hills, Calif., 1981, pp. 65–97.

94 Stuart Hall, "Culture, the Media and the Ideological Effect," in J. Curran et al. (eds.), *Mass Communications and Society*, Arnold, London, 1977, pp. 332–333.

95 Andrew King and Jon Gil, "Muscle for Brains," in the album *Songs of the Free* by Gang of 4, King-Gil, Inc., London, 1982.

96 Emma Goldman and Max Baginski, "The Relationship of Anarchism to Organization," *Mother Earth*, vol. II, October 1907, as quoted in Richard Drinan, *Rebel in Paradise: A Biography of Emma Goldman*, Harper Colophon, New York, 1961, p. 106.

97 See, for instance, Roland Perez, *On An(archy) and Schizoanalysis*, Autonomedia, New York, 1990.

98 For a historical introduction to these diverse strands of anarchist thought, see Richard D. Sonn, *Anarchism* Twayne Publishers, New York, 1992.

99 Larry Tifft and Dennis Sullivan, *The Struggle to Be Human: Crime, Criminology and Anarchism*, Cienfuegos Press, Orkney, Scotland, 1980. See also Larry Tifft, "The Coming Redefinition of Crime and Anarchist Perspective," *Social Problems*, vol. 26, April 1979, pp. 392–402.

100 Tifft and Sullivan, *The Struggle to Be Human*, p. 83.

101 Harold Pepinsky, "Communist Anarchism as an Alternative to the Rule of Criminal Law," *Contemporary Crisis*, vol. 2, 1978, pp. 315–334. See also George Woodcock, *Anarchism: A History of Libertarian Ideas and Movements*, New American Library, New York, 1962.

102 Emma Goldman, *Living My Life*, vol. 1, Dover, New York, 1970, p. 403.

103 Dorothy E. Smith, *The Conceptual Practices of Power: A Feminist Sociology of Knowledge*, Northeastern University Press, Boston, 1990, p. 49.

104 Luce Irigaray, *Sexes et Parentes* and *This Sex Which Is Not One*, as quoted in Margaret Whitford, *Luce Irigaray: Philosophy in the Feminine*, Routledge, New York, 1991, pp. 170, 67.

105 Donna Haraway, "A Cyborg Manifesto: Science, Technology and Socialist Feminism in the Late Twentieth-Century," in Linda J. Nicholson (ed.), *Feminism/Postmodernism*, Routledge, New York, 1985, p. 336.

106 Dorothy E. Smith, *The Everyday World as Problematic: A Feminist Sociology*, Northeastern University Press, Boston, p. 79.

107 Gloria Anzaldúa, "Haciendo Caras, una Entrada," in Gloria Anzaldúa (ed.), *Making Face, Making Soul: Haciendo Caras*, Aunt Lute Foundation, San Francisco, 1990, p. xxv.

108 Trinh T. Minh-ha, *When the Moon Waxes Red: Representation, Gender, and Cultural Politics*, Routledge, New York, 1991, p. 131.

109 Hélène Cixous, "Le Rire," as quoted in Trinh T. Minh-ha, *When the Moon Waxes Red*, p. 131.

110 Teresa de Lauretis, *Technologies of Gender, Essays on Theory, Film, and Fiction*, Indiana University Press, Bloomington, 1987, p. 3.

111 Judith Butler, "Gender Trouble, Feminist Theory, and Psychoanalytic Discourse," in Linda J. Nicholson (ed.), *Feminism/Postmodernism* (2d. ed), Routledge, New

York, 1990, p. 336.

112 Gayatri Chakravorty Spivak, "Feminism and Critical Theory," in *In Other Worlds: Essays in Cultural Politics*, Methuen, New York, 1987, p. 84.

113 Avery Gordon, *Ghostly Memories: Feminist Rituals of Writing the Social Text*, Ph.D. dissertation, Boston College, Chestnut Hill, Mass., 1990, p. 25.

114 Susan Faludi, *Backlash: The Undeclared War Against American Women*, Crown, New York, 1991.

115 Audre Lorde, "Age, Race, Class, and Sex: Women Redefining Difference," in Russell Fergusen, Martha Gever, Trinh T. Minh-ha, and Cornel West (eds.), *Out There: Marginalization and Contemporary Cultures*, MIT Press, Cambridge, Mass., 1990, pp. 282, 286.

116 This is not to suggest that many white feminist responses to the challenges of texts such as *This Bridge Called My Back* have been unproblematic. As Norma Alarcon points out, "Anglo feminist readers of *Bridge* tend to appropriate it, cite it as an instance of difference between women, and proceed to negate that difference by subsuming women of color into the unitary category of woman/women." Norma Alarcon, "The Theoretical Subject(s) of *This Bridge Called My Back* and Anglo-American Feminism," in Anzaldúa, *Making Face, Making Soul*, p. 358.

117 bell hooks, *Yearning: Race, Gender, and Cultural Politics*, The South End Press, Boston, 1990, p. 27.

118 de Lauretis, *Technologies of Gender*, p. 3.

119 Anzaldúa, "Haciendo Caras, una Entrada," p. xiv.

120 Avital Ronell, "Interview with Avital Ronell," in Andrea Juno and V. Vale (eds.), *Angry Women*, Re/Search Publications, San Francisco, 1991, p. 128.

121 Toni Morrison, "The Site of Memory," in Ferguson, Gever, Minh-ha, and West (eds.), *Out There*, p. 302.

122 Monique Wittig, *The Lesbian Body*, Peter Owen (trans.), Avon, New York, 1976.

123 Kathy Acker, *Don Quixote*, Grove Press, New York, 1986, p. 39.

124 Trinh T. Minh-ha, *When the Moon Waxes Red*, p. 84.

125 Luce Irigaray, *Speculum of the Other Woman*, Gillian C. Gill (trans.), Cornell University Press, Ithaca, N.Y., 1985, p. 178.

126 Lorde, "Age, Race, Class, and Sex," p. 282.

127 Anzaldúa, "Haciendo Caras, una Entrada," p. xiv.

128 In using the phrase *radical multiculturalism*, I am following the lead of Wahneema Lubiano and others who make a distinction between the term *multiculturalism* as it is used in critical perspectives and as it is used in various pluralist and often corporate-sponsored contexts. As Angela Davis warns, if the term *multiculturalism* is not connected to struggles against racism, it may suggest cultural diversity but deflect attention from the hierarchical character of contemporary racial formations. Lubiano's and Davis's remarks were made during the symposium Translating Cultures: The Future of Multiculturalism, University of California, Santa Barbara, Nov. 11–14, 1992.

129 Omi and Winant, *Racial Formations in the United States*, p. 58.

130 Ibid., pp. 15–19.

131 Ibid., p. 61.

132 Franz Fanon, *Black Skin, White Masks*, Harles Lam Markmann (trans.), Grove Press, New York, 1967; Homi K. Bhabha, "The Other Question: Difference, Discrimination and the Discourse of Colonialism," in Ferguson, Gever, Minh-ha, and West, *Out There*, pp. 71–87; and Timothy Maliqalim Simone, *About Face: Race in Postmodern America*, Autonomedia, New York, 1989.

133 Toni Morrison, *The Bluest Eye*, Washington Square Press, New York, 1970, p. 7.
134 Anzaldúa, "Haciendo Caras, una Entrada," p. xxv.
135 Ibid., p. xv.
136 Fanon, *Black Skin, White Masks*, p. 18.
137 Henry Louis Gates, Jr., "Talkin' That Talk," in Henry Louis Gates, Jr. (ed.), *"Race," Writing and Difference*, Chicago: University of Chicago Press, 1985, p. 408.
138 My limited knowledge of the material scene in which critical literature is being produced was exponentially expanded by the opportunity to participate in the Coloquio Internaciónal sobre el Imaginario Social Contemporaneo, sponsored by the University of Puerto Rico in February 1991. Most important in making explicit connections between "vernacular" cultural traditions and postmodern critique were the following papers: Aníbal Quijano, "El estudio de lo imaginario en las Ciencias Sociales de America Latina"; Madeline Roman, "Feminismos y post-modernidad: El análisis de la resistencias"; Mirium Muñiz, "El Caribe: Arqueología y poética"; Heidi Figueroa y María Milagros López, "La imagen lábil de la resistencia"; and Antonio Martorell, "Imalabra II."
139 Trinh T. Minh-ha, "Grandma's Story," in Brian Wallis (ed.) *Blasted Allegories*, The New Museum of Contemporary Art, New York, 1987, pp. 3, 2–3.
140 Anzaldúa, "Haciendo Caras, Una Entrada," p. xix.
141 Chela Sandoval, as quoted in Anzaldua, "Haciendo Caras, una Entrada," p. xxvii.
142 Trinh T. Minh-ha, "Not You/Like You: Post-Colonial Women and the Interlocking Questions of Identity and Difference," in Anzaldúa, *Making Face, Making Soul*, p. 375.
143 W. E. B. Dubois, *The Souls of Black Folk: Essays and Sketches*, Fawcett, New York, 1961, p. 17.
144 Cornel West, "The New Cultural Politics of Difference," in Ferguson, Gever, Minh-ha, West (eds.), *Out There*, p. 29.
145 bell hooks, "On Cultural Interrogations," *Artforum*, vol. XXVII, no. 9, May 1989, p. 20.
146 Russell Ferguson, "Introduction: Invisible Center," in Ferguson, Gever, Minh-ha, and West (eds.), *Out There*, p. 13.
147 Cornel West, "The New Cultural Politics of Difference," *October*, no. 53, summer 1990, p. 93.

Shadow Control   By Joseph LaMantia and Stephen Pfohl

CHAPTER 11

CRITICAL PERSPECTIVES:
Social Theory and Social Change

The tradition of the oppressed teaches us that the state of emergency in which we live is not the exception but the rule. We must attain a concept of history that is in keeping with this insight. Then we shall clearly realize that it is our task to bring about a real state of emergency.

Walter Benjamin[1]

Now, it is your turn to imagine a more humane future—a future of justice, equality, and peace. Imagine that young women had exactly the same opportunities as young men. Imagine, indeed, a world without sexism. Imagine a world without homophobia. Imagine that we lived in a world without racism. And if you wish to fulfill your dreams . . . you must also stand up and speak out against war, against joblessness, and against racism.

Angela Y. Davis[2]

INTRODUCTION

Critical perspectives challenge us to make connections between the ritual construction of our everyday lives and the historical organization of power. This is to recognize that we are never fully outside the scenes of deviance and social control which we study. Whether rigorously examining the impetus behind unwarranted police violence against citizens—such as Rodney King— or why reported incidences of rape doubled in the United States in the year following the Gulf War, critical perspectives challenge us to both analyze and change our own historical relations to hierarchical structures of power.

This is why critical perspectives are never merely academic perspectives. As theoretical tools enabling us to diagnose the diverse ways in which class, state, sex and gender, and racialized hierarchies mediate processes of historical inclusion and exclusion, critical perspectives also call upon us to act, so as to uproot the sickening violence that hierarchy begets. In this final chapter, I will explore the implications of critical theorizing for the study and control of deviance, review recent applications of critical thought, and conclude with an overall assessment of power-reflective perspectives.

METHODS OF CRITICAL THEORIZING

Critical approaches to the study of deviance and social control do not privilege any one method to the exclusion of others. Indeed, critical theorists employ a diverse range of methods, including historical, ethnographic, interpretive, social-psychoanalytic, feminist, and even quantitative research strategies. These are used both to deconstruct the taken-for-granted character of hegemonic assumptions about deviance and to reconstruct an image of nonconformity as a contradictory mode of resistance to hierarchical social power. Regardless of the method chosen, all critical researchers are faced with an additional task—the challenge of reflexively situating our own claims to knowledge within and against the dominant structures of power, which constitute our present history. This is the challenge of a *power-reflexive epistemology*, an approach to knowledge that abandons illusions about supposed scientific neutrality in order to bring into the foreground the ways that research inevitably intervenes within the social world it studies.

The reflexive recognition that scientific observers not only describe but also construct the empirical scenes they study has been part of the discourse of theoretical physics since the early years of the twentieth century. What is the best way to theorize the active, if never fully determined, positioning of the observer as a constitutive part of the empirical configurations that she or he observes? While posing difficult problems about the indeterminacy of measurement for physical science, when transposed to social science, such reflexive concerns demand a radical rethinking of how sociological knowledge is filtered by its practitioners' own dynamic relations to power. We social scientists are never really outside the fields of social interactions which we study. To pretend otherwise is to fall prey to the illusions of a positivist viewpoint—a perspective that, while claiming to be objective, fails to examine the ways in which analytic objects are not simply observed but also constructed in the process of being studied.

Critical Theory and the Critique of Positivist Ideology

The affinity between various forms of modern hierarchy and positivism's promise of calculative control over nature has been discussed at numerous points in this text. I have shown—in Chapter 4 and elsewhere—how positivism's supposedly neutral promise of rational control over nature has been instrumental in the historical development of white western imperialism, patriarchal capitalism, and totalitarian state-socialism.

The supposed "facts" of positivist research, like pornographic images of women's bodies, are objectified but not objective. To be truly objective, positivism would have to forsake its desires to blast free of human-animal interdependence and to recognize the socially situated character of all claims to knowledge. This is a central tenet of power-reflexive methods of research: to work within and against the grain of ideological distortions, rather than pretending that one can float free of ideology altogether. This is to rigorously subvert, rather than to naively disavow, the ritual force of ideology. It means that, as power-reflexive researchers, we must labor to locate all claims to truth—our own included—within the contradictory webs of power (and resistance to power) in which these claims are historically founded. Such reflexivity threatens positivism's privileged epistemological standpoint, a standpoint above the actualities of history, looking down. It also undermines the legitimacy that positivism provides to the white-male-dominated economic order which serves as its primary patron.

Convergent attempts to deconstruct the dominance of positivist methods are today being undertaken by power-reflexive Marxist, anarchist, feminist, and radical multicultural theorists. Radical interrogations of positivism are also found in *critical poststructuralism*, a methodological framework emphasizing the material interplay between power and the construction of social knowledge. Critical poststructuralists recognize the centrality of language as a ritual force affecting all claims to knowledge, but language is a selective force as well. As suggested in Chapter 10, whenever language allows us to grasp something about the world, it simultaneously takes our attention away from something else. In this sense, the languages employed by the most dominant theoretical perspectives on deviance exclude or silence other possible viewpoints. This is a basic lesson of poststructuralism, and one that has been with us since the opening pages of this text.

This is not to say that dominant forms of knowledge are ever truly free of the "deviant" forms they exclude. Dominant forms of knowledge are forever dependent on policing the boundaries between what is hegemonic and what threatens the reproduction of hierarchical power. By paying careful attention to such epistemological police work, critical poststructuralism subverts hierarchies of knowledge that are otherwise taken for granted by positivism. It also opens our critical imaginations to forms of resistance and social change which have been repressed in the construction of a positivist viewpoint.

Inspired, in part, by poststructuralism's insistence on ritual links between power and knowledge, contemporary critical theorists raise questions about the experiential pleasures of positivism itself. What pleasures are these and how do they operate? To ask this question is to radically interrogate the methodological claims of positivist neutrality.

In analyzing dominant approaches to the study of deviance, Avery Gordon and I have recently identified three forms of pleasure underlying positivist methods—the pleasures of *sadism, surveillance,* and *the construction of a "normalized" (white male) observer-identity*. Positivism is guided by *sadistic* pleasure because, like the cold, calculating, and dispassionate protagonists of de Sade's pornography, positivists adhere to a disembodied form of rational transcendence. This permits positivists to imagine that they are outside the messy material relations of those they objectify. In this way, positivism penetrates the unruly orifices of the "natural" social world, plugging up its holes and reducing as much variance as possible.

A second pleasure of positivism is surveillance. In this, the positivist researcher gazes endlessly upon *his* captured object of analysis, lest *she* escape *her* master's supposed scientific neutrality and disappear into a space of historical contradiction.[3] When this happens, the paranoid borders of positivism become leaky. Deviant objects of knowledge suddenly begin to show through the disciplinary constraints that positivism places upon them. This both disturbs the masterful gaze of positivism and undermines positivism's third source of pleasure—its claim to a "normal" scientific identity. This is an identity positivism claims for itself, but only by simultaneously subordinating the identities of others to its own supposedly detached scientific laws.

But how can positivism's laws be detached if they are also caught up in the production of such masterful pleasures? It is upon this troubling methodological contradiction that the instrumental promise of positivism stumbles. As Max Horkheimer and Theodor Adorno observe, positivism's claim to represent a universal form of truth holds only within "the court of calculative judgment" in which its methods are historically situated. In reality, positivism "adjusts the world for the ends of self-preservation and recognizes no function other than the preparation of the object from mere sensory material in order to make it the material of subjugation."[4]

Sadism, surveillance, and *the production of the "normalized" (white male) subject* in a discourse that exiles or reductively incorporates difference—these, as I stated above, are the dominant pleasures of positivist research methods.[5] This is a harsh image. If few social scientists recognize themselves in such an image, perhaps it is because the disciplinary confines within which most of us work help to insulate us from grasping positivism's complicity with dominant structures of power. Under the sign of positivist logic, "Being is apprehended under the aspect of manufacture and administration. Everything—even the human individual, not to speak of the animal—is converted into the repeatable, replaceable process, into a mere example."[6]

Positivism fails to reflexively examine the contradictory rituals of power and knowledge that constitute the empirical social categories it seeks to explain. In this way positivist methods "discover" only what has already been hegemonically constructed. Here lies a blind spot at the center of positivism's dazzling promise of enlightenment: A hole around which its quest for reliable measurement and lawful explanation converge. A hole before (or at the blinding center of) positivism's "way of seeing." A hole that remains taboo. A hole that must be wholly covered over (or fetishized) for positivism to work its magic. A white and thoroughly masculinized hole that substitutes what Dorothy Smith calls an "extra-local standpoint" for the fleshy historical contradictions out of which positivism itself emerges.

Power-Reflexive Methods: A Counterhegemonic
Way of Knowing

To recognize positivism as ideological is not to spare critical theory from the charge of being ideological as well. Indeed, certain types of theorizing which claim to be critical are no more free of ideological bias than positivism is. Orthodox Marxists claim that mastery of the dialectical laws of human economic history is needed to attain further rational control over nature. Such instrumental rationality makes orthodox Marxism as ideological as positivism. Orthodox Marxists are no more able to reflexively account for the supposed superiority of their knowledge than are positivists. If the social world (including the world of orthodox Marxism) is determined by fixed economic laws, how is it that orthodox Marxists are able to objectively master the laws by which they themselves are determined? Orthodox Marxism's naive commitment to instrumental mastery makes it ideology under yet another name. Among other things, it fails to examine how its own commitments to a mastery of natural laws make it complicit not only with the imperial daydreams of the modern west but also with patriarchal perspectives that position "man" as if outside nature, gazing down upon "her" unruly materiality.

In attempting to break the hegemony of positivism, orthodox Marxism, and other ideologically shaped modes of knowledge, critical perspectives adopt a *power-reflexive methodology*. This strategy of research refuses the illusory purity of a transcendental vantage point from which to neutrally observe and categorize the world. Power-reflexive methods do not seek knowledge which is detached from power but, instead, recognize the interconnectedness of both power and knowledge. As Michel Foucault points out, "power and knowledge directly imply one another. . . . [T]here is no power relation without the correlative constitution of a field of knowledge, nor any knowledge that does not presuppose and constitute at the same time power relations."[7]

A power-reflexive methodology begins by acknowledging that everything which humans know to be true is conditioned by power. With this in mind, a power-reflexive approach must begin with a process of critical self-scrutiny. Power-reflexive researchers must reflexively double back upon the historical and structural conditions that both empower and limit the ways in which we understand the world. This is no easy task. In Chapter 9 I noted that societal reaction theorists often use verbatim displays of data to permit readers to learn as much as possible about the social contexts in which they conducted their research. As power-reflexive researchers we must do something similar. We must endeavor to make at least partially visible the relations of power which both guide and distort what we theorize.

How can this be done? How are the power-reflexive researchers able to display the partially distortive effects of the social fields in which we labor? The task involves more than simply separating scientific facts from nonscientific ideology. As Michel Foucault points out, "It is necessary to think . . . not in terms of 'science' and 'ideology,' but in terms of 'truth' and 'power.'"[8] The promise of a power-reflexive method is to make partially visible the ritual sceneries of power in which we are situated and, thereby, to increase the objectivity of our research by giving readers access to the material conditions under which our ideas are constructed.

Assuming an intrinsic link between power and knowledge, a power-reflexive researcher must ask herself or himself three basic questions. The first is: How does a person's biography affect the truths that the person is capable of recognizing? A power-reflexive approach assumes that such things as class, gender, ethnic, and age relations influence one's approach to truth. To examine such matters is to reflexively locate a researcher's own biography within history. It is also to recognize that critical research is mediated by a researcher's relations with other people and that such relations involve matters of power. This involves making reflexive connections between the individual's everyday life and the process of research itself.

The second question posed by a power-reflexive researcher is: What do the findings of any particular study suggest about power relations in society as a whole? Whether studying corporate price-fixing, prostitution, or the medical labeling of madness, a power-reflexive approach asks the researcher to make connections between his or her particular topic and more general historical questions about power. In what ways, for instance, do the pressures of corporate competition affect decisions to deviate from fair business practices within a capitalist society? Would the reality of price-fixing be different in some other form of economic system? How are prostitution and other forms of "sex work" related to power differences between men and women? Would such sex work exist—or exist in the same ways—if women had greater power over their own economic destinies? What about mental illness? Does the medicalization of deeply felt emotional problems distract from an understanding of madness as a social response to feelings of powerlessness? To ask such questions is to begin to think critically. It is to search for the social and political meanings of otherwise isolated events. It is also a step toward integrating what we study with how we live.

For critical theorists, a researcher using power-reflexive methodology should pose a third question. Having examined a particular sense of deviance or control, in terms of both biographical and systemic relations of power, the researcher then inquires: Have I learned anything which may help to transform society in the direction of social justice? This question need not be asked at a huge, global level. Perhaps the research has made the researcher more sensitive to some small aspect of everyday behavior which could be changed. Perhaps something has been learned which will help the researcher begin to break down petty obstacles to truly reciprocal power relations. On the other hand, maybe bigger obstacles which affect us all have been identified. How might the researcher best communicate about such matters? How may research be a step toward social justice? By confronting such questions, a power-reflexive methodology attempts to integrate theory with life. If knowledge is always related to power, the final task of a power-reflexive methodology is to guide knowledge toward a greater reciprocity of power. In so doing, a power-reflexive approach seeks to replace old hierarchies of power and knowledge with new modes of self-critical knowledge. This aspect of power-reflexive knowledge is suggested by Foucault, who comments:

> The essential political problem . . . is not to criticize the ideological contents supposedly linked to science, or to ensure that . . . scientific practice is accompanied by a correct ideology, but that of ascertaining the possibility of constituting a new politics of truth. The problem is not changing people's consciousness . . . but . . . the production of truth.
>
> It's not a matter of emancipating truth from every system of power (which would be a chimera, for truth is already power) but of detaching the power of truth from the forms of hegemony, social, economic and cultural, within which it operates at the present time.[9]

CRITICAL PERSPECTIVES ON SOCIAL CONTROL

A fundamental transformation . . . is needed if we are to effectively deal with the problems of crime and deviance.

Sheila Balkan, Ronald J. Berger, and Janet Schmidt[10]

In order to eliminate the use of deviance as a tool of domination it is necessary to radically alter the ritual reproduction of hierarchical social forms. Race, class, and sex and gender inequalities must be replaced by social relations of a more power-reciprocal sort. This is how critical theorists view social control: as a radical restructuring of society toward the ends of social justice.

Structural changes proposed by critical theorists reach far beyond the liberal reforms suggested by other sociological theories. Liberal perspectives, such as anomie, societal reaction, and pluralistic conflict theory, advocate changing existing control mechanisms so as to treat all people more fairly. For critical theorists this is not enough. Insomuch as existing control practices are ritually connected to the hierarchical organization of society as a whole, changes must occur at multiple levels if significant and long-lasting solutions to deviance are to be found. Critical theorists seek a full realization of social justice for all people. This implies a *radical democratization* of all social institutions. Otherwise, attempts to control deviance will be no more effective than placing a patch on a bursting balloon. This may help in the short run, but eventually the patch will explode along with the balloon it reinforces.

But What about Liberal Reform?

Some critical theorists view liberal reform as little more than an effort to bandage broken parts of a system which itself should be abandoned. Such one-sided opposition to reform is problematic. Although often failing to address structural interconnections between powerful social institutions, short-term reforms—such as those aimed at improving schooling, day-care, child support, health services, and environmental safety, as well as curtailing police violence, the overcrowding of prisons, sexual harassment, discriminatory housing and employment practices, and U.S. interference with struggles for justice in the third world—may help take the edge off the most brutal forms of oppression and provide hope for the building of a more just society. Recognizing this reality, most critical theorists provide both modest support for and constructive criticism of liberal reform.

Modest support is provided for three reasons. First, concrete opposition to unnecessary human suffering is a goal worthy of all who claim to care for social justice. Second, by engaging in reform activity, liberals often learn firsthand about the structural resistances which permeate current control systems. Nothing that one learns in the classroom or by reading books about critical perspectives matches the radicalizing effects of the frustrations of co-opted reform work. Third, reform can itself stress or stretch the structural mechanisms of an unjust power hierarchy by exaggerating and exposing contradictions to which it cannot respond.

In addition to providing modest support, critical theorists remind liberal reformers of the dangers of being absorbed by the control systems they seek to change. Due to the time-consuming and emotionally draining character of much reform work, many liberal activists lose sight of the wider structural concerns. As Ron Kramer points out, liberals "may simply not know what specifically they can do to bring about structural change."[11] Although often sympathetic with the tenets of critical theory, liberals may lack a sense of practical strategy about how to connect piecemeal reforms to larger structural concerns. In recent years, critical theorists have become increasingly concerned with assisting change agents in making these connections. Helpful examples include the epilogue to David Simon and Stanley Eitzen's book *Elite Deviance*—in which the authors address such issues as the reorganization of large corporations to better meet public needs, measures to increase democratic participation, fair taxation, progressive income redistribution, and environmental protection—and Elliot Currie's proposals for reducing crime while furthering structural change.[12] These works underscore the need to strategize social change on two fronts: short-term reforms and long-term structural change. Harold Pepinsky's book *Crime Control Strategies* announces a related agenda.[13] Everyone—conservative, liberal, or critical—is a victim of crimes generated by the existing hierarchical order. According to Pepinsky, the challenge for those with a critical perspective is "to promote social justice without sacrificing gains in crime control."[14]

Social Control and Critical Praxis: The Politics of Deconstruction

Critical perspectives on social control are rooted in practical struggles for justice—heterogeneous but convergent efforts to deconstruct hierarchical social institutions so as to reconstruct relations of a more power-reciprocal sort. What specifically does this entail?

In using the term *deconstruction*, I am referring to a form of *critical praxis*—a union of power-reflexive thought and action—that is forever vigilant about the partial and provisional nature of its own ritual relations to power. As articulated in the writings of the critical French philosopher Jacques Derrida, deconstruction connotes an approach to knowledge that reflexively recognizes its own complicity with the ritual operations of language. This is to suggest that whenever language signifies the presence of some object, it does so only by ritually differentiating this object from others. This is a way of saying that all constructions of meaning are relational. We know something only by distinguishing it from what it is not. Objects of knowledge never exist as "things in themselves." They exist only in relation to the ritual field of forces that distinguish them from others. But this field is never neutral. It is ritually charged, so that some objects (here and now) take precedence over others, while the value or significance of the others is deferred, exiled, or postponed.

If this makes the field of language seem like the field of deviance and social control, this, perhaps, is an important sociological implication of Derrida's thought. Language is always a field of control, just as the maintenance of any field of control depends upon language. Within such a field, some objects are hierarchically privileged over others, while other objects are ritually marginalized or silenced. How best to display and counter this ritual process of hierarchy? This question guides deconstructive approaches to criticism.

When applied to literary or philosophical texts, Derrida's deconstructive methods point to *aporias* or material gaps in what makes any text appear singular, or self-contained. No text is ever truly singular or self-contained. All texts depend for their structural identity on dynamic rituals that both differentiate them from others and police the borders of this differentiation against the "deviance" of other possible structural arrangements—arrangements that are exiled from consciousness, arrangements that are denied hegemonic legitimacy, or the status of "common sense." Derrida's deconstructive approach to literature deauthorizes the ritual self-evidency of all textual constructions. This is accomplished by carefully showing that the supposed identity of a text is, in actuality, dependent upon what the text excludes or renders deviant. In a power-reflexive gesture of considerable significance Derrida even doubles back upon his own critical writings, placing "under erasure" the originality of his ideas, while affirming the parasitic, provisional, and always only partial character of his deconstructive claims.

While helping to subvert the self-evidency of certain of the most dominant texts in western literature and philosophy, when translated into critical approaches to social control, Derrida's notion of deconstruction proves to be a powerful ally in countering the institutional violence of hierarchy. To deconstruct structures of power does not mean to overthrow one form of hierarchy and replace it with a new form of privilege. Nor does it mean to fall into the political paralysis of not acting, just because all forms of action partially exclude the immediate realization of other forms. It means, instead, to vigilantly institute something like a process of *radical democracy*, in which actions authorized in one moment are ritually deconstructed in the next. This prevents relations of power from being frozen into timeless images of universal authority. In this sense, deconstruction is never an endpoint of critical praxis. Rather, it is an ethical guide for the ceaseless reconstruction of power-reciprocal relations of social control.

Power-Reciprocal Control: How Do We Get There from Here?

What must be done to begin realizing the radically democratic promise of power-reciprocal social control? Old hierarchies are not about to throw away their power and die. How, then, to introduce a new order of radically democratic economic, cultural, and sexual practices? Antonio Gramsci, whose nonauthoritarian vision of socialism implied participatory control over the ritual organization of everyday life, put the question this way: "How to weld the present to the future, satisfying the urgent necessities of the one and working effectively to create and integrate the other?"[15] According to anarchists Larry Tifft and Dennis Sullivan, we must start by changing our own lives and consciousness. We must begin to experiment with power-reciprocal social forms in the immediacy of our everyday lives. Thus, "If authority, hierarchical, external and rational, is to be replaced, it must happen by the very process in which persons acquire power over their own lives, in which persons 'discover' themselves, their natural relationships to others through mutual aid, and in which they experience the power to be present to self and others in the context of community."[16]

One major difficulty facing those of us who are committed to both deconstruction of hierarchy and reconstruction of more just social relations is a manifest lack of successful models for participatory social change. In part, this is because memories of previous struggles for justice are historically mediated by the people who are most privileged by power. As Walter Benjamin observed, *"even the dead* will not be safe from the enemy if he wins. And this [hierarchical] enemy has not ceased to be victorious."[17] Thus, the resistance of peasant women to patriarchal capitalism was wrongly written as a story of "evil witches," while the resistance of American Indians to the theft of their lands by white Europeans was falsely framed as a story about bringing civilization to the "new world." The lives of over 20 million "native" peoples were taken in this so-called civilizing process. In the words of Benjamin, "There is no document of civilization which is not at the same time a document of barbarism."[18] Even as I write, young U.S. children are being ritually marked by racist myths about Indians and romantic lies about the heroism of white pioneers.

This is not to suggest that there are no precedents on which to model contemporary struggles for justice. "Alternative histories," recounting the struggles of women, nonwhites, the economically impoverished, and the sexually marginalized, are vitally important to the development of critical approaches to social control. These histories, however, have long been marginalized in the "core curriculums" that dominate the west's most important educational institutions. Moreover, official ideologies aside, little support for radical change is found in the failed state-socialist control processes of eastern Europe or in communist-controlled China. While partially undoing previous forms of economic inequality within these supposed socialist countries, a new class of state bureaucratic managers arose to occupy seats of hierarchical power once held by or promised to capitalists.

In criticizing the betrayal of democratic forms of socialism in the former Soviet Union and in China we should not forget the enormous difficulties that both societies encountered in a world dominated by capitalist hierarchies and imperial conquest. This was particularly the case in the early years of the Soviet Union. Hampered by technological underdevelopment and economic hardship, and threatened on all sides by capitalist aggressors, hierarchical-minded Soviet leaders such as Josef Stalin abandoned revolutionary experiments with economic democracy and radical cultural transformation. The result was a reconstitution of class domination, this time by a class of state bureaucrats. Despite this betrayal of certain of socialism's most radical promises and the unpardonable suppression of domestic political dissent, critical theorists should not forget the strategic assistance provided by twentieth-century Communist "regimes" to African, Asian, and other third world nations struggling to rid themselves of western colonial violence.

Not all state-socialist experiments have been so betrayed by bureaucratic hierarchies. In Cuba, for instance, although state courts still preside over major criminal cases and military tribunals try cases of alleged counterrevolutionary activity, "popular tribunals" operate nationwide to handle a wide range of criminal and civil control matters. These "people's courts" are overseen by nonlawyer magistrates, elected by the citizens of a certain district or neighborhood. Well-attended sessions meet in the evenings to solve troublesome disputes and disturbances, resulting in such diverse controls as imprisonment, mandatory agricultural labor, school attendance, and psychiatric therapy. More common is the ritual admonition of offenders, as tribunals draw upon informal mechanisms of neighborhood control rather than upon bureaucratic state policing. In this sense, Cubans "rely as little as possible upon rigid structures and forms, and . . . continue to carry out revolutionary aims."[19]

This is not to romanticize Cuba as a model of nonhierarchical social control. Despite incomparable gains in the areas of real economic equality, education, public health reforms, public safety, and racial injustice—gains so significant that they shame supposedly democratic societies such as the United States— Cubans are today not fully free in the realms of political and cultural expression. In part, this is the result of a continuing war by the United States against Cuba, a war that impoverishes Cuba and places it in a constant state of emergency. What would happen if socialism in Cuba were spared such crises and the country were allowed to enter into relations of unfettered economic exchange with other countries? Would democratic reforms emerge to complement Cuba's revolutionary gains in other areas of social justice? In order to encourage such a possibility and spare Cuba the turmoil and violence that have characterized the collapse of state-socialist hierarchies in many eastern European countries, many critical theorists today urge an end to U.S. initiatives aimed at undermining the independence of this small Caribbean island society.

Cuba is not the only state-socialist society to have experimented with participatory forms of decentralized social control. Although outweighed historically by the totalitarian aspects of these states as a whole, economic decentralization in the former socialist Yugoslavia and community mental health reforms in China were once heralded as critical alternatives to the false "individualization" of social problems in the capitalist west. Nevertheless, the most important historical examples of power-reciprocal control practices involved short-lived experiments in radical participatory democracy. In virtually all cases, attempts to live outside hierarchy were brutally halted by the forces of patriarchal capitalism or a repressive state-socialist regime.

Notable western historical experiments with power-reciprocal control include early modern "pirate utopias," groups that "liberated" both slave ships and the mercantile ships of capitalists, while living according to radical doctrines of liberty[20]; the Paris Commune, a revolutionary assembly of over 30,000 workers who occupied the center of Paris before being captured or killed by Prussian troops from March to May of 1871; the Soviet communes and democratic factory committees organized during the early years of the Russian Revolution; the Hungarian revolts of 1919 and 1956; the Italian factory councils of the early 1920s; and the revolutionary insurrection of Spanish anarchists in 1936. More recent examples include the brief flourishing of democratic socialism in Czechoslovakia before a Russian invasion toppled the reform government headed by Alexander Dubcek in 1968, as well as the festive seizure of sections of Paris by more than a million students and workers in May of that same year[21]; Chile under the reformist leadership of Dr. Salvador Allende, before it was overthrown by a fascist coup which was supported clandestinely by capitalist corporations, including ITT, and the U.S. government; the diffuse efforts of Italian "autonomists," stressing creative cultural transformations and a refusal to work, until they were harassed, framed, and broken by terrorist police tactics in the late 1970s; and Nicaragua following the 1979 revolution, where extensive experiments with participatory economic and political reforms were under way before the U.S.-sponsored "Contra war" pushed Sandinista leaders in the direction of defensive state control. In all these cases, the emergence of radically democratic control processes was quashed by either capitalist or state-social hierarchies.

Despite a long history of suppression, the dream of power-reciprocal control still excites the political imaginations of critical theorists and activists.

Moreover, as contradictory as this may seem, the material conditions for realizing this dream may be nowhere more present than in the United States. Indeed, despite the continuing dominance of white-patriarchal and imperialist-capitalist control structures within the United States, its long tradition of formal legal rights, its high aggregate standard of living, its extensive educational system, its cultural diversity, its advanced technologies, and its (supposed) commitment to democratic social institutions make this country a likely site for significant struggles for justice as we approach the twenty-first century.

The question is how might those who share a dream of power-reciprocal control best participate in such struggles? There is no one answer. Critical perspectives challenge us to reflexively examine and change our ritual complicities with a wide array of racist, heterosexist, and economic hierarchies. Thus, in closing this discussion of power-reflexive approaches to control, it may prove helpful to outline a set of strategies aimed at preparing ourselves to join with others in radically democratic struggles for justice. These involve a set of *strategic refusals* as well as *strategic affirmations*. There is nothing absolute about these suggestions. They are offered simply to stimulate critical thinking and to provoke creative forms of power-reflexive social activism.

Strategic Power—Reflexive Refusals

1. Refuse the legitimacy of efforts to secure "public safety" unless such efforts simultaneously aim at the realization of social and economic justice.

Demands for tougher policing and bigger prisons must be resisted, unless they are accompanied by equally strong demands for the rooting out of the social injustices that make our society such an unsafe place. There is no doubt that serious crime in the United States outdistances the serious crime of all other industrialized nations. This is particularly the case with violent crime. Indeed, the likelihood of being murdered is approximately ten times higher in the United States than in most European countries,[22] while reported rates of robbery are approximately six times higher, and rape three times higher.[23] Also higher are the most visible correlates of severe social inequality. I am here referring to hierarchical structures which make women, the poor, and the racially disenfranchised the most common targets of violence, and which make all U.S. citizens victims of theft, corporate exploitation, and environmental pollution.

In a nation that prides itself on being among the most affluent in history, in 1991 there were over 3 million people who were homeless, while 13.5 percent of all U.S. citizens lived in households with less than $15,000 income per family of four (the official definition of poverty). For African-Americans, the level of impoverishment was far worse, with 31.9 percent of all black families living in poverty. Among Latinos, 28.1 percent were similarly impoverished.[24] While rates of rural poverty remain high, factors such as dein-dustrialization, structural and geographical changes in business (particularly the contracting of cheaper third world labor), an imbalance in employment opportunities between central cities and suburbs, and flight from the inner city by middle-class minorities have led sociologists such as William Julius Wilson to comment upon the persistence of an "urban underclass" in the United States.[25]

The presence of this "underclass" is nowhere more visible than in the worlds of "street crime" and criminal justice. Here poverty sows the seeds of despair, anger, and survival "by any means necessary," while the state takes action against the most powerless, rather than addressing the inequities that underlie high levels of lower-class deviance. Thus, as polarization between the rich and poor grows toward explosive proportions, prisons become over-crowded and the criminal justice system expands to unprecedented levels of control over the lives of the most disadvantaged. Indeed, the U.S. prison population has doubled in a single decade, rising from 500,000 in 1980 to over 1 million in 1990, a rate of 426 per 100,000 and climbing. Nowhere else in the world is the rate of incarceration so high. When measured in 1989, South Africa had the second highest rate of imprisonment, with 333 per 100,000 incarcerated, while the former Soviet Union was third, with a rate of 268. The rate for most other countries was far lower, with England incarcerating 97 per 100,000, France 81, Spain 76, Italy 60, and the Netherlands a meager 40 per 100,000, respectively.[26]

Even more alarming are racial disparities in the rate of imprisonment. Although African-Americans constituted 14 percent of the U.S. population in 1990, they represented over 50 percent of all prisoners in that same year, giving them an incarceration rate more than six times higher than that of whites. One-fourth of all African-American men can expect to go to prison during their lifetime. Moreover, when those on parole or probation are included, there are today more than 650,000 young black men under the control of the criminal justice system, approximately 23 percent of all African-American men between the ages of 20 and 29.[27] For American Indian men, the incarceration rate is already one in every 3.5, while Latinos fill U.S. prisons at double their proportion in the population. Furthermore, as Marc Mauer has recently shown, nonwhites regularly receive sentences that are 30 percent more severe than the sentences which Euro-Americans receive when convicted for the identical offenses.[28]

Despite such manifest connections between social inequality, crime, and harsh criminal justice controls, a great number of Americans today call for even tougher crime control measures, such as more and longer prison sen-tences and more funding for police. From a critical perspective, however, such measures are not tough enough. Only when paired with structural changes that reduce the social inequities that fuel crime will such social control mechanisms stand a serious chance of actually improving the public safety.

2. Refuse all uses of sexist, racist, homophobic, xenophobic, and other cultur-
ally degrading languages—including visual languages, signs, gestures, and
icons.

I am not here advocating state-authorized censorship, but direct and forceful refusals of speech that subordinates the dignity of others. Critical theorists
recognize language as a powerful form of social control. How might we best
refuse languages—including visual languages—that exclude or denigrate
women, gays, lesbians, or racialized minorities? Is it always enough to po-
litely correct those who employ such abusive languages? Or is it sometimes
necessary to seek the assistance of the law to limit the public speech of people
whose only message involves the violent and hierarchical subordination of
others (such as the hateful, racist, or sexist speech of various neo-Nazi and
white male supremacist groups)? Under what conditions, moreover, might
trashing a pornographic bookstore or spray-painting a racist billboard prove
to be a power-reflexive strategy of counterhegemonic control?

3. Refuse to do business with businesses that support social injustice.

While virtually all forms of businesses in capitalist societies are connected
to complex forms of economic inequality, some are more manifestly connected to exploitation than others. Consider businesses that do business with
racist South Africa or contribute money to unjust social causes. What about
companies that discriminate by virtue of race, gender, age, or sexual preference, or that refuse to pay their employees a decent wage or accept union
contracts? What about companies that knowingly manufacture or sell unsafe
products or pollute the environment? By refusing to do business with such
businesses, advocates of power-reflexive social control seek to mobilize both
economic and moral resistance to continuing social injustice.

4. Refuse ignorance of history and of other people's cultures.

Despite enormous educational resources and a relative absence of government censorship, many of us are literally schooled in ignorance of our own
histories and the cultures of others. Such ignorance permits a mystification of
power on the part of the most powerful. By committing ourselves to studying
history and to holding respectful dialogues with others about differences
between their cultures and ours, we refuse the complicities with hierarchical
power that come with ignorance.

This will not be easy. To critically learn history, it is often necessary to also
"unlearn" previously unquestioned assumptions about the world in which
we live. Think, for instance, of the intellectual and moral difficulties posed by
actually facing up to the genocidal history of Euro-Americans' relations to the
American Indians whose lands our ancestors stole and to the African-Americans whose ancestors were put up for sale as slaves. Nor is it easy to establish
dialogues with cultures from which we have become separated not just by
difference but by the violence of hierarchy. Nevertheless, without a reflexive

reconstruction of our historical and cultural sensibilities, we will remain at a powerful distance from one another; we will continue to use deviance as a tool of division, rather than taking the risks involved in ritual reconciliation and radical social change.

5. Refuse the commonsensical character of all authority.

What is most self-evident within hierarchical societies is never purely a matter of common sense. At the moment when things appear most common-sensical, it is because other things—other ways of imagining and acting toward what is real—are being repressed from consciousness. But at what price? Within hierarchical societies, common sense is secured by denigrating more reciprocal forms of power. This is what gives hierarchical social forms their authority. Thus, at the core of all critical approaches to control lies the most basic of deconstructive methods: *questioning authority!*

Strategic Power-Reflexive Affirmations

1. Affirm counterhegemonic forms of community.

I am here referring to both intimate and public forms of community. Communities that challenge us risk reflexive social change. Resisting the status quo is no easy matter. Few individuals are able to do this on their own. At the same time, most contemporary forms of community do little to encourage us in this regard. Quite the opposite: for many people, the elusive promise of the "ideal" nuclear family pales before the reality of broken romantic couplings and the anxieties of betrayal. Patriarchal miscommunications and the terror of psychic and physical abuse are all too common features of modern family life. In addition, while most traditional church, neighborhood, school, and occupational communities offer relief from everyday tensions, they are inadequate to the task of promoting critical thought and action.

As critical scholars, it is important for us not to be nostalgic about the supposed loss of traditional family values and homogeneous neighborhood communities. The community structures that are most likely to support us in future struggles for justice have yet to come into existence. In making transitional moves toward such structures, we need to support a heterogeneity of intimate and public community forms. These we might think of as *temporary autonomous zones*—experimental communities committed to nurturing friendship, love, sustained dialogue, nonpossessive erotic and emotional engagements, economic democracy, political risk taking, patience, mutual sacrifice, careful reconciliations, tolerance, humor, ecstatic spiritual and physical experiences, and a playful diversity of pleasures.[29] Steps in the direction of new forms of community will be neither simple nor graceful, but they should prove exciting. Often mistakes will be made. But if long-term structural changes are ever to occur, it is necessary to first construct new and flexible forms of human engagement and support. Otherwise, we are likely to be either destroyed by change itself or to retreat anxiously to the safety of less power-reciprocal relations.

2. Affirm popular and unpopular cultural subversions.

Subversive cultural practices are not without their contradictions. As Avital Ronell points out, subversion "implies a dependency on the program that is being critiqued—therefore it's a parasite on that program."[30] Subversive acts are, nevertheless, important mobilizers of critical thought and action. By manifestly displaying the contradictory workings of hierarchy, subversive cultural practices may demystify the ritual mechanics of power and engender moral and political outrage. Consider, for instance, the feminist performance art of Karen Finley. When Finley makes "a commodity sandwich" out of her exposed breast while delivering a scathing monologue on the relations between "eating disorders" and our culture's association of women with food, her actions engender a complex mixture of outrage and laughter. Though Finley's subversive art is upsetting to some people, it often provokes strong and power-reflexive responses on the part of her audiences.

Finley is but a single example of the use of subversive cultural tactics on the part of radical artists and political activists. Whether tracing their roots to politicized European avant garde movements, such as the dadaists, the surrealists, or Situationist International, or to the "vernacular signifying practices" of African slaves—whose subtle distortions of their master's language provided linguistic relief and secret means of political communication—subversive cultural work helps to mobilize counterhegemonic dissent.

Cultural subversions are also a way of "performing" critical theory. At their most forceful, they provoke intellectual and emotional reactions against hierarchical power. This makes subversive cultural practices dangerous to the dominant culture they seek to undermine. In response, people in positions of power may attempt to suppress or domesticate the critical messages conveyed by such practices.[31] In this regard, it should be no surprise that Finley's "unpopular" cultural interventions, along with grant proposals by several other politically oriented artists, were denied funding by the National Endowment of the Arts during the conservative Republican administration of former U.S. President George Bush. Politicized rap music has also been the target of widespread conservative criticism, as critical cultural work by Sister Souljah, Ice-T, Paris, Tupac Amaru Shakur, KRS-1, and Public Enemy have all been condemned for subverting the whiteness of "pop" music charts and providing a voice for the anger felt by many African-Americans about continuing racial and economic oppression.

The importance of these and other subversive cultural forms is that they allow us to better recognize the repressive character of many of our everyday cultural rituals while also enabling us to mobilize our minds, emotions, and bodies in ways that free us from the constraints of hierarchy. In the words of Michel Foucault:

> We must free ourselves from . . . cultural conservatism, as well as from political conservatism. We must see our rituals for what they are: completely arbitrary things, tied to our bourgeois way of life; it is good—and that is real theater—to transcend them in the manner of play, by means of games and irony; it is good to . . . have long hair and look like a girl when one is a boy (and vice versa); one must put "in play," show up, transform, and reverse the systems which quietly order us about.[32]

3. Affirm theoretically informed activism.

There is no one form which theoretically informed activism may take. Boycotts, leafleting, strikes, marches, teach-ins, picketing, civil disobedience, guerilla theater, political pranks, pirate radio broadcasts, graffiti and postering campaigns, radical educational projects, organized lobbying, and the occupation and/or disruption of state and corporate spaces are among some of the tactics used today by activist groups. Still, if such actions are to prove critical—as opposed to simply reformist—they must be informed by rigorous theoretical discussion and power-reflexive democratic debate.

It is unfortunate to hear many political activists, including those who identify themselves as members of new social movements, dismiss theoretical analysis as a luxury, or as something that only academics do. We are today living at a moment in history when enormous technological and geopolitical changes are altering the landscape of power, changing matters that once might have been primarily local, into transnational concerns, and bombarding our senses with high-velocity electronic imagery. In order to best counter the power of these hierarchical controls, we need to break down time-worn distinctions between theory and activism, in order that each may be remixed in power-reflexive engagement with the other. At the same time, given the ascendance of various information technologies as forms of social control, it may today be more necessary than ever to recognize that one important site of activism should be academic institutions themselves.

4. Affirm the construction of alternative social institutions.

Deconstructing the hierarchical operations of existing institutions is but a starting point for structural change. Equally necessary are efforts to imagine and implement new economic, political, educational, spiritual, and sexual relations with one another. For this reason, critical theorists actively support reflexive experiments with new styles of work—including cooperatives, worker- and minority-owned enterprises, and job-sharing—as well as innovations aimed at fostering democratic decision making; nonsexist and multicultural approaches to learning; reverence for the sacredness of the earth and its multiple species of animals; and tolerance for a playful diversity of erotic pleasures, freed from the bondage of coercive hierarchy.

As with any experiments with new forms of community, attempts to construct a multiplicity of power-reflexive social institutions will be neither easy nor smooth. Serious efforts to instigate change will have to confront both external and internal resistance—external resistance from the people who are most privileged by power and internal resistance from nearly everybody else, as each of us will be asked to risk exchanging old comforts for the occasional uncertainties, embarrassments, and practical difficulties entailed in the movement from old ritual forms to new (and we hope) more just ways of organizing our lives.

Of particular difficulty will be changes in formal social control policies. Dominant forms of law enforcement, punishment, social welfare, and rehabilitation, though they protect the lives and property of the wealthy and keep a lid on the poor, do little to break current cycles of social injustice. How is it possible to move from reactive police tactics, the violence of imprisonment, dehumanizing bureaucracy, and individual-oriented therapies to publicly accountable rituals of collective responsibility for troubles and tensions that are social in origin? It is toward radical forms of social reconstruction that critical theory directs our attention. Such forms cannot be realized without sacrifices shared by everybody. Although these sacrifices will be difficult, and will require all of us to be able to forgive others and ourselves for inevitable mistakes, to have patience with the inefficiency generated by new ways of acting, and to show respect for the limits of others and ourselves, they will be necessary to support critical struggles for justice. Otherwise, the ritual structuring of sacrifice will remain as it is now—an unequal burden on the disadvantaged and a prod for continued high levels of violence, conflict, and elite deviance.

THE CRITICAL PERSPECTIVE TODAY

A fully mature critical [perspective] . . . has yet to emerge; however a blending of radical criminology and critical sociology . . . would be a significant advance and would contribute to the modification and eventual elimination of those structures that render human freedom and growth subservient to the vested interests of privileged classes.

Raymond Michalowski[33]

Critical perspectives have greatly altered the way in which many sociologists view crime, deviance, and social control. This is not to suggest that critical approaches were readily accepted by the most prestigious institutions of education and research in North America. Indeed—as evidenced by the closing of the School of Criminology at the University of California, Berkeley, in the early 1970s—the advent of critical discourse was often met by political threats and the denial of academic employment. At Berkeley, where radical critiques of the criminal justice system drew the ire of conservative administrators, leading critical scholars were fired and their students branded troublemakers. Nevertheless, by 1973 these new ways of theorizing deviance had become widespread. As William Chambliss observed, "The prevailing consensus that has characterized the past 30 years of sociological and criminological inquiry in theoretical models has been shattered."[34]

The rise of critical approaches was associated with "a growing realization" that crime and deviance deal "with an inherently political phenomenon which should be viewed in the context of power, conflict, and interest groups in our society."[35] In order to assess the impact of this new way of thinking, in 1978, William Pelfry surveyed a sample of 761 members of four well-known professional organizations dedicated to the study of crime and deviance—the criminology section of the American Sociological Association, the American Society of Criminology, the Academy of Criminal Justice Sciences, and the criminal justice section of the American Society of Public Administration.[36] Of 384 respondents, over 57 percent indicated that critical perspectives represented a "viable alternative" to the more traditional approach.[37] This and related responses led Pelfry to conclude that contemporary students of crime and deviance "were inclined towards a critical approach as a perspective with definite potential and one which is seen to be capable of transposing traditional criminology."[38]

By the 1990s, critical perspectives had blossomed so abundantly that these ways of theorizing power came under attack by conservative academics and their political allies as harboring "politically correct" viewpoints on the organization of university life. The term *politically correct* was used to describe the standpoints of critical scholars who argued that, while no forms of knowledge are untainted by power, the dominant organization of power in our society has shaped what we honor as the most valuable forms of knowledge. Rather than intellectually contesting this argument, conservatives labeled critical thinkers politically correct and attacked them for foisting their "ideology" on unsuspecting students. Critical scholars, it was said, were punishing students who refused to toe "the party line." Brought to national attention in the weeks leading up to the 1991 U.S.-led Gulf War against Iraq, scholars who had been branded politically correct were criticized for rejecting patriotism and the supposed neutrality of traditional white male scholarship.

It is not accidental that this attack on critical scholars occurred near the end of the twelve-year rule of the conservative Reagan and Bush administrations. While hardly the bastions of radical thought that conservatives imagine, North American colleges and universities are among the few major social institutions in which reflexive critical discourse is publicly supported. Universities have also been major defenders of *affirmative action* programs, recruitment mechanisms aimed at maximizing the inclusion of groups that have long been denied equal access to educational resources, while enriching the overall learning environment by making academic institutions as diverse and multicultural as society itself. Given the importance of information technologies to transglobal capital and the prominence of universities as sites for the production and dissemination of information, it is not surprising that conservatives would seek to purge the academic influence of critical scholars. Such a purging was high on the agenda of people who complained about political correctness.

In attacking political correctness, conservatives appropriated a term of self-effacement which had been used previously by critical scholars to joke about the impossibility of ever being totally innocent of hierarchical power. Conservatives twisted this term, erroneously using it to picture universities as being run by "left-wing totalitarians" who censored all thought but their own and denied the value of anything white, western, heterosexual, or male. Wherever you go to school, remember that, despite conservative claims about the power of political correctness, most universities remain fairly traditional institutions, administered by relatively hierarchical structures of authority.

Although the alleged specter of political correctness may exist more in the minds of conservatives than in the realities of university life, recent attacks on critical scholarship have pointed to the growing significance of Marxist, feminist, anarchist, gay and lesbian, poststructuralist, and radical multicultural approaches to knowledge. Together, these theoretical orientations call for a radical rethinking of the relations between power and knowledge. This is most evident at the borders between traditional disciplines and within such interdisciplinary fields as critical cultural studies. Here, the theoretical concerns of philosophy converge with literary criticism, sociology, history, women's studies, African-American and ethnic studies, political science, psychoanalysis, communications, psychology, economics, and anthropology. The future of critical research lies in this transdisciplinary zone. What follows is a partial sampling of recent critical thought pertaining to deviance and control.

Critical Studies of Crime

Many critical studies approach from a historical perspective. An excellent example is Michel Foucault's *Discipline and Punish*, a study of the emergence of "delinquency" as a social category and of various disciplinary mechanisms aimed at producing a docile, self-surveillant, and conforming population.[39] A more recent example is Jeffrey Reiman's "pyrrhic-defeat" theory of crime control.[40] Reiman documents the structural roots of crime in a competitive economic system which "refuses to guarantee its members a decent living." This system—the capitalist economic system—"places pressures on all members to enhance their economic positions by whatever means available."[41] Such "economic pressures work with particular harshness on the poor, since their condition of extreme need and their relative lack of access to opportunity for lawful economic advancement vastly intensify for them the pressures toward crime that exist at all levels of our society."[42] Nonetheless, just as the dominant economic system induces crime, so does it generate a host of unworkable crime controls (individual arrests, trials, punishment, rehabilitation, etc.). These individualistic responses to crime are at once doomed to fail and destined to (ideologically) disguise the systemic origins of the criminality.

According to Reiman's pyrrhic-defeat theory, "the criminal justice system fails to reduce crime while making it look like crime is the work of the poor."[43] To be more successful, the criminal justice system would have to overturn the systemic pressures and inequalitites of the capitalist economic system of which it is part. To fight crime in this way, however, would bring criminal justice officials into open confrontation with the richest and most powerful sectors of society. Pressures to avoid such confrontation constrain the vision of crime control agents, who imagine crime as "a threat from the poor." Guided by this image, control agents fight crime but never in a way which "is enough to reduce or eliminate crime."[44] In this sense, crime control strategies typically reproduce the crime they claim to fight.

Other notable critical studies of crime include David Greenberg's analysis of the relation between delinquency and the compound power hierarchies of age, class, and race[45]; Lynn Curtis's analysis of the relationship between inner-city violence and racial and socioeconomic barriers to power[46]; William Chambliss's and Frank Pearce's studies of relations between organized crime and capitalist social institutions[47]; and Jim Brady's provocative investigation of connections between the banking and insurance industries, the redlining of certain "high-risk" (i.e., lower-class and/or racially segregated) urban neighborhoods, and high rates of "arson for profit."[48]

Another important critical study is Don Wallace and Drew Humphries's "Urban Crime and Capitalist Accumulation."[49] Wallace and Humphries used multiple-regression analysis to analyze the impact of capitalist accumulation (the production of higher rates of profit or surplus value when compared to the wage value of labor returned to workers) on rates of urban crime. Controlling for such variables as region of the country, population density, and size of police force, Wallace and Humphries discovered that "in cities that matured as centers of industrial accumulation, high rates of some types of property crime and violence have their origins in individualized and destructive aspects of class struggle. . . . Central city hardship reflects the near colonial status of marginalized groups concentrated in ghettos and subjected to racial oppression."[50]

In addition to the critical criminological studies mentioned above, other areas of deviance subject to recent critical inquiry include madness, rape, and the crimes of the "respectable" business and governmental classes. Critical research on each of these topics is reviewed below.

Madness and Powerlessness

Critical researchers locate the origins of serious mental disturbances within a social context of imbalanced power relations. Since the 1958 appearance of Augustus Hollingshead and Frederick Redlich's *Social Class and Mental Ill-*

ness,[51] sociologists have repeatedly uncovered significant relationships between position in the socioeconomic hierarchy and the likelihood of being diagnosed and treated for a serious mental health problem. Hollingshead and Redlich's survey of persons treated for mental disorders in New Haven, Connecticut, suggested that low-class persons were far more likely to be diagnosed as having serious psychiatric disorders. Relatively powerless patients are also more likely to be subject to the least intensive and most debilitating treatments, such as shock therapy, psychosurgery, and chemical sedation. This means that, once diagnosed, powerless people may be made even more powerless. The harsh realities of this form of double victimization are documented in Robert Perrucci's *Circle of Madness*, an observational study of institutional treatment in an Indiana state mental hospital, while both Robert Menzies and Stephen Pfohl have documented the political character of diagnostic procedures pertaining to judgments of "criminal insanity."[52]

Psychiatric intervention may exaggerate powerlessness, but is the experience of powerlessness itself a cause of mental disorders? Psychiatrist R. D. Laing suggests that this is the case.[53] In a series of in-depth case studies of the significant family and interpersonal relationships of severely disturbed schizophrenics, Laing found consistent evidence that so-called mentally ill persons were victims of a powerful and oppressively distorted communications network.[54] Patients were caught in a power-play of conflicting expectations between people in positions of significant interpersonal influence, authority, or control. When they acted to meet the expectations of one party, they were punished by the other. Anthropologist Gregory Bateson describes this phenomenon as a double bind of contradictory interpersonal relations.[55] In such oppressive situations people may escape into the "crazy" confines of madness. Thus, Laing reads madness as a sensible response to an irrational situation. In a complex, disguised manner, madness may be one way in which people distance themselves from the psychic pains of oppression. In this sense, madness may be viewed as a distorted statement about the unequal structuring of social power.

Critical psychiatric theorists such as Laing decode the political meaning of madness. In *The Politics of Experience*, Laing connects the personal pain of madness to the political-economic conditions of our age.[56] The importance of such a connection is documented by Harvey Brenner.[57] Brenner's analysis of 127 years of U.S. economic cycles suggests that rises in unemployment have been consistently associated with rises in hospitalization for serious mental disturbances. "Loss of employment seems to be the most pervasive source of emotionally destructive pressure within the capitalist economic structure."[58] At a more general level, French critical theorists Gilles Deleuze and Félix Guattari draw connections between the fascistic-like psychic rigidities of patriarchal capitalism and the historical repression of more fluid structures of human-animal relations.[59] In a related manner, critical feminist interpretations of the experience and control of madness in relation to gendered hierarchies of power are found in the work of Elaine Showalter, Hélène Cixous and Catherine Clement, Juliet Mitchell, Jackie Orr, and Janet Wirth-Cauchon, among others.[60]

Rape and the Social Economy of Gender

Many studies of sex and gender hierarchies have also contributed to the development of critical perspectives. Nowhere is this more evident than in the study of sexual violence against women. The gendered filtering of perceptions of deviance has long distorted our society's understanding of rape. According to feminist researchers such as Susan Brownmiller and Susan Caringella MacDonald, rape or the threat of rape has been used throughout history to keep women in their place as the supposed property of men.[61] In an article entitled "Rape: The All-American Crime," Susan Griffin connects violence against women to a culture of male domination in which "eroticism is wedded to power" and rape operates as "a form of mass terrorism."[62] This inhibits a woman's ability to move freely throughout society and perpetuates an unsupported mythology of "victim instigation," the erroneous idea that women cause rape by being unchaste in manner or dress.[63]

Empirical studies of rape find virtually no evidence of victim instigation.[64] Nor does the victimization of women end with the violent act of rape itself. As documented by Lynda Lytle Holmstrom and Ann Wolbert Burgess, the rape victim is victimized a second time by legal and medical institutions, which are supposed to assist her and control her offender.[65] The reality is quite the opposite. As Dorie Klein and June Kress point out, the social control of rape has functioned historically to safeguard men's lawful access to the bodies of "their women," rather than ensuring women's control over their own bodies.[66] The traumatic effects of such male-oriented rituals is particularly acute in relation to rape by "dates" or acquaintances, the terror of which is all too prevalent within contemporary society.

Research by Kurt Weiss and Sandra S. Borges connects such violence to the sexist socialization of both men and women.[67] In a related analysis, Stuart Hills attributes the encouragement of "normal" rape to the imprisonment of males within a mystique of machismo and control over women.[68] Such analyses challenge the stereotype of the rapist as a lone, psychopathic, and disturbed offender. To the extent that rape mirrors hierarchically structured power differences between men and women, its solution must involve more than the punishment or treatment of the rarely convicted offender. As Weiss and Borges point out, "Only liberation from the confines of usual sex-specific role behavior and expectations will lead to less exploitation, less misunderstanding, less hostility, and eventually less rape. For effective social change, it would be necessary to alter the cultural conception of woman as a sexual object and completely change her economic position as an article of male property. . . . Only then will it be possible to free the woman from the status of legitimate victim."[69]

Analyses of the political economy of rape take this analysis one step further. Julia and Herman Schwendinger, for instance, connect the problem of rape in capitalist societies to the hierarchical inequalities of this economic form.[70] The point is not that capitalism causes rape, but that capitalism's viewpoint of people as exchangeable commodities encourages a "fetishism of violence," whereby males who lack control in the economic realm may turn to sexual violence to defend against threats to the false objectification of their own manhood.[71] As in other studies of sexual violence against women, the basic message is this: rape is a terrorist assertion of patriarchal male power.

Corporate and Government Deviance

Crimes by corporations reflect the underlying political economy. . . . Not only is the economy determined by corporate power, but the state itself increasingly serves the corporate economy. Crimes of exploitation inevitably flow from this system of domination.

Richard Quinney[72]

They are coming amongst and in between us. Tapping our phones—you can be sure they've seen us. Are you working for or with the state . . . They are closing down—communications They've taken control—of our situations The forces of control are gathering around our heads.

Au Pairs[73]

The study of the deviance of people in positions of hierarchical power is often traced to Edwin Sutherland's 1939 presidential address to the American Sociological Association.[74] Sutherland's speech, entitled "White-Collar Criminality," was a discussion of the criminal activities of some of America's largest corporations. Sutherland's ideas generated a flurry of sociological interest in the crimes of business people. Notable early studies, each reflecting the influence of Sutherland, include Marshall Clinard's 1952 *The Black Market*, Robert Lane's 1953 "Why Businessmen Violate the Law," and Richard Quinney's 1963 "Occupational Structure and Criminal Behavior: Prescription Violation by Retail Pharmacists."[75]

For the most part, early studies of white-collar criminality paid more attention to the process of differential associations, whereby respectable citizens learn to violate the legitimate rules of business, than to the social or political-economic structures in which deviance by powerful persons operates as a normal feature of the competitive capitalist marketplace. Quinney's concern with how the organizational structure of the pharmaceutical industry fostered differential orientations to lawbreaking and Vilhelm Aubert's 1952 analysis of structured contradictions between the lawful social norms and profit-driven business practices were exceptions to the rule.[76] Yet, even these works did little to explicate the structural environment of "respectable" crime. As Diane Vaughan points out, "Although the work of Aubert, Quinney, and others began to point to the relation between structure and illegal behavior, the . . . classic period of inquiry offered nothing further in elaborated theory."[77]

By the early 1960s this early wave of research on white-collar crime had been pushed aside by a generation of sociologists eager to cash in on the promise of functionalism, learning theory, and the anomie perspective. In order to conduct research on lower-class deviance, this generation of social science professionals busied themselves with obtaining corporate and government grants. Not surprisingly, little corporate or government money was available to study crimes of business or deviance by powerful state agencies. What resulted was "a nearly ten-year hiatus, during which inquiry was practically abandoned."[78] This hiatus was broken during the 1970s, as a new generation of more critical-minded researchers emerged in the wake of the Watergate scandal and increasingly widespread public knowledge of government corruption, business fraud, and illegal deals between government officials, corporate leaders, and organized criminals. Revelations about the crimes of the CIA and other so-called legitimate government agencies in attempting to undermine foreign governments and suppress expressions of public dissent within the United States itself raised troubling questions about the deviance of officials who were charged with preventing deviance.

The 1974 publication of Harold Pepinsky's influential "From White-Collar Crime to Exploitation"[79] foreshadowed new critical approaches to the study of elite deviance, while the writings of Richard Quinney suggested that economic abuses of power were historical by-products of capitalism itself.[80] A similar theme is found in the work of Ronald Kramer, who suggests that reforms aimed at corporate deviance will prove unworkable unless measures are simultaneously directed at "the criminogenic structure" of the capitalist marketplace.[81] A related analysis is developed by Vaughan, who identifies economic competition for scarce resources as a structural inducement to corporate wrongdoing.[82] Vaughan also demonstrates that the interdependence between corporations and government agencies impedes the effective control of corporate deviance. As noted by Richard Quinney, "Crime as an economic enterprise depends on the symbolic alliance between politics and business, which in turn enhances all three realms."[83]

Frank Pearce takes the symbiotic relationship between business and government one step further. In *Crimes of the Powerful*, Pearce documents the collusion of big business, government control agencies, and organized crime syndicates on mutually beneficial projects. These include union busting and fighting Communism.[84] Pearce reviews evidence of CIA sponsorship of international heroin traffic in exchange for Mafia help in "removing" striking Communist workers from the docks of Marseille, France, in 1950; joint plans to assassinate Fidel Castro, whose antiracketeering policies angered gangsters, just as his pro-Soviet initiatives angered government officials; and the maintenance of an anti-Communist vigilance among opium farmers in southeast Asia during the Vietnam war.

More recent work on the crimes of corporate and government elites include David Simon and D. Stanley Eitzen's comprehensive analysis of the structural conditions and multiple forms of "elite deviance,"[85] Raymond Michalowski and Ron Kramer's analysis of the relationship between transnational corporate structures and the production of new forms of business-related crimes,[86] and Kitty Calavita and Henry Pontell's study of the interplay between the structural pressures of "finance capital" and opportunities for unprecedented corporate looting and fraud, following the political deregulation of the savings and loan industry during the 1980s.[87] Also of significance are former U.S. Attorney General Ramsey Clark's analysis of "war crimes" committed by the United States and its coalition partners against the civilian population of Iraq during the 1991 Gulf War and Margot Harry's account of the 1985 bombing of the "Move" community by the Philadelphia police.[88]

Other critical researchers have documented the relationship between stratified political and economic power and the organization of social control. Of particular importance is Ward Churchill and J. J. Vander Wall's careful study of the U.S. government's campaigns of espionage, terrorism, and assassination against the Black Panther Party and the American Indian Movement, and the same authors' subsequent overview of the continuing oppression of U.S. "political prisoners."[89] Important, as well, are studies documenting persistent racial and economic inequities in official social control practices (i.e., in regard to police violence, severity and length of prison sentences, etc.).[90]

Also of significance are Mike Davis's analysis of the relationship between metropolitan power structures and the militarized control of racialized minorities in Los Angeles[91]; Charles Derber's study of the relationship between the cultural glorification of self-interest and the prevalence of institutional and interpersonal forms of violence during the Reagan-Bush era[92]; and work by Edward Herman and Noam Chomsky, as well as Michael Parenti, on elite control of the news and information industries.[93]

Social Control and the Postmodern

In the late 1950s C. Wright Mills used the term *postmodern* to refer to the emergence of a new form of power that was then beginning to transform the cultural landscape of North America. Alert to massive transformations in the "cultural machinery" of "overdeveloped" societies, Mills warned of the increasing power of electronic media as a "kind of scheme for pre-scheduled, mass emotions," whereby it is "impossible to tell the image from the source." Mills viewed the expansion of electronic information not simply as external forces, but as forms of social experience that blur boundaries between "first-hand contact" and prefabricated signs. As such, the media "seep into our images of self, becoming that which is taken for granted, so imperceptibly and so surely that to modify them drastically, over a generation or two, would be to change profoundly modern . . . experience and character."[94] This marked the emergence of a "new society," dominated by the electronic circulation of "mythic figures and fast-moving stereotypes." In this "new society":

> We are so submerged in the pictures created by mass media that we no longer really see them. . . . The attention absorbed by the images on the screen's rectangle dominates the darkened public; the sonorous, the erotic, the mysterious, the funny voice of the radio talks to you; the thrill of the easy murder relaxes you. In our life-situation, they simply fascinate. And their effects run deep; popular culture is not tagged as "propaganda" but as entertainment; people are often exposed to it when most relaxed of mind and tired of body; and its characters offer easy targets of identification, easy answers to stereotyped personal problems.[95]

Like Mills, I am using the term *postmodern* to connote the historical emergence of new forms of social power—power mediated by dense and high-velocity technological rituals; rituals governed by information exchange, electronic imagery, and cybernetic control mechanisms.[96] Mills's concerns have much in common with those of French sociologist Jean Baudrillard. Baudrillard's writings depict the "implosion" of modern forms of experience into the density of fast-moving telecommunicative imagery. Tracing the sociological impact of this new form of social control, Baudrillard underscores the role of mass electronic media as a constitutive feature of contemporary power.[97] According to Baudrillard, telecommunicative technologies at the core of transnational capital are today so transforming everyday social life that we are increasingly controlled by a seemingly endless stream of mass-mediated images.

Is Baudrillard's frightening picture of postmodern control correct? Is the historical project of modernity coming to an end? Is the Enlightenment's white masculine dream of rational control over nature being today superseded by something even worse—technologically administered networks of high-speed fascinations, blurring experiential differences between reality and simulation? Are we entering what Baudrillard calls the "hyper-real," a panicky world in which much of what we experience will be premodeled and sold to us like commodities? Has this "New World Order" of postmodern controls crept upon us so subtly that it today exerts power without many of us noticing? Of the hidden rule of postmodern culture, Baudrillard remarks:

> Disneyland is there to conceal the fact that it is the "real" country, all of the "real" America, which is Disneyland (just as prisons are there to conceal the fact that it is the social in its entirety; in its banal omnipresence, which is [a prison]).[98]

In Chapter 6, in the discussion of functionalist theories of control, the term *cybernetics* was used to describe processes of technology-engineered "feedback," designed to modify human behavior by countering deviant expenditures of energy with information and, thus, keeping humans "on line" with hierarchical systems of power. This is another way of describing the kind of postmodern control mechanisms pictured by Mills and Baudrillard. As a discourse of control, cybernetics originated in wartime. This is underscored by Donna Haraway, who points to historical relations between cybernetics and the militarized organization of advanced patriarchal capitalism. Conceiving of cybernetics as a powerful "theoretical fiction" that forecloses other ways of making sense of the world, Haraway traces this "ideology" to the labor of government-funded "sociobiological" researchers, during and just after World War II.[99] Following the war, cybernetic thinking spread to virtually all fields of administrative knowledge (including sociology), as boundaries blurred between "once artificially separated areas of thought" and vast sectors of the world came to be "seen in terms of information."[100]

Today, given the omnipresence of television and other commercially controlled rituals of telelectronic "feedback," cybernetics exerts control over virtually all walks of social life. This new form of power has enormous implications for the critical study of deviance. From surveillance procedures in criminal justice to technological intervention in our most intimate fears and fantasies, cybernetic forms of power are today altering the sociological meaning of time, space, and subjective human experience. As Les Levidow and Kevin Robins observe, "In diverse realms—the work-place, the school, the training scheme, the home, the video game, as well as the military," cybernetic control mechanisms today "mediate our most primitive emotions, our sense of the natural, the rational and the real."[101]

Signs of postmodern power are everywhere today. Indeed, as Arthur and Marilouise Kroker and David Cook point out, postmodern control mechanisms are "what is playing at your local theater, TV set, shopping mall, office tower, bank machine, or sex outlet."[102] Through facsimile transfer, portable tape players and radios, and omnipresent answering machines, our bodies are increasingly being hooked into fast-moving global networks of information. Fascinating people with the abstract pleasures of appearing to be both everywhere and nowhere at the same time, these new modes of control may seduce and/or terrorize us into losing all but simulated contact with the historical actualities of our contradictory social relations with others. Indeed, as evidenced by the 1991 U.S.-led war against Iraq, as dominant social institutions continue to feed off the bodies of women, the economically disenfranchised, and peoples of color, televisionary mechanisms of power make entertainment out of war and justify the expenditure of billions of dollars on the maintenance of power hierarchies at home and abroad.

The advent of postmodern society significantly alters the environment in which deviance and social control take place. It is vital that critical scholars make links between new rituals of power and the ways in which power is both resisted and amplified in a world mediated by seductive electronic imagery and high-tech surveillance. In addition to the theorists mentioned above, others as diverse as Susan Willis, bell hooks, Frederic Jameson, Patricia Mellencamp, Guy Debord, Jackie Orr, Stanley Aronowitz, William Bogard, David Harvey, Norman K. Denzin, and myself have all recently attempted to make connections between postmodern forms of power and new modalities of hierarchical control.[103] But nowhere are the implications of western culture's immersion in high-tech economies of image making more clearly summarized than by Patricia Williams, when she states:

> Our is not the first generation to fall prey to false needs; but ours is the first generation of admakers to realize the complete fulfillment of the consumerist vision through the fine-tuning of sheer hucksterism. Surfaces, fantasies, appearances, and vague associations are the order of the day. So completely have substance, reality and utility been subverted that products are purified into mere wisps of labels, floating signifiers of their former selves. "Coke" can as easily add life plastered on clothing as poured in a cup. Calculating a remedy for this new-age consumptive pandering is problematic. If people like—and buy—the enigmatic emptiness used to push products, then describing a harm becomes elusive. But it is precisely because the imagery and vocabulary of advertising have shifted the focus from need to disguise. With this shift has come—either manipulated or galloping gladly behind—a greater public appetite for illusion and disguise.[104]

Power-Reflexive Studies of Control: A Final Comment

The critical studies mentioned above suggest that a comprehensive understanding of crime, deviance, and social control must locate these ritual practices within and against the historical reproduction of hierarchy.

In this regard, Patricia Williams's study *The Alchemy of Race and Rights* reads as an exemplar of both power-reflexive methods and a radically historical deconstruction of the uses and abuses of law. Subtitled *The Diary of a Law Professor*, Williams's book gives painstaking and often poetic notice to her own always politicized autobiographical positioning, as an African-American woman law professor and a critial theorist of legal "fictions" that have long operated to shackle the minds, bodies, and economic options of the people the law disenfranchises. Attentive to the subtleties through which rituals of institutionalized legal discourse privatize public inequities and blind those whom they most fascinate, Williams's work critically deconstructs the law's claims to "positivist objectivity" and evokes the possibility of a radically reconstructed notion of human rights—an alchemy of rights shorn of the racism, class bias, and gendered violence that characterize modern legal practice. These are important lessons in the critical study of social control.

ASSESSMENT OF THE CRITICAL PERSPECTIVE

The chief had assured her the officer would be punished if I would identify him. . . . I refused. . . . I told Katherine, much to her disappointment, that the dismissal of her officer would not restore my tooth; neither would it do away with police brutality. "It is the system I am fighting, my dear Katherine, not the particular offender."

Emma Goldman[105]

At the core of critical thinking is an awareness that ritual constructions of power affect the entirety of social life. Critical perspectives recognize that each of our thoughts and actions is laden with power. Each pushes or pulls us in certain directions but not in others. In this sense, the struggle between deviance and social control is a natural struggle, an aspect of our precarious historical existence as a species of social animals who must continuously produce a common sense of collective action simply to survive.

What is not natural is the way in which hierarchical structures favor the control of some classes of people by others. When this happens, social control ceases to be a matter of reciprocal struggle. It becomes, instead, a mode of domination. There is nothing natural about such domination. Hierarchical social forms are the effects of rituals which privilege certain people while excluding others. Nor is there anything natural about forms of deviance which arise in situations of domination. Both deviance and domination are the unnecessary by-products of hierarchical systems of control. To paraphrase Emma Goldman, it is the system we are fighting, not the particular offender.

Critical theorists employ power-reflexive methods to explore the relationship between their ideas and the social contexts of power in which all knowledge arises. A power-reflexive methodology enables us to better approximate objectivity, by taking into consideration the complex ways in which our own relations to power shape the historical standpoints from which we act. This provides an advantage over other perspectives which—despite frequent lip service to objectivity—remain subjected to relations of power which are never made explicit. In addition to the historical sensitivity of power-reflexive inquiry into issues pertaining to the impact of race, class, and gender on the production and control of deviance, I believe that its rigors make critical perspectives the strongest of those reviewed in this text.

This is not to say that critical perspectives represent all there is to know about deviance. Think, for instance, of how someone learns to become a prostitute or explodes in violent rage against a spouse. For critical theorists these are not simply matters of social learning, but learning that takes place within historically specific contexts of power. To understand the actions of female prostitutes (or sex workers) it is necessary to make connections between such persons' immediate biographies and a history of unequal economic relations between men and women. The violent male spouse must, likewise, be understood not simply as a sick individual but as an actor who has been partially shaped by rituals that encourage men to find power in controlling women's bodies.

Self-concept, family background, and educational background—all these things may be involved. But these factors do not exist independently of the ritual structuring of social power. By attending to rituals of power in this way, critical perspectives make the study of deviance both more complex and more uneasy. Recall the discussion in Chapter 1 of the two senses of uneasiness. To view social life within a historical context of power makes the task of studying deviance difficult. This is the first dimension of uneasiness promoted by the critical perspective. Self-concept and family and educational backgrounds—these things may be easier for many of us to grasp than the omnipresent, if often subtle, complexities of power. Critical perspectives enrich our understanding by exploring such complexities.

The second sense of uneasiness also enriches our understanding, but only by sacrificing the detachment that is typical of professional social science knowledge. Unlike perspectives which assume that deviance exists in a world totally separate from our own, critical perspectives suggest that we are structurally connected to deviance and its control, just as we are ritually connected to power. Where do we stand in relation to structures of unequal economic, sex and gender, and racialized power? Where could we stand? How can we get to a more reciprocal place together? These uneasy questions are part of the richness of the critical perspective.

Despite its strengths, the critical theory occasionally fails to realize the full potential of a power-reflexive analysis. Besides the failure of some critical theorists to place their own situated claims to power-reflexive knowledge in the foreground—to address them in a critical framework—there are several common conceptual problems which are encountered in much critical theorizing. These are outlined below. I hope that awareness of these issues will be of assistance to people who are concerned with furthering the development of the critical perspective.

Confusing Structural Affinity with Conspiratorial Motives

Critical theorists contend that hierarchical power differences shape the ritual organization of deviance and social control. This is not to say that the people who are most privileged and most powerful always act self-consciously, nor that they act conspiratorially to secure their interests. To suggest this would be to fall prey to an overly simplistic instrumentalist theory of social control, which would impute deliberate conspiratorial motives to those in greatest positions of power. As suggested previously, power-reflective studies of hegemony recognize that the reproduction of hierarchy is ordinarily more complex and more subtle.

Consider the work of therapeutic control specialists. As discussed in Chapter 4, medicalized control strategies in modern hierarchical societies are typically aligned with structural demands for the individualistic solutions to complex social problems. In such societies, it may seem *as if* therapeutic professionals conspire with other powerful individuals to defend the status quo. But do most treatment agents really conspire to act in this way? There is little evidence that this is the case. Although the structural consequences of their actions may serve to reproduce power hierarchies, most therapeutic control agents feel that they are helping the patients whom they treat.

The issue, then, is less a matter of conspiracy than a case of *ritual affinity*. How is it that particular modalities of control manifest an affinity with certain structures of power? The answer lies in the complex chain of subtle incentives and counterincentives which ritually inform control agents' relations to power. Sometimes conspiracies may be involved. There is evidence, for instance, that during the 1960s the Federal Bureau of Investigation (FBI) self-consciously sought to deviantize Dr. Martin Luther King and waged a secret and illegal war against the Black Panther Party and the American Indian Movement.[106] But even here it is not entirely clear that government officials operated as self-conscious agents of class and racial oppression. Isn't it more likely that some mixture of professional rewards, bureaucratic pressures, cultural fears, masculinized notions of paranoic patriotism, and the racialization of law-enforcement agents' perceptions may have blinded many agents to the structural consequences of their actions? This is not to absolve government agents of wrongdoing. It is to note, with Everett Hughes, that powerful social forces often get good people to do bad things.[107]

This is an important insight. Reduced to the conspiratorial logic of good guys versus bad guys, the critical perspective loses its conceptual richness. The motives of deviants and control agents cannot be inferred from the consequences of their actions. As such, critical theorists must avoid the mere ascription of bad motives, and undertake the much more difficult and complex task of tracing the path of power as it connects to rituals of both power and resistance. Otherwise, like liberal reformers, critical theorists will limit their attention to singling out "bad guys" for public condemnation, rather than working to subvert, uproot, and transform the ritual basis of hierarchical power itself.

Unfortunately, critical theorists have not always avoided the pitfalls of such instrumentalist theorizing. This was a weakness in the early Marxist writings of Quinney and Chambliss.[108] In recent years, critical research has demonstrated a more careful grasp of the relationship between power, control, and historical context.[109] Important studies such as E. P. Thompson's *Whigs and Hunters*,[110] Tigar and Levy's *Law and the Rise of Capitalism*,[111] and Andrew Scull's *Decarceration*[112] shun conspiratorial logic in favor of concrete historical analysis. Scull's work, for instance, examines the relationship between the fiscal crisis of the contemporary capitalist state and the deinstitutionalization of mental patients, prisoners, and delinquents during the early 1970s. Other critical studies which demonstrate a concern for structural consequences rather than conspiratorial inferences include Jim Thomas's study of domestic surveillance,[113] Stuart Hall and his associates' analysis of the political meaning of mugging in racially and economically troubled Britain,[114] and Phil Cohen's "Policing the Working-Class City."[115]

A strong theoretical case against the logic of instrumentalist theory is made by Steven Spitzer.[116] Spitzer faults such logic for failing to account for conflicts between state agents, as well as between control agents and the powerful classes they serve. By contrast, Spitzer directs attention to contradictory structural arrangements that spawn conflicts within and between the controlling classes. It is the historical resolution of these ritual contradictions, rather than an assumed unity of class interest, that represents the proper empirical forces of critical thought.[117] Of related concern is the recent work of William

Chambliss.[118] Chambliss underscores the complex and contradictory dialectic between *historical structuring* and *systemic structuration*. This is to distinguish between the historical activities of people who create structures and structural dynamics which—once ritually established—both constrain and facilitate new patterns of action.

Consensus, Hegemony, and Common Sense

A frequent objection to the critical perspective is brought by theorists who argue that social controls originate not in struggles for power, but in a normative consensus. This issue is raised, for instance, by Graeme Newman in his study *Comparative Deviance: Perception and Law in Six Cultures*.[119] After surveying respondents in six different cultures, Newman reported consistently high levels of condemnation regarding such traditional crimes as robbery. He did not find the same "universal" condemnation for nontraditional forms of deviance, such as factory pollution. From this Newman concluded that, while a conflict or a critical model may be helpful in explaining control strategies related to nontraditional deviance, the more universally condemned traditional crimes are to be understood by a consensus model.

Do high levels of consensus really mean that there is no room for a critical interpretation? Five of Newman's six cultures revealed a consensus (ranging from 70 percent to 95 percent agreement) that robbery should be reported to the police. Does this mean that there is really a universal moral condemnation of robbery (except in Sardinia, where a 50 percent reporting rate is explained away by the atypical presence of what Newman calls a dominant "criminal subculture")?

There are several basic problems with this consensus-by-survey argument. First, Newman's survey abstracts judgments of deviance from the real-world settings in which the actions actually take place. It is one thing to express disapproval of robbery when asked about it by a respectable interviewer. Private property would be looked upon in a very different way, however, were you in a situation of dire poverty in which someone else's well-being appeared to be a theft of your survival. This is not to defend robbing the rich, but simply to point out that any careful study of commonsensical judgments about deviance must consider the play of powerful social forces which make all moral judgments situational.

A second problem with Newman's study is that it is historically uninformed. A consensus may exist, but this does not mean that it has always existed. The category of robbery implies an acceptance of the concept of private property. Recall my discussion of social control in power-reciprocal acephalous societies. Our modern-day concept of robbery would be meaningless to our acephalous ancestors. Acephalous peoples, after all, had no notion of private property. It was only after a long process of political and economic struggle that the capitalist west arrived at its current view of the supposed naturalness of private ownership. Contemporary measures of consensus thus disguise the historical process which has given shape to that which many of us currently take for granted.

A third problem with the assertion of consensus is that it asks no questions about how the consensus came about. People are not born with consensus. What they agree about is a learned agreement. How is the learning accomplished? Does everybody have an equal chance to influence the learning, or is the social organization of common sense mediated by the power of some over others? Does each of us have an equal opportunity to influence school curricula, to organize the news, or to shape the electronic images which daily bombard us with "facts"? Are we truly in reciprocal control of the communicative tools out of which consensus is produced?

The answer, of course, is no! Society does not start with consensus. What consensus exists is ritually nurtured by hegemonic relations of power. Much of what goes on in schools, for instance, subtly shapes how students adjust to the existing order of inequality.[120] The same can be said of the mass media's production of collective representations of what life is and should be.[121]

Schools, news agencies, and television networks are powerful mediators of knowledge. Out of such institutions a relative consensus about the common-sensical nature of deviance and social control may emerge. The social reality of such consensus does not contradict the central theoretical tenets of critical thought. Quite the opposite: in studying the social construction of common sense, critical theorists view consensus as the historical effect of hegemonic rituals of power. This is not to ignore consensus but to analyze the forever contestable conditions of its production. In asking questions about the origins and consequences of consensus, we are thus confronted with the historical realities of power. Consensus doesn't spring spontaneously from the souls of the citizenry. It is manufactured or produced. How is this production achieved? Who guides it? Who benefits and who loses from the social production of particular images of deviance and social control? In exploring such questions, critical theorists deconstruct naive conceptualizations of consensus that are divorced from the historical actualities of power.

Conceptual Links to Other Theoretical Perspectives

A major contribution of critical theory has been to demystify the shortcomings of other perspectives. In this regard, critical theorists have drawn attention to the limits of even such "liberal" viewpoints as anomie and societal reaction. While anomie theorists conceptualize the relation between deviance and structural economic strains, most fail to historicize the basis of such strains. A related criticism is made of societal reaction or labeling perspectives. While generating sympathy for deviant "underdogs," labeling theory often fails to historicize the structures of power in which all labeling occurs.

Despite such theoretical shortcomings, perspectives such as anomie and labeling theory contain important kernels of truth that should not be overlooked by critical theorists. Moreover, many critical studies have been weakest at precisely the points where the anomie and societal reaction perspectives are most insightful—in mapping out the kinds of situations in which people are most likely to be deviant and in analyzing the routine actions of control agents. Thus, in addition to noting the problems of other viewpoints, a more comprehensive critical approach must make conceptual links with the strengths of other perspectives. A good example involves the work of critical theorists such as Carol Warren. Warren's research on the control of madness attends to both labeling processes and the political contexts in which labeling historically occurs.[122] In the words of H. Laurence Ross, the aim is to construct "a [critical] viewpoint premised on an emerging synthesis of these positions."[123]

Thus, although other perspectives often err by failing to analyze the impact of structured differences in power, this is no reason to ignore their contributions to the study of deviance and control. More promising are attempts to build theoretical links between critical thought and other theoretical frameworks. Isn't it possible to construct a critically informed or power-reflexive learning theory? Couldn't the anomie perspective be further developed, so as to include a more rigorous historical consideration of the contradictions engendered by a mix of capitalism, racism, and heterosexism? The construction of such synthetic viewpoints is necessary for a truly comprehensive understanding of deviance and social control.

Structural Determination versus Free Will: A Question of Agency

Structure is both medium *and* outcome *of the reproduction of practices. Structure enters simultaneously into the constitution of the agent and social practices, and "exists" in the generating moments of this constitution.*

Anthony Giddens[124]

Critical theorists view deviance and control within the shifting historical confines of structured social power. This does not mean that human life is strictly determined by impersonal structural arrangements. In emphasizing the reflexive role of ritual in both *constructing* and *constraining* how humans perceive and act toward one another, critical theory views social reality as neither fully determined nor purely willed. Though constraining structures exist, they are never independent of the creative ritual actions that repeatedly bring them into being. Willed actions exist as well, but never independently of the way they are constrained by structures that emerge out of the ritual situations in which these actions meaningfully occur. In this sense, social life is neither fully determined nor freely chosen. It is both partially determined and partially chosen. This doubled character of human historical action is well articulated by Karl Marx, when he states:

> Men [and women] make history, but they do not make it just as they please; they do not make it under circumstances chosen by themselves, but under circum-

stances directly found, given and transmitted from the past. The tradition of all dead generations weighs like a nightmare on the brain of the living.[125]

Unfortunately, not all expressions of critical theory have been as balanced as Marx's. Some have emphasized the importance of structural forces, while neglecting the role of reflexive human agency. This failure to consider the willful or creative side of power was characteristic of dogmatic or orthodox Marxism. Here, the importance of human thought and action was pushed aside in favor of sweeping generalizations about the determining influence of political and economic forces. More recent critical scholarship is less deterministic. As David Greenberg and Drew Humphries point out, the crucial question for a critical Marxism is not to explain social change by reference to invariantly deterministic laws, but to "locate agents of change 'structurally' within the confines of specific historical situations, such that particular courses of action come to be viewed as 'desirable' and 'able or unable' to be achieved."[126]

In this chapter I have taken a similar position. I have argued that, while neither deviance nor control is ever strictly determined, they are also never free of the structured influence of power in history. This is a fundamental paradox of human life. We are, at once, creative and created ritual agents— self-structuring subjects and structurally subjected selves. We are "decentered subjects": subjects who actively assess our situations and make historical choices, just as our choices are limited by the objective possibilities made ritually available to us in our historical relations to others.[127]

A long and shrouded history of hierarchical power has given shape to what we today consider normal and what we control against as deviant. This is what critical theorists mean by *hegemonic social power*: a power which "naturalizes" hierarchy, transforming the material realities of historical struggle into the idealized realities of common sense. By deconstructing the hegemonic bondage of such "common sense," we are able to partially free ourselves from its hierarchical force. This is the power-reflexive potential of critical theoretical activity—to cast light upon the dimly lit hallways of our own lost histories. Fulfillment of this potential will, we hope, enable us to better recognize the economic, sexual, and racialized hierarchies which guide so much current thinking about deviance and social control. In this, we may be partially freed from structures which create us more than we create them. This is the "truth" of critical theoretical standpoints: a deconstructive convergence of Marxist, feminist, anarchist, and radical multicultural perspectives on power. This "truth" may not set us free. It may, however, increase our potential for freedom and encourage us to act together to overthrow the multiple hierarchies which currently imprison us in history.

NOTES

1 Walter Benjamin, "Theses on the Philosophy of History," in *Illuminations*, Harry Zohn (trans.), Schocken Books, New York, 1969, p. 257.

2 Angela Y. Davis, *Women, Culture, Politics*, Vintage Books, New York, 1990, pp. 172, 176.

3 In using masculine pronouns to describe positivism and feminine pronouns in referring to positivism's objects, I do not mean to imply that all positivists are men and that the "objects" of their analyses are women. I mean simply to underscore the patriarchal connotations of a positivist viewpoint.

4 Max Horkheimer and Theodor Adorno, *Dialectic of Enlightenment*, John Cumming (trans), Seabury Press, New York, 1972, pp. 83–84.

5 For an elaboration, see Stephen Pfohl and Avery Gordon, "Criminological Displacements," *Social Problems*, vol. 33, Oct–Dec 1986, pp. S94–S113. 1986. A video-cassette version of this text is also available in VHS format. For a copy, send $10.00 (U.S. currency) to Parasite Cafe Productions, c/o Stephen Pfohl, Boston College, Department of Sociology, Chestnut Hill, MA 02167, USA.

6 Horkheimer and Adorno, *Dialectic of Enlightenment*, p. 84.

7 Michel Foucault, *Discipline and Punish: The Birth of the Prison*. A. Sheridan (trans.), Vintage Books, New York, 1979, p. 27.

8 Michael Foucault, in Colin Gordon (ed.), *Power/Knowledge: Selected Interviews and Other Writings, 1972–1977*, Pantheon, New York, 1980, p. 132.

9 Ibid., p. 133.

10 Sheila Balkan, Ronald J. Berger, and Janet Schmidt, *Crime and Deviance in America: A Critical Approach*, Wadsworth, Belmont, Calif., 1980, p. 316.

11 Ronald C. Kramer, "Teaching Critical Criminology to Criminal Justice Students," paper presented at annual meeting of American Society of Criminology, Toronto, Nov. 4, 1982, p. 11.

12 David R. Simon and D. Stanley Eitzen, *Elite Deviance*, Allyn and Bacon, Boston, Mass., 1982; Elliot Currie, "Fighting Crime," in *Working Papers*, vol. 9, July–August 1982, pp. 16–25.

13 Harold E. Pepinsky, *Crime Control Strategies*, Oxford, New York, 1980.

14 Harold E. Pepinsky, "A Radical Alternative to Radical Criminology," in James A. Inciardi (ed.), *Radical Criminology: The Coming Crisis*, Sage, Beverly Hills, Calif., 1980, p. 310.

15 Antonio Gramsci, quoted in Michael Albert and Robin Hahnel, *Unorthodox Marxism*, South End Press, Boston, 1978, p. 329.

16 Larry Tifft and Dennis Sullivan, *The Struggle to Be Human: Crime, Criminology and Anarchism*, Cienfuegos Press, Orkney, Scotland, 1980, p. 168.

17 Benjamin, "Theses on the Philosophy of History," p. 255.

18 Ibid., p. 256.

19 Balkan, Berger, and Schmidt, *Crime and Deviance in America*, p. 330.

20 See, for instance, Hakim Bey, *T.A. Z: The Temporary Autonomous Zone, Ontological Anarchy, Poetic Terrorism*, Autonomedia, New York, 1991.

21 See, for instance, Rene Vienet, *Enrages and Situationists in the Occupation Movement, France, May '68*, Autonomedia, New York, 1992.

22 Charles Derber, *Money, Murder and the American Dream*, Farber and Farber, Boston, 1992, p. 113.

23 Marc Mauer, "Americans behind Bars—A Comparison of International Rates of Incarceration," in Ward Churchill and J. J. Vander Wall (eds.), *Cages of Steel: The Politics of Imprisonment in the United States*, Maisoneuve Press, Washington, D.C., 1992, pp. 22–37.

24 Katherine O'Sullivan See, "Approaching Poverty in the United States," *Social Problems*, vol. 38, no. 4, November 1991, p. 427.

25 William Julius Wilson, *The Truly Disadvantaged: The Inner City, the Underclass and Public Policy*, University of Chicago Press, Chicago, 1987.

26 Rates based upon combined figures for prisons and jails reported in Marc Mauer, "Americans Behind Bars—A Comparison of International Rates of Incarceration," in Ward Churchill and J. J. Vander Wall, *Cages of Steel*, pp. 22–37.

27 Patricia J. Williams, *The Alchemy of Race and Rights: Diary of a Law Professor*, Harvard University Press, 1991, p. 189.

28 Marc Mauer, *Young Black Men and the Criminal Justice System: A Growing National Problem*, The Sentencing Project, Washington, D.C., February 1990, as discussed in W. Churchill, "The Third World at Home," p. 12.

29 The term *temporary autonomous zone* is borrowed from Hakim Bey. See Bey, *T.A.Z.: The Temporary Autonomous Zone*.

30 Avital Ronell, "Interview with Avital Ronell," in Andrea Juno and V. Vale (eds.), *Angry Women*, Re/Search Publications, San Francisco, 1991, p. 128.

31 See, for instance, Dick Hebdige's excellent analysis of the dominant culture's efforts to contain the subversive effects of British "punk." Dick Hebdige, *Subculture: The Meaning of Style*, Methuen, London, 1979.

32 Michel Foucault, "A Conversation with Michel Foucault," *Partisan Review*, vol. 38, no. 2, (1971), p. 201.

33 Michalowski, "Conflict, Radical, and Critical Approaches to Criminology," in Israel Barak-Glantz and C. Ronald Huff (eds.), *The Mad, The Bad, and the Different*, Heath, Lexington, Mass., 1981, p. 49.

34 William Chambliss, "Functional and Conflict Theories of Crime," *MSS. Modular Publications*, vol. 17, 1973, p. 1. Reprinted in W. J. Chambliss and M. Mankoff (eds.), *Whose Law? What Order?* Wiley, New York, 1976.

35 Charles Reasons, *Criminology: Crime and the Criminologist*, Goodyear, Santa Monica, Calif., 1974, p. 5.

36 William V. Pelfry, "The New Criminology: Acceptance within Academe," in James A. Inciardi (ed.), *Radical Criminology: The Coming Crisis*, Sage, Beverly Hills, Calif., pp. 233–244.

37 Ibid., p. 238.

38 Ibid., p. 241.

39 Foucault, *Discipline and Punish*.

40 Jeffrey Reiman, *The Rich Get Richer and the Poor Get Prison*, Wiley, New York, 1979, p. 7.

41 Ibid.

42 Ibid.

43 Ibid., pp. 5–6.

44 Ibid., p. 6.

45 David F. Greenberg, "Delinquency and the Age Structure of Society," *Contemporary Crisis*, vol. 1, April 1977, pp. 189–223.

46 Lynn Curtis, *Violence, Race and Culture*, Heath, Lexington, Mass., 1975.

47 William Chambliss, "Vice, Corruption, Bureaucracy, and Power," *Wisconsin Law Review*, vol. 4, 1971, pp. 1130–1155; Frank Pearce, "Organized Crime and Class Politics," in David F. Greenberg (ed.), *Crime and Capitalism*, Mayfield, Palo Alto, Calif., 1981, pp. 157–181.

48 James Brady, "Arson, Urban Economy, and Organized Crime: The Case of Boston," *Social Problems*, vol. 31, no. 1, October 1983, pp. 1–23.

49 Don Wallace and Drew Humphries, "Urban Crime and Capitalist Accumulation: 1950–71," in Greenberg, *Crime and Capitalism*, pp. 140–156.

50 Ibid., p. 150.

51 Augustus Hollingshead and Frederich Redlich, *Social Class and Mental Illness*, Wiley, New York, 1958.

52 Robert Perrucci, *Circle of Madness: On Being Insane and Institutionalized*, Prentice-Hall, Englewood Cliffs, N.J., 1974; Robert J. Menzies, *Survival of the Sanest: Order and Disorder in a Pretrial Psychiatric Clinic*, University of Toronto Press, Toronto, 1989; Stephen Pfohl, *Predicting Dangerousness: The Social Construction of Psychiatric Reality*, D.C. Heath, Lexington, Mass., 1978.

53 R. D. Laing, *The Divided Self*, Penguin, Baltimore, 1967.

54 R. D. Laing and A. Esterson, *Sanity, Madness and the Family*, Basic Books, New York, 1964.

55 Gregory Bateson, D. D. Jackson, J. Haley, and J. Weakland, "Toward a Theory of Schizophrenia," *Behavioral Science*, vol. 1, 1956, pp. 251–264.

56 R. D. Laing, *The Politics of Experience*, Penguin, Baltimore, 1967.

57 Harvey Brenner, *Mental Illness and the Economy*, Harvard, Cambridge, Mass., 1973.

58 Balkan, Berger, and Schmidt, *Crime and Deviance in America*, p. 289. See also D. D. Braginsky and B. M. Braginsky, "Surplus People: The Lost Faith in Self and System," *Psychology Today*, vol. 9, no. 3, August 1975, pp. 68–76.

59 Gilles Deleuze and Félix Guattari, *Anti-Oedipus: Capitalism and Schizophrenia*, Robert Hurley, Mark Seem, and Helen R. Lane (trans.), University of Minnesota Press, 1983. See also Brian Massumi, *A User's Guide to Capitalism and Schizophrenia: Deviations from Deleuze and Guattari*, MIT Press, Cambridge, Mass., 1992; Rolando Perez, *On An(archy) and Schizoanalysis*, Autonomedia, New York, 1990.

60 Elaine Showalter, *The Female Malady: Women, Madness, and English Culture, 1830–1980*, Penguin, New York, 1985; Hélène Cixous and Catherine Clement, *The Newly Born Woman*, Betsy Wing (trans.), University of Minnesota Press, Minneapolis, 1986; Juliet Mitchell, *Psychoanalysis and Feminism*, Vintage, New York, 1974; Jackie Orr, "Theory on the Market: Panic, Incorporating," *Social Problems*, vol. 37, no. 4, November 1990, pp. 460–484; Janet Wirth-Cauchon, *Gender and the Disordered Self: The Borderline Case Narrative*, Ph.D. Dissertation, Boston College, Chestnut Hill, Mass., 1993.

61 Susan Brownmiller, *Against Our Will: Men, Women, and Rape*, Bantam, New York, 1975. For a related discussion of rape within a racist social and economic context, see Davis, *Women, Class and Rape*, pp. 171–201.

62 Susan Griffin, "Rape: The All-American Crime," *Ramparts*, vol. 10, September 1971, pp. 28, 35; see also Susan Griffin, *Rape: The Power of Consciousness*, Harper and Row, New York, 1979.

63 See, for instance, Diana Scully and Joseph Morolla, "Convicted Rapists' Vocabulary of Motives: Excuses and Justifications," *Social Problems*, vol. 31, no. 5, June 1984, pp. 530–544.

64 For an analysis of police data on the social circumstances surrounding rape in seventeen major cities, see Lynn Curtis, *Crimes of Violence*, D.C. Heath, Lexington, Mass., 1974.

65 Lynda Lytle Holmstrom and Ann Wolbert Burgess, *The Victim of Rape: Institutional Reactions*, Wiley, New York, 1979. See also Lynda Lytle Holmstrom and Ann

Wolbert Burgess, "Rape: The Victim and the Criminal Justice System," *International Journal of Criminology and Penology*, vol. 3, 1975, pp. 101–110.

66 Dorie Klein and June Kress, "Any Woman's Blues," *Crime and Social Justice*, vol. 5, spring–summer 1975. See also Camile E. Le Grand, "Rape and Rape Laws: Sexism in Society and Law," *California Law Review*, vol. 6, no. 3., 1973, pp. 919–941.

67 Kurt Weiss and Sandra S. Borges, "Victimology and Rape: The Case of the Legitimate Victim," *Issues in Criminology*, vol. 8, no. 2, 1973, pp. 919–941.

68 Stuart L. Hills, "Rape and the Male Mystique," in *Demystifying Social Deviance*, McGraw-Hill, New York, 1980, pp. 57–77.

69 Weiss and Borges, "Victimology and Rape," p. 110.

70 Julia Schwendinger and Herman Schwendinger, "Rape, Sexuality, Inequality and Levels of Violence," *Crime and Social Justice*, vol. 16, winter 1981, pp. 3–31.

71 Ibid., p. 19.

72 Richard Quinney, *Criminology*, 2d ed., Little, Brown, Boston, 1979, p. 197.

73 Au Pairs, "Headache for Michelle," from the album *Playing with a Different Sex*, Human Records/Ideal Home Noise, United Kingdom, 1981.

74 Edwin Sutherland, "White-Collar Criminality," *American Sociological Review*, vol. 5, February 1940, pp. 1–12. See also Edwin H. Sutherland, *White Collar Crime*, Dryden, New York, 1949.

75 Marshall B. Clinard, *The Black Market*, Rinehart, New York, 1952; Robert A. Lane, "Why Businessmen Violate the Law," *Journal of Criminal Law and Criminology*, vol. 44, 1953, pp. 151–165; Earl R. Quinney, "Occupational Structure and Criminal Behavior: Prescription Violation by Retail Pharmacists," *Social Problems*, vol. 11, 1963, pp. 179–185.

76 Quinney, "Occupational Structure and Criminal Behavior"; Vilhelm Aubert, "White Collar Crime and Social Structure," *American Journal of Sociology*, vol. 58, 1952, pp. 263–271.

77 Diane Vaughan, "Recent Developments in White-Collar Crime Theory and Research," in Israel L. Barak-Glantz and C. Ronald Huff (eds.), *The Mad, the Bad, and the Different*, D. C. Heath, Lexington, Mass., 1981, p. 136.

78 Ibid., p. 137.

79 Harold Pepinsky, "From White Collar Crime to Exploitation: Redefinition of a Field," *Journal of Criminal Law and Criminology*, vol. 65, June 1974, pp. 225–233.

80 Quinney, *Criminology*, 2d ed., pp. 141–215.

81 Ronald Kramer, "Corporate Crime: An Organizational Perspective," paper presented at Conference on Trends and Problems in Research and Policy Dealing with Economic Crime, State University of New York at Potsdam, Feb. 7–9, 1980.

82 Diane Vaughan, *Controlling Unlawful Organizational Behavior*, University of Chicago Press, Chicago, 1983.

83 Quinney, *Criminology*, 2d. ed., p. 210.

84 Frank Pearce, *Crimes of the Powerful*, Pluto, London, 1976. See also Morton Halpern et al., *The Lawless State: The Crimes of the U.S. Intelligence Agencies*, Penguin, Middlesex, 1976; Simon and Eitzen; *Elite Deviance*; M. David Erman and Richard J. Lundman, *Corporate and Governmental Deviance*, Oxford, New York, 1982.

85 Simon and Eitzen, *Elite Deviance*.

86 Raymond J. Michalowski and Ronald C. Kramer, "The Space of Laws: The Problem of Corporate Crime in a Transnational Context," in Delos H. Kelly (ed.), *Criminal Behavior, 2nd ed.*, St. Martin's Press, New York, 1990, pp. 344–366.

87 Kitty Calavita and Henry N. Pontell, "Heads I Win, Tails You Lose: Deregulation,

Crime and Crisis in the Savings and Loan Industry," *Crime and Delinquency*, vol. 36, no. 3, July 1990, pp. 309–341.

88 Margot Harry, *Attention, Move! This is America!* Banner Press, Chicago, 1987.

89 Ward Churchill and J. J. Vander Wall, *Agents of Repression: The FBI's Secret Wars Against the Black Panther Party and the American Indian Movement*, South End Press, Boston, 1988.

90 Ivan Jankovic, "Social Class and Criminal Sentencing," *Crime and Social Justice*, vol. 10, fall-winter 1978, pp. 9–16; Alan J. Lizotte, "Extra-Legal Factors in Chicago's Criminal Courts: Testing the Conflict Model of Criminal Justice," *Social Problems*, vol. 25, no. 5, June 1978, pp. 564–580; John Hagan, "The Social and Legal Construction of Criminal Justice: A Study of the Presenting Process," *Social Problems*, vol. 22, 1975, pp. 620–637; Marvin Wolfgang and Marc Riedel, "Race, Judicial Discretion and the Death Penalty," in William Chambliss (ed.), *Criminal Law in Action*, Hamilton, Santa Barbara, Calif., 1975, pp. 365–375.

For analyses of "geographical" discrimination in the justice system, see David Jacobs, "Inequality and the Legal Order: An Ecological Test of the Conflict Model," *Social Problems*, vol. 25, no. 5, June 1978, pp. 515–535; David Jacobs and David Britt, "Inequality and Police Use of Deadly Force: An Empirical Assessment of a Conflict Hypothesis," *Social Problems*, vol. 26, no. 4, April 1979, pp. 403–412; Kirk R. Williams and Michael Timberlake, "Structured Inequality, Conflict and Control: A Cross-National Test of the Threat Hypothesis," *Social Forces*, vol. 63, no. 2, December 1984, pp. 414–431; Michael Timberlake and Kirk R. Williams, "Dependence, Political Exclusion and Governmental Repression," *American Sociological Review*, vol. 49, no. 1, February 1984, pp. 141–147.

91 Mike Davis, *City of Quartz*, Verso, New York, 1991.

92 Charles Derber, *Money, Murder and the American Dream: Wilding from Wall Street to Main Street*, Faber and Faber, Boston, 1992.

93 Edward Herman and Noam Chomsky, *Manufacturing Consent: The Political Economy of the Mass Media*, Pantheon, New York 1988; Michael Parenti, *Inventing Reality: The Politics of the News Media*, 2d ed., St. Martin's Press, New York, 1993.

94 C. Wright Mills, *White Collar*, Oxford University Press, New York, 1951, p. 334.

95 Ibid., pp. 333–336.

96 I am here making a distinction between the postmodern (or postmodernity) as a historical social form and a second term—*postmodernism*. Postmodernism today circulates at the borders of a variety of academic disciplines, political discourses, and artistic practices. It connotes a form of epistemological or aesthetic inquiry marked by a particular style of theoretical or poetic engagement. This style appears to give highest value to a nonlinear and decentered play of language, commentary, and criticism. Frequently associated with the terms *deconstruction* and *poststructuralism*, *postmodernism* is a politically charged term, suggesting a radical overturning of the "master narratives" of white male and western claims to knowledge.

Insomuch as both postmodernity (as a social condition) and postmodernism are being produced (and consumed) together in history, it is important to recognize postmodernism as being, in part, a critical response to postmodernity. In this sense, postmodernism indicates a provisional reaction to the implosion of meaning within a social world where objects of knowledge are rapidly being transformed into contextless bits and pieces of free-floating information. At the same time, postmodernism must be understood as a response to a different crisis altogether—a self-critical response to the political deconstruction of western white male language practices by feminists, peoples of color, postcolonial critics, gays, lesbians, and others who are marginalized in the historical organization and production of modernity. Thus, postmodernism is linked to the critical theoretical perspectives discussed in this text, while postmodernity is itself an object of criticism.

97 Jean Baudrillard, *Selected Writings*, Stanford University Press, Stanford, Calif., 1989.

98 Jean Baudrillard, *Simulations*, Paul Foss, Paul Patton, and Philip Beitchman (trans.), Semiotext(e), New York, 1983, p. 25.

99 Donna J. Haraway, "The High Cost of Information in Post World War II Evolutionary Biology: Ergonomics, Semiotics, and the Sociobiology of Communicative Systems," *Philosophy Forum*, vol. XIII, no. 2–3, winter-spring 1981–1982, p. 249. See also Donna J. Haraway, *Simians, Cyborgs and Women: The Reinvention of Nature*, Routledge, New York, 1991.

100 Sol Yurik, *Behold Metatron, the Recording Angel*, Semiotext(e), New York, 1985, pp. 40, 74, 12.

101 Les Levidow and Kevin Robins, "Towards a Military Information Society?" in Les Levidow and Kevin Robins (eds.), *Cyborg Worlds: The Military Information Society*, Free Association Books, London, 1989, p. 176.

102 Arthur Kroker, Marilouise Kroker, and David Cook, "Panic USA: Hypermodernism as America's Postmodernism," *Social Problems*, vol. 37, no. 4, November 1990, p. 443.

103 Jean Baudrillard, *Selected Writings*, Mark Poster (ed.), Stanford University Press, Stanford, Calif., 1988; Susan Willis, *A Primer for Daily Life*, Routledge, New York, 1991; bell hooks, *Yearning: Race, Gender and Cultural Politics*, Boston, South End Press, 1990, p. 27; Frederic Jameson, *Postmodernism, or, The Cultural Logic of Late Capitalism*, Duke University Press, Durham, N.C., 1991; Patricia Mellencamp, "TV Time and Catastrophe, or Beyond the Pleasure Principle of Television," in Patricia Mellencamp (ed.), *Logics of Television: Essays in Cultural Criticism*, Indiana University Press, Bloomington, 1990, pp. 240–266; Guy Debord, *Society of the Spectacle*, Black and Red Press, Detroit, 1983; Jackie Orr, "Theory on the Market: Panic Incorporating," *Social Problems*, vol. 37, no. 4, pp. 460–484; Stanley Aronowitz, "Postmodernism and Politics," in Stanley Aronowitz, *The Politics of Identity: Class, Culture, Social Movements*, Routledge, New York, 1992, pp. 251–271; Arthur Kroker and Marilouise Kroker (eds.), *The Panic Encyclopedia: The Definitive Guide to the Postmodern Scene*, St. Martin's Press, New York, 1989; Donna Haraway, *Simians, Cyborgs and Women: The Reinvention of Nature*, Routledge, New York, 1991; William Bogard, "Closing Down the Social: Baudrillard's Challenge to Contemporary Sociology," *Sociological Theory*, vol. 8, 1990, pp. 1–15; David Harvey, *The Condition of Postmodernity*, Basil Blackwell, 1989; Norman K. Denzin, *Images of Postmodern Society: Social Theory and Contemporary Cinema*, Sage, Newbury Park, Calif., 1991; Stephen Pfohl, *Death at the Parasite Cafe: Social Science (Fictions) and the Postmodern*, St. Martin's Press, New York, 1992.

104 Williams, *The Alchemy of Race and Rights*, p. 39.

105 Emma Goldman, *Living My Life*, vol. 1, Dover, New York, 1970, p. 308.

106 David Garrow, *The FBI and Martin Luther King Jr.*, Penguin, Middlesex, 1981.

107 Everett Hughes, "Good People and Dirty Work," *Social Problems*, vol. 10, summer 1962, pp. 3–11.

108 For a review of this problem, see Dragan Milovanovic, "Ideology and Law: Structuralist and Instrumentalist Accounts of Law," *Insurgent Sociologist*, vol. X, no. 4–vol. XI, no. 1, summer-fall 1981, pp. 93–98.

109 For a review of other noninstrumentalist Marxist historical research, see Pat O'Malley, "Historical Practice and the Production of Marxist Legal Theory," *Crime and Social Justice*, vol. 19, winter 1982, pp. 53–61.

110 E. P. Thompson, *Whigs and Hunters: The Origin of the Black Act*, Allen Lane, London, 1975.

111 M. Tigar and M. Levy, *Law and the Rise of Capitalism*, Monthly Review Press, New York, 1979.

112 Andrew Scull, *Decarceration: Community Treatment and the Deviant*, Prentice-Hall, Englewood Cliffs, N.J., 1977.

113 Jim Thomas, "Class, State and Political Surveillance: Liberal Democracy and Structural Contradictions," *Insurgent Sociologist*, vol. X, no. 4–vol. XI, no. 1, summer-fall 1981, pp. 47–58.

114 Stuart Hall, Chas Critcher, Tony Jefferson, John Clarke, and Brian Roberts, *Policing the Crisis: Mugging, the State, and Law and Order*, Macmillan, London, 1978.

115 Phil Cohen, "Policing the Working Class City," in B. Fine et al. (eds.), *Capitalism and the Rule of Law: From Deviancy Theory to Marxism*, Hutchinson, London, 1979, pp. 118–136.

116 Steven Spitzer, "Left-Wing Criminology—An Infantile Disorder?" in James A. Inciardi (ed.), *Radical Criminology: The Coming Crisis*, Sage, Beverly Hills, Calif., 1980, pp. 169–189. For an empirical application of this noninstrumentalist approach, see Steven Spitzer and Andrew T. Scull, "Social Control in Historical Perspective: From Private to Public Responses to Crime," in Piers Beirne and Richard Quinney (eds.), *Marxism and Law*, Wiley, New York, 1982, pp. 236–251.

117 For related critiques of instrumentalism, see Peter K. Manning, "Deviance and Dogma," *British Journal of Criminology*, vol. 15, January 1975; Piers Beirne, "Empiricism and the Critique of Marxism on Law and Crime," *Social Problems*, vol. 26, no. 4, April 1979, pp. 373–385; Isaac Balbus, " Commodity Form and Legal Form: An Essay on the Relative Autonomy of Law," *Law and Society Review*, winter 1977, pp. 571–587; David F. Greenberg, "On One Dimensional Criminology," *Theory and Society*, vol. 3, 1976, pp. 610–621.

118 William J. Chambliss, "The Criminalization of Conduct," in H. Laurence Ross (ed.), *Law and Deviance*, Sage, Beverly Hills, Calif., 1981, p. 52.

119 Graeme Newman, *Comparative Deviance: Perception and Law in Six Cultures*, Elsevier, New York, 1976.

120 See, for instance, Samuel Bowles and Herbert Gintis, *Schooling in Capitalist America: Educational Reforms and the Contradictions of Economic Life*, Basic Books, New York, 1976; and Paul Willis, *Learning to Labor: How Working Class Kids Get Working Class Jobs*, Columbia University Press, New York, 1977.

121 See, for instance, Stuart Hall, Dorothy Hobson, Andrew Lowe, and Paul Willis, *Culture, Media, Language*, Hutchinson, London, 1980; Howard Davis and Paul Walton (eds.), *Language, Image, Media*, St. Martin's Press, New York, 1983; Gaye Tuchman, *The Social Construction of News*, Free Press, New York, 1978; Todd

Gitlin, *The Whole World Is Watching*, University of California Press, Berkeley, 1989; Michael Gurevitch, Tony Bennett, James Curren, and Janet Woolcutt, *Culture, Society and the Media*, Methuen, London, 1982.

122 Carol A. B. Warren, "Labeling the Mentally Ill," in Ross, *Law and Deviance*, p. 180.

123 Ross, *Law and Deviance*, p. 10.

124 Anthony Giddens, *Central Problems in Social Theory*, University of California Press, Berkeley, 1980, p. 5.

125 Karl Marx, "The Eighteenth Brumaire of Louis Bonaparte," *The Marx-Engels Reader*, 2d ed., R. C. Tucker (ed.), W. W. Norton, New York, 1978, p. 595.

126 David F. Greenberg and Drew Humphries, "The Dialectics of Crime Control," in David F. Greenberg (ed.), *Crime and Capitalism*, Mayfield, Palo Alto, Calif., 1981, p. 213.

127 For discussions of the term *decentered subject* in poststructuralist theory, see Rosiland Coward and John Ellis, *Language and Materialism: Developments in Semiology and the Theory of the Subject*, Routledge and Kegan Paul, Boston, 1977; and Chris Weedon, *Feminist Practice and Poststructuralist Theory*, Basil Blackwell, New York, 1987.